THE I TATTI
RENAISSANCE LIBRARY

James Hankins, General Editor

BRUNI

HISTORY OF THE
FLORENTINE PEOPLE

VOLUME 2

ITRL 16

LEONARDO BRUNI

✦ ✦ ✦

HISTORY OF THE
FLORENTINE PEOPLE

VOLUME 2 · BOOKS V–VIII

EDITED AND TRANSLATED BY

JAMES HANKINS

THE I TATTI RENAISSANCE LIBRARY
HARVARD UNIVERSITY PRESS
CAMBRIDGE, MASSACHUSETTS
LONDON, ENGLAND
2004

Series design by Dean Bornstein

Library of Congress Cataloging-in-Publication Data

Bruni, Leonardo, 1369–1444
[Historiae Florentini populi. English & Latin]
History of the Florentine people / Leonardo Bruni;
edited and translated by James Hankins.
p. cm. — (The I Tatti Renaissance library; 3)
Includes bibliographical references and index.
ISBN 0-674-00506-6 (v. 1: alk. paper)
ISBN 0-674-01066-3 (v. 2: alk. paper)
1. Florence (Italy) — History — To 1421.   I. Hankins, James.
II. Title.   III. Series
DG737.A2 B813 2001
945'.51 — dc21

Contents

ॐ९१ॐ

Book VI   154

Book VII   284

Book VIII   394

The Dominions of Castruccio Castracani, 1328

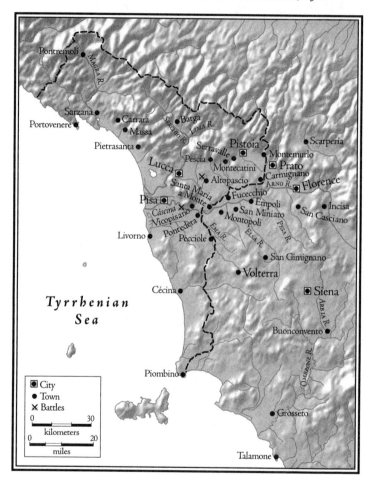

Pontremoli

MAGRA R.

Sarzana

Portovenere

Carrara

Massa

Barga

LIMA R.

SERCHIO R.

Pietrasanta

Serravalle

Pistoia

Scarperia

Pescia

Montemurlo

Lucca

Montecatini

Prato

Carmignano

Altopascio

ARNO R.

Florence

Santa Maria
a Monte

Fucecchio

Pisa

Empoli

Cáscina

San Miniato

San Casciano

Incisa

Vicopisano

Montopoli

PESA R.

Pontedera

ELSA R.

Livorno

Pecciole

EMA R.

San Gimignano

Cécina

Volterra

Siena

Tyrrhenian
Sea

ARBIA R.

Buonconvento

OMBRONE R.

Piombino

Grosseto

◉ City
● Town
✕ Battles

0   30
kilometers
0   20
miles

Talamone

⋄ Eastern Tuscany ⋄

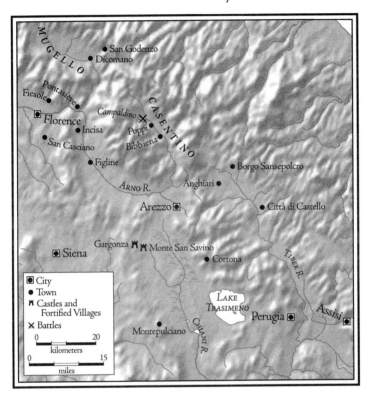

HISTORY OF THE
FLORENTINE PEOPLE

LIBER QUINTUS

1 Commorante adhuc in citeriori Gallia Henrico, Florentini et socii Bononiam copias misere, ut adventum eius, si forte[1] ab ea parte transire in Etruriam conaretur, pro viribus impedirent. Ille, peracta circa Brixiam obsidione, cum singulis fere civitatibus singulos praesides imposuisset, circiter Idus octobris in Ligures transiit. Illic omni honore susceptus, tres fere menses, dum hiems desaeviret, Genuae hibernavit. Inde Tyrrhenum ingressus mare cum triginta navibus longis, quas ei Genuenses[2] Saonensesque paraverant, circiter Nonas martias Pisas devenit.

2 Nec Florentini sociique interea segnes; nam ubi per Ligures iter facere cognoverunt, auxilia nuper Bononiensibus missa in lunensem traduxerunt agrum, ut ex ea parte venienti obsisterent finesque Lucensium tutarentur. Dum Pisis moratur Henricus, crebras incursiones in lucensem[3] miniatensemque agrum praefecti eius fecerunt, sed neque pugna ulla memoratu digna in his locis commissa est, neque oppida ulla grandiora capta.

3 Ipse, paratis quae paranda fuerant, proximi anni principio (is erat annus duodecim supra millesimum trecentesimum) Pisis profectus, iuxta litus inferi maris Romam versus ire contendit. Quacumque incedebat, studia partium ingentesque rerum motus suscitabantur, ut enim quaeque civitas divisa per factiones erat, ita illius appropinquatio alios spe, alios metu concitabat. Itaque Viterbium ingressus est, pulsa diversa factione, eoque praecupide intromisso; et apud Urbevetanos diversa fortuna freti eius fautores,[4] dum res novas attentant, praevalentibus adversariis, urbe pelluntur.

BOOK V

While Henry was still lingering in Lower Gaul,[1] the Florentines 1
and their allies sent troops to Bologna to hinder as much as they
could any attempt on his part to pass from that region into
Tuscany. He, having brought to completion the siege of Brescia,
established garrisons in nearly every city and crossed into Liguria
sometime around the fifteenth of October. He was received there 1311
with full honors and wintered in Genoa for about three months
while the weather was foul. Then he set sail on the Tyrrhenian
Sea in thirty galleys which the Genoese and Savoyards had made
ready for him, arriving in Pisa around the seventh of March.

Meanwhile, the Florentines and their allies had not been idle. 2
For when they learned that Henry was passing through Liguria,
they transferred to the Lunigiana the auxiliaries they had recently
sent to Bologna, so as to resist his coming on that frontier and to
protect the borders of the Lucchesi. While Henry was staying in
Pisa, his commanders made frequent incursions into the territories
of Lucca and San Miniato, but they engaged in no battles worth
recording in these places, nor was any large town captured.

At the beginning of the next year,[2] 1312, having made all neces- 3
sary preparations, Henry set out from Pisa along the coast of the 1312
Tyrrhenian Sea, heading towards Rome. Wherever he marched,
factionalism and tremendous political unrest sprang to life. For as
each city was riven by factions, his coming aroused hope in some,
fear in others. Thus when he entered Viterbo, the faction hostile
to him was expelled and his own installed with great avidity. In
Orvieto his supporters were less fortunate, and were driven from
the city when their adversaries succeeded in defeating their attempted coup.

4 Romae quoque seditiones et tumultus maiorem in modum augentur. Robertum enim Siciliae regem magna pars[5] romanorum civium sectabatur, praecipuae vero auctoritatis Ursinum genus, opibus et gratia longe potentissimum. Et miserat eo Robertus Iohannem fratrem cum valida equitum manu, qui, Ursinis ceterisque eius factionis coniunctis,[6] Capitolio et Ianiculo et Hadriani mole cunctisque trans Tiberim locis et Vaticani occupatis, arcere ab ingressu Henricum suosque constituerant. Altera vero factio, imperatorii fautrix nominis, ducibus Columnensibus Aventinum et Caelium et Quirinalem montes ac totas Exquilias cum Viminali et Subura tenebat, crebraque inter eos proelia committebantur. Ob has contentiones aliquot dies Viterbii commoratus, tandem Romam petens, quia recta introire urbem non dabatur, per Milvium pontem traductis copiis, porta Flaminia ingressus est. Inde, media vadens urbe, in Aventino posuit castra.

5 Florentini, auditis certaminibus quae Romae parabantur, ne communi partium studio deessent, equites quingentos et pedites mille insigni apparatu Romam misere. Miserunt et Lucenses et Senenses et alii socii, ut vires cuique animique fuere. Romae vero crebra proelia commissa sunt: quippe, cum intra unius urbis moenia tantae copiae sibique invicem adversariae clauderentur ac populus ipse romanus intra se divisus, ut cuiusque factionis erat, his vel illis inhaereret, eveniebat singulis fere diebus, ut per vicos et compita pugnaretur. Id certamen tribus fere mensibus duravit. Tandem vero, cum ad basilicam Vaticani, in qua mos erat coronari principes, devenire Henricus nequiret, quoniam hostis potentior longe ab his locis arcebat, contra decus imperii cedens, Laterani coronam assumpsit, pauloque post relicta urbe indignabundus Tibur se contulit.

In Rome, too, there was a considerable increase in sedition and   4
tumult. For a great part of Rome's citizens were followers of Robert, King of Sicily,[3] but the Orsini were of paramount authority,
by far the most powerful clan in wealth and influence. Robert sent
his brother John there with a powerful troop of horse. John, having united the Orsini and members of his own faction, occupied
the Capitol, the Janiculum, Hadrian's castle,[4] Trastevere and the
Vatican with the aim of preventing Henry and his troops from entering the city. The other faction, which upheld the imperial name,
was led by the Colonna and controlled the Aventine, the Caelian
and the Quirinal hills along with all of the Esquiline, the Viminal
and the Subura.[5] The two factions engaged in frequent battles.
On account of these struggles Henry was delayed several days in
Viterbo before setting out for Rome. Since the direct route into
the city was blocked, he brought his troops over the Milvian
Bridge, entering through the Flaminian Gate. Then, making his
way to the center of the city, he pitched camp on the Aventine.[6]

The Florentines heard of the quarrels that were brewing in   5
Rome and sent to the city five hundred knights and a thousand
foot, splendidly equipped, to support their party. The Lucchesi
and the Sienese and other allies also sent such forces as their
strength and spirit allowed. In Rome the fighting was incessant.
Indeed, since such large and mutually hostile forces were confined
within the walls of a single city, and the Roman People itself was
divided, cleaving to the forces of whichever faction they belonged
to, there were battles in the streets and squares nearly every day.
The struggle lasted almost three months. In the end Henry was
unable to make his way to the Vatican basilica, where it was the
custom to crown emperors, having been denied access thereto by
the far more powerful forces of his enemy. To the dishonor of the
imperial cause he gave way and was crowned at the Lateran instead, and shortly thereafter left the City and betook himself in a
rage to Tivoli.

6   Erat imperator pro illatis sibi Romae impedimentis quantum vix dici potest adversariis infensus; praecipue tamen in Robertum regem ac Florentinos, ut principes iniuriarum, illius ardebat animus. Robertum ulcisci e vestigio non videbatur posse, defesso milite ac longis contentionibus afflicto. Itaque in Florentinos conversus, per Sabinos et Umbros ducens, Etruriam ingreditur; inde per perusinum et cortonensem et arretinum agrum Florentiam petere contendit. Dum id molitur iter, universi exules, qui ubique terrarum erant, ad eum confluxerunt.

7   Florentini, simul atque vergere in se totam belli molem intellexere, revocatis propere copiis novoque insuper delectu habito, contra hostem misere, iubentes ut a proelio quidem abstinerent, regionem tantum et oppida tutarentur. Imperator, quo primum die Florentinorum fines intravit, non longe a Varico metatus castra, expugnare oppidum aggreditur. Triduo continuata oppugnatio est et acerrime pro moenibus fossisque dimicatum; tandem, fatigatis oppidanis humilitatique murorum diffissis, oppidum deditur. Cetera subinde oppida eodem terrore capit. Ancisam inde ventum est. In eo loco Florentinorum copiae obviam[7] missae constiterant. Cum igitur in conspectum[8] venisset hostis copiasque adesse cognosset, struxit confestim aciem dimicandique iis[9] fecit potestatem. Florentini pugnae fortunam minime experiundam censebant, satisque putabant fore, si hostem destinerent. Itaque intra munitiones se continentes, iter quod est inter flumen et oppidum tutabantur.[10]

8   Cum neque dimicandi potestas neque transeundi fieret, propterea quod imminens viae castellum praeruptis rupibus facile tran-

Owing to the obstacles they had raised against him in Rome, 6
the emperor was unspeakably furious at his adversaries, but his
spirit burned especially hot against King Robert and the Florentines, the principal sources of his injuries. He did not think he
could avenge himself immediately against Robert, as his own
troops were shattered and exhausted by the long struggles. So,
turning against the Florentines, he marched through the Sabine
and Umbrian lands and entered Tuscany; from thence he pressed
onwards to Florence through the territories of Perugia, Cortona
and Arezzo. Once his expedition had been put in motion, he was
joined by all the [Ghibelline] exiles from every land.[7]

The Florentines realized that the full weight of war was de- 7
scending upon them. Immediately they recalled their troops, and
levying new troops as well, they sent them out against the enemy,
with instructions to avoid battle and to protect the region and its
towns only. On the very day he crossed the Florentine border the
emperor pitched camp not far from Montevarchi and started to
besiege the town. The siege lasted three days, and there was bitter
fighting in the trenches and before the walls, but at last the townsmen were exhausted. Lacking confidence in their humble defenses,
they surrendered the town. After that, Henry captured other
towns in the same way: terror. Then he came to Incisa. There the
Florentine troops sent out to meet him took their stand. When
the enemy came in sight and realized that there were Florentine
troops present, he immediately formed his line of battle and challenged them to fight. The Florentines decided not to try the fortunes of battle, and thought it would be enough to check the enemy. So they stayed inside their defense-works and guarded the
route between the river and the town.

Thus the emperor could neither fight nor pass, since the castle 8
overlooking the road on high cliffs forbade easy passage. So, acting on the information of the exiles, he began to make his way
through the extremely difficult passes in the nearby mountains to

situ arcebat, doctus ab exulibus imperator per proximos ad laevam montes difficillimis saltibus traducere coepit. Quod cum vidissent qui Ancisae erant, veriti ne ipsi post terga ab hoste relinquerentur, signa ilico moventes, citato agmine, Florentiam versus ire contenderunt. Eos superiori de loco conspicati hostes (iam enim pars quaedam oppidum praetervecta erat), magno impetu invadunt. Saltus erat admodum impeditus, et undequaque strepebat hostis superiorique[11] de loco pugnaturus adventabat. At[12] Florentinis nequaquam propositum fuerat pugna decernere, sed rapto agmine ad urbem pervenire. Itaque, ubi ruere in se hostem sensere, confestim verso itinere[13] retulerunt pedem. Accelerata paulo magis est receptio, ut fuga protinus videri posset, et fuit auxilio propinquitas oppidi, ne insignis[14] illa die acciperetur calamitas. Nec sane magnus caesorum aut captivorum numerus fuit, verum ita fractae mentes, quasi ad extremum victi essent.

9   Imperator praetervectus Ancisae oppidum, relictisque post se Florentinorum copiis, non longe ab eo loco nocte illa consedit apud vicum Padule nuncupatum. Postridie vero, luce prima movens, ingenti terrore ad urbem duxit, nec longe a porta casentinati via posuit castra, doctus ab exulibus eam urbis partem minus esse munitam, propterea quod, nondum absolutis novis moenibus vetustisque neglectis, vallo tantum et fossa ab ea parte urbs claudebatur.

10   Trepida quidem primo sub adventu civitas fuit, increbrescente rumore copias omnes nuper contra hostem missas apud Ancisam deletas fuisse. Et sane praesentia hostis ac suorum absentia fidem sinistro rumori videbantur afferre; nam, quo tandem pacto, nisi oppressi, tulissent ad vacuam praesidio urbem hostem venire? Itaque et luctus privatim et publice metus cunctos pervaserat. Sumpsit tamen arma populus et ad tutandas eas urbis partes, quas contra hostis constiterat, sub vexillis concurrit. Ibi distributa loca

the north.[8] When the Florentines at Incisa saw this, they grew afraid that they would be cut off by the enemy. They at once advanced the standards, fell into marching order and headed off towards Florence. Seeing them from the hilltop (for a certain part of the imperial forces had already made their way past the town) the enemy attacked in force. The pass was somewhat obstructed, and the enemy were raising a clamor on all sides as they rushed down the hill to fight. The Florentines, however, had determined not to fight but to march rapidly to the city. Thus when they saw and heard the enemy rushing towards them they at once turned around and returned [to Incisa]. The retreat was somewhat hasty and soon took on the appearance of a rout, but the town was nearby to help them evade any signal calamity that day. There was no great number of killed and captured, but they were mentally shattered as though they had suffered a total defeat.

The emperor bypassed the town of Incisa, and, leaving the 9 Florentine troops behind him, rested the night not far from there at a village called Padule.[9] The following day he set out at dawn and headed for the terrified city. He pitched camp not far from the Casentino gate, having learned from the exiles that this part of the city was less well fortified. The new walls were not yet finished, and the old walls in poor repair, so this side of the city was enclosed only by an earthwork and a moat.

When Henry first arrived the city was in fear, the rumor having 10 spread that all the forces lately sent out against the enemy had been destroyed at Incisa. And indeed the presence of the enemy and the absence of their own troops seemed to give credit to this perverse rumor. For why would they have allowed the enemy to come to the unguarded city unless they had been beaten? Thus private grief and public fear filled every heart. Nevertheless, the people took up arms, and under their standards raced to protect those parts of the city where the enemy was stationed. There each of the gonfaloni was assigned places and sections of the city to

regionesque defendendae singulis societatibus attributae; vallum, neque die neque noctu intermisso opere, instauratum est; ex omni genere contignationis turres et propugnacula debilioribus locis excitatae armatisque hominibus completae.

11   Imperator ab oppugnatione urbis, incertum qua de causa, abstinuit, cum si primum sub adventum trepida adhuc civitate et rumore profligationis suorum consternata tentasset, vix resisti potuisse credatur, praesertim absentibus copiis et murorum tutela ad ea parte deficiente. Sed cunctando ac differendo, cives animos resumpsere, simulque copiae post tergum relictae biduo post diversis itineribus redierunt; quorum adventu sublatis laetitia animis, minas iam hostium longe aspernabantur.

12   Imperatorem vero suae et ipsum spes retinebant. Post adventum siquidem eius et castra apud urbem posita, infinita paene vis hominum ex florentino agro ad eum confluxerat; nec solum imperatorii fautores nominis, verum etiam ceteri permulti, sive metu sive novarum cupiditate rerum, sese illi coniunxerant. Nam et Ancisa, quod oppidum praesens nequiverat obtinere,[15] confestim post recessum copiarum ad imperatorem defecit, ac ceteri ferme omnes populi qui Arnum[16] superiorem accolunt se ultro dediderunt.[17] Per mugellanum quoque casentinatemque agrum multi rebellarant; omissaque urbe, castra hostium frequentabant et commeatum exercitui deferebant. Intra urbem quoque permulti cives praesenti reipublicae statu[18] infensi favere hostibus credebantur.

13   Inter haec sociorum auxilia opportunissime[19] supervenerunt: Lucensium tria millia peditum, equites sexcenti; Senensium totidem equites, peditum duo millia; aliorum quoque sociorum pro cuiusque facultatibus; ex quibus factus est magnus equitum pedi-

defend, and labor on the earthwork was resumed and continued without interruption, day and night. Wooden towers and redoubts were jury-rigged in the more exposed places and filled with armed men.

For some unknown reason the emperor refrained from attacking the city, although if he had made an attempt upon his first arrival, when the city was still in a state of fear and consternation at the rumored rout of its troops, he could scarcely have been resisted, it is thought, especially in view of the absence of the city's troops and the insufficient protection afforded by her walls on the one side. But thanks to his hesitation and delay, the citizens recovered their spirit. At the same time, the troops he had left behind him returned by various routes after a couple of days, and their return brought rejoicing, and soon thereafter, scorn for the enemies' threats.

But it was his own hopes that were holding the emperor himself back, too. For after he had arrived and pitched camp by the city, an almost endless flood of men from the Florentine territory had streamed to him. Not only adherants of the imperial cause, but also many other men had joined him, either from fear or from the desire for revolution. Even Incisa, a city he had been unable to take in person, immediately defected to the emperor after he withdrew his troops. Nearly all the other peoples dwelling in the upper Arno surrendered to him into the bargain. There were also many rebels in the Mugello and Casentino who abandoned the city but frequented the camps of the enemy and brought victuals to his army. Within the city, too, there were many citizens hostile to the current regime who were thought to favor the enemy.

In this situation, help arrived from the allies in a most opportune way. The Lucchesi sent three thousand foot and six hundred horse; the Sienese sent the same number of horse and two thousand men; and other allies sent such troops as their resources permitted. Thus was constituted a large body of horse and foot.

11

12

13

tumque numerus. Castra vero intra urbem contra hostium castra, quo die noctuque praesto foret defensor, per infrequentia aedificiorum loca posuerunt. In his[20] armati cives sociique perstabant; ceterae vero urbis partes sic tranquillae erant, ut ne sentire quidem obsidionem viderentur.

14   Dies continuos quadraginta[21] apud Salvianum templum imperator habuit castra, procul ab urbe non amplius trecentis passibus. Tandem, cum frustra teri ab eo tempus appareret, et quotidie magis in urbe crescerent amicorum auxilia, pridie Kalendas novembris de tertia vigilia[22] retro castra movit, ac transmisso Arno, duobus passuum millibus ab urbe super Emam fluvium castra fecit. Qua nocte hostis recessit, cum ex more tabernacula incensa a militibus et vasa concremata[23] essent, civitas tota, excita eo tumultu, in armis fuit. Ubi vero abire hostem cognovit, tacita resedit, lucemque armata expectavit. Postera mox luce egressi equites proelium leve cum equitatu hostium commisere. Hostis inde secundis castris ad Cassianum pervenit via senensi, octo millibus passuum ab urbe. In his locis cum esset imperator, Pisanorum auxilia[24] ad illum venerunt, peditum tria millia, equites vero quingenti; Genuensium quoque sagittarii expugnationibus utilissimi ad mille. His copiis iterum confirmatus, apud Cassianum obstinatius consedit.

15   Florentini posthac, suburbiis ea ex parte quae ad hostem versa erat (iam enim aedificia longe se extenderant) communitis, sociorumque auxiliaribus remissis, ipsi per se gessere bellum. Hinc discursiones crebro factae ab hostibus, leviaque sunt proelia frequenter commissa; signis tamen collatis nunquam pugnatum est. Verum incendia et clades multipliciter attriverunt agrum, sementesque eo anno impeditae annonae caritatem portendebant futuram.

Camps were set up inside the city in the empty and undeveloped quarters across from the enemy encampment to serve as a round-the-clock garrison. Here the city militia and the allies stood under arms, while the other parts of the city were so tranquil that they hardly seemed to feel themselves under siege.

The emperor encamped for forty consecutive days by the 14 church of San Salvi not more than three hundred paces from the city.[10] Finally, since it seemed to him he was wasting his time in vain, and friendly auxiliary forces were growing in the city day by day, on the thirty-first of October, in the middle of the night, he moved his camp back. Crossing the Arno, he pitched camp two miles from the city above the river Ema. On the night the enemy withdrew, while the soldiers, in accordance with custom, were setting fire to the tents and burning equipment, the whole city was in arms, excited by the tumult. But when it realized the enemy had left, it remained quietly in place, armed, waiting for dawn. Early the next morning the cavalry went out and lightly engaged the enemy cavalry. The enemy then moved to a second encampment at San Casciano on the Via Senese, eight miles from the city. Seeing that the emperor was in this location, the Pisans sent him help: three hundred foot and fifty knights. The Genoese also sent about a thousand archers, extremely useful in sieges. Strengthened by these forces, the emperor held his position at San Casciano with greater resolution.

By this time the Florentines had fortified the suburban zones 15 that had faced the enemy; indeed the construction now covered a large area. So they sent back the auxiliary forces of their allies and waged the war on their own. The enemy made frequent raids, and there were often light engagements, but no pitched battles were fought. Yet the multiplication of fire and destruction caused damage to the countryside, and the difficulties of planting that year portended a future rise in the cost of grain.

16   Supra duos menses apud Cassianum imperator habuit castra, et quidem per mediam hiemem; demum Cassiano profectus, Bonitium petiit. Eo cum pervenisset, pulchritudinem opportunitatemque montis admiratus, oppidum in eum locum restituit, unde a Carolo rege fuerat ante deiectum, in eoque oppido quod reliquum erat hiemis hibernavit. Nec hiberna sane illi quieta fuerunt, cum a Senensibus et Collensibus et Geminianensibus finitimis Bonitio populis lacesseretur sedulo, et ipse ultro in eorum fines omnifariam belli clades inferret.

17   Per hoc tempus Florentini, iampridem vastato circa urbem agro, frequentibus vero oppidis quae nuper ad imperatorem defecerant bellum urbi inferentibus, hosteque ipso praevalido obstinatoque incubante ac, ut fama erat, in proximum annum valentius incubaturo, magnitudine periculorum coacti sunt ad Robertum regem eiusque opem respicere. Oratores ea de causa missi duo: Iacobus Bardius eques florentinus e familia nobili, et Dardanus Acciaiolus, vir per id tempus magnae in republica auctoritatis. Hi Senas primo, inde Perusium profecti, utraque ex civitate legatos sibi coniungi suaserunt, et supervenerunt Lucensium Bononiensiumque legati. Omnesque ad regem una profecti, quanto in periculo forent civitates Etruriae docuerunt subvenirique postularunt. Rex, placide commendata Thuscorum fide, sese ducem futurum civitatibus ac venturum in Etruriam, si modo per negotia regni liceat, pollicitus est; interim vero Petrum fratrem cum equitatu praemissurum.

18   Ea res Florentiam sedulo nuntiata erexit cunctorum animos, et afflictis in rebus lucem quandam optimae spei visa est attulisse.

The emperor remained encamped for more than two months at   16
San Casciano, and that during the mid-winter. Finally he set out
from San Casciano and made for Poggibonsi. Arriving there, he
admired the beauty and convenience of the mountain, and restored the town to the original site, before its relocation downhill
by King Charles.[11] In that town he spent the rest of the winter.
But the winter was certainly not a quiet one for him, as he was
zealously harrassed by the peoples of Siena, Colle Val d'Elsa, and
San Gimignano on the borders of Poggibonsi. He, for his part,
also brought the calamities of war inside their borders in every
possible way.[12]

Around this time the Florentines were compelled by the great-   17
ness of the dangers surrounding them to look to King Robert
for help. The territory around the city had suffered from long devastation; numerous towns that had recently defected to the emperor were making war on them; an exceptionally powerful enemy
was himself obstinately besetting them — and, according to report,
would beset them the following year with still more powerful
forces. For this reason two ambassadors were sent out: Jacopo de'
Bardi, a Florentine knight from a noble family, and Dardano
Acciaiuoli, a man of great authority in the state at that time.
These men went first to Siena, then to Perugia, and persuaded
representatives from both cities to join them, and envoys from
Lucca and Bologna came as well. All of them set out in a body to
see the king. They informed him of the great danger threatening
the cities of Tuscany and asked for help. The king calmly com-
mended the Tuscans for their loyalty, and promised he would act
as their leader and come to Tuscany, provided that the business of
the Kingdom would allow it. In the meantime, however, he would
send his brother Peter ahead with a force of knights.

This news was eagerly announced in Florence and raised every-   18
one's spirits. But a demand for money soon afterwards clouded
this happiness, for the king demanded a three-month's stipend be

Sed turbavit paulo post hanc ipsam laetitiam pecuniarum flagitatio; rex enim pro his quae mittebantur copiis trimestria exhiberi stipendia postulabat. Eorum praestatio multas magnasque difficultates continere videbatur. Primo enim, aerarium publicum longis erat sumptibus inanitum; patrimonia vero singulorum crebra et importuna tributorum pensione exhausta. His accedebat quod Perusini et Bononienses et Lucenses, qui longius aberant ab hoste, non perinde sese oneribus offerebant. Ita ad Florentinos modo tota pensio recidebat. Quaerebatur hoc ipsum a rege mutuum; sed negabat constanter, apparebatque in ea re sane durior. His de causis dilatus est copiarum adventus. Parte denique pecuniarum equitibus persoluta, reliqua expectabatur. Quod, cum in longum traheretur, hostisque in dies formido augesceret, nihil potius tantis ut in malis visum est, quam plenum urbis imperium in regem transferre. Facto igitur populi decreto, in quo potestas, uti e republica existimarent, prioribus dabatur, priores, consilio prius habito, gubernationem dominatumque civitatis regi in quinquennium auctoritate publica tradiderunt.

19   Traditio autem ipsa his verbis facta: 'Cernentes belli pericula prementia nunc et in posterum imminentia, ut populus florentinus urbsque et ager in viam salutis reducatur, solemni deliberatione habita, Robertum regem Siciliae rectorem, gubernatorem, protectorem[25] et dominum civitatis populique florentini in quinquennium deligimus.' Conditiones vero hae adiectae: 'Rex per se ipsum praesens vel per aliquem ex fratribus filiisve civitatem gubernabit; exulem nullum restituet; populum suis legibus uti permittet; prioratus officium, uti nunc est, ita posthac fore in civitate patietur. Haec nominatim excepta, ceterorum ferme omnium regi est potestas permissa.'

provided for the troops he was sending. Paying them seemed to present a great many difficulties. First of all, the public treasury was empty owing to the prolonged expenses [of the war] and individual resources were exhausted from frequent, unseasonable levies. Moreover, the Perugians, the Bolognese and the Lucchesi, being rather far from the enemy, were not offering to assume burdens to the degree that might have been expected. Thus it fell to the Florentines to make the whole payment themselves. They even tried to borrow the funds from the king himself, but he steadily refused, and seemed quite determined in his refusal. That is why the arrival of the troops was put off. At last, part of the money for the knights was paid, and the rest was on account. But since the matter had been dragged out for so long, and fear of the enemy was growing daily, no course seemed better amid such evils than to transfer full power over the city to the king. A decree of the People was therefore passed in which power was given to the Priors to make decisions on behalf of the state. Having first taken counsel, they handed over by public authority the governance and dominion of the city to the king for a five-year period.

The transfer itself was effected using the following words: "In 19 view of the dangers of war currently pressing upon us and in the future threatening us, in order that the Florentine People, its city and territory may be brought back into the path of salvation, we, after solemn deliberation, choose Robert, King of Sicily, to be the rector, governor, protector and lord of the city and People of Florence for a five-year period." The following conditions were added: "The king shall personally or through one of his brothers or sons govern the city; he shall restore no exile; he shall allow the People to use its own laws; and the office of the Priorate shall be permitted to exist hereafter in the city as it is presently constituted. Apart from the named conditions, the king is ordinarily permitted full powers over all other matters."[13]

20   Decretum hoc electionis Iacobo et Dardano oratoribus, tunc
Neapoli commorantibus, offerendum regi transmiserunt. Rex[26]
laetus audivit recepitque. Primum regis factum non magna ex re
benevolentiam sibi civium ingentem paravit. Cum enim priores
ipsi, qui auctores nominandi deligendique regem fuerant, immunitatem sibi fratribusque et parentibus ceteraque privilegia quaedam
praeter populi scitum excepissent, rex, aliis comprobatis quae in
decreto continebantur, hoc unum ita reiecit, ut priorum ipsorum
impudentiam pravitatemque vultu et verbis detestaretur. Ex hoc
regis laus apud cives crevit tamquam[27] iusti principis, nec ad gratiam magis quam ad honestatem proclivis. Et civitatis quidem negotia sic traducebantur.

21   Imperator autem cum Bonitii esset, legati Federici, qui per id
tempus Siciliam tenebat, ad eum venerunt, novam belli materiam
afferentes, de qua paulo superius repetita dicemus. Nuper, dum
Romae esset Henricus ac permultae sibi intra urbem molestiae in-
ferrentur, societas simul et affinitas ab eo inita est cum Federico
Siciliae rege. Id quidem procuratum de industria fuerat, quo Robertum ulciscerentur regnoque spoliarent. Ea siquidem unica per-
agendi via est visa, si Federicus assumeretur socius ac tam validae
potentiae in unum coirent. Federicum vetusta Siciliae controversia
saepiusque iam tentata deiectio, inimicissimum faciebat Roberto.
Convenerat autem in eo foedere, uti proxima aestate terra mari-
que[28] Roberti regnum invaderent; cuius rei gratia pecuniae quaedam a Federico fuerant conferendae.

22   Legati igitur tunc Bonitium venientes pecunias[que][29] a rege tulerunt, ac postularunt ex foedere ut se contra Robertum praepara-
ret. Ob eorum adventum legatorum, novae subinde curae novaque

This decree of election was sent to Jacopo and Dardano, the   20
ambassadors then residing in Naples, for presentation to the king.
The king gladly heard it and accepted the election. His first act,
though no great affair, earned him much good will from the citizens. For the Priors themselves, who had been responsible for
naming and choosing the king, had extracted without the knowledge of the people an immunity for themselves and certain other
privileges for their brothers and relatives. The king approved the
other conditions of the decree, but rejected this single one in such
as way as to show by his words and countenance his detestation of
the Priors' impudence and corruption. From this act the king acquired among the citizens the reputation of a just prince who was
no less disposed to act with honor than with favor. Thus were the
affairs of the city transferred to the king.[14]

While the emperor was at Poggibonsi, legates came to him   21
from Frederick, who controlled Sicily at that time.[15] They brought
new fuel for war—but let us go back a bit to tell the story. Recently, when Henry had been at Rome and was suffering numerous troubles inside the city, he had formed an alliance and a personal bond with Frederick, King of Sicily. He had done this
purposely so as to revenge himself on Robert and despoil him of
his kingdom. Taking Frederick as his ally and combining their
powerful forces seemed the one way of accomplishing his goal.
Frederick had grown hostile in the extreme toward Robert thanks
to the ancient quarrel over Sicily and to Robert's frequent attempts to expel him. A pact was agreed to whereby the following
summer they would invade Robert's kingdom by land and sea. For
this purpose certain monies were to be contributed by Frederick.

That is why legates came to Poggibonsi at that moment bearing   22
monies from the king [of Sicily], and demanding that the emperor
prepare to attack Robert in accordance with the treaty. New concerns and quarrels immediately arose thanks to the arrival of these
legates. The emperor had numerous preparations to make and

certamina suscipiuntur. Imperator, cum multa sibi providenda forent ac eius rei[30] gratia Pisas redire statuisset, Bonitio quidem et his locis Brancham Scolarium exulem florentinum, Ancisae vero ac superioris Arni oppidis Guidonem Caprariam pisanum vicarios praefecit et gubernare populos iussit. Ipse haud multo post Pisas profectus, novas inde copias e Germania convocat; classem Genuensibus permagnam imperat. Dum haec expectat, contra Robertum regem ac Florentinos ceterasque socias civitates edicta gravissima proponit; multos etiam insignes per eam tempestatem homines ab adversariis aemulisque, ut cuique libuit, nominatos sententiis adnotat. Interea quoque, ne torperet otio, miles per praefectos eius, viros militares bellicarumque rerum gnaros, quotidiana prope proelia cum Lucensibus finitimis exercebat.

23 Ea de causa proximi anni principio Florentinorum copiae Lucam transmissae, quamdiu in his locis belligeratum est, auxilio sociis fuere. Calamitates in eo bello maximae a Lucensibus[31] acceptae sunt. Praeter continuas enim incursiones, castella insuper quaedam Lucensium expugnata ab hostibus capiuntur. Miniatensibus quoque non dissimiles inflictae clades.

24 Exercitu classeque paratis, cum tempus constitutum profectioni adesset, praemissis navibus septuaginta (tot enim sibi paraverant Genuenses) ut cum Federici classe iungerentur, ipse, Pisis movens, circiter Nonas Augusti, non satis prospera valetudine iter ingressus est; ducens per miniatensem et florentinum agrum, inde non longe a moenibus Senarum praetervectus, apud Apertum Montem, florentina clade nobilitatum locum, posuit castra. Ibi ingravescens, ad maceretanas aquas divertit. Cum nihilo relevarent aquae, rursus inde movens, ad Bonconventum castra fecit. Hoc demum in loco superante morbo, corruit ac paucis post diebus e vita migravit, in medio cursu rerum maximarum.

decided to return to Pisa for that purpose, appointing Branca Scolari, a Florentine exile, as his deputy in Poggibonsi and nearby places, and Guido Capraia, a Pisan, to be in charge of Incisa and the towns of the upper Arno and to govern their peoples. He himself set out for Pisa shortly thereafter, summoning fresh troops from Germany and demanding a huge fleet from the Genoese. While awaiting their arrival, he published severe edicts against King Robert, the Florentines and their allies. Many distinguished men of the time were proscribed on information provided at will by their enemies and rivals. At the same time his deputy commanders, military men of great experience in war, were putting his soldiers through their paces in almost daily battles with the neighboring Lucchesi, lest they grow soft.[16]

That is why, at the beginning of the following year, Florentine troops were sent to Lucca to help their allies for as long as the fighting lasted in that area. The Lucchesi suffered the greatest disasters in that war. Apart from continual incursions, certain of the Lucchese castles were besieged and captured by the enemy. Similar calamities were visited on San Miniato. 23 1313

Now Henry's army and fleet were ready, and the time fixed for the expedition had come. Sending on ahead to join Frederick's fleet the seventy ships supplied by the Genoese, he himself left Pisa about the fifth of August and set out on his journey in a state of ill health. Making his way through the territories of San Miniato and Florence, he passed not far from the walls of Siena and pitched camp at Montaperti, the place made famous by the Florentine disaster.[17] There his condition became more serious, and he turned aside to visit the baths at Macereto. When the waters failed to bring relief, he again moved on and camped at Buonconvento.[18] Here the disease overcame him and he collapsed, departing this life a few days later, in the midst of his great undertakings. 24

25   Et certe Roberto regi admodum formidatus, quippe Federici copiae iam in Regnum eius traductae, Rhegium urbem, quae contra Siciliam maxime opposita est, occupaverant. Duae insuper validissimae classes tota litora complebant; quibus, cum anxie resisti posse uideretur,[32] addito huius viri tam acris tamque obstinati adventu, in summum discrimen res adducebatur. Sed bellorum eventum nemo satis praedixerit;[33] quippe communis Mars, ut aiunt, magnique saepe terrores parvis momentis in irritum reciderunt.

26   Corpus Henrici magno suorum luctu Pisas relatum est, exercitusque omnis solutus. Classis etiam Genuensium et Federici ac iam traductae citra fretum copiae, audita imperatoris morte, domum irritae redierunt.

27   Qui cum Henrico per Etruriam conspiraverant, eos maxima de spe non minorem in metum inopinatus converterat casus. Praecipua tamen Pisanos formido[34] pervaserat, finitimis Lucensibus Florentinisque ob accepta recens detrimenta gravius irritatis. Itaque, ad curam salutis propriae conversi, ducem quaerebant, cuius ductu auspicioque imminentibus resisterent malis.

28   Uguicio erat Fagiolanus vir ea tempestate in primis acer; ad rei militaris peritiam moderatio quaedam animi et consilium ne in pace quidem aspernandum accedebat; praeterea studio partium vel Pisanis par. Hunc evocare placuit, summamque[35] rerum uni sibi committere. Suscepta igitur[36] civitatis cura, Uguicio ad octingentos equites germanos, ex iis copiis quae nuper cum Henrico militaverunt, ingentis pollicitatione mercedis ad se traduxit, ac cetera

Certainly King Robert had good reason to fear him. For Fred- 25
erick's troops had already crossed into the Kingdom and had occupied the city of Reggio, which is situated just opposite Sicily.
Moreover, two extremely powerful fleets were lining the entire
coast, and although it seemed they could with strenuous action be
resisted, the added approach of this man, so energetic and resolute, was bringing matters to a critical point. But no one can pre-
dict the outcome of wars with certainty, for Mars plays no favor-
ites, as they say,[19] and often great threats fade away in a brief
moment.[20]

Henry's body was carried to Pisa with great mourning on the 26
part of his supporters, and the whole army broke up. The fleet of
Frederick and the Genoese, too, as well as the troops that had already crossed the strait, as soon as they learned of the emperor's
death, returned home in failure.[21]

The unexpected reversal of fortune changed to fear the hopes of 27
the men who had conspired with Henry in Tuscany. In Pisa the
fear was especially pervasive, as the nearby Lucchesi and Florentines were seriously provoked owing to the losses they had recently
sustained. Beginning thus to be concerned for their own safety,
they looked for a military leader whose leadership and authority
would help them resist the evils that threatened them.

Uguccione della Faggiuola was at that time an outstandingly 28
vigorous personage.[22] In addition to his knowledge of war he possessed a commanding spirit, and his wise counsel was not to be
scorned even in times of peace; moreover, his partisan passion was
equal even to that of the Pisans. They decided to summon him
and commit the whole of their affairs to him alone. Uguccione
thus accepted responsibility for the city, and promising enormous
rewards, he brought under his command around eight hundred
knights from the forces that had lately been serving with Henry.
He also oversaw the rest of the necessary preparations with great
resourcefulness. Though previously involved in the war, he now

quae providenda erant sollertissime curavit. Inde Lucenses, bellum ipse prior occupans, sic acriter infestare coepit, ut quae ante fuerant perpessi bella, ludi plane iocique viderentur; usus belli inferendi certissima ratione, ut non semel aut iterum quotannis apparatu facto in hostem exiret (quod superioribus fere bellis fieri consueverat), sed in armis persistens, Pisis ipsis pro castris adversum Lucam propter finitimam propinquitatem uteretur.

29   Lucenses vero, eodem fere tempore quo Florentini, ius ac potestatem sui Roberto tradiderant; quae res, tamquam translata in alterum cura, multum admodum illos ad studium belligerandi reddebat segniores. Nihil denique neque enixe neque fortiter ab illis gerebatur; opem tamen ferebant socii, nec Lucensibus deerant. Verum, quid proderat ea res? Quamdiu enim maiores sociorum copiae Lucae convenerant, Uguicio se Pisis continebat quietemque de industria simulabat; ubi vero abierant, fines hostium pervadebat. Ita magnitudine tandem incommodi perturbatos, quando ceterae deerant viae, ad iniquissimam Lucenses compulit pacem; in qua multum agri et pleraque munita loca Pisanis dimiserunt, exulesque omnis diversae factionis in urbem receperunt.

30   Haec pax initio fere alterius anni ex quo Henricus decesserat firmata est, multum admodum contradicentibus Florentinis et cladem proventuram iam inde vaticinantibus. Cum ergo exules secundum pacem Lucam rediissent, quantum nunquam prius intestina[37] oritur seditio ex bonorum repetitione. Ob quae, cum ad arma tandem[38] itum esset, et intra urbem pugnaretur et alteri Florentinos, alteri Pisanos advocarent, anteveniens Uguicio ab ea parte civium qui suo beneficio redierant in urbem admittitur; quo facto, altera civium pars Luca depellitur; Germani vero et Pisani

began to attack the Lucchesi with such violence that the wars they had previously experienced seemed like mere fun and games. He employed a fixed plan for making war. Instead of equipping the army and going out against the enemy once or twice a year (which had been the practice in most earlier wars), he kept his men continuously in arms and, taking advantage of its proximity, used Pisa itself as a base against Lucca.

But the Lucchesi had handed legal authority and power over themselves to Robert at about the same time as the Florentines had, and this circumstance greatly slackened their warlike zeal, as though their affairs were now someone else's concern. In short, they performed no brave or strenuous deeds. Nevertheless, their allies aided and stood by them. But it was no use. For whenever allied forces were concentrated in Lucca, Uguccione stayed in Pisa, deliberately simulating inaction; when they went away, he would invade his enemy's borders. In the end the Lucchesi were so distressed by their great misfortunes that he compelled them to make an unfavorable peace agreement, since they had no other recourse. In this agreement they gave up to the Pisans much territory and many fortified places, and accepted back into the city all exiles of the opposing [Ghibelline] faction.[23]

This peace was ratified around the beginning of the second year after Henry's death. It was strongly opposed by the Florentines, who predicted that disaster would soon follow from it. And indeed, when the exiles returned to Lucca in accordance with the treaty, civil discord arose as never before from their demands for restitution of property. When at length the matter came to blows, and fighting broke out inside the city, one party called on the Florentines, the other summoned the Pisans. Uguccione arrived first and was admitted to the city by the party of citizens who had been restored owing to his favor, and by this means the other party was expelled from Lucca. But the Germans and Pisans who had entered with Uguccione, once they were victorious, turned to plun-

29

30

1314

qui cum Uguicione intraverant, ubi victores fuere, ad praedam conversi, totam diripuerunt urbem, nec minus amicorum bona quam inimicorum in praedam venere. Hic profecto ludus Fortunae mirificus fuit, ut Pisani, in metu ac desperatione rerum suarum, Luca potirentur, quam tot prosperis ante rebus ne sperare quidem ausi fuissent.

31   Lucenses urbe pulsi, castellis quibusdam circa Nebulam fluvium et per inferiorem Arnum occupatis, ad Florentinorum opes se totos converterant; nam regem incusare quidem haud falso licebat eiusque vel incuriam vel segnitiem carpere. Nec eos sane fefellit spes: erecta siquidem civitas ob sociorum calamitatem, suscepto confestim patrocinio, ad bellum incubuit. Prima fuit cura exules subitaneo tutari milite, ne victoris impetus uno eodemque cursu, trepidis in rebus, castella ipsa quibus sese receperant abduceret. Quare missae eo statim copiae, oppidanis simul exulibusque fecerunt animos ad oppida retinenda. Post haec ad robustiorem apparatum versi, non de repellendo solum, sed de inferendo etiam bello cogitabant. Huiusce rei caput visum est ante omnia cum rege de auxiliis agere ac ducem petere qui bello gerendo praeesset. Cum igitur ea de causa legatos ad regem misissent, permotus rex his rebus quae Lucensibus acciderant, vocibus etiam legatorum compulsus, Petrum fratrem cum equitum manu in Etruriam misit. Hic Florentiam proximo sextili ingressus est, iuvenis summa gratia et populari favore mirum in modum acceptus.

32   Cum de pisano lucensique cogitaretur bello, magna insuper formido, veluti a tergo imminens, consilia perturbabat.[39] Factio enim quae Arretium tenebat palam hostis erat partibusque adversa: et

der and despoiled the whole city, looting the goods of friends as well as enemies. Here surely was a marvelous sport of Fortune: that the Pisans, in fear and desperation for their own situation, should get control of Lucca, which they would not have dared even to hope for earlier, when their affairs had been so prosperous.[24]

Expelled from their city, the Lucchesi [exiles] occupied certain castles around Valdinievole and in the lower Arno region, and depended entirely on the Florentines for help — and indeed they had some right to reproach the king and criticize him for either his lack of oversight or of energy. But they were not deceived in their expectations, for Florence was galvanized by her ally's calamity, and immediately took on the protection of Lucchese interests. They began to hatch plans for war. Their first concern was to scrape together a force to protect the exiles, lest the victor's momentum continue in its onrush and overpower the castles where the men had taken refuge in their fright. The prompt reinforcements gave the townsmen and the exiles the heart to hold onto their towns. Then the Florentines turned their thoughts to building a stronger war-machine, with the intention of prosecuting not only a defensive war, but also an offensive one. The nub of the matter seemed to involve negotiating with the king for help and finding a military leader. So they sent envoys to the king. King Robert, shaken by the fate of the Lucchesi and urged on by the Florentines' speeches as well, sent his brother Peter with a force of cavalry into Tuscany. Peter entered Florence the following August. He was a well-favored youth who was welcomed with extraordinary popular enthusiasm. 31

While he was planning the war against Pisa and Lucca, another great threat, coming as it were from behind, disturbed his counsels. For the faction controlling Arezzo was openly hostile, being of the Ghibelline party. It had caused trouble before Henry's coming, and afterwards had unambiguously taken his side. In short, 32

lacessitam ante Henrici adventum et postea cum illo sensisse non ambiguum erat. Denique Arretinorum et Lucensium ratio par atque eadem esse videbatur. In utraque enim civitate hostes dominabantur; socii vero et amici et earundem sectatores partium exulabant. Illud modo intererat, quod Lucensium recentior erat clades, graviorque ab ea parte hostis Uguicio cum Pisanis imminebat.[40] Itaque, ne bellum arretinum eo conversos intentosque impediret,[41] studia paci adhibere placuit. Quod quidem negotium Petrus regis frater primum fere omnium in Etruria suscepit perfecitque tandem, iniqua licet exulibus conditione, sed tamen eo tempore necessaria.

33 In foedere conventa haec fuerunt: uti Roberto regi gubernatio dominatusque Arretii in quinquennium traderetur, ea tamen exceptione, ne quos exules reducere neve arcem aedificare aut praesidium habere in illa posset; publici reditus civitatis forent, nec ex his quicquam regi poscere capereve liceret; civitas quaterna auri millia singulos in annos[42] regi daret; ipse protegeret bello, in paceque[43] tutaretur. Per hoc foedus, nomen tantum et pecunias rex suscipiebat; gubernatio autem civitatis illis ipsis qui primo tenuerant relinquebatur. Quin etiam deligendi magistratus curam ac potestatem Guidoni praesuli Arretinorum, e familia principe eius factionis, ac Gerio Spinae equiti florentino rex ex foedere permisit. Hi, quamdiu regia duravit potestas, magistratum in annos singulos, Arretinis qui praeforet, regio nomine delegerent.[44]

34 Post foedus cum Arretinis ictum, universa quae per superiorem Arnum sub Henrici adventum rebellaverant, praecisa resistendi spe, ad Florentinos rediere. Ita quietis omnibus ab Arretinis, pisanum dumtaxat bellum restabat.

35 Dum haec a Florentinis regeque providentur, Uguicio nihil intentatum adversus hostes relinquebat. Post captam enim direp-

the Aretine and Lucchesi problem seemed to be one and the same. Enemies were in command of both cities, while friends and allies and their party followers were in exile. The only difference was that the Lucchese disaster was the more recent, and the threat from the direction of the warlike Uguccione and his Pisans was the more grave. So, to keep from being encumbered with an Aretine war while their attention was turned west, it was decided to make an effort to achieve peace. And that is what the king's brother Peter undertook to do and in due course accomplished as almost his first order of business in Tuscany. It was unfair to the exiles, but nevertheless imperative at that moment.

The terms of the treaty were as follows. Governance and lord- 33
ship over Arezzo would be handed over to King Robert for a five-year period, with the stipulations that he could not restore any exiles, nor build a citadel nor have any fort in the city. The public revenue would belong to the city, nor was the king allowed to request or seize any part of it. The city would give the king four thousand gold pieces each year, and he would protect it in war and guard it in peace. By this treaty the king received money and a nominal lordship only; the governance of the city was left in the hands of the same persons who had controlled it before. Indeed, by treaty the king turned over the responsibility and power of choosing magistrates to Guido, bishop of Arezzo, from a leading Ghibelline family, and to Geri Spini, a Florentine knight.[25] These men were each year to choose in the king's name a magistracy to preside over the Aretines for as long as the royal power was in force.[26]

After the treaty with the Aretines was signed, all the towns of 34
the upper Arno that had rebelled at Henry's coming returned to Florentine control, their hope of resistance cut off. Thus all was quiet on the Aretine front, and there remained only the Pisan war.

While the Florentines and the king were taking care of these 35
matters, Uguccione was leaving nothing untried against his ene-

tamque Lucam terribilior inde factus, oppidis quibus se receperant exules infesto quotidie impetu pervadens, nec requiem nec cessationem ullam dabat. Inde mox in alios atque alios traductis copiis, Pistorienses, Miniatenses, Volaterranos omnifariam belli cladibus atterebat. Tandem, maiori vi Catinum adortus, frequentia circum illud praesidia communivit. Ipse vero, modo praesens obsidionem urgebat, modo relictis praesidiis cum parte copiarum agros hostium pervadebat, ut simul obsidere, simul bellum alibi gerere, nec ullis deesse locis videretur.

36   Durante apud Catinum obsidione, cum obsessi magis in dies premerentur, Philippus, alter Roberti regis frater, proxima dehinc aestate Florentiam venit; cuius adventu sublatis laetitia animis, copias undequaque contrahere ac ad obsessos liberandum ire placuit. At Uguicio, audita vi quae contra se parabatur, copiis non modo suis omnibus, verum etiam amicorum impigre contractis, ad Catinum obstinatius consedit. Florentini igitur et socii circiter Nonas sextiles Florentia profecti ad hostem contenderunt. Ducebat autem Philippus[45] regis frater. Erat quoque in exercitu Petrus alter frater,[46] quem primo Florentiam a rege missum ostendimus, sed quoniam is minor erat natu, summa rei apud Philippum habebatur.

37   Transgressi pistoriensem agrum finesque Lucensium ingressi, postquam in conspectu venerunt hostium, castra non longe ab illorum castris posuere. Uguicio munitionibus suos continebat, satis pro gloria existimans, si contra tantos conatus, invitis adversariis, in obsidione perstaret. Itaque levia modo proelia inter utraque castra per singulos ferme dies committebantur, ad totius vero pugnae

mies. Indeed, the capture and sack of Lucca had made him a terrifying figure, and he made daily strikes against the towns where the exiles had taken refuge, giving them neither rest nor respite. Soon, marching his troops against more and more peoples, he wore down Pistoia, San Miniato and Volterra with warlike devastation of every kind. Finally, he assaulted Montecatini with still greater force, surrounding it with a system of forts. Sometimes he would be present personally to press the siege, at other times he would leave the forts behind and invade enemy territories with a part of his forces. Thus he simultaneously laid siege to Montecatini and made war in other places as well. He seemed to be everywhere.[27]

While Montecatini was under siege, and pressure on the besieged was increasing day by day, Philip, another son of King Robert, came, arriving the following summer. His coming raised spirits and was greeted with joy. He decided to collect the scattered troops and go out to relieve the siege. But Uguccione came to hear of the forces being arrayed against him and with great vigor not only pulled together his own forces but also those of his friends, stubbornly maintaining the siege. So the Florentines and their allies set out from Florence around the fifth of August to engage the enemy. The king's brother Philip was in command. His brother Peter was also in the army (the king had sent him to Florence first, as we showed), but since the latter was the younger man, Philip took general command of the expedition.

They crossed Pistoian territory and entered the borders of Lucca. Once in sight of the enemy, they pitched camp not far from his encampment. Uguccione kept his troops inside their forts, believing honor was satisfied by maintaining the siege against the will of his enemies, in the face of so powerful a thrust. Hence there were skirmishes nearly every day between the two camps, but the outcome never came down to a pitched battle. When they had kept at it in this way for several days, Uguccione decided to shift his position back towards Lucca. He was led to this step by

36

1315

37

non descendebatur discrimen. Cum aliquot dies in hunc modum perstitissent, Uguicio, commotus suspicione rerum novarum, quae Lucae per eius absentiam suscitari nunciabantur, castra retro movere constituit, si posset, quieto hoste, sine pugna; sin impediretur, fortunam proelii tentaturus. Structa itaque per noctem acie, primam sub lucem, incensis tabernaculis, movere signa iterque ingredi coepit; quod simul atque e castris Florentinorum animadversum est, confestim rumor attollitur et fugere hostis conclamatur, totis denique castris repente consurgitur.

38   Cum ex hoc palam esset absque pugna abire nequaquam ei licere, Uguicio, versis repente signis, castra ferociter invadit. Senenses et Collenses ab ea parte stationem habebant. In hos, nondum satis paratos prima hostium delata acies, turbavit late ac terga dare protinus coegit; inde, munitiones transgressa, ad intimas castrorum partes dimicando pervenit. Cum totis fluctuaretur castris, Uguicio in perturbatos Germanorum equitatum immittit; ipse cum cetera multitudine subsecutus premebat. A Florentinis primo quidem concursu egregie pugnatum est. Quamquam enim subita res nec struendae aciei, nec alloquendi militem dabat facultatem, tamen ad eam partem qua maior erat tumultus concurrentes, primam hostium aciem quae avidius insecuta fuerat[47] totam paene obruerunt. Sed postquam germanorum equitum procella supervenit, prostratus fortissimus quisque aut vulneratus, patefacere aditum hostibus[48] coepit. Uguicio[49] ipse quadrato agmine sequebatur, nullumque aut se colligendi spatium aut reparandi certaminis dabat. Ita post multam caedem fuga passim fieri coepta. Ceciderunt in ea pugna Florentinorum sociorumque supra duo millia, et cum his Petrus, regis frater, Carolusque Philippi filius; praeterea ex nobilitate florentina optimus quisque fortissimusque oppetiit.

reports of revolutionary agitation taking place in that city owing to his absence. If it were possible, and the enemy kept quiet, he would fall back without fighting. If they offered resistance, he would try the fortunes of battle. So he drew up his order of battle by night. At dawn he burned his tents and began to advance the standards and march on his way. As soon as this was noticed in the Florentine camps, a clamor immediately went up, there was shouting that the enemy was in flight, and in short the whole camp was quickly aroused.[28]

The uproar made it evident that he would not be allowed to get away without fighting, so Uguccione suddenly reversed his standards and fiercely attacked the camp. The men of Siena and Colle were stationed on that side. The first rank of the enemy came down upon them before they had a chance to get ready and scattered them, forcing them immediately to flee. Having passed the defense-works, the enemy forces fought their way to the very center of the encampment. When the whole camp was in turmoil, Uguccione sent his German cavalry against the confused mass of men, while he himself pressed on behind with the rest of the multitude. The Florentines fought with distinction against the first wave. Although the suddenness of the affair had given them no opportunity to form ranks or address the troops, nevertheless they ran to the place where the uproar was greatest and nearly crushed the first rank of the enemy which had been racing eagerly forward. But after the German knights stormed up, the strongest among the Florentines was either knocked over or wounded, and they began to let the enemy through. Uguccione himself followed in a squared-off formation, giving them no opportunity to pull together and get back in the fight. Thus after much slaughter, scattered flights began. More than two thousand Florentines fell in this battle, including Peter, the king's brother, and Charles, son of Philip, and all the best and bravest of the Florentine nobility met their end besides.

33

39   Ceteri dissipatim, ut quemque casus tulit, aufugerunt; multi etiam in ipsa fuga proximis paludibus mersi periere. Philippus, amisso fratre ac filio, inter fugientes evasit, quoniam febri ea die oppressus nec se proelio miscuerat, nec ullum praestiterat ducis officium. Uguicioni quoque non incruenta fuit victoria; nam et Franciscus eius filius qui antesignanis praefuerat in hoc proelio interfectus est, et tota ferme acies prima oppressa.

40   Post hoc proelium qui obsidebantur desperatis iam rebus Catinum victori dediderunt. Funestata proelio adverso civitas, non tam ipsa providebat quam regem intuebatur, sperans illum pro tanto suorum luctu ad ultionem properaturum. Rex autem, sive sapientia sive mollitie quadam, non satis pro voluntate hominum movebatur. Itaque non deerant iam qui carpere palam regem insectarique auderent; denique et culpa suorum ducum acceptam cladem et alium quaerendum principem robustioris animi praedicabant.

41   Quam indignationem paulo post maiorem in modum adauxit Novelli cuiusdam adventus, quem rex praeficiendum bello in Etruriam misit, parvo admodum comitatu, ac, in tanta clade regiae domus, contemnendo. Igitur, principio insequentis anni, crescente in regem odio, Novellum remiserunt, quatuor fere mensibus postquam Florentiam venerat, et dux alter ac princeps quaerebatur. Erant qui Philippum Caroli Valosiani filium e Gallia vocandum; erant etiam qui regem non alienandum, nec post effusum suorum sanguinem ingrate repudiandum censerent. Ex his contentionibus inter cives agitatis, factiones duae resultarunt: una regii fautrix nominis, altera adversatrix; quibus certantibus inter sese, nulla ad bellum adhibebatur provisio.

The rest scattered and fled as chance directed, and many also   39
perished in their flight, drowning in the nearby swamps. Philip,
having lost his brother and his son, got away among the fugitives;
he was suffering from a fever that day and did not take part in the
battle or serve as commander. Nor was it a bloodless victory for
Uguccione, for his son Francesco who had led the skirmishers was
killed in this battle, and almost the whole of his front rank had
been crushed.[29]

After this battle the beseiged, their position now hopeless, sur-   40
rendered Montecatini to the victor. The defeat cast Florence into a
state of mourning, and she looked less to her own resources than
to the king, hoping that, in grief for his own losses, he would has-
ten to take revenge. But he, whether from wisdom or some soft-
ness of character, did not respond as men would have liked. Thus
there were some who dared openly to reproach and criticize the
king, and even declared that the disaster was the fault of his commanders and that they should find themselves another prince of
more robust temperament.

Shortly thereafter, the coming of a certain Novello greatly in-   41
creased their sense of outrage.[30] The king had put him in charge
of the Tuscan war, but with a rather small retinue, and — in view
of the great disaster the royal house had suffered — a contemptible
one. Thus at the beginning of the following year, in growing ha-   1316
tred of the king, they sent Novello back, about four months after his arrival in Florence, and began looking for a new commander and prince. Some thought they should summon from
France Philip, son of Charles Valois; others felt that King Robert
should not be alienated or ungratefully repudiated after the blood
of his own family had been spilt. Out of these quarrels among the
citizens, two factions emerged, one which supported the king, another which opposed him. Thanks to these internal struggles, no
provision was made for the war.[31]

42   Ceterum in hisce malis unica fuit salus: apud hostes quoque coorta dissentio. Pisani siquidem Uguicionis magnitudinem post victoriam metuentes, de abiiciendo illius iugo, securi iam ab hoste,
cogitabant. Ea res ab illo cognita, effecit ut ipse quoque ab hostium persecutione mentem atque animum in cives converteret.
Iamque praestantiores quidam Pisanorum, ab eo proditionis in-
simulati supplicioque affecti, perierant; ceteri vero, perculsi metu,
illius dominatum supportabant inviti. Ipse vero exire in hostem Pisanosque sine praesidio relinquere non satis audebat. Id respiratio-
nem requiemque[50] belli Florentinis dedit, magisque in ea re fortunae beneficio quam ulla proprii consilii providentia fruebantur.

43   Neque vero Fagiolani res, ut cetera violenta, diuturnae fuerunt;
post longas enim suspitiones, tandem Pisis Lucaque simul excidit.
Castrucius erat iuvenis apprime nobilis in ea factione quae nuper,
beneficio ipsius,[51] Lucam redierat, manu audaciaque primarius; aetas ac generis favor sublimem reddebant. Hunc caedem rapinasque
lunensi in agro molitum Nerius Fagiolanus capi iusserat, tru-
susque in carcere pro admissis supplicium expectabat. Id vero Lucenses usque adeo graviter ferre videbantur, ut appareret nunquam
supplicium huius hominis perpessuros. Iam conventiculae coe-
tusque tota urbe agebantur. Cum ea res non dubie ad rebellionem
spectaret, Nerius, ad patrem re celeriter delata, provideri monuit.

44   Quo nuntio excitus Uguicio, confestim cum equitatu Pisis
egressus Lucam versus ire contendit, ea mente ut, poena de reo
sumpta decussisque rerum novarum auctoribus, Pisas e vestigio
remigraret. At Pisani, postquam egressum viderunt, optatam occasionem nacti, corripiunt statim arma, portas claudunt, aedes ac fa-

But one thing saved them in the midst of these evils: that dis- 42
sension had arisen amongst the enemy too. For the Pisans were
afraid of Uguccione's greatness after his victory, and being now
safe from their enemies, they considered how they might throw off
his yoke. Learning of this plot made Uguccione himself also turn
his mind and heart from pursuit of the enemy to the Pisan citizenry. Already, certain leading Pisans had perished, having been
charged by him with treason and executed, while the rest, striken
with fear, unwillingly bore his lordship. But he himself did not
dare go out against the enemy and leave the Pisans without a garrison. That circumstance gave the Florentines rest and respite
from the war. In this they profited more from fortune's favor than
from any foresight or counsel of their own.

But the Faggiuola affair, like other bloody incidents, did not last 43
long, for after a long period of mistrust, he finally lost both Pisa
and Lucca at the same time. There was a youth from the high nobility called Castruccio who belonged to the faction recently restored to Lucca through Uguccione's favor.[32] He returned to Lucca
where he was first in deeds and daring; his age and family influence gave him eminence. Neri della Faggiuola ordered him seized
for plotting slaughter and plunder in the Lunigiana, and he was
thrown into prison for his offenses, awaiting punishment. But the
Lucchesi were so offended at this that it was obvious they would
never allow the man to be punished. The whole city at that point
was seething with secret meetings and plots. Since the matter defi-
nitely looked as though it would lead to rebellion, Neri quickly informed his father, warning him to look out.

Uguccione was stirred to activity by the news, and leaving Pisa 44
immediately with his cavalry, he headed to Lucca. His plan was to
punish the guilty party and put down the leaders of the revolt,
then immediately return to Pisa. But the Pisans, observing his departure, snatched the hoped-for opportunity. At once they fell to
arms, shut the gates, and attacked Uguccione's house and family

miliam eius igne ferroque adoriuntur. Advolat pisanae defectionis fama ad Lucenses: corripiunt et illi arma, aedes communiunt, impedimenta per vias iactant. Haec eo intentius agunt, quod illum in suam perniciem intelligebant venisse. Quibus tandem conterritus Fagiolanus, cum a tergo et a fronte praeclusus, nullam obtinendi spem superesse videret, recepto modo filio, in lunensem abiit agrum.

45   Triennio fere Pisanis Uguicio praefuit. In hoc brevi tempore multis ac praeclaris rebus gestis, ad extremum, tamquam fortunae ludo iactatus, una atque eadem die utriusque civitatis imperium amisit.

46   Proximo dehinc anno Pisani, legatione ad regem missa, fratris ac nepotis casum suppliciter deplorarunt, culpam omnem facti in Fagiolanum referentes: se quidem ab initio, sui tutandi causa, quod fas et iura permittunt,[52] illum sibi praefecisse, atque eo usque illius imperio laetatos, donec, icto cum Lucensibus foedere, se ab illorum iniuriis vindicassent; quidquid posthac accesserit, id quidem Fagiolani iam esse, non Pisanorum; hominem durum atque saevum lites ex litibus, certamina ex certaminibus serentem, nihil de pisani commoditate populi, plurimum de propria tyrannide cogitasse; quod Luca direpta fuerit, quod amici regis pulsi, eiusdem facis atque incendii esse; implicatum deinde ab illo de industria bellum obsidione Catini, et crebra in Pistorienses Volaterranosque incursione; facta eius viri quam sibi displicuissent exitum docere, quod non prius se quieturos putassent quam, raptis contra illum armis, urbe pepulissent; obsecrare, ut iram, si qua forte regium in pectus ea ob facta altius descenderit,[53] cognita veritate leniret; Pi-

with fire and sword. Reports of the Pisan defection flew to Lucca, and they too seized arms, fortified their houses, and threw up barricades in the streets. They did this the more strenuously as they recognized that Uguccione was finished. Finally Faggiuola took fright at these developments. Seeing that his position was hopeless, as he was cut off in front and behind, he left for the Lunigiana, pausing only to recover his son.

Uguccione ruled Pisa for almost three years. In that brief time   45 he performed many famous deeds, but in the end, as though by a throw of Fortune's dice, he lost control of both cities on one and the same day.[33]

The following year the Pisans sent a legation to the king which   46 in an attitude of humble entreaty lamented the loss of his brother and nephew, blaming everything on Faggiuola. For their part (they   1317 said) they had from the beginning made him their leader in self-defense, as right and law permitted, and they had been pleased with his command up to the point where they had signed the treaty with Lucca and avenged themselves for the injuries suffered at Lucchese hands. Whatever had happened after that was Faggiuola's fault, not the Pisans'. He was a hard and ferocious man who sowed quarrels from quarrels and fights from fights. He had given no thought to the good of the Pisan people, but had regard only for his own tyranny. That he had seized Lucca and expelled the king's friends were matters of his own brand and burning. Then he had deliberately involved them in the war to besiege Montecatini and to raid Pistoia and Volterra. How much this man's deeds had displeased them might be learned from the outcome, for no sooner had they believed themselves to be on the point of achieving peace than they had taken up arms against him and expelled him from the city. They beseeched the king, now that he had learned the truth, to soften his wrath, if perchance some had lodged deep in the royal breast owing to these events. The Pisans asked that he would grant them peace, now that the

sanisque rogantibus, pulso tandem tyranno, malorum omnium turbarumque auctore, pacem daret.

47   Hac oratione regem, nec prius quidem asperum, ad pacem flexerunt. Conditiones dictae: ut captivi omnes Florentinorum sociorumque dimitterentur; immunitatem, uti[54] prima in pace convenerat, Florentinus Pisis haberet. Lucensibus quoque iisdem conditionibus pax data: illud modo additum in foedere, uti castella omnia Lucensium quae exules tenebant, illis ipsis quorum in manibus erant remanerent. Pax fere ab omnibus improbata est, ut a rege mollioris animi contra decus sui nominis concessa; sed praesertim Florentinis molesta fuit, cupientibus catinensem ignominiam ulcisci. Verum, ne regiae auctoritati derogare viderentur, aegre ad extremum ratam habuere.

48   Eodem anno constitutum est ut qui in expeditionem proficiscerentur equites, haec arma deferrent: calvariam galeamque insuper cristatam, thoracem, manicas, femoralia, ocreas, omnia ex ferro. Hoc ex eo provisum, quia levis armatura multis nocumento fuisse superiori adverso proelio videbatur.

49   Per hoc tempus gratia Roberti regis ob varias incusationes Florentiae vacillans, opera maxime unius praefecti redintegrata est: post indignationes enim superiori tempore coortas, rex Guidonem comitem urbi praefecit. Is, quoniam finitimus ac paene civis, nec solum morbos civium, sed causas etiam originesque cognorat, ad pacandam civitatem animum intendit. Supra quinquaginta capitales inimicitiae familiarum ex nobilitate plebeque in civitate vigebant: quae omnes, per huius providentiam, adiuvante republica,

tyrant, the source of all evils and disturbances, had at last been thrown out.

This oration inclined the king towards peace, who even before 47
it had not indeed been bitter. It was stipulated that all Florentine and allied prisoners should be released, and that Florentine citizens in Pisa should enjoy immunity, as had been agreed in the first peace treaty. The Lucchesi were granted a peace on the same conditions, with the further stipulation that all Lucchese castles being held by the exiles should remain in exile hands. The peace was condemned by nearly everyone as a concession on the part of a weak king, one that dishonored his name. But it was particularly distressing to the Florentines, desirous as they were of avenging their ignominious defeat at Montecatini. But so as not to seem to derogate from the royal authority, in the end they grudgingly ratified it.

In the same year it was ordained that knights setting out on an 48
expedition should bear the following arms: a cervèllaire, a crested helmet, a cuirass, greaves, and armor on the arms and legs, all of iron. This provision was made because it appeared that light armoring had been a source of harm to many men in the late unhappy battle.

Around this time, good will towards King Robert, which had 49
wavered owing to the various charges made against him in Florence, was restored, thanks most of all to the efforts of a single royal deputy. For after the angry reactions that had he had previously aroused, the king put Count Guido[34] in charge of the city. He, being a neighbor and practically a citizen, understood not only the diseases of the citizens, but also their origins and causes, and put his mind to pacifying the city. More than fifty deadly feuds were raging in the city amongst families of nobles and commoners. With the help of the state and his own foresight, these were all suppressed. Arms were laid down as though peace had come after war. These private acts of friendly reconciliation among

sublatae sunt, et, quasi ex bello pax esset, arma deposita. Has privatas civium amicitias mox publica insuper consensio secuta est, cum omnis ante dissensio in republica ex privatis simultatibus oriretur. Itaque tranquilla omnia publice privatimque huius praecipue diligentia effecit. Nihil est tam hebes quod non beneficentia moveatur. Civitas enim nuper infensa, beneficio praefecti rursus in regem conversa est; et qui paulo ante de abrogando imperio ante finitum tempus cogitabant, repente mutati, in triennium prorogarunt.

50   Eodem anno, Cremonensium exulibus tradita auxilia sunt a civitate, et Parmensibus subsidia quaedam missa, quo adversariis resisterent.

51   Altero post hunc anno neque domi neque foris gestum quicquam memoria dignum reperio, praeterquam quod missa regi auxilia sunt, tunc Genuae commoranti. Genuensibus enim nuper civili discidio agitatis, alterius factionis homines armis praevalidi adversarios expulerant, ac in regis manus se urbemque tradiderant. Pulsi vero contra[55] ad suarum partium fautores per Galliam et Liguriam confugientes, vi redire in urbem conabantur. Id certamen regem eo traxerat, praesensque ipse bellum administrabat. Missa igitur tunc his de causis Florentinorum sociorumque auxilia, regi multis in locis usui fuere. Contentio autem ita crevit, ut non Ligures modo, sed tota cis Alpis[56] Gallia studio partium scinderetur, ac Etruria, mox eundem secuta motum, bella gravissima integraret. Admiscuit se quoque his certaminibus Iohannes pontifex romanus, qui, cum regi suisque faveret, litem antiquam contra fautores imperii renovavit.

52   Cum igitur tamquam incendium quoddam dilataretur bellum ac Genuae simul et per Galliam certaretur, Florentini vero magna

the citizens led as well to public consensus, since all the previous dissension in the state had arisen from private feuds. Hence, Guido's exertions brought about universal tranquillity, public and private. There is nothing so inert that it may not be moved by good deeds. Indeed the city, which had lately been hostile to him, turned once again to Robert, thanks to the good offices of his deputy. And those who shortly before were thinking of ways to terminate his powers before the appointed time suddenly changed their minds and extended it for three years.[35]

In the same year, the city gave help to exiles from Cremona, 50 and subsidies were sent to the citizens of Parma so that they might resist their adversaries.

For the next year after that I find no deeds done at home or 51 abroad worth recording, except that reinforcements were sent to 1318 the king, who was then dwelling in Genoa. That city had lately been disturbed by civil discord. The men of the faction that was the stronger in arms had expelled their adversaries and surrendered themselves and the city into the hands of the king. Those who had been expelled, on the other hand, fled to the supporters of their party in Gaul and Liguria, and tried to reenter the city by force. That struggle had brought the king thither, and he was prosecuting the war himself, in person. That is why the Florentines and their allies sent reinforcements at that time, which were of use to the king in many places. The struggle grew to the point where not only Liguria, but also all of Cisalpine Gaul was riven with partisanship, and its momentum soon spread to Tuscany, where fierce wars were resumed.[36] John, the Roman pontiff, also involved himself in these struggles.[37] Being favorable to the king and his supporters, he renewed his ancient quarrel with the supporters of the empire.

Thus the war began to spread like fire and there was fighting si- 52 multaneously in Genoa and throughout Gaul. The Florentines sent large reinforcements there. To check the Florentine forces,

eo auxilia submisissent, ad impediendam eam manum, adversarii Castrucium (is enim post eiectum Fagiolanum Lucae dominabatur) excitarunt, magnisque pellexerunt praemiis, uti rupto foedere bellum adversus Florentinos in Etruria suscitaret. Castrucius ergo, biennio fere[57] post pacem, nulla ipse prius[58] lacessitus iniuria, infesto agmine florentinum agrum ingressus, Emporium usque populabundus pervenit et quaedam munita loca improviso cepit impetu. Ob hunc tumultum, mille equites nuper a Florentinis in Galliam missi domum confestim revocati sunt.

53   Auxit quoque in Etruria suspicionem, quod Guido praesul Arretinorum, per factionem sublevatus, Arretii susceperat dominatum. Is erat vir egregius quidem, sed e familia diversarum partium ac maxime florentino nomini adversa. Itaque, huius sublevatio ab iisdem impulsoribus quibus et[59] castrucianum bellum fluxisse credebatur.

54   Castrucius, cum e Gallia Florentinorum equites opera maxime sua revocatos gauderet, quo potentiam magis audaciamque ostentaret suis, coacto exercitu, Genuam versus ducere coepit, ut non solum detractione hostilium copiarum, verum etiam sui praesentia partibus opitularetur. Florentini autem, quo vice versa illum revocarent, haud multo post eius profectionem[60] fines Lucensium ingressi, magno tumultu Lucam circumsederunt; quo tandem metu, Castrucius retro respicere copiasque reducere e vestigio compulsus est. Sed Florentini, ubi hostem ex reditu appropinquare senserunt, populato infestius agro, Fucetium se recepere. Castrucius vero, simul atque reversus est, ad eos duxit, nullam confligendi moram, si per illos liceret, facturus. Sed neque propositum fuerat pugna decernere Florentinis, neque eam ob rem ingressi fuerant hostium agrum, sed ob revocandum hostis iter; quod iam plane assecuti cum essent, nil aliud in praesentia flagitabant.

their adversaries stirred up Castruccio (who was lord of Lucca after the expulsion of Faggiuola) and offered him vast rewards if he would break the treaty and provoke a war against the Florentines in Tuscany. Hence Castruccio, just two years after the peace treaty and having suffered no prior injury, invaded Florentine territory with an offensive force, bringing devastation as far as Empoli and seizing certain fortified places in a surprise attack. Owing to this uproar a thousand knights the Florentines had recently sent to Gaul were hastily recalled. [38]

1320

Apprehension in Tuscany also grew because Guido, the bishop of Arezzo, had been raised up by a faction to take over the lordship of Arezzo. He was a distinguished man, but from a Ghibelline family and extremely hostile to the Florentine name. Thus his elevation was believed to be the work of the same forces that were behind the war with Castruccio.

53

The lord of Lucca, delighted that the Florentine knights had been recalled from Gaul through his efforts, mustered his army and began to lead them towards Genoa, so as to give his party still more proof of his power and audacity. He would help them not only by diminishing the number of their enemies, but also by his personal presence. The Florentines, however, to force his return, entered Lucchese territory shortly after his departure and with great uproar surrounded Lucca. At this threat, Castruccio was compelled to look over his shoulder and bring his troops back immediately. But the Florentines, when they learned the enemy had returned and was approaching, aggressively devastated Lucchese territory and took refuge in Fucecchio. Castruccio marched out towards them as soon as he returned, and would have engaged them immediately if they had allowed it. But it was not the Florentines' purpose to have a decisive battle; that was not why they had invaded their enemies' territory. They had done it to force his return, and having achieved that, they sought nothing else for the moment. [39]

54

55   Diu[61] in his locis uterque exercitus constitit, cum palus tantum, nec ea quidem lata, dirimeret castra, tandem irrita expectatione, sine proelio est digressum, ea tamen opinione hominum, ut in congressu ipso collationeque castrorum hostis superior haberetur, nec tantum copiarum multitudine, quantum audacia et decertandi cupiditate. Tunc igitur, non prospera satis fama cum digressum foret ab hoste, Florentini, quo id emendarent, bello valentius incumbentes, bifariam adoriri statuerunt, rati per hunc modum facilius domitari hostis audaciam posse, si duplici bello idem sub tempus distraheretur.

56   Quamobrem proxima aestate partem copiarum lunensem in agrum misere ad Spinettam principem eius regionis, qui a Castrucio per superiora vexatus tempora et castellis possessionibusque exutus, armis sua repetebat. Cum hoc igitur icto foedere, partem copiarum ad eum misere. Ipsi vero, cum reliquis copiis alia ex parte profecti, agrum lucensem ingrediuntur, et ad Victolinum castrametati, obsidere id castrum[62] perrexerunt. Et praemissa quidem in agrum lunensem[63] manus, cum sese sociis coniunxisset, hosti permagna intulit detrimenta, cunctaque prius in his locis recuperavit amissa: Victolinum autem obsidebatur infeste.

57   At Castrucius, quamquam bipartito adoriretur hostis,[64] non ea de causa se quoque distrahendum putavit, neque sese suasque vires sciscidit;[65] sed coactis in unum copiis ad Victolinum duxit, certissimo pugnandi animo, si hostis non detrectaret. Nostri, cognito Castruci adventu, quia longe praestare equitatu intelligebant,

Both armies remained fixed in their positions for some time, al- 55
though only a swamp, and not a large one, separated the two
camps. Finally, disappointing expectations, they departed without
a battle, though the general opinion was that the enemy had had
the best of it in that encounter, not so much from superior forces
as from his greater audacity and readiness to fight. Then the Florentines, to counteract the unfavorable reputation they had acquired by retreating before their enemy, formulated a more vigorous war plan. They decided to attack on two fronts. They believed
that in this way they could more easily tame the enemy's audacity,
distracting him by two wars at the same time.

Hence the following summer they sent part of their forces into 56
the Lunigiana to Spinetta, the lord of that region,[40] who at some 1321
earlier point had been harrassed by Castruccio and stripped of his
castles and possessions, and was trying to recover them by force of
arms. The Florentines therefore made a pact with him and sent
him part of their forces. They themselves with the rest of their
troops set out from the other direction and entered Lucchese territory. They pitched camp by Montevettolino, aiming to besiege that
castle. The force sent ahead into the Lunigiana, joined with its allies, caused enormous damage to the enemy, and recovered everything that had earlier been lost in that region. Montevettolino was
besieged aggressively.

But Castruccio, though set upon by a double enemy, did not 57
for that reason think that he too should separate his forces or divide them in parts. Rather, he collected his forces together and
marched out to Montevettolino with the fixed intention of fighting, if his enemy did not withdraw. Learning of his advance, our
forces recognized the great superiority of his cavalry, and fearing
lest their supply-lines should be cut off, they abandoned the siege
of Montevettolino and withdrew their army, taking refuge within
their own borders. The enemy immediately set out after them.
When he had moved his army right up to theirs and with arrogant

veriti ne commeatus intercluderentur, deserta Victolini obsidione retro moverunt castra et se suis finibus receperunt. Hos e vestigio secutus hostis, cum castra castris admovisset pugnamque iactantius flagitaret, simulata pugnandi in posterum voluntate apparatibusque ad speciem factis, per mediam noctem, frustrati hostem, Fucetium se incolumes receperunt copiasque omnes intra oppidum induxerunt. Eo quoque Castrucius secutus, aciem ante oppidum struxit et classica in conspectu occinere fecit; demum, quia pellicere[66] ad pugnam nequibat, omnia circa oppidum igne ferroque populatus est. Inde, in cetera Florentinorum sociorumque conversus loca, terribilis imminebat. Ob id, revocatae e lunensi agro copiae redierunt, et castella ibi de hoste capta post recessum earum pari facilitate Castrucius recuperavit. Ita, conatus civitatis ad bellum eo anno adhibiti, contra quam creditum est, ad extremum reciderunt; nam nec lunensi in agro quicquam profectum est, et ad Victolinum ceterisque locis, ubi maiores copiae fuerunt, longe superior quam unquam hostis apparuit.

58   Eodem anno magnitudine belli commota civitas duodecim viros primum creavit, qui prioribus in consilio adessent, cum illi haud satis sufficere tantae rerum moli viderentur. Creatus est autem is magistratus anno vigesimo primo supra millesimum trecentesimum; idque postea[67] in republica servatum[68] est. Turres etiam quaedam et murorum partes eo anno perfectae.

59   Proximo dehinc anno, Pistorienses, assiduis belli calamitatibus a Castrucio vexati, pacem cum illo fecerunt, antiqua Florentinorum societate deserta. Ad quam impediendam cum frequentes legati a Florentinis mitterentur, pervicit falsa utilitatis ratio, ut quieti potius quam honestati consulerent.

60   Per idem fere tempus, rumor fuit Castrucium partem copiarum per agrum senensem Arretium transmittere. Et simul apud Senen-

ostentation challenged them to battle, the Florentines pretended
they were willing to fight the next day and drew up their formations so as to give that impression. But this was a trick, for they
took refuge in the middle of the night in Fucecchio and marched
all their forces inside that town. Castruccio pursued them there,
too, formed ranks in front of the town, and caused the trumpets
to be sounded in full view. Finally, unable to induce them to give
battle, he devastated everything near the town with fire and sword.
Then he turned to other places belonging to the Florentines and
their allies and terrorized them. On this account the Florentines
recalled their troops from the Lunigiana, and after their departure
Castruccio recovered the castles captured by his enemies there
with equal facility. Thus the city's war effort that year, unbeliev-
ably, rebounded in a disastrous way. They had achieved no results
in the Lunigiana, and at Montevettolino and other places where
their main forces had been, the enemy looked more powerful and
effective than ever.[41]

In the same year, shaken by the scale of the war, the city for the
first time created the board of Twelve Men to advise the Priors, as
the latter seemed inadequate in the face of such massive challenges. This magistracy was created in 1321 and in due course became a fixture in the state.[42] In that year certain towers and parts
of the wall were finished.[43]   58

In the following year the Pistoiesi, afflicted by Castruccio with   59
continuous military disasters, made peace with him, abandoning
their old alliance with Florence. Although the Florentines sent nu-   1322
merous envoys to stop it, a false argument from utility won the
day, to the effect that the Pistoiesi should consult the interests of
peace rather than of honor.

At around the same time there was a rumor that Castruccio   60
was sending part of his forces through Sienese territory to Arezzo.
Simultaneously a revolution was feared in Siena owing to a feud
between two powerful clans, the Tolomei and the Salimbeni,

ses res novae timebantur ex duarum potentissimarum gentium, Tolomeorum[69] Salimbeniumque, inimicitiis, quae totam diviserant civitatem. Itaque missa propere Senas auxilia, trepidis in rebus populum confirmarunt. De copiis vero Arretium missis falsus rumor fuerat allatus; non enim copiae ullae, sed magistratus tantum, qui peregrinus eligi consuevit, ex urbe Luca[70] Arretium transierat. Is, quia comitatior ingrediebatur, rumorem praebuit falsarum copiarum.

61   Eodem anno Guido Arretinorum praesul, de cuius novo dominatu supra diximus, armata multitudine Fronzolae arcem Pupio imminentem obsedit cepitque. Inde positis ad Voconianum castris, expugnare oppidum nitebatur. Causa vero huius conatus erat, quod incolae eius oppidi diversarum partium habebantur, et superiori certe bello Florentinis exulibusque arretinis semper cohaeserant. Cum igitur[71] his de causis obsiderentur[72] oppidani, missis Florentiam nunciis, subvenire sibi precabantur. Florentini vero, etsi detrimentosum putabant ad bellum lucense arretinum simul[73] adiungere, tamen, ne deessent fidelissimorum hominum precibus, et simul quia existimabant praesulem, si id oppidum cepisset, maiora inde moliturum, ferre auxilium decrevere. Ac[74] primo subitanea manu[75] equitum casentinatem in agrum ad spem obsessorum praemissa, mox, convocatis sociis, maiores copiae parabantur. Sed praesul, inter hunc apparatum die noctuque obsidionem urgens, oppidum antecepit ad solumque evertit. Itaque intermissi apparatus Florentiae sunt, et praesul ipse post eversum Voconianum nihil ultra molitus, Arretium copias reduxit.

62   Cum hinc Arretinorum suspicio, illinc bellum castrucianum urgeret iamque e sociis Pistorienses defecissent, placuit ad inspicien-

which had completely divided the city. In these parlous circumstances reinforcements were instantly sent to Siena to strengthen the popular party. The rumor about the troops sent to Arezzo, however, proved false: there weren't any troops, only a magistrate, a foreign one elected in accordance with custom, who had been travelling from Lucca to Arezzo.[44] He had made his entrée with a larger retinue than usual, thus giving rise to the false report about the troops.

In the same year, Guido, bishop of Arezzo, of whose freshly-minted lordship we have already spoken, armed a host, and besieged and captured Fronzole, the citadel that overlooks Poppi. Then, pitching camp at Castello Focognano, he set about reducing the town. The reason for this attack was that the inhabitants of the town were believed to be Ghibellines — and, certainly, in the late war they had sided with the Florentine exiles and Aretines. Well then, despite this having been the grounds for the siege, the townsmen sent messengers to Florence imploring her help. The Florentines, although they believed it would be not be in their interest to add an Aretine war to the Lucchese one, nevertheless decided to send military aid so as not to ignore the pleas of men who had been extremely loyal, and at the same time because they calculated that the bishop, if he were to capture the town, would then make bigger plans. First they sent out a rapid striking force of knights into the Casentino to give hope to the besieged; then, summoning their allies, they prepared larger forces. But the bishop, by pressing forward with the siege day and night in person, captured the town first, razing it to the ground. Hence the war preparations in Florence were suspended and the bishop himself, after sacking Castello Focognano, marched his troops back to Arezzo.[45]

With apprehension about the Aretines on one flank, the Castruccian war pressing them on the other, and the recent defection of the Pistoiesi, it was decided to muster the army in order to test

61

62

dos reliquorum animos exercitum indicere. Igitur quasi magna quaedam res arcane subesset, omnes copiae ad nonas quintiles in armis fore iubentur, et auxilia sociorum arcessuntur. Convenerunt frequentius socii quam unquam ante, adeoque invaluit studium, ut peditum equitumque permulta millia ad praescriptum convenirent. Quae res sic animos civium erexit, nihil ut iam formidarent; sic adversarios conterruit, ut audito hoc apparatu, cum cuius gratia cogeretur ignotum esset, et alii Pisas, alii Arretium, alii Lucam prodi circumferrent, omnes sibi metuere invigilareque cogerentur. Sed auxilia sociorum collaudata, paulo post, quasi rebus non procedentibus, domum remissa sunt.

63   Per extremum eius anni, Iohanne romano pontifice rogante, Florentini rursus auxilia equitum in Galliam miserunt. Implicatis enim rege simul et pontifice genuensi bello, cum de communi studio partium ageretur, tota cis Alpis Gallia mirum in modum fluctuabat. Nec bellum quidem etruscum alienum ab illo putabatur; nam et Castrucium inimici regis pontificisque pepulerant ad bellum in Etruria concitandum, et Guido Arretinorum praesul, etsi non aperte inferebat bellum, tamen multa quotidie moliri adversus amicos sociosque florentini populi cernebatur, et a[76] favore plane diversarum partium hominum totus pendere.

64   Missa igitur tunc in Galliam auxilia iisdem rationibus impetrarunt, ut proxima secutura aestate Genuenses cum classe in lucensem agrum descenderent; Florentini vero et socii omnibus copiis alia ex parte eundem agrum pervaderent: fore enim, ambobus uno

the attitude of the other allies. Thus, as though some great campaign were secretly afoot, all troops were bidden to be present in
arms on the fifth of July, and the allied auxiliaries were summoned. The allies came in far greater numbers than ever before,
and their zeal was so strong that many thousands of horse and
foot assembled on the prescribed date. This encouraged the citizens so that they now feared nothing. And it so frightened their
adversaries that, learning of this army, whose purpose in assembling was hidden from them, and hearing reports of betrayals in
Pisa, Arezzo and Lucca, they were all compelled to fear and keep
watch over for each other. But after commending the allies for
sending troops, the Florentines sent them back home, as though
the campaign was not going forward.[46]

At the end of this year, at the request of John [XXII], the Ro-   63
man pontiff, the Florentines once again sent cavalry reinforcements into Gaul. The king and the pope were involved simultaneously in the Genoese war, and all of Cisalpine Gaul was in flux
to an extraordinary degree, as it was a matter of partisanship on
both sides. Nor was the Tuscan war regarded as unrelated, for the
enemies of the king and the pontiff were pressuring Castruccio to
stir up war in Tuscany, and Guido, bishop of Arezzo, although
not making war openly, was nevertheless seen to be hatching numerous plots against the friends and allies of the Florentine People
and was wholly dependent, plainly, on support from the opposing
party.

Hence, the reinforcements sent at that time to Gaul were re-   64
quested on the same grounds: so that the following summer the
Genoese might descend upon Lucchese territory with their fleet,
while the Florentines and their allies would attack the same territory from the opposite side with all their troops. With both forces
attacking Lucca at one time, Castruccio himself would be overwhelmed. While they were gathering the forces and equipment for
this campaign, a certain captain of the cavalry from Friuli, who up

tempore Lucam adorientibus, ut Castrucius ipse opprimeretur.
Cum ad eam rem apparatus fierent, praefectus quidam foroiulia-
norum equitum, qui vel integerrima fide ad eam usque diem apud
Florentinos stipendia faciebat,[77] corruptus pecunia, ad Castrucium
transfugit. Id quidem factum multorum turbavit animos, nec tam
pro subtracta copia (non enim supra ducentos equites praefectum
in transfugio secuti fuerant), quam quod de corruptela ceteri formidabatur exercitus. Ob eam rem irrumpere (uti constitutum fuerat) in lucensem agrum supersederunt, et apparatus ad id factos
dissolverunt. At Castrucius ob hoc ipsum elatus, cum iis quas resistendi causa paraverat copiis, ultro iam in hostilem profectus, ad
Fucetium posuit castra. Inde transmisso Arno in miniatensem to-
porianumque agrum duxit, belli cladibus et terroribus cuncta in-
volvens. Post haec magno applausu Lucam rediit, iis in hostem
editis quae hostes in eum sese facturos minabantur.

65   Dum a Castrucio ista geruntur, Guido praesul, armata Arretinorum multitudine, Fagiolam et alia quaedam[78] castella filiorum
Uguicionis Fagiolani obsedit. Causa vero obsidendi fuit quod illi,
etsi studio partium similes, tamen dominatum eius praesulis haud
aequo animo videbantur perferre. Guido igitur, ubi plerasque illorum arces asperis quidem in locis subegit (sunt enim in finibus arretini agri circa Apennini iugum), reducto exercitu Rondine cir-
cumsedit. Id oppidum in fide florentini populi erat iam inde a
superioribus bellis. Itaque oppidani, statim ab initio obsidionis
missis Florentiam legatis, subveniri sibi postularunt. Movebant
cunctos optimorum ac[79] fidelissimorum[80] hominum preces; sed
implicata castruciano bello civitas, ne alias insuper lites ab Arretinis concitaret, neque ferre opem neque rursus negare ob verecun-
diam audebat. Itaque, inter spem metumque pertracti Rondinen-
ses, aliquot mensibus obsidionem pertulere. Tandem, ubi sese

to that time had served the Florentines as a mercenary with the utmost loyalty, was bribed and fled to Castruccio. This act troubled many, not so much for the loss of his troops (for no more than two hundred knights had followed their captain in his flight), but because they feared the corruption of the rest of the army. Owing to this incident the Florentines abandoned the invasion of Lucchese territory they had agreed to make and disbanded the army put together for the purpose. But Castruccio was encouraged by the same incident, and with the troops he had readied to resist the Florentines he now set off into hostile territory and pitched camp at Fucecchio. Then he crossed the Arno and marched into the territory of San Miniato and Montopoli, roiling everything in the terror and destruction of war. After this he returned to Lucca to great applause, having done to the enemy what the enemy had been threatening to do to him.[47]

While Castruccio was performing these deeds, Bishop Guido 65 had armed a host of Aretines and was laying siege to Faggiuola and certain castles belonging to the sons of Uguccione della Faggiuola. They were being attacked because, despite belonging to the same party, they seemed to find unbearable the lordship of that prelate. So Guido, having subdued numbers of their strongholds in rugged terrain (they were located within Aretine territory near the ridges of the Appenines), marched his army back and lay siege to Rondine. This town had been loyal to the Florentine people from the time of the late wars. Hence as soon as the siege started the townsmen sent envoys to Florence requesting aid. Everyone was touched by the pleas of these excellent men of great loyalty, but the city, involved as it was in the Castrucian war, did not dare to provide aid, lest they give the Aretines further grounds for disputes, nor on the other hand did they dare deny it, out of shame. While they were being racked between hope and fear, the Rondinesi endured the siege for several months. Finally, when the

urgeri in dies magis vident,[81] nec ulla sibi auxilia praestabantur, seque et oppidum Arretinis dediderunt.[82]

66   Eodem anno Castrucius, praeter omnium expectationem cum exercitu profectus, non longe a Prato minabundus consedit. Ob repentinum eius adventum, cum tumultus maior concitus fuisset ac fuga agrestium passim fieret, Prato quoque metueretur, Florentini, iustitio indicto tabernisque tota urbe clausis, populariter fere sunt contra illum egressi, ut essent intra paucas inde horas in armis peditum supra viginti millia, equites vero urbani ad duo millia. Haec omnis multitudo raptim Pratum deducta contra hostem opposita stetit. Castrucius apud Areolum vicum habebat castra; qui, postquam tantam multitudinem tam subito adversus se venisse[83] conspexit, etsi longe impar tantis copiis erat, tamen, simulata fiducia, quasi in crastinum pugnaturus, hostem distinuit. Mox, per noctis silentium, transmisso Umbrone amne, per agrum pistoriensem abiit, nec prius intermisit iter quam ad Serram oppidum se recepit.

67   Cum exorta lux vacua hostium castra patefecisset, variis apud Florentinos sententiis certatum est. Plebs enim ac urbana omnis multitudo sequendum e vestigio hostem censebat; nobilitas autem, sive indignatione adversus plebem sive quod experta et bellorum gnara, in subitaneo collectitioque milite non multum spei collocandum putabat, reducendas tunc domum copias,[84] et alio, si videatur, tempore sociis convocatis apparatuque solemniter facto, vadendum in agros hostium suadebat. Cum varietas sententiarum discordias induxisset, ac plebs fidem nobilitatis, nobilitas vero temeritatem ac vaesaniam plebis incusaret, odia graviter exarsere. Itaque mittere Florentiam placuit, et ad priorum voluntatem rem

latter saw themselves under more pressure each day, and no help being offered them, they surrendered the city to the Aretines.[48]

In the same year Castruccio, to everyone's surprise, set out with his army and encamped not far from Prato in a threatening manner. His sudden coming provoked a great uproar: countrymen were in flight everywhere, and Prato too was in a state of fear. The Florentines declared a state of emergency and closed all the shops in the city. The people went out against him practically in a body, so within a few hours there were more than 20,000 infantry in arms and up to 2000 urban knights. This whole host marched out rapidly to Prato and took up position opposite the enemy. Castruccio had his camps near the village of Aiuolo. Seeing such a large host come against him so quickly, he nevertheless made a show of confidence — even though his own forces were vastly inferior — and fended off the enemy as though he were going to fight on the morrow. Then, in the silence of the night, he crossed the Ombrone and departed via Pistoian territory, and didn't stop until he had taken refuge at the town of Serra.

66

1323

When the rising sun revealed the empty enemy camp, there was a battle of opinions among the Florentines. The plebs and the urban multitude were for setting off immediately after the enemy. But the nobility, whether from resentment at the plebs or because of their own expertise and knowledge of war, believed that they should not place too much confidence in a ragtag collection of inexperienced soldiers, but urged that they should now march the troops back home, and, if it seemed advisable, invade the enemy's territory another time after summoning the allies and mustering the army with the proper formalities. The variety of opinions led to discord, with the plebs accusing the nobility of disloyalty, and the nobility accusing the plebs of recklessness and madness, and deep hatreds were inflamed. Thus it was decided to send to Florence and submit the whole matter to the will of the Priors. This action ignited quarrels in the city, too, amongst those who had re-

67

integram referre. Ea relatio in urbe quoque apud eos qui domi remanserant contentiones accendit, variantibus sententiis non priorum modo sed et aliorum civium, donec, insurgente puerorum[85] multitudine ac minima de plebe turba per forum et compita exclamante, profectio decernitur.

68   Profectus est igitur exercitus incredibili multitudine; nam, praeter urbanam turbam quae totam[86] se ad id effuderat, ex agro passim omnes eo properabant, et sociorum auxilia frequentissima ad primum adventum hostis percita supervenerant. Cum circa Fucetium pervenissent et nobilitas quae dissuaserat tantummodo sequeretur signa, curam vero ac studium commeatus ceterarumque rerum auctoribus profectionis relinqueret, nec opportune quicquam ageretur, re ipsa iam vanitatem coepti arguente, suscepta temere expeditio irritatur. Itaque tantae simul copiae nec hostile intrarunt solum, nec quicquam omnino perfecerunt,[87] sed pleni incusationum iniuriarumque, alii alios culpantes, domum reversi sunt.

69   Domi quoque contentiones vehementissimae ab exercitu haustae ex data exulibus fide. Sub primum enim Castruci adventum, cum Prato[88] imminere nunciatum esset, ac proelium futurum crederetur, exulibus promissa reductio est, si modo in castris armati contra hostem adessent. Ob eam rem ingens manus exulum in castra confluxerat. Ortis mox inter cives discordiis et usque Fucetium exercitu perducto, cum inde Florentiam male concordes remearent, iniecta exulibus suspicio est ne promissa eis servarentur; nec deerant qui commonefacerent, ut sibi ipsis prospicerent. Quamobrem commoti exules antevenire exercitus reditum[89] statuerunt. Itaque, sub vexillo celerius profecti, ad urbem contenderant eo consilio, ut armati ingrederentur.

mained behind. Opinions fluctuated not only among the Priors but also among the other citizens. A crowd of boys rose up in revolt and the lowest classes of the plebs, in a mob, began shouting in the Piazza Signoria and on streetcorners. After this, an expedition was decreed.[49]

Thus the army set out in unbelievable numbers, for in addition 68 to the urban mob, which poured out in a body for the purpose, everyone throughout the territory hastened there, and numerous allied reinforcements had been coming in as well, having been stirred to action by the initial coming of the enemy. They reached Fucecchio. The nobility which had been against fighting were merely following the standards, leaving to the authors of the expedition the responsibility and oversight of provisioning and other matters. Everything was disorganized, and this circumstance itself being proof that the undertaking was in vain, the expedition so rashly undertaken led to no result. So this great combination of forces neither invaded enemy soil nor accomplished anything at all, but returned home, seething with accusations, outrage and mutual recrimination.

At home the army had its fill of intense strife owing to an 69 agreement made with the exiles. For when Castruccio first arrived, it was reported that Prato was under threat. In the belief that a battle was imminent, restoration was promised to the exiles provided they would present themselves in the camps, armed against the enemy. On this account a huge number of exiles had streamed into the camps. Then, when discord arose among the citizens, and the army had marched as far as Fucecchio only to return to Florence in a state of discord, the exiles began to suspect that the promises made to them would not be kept. There were some who advised them to look out for themselves. So the excited and nervous exiles decided to anticipate the army's return, and set out swiftly under their banner, heading for the city with the idea of entering it in arms.

70   Civitas, discordiarum contentionumque exercitus gnara, statim atque venire exules nuntiatum est, verita ne ad res novandas essent praemissi, sumpsit arma, ac[90] venire in urbem prohibuit. Quare exclusi exules ante portam consedere. Tandem postera die, cum reliquus exercitus adventaret, veriti civium vim, retro abiere; Pratique consistentes, rogare iam inde verbis coeperunt quod ante flagitaverant armis. Eius rogationis gratia octo exulum legati fide publica in urbem venerunt. His nobilitas favebat; nam et erant quidam inter exules ex praecipuis familiis, et magna clientium[91] manus, hominum facinorosorum, quis plurimum nobilitas utebatur. His de causis favor erat nobilitatis in reducendis exulibus propensissimus. Priores quoque, qui auctores pollicendi fuerant, repraesentandum exulibus promissum, neque fraudandos frustrandosque homines publica fide clamitabant. At plebs infensa, partim consuetudine obtrectandi,[92] partim ira turpiter reducti exercitus, postulationem adversabatur. Denique cum his de rebus magistratus referret, introducti exulum legati huiuscemodi orationem habuere:

71   'Si aut de exilio nostro aut de conditione singulorum disserendum foret, alia nobis dicendi ratio aliaque oratio proponeretur. Nunc autem cum, qualescumque tandem ipsi simus, talibus promiseritis, simplex admodum postulatio nobis sufficiet. Fidem publicam, quam sub adventum hostium nobis spopondistis, nunc demum illis admotis omnique terrore depulso, praestari nobis flagitamus. In hac vero postulatione nostra, si quis forte subsistit, necesse est eo adduci quod aut promissum neget, aut a nobis impletum; aut quod, etiamsi utrumque[93] factum sit, tamen servanda non esse promissa civitatis contendat. Horum duo prima docere nostrum erit; tertium in vestra aequitate ac in civitatis pudore repositum est.

The city was aware of the discord and quarrels in the army, and 70
as soon as the exiles' coming was announced, fearing that they had
come to engineer a coup, it took up arms and forbade them to enter. Hence the excluded exiles encamped by the gate. Finally, on
the following day when the rest of the army arrived, the exiles
withdrew, fearing violence from the citizens. Stopping at Prato,
they now started to request in words what previously they had demanded in arms. To make this request eight exile envoys entered
the city under a safe conduct. The nobility showed them favor, as
some of the exiles were from leading families, and they had a large
body of clients, criminal types whom the nobles found extremely
useful. For these reasons the nobility were strongly inclined to restore the exiles. The Priors, too, who had been responsible for the
offer, clamored for the promise to be put into effect, saying that
men should not be defrauded and deceived by a public agreement.
But the plebs were hostile and opposed the request, partly from
their customary tendency to malicious criticism, partly from anger
at the shameful retreat of the army.[50] Finally the magistrates took
up the matter. The envoys of the exiles were brought in and made
a speech something like this:

"If we had to discuss our exile and the situation of individuals, 71
we would speak in a different way and deliver another speech. But
since you have made promises of this nature to us, irrespective of
our situation, a simple request will suffice us. The public agreement you solemnly made with us when the enemy came we are
asking you to fulfill now that he is gone and the peril has been
averted. If someone perhaps opposes our request, he must necessarily allege either that the promise was not made or that we did
not fulfill it — or he must maintain that the city's promises should
not be observed even when both conditions have been observed.
We shall address the first two possibilities; we leave the third to
your sense of justice and the city's sense of shame.

72 'Quamquam, quis est qui de horum aliquo ambigere possit?
Quis nescit promissum, quis non publicatum, quis non ita procla-
matum, ut non Florentiae modo, sed per finitimas quoque urbes
vox civitatis exaudiretur? Atqui in rebus agendis quandoque alterius ad alterum promissio fit secreta quidem ac minime vulgata,
quae, etsi est aeque servanda, potest tamen a multitudine ignorari.
Hic autem nihil est cur civis ignoret quod in civitate factum peregrini etiam sciunt. Sed quid in eo moramur quod et priores, viri
clarissimi, fatentur, et civitas conscia veritatis non negat? Illud,
credo, est dubium in castris ne fuerimus adversus hostem, quae
fuit conditio in promissione[94] adscripta. Id nos et literis sigillis-
que[95] vestrorum ducum et mille insuper testibus docemus. Et quis
fuit in exercitu civium vestrorum cui ulla modo sit patriae cura,
qui nos non viderit in fronte contra hostem collocatos, qui non
proeliandi cupidos, qui non pro victoria devotos, cum pro tanto
beneficio in nos collato,[96] etiamsi oppetendum foret, vix satisfactum merito de nobis vestro putaremus? Nos enim vitam pro
patriae victoria (ni hostis fugere quam experiri virtutem maluisset)
non forti modo verum etiam libenti animo impensuri eramus, ac
neque corporibus neque animabus nostris parsuri. Post foedam
vero illam degeneremque hostis fugam et confessionem timoris
sui, signa publica secuti, quocumque duxerunt duces vestri, nusquam discessimus. Quod[97] si duces ipsi non eo profecti sunt quo
proficisci optastis, quis nobis id succenseat? Neque enim nostrum
erat ducibus praecipere, sed eorum praecepta spectare et sequi.
Quod si desiderium certe nostrum valuisset, etiam hodie solum
hostile calcaremus. Quare, cum et promissum a civitate et a nobis
quae in conditione fuerunt impleta constet, vos iam quid fides ves-

"To be sure, no one can have possibly have doubts about either of the two cases. Who doesn't know about the promise? Who doesn't know that it was published and proclaimed in such a way that the city's word was heard not only in Florence but also in neighboring cities? To be sure, it sometimes happens in the conduct of affairs that someone makes a promise to somebody else in secret and without public knowledge which can go unrecognized by the multitude, even when it is observed with justice. In this case, however, there is no reason why a citizen should fail to take cognizance of what even foreigners know to have been done in the city. But why dwell on what even the Priors, those distinguished men, confess, and the city, knowing the truth, does not deny? There existed in the ranks, I believe, a doubt as to whether we exiles opposed the enemy, which was a condition explicitly specified in the promise. In proof of our opposition we cite the letters and seals of your commanders and a thousand witnesses besides. And who is there in your citizen army with any concern for his country who did not see us in the front line against the enemy, spoiling to fight, committed to victory? Indeed, we thought that, even if we perished, we would scarcely recompense what you deserved of us in return for the great gift you gave us. With strong and even willing spirits we were ready to spend our lives for our country's victory, if the enemy had not preferred flight to a trial of courage; we were prepared to spare neither life nor limb. After the foul and base flight of the enemy and his admission of fear, we followed the city's standards and never disengaged wherever your commanders led. And if the commanders themselves did not set out in the direction you wanted them to go, why should someone be angry at us? It was not our role to give orders to the commanders, but to observe and follow their orders. Certainly, if our own desires had had any effect, we should be treading on enemy soil at this very moment. Therefore, since it is evident that the city made a promise and that we fulfilled the conditions contained therein, you

tra ac gravitas exigat videtote. Nam nos quidem in hac parte loqui pudor impedit, cum iniuriosum sit vel dubitare solum de civitatis fide.'

73 Postquam legati exulum auditi sunt, curia excedere iussis, consultari est coeptum. Nobilitas ferme[98] omnis et magistratus servandam fidem publicam suadebant, et cum precibus exulum, tum propinquorum intercessionibus permulti movebantur. At quidam ex his qui in consilio aderant, vir severitatis priscae, cum tandem locum[99] dicendi nactus est, ita fertur dixisse.

74 'Si reductionem tantummodo postulassent exulum legati, nihil equidem plus eorum postulationi quam tabellam mei testem iudicii respondissem. Nunc autem, cum eo spectet oratio illorum,[100] ut et notam finitimis promissionem iactent et dedecus perfidiamque civitatis redarguere pergant, non tabella respondere sat est, sed et voce quoque eorum calumnia videtur refutanda. A civitate promissam reductionem aiunt. Quo tandem modo? Quia priores, inquit, promiserunt, publicarunt, proclamarunt, ut etiam finitimi exaudirent. Mitte, quaeso, hanc verborum pompam; ad solidum, ut ita dixerim, accede. Fateor promissum a prioribus; a civitate tamen promissum nego. Date veniam, quaeso, optimi praesides; consulendi enim facultas libera esse debet; nec ego quicquam minuo ex maiestate vestra, sed maiestatem populi adversus calumniam defendo.

75 'Nego, inquam, esse idem priores ac civitatem, nec idem sane eorum[101] decreta valere. Legibus enim sic reipublicae gubernatio a maioribus nostris temperata est, ut civitas quidem sine ulla excep-

should now provide for what your own guarantee and gravity demand. Shame prevents us from speaking on this latter topic, as it is an act of injustice even to doubt the good faith of the state."

After the exiles' envoys had been heard, they were bidden to 73 leave the court, and consultation began. Practically all of the nobility and the magistrates argued for observing the public guarantee, and very many were affected by the pleas of the exiles and the intercessions of kinsmen. But one of those present in the council, a man of old-fashioned severity, when finally given a chance to speak, is said to have spoken as follows:

"If the exile envoys had requested nothing more than return 74 from exile, I should certainly have answered their request with nothing more than a written vote indicating my own judgment. But now, since their oration makes reference to their boast that the promise was known to our neighbors and goes on to make a case based on the city's disgrace and perfidious behavior, it is not enough to respond with a written vote; their calumny also requires verbal refutation. They say that the city promised them restoration. But how, pray? Because the Priors, they say, promised it, published it, proclaimed it so that even our neighbors heard it. But please, put away this show of words; let's get down to the facts of the matter. I admit the Priors made a promise; I deny the city did. Please forgive me, most excellent judges, but one should enjoy freedom in giving counsel. I would not detract in the least from your majesty, but I do defend the majesty of the People against calumny.

"I deny, I say, that the Priors and the city are the same; nor, 75 surely, do their decrees have the same validity. Our ancestors tempered the government of the state with laws in such a way that the city had full power without exceptions, while the Priors had only that power which the city allowed them. I ask, then, whether the Priors were really allowed to restore the exiles. The laws themselves will reply that this was not allowed. Therefore, if a solemn

tione omnia possit, priores vero ea tantum quae civitas permisis-
set. Quaero, igitur, numquid prioribus permissa sit reductio exulum. Respondebunt ipsae leges non esse permissam. Qua ergo de
re decretum solemne si a prioribus fieret, invalidum esset; ea de re
nuda pollicitatio valida erit? Et si decretum foret,[102] nemo serva-
ret; promissum autem, nisi servetur, civitatis fama laedetur? Natura ita comparatum est, ut factum sit quam promissum longe ro-
bustius. Quorum igitur factum civitas[103] sine ullo dedecore habere
irritum debet, eorum promissum nisi ratum habuerit, quae tandem infamia erit? Maiores nostri in finiendo exilio non magistratus nutum, sed populi decretum spectari voluerunt; multis denique locis rem discussam et comprobatam esse prius. Magnum,
credo, visum est atque arduum, ut quem civitas ut facinorosum ac
malum civem abiecerat, is paulo post reduceretur ut bonus. Tum
ut metu homines a maleficiis deterrerent, difficultates permaximas
reductioni opposuerunt, ut praeter publica populi decreta consensus etiam inimicorum spectaretur. Quae omnia mehercle salutaria
ad civium quietem stabilita legibus, usu comprobata, moribus in-
veterata, isti una promissione evertenda putant, nec in uno aut altero exulum, sed in[104] universa penitus multitudine.

76   "'At in exercitu fuerunt, contra hostem steterunt armati!" Non
hoc quaero, fuerint in exercitu, sed illud quaero, reducendine sint
secundum leges. Hoc tu prius mihi[105] ius proba; ego tibi quod
reliquum est perquam facile concedam. Quamdiu vero id a te pro-
batum non sit, etsi millies in exercitu fueris, nihilo magis censebo
reducendum. Etenim si fuisse in exercitu tanti per se ipsum existi-
mari debet, ut etiam contra leges sint exules reducendi, quid dabi-
mus, quaeso, civibus nostris qui nullo prius admisso nec cuiusquam noxae rei, eodem in exercitu populariter affuere?

77   'Atque adhuc eo spectat oratio mea ut, et si omnia cum laude
sint ab exulibus facta, tamen reducendi non videantur. Quid, si

decree that the Priors might make would be invalid, shall a mere promise on that same matter be valid? Even if it were a decree, no one would observe it; will the city's good name be harmed by not observing a promise? By nature deeds are evaluated much more robustly than promises. When the city is obliged to hold someone's deeds useless, what infamy will there be, pray, in holding a promise made to them as other than valid? Our ancestors intended that exile should be terminated by popular decree, not by a magistrate's approval; they intended that the matter should be widely discussed and approved first. It seemed to them a great and difficult matter, I believe, that a criminal, evil citizen whom the city had ejected should shortly thereafter be restored as though he were a good citizen. At that time they put extraordinary obstacles in the way of restoration in order to deter men from evildoing through fear. They required the consensus of their enemies in addition to a public decree of the People. All this was established by law as salutary to the tranquillity of the citizens; it was approved through usage and rooted in custom. These men now think to overturn all this by a single promise, not in the case of one or another exile, but of the whole lot of them!

"'But they served in the army, standing armed against the enemy!' I'm not asking whether they served in the army, I'm asking whether their restoration is legal. If you can prove to me that it was legal, I shall readily concede to you the rest. So long as you do not prove this, I shall no more agree to their restoration, even if they served in the army a thousand times! And if their service in the army is to be valued at such a price that exiles can be restored even against the laws, what, pray, shall we grant to those of our citizens who served as *popolani* in the same army, having never before participated in it, and being guilty of no wrongdoing? 76

"Thus far, my speech has considered only the fact that the exiles need not be restored, even if all their actions were laudable. But what if, as a result of this promise, they come armed against 77

post eam promissionem armati contra patriam venerunt, si obsiderunt portas? An huius populi memoria tam cito excidisse putant,
quo die illi, relicto post se exercitu optimorum civium, ad patriam,
quam defensoribus reperire vacuam[106] existimabant, occupandam
expugnandamque properarunt? Adeo parum apud eos interfuit inter civem et hostem! Quos nisi portae ac moenia arcuissent, non
verbis, ut nunc, sed vulneribus et armis fuisset a nobis disceptandum. Et hi, nisi reducantur, fore civitatem in dedecore audent dicere; qui, si reducerentur, maximum esset dedecus civitatis. Ego
igitur, ut sententia mea breviter[107] complectar, reducendos nequaquam censeo, vel quia invalida fuit promissio, vel quia, si valida esset, illi novo crimine quo minus reduci debeant effecerunt.'

78   Cum haec pro exulibus contraque exules dicta essent, magistratus, quo voluntas singulorum eliceretur, tabellas consultoribus dari
iussit. Quae cum[108] non satis prospere exulibus responderent, et
urna iam saepius in cassum circumlata homines fatigasset, dimissum consilium est, magna cum eorum querela qui, utcumque promissum esset, repraesentandam[109] exulibus fidem publicam suadebant. Cum igitur dissentire inter se cives in ea re haud obscurum
esset vocesque liberius iactarentur, exules, sumpto ex favore animo,
vi redire in urbem constituerunt. Ad hoc securium magna vis
praeparatur, et tempus locusque[110] facinori deligitur. Tempus maxime illis placuit intempesta nox; locus autem faesulana porta, per
quam effractam irrumpere parabant. Quae ubi mature composita
sunt, dato inter se signo, pluribus ex locis ad urbem venerunt. Sed
res permultis nota clam esse non potuit. Itaque occaso iam sole,
cum eius rei fama incidisset, murmur primo fuit, mox et arma
sumpta, vigiliaeque tota nocte per urbem actae, et singulis porta

their country? What if they laid siege to its gates? Do they think this People has so quickly forgotten the day when they abandoned an army of excellent citizens and rushed to capture and occupy a country which they thought they would find empty of defenders? So slight was the difference for them between a enemy and a citizen! If the gates and walls had not repelled them, we should have disputed the matter with wounds and arms, not, as now, with words! And these men dare say that the city will be disgraced if they are not restored — the same men who would be the greatest disgrace to the city if they *were* restored! For my part, then — to give my view in a nutshell — I hold that they should by no means be restored, either because the promise is invalid, or, even if it were valid, because they have committed a new crime invalidating their restoration."

After these speeches in favor of and against the exiles, the magistrate bade the counselors hand over their ballots so that the will of each might be known. When the result was less than favorable to the exiles, and the urn had gone round in vain a number of times, wearying the men, the council was dismissed. The men who had argued for giving effect to the public guarantee just as it had been promised to the exiles complained bitterly. Since the disagreement among the citizens over this matter was hardly secret, and opinions were being thrown around with great freedom, the exiles, encouraged by the goodwill they enjoyed, decided to return to the city by force. For this purpose a great quantity of axes was readied, and a time and a place for the deed were selected. The time they liked best was the dead of night, the place the Faesulan Gate. This they hacked to pieces and prepared to burst through it. When everything was ready, they gave the signal and came up to the city from many places. But a thing known to many cannot be kept secret. Thus, after sunset when the matter was reported, a murmur went up, then there was a rush to arms. Vigil was kept throughout the city the whole night, and torches were placed with

78

rum turribus faces cum praesidio armatorum impositae. Quare adventantes paulo post exules, cum detectam fraudem cognovissent, irrito coepto abiere. Fuit autem exulum numerus supra mille quingentos.

79   Rem ab exulibus compositam non sine consensu nobilitatis creditum fuit, et certe pro vero habitum. Quocirca, post repulsos exules, agitatum est de coniuratis puniendis; in quibus, cum universa nobilitas in periculum vocaretur, nec punire omnes nec impunitos relinquere placuit, sed in principes tantum eius motus animadvertendum fore. Hos cum privatim accusare nemo[111] auderet,[112] concione populi advocata, inaudito hactenus exemplo indictum est, ut singuli quem maxime putarent sontem ex nobilitate schedulis adscriberent, sine auctore, sine nomine. Quibus tandem receptis lectisque, compertum est nomina trium nobilitatis principum a pluribus delata: Amerigi Donati, Tegghiae Frescobaldi, Lotteringi Gherardini. Hi vocati ad magistratum, sub fiducia paruerunt. Interrogati autem de coniuratione, requisitos quidem se ab exulibus dixerunt, assensum tamen nunquam praestitisse. Ita non quasi coniurassent, sed quasi non patefecissent, duobus millibus aeris singuli eorum multati, ad breve insuper tempus relegantur. De ceteris vero conniventibus oculis transitum, ne infinita discordiarum inter cives suscitaretur materia. Ex hoc popularium studiis ad rempublicam tuendam erectis, minora vexilla, quos pennones vocant, maioribus adiunxerunt et in populum dederunt; experti nocturno illo tumultu percommodum incidere, ut manente vexillo pars aliqua societatis in opportuna loca sub minoribus signis mitti posset.

armed garrisons in each gatetower. Thus, when the exiles arrived a little later, they saw that their trick had been detected, and they went away, their plan foiled. The number of exiles involved was more than 1500.

It was believed, and certainly accepted as a fact, that the affair 79 had not been planned without the assent of the nobility. On this account, after the exiles had been repulsed, there was discussion about punishing the conspirators. Although the whole of the nobility was implicated, it was decided neither to punish all of them nor leave them unpunished, but to proceed only against the leaders of the disturbance. Since no one dared accuse them as a private individual, a popular assembly was summoned, and, in an unprecedented act, it was proclaimed that anonymous individuals might write down on pieces of paper the names of those members of the nobility whom they thought most guilty. When these papers were collected and read, it was found that three noble leaders had been denounced by numerous people: Amerigo Donati, Tegghiaio Frescobaldi, and Lotteringo Gherardini. These were summoned before the magistrate and complied under surety. Interrogated about the conspiracy, they said that they had indeed been approached by the exiles, but that they had never given their assent. So they were fined two thousand lire each, not as conspirators, but for failure to disclose information, and were also banished for a short period. The others who had connived in the conspiracy were passed over, lest endless fuel for civic discord be supplied. As a result of this affair, popular zeal for safeguarding the state was at a high pitch, and lesser standards, known as "pennons", were added to the greater ones and handed over to the People. They had learned during the recent nocturnal disturbance that it was highly useful on occasion for some part of a militia company to be sent to convenient places under lesser standards while the greater standards remained behind.[51]

80   Per hoc ipsum tempus sortitio magistratuum noviter instituta
est, cum antea semper electio per suffragia obtinuisset. Ea mutatio, etsi parva tunc res opinione hominum visa sit, maximam tamen inclinationem reipublicae attulit, mutata penitus gubernandae
civitatis forma. Sortitio autem per hunc modum instituta: prioribus et collegiis data potestas, ut eorum civium, qui digni eo mu-
nere viderentur, nomina schedulis scripta comprobataque loculo
includerent; inde, cum tempus adesset magistratus deligendi, tunc
sorte nomina promerentur; cuius depromptum nomen esset, is foret magistratus, nisi lege vetaretur. Vetitum autem erat, si aut intra
triennium eundem gessisset aut frater cognatusve aliquis in magistratu esset. His casibus, unde nomen promptum[113] esset, retrude-
batur.[114] Prima sortitio in triennium et sex menses constituta;
resque ipsa probavit utilem esse hanc legem ad tollendas civium
contentiones, quae per procurata crebro oriebantur suffragia.

81   Sed quantum in illo prodest reipublicae, tantum obest, vel
etiam magis, quod indigni plerumque ad magistratum ex sorti-
tione sumuntur. Neque enim pari diligentia providetur praesenti
officio et multis secuturis; sed remota quidem illa et an futura sint
minime certa hebetiori intuemur oculo; praesentia vero acriter et
argute. Extinguit praeterea virtutis studium, qua si suffragiis cer-
tandum foret et aperte in periculum famae veniendum, multo magis sese homines circumspicerent. Morem igitur primum longe
probabiliorem utilioremque reipublicae fuisse non ambigo, quo et
populus romanus semper usus est in magistratibus creandis. Florentiae tamen hic sortitionis mos tunc primo inductus ad nostra
usque tempora devenit, popularitate[115] quadam in republica servatus.

During this time sortition of magistrates was instituted for the 80
first time; hitherto, election by voting had been the practice. This 1323
change, although the general view regarded it as a small one at
the time, nevertheless brought about a great alteration in public
affairs, changing entirely the form of the city's government. Sortition was established in the following way: power was given to the
Priors and Colleges to store the names of those citizens who
seemed worthy of office in a bag, after they had been written
down and approved; then, when the time came to choose magistrates, names would be drawn by lot. Whoever's name was drawn
would be a magistrate unless barred by law. He was barred if he
had held the same office within the previous three years, or if
some brother or cousin of his was in office. In these cases, names
would be put back in the bag. The first sortition was fixed for
three and a half years; circumstances themselves had proven that
this law was useful to prevent quarrels among the citizens, which
often arose from the administration of voting.

But however much this procedure benefits the state, sortition 81
harms it as much or even more, in that most of the time unworthy
persons are assumed into the magistracy. For we do not use the
same care in providing for the numerous tasks that lie in the future as we do for the one task at hand; remote, contingent, and
dubious matters we regard with dimmer eyes, while present concerns are treated with close attention and shrewdness. Moreover it
extinguishes zeal for virtue, as men are much more careful in their
behavior if there is a contest for votes and their reputation may
openly be put in danger. I have no doubt, therefore, that the earlier practice [of voting] was much better and more useful to the
state. It was also a practice that the Roman people always used
in choosing its magistrates. In Florence however this custom of
sortition, first introduced at that time, has come down to our own
age, being maintained in the state by a measure of popular favor.[52]

82　　Dum haec domi geruntur, bella interim ab hostibus inferebantur gravissima. Castrucius enim, vir ingenio acri, in florentinum agrum quotidianas prope incursiones faciebat. Altera vero ex parte Guido Arretinorum praesul, impigri et ipse vir animi, socios et amicos[116] florentini populi cunctis belli cladibus infestabat. Qui cum oppida pleraque arretini agri, quae dudum una cum exulibus in societatem Florentinorum devenerant, expugnasset, nonnulla etiam funditus diruisset, maiora iam inde audens, Tifernum, urbem sociam et amicam florentini populi, vi et armis invasit, pulsisque diversarum partium hominibus, potestati ditionique suae civitatem[117] subegit. Ob eam rem Perusini et aliae quaedam finitimae civitates, quae sibi pergravem Arretinorum vicinitatem suspicabantur fore, novam societatem cum Florentinis inierunt pro Tiferni recuperatione. Societas ea in triennium constituta est.

83　　Per extremum eius anni Castrucius, magnam rem ausus, in sua paene audacia corruit. Fucetium erat oppidum nobile in finibus lucensis agri. Id Florentini per superiora bella traditum in potestate continebant, eaque per id tempus sedes erat belli adversus Castrucium et Lucenses. Cum itaque cunctas, ut par erat, vias pro abducendo eo oppido Castrucius scrutaretur, tandem proditores sibi magna comparat pecunia. Inde procellosa nocte, quo minus sentiretur, profectus, ut compositum erat, antiquo poste, quem ad hoc ipsum proditores demoliti fuerant, ingreditur, habens equites delectos non amplius centum quinquaginta, pedites vero circiter quingentos. Cum oppidum pervadere locaque occupare opportuna coepisset, exciti oppidani arma corripiunt, factoque suorum globo fortiter repugnant.

While this was taking place at home, the enemy was meanwhile 82
waging wars of the most intense and threatening kind. For Castruccio, a man energetic by nature, was making almost daily incursions into Florentine territory. From the other direction Guido,
the bishop of Arezzo, who was himself an active spirit, was harrassing allies and friends of the Florentine people, inflicting all the
disasters of war upon them. He captured most of the towns in
Aretine territory which together with the Aretine exiles had previously been allied to the Florentines, and some of them he razed to
the ground. His audacity increasing, he then attacked with armed
violence Città di Castello, a friend and ally of the Florentine
people. Having expelled the members of the opposing party he
subjected the city to his power and sway. On this account the
Perugians and certain other nearby cities, seized with fear of their
Aretine neighbors, entered into a new alliance with the Florentines
for the recovery of Città di Castello. The alliance was fixed for
three years.[53]

At the end of this year Castruccio undertook an enterprise of 83
great daring and was nearly ruined by his audacity. Fucecchio was
a fine town within the borders of Lucchese territory. It had been
turned over to the Florentines in previous wars and they had kept
it in their hands, using it at that time as a base for the war against
Castruccio and the Lucchesi. Understandably, Castruccio investi-
gated every possible way to take back the town, and at last discovered persons who would betray it to him for a large sum of money.
Thither he set out, choosing a stormy night to cover the sound of
his entry, and as had been agreed he entered by an old postern
gate which the traitors had knocked down for this purpose. With
him were no more than 150 picked knights and about five hundred
infantry. After his forces had begun to infiltrate the town and seize
the key places, the townsmen woke up, seized their arms, and
forming themselves into a single body fought back bravely.

84   Raro unquam atrocius quam ea nocte proeliatum ferunt; atque
ea conditio fuit pugnae, ut neutri ad summum praevalerent. Nam
neque Castrucius pervincere quasdam oppidi regiones potuit,
neque oppidani illum suis locis expellere. Primam sub lucem subsidia proximis e castellis, re per noctem ex ignibus cognita, supervenerunt, quae alacri clamore ab oppidanis excepta in Castrucianos feruntur. Ille, ubi nova supervenire auxilia cognovit, iactis per
vias impedimentis sese in superiori parte oppidi saepsit. Ibi[118]
adventum suarum copiarum quas maiores arcessiverat, expectare
constituit. Verum fatigatus nocturno proelio miles, ubi maior impetus fit[119] et integri fessum urgent,[120] locum tutari non potuit.
Itaque transgressi munitiones, foedam caedem edidere. Castrucius
ipse, dum cominus pugnat, accepto in faciem vulnere aufugit; eorum vero qui secum intraverant multi caesi, plures etiam capti, reliqui, sese ex oppido praecipites dantes, evasere. Haec domi forisque eo anno gesta.

85   Principio insequentis anni nulla fere primo res acta quam equites, ut in foedere convenerat, Perusinis traditi, quo adversus Arretinos bellum inferrent. Dux ex sententia civitatis his equitibus
praefectus est Amerigus Donatus, Cursii filius, eques florentinus.
Miserunt et Senenses et Bononienses et aliae civitates quae erant
in foedere. Conditio eius[121] belli ista fuit, ut fere ad Tifernum circumque ea loca[122] belligeraretur; inter Florentinos vero et Arretinos tacito quodam consensu quies esset, nec aut hi aut illi alterutrius agros invaderent. Ita auspicio magis Perusinorum contra
Arretinos bellum gerebatur: auxilia tantummodo, ne deessent
causae, a Florentinis submissa.

86   Per idem tempus gravis suspicio civitatem habuit, ne Pistorienses ad Castrucium deficerent. Philippus erat Tydicius,[123] magna

There can have been few battles as ferocious as the one fought 84
that night. The fight was such that neither side was able to get
the upper hand. For neither could Castruccio gain control of certain parts of the town, nor could the townsmen expel him from
the parts he had occupied. At dawn reinforcements arrived from
nearby castles which had learned of the affair during the night
thanks to the fires. The townsmen welcomed them with cheers as
they bore down on Castruccio's men. When Castruccio saw that
reinforcements were arriving, he set up barriers in the streets and
barricaded himself into the upper part of the town. He decided to
wait there for the arrival of the larger forces he had summoned.
But his soldiers were exhausted by the nocturnal battle and when
a new attack started, with fresh troops coming down upon the
tired men, they could not hold the position. So they crossed the
fortifications and engaged in foul slaughter. Castruccio himself,
fighting hand-to-hand, was wounded in the face and fled. Many of
those who had entered the town with him were killed, most were
captured, while the rest jumped down from the walls and escaped.
Such were the deeds of that year at home and abroad.[54]

At the beginning of the following year, almost the first thing 85
that happened was the consignment of cavalry to the Perugians in
accordance with the treaty, so as to make war against the Aretines.
The city appointed Amerigo Donati, son of Corso and a Floren- 1324
tine knight, to command the cavalry. The Sienese, Bolognese and
other cities in the league also sent troops. The war was conducted
in such a way that it was mostly fought near Città di Castello and
its environs. By a kind of tacit consent there was no hostile activity
between the Florentines and the Aretines, and neither one invaded
the others' land. Thus the war against the Aretines was waged
more under the auspices of the Perugians; the Florentines only
sent reinforcements in support of the cause.[55]

At this same time there was real fear in the city that the 86
Pistoiesi might defect to Castruccio. A powerful man called

vir potentia, qui dominatum Pistorii affectabat; eamque ob causam, praefectum regis, multis iam ante iniuriis[124] lacessitum, excedere urbe compulerat. Mox a civibus revocatum, cum Pistorium versus iter faceret,[125] privata latronum manu spoliandum vexandumqae curavit, ratus per huiuscemodi iniurias praefecto illatas regem quasi infensum civitati in suspicionem venturum, cives autem in se atque suos omnino converti. Hac igitur mente, cum ea perfecisset, Novellus, quem nuper ad Florentinos rex cum manu equitum miserat, commotus indignitate flagitii, Carminianum, pistoriensis agri oppidum, repentino impetu invasit. Quod postquam Pistorii auditum est, nulla fuit mora, quin Castrucius arcesseretur. Ille vero praesto adfuit[126] Pistoriensibus opem laturus; quo territi metu Florentini reddere Carminianum eos ipsos qui invaserant compulerunt. Sed haud multo post Philippus, Castruci favore fretus, tyrannidem invasit, foedusque cum illo aperte coniunxit; bellum tamen Florentinis nullum inferebat, sed quasi medius ita perstabat, ut alterutrius videretur potentiam formidare. Cum ergo tergiversaretur et ad hos modo, modo ad illos inclinaret, neutrae parti fidus, sed omnibus suspectus habebatur. Tanta vero Pistorii opportunitas erat ad bellum, ut utrique magnopere illius commodo moverentur.

87   Domi quoque eodem anno res innovatae; et superiore quam primo factam diximus antiquata, nova est sortitio instituta non priorum modo, sed et minorum magistratuum. Ex hac mutatione in republica, qui ante plurimum potuerant, ii minus valendi reman-

Filippo Tedici[56] aspired to the lordship of Pistoia and for that reason had compelled the king's lieutenant to leave the city, having provoked him with numerous insults and injuries. The man was soon recalled by the citizens, but as he made his way back to Pistoia, Tedici saw to it that he was harrassed and robbed by a private band of robbers. His idea was that this kind of injury would make the city apprehensive and fearful of the governor's hostility, and that the citizens would have recourse to himself and his supporters. When he had executed this plan, Novello,[57] who had recently been sent by the king to the Florentines with a body of knights, became outraged at this disgraceful crime, and swiftly attacked and seized Carmignano, a town in Pistoiese territory. As soon as this was known in Pistoia, they immediately summoned Castruccio. He was soon on the spot, ready to bring aid to the Pistoiesi, at which the frightened Florentines forced the very men who had seized Carmignano to surrender it. But soon thereafter Filippo, relying on Castruccio's influence, set up a tyranny and allied himself openly with the Lucchese leader. Yet he did not wage war against the Florentines, but stood as it were in the middle, seemingly fearful of the power of both sides. While he hesitated, inclining now to this side, now to that, he was trusted by neither party and suspected by everyone. But Pistoia's strategic importance was such that both sides were greatly attracted by its advantages.[58]

At home, too, in the same year there were constitutional 87 changes. The innovation we described earlier was nullified as soon as it was passed, and a new form of sortition was instituted including the minor magistrates as well as the Priors. Thanks to this change, those who before had been most powerful in the state became less strong, and, as is usually the case, they aroused great envy and persecution owing to their former power. Nardo Boldoni had been one of the leaders who had previously governed the state. In order to destroy him he was called before a magistrate on

serunt, magnaque, ut fit, invidia ob priorem eos potentiam exagitabat.[127] Nardus erat Berdo[128] unus e principibus qui ante rempublicam gubernarant. Huic cum dies apud magistratum dicta esset et causae pervertendi cupidius quaererentur, priores, quo illum periculo eriperent, gratia, ut fit, hominis, per legationis speciem dimiserunt, quasi reipublicae causa abesset. Cum praeses nihilominus damnare pergeret, nec ullam absentis rationem haberet, Michael huius frater et cum eo apparitores priorum pro tribunali adeuntes, reipublicae causa absentem allegabant ex priorumque auctoritate damnare prohibebant. Ibi, cum verbis certaretur, rixa tandem exorta est inter praesidis priorumque apparitores. Fit civium concursus et alterutris faventium atria complentur. Pervicit tandem obstinatio praesidis, nec absentem modo damnavit, verum etiam fratrem, qui cum apparitoribus priorum ad tribunal venerat, relegavit ad tempus. Quosdam etiam e prioribus, quod huic reo favissent, gravissima post multatione afflixit.

88   Altero dehinc anno, Philippus Pistoriensium tyrannus quod diu parturierat aliquando tandem peperit. Cum enim haud multo prius ad Florentinos conversus, eorum auxilia in urbem recepisset, inito mox cum Castrucio foedere intromissisque per noctem copiis, Pistorium illi tradidit. Quo facto omnes Florentinorum copiae, quot auxilii causa intra urbem fuerant, opprimuntur.

89   Huius vero rei nuntius ubi Florentiam perlatus est, priores e publico, quod forte ea die agebatur, convivio assurgentes, profectionem subitaneam indixere, nondum proditionis gnari, sed putantes aliquam urbis partem adversus Castrucium defendi. Ita Pratum usque rapto agmine profecti, eo tandem in loco perditas res tyranni fraude cognoverunt. Inde, quoniam vanum erat conari, Florentiam revertuntur. Post haec maiori nixu cogere exercitum ac

trumped-up charges, whereupon the Priors, taking account (as usual) of the man's rank, sent him out on a specious legation to remove him from danger, as though public duties were causing his absence. Nevertheless the royal governor continued to seek his condemnation and would not accept any excuse for his absence. His brother Michael and the clerks of the Priors then appeared before the tribunal and alleged that he was absent on public service and by the authority of the Priors forbade his condemnation. A dispute then arose. It began with words but ended in a brawl between the clerks of the priors and those of the governor. The citizens ran to look and the loggias filled with the supporters of both sides. Finally, the governor's obstinacy was victorious, and he not only condemned the absent Nardo, but banished for a time his brother who had come to the tribunal with the Priors' clerks. He also inflicted a heavy fine on some of the Priors because they had shown favor to the defendant.[59]

The next year Filippo, the tyrant of Pistoia, finally gave birth to what he had long conceived. For although he had turned to the Florentines not long before and had admitted their auxiliaries into the city, he now entered into a pact with Castruccio. He allowed Castruccio's troops to be brought in by night and delivered Pistoia to him. Whereupon the full complement of Florentine troops that were inside the city as auxiliaries were killed. 88 1325

When news of the slaughter was brought to Florence, the Priors, just then rising from a public dinner that happened to be held on that day, declared that an expedition should set out immediately. They were not yet aware of the betrayal, but thought that some part of that city would be defended against Castruccio. Thus a flying column was sent as far as Prato, where at last they learned that all was lost owing to the tyrant's trickery. Since effort was vain, they returned to Florence. Then it was decided to raise a more powerful army and send it against the enemy. A war-ma- 89

mittere in hostem placuit. Apparatus ad hoc non magnifice solum, verum etiam celeriter facti.

90   Dux exercitui praefectus est Ramundus Cardonius, qui magnos ante exercitus suo auspicio in Gallia ductaverat; ubi post res bello egregie gestas, tandem adverso proelio a Mediolanensibus captum redemptumque, Florentini castruciano bello delegerant ducem; casusque ita tulerat, ut altero post defectum Pistorii die, cum manu quadam equitum Florentiam pervenisset, praesentiaque et auctoritate mentes hominum extulisset ad bellum valentius capessendum. Cum igitur res subita et improvisa festinato indigere videretur, dux cum parte equitatus Pratum se propere contulit; reliquas vero copias ad eum convenire iussit. Cum omnes convenissent, movens inde dux, structa atque composita acie ad hostem pervenit. Castrucius fortunam pugnae experiri non ausus, intra moenia suos continebat, satis existimans fore, si urbem tutaretur. Quod exploratum cum esset, ad vastationem conversi, omnia circa urbem hostilem in modum popularunt, motis etiam saepius de industria castris, quo nulla regionis pars remaneret incolumis.

91   Post haec retro profecti, Titianum circumsederunt. Aliquot dies circa illud commorati, vineas agere, machinas instituere cuniculosque deducere coeperunt. Ea cuncta iussu ducis vel enixe fiebant, quo mentes hostium eo maxime converterentur. Ipse tamen longe alia cogitans, praefectum arcane instructum cum parte equitatus de prima vigilia praemittit,[129] et occupare transitum paludis iubet. Eadem ipsa nocte, quo magis avertat hostem, aliam equitatus partem circa Pistorii moenia magno cum tumultu praedatum mittit. Agrum lucensem a pistoriensi agro, a superiori quidem parte, montes asperrimi dirimunt Apennini[130] dorso connexi, adi-

chine was assembled for the purpose that was as swift in its formation as it was magnificent in appearance.

As captain they chose Ramondo di Cardona, who had previ- 90
ously led a great army in Lombardy under his own auspices.
There, after distinguishing himself in the war, he had been taken
captive by the Milanese during an unsuccessful battle. The Florentines ransomed him and chose him their as their captain in the
Castrucian war. As chance would have it, he had come to Florence
with a force of cavalry on the day after Pistoia defected, and his
presence and authority encouraged men's hearts to conduct the
war more vigorously. Since this sudden and unexpected event
seemed to demand haste, the captain with part of his cavalry rode
hastily to Prato, ordering the rest of the forces to meet him there.
When all the troops had been assembled, the captain set out from
Prato and marched towards the enemy in full battle array. Castruccio did not dare try the fortune of war, but kept his forces inside the city, believing it would be enough if he defended the city.
When his plan was discovered, the Florentine troops turned to
devastation, and they destroyed the environs of the city in hostile
fashion, purposely moving their camp often so that no part of the
region would remain unharmed.[60]

After this they withdrew and besieged Tizzano. They remained 91
there several days, and began to dig tunnels and bring up siege engines. All this was done with great activity at the order of the captain, so as to fix the attention of the enemy on that point. His real
plans were far different. In the first watch he sent out a lieutenant
with a detachment of calvary, bearing secret orders to occupy a
crossing through the swamp. The same night, to distract the enemy still further, he sent another party of cavalry near the walls of
Pistoia on a noisy mission of plunder. On its northern frontier the
Pistoian territory is separated from the Lucchese by forbidding
mountains, a spur of the Apennines, and its passes are almost all
guarded by fortresses. On the other side a broad swampland inter-

tusque ferme arcibus tenentur; altera vero ex parte palus latissima et impeditissimo ubique gurgite, praeter unum aut alterum aditum in quo se admodum coarctat, planitiem intersecat. Haec rursus arcta castellis praesidiisque hostes tutabantur. Ad haec igitur loca improviso occupanda missus praefectus, cum Fucetium pervenisset, pontem ligneum de industria paratum ad arcta paludis[131] nocte defert, ignaroque hoste, copias traducit; de hoc ipso ducem certiorem facit.

92 Ramundus, ubi haec intellexit, magna perfusus laetitia, confestim signa movit, desertaque protinus oppugnatione, vestigia praefecti secutus, ante paene quam hostis sentiret, cum omnibus copiis paludem transmisit. Inde Cappianum proximum castellum expugnare adortus, octavo fere post coeptam oppugnationem die, in deditionem accepit. Post haec, Falconium exercitu ducto (id quoque castellum paludi adiacet), pari tenore capit. Cum fama Florentinis prospera in dies vulgaret et[132] hostis iacere premique videretur, amici sociique, opitulandi studio conciti, eo decucurrerunt. Senenses enim, supra ducentos equites quos ab initio miserant, totidem alios equites et sagittarios sexcentos oppugnationibus utiles adiunxerunt. Miserunt et praecipuae Senarum familiae suo privatim nomine equites ducentos. A Perusinis quoque et Bononiensibus et Volaterranis aliisque sociis auxilia eodem rumore excita supervenerunt. Ex quibus omnibus permagna equitum copia in exercitu erat, peditum vero ad viginti millia.

93 Florentini, captis proximis trans paludem arcibus, demum ultra profecti, Topalsium obsedere. Id castellum, praeterquam fossis et turribus munitissimum erat, quingentorum insuper militum praesidio tenebatur. Stativis igitur circa illud positis, cum oppugnatio longius traheretur, exercitus, palustri humore ac insolita coeli gravitate confectus, aegrotare coepit, passimque languentium catervas erat inspicere, moriebanturque frequentes; missionem vero ple-

sects the plain, blocking access with deep waters everywhere except in one or two places where there are narrow passes. The enemy guarded these passes, too, with castles and fortresses. It was these places, therefore, that Ramondo unexpectedly sent his lieutenant to seize. The latter, arriving at Fucecchio, threw a specially prepared wooden bridge across the narrow passes of the swamp by night, and unbeknownst to the enemy brought his troops across them. Then he informed the captain of his success.[61]

Ramondo was overjoyed when he heard the news, and at once 92 abandoned the siege and marched away, following the trail of his lieutenant. He crossed the swamp with all his troops almost before the enemy knew it. Then he set about capturing the nearby castle of Cappiano, which surrended about eight days later. Then he marched the army to Montefalcone, another castle near the swamp, which he captured with equal speed. As the reports spread each day of the Florentines' good fortune, and their enemies seemed to be helpless, friends and allies hastened to them, motivated by zeal to be of service. The Sienese, in addition to the two hundred horse they had sent at the beginning, added another two hundred, plus six hundred archers, useful in sieges. The principal families of Siena, too, sent two hundred cavalry privately in their own names. Excited by the same rumor, reinforcements also arrived from Perugia, Bologna, Volterra, and other allies. Altogether there was an extremely large number of cavalry in the army and around 20,000 infantry.

Having captured the nearby strongholds near the swamp, the 93 Florentines then moved beyond it to besiege Altopascio. This castle, besides being heavily fortified with moats and towers, was guarded by five hundred soldiers. Having pitched camp nearby, when the siege began to drag out somewhat longer, the army began to suffer from a sickness contracted from the swampy humors and the unusual heaviness of the air. Everywhere you could see troops of sick and often dying men, and many men requested

rique valetudinis causa flagitabant. Ea primo res vigorem exercitus florentini populi attrivit. Permansit tamen in obsidione dux, et quasvis difficultates superare constituit.

94   Obsessos vero cum munitio egregia, tum multo magis Castruci spes et praesentia sustentabat; nam ille, ubi a Titiano subitum discessum nostrorum transmissasque paludes intellexit, cura simul et dolore anxius, Lucam redire constituit. Pistoriensibus igitur cunctis, de quorum fide ambigebat, profectione indicta, nobilitatem omnem ac optimum quemque e plebe secum eduxit;[133] ad tuendam vero urbem alias suorum copias dereliquit. Ipse, transgressus Montium Fauces per Nebulam fluvium, brevissimo itinere hostis antevenit, mediumque inter Lucam et florentinum exercitum, dextra ex parte, collem excelsum occupavit, ex eoque ad paludem militari opere fossam deducere[134] aggressus est. Amicorum praeterea undequaque auxilia rogat, neque die neque noctu agere multa conarique desistit.

95   Interea, quo hostis averteret, crebras incursiones a suis qui Pistorii remanserant in pratensem florentinumque agrum fieri providebat, incendiisque et rapinis cuncta misceri. Adversus eam manum ducentos equites bononienses, qui auxilii causa venerant, retinere circa urbem placuit, hominesque ex agro adiungere, qui parati intentique incursionem hostium observarent. Itaque, aliquotiens ante feliciter ausi Castruciani, tandem, cum licentius agerent, circumventi a bononiensi equitatu, concursu etiam agrestium oppressi, paene ad internecionem occiduntur.

96   Hoc detrimento accepto, rursus Castruci spes debilitari est coepta, simulque obsessi, ubi fractas Castruci vires deletasque copias in agro florentino, qua una spe maxima tenebantur, cognove-

leave for reasons of health. At first this situation wore down the strength of the Florentine People's army. Yet their captain persisted in the siege, resolved to overcome all difficulties.

The hopes of the besieged, meanwhile, were sustained by their 94 fine fortifications and still more by Castruccio's presence. He, to be sure, when he learned of the sudden departure of our forces from Tizzano and their crossing of the swamp, became anxious and upset, and decided to return to Lucca. Having commanded all the Pistoiesi whom he distrusted to depart, he marched out with all the nobility and the best of the commoners, leaving behind other forces of his to guard the city. Crossing through Serravalle by the shortest way, through Valdinievole, he arrived before the enemy did, and took up position between Lucca and the Florentine army, on a high hill on the right hand side. There he set about constructing a moat down to the swamp, using his soldiers as laborers. In addition he sent for reinforcements from his friends from every quarter, and worked ceaselessly, day and night, on numerous plans and projects.

Meanwhile, to distract the enemy, he saw to it that the troops 95 he had left behind in Pistoia should make frequent raids into Pratese and Florentine territory, throwing them into confusion with fire and pillage. To defend against this force the Florentines decided to keep near the city two hundred Bolognese cavalry who had come to help, adding a body of rustic folk who were prepared and ready to keep watch for enemy raids. Thus, after enjoying success with a number of daring raids, Castruccio's men at last took too great a chance. Surrounded by the Bolognese cavalry, and hemmed in, too, by a throng of rustics, they were cut down almost to a man.[62]

Having suffered this loss, Castruccio's hope began once again to 96 fade. At the same time, when they learned that Castruccio's forces had been broken and his troops, their single greatest hope, had been wiped out, the besieged lost confidence in the situation and

runt, rebus iam diffisi castellum dediderunt, incolumes inde abire pacti.

97　　Recepto Florentini castello munitissimo[135] praesidioque imposito, quid iam agendum foret consultabant. Erant quibus optimum videretur exercitum reducere, praesertim morbis gravitateque coeli laborantem, et longa difficilique militia per aestatis autumnique ferventissimos ardores insalubribus locis confectum, missione etiam multorum a duce concessa diminutum: nam postquam diutius in his locis commoratum est, multi, vel taedio castrorum vel metu valetudinis adversae, commeatum a duce postulaverant. Ea plane res perfacile concessa maiorem in modum attenuaverat castra; quae prospicientes quidam graviores exercitum reducendum suadebant. Alii, iactantia magis[136] quam ulla probabili ratione ducti, non prius reducendum victorem exercitum praedicabant quam Lucae moenia pulsassent. Haec tandem, quae minus sapiens, ceterum ferocior ac[137] iactantior erat, ad extremum vicit praevaluitque sententia. Cum ergo Lucam petere statuissent, dux postridie signa movens, ad sextianam paludem fecit castra. Biduo in his locis commoratus, cum ad superiora contendere loca statuisset, cohortem praemisit, quae saepta intercisaque complanaret. Huic centum non amplius equites in praesidio attribuit.

98　　Castrucius, ubi adventare cohortem sensit, superiori de loco partem equitatus in illam mittit. Concurrunt equites qui in praesidium[138] ierant cohortis, proeliumque equestre in subiecta valle conseritur, non magnum ab initio, sed tempore augescens. Quod enim propinqua erant castra, continue plures ad strepitum vociferationemque proeliantium concurrebant. Pugna fuit egregia sine ullo pedite, ac supra tres horas sic acriter dimicatum, ut misceren-

surrendered the castle, it having been agreed that they could leave unharmed.

The Florentines took possession of this well-fortified castle 97 and, mounting a guard, took counsel as to what they should do next. Some thought it would be best to withdraw the army, citing particularly its sufferings with disease and the heavy air, the long and difficult campaign in the boiling heat of summer and autumn in unhealthy places, and also how it had decreased in size thanks to the many leaves the captain had granted. For after a good deal of time had been spent in these places, many had requested a furlough from the captain out of boredom with camp life or from fear of bad health. The readiness with which leave had been granted had much reduced the army's size, and seeing this, certain men of the graver sort argued for withdrawing the army. Others, influenced more by bravado than sound reasoning, urged that the victorious army should not be withdrawn until it had assailed the walls of Lucca. The latter view — less wise but more bellicose and boastful — in the end prevailed. So, it having been decided to head for Lucca, the captain on the following day sent forth the standards and made camp by the swamp at Sesto. He spent two days in this place before deciding to make for higher ground, sending out a party to knock down the palisades and barriers. This party was given a guard of no more than a hundred cavalry.[63]

When Castruccio heard that the party was coming, he sent a 98 detachment of horse out against it from higher ground. The knights who had come to guard the party rode up and a cavalry battle was joined in valley below. It was a small one at first, but it grew. Since the camps were near each other, more men were continually drawn into the battle by the noise and clamor of the combatants. In due course whole battle formations were often involved, each crushing the other and being crushed in turn. Finally Castruccio himself with the rest of his cavalry made a sudden descent into the battle. Since he had stormed down to the attack

tur saepe acies totae ac invicem profligarent profligarenturque. Tandem Castrucius ipse cum reliquo omni equitatu repente in pugnam descendit; qui, cum de superiori loco impetum procellamque dedisset ac longe numero praestaret, premere iam Florentinorum equitatum coepit. Ramundus quoque cum reliquo equitatu ad ipsa iam saepta pervenerat aliquanto infra eum locum ubi pugnabatur, coniectusque in difficiles aditus, cum haud facile expedire agmen posset, superati interea equites qui adversus Castrucium dimicabant, terga dederunt. Ne detrimentum in fuga acciperetur, propinquitas maioris agminis ad saepta ipsa expectantis effecit. Ceterum in proelio optimus quisque aut interfectus est aut graviter vulneratus; capti etiam complures. Hosti quoque non incruenta fuit victoria, multis suorum amissis, et ipso quoque Castrucio duce, dum cominus pugnat, vulnerato. Post haec ad speciem commorati cum utrinque tubae canerent, tandem, nocte dirempti, in sua quique[139] castra rediere.

99 Hoc proelium Florentinos longe segniores quam antea reddidit ad studium concertandi. Contra vero hostis, spe sublatus, victoriam meditari copiasque amicorum instantius arcessere, praesertim mediolanensium principum, quorum equitatus in agro parmensi bellum per id tempus gerere ferebatur. Igitur favore partium ac praemiorum pollicitatione obtinuit ut Accius Vicecomes, iuvenis et natura acer et multis bellis exercitatus, cum octingentis equitibus Apenninum transcendat ac Lucam, quam ocissime possit, approperet. Interea[140] non insolito astu providit, ut quaedam circum oppida per falsas proditionum spes ducem exercitumque demorarentur; arcane colloquia apud primores sererent, quibus factum est ut dux, falsa delusus spe, malo quidem consilio, in his copias locis contineret diutius. Sed cum fama adventare Accium vulgaret, Florentini primo falsum rumorem credere ab hoste diffusum. Enim-

from higher ground and his forces were far greater, he began to bring pressure on the Florentine cavalry. Ramondo, too, with his remaining cavalry had by now come up to the palisade, just below where the battle was being fought, but the approach was difficult from his position and it was no easy matter for him to extricate his column. Meanwhile, the cavalry who had been fighting Castruccio were defeated and put to flight. The propinquity of the army's main body, which was waiting by the palisade, prevented them from suffering further harm in their flight, but there was no excellent knight in the battle that was not either killed or gravely wounded, and many, too, were captured. The victory was a bloody one for the enemy also, for they lost many of their men, and even Castruccio himself was wounded in hand-to-hand fighting. For appearance's sake both armies lingered with trumpets blowing on both sides, but at last, as night fell, each returned to its own camp.[64]

This battle made the Florentines far less eager to fight than they had been before. The enemy, on the other hand, grew hopeful and began to think about victory. He urgently besought troops from his friends, especially from the Milanese princes, whose cavalry were said to be waging war in the territory of Parma at that time. By appeals to partisanship and promises of reward he arranged to have Azzo Visconti, a ferocious youth with much experience in war, cross the Apennines with eight hundred knights and come to Lucca without delay. Meanwhile, he saw to it with his accustomed shrewdness that certain nearby towns should detain the Florentine captain and his army with false hopes of betrayals, and secretly they engaged in parleys with their leaders, thanks to which it transpired that the captain, deluded with false hope and bad counsel, kept his troops still longer in that unhealthy spot. When the report began to circulate that Azzo was coming, the Florentines at first thought it was a false rumor spread by the enemy. Of course when they learned that he had indeed crossed the

99

vero ubi exuperasse Apennini iugum et iam Lucae appropinquare cognoverunt, retro moventes castra, Topalsium rediere. Muniendo eo castello cum diem integrum absumpsissent, motis postridie signis, Fucetium versus remeabant.

100 Haec primum sub ortum solis agebantur, eo die Accius cum equitatu venturus erat in castra. Itaque dolens Castrucius Florentinorum copias sine pugna abire speratamque victoriam in ipso articulo e manibus praeterlabi, ipse cum suis e colle quem occuparat descendere ac impedire agmen distinereque[141] constituit. Id cum ardentius faceret, magnam nostris difficultatem iniecit et quasi incertos consilii reddidit. Properarentne abire? At id, praeterquam turpe et dedecoris plenum, insuper quoque periculosum videbatur. Starent ac resisterent? At novi equitatus formidabatur adventus, qui, si hosti adiungeretur, desperationem penitus afferebat. In his difficultatibus vicit id consilium quod magis decorum videbatur, conversisque in hostem signis (quae unica erat salus), profectionem intermiserunt. Et levia quidem proelia statim committi sunt coepta. Duces vero, quasi mox totis agminibus conflicturi, se ad pugnam comparabant. Castrucius tamen e colle non penitus descendebat, sed minabundus et quasi mox aggressurus rem in longum protrahebat. Inter haec Accius cum equitatu supervenit, qui cum se Castrucio iunxisset, nulla fuit mora quin signa inferrent.

101 Florentini, etsi adventus novi equitatus turbabat animos, tamen aciem struxerunt et ad fortunam proelii se pro tempore compararunt. Acies triplici subsidio firmata fuit. Ceterum in congressu qui in fronte stabant fortissime dimicarunt, sed ubi pugna ad secundam pervenit aciem, praefectus Ramundi, qui eidem praeerat aciei,

Apennine passes and was now approaching Lucca, they withdrew their forces and returned to Altopascio. Having spent a full day strengthening that castle, they retreated the following day in the direction of Fucecchio.

This happened at sunrise on the day that Azzo was to have 100 come to the Lucchese camp with his cavalry.[65] Castruccio was naturally unhappy that the Florentine troops were leaving without a fight and that his hoped-for victory was slipping out of his hands at the critical moment. So he decided to come down with his troops from the hill he was occupying and to block and delay the Florentine column. His fierce assault created a great problem for our troops and cast their plans into uncertainty. Should they make a run for it? But that course, in addition to being shameful and thoroughly unseemly, seemed to be perilous as well. Should they stand and fight? But they feared the arrival of Azzo's cavalry, which if joined to that of the enemy would put them in a desperate position. In these difficult circumstances the more honorable advice triumphed, and they turned their standards against the enemy, postponing the march home (which was their one hope). Skirmishes immediately began, but the captains prepared for battle as though the conflict was going to take place in full battle formation. Castruccio, however, had not completely abandoned his position on the hill, but dragged out the situation by acting in a threatening manner, like someone about to attack. While he was doing so Azzo arrived with his cavalry, and when he had joined up with Castruccio, they immediately began the attack.

The Florentines, though worried by the arrival of fresh cavalry, 101 nevertheless set up their line of battle and prepared themselves for the fray insofar as time allowed. The battle line was strengthened by triple ranks. In the first onslaught the men standing in the front rank fought with extreme bravery. But when the battle reached the second rank, Ramondo's lieutenant, who was in command of it, whether through cowardice or treason (for both expla-

sive ignavia sive proditione (nam utrumque de illo proditum est),
referre illico pedem ac signa convertere coepit. Ea res non agmen
quod ab eo ductabatur solum, sed tertium quoque quod in subsidio stabat trepidare ac de fuga magis quam de victoria cogitare
perpulit. Ita prementibus hostibus, tandem omnes profligantur. In
hac pugna non multi ceciderunt[142] ob breve admodum certamen;
in fuga vero longe sunt maiora[143] detrimenta suscepta. Nam Castrucius, misso confestim equitatu, transitum paludis, quo[144] eva-
dendum fuerat, occupavit, his qui in praesidio pontis erant sponte
sua deserentibus. Ibi oppressi permulti mortales, capti etiam complures; Ramundus ipse dux cum filio impedimentaque omnia in
potestatem victoris devenere.

102   Victor triduo fere in his locis commoratus, amissa prius castella
recuperavit; spoliis mox captivisque Lucam missis, ipse cum omnibus copiis Pistorium rediit. Inde florentinum agrum magno terrore
ingressus, sexta post proelium die apud Signiam castra fecit.
Opportunitas eius loci, qui bello urbi inferendo aptissimus est,
studia civium commoverat ad Signiam muniendam. Ea de causa
equites peditesque eo missi in praesidio erant; qui postquam adventare Castrucium intellexere, praesentia victoris conterriti diffi-
sique munitionibus aufugerunt.

103   Hostis capta Signia secundis inde castris ad Piretolam constitit,
duobus passuum millibus ab urbe. Mox ad moenia profectus,
cuncta tumultu ac terrore complevit, refugientibus in urbem agres-
tibus, et pecora simul parvosque natos pavore insolito, quasi perdi-
tis rebus, una trahentibus. Structa contra portam acie, nemo cum
obviam prodiret, ad vastationem conversus, quidquid villarum ae-
dificiorumque fuit ab ea parte incendit. Ludicrum etiam cursus
edidit a solito civitatis carcere Piretolam versus. Primum equites,

nations have been reported) began to withdraw and reverse the standards. This act spread fear not only in the rank he was leading, but also in the third rank which was standing in reserve, and it turned men's thoughts to flight rather than victory. Hence, under pressure from the enemy, the whole army was overwhelmed. Not many fell in the battle itself owing to its brevity, but much greater damage was sustained in the flight. For Castruccio quickly sent out cavalry which seized the pass through the marsh; those who were guarding it deserted of their own accord. Many men died in that place, and many more were captured. Captain Ramondo himself with his son and the entire baggage train fell into the hands of the victor.[66]

After spending three days there the victor recovered the castles   102
he had lost and, sending the spoils and prisoners to Lucca, he himself returned to Pistoia with all his forces. From there he entered Florentine territory, causing great terror, and pitched camp at Signa on the sixth day after the battle. The convenience of this place for making war against the city aroused the zeal of the citizens to fortify it. For this reason horse and foot were sent there to guard it, but when these forces learned that Castruccio was coming they fled, terrified by the presence of the victor and lacking confidence in the fortifications.

Having captured Signa, the enemy established from that base a   103
second camp at Peretola, two miles from the city. From thence he set out for the city walls, spreading alarm and confusion everywhere. Countrymen in unaccustomed panic were streaming into the city, taking with them their farm animals and small children as though all was lost. Castruccio set up his battle line before the gate, but when no one came out to meet him he turned to devastation, burning all the villas and buildings on that side of the city. He set up a racecourse between what was normally the city jail and Peretola. First the cavalry, then the infantry, then the prostitutes ran it. Silken favors were given to the victors in each of

inde pedites, mox scorta decurrerunt.[145] Horum singulis certaminibus singula pallia siricea victori proposuit. Triduo apud Piretolam hostis habuit castra. Inde in viam pratensem deflectens, regionem amoenissimam insigni villarum celebritate, a moenibus paene
urbis ad Marinam fluvium uno tenore[146] vastavit. Trans Arnum
post haec missis copiis per proximum Signiae pontem, a sinistra
fluvii ripa usque ad urbem ac laevos montes omnia populatus est.
Ea cum perfecisset, onustum praeda militem inaestimabilique rapina locupletatum Lucam reduxit, ut promissam Accio pecuniam
solveret. Fuit autem summa auri viginti quinque millium.

104   Quae cum ex fide persoluta esset, Accius, militibus suis in
unum vocatis, 'Exegimus', inquit, 'commilitones, rem praeclaram.
Amico enim nostrarumque partium homini suis in periculis opem
strenuam ferentes, unaque cum illo adversus hostem[147] dimicantes,
facilem ac locupletem victoriam nacti, gloriam belli cum opulentia
praedae coniunximus. Nunc autem tempus est per eandem qua ve-
nimus viam in Galliam remeandi. Quod ita laeto faciemus animo,
si non iam Castrucio, sed mihi duci vestro concedetis, ut nostro
ipsi nomine unam modo diem florentina moenia pulsemus. Civitas enim est non diversarum modo partium, sed nostro quidem
generi atque familiae peculiariter inimica. Quotiens illa adversariis
nostris submisit auxilia! Quotiens inimicos fovit! ut etiam huius
vexilla e mediolanensi arce spectare cogeremur. Quare, agite nunc!
parenti generique et mihi vestram operam navate. Cernat Florentinus e muro Accium Vicecomitem iniurias parentis suasque ulcis-
centem, ac discat parcius nocere generi nostro.'

105   Ad haec laetum clamorem cum tota simul agmina extulissent,
collaudata eorum fide postridie in armis esse iubet, ac prima luce
movens Signiam rediit. Secuti sunt etiam castruciani milites,

the contests. The enemy remained encamped for three days at Peretola. Then, turning down the Via Pratese, he devastated the whole area practically from the walls of the city to the Val di Marina, a lovely region celebrated for its fine villas. Afterwards, crossing the Arno by the bridge of Signa, he ravaged the whole region on the left side of the river and the mountains to the south, right down to the city. When he had finished, he led his troops back to Lucca, loaded with plunder and enriched with countless spoils, so that he could pay Azzo the money he had promised him. The sum was 25,000 florins.

When this had been paid him in accordance with the agreement, Azzo called his soldiers together and addressed them: "We have accomplished, fellow soldiers, a famous deed. We have brought vigorous help to a friend and fellow partisan in the moment of his peril, and we have fought alongside him against his enemies, achieving an easy and highly profitable victory. We have acquired glory in war and rich plunder. Now it is time to return to Lombardy the same way we came. I shall return there happily if you will agree, not now for Castruccio's sake but for the sake of me, your commander, to make a strike of a single day only against the walls of Florence in our own name. For that city not only belongs to the opposing party, but is also particularly hostile to my kin and family. How often has it sent aid to our adversaries! How often has it fostered our enemies! We have even been compelled to watch its banner from the Milanese citadel. So ride now! Spend your energies for my father, for my kin, and for me. Let the Florentine see from his walls how Azzo Visconti avenges the injuries done to him and his father, and let him learn to be more careful about harming one of my kin!"[67]

The whole column greeted his words with a happy cheer, and commending their loyalty, he ordered them to be in arms the next day. Setting out at dawn, he returned to Signa. Castruccio's soldiers, too, followed him, both from respect for the young man and

tum[148] ob gratiam iuvenis, tum ob praedarum cupiditatem. Apud
Signiam nocte una commoratus, postera die, structa insigniter
acie, ad urbem venit. Ibi, cum se vexillaque e proximo ostentasset,
nemine obviam prodeunte, in ipso fluminis alveo per multas commoratus horas et ludicris quibusdam militari more factis, incli-
nante iam sole, Signiam rediit. Mox inde profectus, Lucam primo,
post[149] in Galliam transiit.

106　　Post Accii discessum, Castrucius iam ipse per se copias omnes
circa Pratum deduxit. Cum frustra eius oppidi oppugnationem[150]
tentasset, ad vastationem conversus, omnia ferro igneque popula-
vit. Novem fere[151] diebus circa Pratum consumptis, Signiam cum
exercitu regressus, ultra citraque Arnum infesto agmine rursus[152]
portas adusque discurrit, ac si quid incolume superfuerat[153] a
priori vastitate, incendit.

107　　In tanta civitatis clade illud etiam turbabat, quod multitudo
agrestium cum pecoribus ac semirapta supellectile in urbem re-
fuga, per vias[154] passim complebat omnia.[155] Hanc sive ob insolentiam urbis sive ob anxietatem incommoditatemque rerum suarum,
morbus invaserat malique huius contagio cives etiam apprehende-
rat, et moriebantur multi, et plena aegrotantium cuncta cernebantur. Caritas quoque annonae consecuta est, raptis aut incensis fru-
mentis, ac spe in futurum deterrima. Augebat insuper civitatis
metum, quod vulgo ferebant Guidonem Arretinorum praesulem
magno cum exercitu e superiori parte ad urgendam obsidionem
esse venturum; rogatumque a Castrucio multis nunciis constabat,
veterem Arretinorum cladem apud Campaldinum acceptam me-
morante ac tempus ad delendam inimicorum potentiam ostende-
nte, fore quidem, si ille superiori de loco adventaret, ut Florentia

out of desire for plunder. After spending the night at Signa, on the following day he arranged his men in splendid formation and went to the city. There he displayed himself and his flag at close quarters, but no one came out to meet him. He stayed many hours by the river bed, his troops amusing themselves after the military fashion, and when the sun went down he returned to Signa. Soon he left that place and passed first to Lucca, then Lombardy.[68]

After Azzo's departure, Castruccio himself now brought all his 106 troops down to Prato on his own account. After trying in vain to take that town, he turned to devastation, and ravaged everything with fire and the sword. Having spent almost nine days near Prato, he withdrew to Signa with his army and scoured once again the whole area up and down the Arno with plundering parties, right up to the gates of the city, and burned whatever had been left over from the earlier devastation.

In the midst of this great civic disaster, another source of con- 107 fusion was the large number of country folk who had taken refuge in the city with their cattle and hastily-seized possessions. The streets and the whole city was full of them. Whether because they were unused to city life or owing to anxiety about the state of their affairs, disease attacked them; and the citizens, too, caught the sickness from them, dying in droves. The whole city appeared to be full of the sick. Thanks to the seizure and burning of their crops, famine, too, soon followed, and the outlook for future harvests was extremely poor. The city's apprehension was further increased by the widespread report that Guido, bishop of Arezzo, was coming with a large army from the upper Arno to take up the siege. Castruccio had evidently entreated him through multiple messengers to remember the old defeat suffered by the Aretines at Campaldino, and had pointed out this opportunity to destroy the power of his enemies; if he would come from the upper Arno, Florence would be besieged on all sides, and its enormous popula-

undique obsideretur, multitudinem vero populi absque importato victitare non posse.

108   Ob hunc obsidionis metum, viri creati sunt duo ad moenia urbis ceteraque munimenta inspicienda instaurandaque: Nerius Angeli filius Albertus et Ianus Landi filius Albicius. Ab his vallum aliquot locis factum; in arce autem[156] fesulana, ne eam occuparet hostis, praesidium communitum est; alterum quoque praesidium in colle urbi imminente ad Miniatis aedem. Ceterum neque preces neque monita Castruci Guidonem praesulem movere potuerunt, sive quod eius odium in Florentinos minime acerbum erat, sive quod Castruci gloriae invidebat, sive quod eius magnitudinem formidabat. Castrucius certe semper prae se tulit praedicavitque per praesulem stetisse, quo minus Florentia malo domita caperetur.

109   Tunc autem per se bellum gerens, omnia vastationibus incendiisque foedavit. Post hoc per Marinam fluvium transire in agrum mugellanum conatus, cum ab accolis, concursu ad Comblate vetustum oppidum facto,[157] arceretur, circa fluvium diffusus, hominum pecorumque magna coacta praeda, nocte una in his locis commoratus est. Id Florentiae nunciatum cum esset, missi equites ducenti et peditum duo millia fauces ipsas fluvii qua redeundum erat praeoccupare constituerunt; quod si fecissent, videbatur hostis evadere non posse. Sed Castrucius, parvo anteveniens spatio, cum omni praeda ac longo captivorum agmine praetergressus est. His peractis, cum quantum nullus antea regionem afflixisset, relicto apud Signiam satis grandi praesidio, Lucam rediit. Ibi suorum operum ostentator speciem quandam triumphi egit; apud Signiam quoque monumentum victoriae nummum percussit.

110   Dum haec a Florentinis Castrucioque geruntur, Guido Arretinorum praesul magnis equitum peditumque copiis Laterinum ob-

tion could not be victualed without food brought in from outside its walls.[69]

Fearing such a siege, two citizens were elected to inspect and restore the walls and the city's other fortifications: Neri d'Agnolo degli Alberti and Giano di Lando degli Albizzi. They built earthworks in several places and erected a stronghold within the citadel of Fiesole to prevent its being taken by the enemy, and another on the hill overlooking the church of San Miniato al Monte. However, neither Castruccio's prayers nor his threats were able to influence Bishop Guido, whether because his hatred of the Florentines was not overly bitter, or because he envied Castruccio's glory, or because he feared his greatness. Castruccio, certainly, always maintained and declared openly that it had been the bishop's fault that he had not captured Florence when it had been mastered by disease. 108

But he continued to wage war on his own at that time, befouling everything with fire and destruction. Afterwards he tried to pass into the Mugello through the Val di Marina, but his way was barred by the inhabitants who had gathered at the old town of Combiata. Compelled by his great plunder of men and animals to spread out by the river, Castruccio spent a night in this area. When news of this came to Florence, two hundred horse and two thousand foot were sent out to block the mouth of the riverbed where Castruccio would have to exit. And if they had accomplished this, it seems the enemy could not have escaped. But Castruccio beat them handily and came out with all his plunder and a long line of prisoners. This done, he returned to Lucca, leaving behind at Signa a considerable garrison and having devasted the region as no one before him had ever done. In Lucca, in order to show off his deeds, he held a kind of triumph, and at Signa he also struck a coin to commemorate his victory.[70] 109

While these events were taking place between the Florentines and Castruccio, Guido, bishop of Arezzo, laid siege to Laterina 110

sedit. Causa vero obsidendi ista fuit. Pontifex romanus, commotus ob Tiferni occupationem a praesule Arretinisque nuper factam, cum frustra adversus eos minas censurasque exercuisset, tandem Cortonam antiquum oppidum a praesulatu Arretinorum abscidit, ac proprium illi episcopum dedit Rainerium Beordi filium e familia nobili. Is ergo cum in diminutionem civitatis procurasse abscissionem eius oppidi videretur, tanta repente indignatio apud Arretinos coorta est, ut domos ubertinae gentis, ex qua is erat, everterent, et castella quae ab illis tenebantur infesto milite pervaderent. Cum itaque Laterinates propter vicinitatem gentis ad favorem eius inclinare viderentur, et aliae quoque indignationis causae subessent, ad illud obsidendum cum multitudine Arretinorum profectus praesul, tandem oppidum cepit et ad solum evertit.

III Post haec Sabinum exercitus a praesule traductus. In id oppidum nulla iam Cortonae iniuria, sed partium ducebat studium. Admotis itaque copiis, cum Sabinum quoque obsedisset ac tandem expugnasset, pari tenore ad solum evertit.

II2 Eodem anno, per extremum fere autumni tempus, Castrucius per proximos agnatosque captivorum de pace cum Florentinis agere coepit. Eius rei causa, cum parentes propinquique multa per gratiam conarentur, ac per se quisque operam navaret, in suspicionem vertere ne per speciem pacis colloquia proditionis quaererentur. Itaque suppressa eius rei mentio est salubrique civitatis decreto provisum ne cui proximo agnatove captivi alicuius arcis aut

with a great force of cavalry and infantry. The reason was as follows. The Roman pontiff, who was upset by the recent occupation of Città di Castello by Guido and the Aretines, had been hurling threats and censures against them in vain. Finally, he detached the ancient town of Cortona from the bishopric of Arezzo and gave it its own bishop, Rinieri di Biordo, of a noble family. Since it appeared that Rinieri had obtained the separation of that town to the detriment of their own city, the Aretines were immediately outraged, and, having knocked down the dwellings of the Ubertini (for Rinieri belonged to that family), they sent a military expedition to attack the castles that family controlled. The Ubertini being their neighbors, the people of Laterina seemed to favor the family, and there were other grounds for being angry at them besides. Hence the bishop set out with a multitude of Aretines to besiege the place, which at length he conquered and razed to the ground.

After that, the bishop brought his army to Monte San Savino. III It was not now the injury in regard to Cortona, but partisanship that led him against that town. So he brought his troops up there and besieged Monte San Savino too, took it, and razed it to the ground in the same way.[71]

In that same year, almost at the end of the autumn, Castruccio 112 began to negotiate peace with the Florentines through kinsmen and male relatives of his prisoners. Owing to this circumstance — since the relatives and kinsmen were attempting many things through influence and everyone was looking out for themselves — they aroused the suspicion that they were aiming to discuss betrayal under the cloak of peace negotiations. So talk of the peace was suppressed, and the city passed a salutary decree prohibiting any stronghold or town from being committed to the custody of any kinsman or male relative of a captive. And lest the enemy be able to roam at will making open war with too great freedom, the Florentines reinforced two forts, one at Combiata and the other at

oppidi custodiam liceret committi. Ne autem aperto bello vagari licentius quiret hostis, unum apud Comblate, alterum apud Bonum Montem praesidia communiverunt ac stationibus militum firmarunt, quo nec per mugellanum agrum, quod iam prius tentaverat, nec per Gravem fluvium pervadere posset. Vectigalibus quoque adauctis, novos pecuniarum reditus novumque delectum habere constituerunt. Praeterea in his ipsis difficultatibus, ne inferiores beneficentia viderentur, Bononiensibus gravi tunc bello laborantibus ducentorum equitum misere subsidium. Ita, iam dempto metu, maiori cum animo res a civitate gerebantur.

113   Inter haec hostis reductis copiis Murlum oppidum non longe a Prato obsidere constituit; eius rei gratia, cum exercitum admovisset, machinis et cuniculis ac omni expugnandarum arcium apparatu pervincere adortus est. Erant in praesidio milites centum quinquaginta, duoque cum his praefecti e nobilitate florentina, Iohannes Adimar et Rainerius Pactius. In his tanta providentia ac magnitudo animi fuit, ut hostium conatus longo tempore frustrarentur. Castrucius ergo saepe incassum expugnationem adortus, cum immorandum esse videret, quaedam circum oppidum praesidia communivit; cuniculos vero in ipsam arcem agere perrexit. Crebro insuper adortus per diem plurimum, nonnunquam etiam noctu, nec spatium somni nec ullam requietem obsessis dabat. Quare, tandem lassitudini militum timentes praefecti, quod magni murorum ambitus assidua incubatione tuendi erant, re Florentiam nunciata, subvenire postularunt. Id cum negligenter fieret, hostis interea de praesidio in praesidium fossam vallumque circumduxit ac omnem ferendae opis spem obsessis praecidit.

114   Durante apud Murlum obsidione, castruciani,[158] qui apud Signiam erant, florentinum agrum assiduis[159] incursionibus infesta-

Montebuoni, strengthening them with military garrisons, so that Castruccio could not pass through the Mugello, which he had already tried, nor via the river Greve. Customs income[72] having also increased, they decided to raise more cash receipts and have a fresh levy of troops. Moreover, despite the difficult straits they were in, they sent aid in the form of 200 knights to the Bolognese, who were involved at the time in a serious war, lest Florence should appear behindhand in conferring benefits. Thus, having now laid aside its fear, the city began to conduct its affairs with greater spirit.[73]

Meanwhile the enemy brought back his forces and decided to besiege the town of Montemurlo, not far from Prato. With this object in view, he encamped his army and set about attacking the town with siege engines, tunnels, and all the apparatus for reducing strongholds. In the fort were 150 soldiers led by two Florentine nobles, Giovanni Adimari and Rinieri de' Pazzi.[74] These men possessed such great foresight and strength of character that the enemy's endeavors were long frustrated. Having tried to storm it numerous times without result, Castruccio, seeing that there was going to be some delay, built several bastions around the town and set about digging tunnels underneath the citadel itself. Moreover he frequently attacked the town through most of the day, sometimes also at night, and never gave the besieged a moment for sleep or rest. Finally, the Florentine commanders grew frightened at the exhaustion of their troops, since the vast circuit of the walls needed to be guarded continually. Informing Florence of this threat, they asked for help. But the matter was treated carelessly and the enemy in the meantime surrounded the town with trenches and earthworks, stretching from bastion to bastion, and so cut off any hope of aid being brought to the besieged.

While the siege of Montemurlo was taking place, Castruccio's troops based at Signa were harrassing the Florentine countryside with continual raids. Finally, when they had galloped down the

bant. Demum pisana via discurrentes, cum ad ipsas paene urbis portas magno tumultu devenissent, irritati maiorem in modum cives, in eosque egressi quatuor passuum millibus, ita praecipites egerunt, ut effusa semper fuga uterentur, nec ulla arte praeterquam celeritate pedum evaderent. Ex hoc hostes appropinquare urbi formidarunt; sed remotiora vexantes loca, omnifariam belli clades inferebant.

115   Obsessi vero apud Murlum in dies magis premebantur, ac iam partem murorum cuniculi quassarant. Quae cum in praesentia forent gravia et in futurum graviora timerentur, ad extremum iam auxilium respiciens civitas, Carolum Roberti regis filium in Etruriam evocare ac ei civitatis imperium tradere constituit. Huius[160] rei gratia, legati quinque creati: Franciscus Scala, Alexius Rinutius, Donati duo, alter Acciaiolus, alter Perutius, Philippus Bartoli filius. Hi decretum populi ferentes, cum ad Carolum venissent, Alexius (is enim scientia iuris clarus ea tempestate habebatur), 'Quod faustum', inquit, 'felixque sit tibi, Carole, parentique tuo nobisque omnibus, florentinus populus te in decennium his conditionibus dominum gubernatoremque civitatis deputat.' Conditiones inde[161] ex pagella recitatae sunt, non dissimiles his quae fuerant dudum in traditione regi descriptae, nisi quod hic certus pecuniarum militumque modus erat praescriptus, ibi vero cuncta regis arbitrio permissa. Iuvenis igitur ex sententia patris civitate suscepta sese copiasque parabat, proxima aestate in Etruriam transiturus.

116   Castrucius vero,[162] dum haec agebantur, Murlum summa vi oppugnabat; iamque murorum partem cuniculi everterant; reliquas

Via Pisana and arrived with great uproar practically at the very gates of the city, the citizens, exceedingly provoked, came out four miles against them, acting with such suddenness that the enemy troops took off in disorderly flight and got away by employing the simple tactic of taking to their heels. After this the enemy were afraid to come near the city, but harrassed more remote places, visiting upon them in every way the disasters of war.

But the siege of Montemurlo grew more desperate by the day, 115 and by now the walls had begun to tremble owing to the tunnels beneath them. Since the situation was grave and it was feared that it would become graver still, the city now looked to its last source of aid, and decided to recall into Tuscany Charles, the son of King Robert, and turn over command of the city to him.[75] For this purpose, five ambassadors were chosen: Francesco Scali, Alessio Rinucci, Donato Acciaiuoli, Donato Peruzzi, and Filippo di Bartolo. These men conveyed the people's decree, and when they had come to Charles, Alessio (who at that time had a great reputation for legal knowledge) said: "The Florentine People appoints you lord and governor of the city for ten years on these conditions, and may this bring you prosperity and good fortune, Charles, and also your father and us all."[76] The conditions were read out from the document, which were not dissimilar to the ones that had been prescribed to the king when he had been granted power earlier, except that on this occasion a fixed amount of money and troops was specified, whereas previously everything had been left to the king's discretion. The young man thus took possession of the city on his father's advice and prepared himself and his troops to pass into Tuscany the following summer.

In the meantime Castruccio was besieging Montemurlo with 116 the greatest violence, and by now the tunnels had knocked down part of the walls, while the rest were crumbling under the siege engines. The garrison was exhausted and suffering from wounds, and since no reason remained for them to hold out, the town was

vero machinae quassarant. Defessis militibus ac vulneratis, nulla cum ratio durandi superesset, oppidum Castrucio deditur, his qui intus erant incolumibus abire pactis. Murlo recepto, hostis moenia refecit ac praesidio militum communivit.

117 Per haec ipsa tempora Petrus quidam gallus copiis Florentinorum praefectus, cum suae gentis hominibus qui apud hostem militabant clam tractatu habito, necem Castruci ac Signiae receptionem multis ac magnis pollicitationibus agitabat. Ea res demum patefacta sortiri effectum nequivit. Ceterum, captis plerisque auctoribus supplicioque affectis, ita turbavit Castruci exercitum, ut cuncta suspicionibus implerentur. Et auxit mox eum timorem, quod Petrus cum subitaneis equitibus solito audacius ad Signiae portas accessit. Itaque ipse, duobus peditum millibus, equitibus vero[163] septingentis Pistorio movens, Signiam petiit. Ibi, amotis e[164] praesidio iis de quorum fide dubitabatur, cum his copiis florentinum agrum ingressus, via senensi Cassianum usque pervenit, et quo dolorem augeret, incendia late exercuit.

118 Iam fama vulgarat Caroli regis filii apparatum; nec ambiguum erat illius adventum proxima aestate esse futurum. Quam rem secum agitans Castrucius, Signiam deserere statuit; ante tamen quam id faceret, quo metus suspicio abesset, structo agmine, ad Piretolam venit. Ibi aliquanto commoratus, nemine prodeunte obviam, reductis Signiam copiis, postera die oppidum incendit copiasque a Signia Carminianum traduxit. Ea posthac sedes fuit belli. Inde pratensem florentinumque pervadens agrum, cuncta belli cladibus reddebat infesta.

119 Principio insequentis anni Castrucius, quo Petrum Florentinorum praefectum pro tentata nuper in se proditione ulcisceretur,

surrended to Castruccio on condition that those within should be allowed to leave in safety. Having taken possession of Montemurlo, the enemy rebuilt the walls and strengthened it with a military garrison.[77]

In this same period, a certain Peter the Frenchman who was commanding the Florentine forces formed a secret pact with some of his kinsmen, who were fighting for the enemy, to kill Castruccio and turn over control of Signa in return for many great rewards. The plot was at length discovered and came to nothing. Yet though most of those responsible were captured and punished, Castruccio's army was thrown into turmoil and filled with suspicion. And their fear soon grew, for Peter with a flying column of horse approached the gates of Signa more daringly than usual. Hence Castruccio himself set out from Pistoia with two thousand foot and seven hundred horse and headed for Signa. There he expelled from the garrison those whose loyalty was suspect, and entering Florentine territory with his troops, he took the Via Senese as far as San Casciano, setting fires far and wide so as to increase the Florentines' suffering.[78]

By now reports were spreading of the preparations Prince Charles was making for war, and there was no doubt that he would be coming the following summer. Castruccio, pondering this fact, decided to leave Signa behind; but before he did so, in order that he not be suspected of fear, he arrayed his forces for battle and went to Peretola. Tarrying there awhile, when no one came out to fight him, he brought his troops back to Signa, and on the following day burned the town and transferred his troops from Signa to Carmignano. Thereafter that became his base for the war. From that place he would invade the territories of Prato and Florence, exposing them to all the disasters of war.[79]

At the beginning of the following year, to avenge himself on Peter, the Florentine commander, for the recent attempt on his life, Castruccio made the following plans. Thinking that the man

117

118

119
1326

haec machinatur. Ratus enim, ut nuper Signiam, sic etiam alia oppida fraude tentaturum, homines subornat, qui clam cum Gallo serant colloquia, et re arcane composita, tradere Carminianum paciscantur. Gallus, ad haec natura pronus, cum desertam ab hoste Signiam ob sui unius putaret factum, cupide magis quam caute in re periculosa incessit. Pactus enim proditionem sine ullo consilio, ipse unus conscius cum aliqua delectorum manu ad recipiendum oppidum profectus, in insidias ad hoc ipsum institutas praecipitatur. Ibi repente circumdatus ab hoste, ac tandem, cum resisteret, profligatus, cum multis suorum capitur; quem mox Castrucius ad se ductum securi percuti iussit.

120   Eam ob rem accelerata Caroli evocatio est[165] atque iterato imperium illi decretum. Conditiones insuper quaedam largiores additae: ducenta auri millia in annos singulos durante eo bello florentinus populus exhibebit; stipendia insuper equiti conducto et pediti. Horum numerus erat ad sex millia militum. Oratores cum his conditionibus ad accelerandum illius adventum missi Alamannus Acciaiolus, Spinellus Primerani, Petrus Nardi.

121   Eodem anno Signia reposita est, quam superiori anno Castrucius everterat. Et quo habitatoribus compleretur, data cunctis immunitas est qui in eam coloniam migrarent. Inexhausta quaedam[166] erat per id tempus tributorum pensio. Ob ea fugienda onera, complusculi id se in oppidum contulerunt.

122   Per idem tempus pontifex legatum[167] in Etruriam misit Iohannem Ursinum romanae ecclesiae cardinalem. Is ergo, Pisas mari

might be ready to make a treacherous attempt on other towns as he had recently in the case of Signa, Castruccio suborned some men to parley clandestinely with the Frenchman and bargain with him for the betrayal of Carmignano, settling the matter secretly. By nature disposed to such schemes, and believing as he did that the enemy had abandoned Signa on account of him alone, the Frenchmen stepped into a perilous situation with more greed than caution. Having arranged for the betrayal without taking any counsel, he himself, the only one privy to the scheme, set out with a picked force to receive the town's surrender, and fell headlong into the trap that had been set for him. He was surrounded suddenly by the enemy and eventually fled after some resistance. He was captured with many of his men and soon thereafter was brought before Castruccio and beheaded.[80]

Thanks to this affair, the summoning of Prince Charles was accelerated, and he was decreed power for a second time. More generous conditions were added besides: that the Florentine People should furnish 200,000 florins every year for the duration of the war and that it should provide stipends in addition for the horse and foot that would be hired. These soldiers should number up to six thousand. The ambassadors sent out with these codicils for accelerating Charles' arrival were Alamanno Acciaiuoli, Spinello di Primerano, and Piero di Nardo. 120

In the same year Signa was recovered, after having been destroyed by Castruccio the previous year. To fill it with inhabitants, a tax exemption was given to everyone who should emigrate to that colony. In that period there was no end to the taxes that had to be paid. So there were quite a few people who betook themselves to that town in order to flee the burden of taxation.[81] 121

Around the same time the pope sent to Tuscany as his legate Giovanni Orsini, a cardinal of the Roman church.[82] He then was carried by sea to Pisa, setting out from thence to Florence to await the arrival of Charles, who was reported to have entered Tuscany 122

advectus, inde Florentiam petens, Caroli adventum, qui eodem fere tempore ingressus in Etruriam ferebatur, expectavit. Carolo autem complusculos dies Senis mora fuit, ad componendas familiarum discordias civitatemque in suum arbitrium redigendam. Quod cum tandem ex sententia perfecisset, mense fere post legati ingressum Florentiam venit. Satis constat neminem unquam ante, quod quidem memoria extaret, tanto procerum comitatu tantaque insigni pompa in Etruriam venisse. Ceterum, in bello gerendo nequaquam ferventi animo deprehensus est, seu id tarditate mollitieque naturae, seu a patre monitus; nequaquam ita se strenuum praebere visus est, ut magnitudo nominis copiarumque poscebat.

123   Tantis igitur viribus apud Florentiam crescentibus, cum regis simul pontificisque robur supra quam ferri posset, insurgere videretur, conterriti diversae factionis principes sibi prospicere perrexerunt, sollicitati maxime a Galeactio Vicecomite Mediolanensium tyranno, qui iam pridem a pontifice regeque lacessitus bello castrucianum in Etruria tumultum concitarat, et crescere adversariorum potentiam haud quieto spectabat animo. Is igitur, sollicitando atque monendo, tandem auctor fuit ut principes diversae[168] factionis, contrario insurgentes nixu, Ludovicum Bavariae ducem ad imperatoriam dignitatem electum in Italiam evocarent. Erat iam pridem Ludovicus pontifici romano infensus, quod nuper, ob favorem genuensi gallicoque bello inimicis praestitum, pontifex indignum pronunciarat imperio ac censuras in illum severissime exercuerat. Igitur, ubi de mente Italicorum certior factus est, superatis confestim Alpibus, Tridentum pervenit, ut praesens de re proposita cum proceribus loqueretur, modumque sui transitus tempusque com-

at around the same time. Charles, however, was delayed a few days in Siena in order to compose some quarrels between the clans and bring the city under his control. When he had finally accomplished this task to his satisfaction, he arrived in Florence about a month after the legate. It is evident that no one in living memory had ever before come into Tuscany with so great a retinue of barons and such splendid pomp and circumstance. Yet in the conduct of war he was by no means found to be an ardent spirit, whether this was owing to some slowness or weakness of nature or to the instructions of his father; by no means did he act with the energy that the greatness of his name and his forces would seem to demand.

With such large forces being amassed in Florence, the power of 123 the king and the pope seemed to be rising more than could be borne, and the leaders of the opposing faction grew terrified and exerted themselves to look out for their interests. They were roused to action most of all by Galeazzo Visconti, the tyrant of Milan, who having been for a long time harrassed in war by the king and the pope, had stirred up the tumult involving Castruccio in Tuscany. He regarded the growth in his adversaries' power with no tranquil eye. Thus it was he who by his agitation and advice was ultimately responsible for the Ghibellines' rising up in reaction and calling into Tuscany Ludwig, Duke of Bavaria, who had recently been elected to the imperial title.[83] Ludwig for some time had been hostile to the Roman pontiff because lately, owing to the support he had given the popes' enemies during the war in Genoa and Lombardy, the pontiff had declared him unworthy of the empire and subjected him to the severest of censures. Hence, once informed of the Italians' intentions, he immediately crossed the Alps and arrived in Trent, so that he might speak with the principals in person about the project and establish the timetable and manner of his expedition. A council was therefore proclaimed at Trent, where Ludwig was joined by the tyrants of Milan, Mantua and

poneret. Tridenti igitur indicto conventu, Mediolanensium, Mantuanorum Veronensiumque tyranni, aliique ex Gallia et Etruria
principes eius factionis ad eum convenerunt, magnisque demum
pollicitationibus effecerunt, ut omisso in Germaniam reditu, copiis vero evocatis, Italiam Romamque pervadat. Ea res fama rumo-
reque populorum diffusa mentes omnium[169] erexit, ac futura, ut
fit, expectatione suspendit.

124   Igitur insequentis anni principio Ludovicus, contractis ad aliquem modum copiis, Tridento movens, per dexteros montes
Brixiam primo, inde Mediolanum pervenit. Ibi, ut mos est, magno
concursu hominum per manus Guidonis Arretinorum praesulis
coronatur. Hunc enim pontifex romanus ob Tiferni, de qua supra
diximus, invasionem primo censuris vexatum, quoniam et censuras et pontificem contemnebat, tandem omni dignitate privarat; in
eiusque locum Bosum quendam Ubertini generis praesulatus titulo substituerat, qua indignatione ac simul studio partium accen-
sus,[170] cum Arretinis dominaretur, magno equitatu ad Ludovicum
accesserat, nec erat[171] fere per id tempus maior incendii fax. Huius
igitur manibus tunc apud Mediolanum Ludovicus[172] coronatus
est.

125   Post coronationem vero mora longior fuit pecuniis comparan-
dis, quarum non avidissimus tantum, sed etiam indigentissimus
erat. Atque eo in genere hic primum illius improbitas patefacta
est. Cum enim opera maxime Galeactii Vicecomitis in Italiam arcessitus esset ac summo cum honore Mediolani receptus, usque
adeo perverse ingratus fuit, ut pecuniarum cupiditate dominatu
eum spoliaret et in carcerem truderet; Actium vero huius filium,
quem castruciano proelio interfuisse diximus, ac Luchinum fratrem una captos ad redemptionem sui magna pecunia compelleret.
Imposito deinde Mediolanensibus novo praeside, ac viginti qua-

Verona, as well as by the other leaders of that faction in Lombardy and Tuscany. By making large promises the Italian Ghibellines secured his decision not to return to Germany, but to summon hither his troops and invade Italy and Rome. This decision spread abroad among the peoples in report and rumor, occupying everyone's thoughts and keeping everyone in suspense, as usual, wondering what was going to happen.[84]

Thus, at the beginning of the following year, Ludwig scraped together some troops and left Trent, coming down by the western mountains first to Brescia, then to Milan. Here in accordance with custom he was crowned by the hand of Guido, bishop of Arezzo, amidst a great throng of men.[85] The Roman pontiff had finally deprived Guido of all his offices after having first harassed him with censures because of the afore-mentioned invasion of Città di Castello—censures which Guido had treated with contempt, as he had the pope himself. The pope had appointed a certain Boso, of the house of the Ubertini, to be bishop in his place. Enraged by this act as well as by partisanship, and being lord of the Aretines, Guido rode off to meet Ludwig with a large force of cavalry, and practically no one was a more of a firebrand than he at that moment. Thus his was the hand that crowned Ludwig in Milan. 124 1327

After the coronation there was a long delay to gather money, of which Ludwig was not only extremely covetous, but also extremely needy. It was in the matter of money, in fact, that his wickedness was first revealed. For although it had been primarily through the efforts of Galeazzo Visconti that he had been summoned to Italy and received with highest honors in Milan, the Bavarian was so perverse in his ingratitute as to despoil Visconti of his lordship and throw him into prison out of greed for money. He then compelled Visconti's son Azzo (who took part, as we said, in the battle with Castruccio) and his brother Luchino, who had been taken captive together, to pay a large ransom. Then he imposed a governor on Milan with a council of twenty-four citizens, and making a 125

tuor civibus in consilio adiunctis, cum speciem quandam libertatis subostentasset, quasi collati beneficii pretium, ingentem pecuniarum vim ab illis extorsit.

126 Dum haec in Gallia geruntur, Carolus et Florentini adversus Castrucium paratas copias circa maturationem segetum in hostes misere. Non enim profectus est in exercitu Carolus, sed Florentiae remanens, Novellum quendam e suis proceribus exercitui praefecit. Is igitur cum exercitu profectus, prima non longe a Signia fecit castra, triduoque in his locis commoratus est, nemine penitus gnaro quas hostium partes foret invasurus. Demum noctis silentio movens, tabernaculis etiam quo minus sentiret hostis ad speciem relictis, per sinistram Arni ripam Fucetium pervenit. Inde, subitaneo ponte transmissis paludibus, ad oppidum eius regionis munitissimum (Montem incolae vocant) copiis omnibus[173] consedit. Expugnationem eius aggressus, cum certatim equites peditesque niterentur ac, sine ulla sui cura per fossas ac praerupta evadentes loca, scalas moenibus admoverent, multitudoque sagittarum tamquam nimbus quidam hostis vulneraret, tandem nudata defensoribus moenia[174] capit. Oppidani ex primis moenibus in secunda refugerunt, nam triplici muro oppidum circumdabatur. Verum secunda quoque[175] eadem virtute expugnata capiuntur. Restabat arx. Ea minime tunc tentanda est visa; sed ad praedam caedemque oppidanorum versi milites, cum rixae contentionesque inter domesticos conductosque orirentur, qui minus poterant, ignem temere[176] iniecerunt. Id pluribus locis factum omnia comprehendit, ut nemo fere cuiusquam aetatis aut sexus eo ex oppido superforet; nam et latentes flamma ruinaque domorum et[177] deprehensos gladius iraque absumpsit. Qui in arce erant, dierum octo inducias pacti, ni

little boast of this specious liberty, he extorted an enormous sum of money from them, as though this were the price of the benefit he had conferred upon them.[86]

While this was happening in Gaul, Charles and the Florentines 126 sent the troops they had readied against Castruccio out against the enemy at harvest-time. Charles did not set out in the army himself, but remained in Florence. He put a certain Novello, one of his barons, in command of the army.[87] So it was Novello who set out with the army, and pitching his first camp not far from Signa, he remained three days in that place. Almost no one knew from what direction he was going to strike the enemy. Finally he set out in the silence of night and, leaving behind his tents to deceive the enemy, he came along the south bank of the Arno to Fucecchio. From there he crossed the swamps with pontoon bridges and came to a halt with all his troops near the most highly fortified town of the region, which the inhabitants call Santa Maria a Monte. They began the assault, cavalry and infantry striving together in rivalry, and with total disregard for their own safety they crossed trenches and broken ground, threw ladders against the walls and wounded the enemy with a thunderstorm of arrows. At last, having denuded them of defenders, they captured the walls. The townsmen fled from the first set of walls to the second, for the town was surrounded by triple walls. But the second wall, too, was attacked and taken with equal courage. There remained the citadel. It seemed right not to attempt it at once, and the soldiers turned to plunder and slaughter of the townsmen. When fights and disputes arose between our own troops and the mercenaries, the weaker side rashly began to set fires in many places, which soon consumed everything. No one of any age or either sex escaped the town, for those who hid were consumed by fire and falling buildings, while those who were caught were killed by wrath and the sword. Those in the citadel agreed to a truce of eight days, promising to surrender the citadel unless Castruccio

intra eos dies opem attulisset Castrucius, arcem dedere promiserunt. Ea de causa Castrucius ad ea loca profectus, cum procul a Florentinis editiori loco constitisset atque impar esset numero copiarum, ferre auxilium nequaquam suis[178] est ausus. Ita arx tandem ab his qui intus erant pactione deditur. Florentini, potiti integre oppido, moenibus propugnaculisque reparatis, praesidium in eo posuerunt.

127 Inde ad hostem profecti nec longe ab eo castrametati, pugnae se obtulerunt; quam cum detrectaret Castrucius ac intra munitiones copias detineret,[179] triduo commorati, retro moverunt castra, transmissisque paludibus et agrum pistoriensem ingressi, Arteminum obsederunt. Id quoque castellum per ea tempora munitissimum erat. Aliquot dies circa illud commorati, tandem incredibili virtute expugnare adorti sunt. Cum egregie resisteretur, ingenti materiae vi circa muros congesta incensaque, vallum simul portaque crematur. Neque die neque noctu oppugnatione intermissa, qui intus erant, desperatis ad extremum rebus, incolumes abire pacti, castellum dedidere.

128 Cupientes post haec eodem vincendi ardore Carminianum adoriri, Carolus Florentiam revocavit, certior factus de Ludovici adventu. Ille enim, post Mediolanensium principes deceptos pecuniasque exactas, cum ceterorum principum tyrannorumque animos ab se ob id alienatos sentiret, conventum iterato indixit[180] Urceis in oppido brixiensis agri. Ibi vel purgato vel attenuato crimine, erectis iterum animis, Etruriam petiit, superatoque Apennini iugo, cum omnibus copiis per agrum lunensem Pisas versus adventabat. Ob eam rem exercitus a Carolo tunc Florentiam revocatus est.

129 Castrucius, ubi appropinquare Ludovicum intellexit, obviam cum equitatu profectus, summo honore illum excepit, donisque et

should bring aid within that time. With that end in view Castruccio set out for the place, taking up position on a height at some distance from the Florentines. As his forces were numerically inferior he did not dare to bring aid to his men. Thus, in accordance with the agreement, the citadel was finally surrendered by the men inside. The Florentines took full control of the town, repaired the walls and outworks, and placed a garrison in it.

From thence they set out for the enemy and camped not far 127 from him, offering battle. Castruccio declined and kept his troops inside their fortifications. The Florentines waited three days and withdrew, crossed the swamps and, entering Pistoiese territory, laid siege to Artimino. This castle, too, was extremely well fortified in those times. They spent several days nearby, then finally, with incredible courage, set to work to capture it. Meeting with extraordinary resistance, they laid a great mass of fuel around the walls and set fire to it, burning down the gates and the palisade at the same time. The siege went on day and night until those within, their situation at last growing desperate, surrendered the castle on condition that they be allowed to leave unharmed.[88]

Afterwards, though desirous of attacking Carmignano with the 128 same conquering zeal, the troops were recalled to Florence by Charles, who had been informed of Ludwig's coming. The latter, realizing that he had alienated the minds of the other princes and tyrants by deceiving the princes of Milan and extracting their money, called a meeting once again at the town of the Orci in the territory of Brescia. There he either excused or asked forgiveness for his crime, and having raised their spirits again he headed for Tuscany. Crossing the Apennines, he entered with all his troops through the Lunigiana, going in the direction of Pisa. That was why Charles recalled the army to Florence at that time.[89]

Castruccio, when he learned that Ludwig was approaching, 129 went out to meet him with his cavalry and received him with the greatest respect, showering him with gifts and honors. But the

muneribus magnifice fovit. At Pisani, etsi primo illius adventu in Galliam[181] laetati fuerant legatosque suos in primo illo conventu ad eum miserant, tamen postea, vel hominis improbitatem avaritiamque formidantes vel contentionem romanae sedis contra quam hic aperte nitebatur perhorrentes, excludere portis[182] statuerunt. Itaque dudum coronatione eius nunciata focos et cetera laetitiae exultationisque indicia fieri Pisis vetuerant; et tunc illo appropinquante urbem communiverant germanosque equites mercede apud se militantes ob generis suspicionem ablatis equis pepulerant urbe; denique, si vi conaretur, vocare auxilia Caroli Florentinorumque cogitabant. At Ludovicus, si ab ea civitate vel unica per Etruriam[183] imperatorii nominis fautrice reprobaretur, gravissimum sibi ad cetera conficienda ratus, curam maxime verterat in Pisanos, nec quicquam intentatum relinquere constituerat, quo suae illos adiiceret potestati. Misit igitur oratores, qui pisanum alloquerentur populum benignisque pollicitationibus conciliarent animos. Sed ii[184] qui rempublicam tenebant, sapientissimi et gravissimi[185] viri, mobilitatem plebis veriti, eos in urbem recusarunt admittere.

130 Restabat igitur vi conari; sed inerat periculum, ne ad Carolum Florentinosque confugientes, auxilia inde quaererent aperteque desciscerent. Horum igitur mediam quandam placuit viam tentare per Guidonem Arretinorum praesulem, cui publica cum Pisanis erat amicitia, an a proposito divelli possent. Praesul igitur, legatis Pisanorum principibus civitatis ad se fide publica vocatis, apud Libramfactam oppidum colloquium instituit. Denique post multa

Pisans, though they had been delighted upon his first arrival in Lombardy and had sent ambassadors to that first council [in Trent], afterwards decided to close their gates to him, either fearing his wickedness and avarice or dreading contention with the Holy See, against which Ludwig was opening striving. Thus, once his coronation was announced, they forbade fireworks and other signs of happiness and rejoicing. Then, as he approached, they fortified the city and expelled from it some German knights who were serving with them as mercenaries, taking away their horses, because they suspected men of that nation. Finally, they gave thought to calling on Charles and the Florentines for aid if he should attempt some violence against them. But Ludwig, judging that it would be a serious blow to his other enterprises if he were rejected by the city that was unique in Tuscany for its advocacy of the imperial name, concentrated all his attention on the Pisans, and decided to leave nothing untried which might attach them to his power. Thus he sent ambassadors to address the Pisan people and reconcile their minds to him with promises of goodwill. But the men who controlled the state, being wise and serious men, refused to allow them in the city, fearing the fickleness of the common people.

The remaining option, therefore, was violence. But that way lay 130 the danger that they would flee to Charles and the Florentines and seek help from them, openly defecting from the imperial cause. So he decided to try a middle way between these alternatives, using Guido, the bishop of Arezzo, with whom the Pisans had public ties of friendship, to see whether he could shake them from their position. Hence the bishop summoned to himself under a safe conduct representatives of the Pisans, all leading citizens, and fixed a parley with them at the town of Librafatta. In the end, after the matter had been discussed backwards and forwards, they returned to this conclusion: the Pisans promised to give the new emperor 60,000 florins to leave and not launch a war against

ultro citroque agitata, res huc redibat: Pisani sexaginta auri millia
novo principi dare promittebant, ut inde abiret nec eos bello adoriretur; in urbem vero uti reciperent, nulla suasione poterant adduci.
Ea conditione per Ludovicum repudiata, cum legati re infecta Pisas reverterentur, Castrucius, traiecto confestim Auseri[186] fluvio
(nam castra Ludovici cis amnem erant), legatos contra fidem eis
datam intercipit; et Ludovicus, simul atque captos Pisanorum legatos cognovit, subitaneo impetu, traiecto amne Pisis copias admovit.

131   Ceterum ea captivitas legatorum magnas in exercitu contentiones peperit. Guido enim praesul ad dedecus sui nominis pertinere
arbitratus legatorum oppressionem, quos ipse data fide in colloquium iussu principis evocasset, iniuriam sibi a Castrucio in-
flictam vociferabatur; non enim tam Pisanos quam suam fidem
esse violatam. Peracta denique inter eos contentio est cognoscente
Ludovico. Praesul legatos Pisanorum liberandos remittendosque
in urbem clamitabat, aperteque prae se ferebat hanc iniuriam non
esse laturum. Castrucius minime se mirari[187] aiebat, si ille hostes
vinci doleret; ex matre siquidem florentina genitum, neutra ex
parte integrum esse; itaque hos sectari, illis favere; ut enim generis
diversitatem, sic animi inconstantiam miscuisse.

132   'Neque vero haec eius vacillatio,' inquit, 'nova est, nec primum
nunc deprehensa; nam, quod Florentia stat ac non malo domita
iam pridem concidit, hic unus est causa. Urbem enim adverso
proelio fractam cum ipse ad portas urgerem, multitudo autem inclusa nec frumentum haberet nec famem tolerare diutius posset, et
obsideri et capi nullo negotio potuisse si hic a me quaesitus roga-
tusque ad urgendam obsidionem[188] e superiori parte[189] venire[190]
voluisset.' Eam tunc rem ab hoc desertore proditoreque suarum
partium recusatam, has nunc molestias novo principi afferre atque,

them, but no persuasion could bring them to accept Ludwig into the city. That condition was rejected by Ludwig and the legates turned back towards Pisa without the matter being settled. Thereupon Castruccio immediately crossed the Serchio river (for Ludwig's camp was on this side of that stream) and intercepted the legates in contravention of the safe conduct given them, and Ludwig, as soon as he learned that the Pisan legates had been captured, in a rapid strike crossed the stream and brought his troops up to Pisa.[90]

But capturing the legates led to great contention in the imperial 131 army. For Bishop Guido regarded the capture of the legates as a disgrace to his own reputation, since he had himself summoned them at the emperor's command and had given them his word. So he complained bitterly about the injury that Castruccio had inflicted on them, saying that it was his own word of honor that had been outraged, not the Pisans'. The dispute was finally heard formally with Ludwig acting as judge. The bishop called for the legates to be freed and returned to Pisa, making it plain that he would not bear this injury. Castruccio said he was not at all surprised that the bishop was grieved to see the enemy beaten. Seeing that his mother was a Florentine, he was a full member of neither party. Hence he followed this one, showed favor to that one, the inconstancy of his mind reflecting the mixture in his blood.

"And this vacillation of his is nothing new," he said, "nor has it 132 only now been made manifest, for he alone is the reason why Florence stands and has not long since fallen, mastered by an evil fate. When I myself was pressing hard at the gates of that city, then broken by defeat in battle, when her multitude trapped within was without food and starving, she could have been besieged and captured without effort if this man, whom I implored to come from the other direction to press the siege, had so wished. Having refused this task at that time, this deserter and betrayer of his party now heaps these troubles upon the new emperor; and just as be-

ut Florentiam tunc salvam esse voluit, ita nunc Pisanos in potestatem venire permoleste fert. 'Tu,' inquit, 'princeps, non quid Guido praesul velit, sed quid tibi conducat spectare debes.'

133 Ad haec praesul se quidem sui generis nequaquam poenitere, nec sane ignotum esse posse Castrucio, cum ille nuper apud Arretinos egenus et miser sustentamenta vitae ab eodem genere reportarit; ad obsidendam vero Florentiam ea de causa non venisse, quia tunc sibi pax fuerit cum Florentinis, quam salva fide frangere non licebat; se[191] ita semper animatum fuisse, ut iuris iurandi religionem fidemque etiam hosti datam putaverit conservandam. 'Neque enim', inquit, 'si tu, Castruci, ut proditor et improbus, pacem Florentinis fregisti, ego quoque frangere debui. Nam Pisanorum quidem facto nil magis obstitit obstatque quam tui unius praesentia. Iam enim certe scio principi huic portae illae paterent, nisi te omnium fraudum[192] proditionumque auctorem Pisani vererentur.'

134 Haec et huiusmodi altercantes Ludovicus separavit et ad Castruci favorem inclinare aperte[193] visus est. Aggressus igitur obsidionem Pisarum, urbem undequaque cinxit, ac mense fere toto circa illam commoratus pactione tandem recepit.

135 Per haec ipsa tempora Guido Arretinorum praesul[194] ob superiorem indignationem a Ludovico discessit, quasi negotiis in Arretinos vocantibus. Cum per maritimam iter faceret, apud Nigrum montem correptus morbo interiit. Vir magnus quidem atque gloriosus, nisi quod adversus pontificem rebellis. Quem tamen errorem ante obitum recognovisse ac, si vita suppeteret, pro eodem pontifice adversus hostis militaturum se promisisse quidam literis tradidere. Post huius mortem Petrus cognomento Sacon, huius Guidonis frater, tyrannidem Arretinorum excepit.

fore he wanted Florence to be saved, so now he objects strenuously to capturing the Pisans. My emperor, you ought to consider your own interest, and not what Bishop Guido wants."

The bishop responded that he was by no means ashamed of his 133 lineage, nor indeed could that lineage be unknown to Castruccio, since the bishop's family had supplied him with the means of survival when he had lately come to Arezzo, miserable and needy. Guido himself had not come to besiege Florence because he had a peace treaty with the Florentines at that time which he could not break without sacrificing his word of honor. He had always held the conviction that one should keep one's sworn oath and promise, even when given to an enemy. "Your treachery and wickedness in breaking the peace with Florence, Castruccio, did not oblige me to break it as well. Indeed, the greatest obstacle in this Pisan affair has been and is your own presence alone. For I know their gates would have already opened to this emperor if they had not been afraid of you, the author of every act of deceit and betrayal."

Ludwig weighed this and similar points of dispute, and seemed 134 openly to favor Castruccio. Thus he set about besieging the Pisans, surrounding the city on all sides, and after he had stayed there almost a whole month, he took possession of it by means of a negotiated settlement.[91]

During this time Guido, the bishop of the Aretines, took his 135 departure from Ludwig because of his outrage at what had transpired, alleging that Aretine affairs demanded his attention. While journeying along the coast, he took sick at Montenero and died. He was a great and glorious man apart from his rebellion against the pope. Some writers record, however, that he recognized his error before his death, and promised to fight for that same pope against the enemy if he should survive. After his death, Guido's brother Peter, whose surname was Saccone, took over as tyrant of the Aretines.[92]

136 Ludovicus, receptis Pisis, duobus fere mensibus ibi commoratus est, pecuniis exigendis ac ceteris parandis quae ad iter pertinebant. Constituerat enim non solum Romam[195] petere, verum etiam Roberti regnum invadere. Sed dum Pisis moram trahit, a Castrucio rogatus, Lucam primo, mox inde Pistorium accessit, ut Florentiam ex propinquo videret. Reversus Pisas, cum omnia tandem parata forent, iter per maritimam regionem Romam versus ingreditur, habens equitum peditumque pergrandem exercitum. Castrucius, cum sibi quoque eundum foret, praesidio mille equitum Lucae relicto, ipse cum quingentis equitibus ac mille sagittariis post Ludovicum secutus, Viterbii se cum illo coniunxit. Carolus vero, quamdiu hostium copiae Pisis constitere, cum suis ipse copiis Florentiae commoratus est. Sed ubi Ludovicum Castruciumque arripuisse iter cognovit, Florentinis in concionem vocatis, necessitatem profectionis suae ostendit ac Philippum quendam e suis praefectis cum mille equitibus in praesidio se relinquere pronuntiavit. Cohortatus deinde cives ad fortitudinem et constantiam, cum ceteris copiis Senas primo, inde Perusiam, post in regnum abivit.

137 Romani, iam pridem audito Ludovici adventu, in seditione gravissima versabantur; et praevalebat factio regi pontificique adversa. Ab ea tandem receptus in urbem Ludovicus, haud multo post magno applausu populi coronatur. Ceterum nullus in coronando solitus ordo, nemo legatus, nulla pontificis auctoritas adfuit. Imposita est illi corona populi nomine[196] a Sciarra Columnensi, principe diversae factionis; in cuius rei memoriam ipse posterique eius ad antiquum gentis insigne coronam addidere, quasi praeclarum fuerit scelerate fecisse.

138 Castrucio quoque permaximi Romae sunt honores impensi, nec a Ludovico solum, qui cuncta illi eximia tribuebat, sed a populo

Ludwig, having taken possession of Pisa, remained there about 136
two months to extract money and make other preparations for his
journey. He had decided not only to head for Rome, but also to
invade the kingdom of Robert.[93] During his stay in Pisa he came
at Castruccio's request to Lucca, then Pistoia, to observe Florence
close up. Returning to Pisa, when everything was finally ready, he
set out on his journey for Rome by the coast road with a great
army of horse and foot. Castruccio was also obliged to go, so he
left a guard of a thousand knights at Lucca and himself set out after Ludwig with five hundred knights and a thousand archers,
joining him at Viterbo. While the enemy was gathering his forces
at Pisa, Charles stayed in Florence with his troops. But when he
learned that Ludwig and Castruccio were on the march, he summoned the Florentines to a council and represented to them the
necessity of his setting out, declaring that he would leave behind
one of his commanders, a certain Philip, with a guard of a thousand knights.[94] Then, urging the citizens to remain brave and
steadfast, he went away with the rest of his forces, first to Siena,
then to Perugia, and after that into the Kingdom.

The Romans had long since heard of Ludwig's coming and 137
were in a grievous state of rebellion; the faction opposed to the
king and the pontiff held the upper hand. This faction at length
received Ludwig into the city, where shortly thereafter he was
crowned to great popular applause. But the usual coronation ceremony was not observed, and no legate or papal authority was present. A Ghibelline prince, Sciarra Colonna, crowned him in the
name of the people, in memory of which he and his posterity
added a crown to their ancient family device, as though to have behaved with such wickedness were a mark of distinction.[95]

To Castruccio, too, the greatest honors were paid in Rome, not 138
only by Ludwig, who granted him every distinction, but also by
the Roman people. After the emperor he enjoyed unique respect,
and all decisions were referred to him alone; on him alone, it

etiam romano. Unus post principem hic spectabatur; ad hunc unum[197] omnia referebantur consilia, hic denique unus erat a quo res tota pendere videretur. Concursus maximi tota ex Italia Romam fiebant. Omnes enim qui pontificem oderant vel studio partium diversa sequebantur, exultanti laetitia properabant, iamque Roberti regnum, tamquam partium caput, pervadendum occupandumque dictitabant. Et virium certe armorumque sat esse videbatur, apparatusque ea de causa propalam fiebant.

139 Versis igitur in principem animis ac omnium sermone illius famam celebrante, splendida memorabilisque res in Etruria gesta mentes in se animosque convertit. Philippus enim, quem praefectum copiis Florentiaeque[198] relictum[199] ostendimus, rem magnam audacemque adortus est, Pistorium capere, secutus in ea re duorum exulum cohortationem, qui locorum gnari intromittere copias promiserunt. Igitur scalis machinisque in pratensi arce secreto fabricatis, ubi tempus rei gerendae visum est,[200] Philippus, cum equitibus primis fere tenebris Florentia egressus, Pratum concessit, nemine florentinorum civium gnaro, praeter unum Simonem Tosam, splendidum equitem e suprema nobilitate, quem in partem huius consilii iam pridem susceperat. Cum Pratum venisset, sumptis celeriter machinis profectioneque indicta, cum duobus peditum millibus, equitibus sexcentis ad Pistorii moenia illa ipsa nocte pervenit. Ibi exules per glaciem (asperrima namque erat hiems) fossas transgressi, partem murorum maxime neglectam scalis ascenderunt ac centum fere milites secutos exceperunt; complures quoque, pedetentim transgressi fossas, moenia perfodere aggressi sunt.

140 Dum ista fierent, praefectus forte vigilum ambita cetera urbe in haec ipsa loca devenit. Cum, ut fit, custodes excitaret, deprehenso strepitu accurrit clamoremque extollit. Ad eam vociferatio-

seemed, the whole business depended. A great concourse of persons came together in Rome from all of Italy. All those who hated the pope or adhered to the Ghibelline party hastened there in a state of exultation and joy, and already there was much talk about how Robert's kingdom, as the chief Guelf power, should be invaded and occupied. There certainly appeared to be forces and arms enough, and equipment was being openly prepared for the purpose.

While every thought was bent on the emperor and every voice celebrated his fame, a splendid and memorable deed in Tuscany diverted the attention and spirits of men. For Philip, who had (as we showed) been left in charge of the troops in Florence, undertook a great and audacious deed, the capture of Pistoia. In this he followed the urging of two exiles who knew the local situation and promised to bring his forces inside the city. Thus, having constructed ladders and siege engines secretly in the citadel of Prato, when the moment for the attempt seemed right, Philip around dusk left Florence with his knights and withdrew to Prato. Not a single Florentine citizen knew of it save one Simone della Tosa, a distinguished knight from the highest nobility, who had long been privy to the plan. Arriving in Prato, Philip swiftly gathered the siege equipment and ordered his troops to march; he arrived that same night by the walls of Pistoia with two thousand foot and six hundred cavalry. There the exiles crossed the frozen moat (for it was a severe winter) and climbed up the most neglected part of the walls on ladders. They brought with them about a hundred soldiers. Many others, too, crossed the moats cautiously and set about digging through the walls.

While this was going on, the commander of the watch, having made the rounds of the rest of the city, arrived in the area. Whilst bestirring the guards in the usual way, he heard the noise, ran out and raised the alarm. The men living nearby were roused by his shouts and realized what was happening, and the clamor spread

139

1328

140

nem experrecti qui loco vicini erant, rem persenserunt celeriterque diffusus per urbem clamor homines excitavit. Philippus inter haec, ponte super fossas iniecto, frequentes transmiserat, et simul moenia iam binis locis effracta transitum non pediti modo, verum etiam equiti dabant. Ipse quoque²⁰¹ Philippus iam introierat summaque constantia rem exequebatur. Quin etiam, qui pro moenibus erant in proximam evadentes turrim, custodibus vi oppressis ignem in subiectam coniecerant portam, quo facilior multitudini foret ingressus.

141   Erant Pistorii in praesidio milites castruciani circiter septingentos. Hi, cum ingressum hostium ex clamore sensissent, trepidi primo convenerunt, voluntatem civium ac proditionem formidantes. Sed postquam cives integris animis corripere arma adversus ingressores viderunt, spem bonam complexi, parte suorum apud forum relicta, ceteri ad arcendos hostes cum multitudine civium properarunt. Proelium atrox fuit quantum nunquam ante. Tandem²⁰² praevalentibus Castrucianis, ad fracturas usque ipsas murorum qui ingressi fuerant repelluntur, multique conterriti excedebant urbe, multi etiam eorum qui pro moenibus stabant quasi re desperata locum deserentes, ad suos qui extra urbem constiterant refugerunt; eratque incertitudo quaedam et vacillatio per fossas et praepedita loca, aliis intrare, aliis evadere properantibus. Sed restituebat proelium ipse dux, qui cum turma equitum ante fracturas ipsas consistens, ubi appropinquabat hostis, procellam equestrem in eos dabat ac pedem referre compellebat.

142   Ita saepius fluctuante proelio, cum acriter tamen Castruciani pugnarent praevaliturique tandem viderentur, porta interim cremata ac refracta,²⁰³ multitudo equitum peditumque irrupit, tu-

quickly through the city, waking up the people. Philip meanwhile had thrown a bridge across the moat and had sent across it a throng of soldiers, while at the same time the walls, now breached in two places, gave passage not only to foot soldiers but even to cavalry. Philip himself now also entered and carried forward his enterprise with great resolution. Furthermore, the men who were now inside the walls broke into a nearby tower, crushed the guard, and threw fire down on the gate below to make it easier for the mass of men to enter.

There were about seven hundred of Castruccio's soldiers on 141 guard in Pistoia. When these men realized from the clamor that their enemies had entered, they at first met together in trepidation, fearing ill-will and treachery on the part of the citizens. But after they saw the citizens wholeheartedly taking up arms against the invaders, they regained their hope and, having left a part of their forces in the main square, the rest rushed off along with the mass of the citizens to ward off the enemy. The battle was of unprecedented ferocity. At length, Castruccio's men began to get the upper hand, and drove the invaders back to the breaches in the walls, and many fled the city in terror, while many of those standing inside the walls also lost hope, abandoned their posts, and took refuge with their fellows outside the city. There was uncertainty and indecision in the moats and the obstructed areas, with some men trying to enter, others running to get out. But the commander himself stopped the rout by standing fast with a troop of horse in front of the breaches in the walls. When Castruccio's men approached, he brought down a storm of cavalry upon them and forced them to retreat.

The battle continued to go back and forth in this way. Cas- 142 truccio's men fought bitterly and it seemed they would prevail, but in the meantime the gate was burned and broken down, and a mass of horse and foot burst through it. At that moment Castruccio's men broke, hearing the louder din of horns and trumpets

baeque simul classica armorumque[204] clamor maiori tumultu ab ea
parte exaudita, Castrucianos fregere. Quare paulatim cedentes in
forum revertuntur. Ibi susceptis Castruci filiis (duo quidem erant)
ad arcem, quam in extrema urbis parte communiverat, aufugerunt.
Cives autem omisso certamine domos suas reversi posuerunt arma
victoremque per urbem discurrere passi sunt.

143   Nec posthac nisi ad arcem proeliatum est, nec quidem[205] sine
periculo eorum qui vicerant. Philippus enim vestigia secutus hostium contra ipsam arcem signa constituerat; milites autem ad
praedam dilapsi, ducem nudatum paene omnibus copiis derelique-
rant. Eam igitur paucitatem conspicati hostes, eruptionem subito
faciunt, magnoque ruentes impetu non multum abfuit quin ducem
ipsum signaque opprimerent. Nec usquam ea nocte maiori periculo res stetit; nam profligatis qui cum duce remanserant, ceteros
per urbem sparsos praedaeque intentos[206] opprimere nullum erat
negotium. Sed egregia virtute ducis hostium vis sustentata est, et
simul aurora iam affulserat, militesque intellecto periculo ad signa
recurrebant. Quare desperatis ad extremum rebus Castruciani, relicta penitus urbe, arce quoque ipsa deserta, aufugerunt. Urbs tota
a militibus direpta est sine ulla exceptione, amicarumne partium
an inimicarum quis esset; a civium tamen corporibus temperatum.

144   Post haec Philippus, compositis ad aliquem modum rebus, decimo fere post die Florentiam rediens, tanto honore susceptus
est, ut triumpho similis eius ingressio videretur, societatibus cum
vexillis obviam prodeuntibus, magistratuque et ceteris ordinibus
certatim se ad eius honorem effundentibus.

145   At Castrucius postquam amissum Pistorium cognovit (celeres
enim nuntii mare delati, neque die neque noctu intermissa naviga-

and the clash of arms coming from that direction. They gave way little by little, turning back to the main square. There they snatched up Castruccio's two sons and took refuge in the citadel he had constructed on the far side of the city. The citizens abandoned the fight, went home and laid up their arms, allowing the victor to run freely through the streets.

After that the only fighting was at the citadel, and it was not without peril to the winners. For Philip, hard on the footsteps of the enemy, had set up his standard opposite the citadel, while his soldiers abandoned themselves to pillage and left their commander almost denuded of all his forces. The enemy took note of this and made a sudden sortie, rushing towards him with great force, and the commander and his standard were very nearly taken. This was the moment of greatest peril during that night, for it would have been a simple matter to crush the rest of his men, who were spread out through the city intent on plunder, once the men who had remained with Philip were put to flight. But thanks to his extraordinary bravery the commander was able to bear up under the onslaught of the enemy, and as soon as dawn came the soldiers realized the danger and returned to their standards. With their situation at last desperate, Castruccio's men fled, leaving the city behind entirely, even the citadel. Philip's soldiers sacked the whole city, sparing neither Guelf nor Ghibelline, although the persons of the citizenry were spared.[96] 143

After this, Philip restored order after a fashion and returned on the tenth day to Florence. He was received with such honor that his entrance seemed like a triumph. The militia companies came out to meet him with their standards, and the magistrates and all the other ranks of the citizenry poured out, competing to do him honor. 144

But after Castruccio learned of the loss of Pistoia (the news was brought swiftly by sea, coming to him three days later after a sea voyage that continued day and night without interruption), he 145

tione triduo rem ad eum tulere), ad Ludovicum profectus, gravissime questus est, quod se pericula sua providentem Romam invitum traxisset. Inde festinato recessu cum his quas adduxerat copiis (erant hae sexcenti equites delecti et mille sagittarii), Pisas versus redire properavit. In itinere ipso, quoniam sollicitudo animi tarditatem corporis anteibat, relictis post se copiis, ipse cum duodecim comitibus, die noctuque fatigatis equis, per infestas latrociniis vias Pisas pervenit. Ibi praesentiam suam ostentans animumque afflictis addens rebus, cetera in fide continuit. Post haec contractis copiis in agrum pistoriensem profectus, Murli in arcem, quae media inter hostes relicta erat, frumentum simul praesidiumque induxit. Lucam mox Pisasque regressus, rempublicam Pisanorum suo pro arbitrio, quasi communi utilitate id exigente, administrabat, pecuniasque ad bellum inde sumebat.

146   Ludovicus inter haec nefariam rem[207] aggreditur: falsum pontificem romanum facere, privato sua sententia Iohanne XXII, eiusdem sedis vero antistite. Quod ludibrium barbari vesanique hominis sacra fidelium ecclesia nequaquam recepit; tantum fautores quidam eius perfidiae receperunt, qui merito ab unitate fidelium sequestrati sunt. Addixerunt se quoque huic furori complures apostatae rebellesque[208] religionum ac omnis sentina reproborum clericorum. Ipse vero falsus pontifex sibi cardinales creavit, ac cetera veri pontificis officia aemulatus, Ludovicum in imperio confirmavit. Ita falsus imperator falsusque pontifex sibi invicem auctores dignitatis fuerunt, altaria sacrasque urbis sedes mutuo profanantes.

147   Dum ea Romae geruntur, Castrucius neque diem neque horam intermittens cum omnia sagaci scrutaretur animo, tandem in spem

came before Ludwig and complained bitterly that he had been drawn unwillingly to Rome, though foreseeing his own peril. Then he beat a hasty retreat with the troops he had led there (six hundred picked knights and a thousand archers) and hastily returned in the direction of Pisa by the same route. As his mental anxiety outran his physical pace, he left his troops behind and with twelve companions made his way to Pisa through bandit-infested roads, riding day and night on exhausted horses. Once there, he preserved the loyalty of his other forces by showing himself and inspiring courage in the midst of affliction. Then he gathered his troops and set out into Pistoiese territory, bringing corn and reinforcements to the citadel of Montemurlo that had been left isolated in the midst of enemies. Then he marched back to Lucca and Pisa and subjected the Pisan state to his personal governance, as though the common utility required it, and extracted money from the city for the war.[97]

Ludwig, meanwhile, undertook an act of unholy wickedness: he 146 set up a false Roman pontiff,[98] using his authority to depose John XXII, the true priestly occupant of that see. The Holy Church of the faithful by no means accepted this act of mockery on the part of a barbarous madman; only certain supporters of his treachery accepted it, those who were excommunicates (and rightly so). A large number of apostates and rebels against their vows, all the dregs of a debased clergy, also associated themselves with this madness. But the false pope created cardinals and, mimicking other duties of the true pontiff, he confirmed Ludwig as emperor. Thus the false emperor and the false pope authorized each other's rank, together profaning the altars and holy sites of Rome.[99]

While this was taking place in Rome, Castruccio passed neither 147 a day nor an hour without his keen intelligence examining every possibility. At last he began to have hope of recovering Pistoia. His hopes were aroused for the following reasons. After Pistoia had been captured and sacked, when the city had been stripped

venit Pistorii recuperandi. Afferebant vero ei spem huiuscemodi causae. Post captum direptumque Pistorium, cum urbs plane rebus omnibus spoliata fuisset, contentio quaedam inter Philippum Caroli praefectum et Florentinos erat coorta. Iubebat ille frumentum ceteraque ad eius urbis tutelam necessaria Florentinos publico sumptu inferre. Illi vero non sibi sed Carolo quaesitam urbem Pistorium respondebant: se quidem ducenta auri millia praestare in annos singulos certa pactione promisisse, quae iam plane essent persoluta; nec esse aequum supra id quod semel conventum pactumque sit populum onerari; magis vero illum ipsum, qui urbem Pistorium omnibus rebus exuerit, necessaria ad eius tutelam resarcire debere. Quid enim indignius quam, cum ipse vacue fecerit, praedam quidem sibi habere, iubere autem alios replere? Philippus contra iure belli parta militum esse consuesse; satis profecisse videri, quod hosti illam suo periculo ademisset; praedam vero quam miles ceperit ut iam restituat petere, ingratissimum simul iniquissimumque videri. His contentionibus neque frumenti quantum sat erat importabatur neque cetera opportuna fiebant.

148   Castrucius ergo gnarus istarum rerum, cum hostium contentiones lucrum existimaret suum, exercitu Pisanis Lucensibusque indicto, magnis repente copiis Pistorium obsedit. Erat intra urbem Simon Tosa eques florentinus a Philippo relictus, habens in praesidio milites circiter mille et cum his equites trecentos, praeterea cives pistorienses eiusdem factionis. Cum iis²⁰⁹ urbem egregie tutabatur, interdumque eruptione facta hostes invadere ac turbare opera non dubitabat. Alia vero manus equitum Prati consistens saepe Castrucianos pervadebat, ut neutra ex parte sibi quies esset. Castrucio unica spes erat in commeatus defectu, docto intra

utterly of all its goods, a degree of contention arose between Philip, Charles' commander, and the Florentines. Philip demanded that corn and other things necessary to guard that city should be supplied by the Florentines at public expense. They replied that Pistoia had been acquired for Charles' sake, not theirs; they had promised him expressly by agreement to supply 200,000 florins each year, which had already been paid; it was not fair to burden the people beyond what had already been settled and agreed to; rather, it was he himself who — having stripped Pistoia of all its wealth — should make good the necessary expenses for its defense. What could be less fitting than for him to ask others to replenish a city that he had himself emptied, taking the plunder for himself? Philip replied that by the laws of war spoils customarily belonged to the soldiers; it seemed to him that he had contributed enough by capturing the city from the enemy at his own peril; he thought it would be an act of the greatest ingratitude and injustice to ask the soldiery at this point to restore the plunder they had seized. Owing to these quarrels insufficient food was brought into Pistoia and other preparations were not made.

Castruccio, therefore, having learned of this situation, and believing that the quarrels of his enemies were a source of profit to himself, ordered the Pisan and Lucchese armies to assemble, and besieged Pistoia with large forces. Simone della Tosa, the Florentine knight, had been left inside the city by Philip and had a garrison of about a thousand soldiers and three hundred knights as well as some Pistoiese citizens belonging to the Guelf faction. With these forces he distinguished himself in the defense of the city, and from time to time did not hesitate to make sorties to attack the enemy and disrupt the siege-works. Another force of cavalry based in Prato often attacked Castruccio's men, so that he had no peace on either front. Castruccio's one hope was to starve his enemies out, as he had learned that there was no more than two months' supply of grain inside the city. Thus he gave up all

148

urbem duorum non amplius mensium annonam inesse. Itaque omissa per vim expugnandi cura ad hoc unum intendebat, urbem undique cingere ac facultatem commeatus obsessis auferre.

149   Florentini vero, etsi iusta quidem, ceterum damnosa indignatione fuerant prius commoti, tamen, ubi Castrucium tantis copiis Pistorium circumsedisse viderunt, sero quidem meliora susceperunt consilia. Nec iam ullus sumptuum aut pecuniarum erat respectus; ultro facere omnia; pecunias affatim promere; et qui prius parvo in dispendio renitentes fuerant, magna iam dispendia volentes subibant; quae est ferme natura populorum. Igitur impigre contractis copiis equitum ad tria, peditum vero supra viginti millia coegerunt; frumentum praeterea et commeatum summo labore summaque impensa parant, per vim et arma Pistorio inferendum. Philippus omnibus affatim paratis cum Prati convenire copias iussisset, inde profectus ad hostem duxit, nec longe ab illo metatus castra proelio rem decernere flagitavit.

150   Castrucius vero, etsi minime tentandum sibi fortunam pugnae constituerat, tamen simulata re quasi pugnaturus foret, aliquamdiu hostem spe vana distinuit.[210] Interim vero, neque die neque nocte intermisso opere munire castra, opportuna subinde loca fossis arboribusque excisis praepedire contendebat. Quod cum tandem animadverterent Florentini, per vim conandum rati, structa confestim acie, crebros posthac impetus ad munitiones hostium facientes, perrumpere conati sunt. Conantes vero fossae impedimentaque prohibebant, et arcebant praesidia armatorum pro fossis valloque ab hoste disposita. Tandem frustra conati, cum neque pellicere ad pugnam neque pervadere munitiones valerent, inopes consilii residebant. Ita complures dies frustra moratis, tandem abs-

thought of reducing it by force, and concentrated on the one goal of surrounding the city on all sides and preventing the besieged from receiving provisions.

But the Florentines, despite their earlier outrage — justified, but costly — in the end took better counsel when they saw that Castruccio had surrounded Pistoia with large forces. Now no money or expense was spared; the utmost was done in everything; the florins simply poured out; and the same men who before had balked at a small outlay now voluntarily assumed a large one — such being, as a rule, the way of popular regimes. Thus they tirelessly assembled troops and brought together 3000 horse and more than 20,000 foot; in addition they readied corn and provisions with the greatest effort and expense so as to deliver them to Pistoia by force of arms. After all these preparations had been exhaustively made, Philip ordered the troops to muster at Prato, and setting out from thence, led them towards the foe. He pitched camp not far from him and challenged him to battle.

149

But Castruccio, although he had decided to avoid the fortune of battle at all costs, nevertheless pretended he was going to fight, distracting the enemy for a while with vain hopes. Meanwhile, he worked continuously day and night to fortify his camp, trying to block the approaches to it with trenches and felled trees. When the Florentines finally noticed this, they decided to make an armed thrust. Hastily forming ranks, they made a rapid series of strikes on the enemy's defense-works, trying to break through them. But the trenches and obstacles kept the attackers at bay, and the armed garrison positioned in front of the moat and earthwork held them off. The strikes having failed, the Florentines at last returned to base, being unable either to induce the foe to give battle or to penetrate his defenses. At a loss for what to do, they wasted many days there before finally deciding to leave and invade the territory of Pisa and Lucca. Perhaps (they thought) the threat to his own property would frighten the enemy into raising the siege. To

150

cedere placuit, ac pisanum lucensemque agrum invadere, si forte ea
re deterritus hostis suarum metu rerum ad solvendam obsidionem
quiret[211] compelli. Quo autem speciosior esset discessus, structa in
conspectu acie, tubas[212] canere iusserunt et ad proelium hostes
provocarunt. Postquam nemo extra munitiones prodibat, signa
moventes, pars quaedam Pratum reversa, ibi[213] cum frumento ac
cetero commeatu restitit ad omnem motum hostis intenta; alii Pisas versus profecti infesto agmine portas adusque pervenerunt.
Fuerunt etiam qui agrum lucensem ingressi, eundem Lucae terrorem inferrent. Castrucius ob hoc nihilo magis obsidionem dissolvit, ratus (id quod erat) praeter damnum praedamque nihil periculi subesse, quando non tam spes quam desperatio hostis ad ea
loca ducebat.

151   At hi qui Pistorii obsidebantur, absumpto iam omni quod intus
erat frumento, cum fames premeret suosque paulo ante frustra co-
natos[214] re infecta abire conspexissent, desperatis ad extremum rebus Pistorium dedunt, tertio fere postquam obsideri coeptum fuerat mense. Praesidium incolume ex pactione deductum est. Fama
quidem Castruci nulla umquam[215] ex re tantum enituit quantum
ex hac una obsidione. Admirabile porro visum est longe adeo pau-
cioribus copiis circa urbem magnam per loca plana circumfusis et
intus simul extraque oppugnatis, industria solum ac scientia rei
militaris ita perstitisse, ut adversariorum conatus omnis impe-
tusque arceret ac victor tandem urbe in oculis paene tantarum
hostium copiarum potiretur.

152   Fractis civium animis ob Pistorii amissionem ac bellum ex propinquo magis quam unquam horrentibus, periculum insuper novum tremendumque nunciatur. Ludovicus enim, frustra tentato
contra Robertum regem progressu, tandem Roma abiens in Etru-

make their departure more impressive, they arrayed themselves in battle-formation in full sight of the enemy, caused the trumpets to sound, and challenged the foe to battle. When no one came forth from the defenses, they began to march. Part of their forces returned to Prato, where they remained with the corn and provisions, watching the enemy's every move. Others in a striking force set out in the direction of Pisa, coming to the very gates of the city. There was also a party that entered the territory of Lucca and brought the same terror to that city. These moves were equally ineffective in making Castruccio raise the siege, for he reckoned—correctly—that he was not in any real danger apart from the destruction and plunder; it was not so much hope as despair that had led his enemies to those places.

But those under siege at Pistoia by now had consumed all the corn within the city and were starving. Having observed the failure of their side's attacks and their departure, they despaired and surrendered the city, about three months after the siege had begun. By agreement the garrison was withdrawn unmolested. Nothing ever cast greater luster upon Castruccio's reputation than this single siege. It seemed truly a wonderful thing to have surrounded a large city in the midst of a plain with vastly inferior forces which were under attack both from within the city and from without, and yet to have so persevered through hard work and knowledge of military affairs alone that he was able to ward off every thrust and attack of his adversaries and in the end victoriously get control of the city, practically before the very eyes of such large hostile forces.[100]

The spirits of our citizens were shattered by the loss of Pistoia, and they were dreading the war, now closer to them than ever before, when a new and fearful danger was announced to them besides. Ludwig, his planned expedition against King Robert having come to nothing, was at last leaving Rome, and he had decided to come back into Tuscany. He had journeyed as far as Todi with the

riam redire constituerat; eoque animo Tudertum usque iter fecit, ut palam dictitaret se Florentiam petere; eratque ad eum concursus exulum et omnifariam adversariorum. Res tota sic ferebatur composita: uti Ludovicus cum exercitu per perusinum cortonensemque agrum veniret Arretium, inde paratus structusque Florentiam invaderet; Castrucius e diversa regione victor a Pistorio cum omni suorum manu superveniret; Ubaldini vero ac ceteri diversae factionis tyranni, qui circa Apenninum incolunt arces, alia rursus manu per mugellanum agrum descendentes, ab ea quoque parte obsidionem urgerent.

153   Erant haec formidolosa ac plena sollicitae expectationis, ita ut plerisque nullam superesse spem a periculo videretur. Quippe vel Castrucius ipse per se satis robustus hostis terrere poterat; quid, addito Ludovici exercitu atque praesentia cum omnium[216] simul[217] inimicorum coetu? Exanimata igitur metu urbana multitudine ac futurum anxie expectante, horror primo velut attonitos habebat cives; mox se respicientes ultroque cohortantes, nihil facere providereque omiserunt, quo ab imminenti periculo servarentur.[218] Igitur, Varicum ceteraque superioris Arni oppida quae ad Arretinos spectant affatim communire ac validis praesidiis firmare placuit. Ad hoc binos per singula oppida florentinos cives cum manu militum sagittariisque posuere. Idem factum est per alia castella, quorum aut de fide aut de imbecillitate timebatur; urbis insuper munimenta undique instaurata. Admoniti praeterea socii, ut quasi ad extremum opus quanta maxima[219] possint[220] auxilia mitterent. His provisis, forti iam animo discrimen expectabant, futurum certe maximum, ni Dei benignitas avertisset.

154   Ludovicum Tuderti aliquot dies commoratum, cum omnia iam[221] ad iter in Etruriam parata essent, novae coortae spes ad in-

intention of broadcasting his march on Florence, and exiles and adversaries of every kind flocked to him. It is said that the whole affair was arranged in the following way. Ludwig would come with his army via the territory of Perugia and Cortona to Arezzo, where he would make his preparations to invade Florence. Castruccio, fresh from his victory, would advance on the city with all his forces from Pistoia on the other side, while the Ubaldini and the rest of the Ghibelline tyrants dwelling in their Apennine fastnesses would come down with another force into the Mugello, pressing the attack from that direction, too.

These tidings were fraught with fear and anxiety, and to many 153 it seemed that there was no hope of escaping the danger. Castruccio by himself was an enemy powerful enough to strike terror into their hearts; what would be their fate when Ludwig's army and his personal presence was added to a simultaneous gathering of all their enemies? So the urban multitude cowered in fear and awaited the future with anxiety. The citizens at first, as though thunderstruck, were seized with horror, but soon they recovered their self-respect and spontaneously began to encourage one another, neglecting no provision or activity that might save them from the peril hanging over them. Thus they decided to fortify fully Montevarchi and the other towns of the upper Arno that looked towards Arezzo and to strengthen the garrisons in those places. For this purpose they placed two Florentine citizens in each town with a force of soldiers and archers. They did the same in the case of other castles whose loyalty or strength was suspect, and the fortifications on all sides of the city were restored. In addition, the allies were urged to send as many reinforcements as they could, as in a case of extreme need. Having taken these steps, they now awaited the crisis with brave hearts, and it surely would have been the greatest of crises had not the good will of God averted it.

Ludwig had spent several days in Todi and had already made 154 all his preparations for the journey to Tuscany when a new hope

ferum mare diverterunt. Classis enim Siculorum, quae regnum Roberti invadere constituerat, tardius comparata, demum eo tempore advenit, cum iam Ludovicus coeptum Regni negotium omisisset. Praeerat autem classi Petrus Federici regis filius, erantque cum ea classe naves genuensium exulum qui regi adversabantur. Hi omnes, cum ad tiberina ostia pervenissent, cognito Ludovici ex Urbe discessu, per nuncios illum multis precibus arcessiverunt.[222] Ea de causa Tuderto profectus Viterbium rediit, relictoque ibi pontifice atque impedimentis, ipse cum equitatu delecto Cornetum (ibi namque praestolabatur classis) profectus est. In colloquio magis querelae effusae quam ulla provisio aut reparatio facta. Illi frustra paratam classem magnamque vim pecuniae incassum absumptam, hic tarditatem adventus ac res simul spesque suas ob id frustratas querebatur. Ad reditum autem in Regnum, quod illi postulabant, mussare videbatur, fatigato milite ac urbe Roma, quae statim post illius discessum amicos fautoresque illius disperserat, adversante,[223] aditibusque in Regnum firmo regis praesidio custoditis. Ludovicum igitur a cogitato in Florentinos impetu huiusmodi causae vel averterunt vel certe retardarunt.

155   Castrucium autem per haec ipsa tempora mors opportuna oppressit. Post receptum enim Pistorium et quibus erat opus firmatum, cum Lucam ad cetera paranda rediisset, in valetudinem incidit adversam ac post paucos dies e vita decessit. Causam vero eius morbi ex labore castrensi immodico nimiaque corporis animique fatigatione provenisse putant. Obiit quoque per idem fere tempus Galeactius Vicecomes, qui dudum in Mediolanenses ceterasque Galliae civitates amplum ac regno simile tenuerat imperium. Is enim, post res amissas ac perditas opes, ad Castrucium confugerat ac in pistoriensi obsidione cum illo fuerat. Ibi contracto morbo Pisciae in oppido e vita decessit.

arose that diverted him to the Tyrrhenian Sea. For the Sicilian fleet which was to have invaded Robert's kingdom had been assembled so late that it arrived at a point when Ludwig had already abandoned his projected conquest of the Regno. The fleet was commanded by Peter, son of King Frederick,[101] and with him were the ships of the Genoese exiles who were opposed to the king [Robert]. When all these forces arrived at Ostia, they learned of Ludwig's departure from Rome and sent messengers begging him to return. That is why he left Todi and returned to Viterbo, leaving there his baggage and the [false] pontiff, while he himself with a force of picked knights made for Corneto, where the fleet was waiting. The colloquy that ensued was marked more by a flood of grievances than by any planning or renewed purpose. The Sicilians complained of having readied a fleet in vain and of the enormous amount of money they had wasted to no purpose; Ludwig grumbled at their late arrival and the consequent frustration of his plans and hopes. Yet he seemed to demur at the return to the Regno they were seeking: his soldiers were tired; the city of Rome had dispersed his friends and followers after his departure; and the approaches to the Regno were guarded by strong royal garrisons. Causes of this kind thus averted or at least retarded Ludwig's planned attack on Florence.[102]

At this convenient moment death overtook Castruccio. After 155
recovering Pistoia and strengthening its defenses, he had returned 1328
to Lucca to make further preparations when he took sick and, after a few days, departed this life. It is thought that his sickness was the result of his excessive exertions in the field and of extreme fatigue of body and spirit. Galeazzo Visconti also died around the same time. He had long held vast power, similar to a kingdom, in the territory of Milan and in other cities of Lombardy. After the wreck of his affairs and the loss of his resources he had taken refuge with Castruccio and was with him at the siege of Pistoia. There he took sick, and departed this life in the town of Pescia.[103]

156   A Castrucio filii duo superstites relicti, Arrigus et Galeranus. Eos, quia tenera adhuc aetas tantae moli impares reddebat, sub matris amicorumque tutela pater dimiserat. Hi igitur celato obitu Pisas novis copiis occuparunt, veriti ne Pisani re cognita rebellandi consilium sumerent. Neque vana erat suspicio; nam Pisani dominatum Castruci haud satis aequo ferebant animo, facultatem omnem arrepturi. Decursa igitur urbe ac populo aliquot locis fuso, cum dominatum vi et armis adulescentulis confirmassent, tunc demum patefacta mors et funus omni magnificentia peractum. Nuntius de Castruci obitu ad Ludovicum pervenit, cum adhuc in colloquio classis esset. Ex hoc mutato repente consilio, omnibus posthabitis curis, per maritimam Pisas contendit. Ita imminens civitati periculum non tam humana ope quam divino est beneficio sublatum.

157   Florentiae auditus Castruci obitus inter spem ac metum vix credibilis videbatur. Mox, ut magis ac magis confirmatus est, versis in laetitiam animis, non iam de repellendo, sed de inferendo bello cogitabant. Hoc enim uno acerrimo sublato hoste, et Ludovicum iam et ceteros longe contemnebant. Igitur eductis repente copiis expugnare Carminianum adorti, in quo satis validum erat praesidium, cum signo dato unum sub tempus ad moenia subiissent, incredibili tandem virtute munitiones transgressi, oppidum expugnarunt et usque ad arcem cum magna hominum caede pervicerunt. Arx deinde octo continuos dies machinis ballistisque oppugnata est; nec diuturnam promittebat moram inclusorum in ea hominum multitudo quamvis magnam vim annonae brevi consumptura. Ve-

Castruccio was survived by two sons, Arrigo and Galerano. 156
Since they were still of tender years and unequal to great burdens,
he had left them under the tutelage of their mother and his
friends. So the boys' tutors concealed his father's death and occupied Pisa with fresh troops, fearing that, once the Pisans learned
of his demise, they would decide to rebel. This was no empty suspicion, for the Pisans had by no means endured the lordship of
Castruccio with tranquillity, and would seize every chance to end
it. So the tutors made a show of force in the city, breaking up
gatherings of the people in some places. Only when they had reinforced the boys' lordship with armed violence did they disclose
Castruccio's death, and funeral rites were performed with full ceremonial. The news of Castruccio's death came to Ludwig when
he was still in colloquy with the fleet. Hearing it, he suddenly
changed his plans and, putting aside all other concerns, pressed on
to Pisa by the coastal road. Thus the imminent danger to the city
was removed less by human aid than by divine beneficence.[104]

In Florence, living between hope and fear, the reports of Cas- 157
truccio's death seemed scarcely credible. But soon, as the reports
were confirmed over and over, their spirits were filled with joy, and
they began to think, not of warding off war, but of waging it.
With this bitterest of foes removed from the scene, they now despised Ludwig and the rest of their enemies. Thus they suddenly
marched out their troops and began to lay siege to Carmignano,
which had a fairly strong garrison. Sounding the charge, they
made for the walls all at once and at last, with incredible bravery,
broke through the defenses, captured the town, and prevailed
with great slaughter all the way to the citadel. Then for eight days
without interruption they attacked the citadel with siege engines
and catapults. The great multitude of men shut up inside would
shortly consume any corn-supply, however large, and this assured
that resistance would not last long. But since it was now being reported that Ludwig was approaching Pisa, to prevent some new el-

rum, quia advenisse iam Pisas Ludovicus ferebatur, ne quid forte novi emergeret, pacti ut[224] cum his quae asportare singuli possent incolumes abirent, et pauca insuper pecunia equitibus addita receperunt arcem.

158   Ludovicus, ubi Pisas advenit, summa gratulatione populi receptus, quo benevolentiam sibi conciliaret ac spem dominatus Castrucianis auferret, Tarlatum equitem arretinum, fratrem Guidonis praesulis, cui amicitiam cum Pisanis et odium adversus Castrucium fuisse diximus, civitati praefecit. In ceteris quoque non satis placato corde in Castruci filios videbatur esse. Quamobrem illi primo timentes Lucae portas claudebant, nec quemquam ab illo proficiscentem intrare urbem patiebantur. Demum lenita ira, cum adolescentium mater, grandia ferens munera, Pisas ad eum venisset natosque suos illius fidei commendasset, Lucam proficiscitur. Ibi per eius praesentiam insurgente plebe ac tyrannidem Castrucianorum incusante, gubernationem adulescentibus ademit, et quendam e proceribus suis Lucae praesidem imposuit, simulque magnam pecuniae vim Pisanis Lucensibusque imperavit, quasi mercedem tyrannidis sublatae.

159   Dum haec in Etruria geruntur, Carolus, Roberti regis filius, morbo correptus apud Neapolim obiit diem, civesque,[225] illius imperio liberi, rempublicam ex integro capessentes, bona iam spe gubernationi incubuerunt. Et sane iampridem odio fuerat Apulorum Campanorumque avara cupiditas, cuncta ad rem pecuniariam referentium. Quamquam profuit in multis regiae domus favor, attamen (quod negari non potest) inexhausta quaedam pecuniarum

ement of chance emerging, it was agreed that the defenders could leave unmolested with whatever they could carry, and the Florentines took possession of the citadel, having paid a small additional sum to the knights defending it.

When Ludwig arrived in Pisa he was received by the people 158 with great festivity in order that they might recover his good will and destroy any hope of domination on the part of Castruccio's followers. Ludwig appointed as governor of the city Tarlato, an Aretine knight, the brother of Bishop Guido, whose friendship with the Pisans and hostility towards Castruccio we have described. In other matters, too, he seemed to be less than well disposed to Castruccio's sons. On this account they at first shut the gates of Lucca in fear of him and did not allow anyone coming from him to enter the city. At length their anger softened, and after the mother of the boys came to him in Pisa, bearing ample gifts and commending her sons into his tutelage, he came to Lucca. There, his presence encouraged the plebs to rise up and accuse Castruccio's followers of tyranny, whereupon he removed the boys from power and appointed one of his own barons as governor of Lucca. At the same time he demanded a large sum of money from the Pisans and Lucchesi, as though he deserved a reward reward for putting down tyranny.[105]

While these events were taking place in Tuscany, Charles, the 159 son of King Robert, was taken ill and died in Naples. The citizens [of Florence], freed of his power, took charge of the state once more, and now with fair hope devoted themselves to its governance. Indeed, they had long hated the insatiable greed of the Apulians and Campanians, who reduced everything to money. Although the favor of the royal house was advantageous in many ways to the Florentines, nevertheless, it cannot be denied that for the Angevins, Florence constituted a kind of exhaustible stock of money. If anyone should reckon up the money paid from the time of Charles, the first king of Sicily, down to the other Charles of

materia Florentia illis fuit; ut, si quis a Carolo primo Siciliae rege ad hunc alterum quem modo diximus Carolum pecunias numeret, supra fidem supraque modum videatur populum unum tantis oneribus suffecisse. Igitur, liberam tunc cives reipublicae administrationem complexi, quae necessaria fuerant providerunt; magistratuum sortitiones ex delectis comprobatisque hominibus in biennium destinatae; consilia duo rebus maioribus decernendis constituta, alterum merum populare, alterum[226] mixtum ex nobilitate et plebe, quod commune vocitatum est. His simul ac vexilliferis societatum[227] tempus taxatum est mensium quatuor, cum primo sex durare consuesset.

160 Per hoc ipsum fere tempus coorta in Ludovici exercitu seditione, ad octingentos germani equites ab eo defecere, qui Pisis egressi, cum Lucam occupare constituissent, parvo temporis momento, re ante cognita, prohibiti ianua sunt. Exclusi itaque Luca ac spe frustrati, cuncta circa urbem loca hostili rapina foedaverunt. Mox in proximum evadentes collem apud Cerulium, munitum quondam a Castrucio locum, stativa posuerunt; gravis profecto vicinitas et amicis pariter inimicisque formidata. Hi, missis Florentiam legatis, fidem operamque suam pollicebantur. Frequenter de his consultatum est, tandemque res infecta relicta, illa maxime ratione quod periculosum credebatur[228] germanis hominibus et sub hoste militare solitis rem civitatis committere.

161 Ceterum horum transfugium ac diuturna iisdem in locis incubatio maximarum posthac novitatum semina pepererunt. Ludovicus enim horum discessu sollicitus, lenibus primo verbis iram Germanorum placare nixus, ubi duriores sensit, Lucae cui illi imminebant timere, praesides mutare, Castruci filios amovere, omnia denique suspicionibus replere perrexit. Tandem vero convenit ut

whom we have just spoken, it would seem to him beyond belief
and measure that one people could have endured such enormous
burdens. So the citizens embraced the free administration of the
state and made the necessary provisions. Sortitions of magistrates
from selected and approved men were fixed for a two-year period,
and two councils were established to decide important matters.
One was a purely popular council; the other was a mixed council
consisting of nobility and plebeians, and was called the "Council
of the Commune".[106] The term for these councils and for the standard-bearers of the militia companies was fixed at four months,
whereas before it had customarily lasted for six.[107]

Around this same time sedition arose in Ludwig's army, and up   160
to eight hundred German knights defected from him. These men
left Pisa and decided to occupy Lucca, but their intentions were
quickly discovered, and the doors were closed against them. Shut
out of Lucca and frustrated in their expectations, they befouled
and pillaged the whole area around the city. Then they went up a
nearby hill near Ceruglio, a place once fortified by Castruccio,[108]
and pitched camp. Their proximity was a grave cause of fear to
friend and enemy alike. They sent envoys to Florence, offering
their loyalty and services. There was much discussion of the offer,
but in the end the matter was left unsettled, mostly because it was
believed perilous to entrust the city's affairs to Germans who usually fought on the side of the enemy.

Yet their flight and continuing presence in that location sowed   161
the seeds of the greatest political changes thereafter. For Ludwig,
anxious at their departure, at first tried to placate the Germans'
anger with soft words, but then, when they remained obdurate,
proceeded to change the governors of Lucca (the city they were
threatening); he sent Castruccio's sons away, and ended by spreading paranoia everywhere. Finally it was agreed that Azzo Visconti,
restored to his paternal tyranny for this very purpose, should pay
the money the Germans were asking for. To this end certain en-

Accius Vicecomes, in paternam tyrannidem ob hoc ipsum restitutus, postulatas ab his pecunias exsolveret. Huius rei gratia legati quidam Germanorum cum Accio profecti sunt, militum nomine pecunias excepturi. Verum hi[229] ipsi legati, ubi pecunias[230] susceperunt, et fidem et commilitones valere sinentes, diverso itinere in Germaniam abiere. Ita spe frustrata res ad irritum recidit, castraque iisdem in locis[231] Germani tenebant, Ludovico infensi ac nocendi occasionem expectantes.

162   Per extremum huius anni Castruci filii, quos in privatam formam redactos a Ludovico diximus, militibus centurionibusque qui sub patre militaverant magno numero coactis, Pistorium occupare conati sunt. Praesidium Ludovici intra urbem erat, non tamen ita validum, ut esset pertimescendum. Ingressi itaque Pistorium Castruciani, cum pleraque improviso pervasissent loca insurgentibus civibus urbe repelluntur.[232]

163   Eodem anno coniuratio Florentiae deprehensa est facinorosorum hominum, qui incendere urbem ac prodere[233] hosti cogitaverant. Res tota ita composita ferebatur, ut constituta nocte quatuor urbis locis de industria incensis, dum ad illa restinguenda intenti cives essent, coniurati portam effringerent hostemque ad hoc ipsum ex composito paratum arcessitumque reciperent. Id excogitatum compositumque fuerat per id tempus, quo Ludovicus et Castrucius venturi ad urbem credebantur. Et perminima de plebe homines ad facinus patrandum comparata manus, repertaeque sunt aedes aliquot malleolis constipatae, quo promptius validiusque corriperentur incendia. Quare supplicio de proditoribus sumpto civitas conquievit.[234]

voys of the Germans were given a safe-conduct with Azzo to accept the monies on behalf of the soldiers. But these same envoys, once they had received the monies, bade farewell both to their loyalty and to their fellow soldiers, and went off to Germany by a different route. Thus their hopes were frustrated and the affair came to nothing. The Germans remained encamped in the same place, hostile to Ludwig and looking for a chance to do him harm.[109]

At the end of this year, Castruccio's sons, whom (as we said) Ludwig had reduced to the condition of private individuals, assembled a great number of soldiers and officers who had served under their father, and tried to occupy Pistoia. Ludwig had left a garrison inside the city, but it was not strong enough to inspire fear. So Castruccio's followers entered Pistoia and prevailed in many places owing to surprise, but the citizens rose up and drove them out of the city.[110]

162
1328

In the same year a criminal conspiracy was uncovered in Florence. The criminals planned to set fire to the city and betray it to the enemy. It is said that the whole plot had been so arranged that, on the appointed night, fires would be set on purpose in four places in the city, and while the citizens were intent on putting them out, the conspirators would break down the gate and let in the enemy who would have been deliberately summoned and ready to make an assault. The plot had been devised and arranged at the time when it was thought that Ludwig and Castruccio were coming to the city. A band of men from the lowest classes had been ready to carry out this crime, and a few buildings were found packed with incendiary materials so that the fires would catch more swiftly and strongly. The traitors were put to death and the city enjoyed quiet.[111]

163

LIBER SEXTUS

1 Principio insequentis anni Ludovicus, quoniam germani equites qui ab eo transfugerant omnibus coeptis cogitatisque suis obsistere videbantur, nec promissae ab Accio pecuniae comparebant, quo his[1] prospiceret incommodis, transire in Galliam statuit. Relicto itaque Pisis falso pontifice cum omni haereticorum apostatarumque sentina, ipse, cum his quae supererant copiis, superato Apennini iugo, per agrum parmensem descendit in Galliam. Atque haec omnia sic ab eo gerebantur, quasi prope diem Pisas ad pontificem reditturo. In Gallia vero maiora longe quam putabat impedimenta offendit. Accius enim illius perfidiam in paterna dudum eversione expertus, parere noluit adventanti, sed Mediolano ceterisque oppidis longe exclusit. Quare bello est in his locis necessario implicatus. In Etruria vero post eius discessum varios casus variosque eventus res susceperunt. Germani siquidem, quos in colle imminenti Lucae diximus consedisse, haud multo post eius transitum in Galliam, Marcum Vicecomitem, quem a Ludovico missum pro obside retinebant, sibi ducem praefecerunt. Huius maxime opera atque ingenio freti, tandem Lucam occupant, intromissi per arcem a veteranis qui custodiae praeerant. Mox per legatos Florentiam missos obtulerunt eam se urbem dedere velle. Duo ab his postulabantur: stipendiorum antiquorum dissolutio (ea summa erat auri millia circiter octoginta); secundum, pro Castrucii filiis praecipua quaedam. His namque et amicitia erat paterna cum Marco Vicecomite et ingressum Germanorum in urbem Lucam odio praesentis dominatoris curavisse videbantur.

BOOK VI

At the beginning of the following year, the German knights who 1
had deserted Ludwig seemed to be standing in the way of all his 1329
plans and projects and the monies promised by Azzo had gone
missing. So Ludwig decided to pass into northern Italy to attend
to these problems. Leaving behind in Pisa the false pontiff with all
his worthless heretics and apostates, he himself, with what was left
of his forces, crossed the Apennines and descended into northern
Italy via the territory of Parma. He conducted himself in all things
as though he was soon going to return to the pontiff in Pisa. But
in northern Italy he encountered more obstacles than he had
thought. For Azzo, having had experience of Ludwig's perfidy in
deposing his father some time before, did not wish to obey the
new arrival, but shut him out of Milan and other towns. Hence
Ludwig necessarily became involved in war in these places. In
Tuscany events took various twists and turns after his departure.
For not long after Ludwig passed into northern Italy, the Germans — who had, as we said, taken up position on a hill overlooking Lucca — chose as their leader Marco Visconti, an envoy of
Ludwig's whom they had kept with them as a hostage. Relying
chiefly on his services and intelligence, they at length occupied
Lucca, having infiltrated the citadel with the help of veterans in
command of the guard. Then they sent envoys to Florence indicating their willingness to hand over the city. They made two demands: [first], that their long-overdue stipends be paid (the sum
was about 80,000 florins); second, that a special sum be set aside
for the sons of Castruccio. For the latter shared their father's
friendship with Marco Visconti, and they seemed to have facili-
tated the Germans' entrance into Lucca out of hatred for its current lord.[1]

2   Re igitur Florentiam delata, varie consultatum est a civitate. Erant quibus sine ulla cunctatione[2] suscipiendam a florentino populo Lucam ac Germanis pecuniam[3] exsolvendam; erant etiam qui totam huiusmodi oblationem repudiandam censerent. Oberantque utilitati publicae simultates privatae; quod enim praecipui quidam cives ferebantur auctores repertoresque huiusce facti Germanis fuisse, horum successibus renitentes adversarii contra pugnabant. Cum igitur ad populum magistratus de his[4] referret ac variae pro cuiusque ingenio dicerentur sententiae propiusque ad repudiandum res inclinaret, Pinius Tosa eques florentinus, qui unus ex auctoribus fuisse Germanis ferebatur, in hunc modum sententiam dixit:

3   'Si quemadmodum leges domi, spectatissimi cives, quas tempus experientiaque rerum magistra inutiles arguit, sic etiam detrimentosa foris consilia corrigere vobis liceret, non multum aut mihi aut alteri cuiquam patriae amatori in hac deliberatione vestra putarem laborandum; quippe, tempore ipso comprobante, quid factu sit optimum sequeremini. Nunc autem ea quoniam est natura rerum propositarum ut male suscepto consilio poenitere nil prosit, omnes et adniti et conari oportet quo reipublicae commodum amplectamur. Res enim haec, ni fallor, permagna agitur, et in qua plurimum referat hoc vel illud eligatis. Ac me quidem aut error habet ingens aut permulta simul ad suscipiendam Lucam vos hortari videntur, quae cum ante oculos posita sint, miror esse quosdam qui se haec videre intelligereque dissimulent.

4   'Ipse breviter quae intueri videor singulatim discurram. Utilitatem Lucae susceptio nobis[5] duplicem affert; nam et sedes illa per

The matter was therefore brought to Florence and the city was   2
given a variety of advice. There were those who held that the Florentine People should accept Lucca and pay the Germans their
money without delay; there were also those who held that the
whole offer should be rejected. Private feuds became an obstacle to
public utility, for as certain leading citizens were reported to be advocates and sponsors of the German offer, their adversaries fought
on the opposite side to prevent them from enjoying a political victory. So the magistracy brought the matter before the People and
various opinions were voiced according to each man's disposition.
As the offer moved closer to being rejected, Pino della Tosa, a
Florentine knight and one of those reported to be an advocate of
the Germans,[2] gave his views in the following manner:

"If, distinguished citizens, it were allowable to correct damaging   3
advice in foreign affairs just as we do in the case of domestic laws
which time and experience, mistress of affairs, have shown to be
profitless, neither I nor any other patriot, I should think, would
have to exert himself in this debate of yours; indeed, time itself
would confirm the best course of action for us to follow. As it is,
however, such is the nature of the affair before you that once ill
counsel has been taken it will be useless to repent. So we should
all try and strive to embrace the good of the republic. For unless I
am mistaken the affair we are discussing is of the highest importance, and a great deal depends on whether you choose one course
or the other. Either I have made a great error indeed or there
would seem to be numerous reasons that together urge you to take
possession of Lucca. Since these are in plain view, I wonder that
there are certain men who pretend not to see and understand
them.

"I shall briefly run through them one by one, as they appear to   4
me. For you to take possession of Lucca would serve a double purpose: that base, once occupied by you, would not lie open for enemies to use, and you would find it highly convenient to use against

vos occupata hostibus non patebit, et ipsa vobis contra hostem peropportuna erit. Scitis enim quot bella per hosce annos gravia quidem et aspera pertulistis, ea omnia ab iis[6] qui Lucam tenuerunt vobis esse illata. Haec igitur facultas adempta hosti permagnam reipublicae nostrae securitatem pariet nocendique cupidos longius submovebit, ut iam ab ea parte nihil sit amplius formidandum. Nulli vero nobis neque animis inimiciores neque opibus infestiores sunt quam Pisani: nil porro opportunius ad eos comprimendos quam Luca urbs finitima, paene in vestibulo eorum posita, ut sive inferendum adversus eos sive repellendum sit bellum, permagnam exinde opportunitatem ad utrumvis habeamus.

5   'Age vero, ipsa per se quanta potentiae erit accessio pulcherrimam munitissimamque urbem, tantum agri, tot oppida, tot arces, in potestatem vestram devenire? Quid autem, gloria et amplitudo nominis maiestasque florentini populi quantum augescet, si civitas, dudum nostrae opibus et potentia paene par, nobis[7] subiiciatur? Equidem, ut ista communi vita moribusque hominum utor, ita illis me moveri fateor quae bona apud homines putantur: extendere fines, imperium augere, civitatis gloriam splendoremque extollere, securitatem utilitatemque asciscere: quae nisi expetenda dicamus, et cura reipublicae et pietas in patriam et tota paene haec vita nobis fuerit pervertenda. Haec si illi qui suscipiendam vobis dissuadent contemnunt ac pro nihilo censent, novas porro vivendi normas in vitam adducunt; sin illa probant ac in bonis existimant, hanc suscipiendam putent necesse est, unde tot simul bona commodaque proveniunt. Mihi quidem divino quodam beneficio haec oblata facultas nobis videtur, ut ex qua urbe primo Fagiolanus, postea Castrucius non sine clade nobis intulerunt bellum, eam

an enemy. You are aware how many harsh and formidable wars you have endured in recent years, and how all of them were launched by men in control of Lucca. Removing this base from enemy hands will bring the greatest security to our republic; it will keep at a much greater distance those who desire to do us harm, so that there will no longer be anything to fear from that quarter. Indeed, we have no more hostile and resourceful foe than the Pisans, and nothing would be more suitable for restraining them than the nearby city of Lucca, placed as it is practically on their doorstep. Whether attacking them or defending ourselves against them, we would henceforth have an extraordinary advantage in both defensive and offensive war.

"And just think, too, how much your power will increase when 5 you get control of this most beautiful and well-fortified city-state, with such a large territory and so many towns and citadels! Think how much the glory, fame and majesty of the Florentine People will grow if a city which has long been nearly our equal in wealth and power should be made subject to you? For my part, I confess, as one who practices the common life and moral customs of mankind, I am moved by the things that men hold to be goods: extending borders, enlarging empire, raising on high the glory and splendor of the state, assuring our own security and advantage. If we say that these are not desirable things, then the welfare of the republic, patriotism and practically this whole life of ours will be overthrown. If those who would dissuade you from taking Lucca despise such things and think them of no account, they are in their turn introducing new moral standards into life; if they approve of them and consider them goods, then they must necessarily believe that Lucca should be taken, for so many goods and advantages follow together therefrom. In my view this opportunity has been offered us by a kind of divine beneficence, that we are now able to subdue to our power without danger or suffering the city from which first Uguccione della Faggiuola, then Castruccio,

nunc urbem sine periculo, sine vulnere potestati nostrae subdere valeamus. Quod si hanc facultatem nobis oblatam[8] nunc praetermiserimus, deinde a quibusdam huius populi adversariis Luca suscipiatur, bellumque inde tumultusque[9] insurgat, quis non merito nos culpabit? Quis non carpet? Quis non iustas ignaviae poenas subire nos dicet, quod, dum liceret illam accipere, tam socordes ignavique fuerimus? Damna, o cives, et incommoda omnia pergravia[10] sunt, sed illa maxime quae nostra proveniunt culpa. Nam sua quidem ignavia incidere in mala, praeterquam damnosum, turpe insuper est ac sibi ipsi qui commisit acerbum. Itaque sapientes culpam modo ab hominibus praestandam putant, eventum autem rerum non praestandum: illud enim nostrae, hoc[11] vero fortunae potestatis est.

6   'Duo contra haec dici maxime video. Nam sunt qui satis vos habere monentes, id quod est tuendum censeant, et nec impensis nec coeptis sese novis onerandum. Alii susceptionem eius urbis non improbant quidem, sed absque ullo impendio venturam demum in potestatem nostram arbitrantur. Hi divinare mihi videntur: superiores vero longe aberrare. Tuendum quod est solum censent, quasi vero ista susceptio non pro tutela fiat eorum quae possidemus, aut superiora bella inde nobis illata non in periculum haec ipsa amittendi coniecerint! Non eadem isti mente in patrimonio proprio ac in republica versantur. Patrimonium quidem semper augere quaerunt atque in eo die noctuque anhelant; reipublicae vero acquirere interdicunt. Populus romanus, parens noster, nunquam orbis imperium nactus esset, si suis rebus contentus nova coepta impensasque refugisset. Nec sane idem propositum est homini publice et privatim. Nam publice quidem magnificentia proposita est, quae in gloria amplitudineque consistit; privatim vero

made disastrous war against us. If we now pass up this opportunity that is being offered us, and Lucca is taken by some of the adversaries of this People, and war and tumult should arise therefrom, who will not hold us culpable, and rightly so? Who will not criticize us? Who will not say that we should suffer just penalties for sloth and weakness because we were faint of heart when we were permitted to take it? All losses and evils are serious, my fellow citizens, but the worst are those that proceed from our own fault. To fall into evils through one's own sloth is shameful as well as damaging, and a bitter thing to the man responsible. Thus the wise believe that men should be answerable only for their faults, not for outcomes, as the former is in our power, the latter in fortune's.

"I see two main arguments against taking Lucca. There are   6
those who tell you you have enough to take care of already, and that you should not burden yourselves with new expenses and enterprises. Others do not object as such to the taking of the city, but think that it will come into our possession eventually without any expense. The latter are practicing divination, the former are seriously in error. They think only of protecting what we have, as though the taking of Lucca would not be done for the protection of what we possess; as though the recent wars waged against us from that quarter did not place our possessions in danger! These men adopt an attitude towards conducting public affairs different from the one they hold in the case of their own patrimonies. They are always seeking to extend their patrimony and labor to do so day and night; but they forbid the state from expanding. The Roman People, our forebears, would never have achieved world empire if it had rested content with what it had and had fled from new enterprises and expense. In any case, man does not have the same goal in public and private affairs. In public affairs the goal is magnificence, consisting in glory and greatness; in private affairs the goal is modesty and frugality. Thus, those who consult the in-

modestia et frugalitas. Itaque qui de republica consultant grandio-
rem animum celsiusque propositum assumere debent, nec tam de
impensis et laboribus quam de gloria splendoreque cogitare.

7   ' "At sine ullo impendio ad nos deveniet."[12] Quam vereor ne, si
nunc non accipimus,[13] longe post haec maiora et frustra quidem
impendere cupiamus! Occasionem poetae tradunt crines a fronte
proferre, pone vero calvitiem habere, ut, dum te adit, apprehendere
queas, sin vero neglexeris, nullam post ansam nanciscare. Haec
ego metuo ne nobis[14] eveniant, cives, si nunc Fortunae ad nos
conversae munus facultatemque non apprehendamus. Mea igitur
sententia est Lucam sine ulla mora suscipiendam, et hanc facultatem nobis oblatam nullo modo negligendam esse, cum susceptio
nobis utilitatem securitatemque et gloriam afferat, reiectio autem
periculum et infamiam comminetur.'

8   Pinius[15] quidem ita. Cives autem, partim invidia, partim tributorum formidine, id consilium neglexerunt, vana opinione detenti
quasi Luca tandem ad eos nullis foret pecuniis perventura. Itaque
post longas consultationes res infecta dimissa est, malo admodum
consilio civitatis.

9   Per idem tempus Pistorienses, Ludovici rem in deterius labi
cernentes, pacem a Florentinis quaesiverunt, quae illis vel cupien-
ter concessa est. Per eam pacem exules ferme omnes Pistorium rediere. Praeterea Murlum per eandem pacem Florentinis restitutum, et Carminianum Arteminumque, pistoriensis agri castella, ut
Florentini retinerent concessum. Quoque pax ea stabilior esset,
quatuor ex praecipuis Pistoriensium familiis equestri dignitate a
populo florentino insigniti sunt. Insignivit autem populi nomine
Iacobus Stroza eques florentinus, ad hoc ipsum cum potestate publica Pistorium missus, donoque his dati in singulos aurei nummi
quingenteni. Insuper, ludi equestres grandiori magnificentia ob

terests of the republic ought to endow themselves with greatness of spirit and a more exalted purpose, and to take thought less for expense and effort than for glory and splendor.

"'But it will come into our possession without any expense'. 7 How I fear that, if we do not take it now, we may yearn to pay far more for it hereafter, but in vain! The poets say that opportunity has hair in the front and is bald from behind: when it approaches you, you can seize it, but if you let it pass, it offers you no purchase afterwards.³ I fear this may happen to us, citizens, if we do not seize this chance, this gift Fortune, facing us, holds out. In my view Lucca should be taken without delay, and we should by no means pass up this chance that is offered us, since taking it means advantage, security and glory, while refusal threatens danger and infamy."

Thus Pino. But the citizens, partly through envy, partly 8 through fear of taxes, ignored this advice, held in check by the empty belief that Lucca would in the end come into their possession without expenditure. Thus after long discussion the matter was dropped without result, an extremely bad decision on the city's part.⁴

In the same period the Pistoiesi, observing how Ludwig's situa- 9 tion was growing worse, sought peace from the Florentines, which was granted with alacrity. As a result of that peace nearly all the exiles returned to Pistoia. By the terms of the peace Montemurlo was also returned to the Florentines and they were allowed to keep Carmignano and Artimino, castles in Pistoiese territory. To make the peace more stable, four men from leading Pistoiese families were decorated with knightly rank by the Florentine People. Jacopo Strozzi, a Florentine knight, decorated them in the name of the People, having been sent to Pistoia with public authority for this very purpose; and five hundred gold florins was given to each of them as a gift. In addition, a tournament was held in Florence of still greater magnificence to celebrate the peace. The castles in

eam pacem Florentiae celebrati. Hanc Pistoriensium pacem proxima Lucensium castella quae sunt circa Nebulam amnem consecuta sunt, interponentibus sese Pistoriensibus pacemque suadenti-
bus. Pisani quoque sub idem fere tempus ad libertatem spectantes,
repellere Ludovici iugum perrexerunt. Eius rei causa, Marco Vicecomite cum Germanorum aliqua manu clam arcessito et intra
urbem recepto, arma populariter corripiunt; depulsoque demum
Tarlato praeside cum omni Ludovici praesidio, rempublicam libe-
ratam suo iam ipsi auspicio gubernarunt. Ita mutatis undique rebus Etruriae status novabatur.

10   Marcus Vicecomes, ob navatam Pisanis operam magnifice ab illis donatus, haud multo post Florentiam venit, receptusque eximie
ac publice honoratus, negotium lucense iterato induxit,[16] proposi-
tis iisdem conditionibus quae ab initio fuerant civitati oblatae. Eas
ob res consultatio iterata, eundem quem primo habuerat exitum
habuit. Itaque Marcus ad extremum re infecta cum paucis equitibus in Galliam abiit. At Germani Lucae relicti, cum pecunias
quaererent, eamque urbem non secus atque mercem quandam lici-
tationi offerrent, tandem ad Pisanos rem detulere. Nec vero cunc-
tati sunt Pisani illam capessere; quippe iampridem solliciti ne tam
finitima urbe potiretur Florentinus, haud cunctanter pecunias solvere urbemque suscipere paciscuntur. Id postquam Florentiae auditum est, nulla fuit mora quin bellum inferretur Pisanis, quod
post praesidium Ludovici eiectum tacito magis consensu quam
aperta pace fuerat intermissum. Ea de causa profecti equites peditesque ad Pisarum usque moenia repentino impetu pervasere.

11   Sub idem fere tempus, Catinum oppidum, quod nuper in fidem
florentini populi devenerat, ad hostes defecit. Oppidani siquidem

the Valdinievole nearby followed suit, with the Pistoiesi acting as intermediaries and advocates of the peace.[5] The Pisans also, around the same time, had liberty in view, and took steps to throw off Ludwig's yoke. For this purpose they secretly summoned Marco Visconti with a band of Germans and brought them within the city as the people ran to arms; and expelling the governor Tarlato with all of Ludwig's garrison, they themselves governed a liberated republic under their own auspices. Thus, with things changing on all sides, the political situation in Tuscany was recast.[6]

Marco Visconti, having been magnificently rewarded by the   10
Pisans for his devotion, came shortly thereafter to Florence, where he was received with distinction and given public honors. Once again he brought up the business of Lucca, proposing the same terms under which it had originally been offered to the city. Whereupon there was renewed discussion, but the matter ended as before. Thus in the end Marco went off to northern Italy with a few knights, the matter unsettled. But the Germans left behind in Lucca, since they were still in search of money, were offering the same city up to bid like merchandise, and finally brought the business to the Pisans. The Pisans hastened to seize the opportunity; they had indeed long been worried that the Florentine would get control of this neighboring city, and immediately reached an agreement to pay the money and acquire the city. After the news came to Florence, war was resumed against the Pisans without delay— a war that, after the expulsion of Ludwig's garrison, had been stopped by tacit consent rather than by an open peace. For this reason the infantry and cavalry set out and made a surprise attack right up against the walls of Pisa.[7]

About the same time, the town of Montecatini, which had re-   11
cently sworn fealty to the Florentine People, defected to the enemy. For the townsmen, having expelled the sponsors of the peace with Florence and taken in soldiers of Castruccio (a large band of

pulsis florentinae pacis auctoribus castrucianisque militibus (adhuc enim ingens per ea loca supererat veteranorum manus) receptis subito extulerunt bellum. Cum cetera quoque illius regionis oppida eundem secutura motum viderentur, mittere confestim copias placuit. Dux autem his[17] praefectus est Amerigus Donatus Cursi filius eques florentinus, qui cum ingenti equitum peditumque manu ad ea loca profectus, rebelliones suo adventu compescuit; nec multo post Victolinum eadem meditatum, interceptis principibus qui per colloquia profecti ad hostes fuerant,[18] occupavit. Inde Catinum circumsistens urgere coepit impigre adeo atque infeste, ut neque commeatus importari neque ingredi quisquam aut egredi quiret. Inter haec Pisani, spe potiundi Luca[19] ob coortas difficultates exclusi, pacem cum Florentinis fecerunt. Conditiones fere dictae eaedem quae fuerant in priori pace.

12 Saepius deinde temptata Lucae deditio cum a civitate reiiceretur, Spinulae tandem genuensi, viro nobili divitiisque supra privatum modum abundanti, suscepta pecunia, Germani illam tradidere, venientemque cum praesidio in arcem validissimam, quam in ea urbe[20] Castrucius muniverat, induxere. Spinula igitur, recepta urbe, civibusque in suam voluntatem benigne traductis, pacem agere cupiebat. Florentinis autem longe diversa erat mens; spes enim simul cupidoque incesserat Luca potiundi. Itaque nec Pisanos nuper tulerant se ingerentes, neque tunc Spinulae factum aequo ferebant animo. Quamobrem reiecta pacis flagitatione Catinum acrius premere aliaque lucensis agri castella ad defectionem hortari auxiliaque rebellantibus polliceri coeperunt.

13 Spinula igitur et Lucenses cum se bello haud dissimulanter impeti viderent, audendum aliquid rati, in proximum castellum,

his veterans being still in the area), suddenly revealed themselves to be hostile. Since the rest of the towns in this region seemed likely to follow the same movement, the Florentines decided to send troops at once. The commander in charge was Amerigo Donati, son of Corso, a Florentine knight, who set out for the area with an enormous body of horse and foot. His arrival checked the rebellions, and when shortly thereafter Montevettolino was considering the same course of action, he intercepted the leaders who had left for a parley with the enemy and occupied the town. Then he surrounded Montecatini and began energetically to put hostile pressure on it, allowing no provisions to be brought inside and forbidding anyone to enter or exit. Meanwhile the Pisans, owing to the difficulties that had arisen, put aside their hope of getting hold of Lucca and made peace with the Florentines. The terms were nearly the same as had obtained in the previous peace.

The surrender of Lucca was again explored numerous times 12 and again rejected, whereupon the Germans finally received their price and handed the city over to a Genoese, Spinoli,[8] a nobleman possessed of riches beyond those of a private person. When he came with his guardsmen the Germans brought him inside the extremely strong citadel that Castruccio had built in that city. Spinoli then took possession of the city, won its citizens over to his lordship through generous treatment, then wished to make peace. But the Florentine attitude was quite different, for the hope and desire of controlling Lucca had been growing, so that they could neither endure the Pisans pushing their way in, nor could they view calmly what Spinoli had done. On this account they rejected the appeal for peace and began to put still heavier pressure on Montecatini, and to exhort the other castles in the territory of Lucca to defect, promising aid to the rebels.

Spinoli and the Lucchesi, therefore, seeing that open war was 13 upon them, decided to perform some act of daring and to march their troops against a nearby castle which happened to have re-

quod forte per eos defecerat dies, copias educunt. Adfuit[21] fortuna coeptis: multa cum inimicorum caede castellum ipsum vi expugnatum receperunt. Inde gratulabundi Lucam reversi, opem ferre obsessis ad Catinum statuunt. Ad haec maiora equitum auxilia convocare ac peditem cogere magnasque ad eos copias ex Gallia venire a Ludovico rumor erat. Ob eum rumorem validioribus praesidiis obsidionem firmare placuit atque ita Catinum circummunire ut, quamvis potentissimus adventaret hostis, undique tamen excluderetur. Ad hoc vero non tam Catini utilitas quam generosa quaedam celsitudo impellebat animi, quod magnum aliquid de se ipsis opinantes alienum protinus a dignitate existimabant, si hosti concedere viderentur. Huius igitur rei causa longum atque anxium opus aggrediuntur.

14   Catinum est oppidum in monte edito, planitiesque sub eo meridiem versus patescit; ceteris vero ex partibus undique colles cingunt. Florentini igitur per planitiem primo,[22] quod ab ea parte maxime accessus erat hosti, fossam latam profundamque deduxerunt, aggeremque post eam atque vallum crebris cum turribus propugnaculisque exstruxerunt. Fossam autem ipsam aqua ex flumine derivata explebat; externus vero fossae agger truncis ac praeacutis arborum ramis crebro multiplicique inter se nexu dispositis et ab stipite sub terra dimissis muniebatur. Erat huius fossae longitudo passuum millia circiter sex, atque ita ab radicibus montium reducta, ut inter eos ac vallum castris spatium sat esset. Inde per colles munimenta producentes, opportunis locis occupatis recisisque aditibus et castellis praesidiisque impositis, undequaque Catinum cinxerunt, ut esset hic ambitus castrorum munitionumque supra duodecim millia passuum: mirifica certe res ac vel apud romanum populum memoranda.

belled in recent days. Fortune favored their undertaking, for they assaulted and captured this same castle with vast slaughter of their enemies. From there they returned rejoicing to Lucca, and decided to bring help to the besieged at Montecatini. The rumor was that for this purpose greater forces of cavalry were being called together, infantry collected, and large forces were coming to them from northern Italy, sent by Ludwig. On account of this rumor it was decided to reinforce the siege with stronger defenses, and so to surround Montecatini with defenseworks that, however powerful an enemy should come, he would be shut out on every side. Their motive in this was not so much the value of Montecatini as a certain noble high-mindedness: believing in their own greatness, they thought it beneath their dignity to seem to give way before the enemy. So thanks to this spirit they embarked upon a long and anxious enterprise.

Montecatini is a town placed on a mountain, with a plain 14 spreading beneath it towards the south; on all other sides, however, it is girt about with hills. The Florentines therefore first dug a broad and deep moat across the plain, as the enemy had the most access on that side. They then erected an earthwork behind it with palisades, numerous towers, and bastions. The moat was filled with water diverted from the river, and an earthwork outside the moat was fortified with the branches of trees, cut off and sharpened and bound close together in a line with their stumps sunk in the earth. This moat was about six miles long, and led from the roots of the mountains in such a way that there was enough room for the camp between the mountains and the earthwork. Thereafter they extended the fortifications through the hills, occupying the key places, cutting off the approaches, and establishing castles and defenseworks. Montecatini was surrounded on all sides with a ring of encampments and fortifications more than twelve miles long. This was surely a marvelous achievement, one that would have been memorable even for the Roman People.[9]

15   Hostes parato exercitu, cum ex Gallia equitatus supervenisset, Luca profecti, ad oppidum Pisciam constitere. Inde proxima arce cui Uzano nomen est occupata, ex eo rursus loco per superiores colles irrumpere conati, Florentinorum concursu ad eas munitionum partes facto, repelluntur ac irrito coepto pedem referre coguntur. Saepius post haec improviso conati, cum eodem modo prohiberentur, maiores subinde copias parant. Ad superiorem equitatum quingentos equites germanos belli[23] expertos adiungunt; peditum vero multitudinem ex pisano lunensique[24] agro vel praemiorum pollicitatione vel studio partium maximam cogunt.

16   Cum satis parata essent, non clam neque per colles, sed apertis campestribusque[25] locis ad munitiones pervenerunt. Florentini toto castrorum robore ad ea conversi loca contra hostes stetere, atque ita primo die castra sunt facta, nihil ut praeter vallum fossamque[26] interesset. Hostes pugna decernere cupiebant, idque iactabundi flagitabant. Florentini vero neque deducere copias ex praesidiis munitionum poterant, ne tantus dudum labor susceptus irritaretur, neque pugnandum existimabant nisi integro milite. Itaque satis putabant si munitiones tutando hostium impetum conatumque repellerent. Igitur hostes ex composito armata multitudine et fortissimo quoque milite cohortato loca distribuunt, partes consignant, unoque impetu pluribus simul locis succedunt ad munitiones oppugnandas. Eodem fere ordine Florentini ad tutandum festinant, et clamor ingens utrinque attollitur; sed qui subibant hostium non sagittis modo et tragulis sed saxis quoque e vallo propugnaculisque feriebantur, et cum ad aggerem ventum erat, acutis

The enemy prepared an army, and when the cavalry from 15
northern Italy had arrived, they set out from Lucca, stopping at
the town of Pescia. Then they occupied a nearby citadel called
Uzzano and from that place tried to break into Montecatini
through the upper hills. The Florentines rushed to that part of the
fortifications, and the enemy was driven back and compelled to retreat in failure. After this they very often made surprise attacks
and, being shut out in the same way, they then assembled larger
forces. To their existing cavalry they added five hundred German
knights, expert in war, and they collected an enormous mob of infantry from the territory of Pisa and the Lunigiana, who were motivated either by promise of reward or by partisanship.

When they had readied these forces, the enemy came, not se- 16
cretly through the hills, but through the open countryside, right
up to the defense-works. The Florentines concentrated the whole
strength of their encampment on that place and stood against the
foe, and on the first day pitched camp so that there was nothing
between them and the enemy except the earthwork and the moat.
The enemy wanted a decisive battle, and with noisy braggadocio
demanded one. But the Florentines could not march their troops
out of the defense-works without wasting their long and mighty
labors, nor did they believe they should engage the enemy except
with their full forces. They thought it would be enough if they defended their positions and repelled the assaults and strikes of the
foe. So the enemy, according to plan, summoned the armed multitude and their powerful force of trained soldiers, marching them
into their assigned positions, and in a single, simultaneous assault
from many directions they moved forward to attack the defense-
works. The Florentines hastened to protect them with almost the
same good order, and a great clamor arose on both sides. The advancing enemy forces were stricken not only with arrows and
spears but also with rocks flying down from the earthwork and
the bastions. And when they arrived at the earthwork they were

ramis sese induebant, fossaeque altitudo et aqua conspecta omnem
conatus adimebat spem.

17   Quibus difficultatibus repulsi, tandem omissa per vim irrum-
pendi cura ad ingenium convertuntur. Erat fossae, ut diximus, longitudo per planitiem circiter sex millia passuum; caput autem ab
ea parte quae Pistorium versus aspicit, a colle qui est sub castello
Serra, incipiebat. Id quo magis aberat ab hoste, eo custodiebatur
minus. Hostes igitur re per exploratores cognita partem copiarum
per noctem dimissam ea improviso loca invadere iubent. Ipsi autem, quo magis a suspicione divertant, prima luce ad munitiones
succedunt, et maiorem quam unquam conatum de industria osten-
tant. In hanc pugnam intentis omnium animis, copiae hostium,
quas per noctem missas diximus, repente ex insidiis egressae[27] munitiones invadunt, nactaeque locum defensoribus vacuum, intro
penetrarunt. Inde ad laevam secus vallum discurrentes, fugam trepidationemque edidere delataeque in proximum praesidium, brevi
momento expugnant; praefectum eius Iacobum Medicem florentinum equitem capiunt; praedam ingentem nanciscuntur. Lucenses,
qui ad alias munitionum partes Florentinis oppositi stabant, ubi
suorum ingressum cognovere, omissa oppugnatione, citato agmine
ad ea loca contenderunt, quo per priorum[28] vestigia penetrarent;
simulque Florentini re intellecta omnem confestim equitatum ac
levis armaturae militem effuso cursu eo dimisere. Cetera vero acies
structa et composita secus vallum aequis ferme regionibus cum
hostium acie procedebat. Sed equitatus a Florentinis praemissus
interiori atque eo compendiosiori via profectus longe antevenit
proelioque[29] cum his qui intraverant hostibus implicatur. Et succe-
debat proelio levis armaturae miles, qui equitibus permixtus rem

caught on the sharp stakes, and seeing the depth of the moat and the water they lost all hope of success.

Thrown back by these obstacles, they put aside all thought of 17 breaking through by force, and resorted to ingenuity. As we said, the length of the moat through the plain was about six miles. The moat started on the side facing Pistoia, on a hill beneath the castle at Serra. As this end was furthest from the enemy, it was less well guarded. Having learned of this circumstance through spies, they sent away part of their forces by night to make a surprise attack on the area. To further divert suspicion, they marched [their main forces] on the defenses at dawn, and of set purpose they made a greater effort than ever. While everyone's attention was on this battle, the enemy troops that had (as we said) been sent out by night emerged suddenly from their hiding places and attacked the defense-works. Finding a place empty of defenders, they made their way inside. Then, running along the inside of the earthwork, they produced fear and flight, and coming to the next stronghold they captured it in a moment, taking prisoner its commander, Jacopo de'Medici, a Florentine knight, and seizing a large amount of plunder. The Lucchesi, who were stationed opposite the Florentines in another part of the defenses, having learned that their forces were inside, abandoned the siege and, marching quickly, made for the point of the breach, with the purpose of following in the footsteps of the first troops to enter. The Florentines learned of the breach at the same time and immediately sent out their knights and lightly armed troops in a loose charge. Another battle-line was set up and positioned which marched along the earthwork almost exactly opposite the line of the enemy on the other side. But the cavalry the Florentines had sent ahead by the shorter route inside the earthwork arrived far in advance, and engaged in battle the enemy who had entered. The lightly-armed troops then joined the battle and, mixed together with the knights, performed outstandingly that day. At last they drove back the enemy inside

ea die gessit egregie. Ab his pulsi, tandem hostes qui munitiones intraverant ad Catinum refugerunt. Reliqua vero Florentinorum acies ad munitiones concurrens, facile eas tutata est a cetero hostium ingressu. Ita pars una hostium inclusa, reliqua vero[30] exclusa remansit.

18   Secutis post haec diebus acerrimum fuit certamen, cum ab externo hoste summa vi munitiones oppugnarentur, intus vero inclusi idem sub tempus ab oppido acriter invaderent. Adversus eam vim Florentini bifariam partiti copias resistebant, ut equitatus cum aliqua peditum[31] manu ab radice montium repugnaret, ceterae vero copiae munitiones ab externo tutarentur impetu; pugnabaturque eodem tempore a fronte et a tergo, et simul turres munitionesque toto ambitu tutandae erant: in quibus, cum magna necessario distineretur manus, summum in periculum res veniebat, et quo magis sperabant hostes, eo acrius nitebantur. Sed contra haec omnia incommoda peropportunum remedium fuit, quod, intellecto periculo, tota paene civitas se in castra diffudit. Ita multitudine virorum suppeditante spem conatus hostibus ademere.

19   Spinula igitur Lucensium dux multos dies frustra conatus, retro tandem movit castra ad oppidum Pisciam. Obsessi vero, cum antea necessariorum angustia laborabant, tum[32] addito novarum copiarum adventu maiori inopia premebantur. Afferebat desperationem recessus suorum; erumpendi nulla penitus videbatur facultas; expectare autem ac diuturniorem experiri moram defectus commeatuum prohibebat. Quibus ad extremum difficultatibus victi, deditionem facere constituunt. Pacti ut incolumibus abire sibi liceret, deducto vetere novoque praesidio vacuum Florentinis oppidum reliquere. Per hunc modum Catinum receptum est longo quidem certamine, sed admodum glorioso. Agmina paene trium-

the fortifications, who took refuge in Montecatini. The rest of the Florentine battle line then rushed to the defenses and easily saved them from being entered by the rest of the enemy forces. Thus one part of the enemy army was shut up inside, while the rest remained outside the defenses.[10]

On the following days there was the bitterest of struggles, since 18 the enemy outside was attacking the defenses with the great violence, while at the same time the enemy within was assaulting them hard from the town. The Florentines resisted, dividing their forces into two parts, so that the cavalry with a force of infantry fought back from the root of the mountains, while the rest of the troops guarded the defense works from external attack. There was simultaneous fighting at the front and at the rear, and the towers and fortifications had to be protected along the whole circle, all at the same time. Since this meant spreading out a large force, the situation became extremely perilous, and the more hope the enemy had, the harder he fought. But against all these disadvantages there was one most opportune remedy: the fact that practically the whole city, having learned of the danger, had poured out into the camps. Thus with the aid of a multitude of men, the enemy lost hope in their enterprise.

So Spinoli, the Lucchese leader, after many days of fruitless 19 effort, finally withdrew his army to the town of Pescia. The besieged were already suffering from lack of necessities before, but with the arrival of the new forces they were beset with still greater want. The withdrawal of the Lucchese army added to their desperation. There seemed to be no way at all to break out, and lack of provisions prohibited any thought of waiting out the siege. Overcome by these difficulties, they finally decided to surrender. Having made an agreement allowing them to leave unmolested, the old and new garrison withdrew, leaving the town empty for the Florentines. In this way, after a long but glorious struggle, Montecatini was taken. In formation, almost as though they were cele-

phantia in urbem coronatique fronde milites domum ad coniuges et liberos suos eximia omnium gratulatione redierunt. Consultatum post haec de Catino evertendo, pervicitque tandem eorum sententia qui retinendum censebant, propter eximiam eius opportunitatem ad bellum.

20 Haud multo post reductas in urbem copias, Bugianum (quod antea castellum in potestate[33] florentini populi fuerat) ad Lucenses defecit. Cum eius rei causa maiores copiae subito advenissent, egressi repente oppidani cum adventitio milite, vicum ei castello subiectum invadere perrexerunt. Erat in eo aliquantulum copiarum, quae ubi fraudem oppidanorum ac novum clam praesidium receptum vident, raptis confestim armis, non solum egregie tutati sunt locum, verum etiam fractos hostes magno sui detrimento persecuti sunt.

21 Multa iam suadere videbantur Lucam ipsam obsideri atque capi posse: primum, quod ipsi per se Lucenses imbecilli sane atque impares erant, praesertim civitate divisa magnaque exulum manu in hoc ipso bello Florentinos sectante. Externi vero nulli videbantur opem laturi, nam Pisani quidem, nova pace obligati, nihil contra molituri credebantur. Ludovicus autem, romani nominis invasor, unica partium spes, fractus ac debilitatus gallico bello, tandem in Germaniam trans Alpisque abierat; falsusque pontifex ab eo Pisis relictus, post Pisanorum rebellionem ad verum pontificem ductus, veritatem agnoverat. Nihilque supererat in praesentia[34] quod videretur formidandum. Quas ob res Florentini magna spe versi ad bellum, non iam levia consectari, sed Lucam ipsam, caput atque arcem belli, obsidere constituunt.

22 Ad hoc, ubi satis omnia parata structaque sunt visa, egressi in arma contra hostes duxere, ac primum Cerulio Viminariaque ac

brating a triumph, the soldiers returned home to their wives and children, crowned with the victor's wreath, to universal rejoicing. Afterwards there was a debate about destroying Montecatini, but in the end the view prevailed of those who thought it should be retained owing to its extraordinary military advantages.[11]

Soon after the return of the troops to the city, Buggiano (which 20 before had been a castle in the power of the Florentine People) defected to the Lucchesi. On this account the latter quickly sent more troops, who with the townsmen suddenly went out and tried to invade the countryside surrounding the castle. A small force of Florentine troops observed the treachery of the townsmen and the clandestine arrival of a new garrison. Instantly seizing arms, they not only defended the area with distinction, but also pursued the shattered enemy forces, inflicting great damage on them.

There now seemed to be many arguments for besieging and 21 capturing Lucca itself. First, the Lucchesi were intrinsically weak and inferior, especially with the city divided and a large band of exiles taking the Florentine side in the war. It appeared that no external powers could bring them aid, for it was believed the Pisans would not take any hostile action, bound as they were by the recent peace treaty.[12] Ludwig, the usurper of the Roman name and the one hope of his party, shattered and weakened as he was by the war in northern Italy, had at last gone away through the Alps to Germany; the false pontiff he had left in Pisa had been brought before the true pontiff after the Pisan rebellion and had recognized the error of his ways. It seemed that for the present there was nothing left to fear. Hence the Florentines with great hope turned again to the war, and decided they would pursue no insignificant objects but attack Lucca itself, the head and citadel of the war.

When everything had been prepared and set in order for this 22 purpose, they marched out in arms against the enemy. First occupying Cerruglio and Vivinaia and the rest of the strongholds over-

ceteris imminentibus Lucae arcibus occupatis, inde mox descendentes, urbi ipsi admoverunt castra, primo ab una urbis parte, mox, crescentibus copiis et amicorum auxiliis confluentibus, alia subinde appetendo loca, undequaque illam cinxere. Cum durior in dies redderetur obsessorum conditio, nec futuri spes praesentia sublevaret mala, Spinula, rebus diffidens, modo pactiones tentare cum Florentinis, modo alienum refugium circumspicere, scrutari denique omnia indagarique incepit.

23   Magnam in bello vim habet fortuna, ut nihil tam exploratum videri possit, de quo non ante supremum sit eventum rei dubitandum. Obsessis enim tunc penitus fractis et quo se verterent nescientibus, cum neque spes neque consilium superesset, fortuna ipsa, quod nemo prius suspicari poterat, subministravit auxilium. Johannes erat Bohemiae rex, Herrici eius qui dudum imperator in Etruria decesserat filius. Hunc aliis de causis Italiae finibus propinquantem Brixiani seditione domestica advocarunt. Qua de causa Brixiam cum equitatu ingressus, haud multo post[35] Bergomates quoque vicinos eadem ferme ratione suscepit ac per amicos paternos vires extendit. Ad hunc igitur Spinula et Lucenses legatione missa, Lucam dedidere. Ille opem ferre obsessis periculoque liberare pollicitus est. Id etsi armis agendum existimabat, tamen viam primo humaniorem ingressus, legatos Florentiam misit, qui sui iuris esse Lucam docerent ac benigne postularent obsidionem dissolvi. Quod negatum cum esset, ad vim conversus et arma, copias parat, expeditionem in Etruriam indicit.

24   Florentinos praeterquam quod inopinata res turbabat animos, illa insuper afficiebat cura, quod orta nuper in castris seditione

looking Lucca, they then came down and camped right next to the city itself. At first they positioned themselves on one side of the city, but later, as their troops increased in number and reinforcements flowed in from their friends, they occupied other places as well, surrounding the city on all sides. As the condition of the besieged worsened with each day, and there were no hopes for the future to relieve present evils, Spinoli lost confidence in his project, and now tried to reach agreement with the Florentines, now looked around for a foreign refuge, and in short began to investigate and hunt down every possibility.

Fortune has great power in war, and there is no course of action so judiciously chosen that it will not be thrown into doubt before reaching its final outcome. For at that moment, when the besieged were entirely broken and knew not where to turn, when they had no hope and no plan, Fortune herself brought them aid from a quarter no one had previously suspected. The king of Bohemia was John, son of the emperor Henry who had died in Tuscany some time before.[13] He had been approaching the borders of Italy for other reasons when the Brescians called him in to put down a domestic rising. For this reason he entered Brescia with his knights, and shortly thereafter took under his protection the neighboring citizens of Bergamo for much the same reason, extending his power by means of his father's friends. Spinoli and the Lucchesi sent a diplomatic mission to him handing over Lucca. He promised to aid the besieged and to liberate them from danger. Although he reckoned this would have to be accomplished by arms, he at first took the more humane route and sent envoys to the Florentines, informing them that Lucca was now his and kindly requesting that they would put an end to the siege. This request denied, he had recourse to violence and arms; and marshalling his troops he announced an expedition to Tuscany.

The Florentines, apart from being thrown into disarray by this unexpected event, were also anxious about a revolt that had re-

conducti milites nulla ducis reverentia caedes et incendia foede pa-
traverant. Ob quae suspecti simul contumacesque nec ipsi se duci,
nec dux illis se satis credebat. Et iam transfugia quaedam ex castris
facta erant conductorum. Quamobrem periculosum rati expectare
hostem, ubi appropinquare praefectus regis cum equitatu nuncia-
tus est, obsidione omissa copias reduxere, quinto fere mense postquam obsideri fuerat[36] coeptum. Per hunc modum primus florentini conatus populi ad Lucam, plenus dudum bona spe, in irritum
recidit, ac maiora subsecuta certamina dispendiis et periculis, mali
poenas consilii, a populo exegerunt.

25   Aliquot dies postquam Lucam venerat regis praefectus, florentinum populabundus ingreditur agrum, habens equites ad mille ducentos, peditum autem ad duo millia. Temeraria procul dubio res,
attamen sortita successum. Cum enim faciliter intercludi possent,
triduo agros populati, magnas inde praedas abegere. Per idem fere
tempus Iohannes rex Parmam et Regium et Mutinam, Galliae urbes, se ultro dedentis,[37] accepit. Ita propinquior potentiorque factus, in dies magis formidabatur.

26   Proximo dehinc anno plurimum aucta suspicio est ob colloquium congressumque regis et legati romanae sedis qui Bononiae
praeerat; in quo perquam amice sese receperant contra omnium
expectationem, ut non modo non succenseret legatus regi pro occupatis Galliae civitatibus, verum etiam sibi gratias videretur habere. Et secuta mox convivia arctaeque amicitiae signa moverunt
hominum mentes et in suspicionem verterunt; quibus est de rebus,
quo clariores sint, paulo altius repetendum.

27   Bellum gallicum originem traxit a genuensi bello. Pulsi enim
dudum Genua cives diversarum partium, se ad Mediolanenses

cently arisen in the camps. Some mercenaries had been commit-
ting murders and acts of arson. The suspects were contumacious
into the bargain and did not trust their commander, or he them.
Already there had been some desertions from the camps of the
mercenaries. So, thinking it would be perilous to await the enemy,
when it was announced that the king's lieutenant was approaching
with his cavalry, they abandoned the siege and withdrew their
troops, about five months after the operation had begun. In this
way the first campaign of the Florentine People against Lucca, an
enterprise once full of hope, broke off in failure, and still greater
struggles, expense and danger would be demanded of the People,
in punishment for their bad decision.[14]

Several days after the arrival of the king's lieutenant in Lucca   25
he entered Florentine territory to devastate it, having with him
around twelve hundred knights and two thousand infantry. Undoubtedly this was a rash undertaking, but it turned out success-
fully. For although they could have been easily barred, they ravaged the fields for three days, making off with large amounts of
plunder.[15] About the same time King John took over Parma,
Reggio and Modena, Lombard cities that had turned themselves
over to him voluntarily. Thus with each passing day he was more
formidable, more powerful — and closer.

The next year there was a great increase in tensions owing to a   26
parley and meeting between the king and the legate of the Roman   1332
see who ruled Bologna. At this meeting both sides received each
other in a very friendly way, contrary to everyone's expectations.
For not only was the legate not angry with the king for having occupied the Lombard cities, he even appeared to be grateful to him
for it. There followed banquets and signs of close friendship which
created suspicions in men's minds. In order to clarify this situation, we must go back a bit earlier.[16]

The Lombard war originated in the Genoese war. The Ghibel-   27
lines who had been expelled from Genoa some time before betook

contulerant, eorumque freti opibus redire in urbem conabantur. Altera vero factio, Roberto rege advocato, sese et urbem illi dediderat, cuius freta viribus contra adversarios repugnabat. Admiscuit se tunc his certaminibus pontifex romanus legatumque suum misit in Galliam. Crescente igitur romanae sedis potentia, ita complures annos gerebatur bellum, ut appareret[38] mera partium studia in illo versari. Robertus enim rex Florentinique ac tota illiusmodi factio legato in Galliam, legatusque ipse, cum opus erat, in Etruriam submittebat auxilia. Mediolanenses autem Veronensesque et[39] Mantuani ceterique imperii fautores contra nitebantur.

28   Post discessum igitur Ludovici ex Gallia, legatus Bononiae consistens, Mutinam et Regium et Parmam, quae dudum urbes ab eo defecerant, gravissimo urgebat bello; quo metu hae civitates sese Iohanni regi dediderunt. Secuta ergo colloquia et amicitiae signa regem inter legatumque, cum ante his de causis crederentur hostes, querelas simul suspicionesque peperere. Robertus enim rex, quod paternam inimicitiam adversus Iohannem exercebat, legati factum indignabatur; Florentini vero ob ereptam e faucibus paene Lucam et antiquam Henrici patris obsidionem infensissimi erant; eodemque modo per Galliam mediolanenses, veronenses mantuanique principes, legati veteres hostes, Iohannem, etsi a stirpe suarum partium fautorem, tamen ob hanc ipsam legati coniunctionem suspectum habuere. Ita paene contra[40] naturam rerum coniunctio quaedam animorum inita est inter principes Galliae Robertumque regem et Florentinos contra Iohannem et legatum; quae haud multo post hos ipsos omnes in unum et apertum foedus coniunxit.

themselves to the Milanese, and with their aid were trying to return to their own city. But the opposing faction summoned King Robert and handed themselves and the city over to him, and supported by his forces fought back against their adversaries. At that point the Roman pontiff became mixed up in these struggles, sending his legate into northern Italy.[17] So, as the power of the Roman see waxed, war was waged for many years in such a manner that it seemed a matter of pure partisanship, hinging on the legate. For King Robert and the Florentines and that whole faction would send aid to the legate and the legate himself would send aid to Tuscany when the need arose. The Milanese, Veronese, the Mantuans and the other imperial supporters fought on the opposite side.

After Ludwig's departure from northern Italy, therefore, the 28 legate, now based in Bologna, made war ferociously against Modena, Reggio and Parma, the cities that had rebelled against him some time before. In fear of him these cities turned themselves over to King John. Thus the discussions and signs of friendship between the king and the legate, who before had been thought enemies for the aforesaid reasons, gave rise at once to complaints and suspicions. King Robert, indulging his ancestral animosity towards John, was indignant about the legate's action, while the Florentines were extremely hostile owing to his having practically snatched Lucca out of their maw, and also because of the siege laid by his father Henry long before.[18] In the same way, in northern Italy the lords of Milan, Verona and Mantua, the legate's inveterate enemies, held John suspect on account of this association with the papal representative, even though by descent John was a supporter of their party. Thus, an almost unnatural sympathy developed between the lords of northern Italy and King Robert and the Florentines against John and the legate. Soon thereafter this sympathy joined them all together in a single, undisguised confederation.[19]

29   Per idem tempus Pistorienses arbitrium potestatemque civitatis florentino populo tradidere, commoti ob discordias civium, quod ii[41] qui dudum pulsi a Castrucio per florentinam pacem redierant in urbem, plus posse adversarios permoleste ferebant, videbanturque ob eam indignationem res novas molituri. Quare praevenientes familiae dudum in florentina pace honoratae dedendi protinus urbem auctrices fuere; neque posthac ut foederati neque rursus ut subditi, sed ut subiecti Pistorienses sunt habiti, etsi ad speciem ius deligendi magistratus ceterasque huiusmodi,[42] liberi populi simulacra, eis[43] in deditione reservata sunt.

30   Eodem anno, Bargam, oppidum lucensis agri quod in potestate florentini populi erat, obsederunt hostes. Eam obsidionem quo dissolverent, Florentini cum exercitu ingressi lucensem agrum, ad Cerulium castra fecere, sperantes metu Lucae obsidionem deserturos. Cum nihilo magis ob id moverentur, omnibus copiis Bargam petiere. Hostes munitissimis castris se[44] circa oppidum continebant, atque ita reciderant aditus ut importari nil posset; pugnam vero detrectabant. Quare, frustrati a spe opis ferendae, nostri domum irriti rediere, Bargaque paulo post inopia frumenti Lucensibus redditur.

31   Altero dehinc anno crescente legati suspicione, quoniam Iohannes, relicto in Italia equitatu cum Carolo eius filio, ipse trans Alpis ad maiores comparandas vires abierat, magno consensu foedus initum est. Fuerunt in eo foedere Veronensium Mantuanorumque tyranni, praeterea Accius Vicecomes, qui nuper castruciano bello

Around the same time the Pistoiesi handed legal supervision of   29
their city over to the Florentines, having been moved to do so by
civil discord. The persons expelled by Castruccio had returned
thanks to the peace treaty with Florence. They found it unbearable that their enemies had more power than they, and it appeared
they were plotting a coup on this account. Hence those families
that had been honored some time previously in the Florentine
peace advocated handing the city over forthwith. After this the
Pistoiesi were considered to be neither a federated nor a subject
people, but rather dependents and subordinates,[20] although for appearance's sake they reserved in the act of donation the right of
choosing magistrates and other rights of this kind, the simulacra
of a free people.[21]

In the same year the enemy besieged Barga, a town in Lucchese   30
territory which was under the control of the Florentine People. To
break the siege, the Florentines entered Lucchese territory with
their army and pitched camp at Cerruglio,[22] hoping that the enemy would abandon the siege out of fear for the safety of Lucca.
When the enemy refused to budge, the Florentines headed for
Barga with all their forces. The enemy had stationed themselves in
well-fortified positions around the town, and had cut off access so
that nothing could be brought inside. But they shrank from battle,
so our forces, frustrated in their hope of bringing aid to Barga, returned home in failure. Shortly thereafter lack of provisions made
Barga surrender to the Lucchesi.[23]

The following year, suspicion of the legate continued to grow, as   31
John, leaving his cavalry behind in Italy with his son Charles, him-   1333
self went away across the Alps to gather greater forces. So by
broad consent a league was formed. In the league were the tyrants
of Verona and Mantua[24] as well as Azzo Visconti, who had recently struck the walls of Florence in the Castruccian war. Such is
the power wielded by indignation and hope of advantage that it
joins together in friendship and association even the bitterest of

florentina pulsaverat moenia: tantumque indignatio potuit et utilitatis spes, ut acerrimi quondam hostes in unum amicitia societateque iungerentur. Conditiones vero adscriptae hae: totis ut viribus, cum opus esset, sibi invicem opitularentur; interim vero belli gerendi causa equitum tria millia in armis haberent;[45] horum Florentini sexcentos conferrent, totidem Robertus rex, Mastinus autem Veronensium tyrannus octingentos, Accius Mediolanensium sexcentos, Ferrariensium principes (nam hi quoque in foedus venerant) ducentos, totidem Mantuanus.

32   Legatus per haec ipsa tempora Ferrarienses bello persequebatur castraque habebat apud Argentam oppidum. Qui ubi initam societatem a florentino populo cum hostibus intellexit, ira et indignatione commotus, oratores Florentiam questum misit. Hi, consumpta pleraque oratione veteribus inimicitiis refricandis damnandoque foedere, ab illo ut[46] se diiungeret civitas postularunt. Ad haec responsum est florentinum quidem populum romanae sedis fautorem in primis fuisse, atque eo magis indignari si quis adversariorum suorum ab sede illa foveatur; nec vero cuiquam admirationi[47] esse debere, si adversus Iohannem Herrici filium, quem et paterna vetus inimicitia et nova Lucae iniuria infestum reddat, sese putaverint muniendos. Sub hoc responso oratores dimissi. Et constabat plus intelligi a civitate quam verbis exprimeretur: nam conciliatus quidem pontifici Iohannes rex per Francorum regem, quem arctissimo consanguinitatis attingebat gradu, credebatur hoc totum Italiae coeptum non invito pontifice adoriri.

33   Per hoc tempus Carolus Iohannis filius Lucam accessit, fuitque metus ne maiori aliqua re invitatus Apenninum transisset. Ceterum paucos dies Lucae commoratus, audito patris reditu, in Galliam properans, Parmae illi occurrit. Venerat cum Iohanne haud magnus equitatus, verum optimus quisque et belli cupidissimus,

former enemies. The terms of the league were as follows. They should help each other in case of necessity with their entire strength, but in the meantime they should maintain three thousand knights in arms in order to conduct a war. Of these the Florentines would contribute six hundred; [King] Robert an equal number; Mastino, tyrant of Verona, eight hundred; Azzo of Milan six hundred; the princes of Ferrara (who had also joined the league)[25] two hundred; and the prince of Mantua an equal number.[26]

At this time the legate was making war on the Ferrarese and   32
had encamped by the town of Argento. When he learned that the Florentine People had joined forces with his enemies, he was infuriated and sent ambassadors to Florence to complain. These men, having consumed most of their oration rekindling old hostilities and condemning the league, demanded that the citizens sever themselves from it. The response to this was that the Florentine People were the principal supporters of the Roman See, and for that reason were the more indignant when one of their adversaries was favored by that See; that it should be a cause of wonder to no one if they took measures to protect themselves against John, Henry's son, whom the ancient enmity of his father and the fresh injury of Lucca had made their foe. Directly after this response the ambassadors were dismissed. It was evident that the city understood more than it would express in words, for it was believed that this whole Italian enterprise had arisen not without the approval of the pontiff, who had been reconciled with King John through the offices of the latter's close relative, the king of France.[27]

At this time Charles, son of John,[28] came to Lucca, and there   33
was some fear that he had been invited to cross the Alps for some larger purpose. But he remained only a few days in Lucca, for hearing of his father's return, he made haste to northern Italy, meeting him in Parma. No great force of knights had come with John from Germany and France, but each one of them was out-

ex Germania et Gallia, plurimumque viri nobiles et principes quidam cum illo advenerant. Sed ex civitatibus quae ante discessum
in fide erant regis, per medium hoc tempus Brixiam et Bergamum
Mastinus averterat; Accius vero Ticinum abstulerat. Ticini tamen
arx tunc[48] etiam a suis tenebatur; quare profectus Ticinum rex
ferre obsessis auxilium tentavit, sed ita fossis castellisque circum-
muniverat[49] Accius, ut nihil ad extremum rex proficere posset.
Itaque populato infestius mediolanensi agro Parmam copias reduxit.

34   Legatum apud Argentam oppidum habuisse castra diximus, nec
longe ab his Ferrariensium constiterant copiae. Proelio itaque
commisso, profligati sunt Ferrarienses, unusque e principibus eorum, Nicolaus, eo in proelio captus. Propius deinde admotis castris, Ferraria obsidebatur. Ad hanc obsidionem praeter victrices
copias magna Bononiensium multitudo et cuncti Flaminiae proce-
res legati iussu coierant in castra. Ferraria ita secus Padum amnem
sita est, ut moenia paene fluvio abluantur. Statim infra[50] urbem
scissus gurges insulam facit, in qua vetustum fuit oppidum. Id oppidum, cum a Ravennatibus impeteretur bello, desertum creditur,
et trans amnem multitudo traducta urbem condidisse. Hostes igitur primo in ea insula contra urbem, post haec transmisso amne
moenibus admoverunt[51] castra, valloque et fossa muniti, terribiles
assidebant.

35   Fracti iam ante proelio Ferrarienses, urgente ad portas hoste,
gravissimo in discrimine versabantur. Ob hoc igitur sociorum periculum, Florentini auxilia mittere constituerant. Sed inerat difficultas maxima, quod neque per Flaminiam neque per bononiensem agrum, omnia tenente legato, neque rursus per Mutinensem
aut Parmensem, regis impedientibus copiis, transmitti auxilia po-

standing and warlike, and the greater part of those who had accompanied him were nobles and princes. But in the meantime, of the cities previously loyal to the king, Brescia and Bergamo had switched to Mastino, while Azzo had seized Pavia. The citadel of Pavia was still being held by John's men, so the king set out for Pavia in an attempt to relieve the besieged. But Azzo had surrounded the city with moats and strongholds so that in the end the king was unable to make any headway. So he ferociously pillaged the territory of Milan and withdrew his troops to Parma.[29]

As we said, the legate had encamped by the town of Argento, 34 and the troops of the Ferrarese were stationed not far from them. Thus a battle was joined, and the Ferrarese were put to flight. One of their princes, Niccolò,[30] was captured in the battle. The papal camp was then moved closer and Ferrara was besieged. In this siege the victorious troops by order of the legate were joined in the camps by a great multitude of Bolognese and all the leading men of the Romagna. Ferrara is situated so close to the river Po that its walls are practically washed by that river. Immediately below the city the waters divide, forming an island, on which the old town was situated. It is believed this town was abandoned after being attacked by Ravenna, and the population moved across the river and founded the [present] city [of Ferrara]. So the enemy first camped on the island opposite the city, then crossed the river and made camp right next to the walls of the city. Protected by an earthwork and a fosse, they invested the city, terrible to behold.

The Ferrarese were already shattered by the earlier battle, and 35 with the enemy at the gate, they were entangled in the gravest of crises. So because of this danger to their allies, the Florentines decided to send reinforcements. But this decision presented a serious difficulty, in that reinforcements could not be sent either through the Romagna or Bolognese territory, those being controlled by the legate, nor again through the territories of Modena and Parma, blocked by the king's troops. So as not to fail their allies they de-

terant. Ne tamen deessent sociorum saluti, longo anfractu per Genuensium et Mediolanensium fines copias mittere statuerunt. Tantum longitudo itineris breviores modo copias fecit, delectique solum missi equites quadringenti; cumque his[52] praefecti duo ex nobilitate praestantissimi per ea tempora iuvenum, Franciscus Pallae filius Stroza et Ugo Vieri filius Scala. Hi Genuam primo, inde pedestri itinere Mediolanum pervenere, urbemque ingressi sunt sub vexillo florentini populi, non conquerente modo Accio Vicecomite, verum etiam omni liberalitate obviam prodeunte. Ex Mediolano Veronam petentes, recepti sunt pari magnificentia a Veronensium tyranno. In hoc tandem loco, quia reliquus cogebatur exercitus, aliquandiu constitere.

36   Per haec ipsa tempora Iohannes Bononiam ad legatum profectus, cum de communi bello consultarent, statuit quam primum cum omni equitatu ad urgendam obsidionem se in castra conferre. Ea de causa rex parte copiarum praemissa, ipse Parmam reversus est ad cetera comparanda. Haec res impulit auxilia sociorum quae Veronae coacta erant,[53] ut praevenire maturarent. Verona igitur profecti equites Ferrariam ingressi sunt, nec ulla posthac fuit mora quin castra adorirentur.

37   Armata ergo multitudine urbana omnibusque paratis, cum duabus simul portis eruptionem fecissent, castra hostium adoriuntur. Naves etiam, quarum ad triginta habebant, per flumen ad castra oppugnanda dimittunt. Florentini, multis id munus detrectantibus, eam sibi partem in distributione locorum susceperant, ut pone castra aggrederentur. Et coniunxerant se his[54] veronensium equitum ad centum quinquaginta et in his plerique florentini exules, qui antiquo partium aestu iactati, apud veronenses tyrannos tamquam in portu aliquo tranquillitatis constiterant. Hi omnes circumdatis hostium castris e diversa ab urbe regione vallum re-

cided to send the troops by a long detour through the borders of Genoa and Milan. The length of the journey imposed reductions in the number of troops, so only 400 picked knights were sent, and with them two outstanding commanders of the day, the young noblemen Francesco di Palla Strozzi and Ugo di Vieri Scali. This force went first to Genoa, then travelled by land to Milan, entering the city under the banner of the Florentine People. Azzo Visconti made no objection and indeed came out to meet them with every mark of liberality. From Milan they headed for Verona and were received with equal magnificence by the Veronese tyrant. In this place they finally stopped, since the rest of the army was being marshalled.[31]

At this same time, John went to meet the legate in Bologna, 36 and having taken counsel together over their mutual war, John decided to join the legate's camp with all his knights to press the siege of Ferrara. For this purpose the king sent part of his forces ahead, and himself returned to Parma to collect more. This circumstance impelled the league's reinforcements, mustered in Verona, to make haste so as to get there first. So the knights left Verona, entered Ferrara, and set up their camp without delay.

Thus when the city population had been armed and all was 37 prepared, they sallied forth simultaneously from two gates and attacked the enemy camp. They also sent ships, of which they had about thirty, down the river to attack the camp. After many others had balked at this task when posts were being allotted, the Florentines undertook to attack the camp from behind. They were joined by about 150 Veronese knights, among them many Florentine exiles whom ancient seas of partisanship had washed up there, and who had remained with the Veronese tyrants as though in some tranquil port. All these forces, having gone round the enemy camp, suddenly attacked the earthwork from a different area of the city, and since the enemy were less vigilant on that side, they pene-

pente invadunt, ac minus ab ea parte intento hoste, quamquam
difficillimo aditu, intro munimenta[55] penetrarunt.

38   Atque fortuna ita fuit, ut non longe ab eo loco vexilla regis
equitatumque ab eo praemissum in castra offenderet. Laetati igitur
eam potissimum pugnam sibi oblatam, in qua, praeter communem
causam, privata insuper ultio exposcenda esset,[56] cohortati suos, in
vexilla regis feruntur. Regii equites proeliorum gnari pugnam fortiter exceperunt. Certamen atrox fuit atque aliquandiu ita pugnatum ut neutram in partem inclinaret victoria. Sed praecipua eo die
pugnandi laus penes duces ipsos Florentinorum fuit, cum ambo
pari ardore in prima versarentur acie; viri militares et magna domi
fama extendere factis gloriam properabant, magisque exemplo
quam verbis adhortabantur suos. His bonis artibus impigre freti,
tandem hostes exsuperant ac referre pedem compellunt, simulque
refracta pluribus locis munimenta castrorum pervaduntur. Addi-
tur praeterea terror hosti, quod, cum magna effusaque esset fuga
ad ulteriorem fluminis ripam, pons nimio pondere delapsus est.
Quo facto omnis hostium equitatus et maxima peditum pars in-
tercipitur. Per hunc modum victoria Ferrariensibus sociisque parta
cum magna adversariorum strage.

39   Ob hanc victoriam cuncta paulo post Flaminia defecit a legato,
et Bononiae ita trepidatum ut, nisi Iohannes rex cum equitatu advenisset, populus arma fuisset capturus. Illius praesentia res novas
compescuit.

40   Eodem anno rex Lucam subito accessit, huiusmodi causa per-
tractus. Cum ob adversum proelium afflictae legati simul[57] re-
gisque opes viderentur, Castruci filii, quos obsidum loco rex secum
habebat, clam arrepta fuga, ex clientelis paternis magno numero

trated inside the defenses, although they were extremely difficult to enter.

As luck would have it, not far from the breach they encoun- 38 tered the standards of the king and the knights whom he had sent ahead to the camp. They were delighted that this fight in particular had come their way, in which they might exact private vengeance above and beyond the common cause; and summoning their fellows they advanced on the royal standard. The royal knights were experienced in war and met them bravely. The struggle was bitter and for some time fought in such a way that victory inclined towards neither side. But on that day the Florentine commanders earned exceptional praise for their prowess in battle, as both men with equal ardor were found in the front rank. Military men of great fame at home, they made haste to extend the glory of their deeds abroad, exhorting their troops more by example than by words. With their tireless and skilful support, the enemy was finally overcome and compelled to retreat, and the camp's defenses, broken simultaneously in many places, were overrun. Adding to the enemies' terror, when they were fleeing in a large and disorderly body to the opposite bank of the river, the bridge collapsed under the excessive weight, whereupon all the enemy cavalry and the largest part of his infantry were cut off. In this way the Ferrarese and their allies achieved victory with great slaughter of their enemies.

Thanks to this victory all of the Romagna shortly thereafter de- 39 fected from the legate, and such was the state of alarm in Bologna that, had King John not come with his cavalry, the people would have taken to arms. His presence quelled a revolt.[32]

In the same year, the king suddenly visited Lucca for the follow- 40 ing reason. Since the resources of both legate and king seemed depleted by their defeat in battle, the sons of Castruccio, whom the king had with him as hostages, secretly fled and suddenly entered Lucca, having mustered a great number of their father's clients.

coacto, Lucam subito ingressi sunt, urbemque in suam potestatem redegerunt, praeter arcem, in qua praesidium erat regis. Ea res effecit ipse ut rex cum duobus fere millibus equitum Lucam propere accederet. Ibi, pulsis adolescentibus urbeque recepta, magnam vim pecuniae Lucensibus imperavit, et, quasi pertaesus Italiae, trans Alpis abire constituit.

41 Laetam victoria civitatem diluvium aquarum paene submersit. Circiter enim Kalendas novembris quatuor diebus totidemque noctibus continuato imbre, incredibili aquarum multitudine amnes per casentinatem arretinumque agrum egressi alveis, instar aequoris omnia texere. Inde passim descendentibus, cum Seva quoque fluvius inundato mugellano agro plena decurreret valle, Arnus autem nullis neque ripis neque terminis coerceretur, omnia supra urbem loca complentur. Ea vis aquarum in muros perlata urbis partem illorum ad orientem versam prostravit; inde per urbem quasi captam expugnantamque discurrens, trepidis ac fugientibus civibus, cunctam occupavit, ut ad templum Martis supra dimidium porphyrearum columnarum, humilioribus vero locis supra duodecim pedes altitudo ascenderet. Nec prius increscere destitit aquarum moles quam ad occidentem quoque, non capiente iam urbe aquam, moenia subvertit. Tunc demum egesta vis et decrescere pelagus coepit. Tres urbis pontes deiecti, et proxima secus fluvium aedificia multaeque per urbem domus concidere.

42 Cessante aquarum metu, cum homines velut attoniti remansissent, novus iterato metus incidit a nobilitate. Robustissimae trans Arnum familiae nobilium erant; pontes autem disiecti eas separaverant, ut iam duae urbes ex una factae viderentur. Et rixae quaedam coortae suspicionem augebant. Ob hunc metum pontes duo

They brought the whole city under their control except the citadel, where the king's garrison was. This event caused the king himself to come hastily with around two thousand horse to Lucca. There he expelled the young men and took charge of the city, demanding a large sum of money from the Lucchesi. Then, as though tiring of Italy, he decided to go away across the Alps.[33]

The city, rejoicing in victory, was then nearly drowned in a 41 flood. For around the first of November it rained continuously for four days and nights, and the rivers throughout the Casentino and the territory of Arezzo overflowed their beds and everything was covered like the sea with an incredible abundance of water. Then the waters washed down everywhere, and when the river Sieve also rushed down its flooded valley, having inundated the Mugello, the river Arno could be contained by neither banks nor bounds and flooded all the areas above the city. The force of the waters dashing against the walls of the city knocked down the part of them facing east, and from thence they rushed through the city like a conquering army, putting to flight the terrified citizens and occupying everything, so that they came halfway up the porphyry columns at the temple of Mars,[34] and in lower-lying places rose to a height of more than twelve feet. The mass of waters did not cease growing until the city was no longer able to contain them and they knocked down the walls on the western side. Not until then did their force abate and the floodwaters begin to subside. Three of the city's bridges were thrown down, and the buildings nearest the river as well as many houses throughout the city collapsed.

The fear of flood was receding (although people remained 42 stunned by it), when they met with a new source of alarm, this time from the nobility. The families in Oltrarno were extremely powerful, and with the bridges down they were separated off, so that two cities now seemed to have been made from one. Certain fights that broke out increased suspicion. On account of this fear two pontoon bridges were constructed so that aid could be

ratibus facti, quo transarninae plebi, si opus foret, succurreretur. Tunc demum timere desitum est.

43   Eodem anno Florentinorum sociorumque oratores communi de re apud Hericem in Liguribus convenere. Movebat autem quia, legato gravi plaga perculso Iohanneque rege trans Alpes relicta Italia digresso, prosperis secundisque rebus, de praeda iam inter socios oriebatur contentio, discordiam paritura, ni obviam iretur. Itaque prospicere iam inde et antevenire placuit. Re igitur discussa, ita tandem convenit uti Cremona Mediolanensi, Parma Veronensi, Regium Mantuano, Mutina Ferrariensi, Luca Florentino destinaretur; haec bona fide procuranda adiuvandaque quoad urbes istae in potestatem venirent.

44   Bellumque posthac acrius coeptum. Prima hostium ruina ab eo qui caput fuerat malorum omnium legato incepit. Hic erat vir gallus intollerabili superbia atque fastidio. Et auxerat naturae vitium prosperitas fortunae, nihil ut iam minus ferendum quam eius protervia videretur. Cum ergo Ferrarienses, capta post proelium Argenta, bononiensem in agrum copias traduxissent lateque omnia vastarent, cives, per eam occasionem sumptis armis, verterunt impetum in legati satellites; quibus varie per urbem oppressis, ipse trepidus in arcem munitissimam, quam sibi construxerat, refugit. Bononienses arcem obsessam die noctuque oppugnabant.

45   Quae cum Florentiae audita essent, etsi populus non invito animo hanc legati ruinam[58] percipiebat, tamen vicit humanitatis respectus, ut pro reverentia sedis romanae de legati salute cogita-

brought to the plebs of the Oltrarno if need arose. Not until then did the fear come to an end.[35]

In the same year ambassadors of the Florentines and their allies 43
conferred at Lerici in Liguria on matters of common concern. Their motive was that, with the legate staggering from a heavy blow, King John departing across the Alps, leaving Italy behind, and affairs taking a prosperous course, contention had arisen among the allies concerning the spoils, a contention that would lead to discord if it were not resolved. So they decided to take thought for the future and head off any trouble. After discussions it was decided that Cremona should fall to the Milanese, Parma to the Veronese, Reggio to the Mantuans, Modena to the Ferrarese and Lucca to the Florentines; this settlement was to be observed and promoted in good faith so that these cities should come under their control.

After this the war started, more bitter than ever. The first col- 44
lapse of the enemy began on the part of the legate, the man responsible for all the evils. He was a Frenchman of intolerable arrogance and pride. His good fortune had augmented his natural vice, so that nothing seemed more unbearable than his highhandedness. So when the Ferrarese, having captured Argento after the battle, marched their troops into the territory of Bologna, causing general devastation, the citizens used this as an excuse to seize arms, then turned them on the satellites of the legate. With his men crushed severally throughout the city, the legate himself ran in fear to an extremely well-fortified stronghold that he had built for himself. The Bolognese attacked the besieged citadel day and night.

When the news came to Florence, although the people were by 45
no means reluctant to learn of the legate's ruin,[36] nevertheless humane concerns prevailed, and out of reverence for the Holy See they took thought for the legate's safety. So they immediately sent out four ambassadors to Bologna with three hundred cavalry and a large number of infantry from the Mugello. By advice and entreaty

rent. Ita missi confestim Bononiam oratores quattuor et cum his equites trecenti ex mugellanoque agro magnus peditum numerus. Hi rogando atque monendo sequestres tandem fuere, ut legatus reddita civibus arce incolumis abiret. Id tanta difficultate impetratum, ut aliquot dies adversus eorum preces resisterent Bononienses; et post rem impetratam, cum extra moenia legatum deducerent, vix a populi impetu in eum ruentis defendere illius salutem potuerint. Magna demum vi Florentiam perductus, mox Pisas, inde mari delatus ad pontificem abiit.

46 Altero dehinc anno Florentini Lucam obsidere constituerant, atque ita convenerat[59] ut ex sociorum copiis quae circa Parmam erant in castris, pars Apenninum transiret ad Lucae obsidionem perurgendam. Haec itaque auxilia expectantibus Florentinis, insidiae in castris ad Parmam deteguntur. Equites enim germani, pecunia corrupti, seditionem in exercitu facere ac Mastinum ceterosque duces qui praeerant castris interficere constituerant. Hoc a legato, quo iniurias ultum iret, procuratum credebatur. Igitur ea re detecta plerique Germanorum Parmam transfugere; turbatioque ista effecit confestim, ut Parmae solveretur obsidio, deficientibusque auxiliis, Luca quoque quo minus obsideretur impedimento fuit.

47 Per hoc tempus marmorea turris quae est ad Reparatae templum fundari coepta est, architectata quidem a Iotto, insigni per eam tempestatem pingendi magistro. Is et fundamentis iaciendis praefuit et formam, qualem nunc videmus, praestanti magnificentia operis designavit.

48 Eodem anno copiae sociorum, duce Mastino veronensi, in agrum parmensem reversae obsidionem ex integro incoharunt, fuitque in his Florentinorum equitatus ex foedere constitutus. Aliae insuper copiae circa Lucam deductae cuncta belli terroribus

they finally became the intermediaries through whom the legate left unharmed, having surrendered his stronghold to the city. The Florentines obtained their request with the greatest difficulty, the Bolognese resisting their entreaties for several days. Even after their request had been obtained, while they were bringing the legate outside the walls, they could hardly protect his life from the populace rushing to attack him. Using overwhelming force they finally brought him to Florence, then to Pisa, whence he returned by sea to the pope.[37]

The next year the Florentines decided to besiege Lucca, and it 46 was agreed that part of the allied troops encamped near Parma 1334 should cross the Apennines to press the siege of Lucca. While the Florentines were awaiting these reinforcements, plots in the camp at Parma were uncovered. The German knights had been bribed and were causing sedition in the ranks; they had decided to kill Mastino and the other commanders in charge of the army. It was believed that this was arranged by the legate, to avenge his injuries. Thus when the affair was exposed, many of the Germans took refuge in Parma. The effect of this disturbance was that the siege of Parma was immediately raised, and the absence of reinforcements proved an obstacle to besieging Lucca as well.[38]

At this time the foundations of the marble tower next to the 47 church of Santa Reparata were laid. The architect was Giotto, a distinguished master of painting of that period. He both oversaw the laying of the foundations and designed the form, as we now see it, of this work of extraordinary magnificence.

In the same year the troops of the League, under the command 48 of Mastino of Verona, returned to the territory of Parma and began the siege all over again. Florentine cavalry were among them as stipulated in the treaty. Other troops beyond these were marched around Lucca, afflicting the whole countryside with the terrors of war. On this account King John, who had gone to France, gave Lucca as a gift to the French king in order to ward off the threat to

infestabant. Ob haec Iohannes rex, qui in Galliam ulteriorem abierat, quo imminens Lucae periculum depelleret, regi Francorum dono illam dedit. Ipse autem rex, accitis florentinis civibus, quorum multitudo ingens in regno eius negotiabatur, donationem factam ostendit, suamque esse Lucam protestatus est; proinde abstineret Florentinus ab inferendo bello. Ea res Florentiam a negotiatoribus perscripta, nequaquam retardavit populi coeptum. Nec plane rex ipse rem[60] persecutus est, certior factus a Roberto rege Lucam ad Iohannem nunquam iure pertinuisse,[61] sed sua dudum cum esset, a Fagiolano primum, mox a Castrucio occupatam.[62]

49   Hoc anno Iohannes pontifex romanus e vita migravit. In eius locum Benedictus successit. Proxima dehinc aestate, fervente in Gallia bello Parmaque obsessa, novum rursus bellum in Etruria concitatur. Arretinorum enim post mortem Guidonis praesulis Petrus cognomento Sacon acceperat dominatum. Hic fuit vir bello quidem admodum praestans, ad urbanas vero conversationes[63] non satis aptus. Cum tamen opes a fratre partas suscepisset, non solum tenuit eas armis, verum etiam extendit, praecipue tyrannis et his quidem suarum partium infestus, quos castellis arcibusque exutos longe lateque disperserat. Florentini cum hoc pacem agebant, intenti lucensis belli[64] curis; Perusini vero pro occupato dudum Tiferno ita se habebant, ut odia potius occulta quam apertum superesset bellum.

50   Rebus in hunc se modum[65] habentibus, arcana quaedam coniunctio fit Perusinos inter et tyrannos Sacone eversos, quorum longe princeps adversarius erat Nerius Fagiolanus, eius qui dudum Pisas Lucamque tenuerat filius. Is ergo acceptis clam copiis, nullo

the city. The [French] king summoned the Florentine citizens who in great numbers were engaging in business in his kingdom and showed them the act of donation. He protested that Lucca was his, and that the Florentine should henceforth abstain from making war against it. Although the merchants informed Florence in writing of this circumstance, it by no means inhibited the People's undertaking. The king clearly did not follow through with his claim, being informed by King Robert that Lucca had never rightly belonged to John, but had been his own all along, although occupied first by Uguccione della Faggiuola and afterwards by Castruccio.[39]

In this year the Roman pontiff John departed this life. Benedict succeeded to his place.[40] The following summer, with war growing hotter in northern Italy and Parma under siege, a new war again burst into flame in Tuscany. Pietro Saccone had taken over the lordship of the Aretines after the death of Bishop Guido.[41] This man was truly outstanding in matters of war, but was less well adapted to civil behavior. He had received the resources acquired by his brother and not only kept them by arms, but also extended them, being particularly hostile to tyrants—even to those of his own [Ghibelline] party—whom he had stripped of their castles and strongholds, scattering them far and wide. The Florentines maintained peace with him, being intent on the Luccan war, but the Perugians, owing to his occupation of Città di Castello some time earlier, behaved as though they preferred hidden hatreds to open war.[42] 49 1335

With affairs in this state, a kind of hidden pact was made between the Perugians and the tyrants Saccone had deposed. Of the latter, by far his principal adversary was Neri della Faggiuola, the son of the man who some time before had controlled Pisa and Lucca.[43] Neri, then, secretly acquired forces and without exciting suspicion entered Borgo (a town along the Tiber fourteen miles from Arezzo) by means of treachery.[44] Nonetheless, the citadel 50

tale aliquid suspicante, Burgum (id est oppidum secus Tiberim quatuordecim millibus passuum ab Arretio) per proditionem invadit. Cum arx nihilominus praesidio teneretur, Sacon re audita eo raptim copias duxit opique ferendae intentus omnia rimabatur. Inter haec Perusini, ut compositum erat, omnibus repente copiis via cortonensi, quae est a Burgo diversissima, in agrum Arretinum supervenere. Quod postquam a Sacone intellectum est, omissa Burgi cura Arretium rediit. Ibi armata populi multitudine et sub signis structa, certissima dimicandi spe, ad hostes contendit. Nec Perusini quidem detrectarunt certamen, sed utpote viri fortes se ad pugnam compararunt. Ubi autem signo dato concursum est, anceps atroxque proelium fuit. Tandem, superantibus Arretinis et animis viribusque praevalentibus, Perusini multa suorum caede in fugam vertuntur. Quos turbatos prostratosque persecuti victores, magnam ediderunt stragem, ac viginti ex hostibus signa eo proelio capta retulerunt. Inde agrum perusinum ingressi, non longius ab urbe quam duobus passuum millibus fecerunt castra, omniaque circum moenia igne ferroque popularunt.

51 Florentini autem cognito Perusinorum casu memores pristinarum amicitiarum, confestim auxilia equitum illis misere, quibus ex gravi conflictatione sustentati sunt. Nec multo post Genuensium auxilia quaedam Saconi missa (erat namque sibi uxor genuensis), dum prope urbem pacate faciunt iter, iuventutis concursu invaduntur, armisque et impedimentis direptis, iter retro vertere coguntur. Ita civitas, etsi nondum apertum susceperat bellum, partes tamen Perusinorum animis praeferebat, quae res[66] multum valuit ad cursum victoriae compescendum.

52 Per idem fere tempus Parma, iampridem oppugnata, cum amplius resistere nequiret, ad extremum capitur; eam, ut convenerat in foedere, Mastinus suscepit. Mutina quoque ac Regium paulo post eodem tenore in victoris manum devenere. Una restabat Luca, Florentinis belli praemium destinata, eademque semper

was still being held by a garrison, so Saccone, hearing of the attack, rapidly marched troops there and was exploring every avenue, intent on bringing succor [to the garrison]. Meanwhile the Perugians, as agreed, suddenly came up the Via Cortona, quite far from Borgo, and into Aretine territory. Once Saccone learned of this, he forgot about Borgo and returned to Arezzo. There he armed the populace and marshalled them under standards; then in the certainty of coming to blows he went out to meet the enemy. Nor did the Perugians shrink from the contest, but like brave men readied themselves for battle. The charge was sounded and the clash began; it was a ferocious battle on both sides. Finally the Aretines prevailed, being superior in strength and spirit, and the Perugians were put to flight with great bloodshed. The victors pursued the scattered and defeated enemy, slaughtering them in great numbers, and they brought back twenty battle-standards captured from the enemy in that battle. Then, entering Perugian territory, they encamped not more than two miles from the city, devastating the whole area around the walls with fire and sword.

But the Florentines, learning of the Perugians' misfortune, re- 51 membered their ancient friendship and immediately sent them mounted reinforcements who sustained them in their struggle. Soon thereafter, some reinforcements the Genoese had sent to Saccone (whose wife was from Genoa), passing peacefully near Florence, were set upon by a mob of Florentine youths, stripped of their weapons and baggage, and compelled to return home. Thus, although Florence did not engage in open war, it nevertheless took the side of the Perugians in its heart, a circumstance of great value in checking the onrush of [the Aretines'] victory.[45]

At about the same time, Parma, long under siege, was unable to 52 offer further resistance and was taken. As agreed in the treaty, Mastino took control of it. Modena, too, and Reggio shortly thereafter, came, through the same course of events, into the hands of the victor. There remained only Lucca, assigned to the

quasi fato quodam novi certaminis inexhausta materia. Lucae siquidem causa in gallicum bellum se coniecerant Florentini; eiusdem Lucae causa aliud rursus bellum adversus Mastinum susceperunt; Lucae etiam causa pisanum postea bellum exarsit; de quibus iam dicere aggrediemur.

53   Tres erant fratres Ruffi parmenses, nati summo loco, quibus Iohannes rex Parmam et Lucam abiens reliquerat gubernandam. Horum duo, coacti bello, cum Parmam tandem dedissent, multa ultro citroque pacti sunt, et illud in primis, ut is qui Lucae praeerat frater certa pactione Mastino illam dimitteret. Id factum non repugnantibus Florentinis fuerat, ductis vana spe quod faciliorem hanc fore viam arbitrabantur, si rem in suam fidem Mastinus suscepisset, praesertim cum fratres illi in eius potestate essent futuri. Ipse vero tyrannus palam dictitabat Florentinis sese id negotium facessere; eorum quidem auxilia omnibus victoriis obsidionibusque per Galliam affuisse; ceteros vero socios praemia belli consecutos, florentinum populum unum restare, cui Luca ex foedere debeatur; id non magis ad populi florentini studium quam ad fidem suam ceterorumque sociorum pertinere. Haec et huiusmodi praedicanti fides adhibita erat, eo magis quo consona vero honestoque profari videbatur. Itaque illi permissum negotium est, eiusque ab opere civitas dependebat.

54   Re igitur aliquanto protracta, Lucam, dante illo qui tenebat fratre, Mastinus suscipit, ac suo praesidio communit. Florentini, missis confestim ad eum legatis, secundum promissa Lucam postularunt. Tyrannus autem primo[67] benignis affatibus, dum rem

Florentines as spoil of war, and as always, as though by a kind of fate, an inexhaustible source of fuel for new struggles. It was because of Lucca that the Florentines had thrown themselves into the Lombard war; it was because of Lucca that the Pisan war afterwards broke out. These matters we shall now try to describe.[46]

There were three brothers of the Rossi family of Parma,[47] of   53
noble stock, whom King John on his departure had left to govern Parma and Lucca. Two of them, when war finally compelled them to surrender Parma, negotiated back and forth on a number of terms, but the principal one was that the brother principally in charge of Lucca should deliver the city by fixed agreement to Mastino. The Florentines, deluded by vain hope, did not oppose this because they thought it would be easier if Mastino would handle the matter in trust, especially since the brothers were going to be in his power. The tyrant himself openly declared that he was taking on this business for the sake of the Florentines; their troops had indeed been present at all the victories and sieges throughout northern Italy; the other allies having received their rewards, the Florentine People alone remained, to whom Lucca was due by treaty; the matter touched his own honor and that of the other allies as much as the desires of the Florentine People. They trusted the tyrant when he said this and similar things, the more so as he seemed to be stating things consonant with the truth and with honor. So the business was entrusted to him, and the city depended on his agency.

And so the matter began to drag out. Lucca was handed over   54
by the Rossi brother; Mastino received it and fortified it with his own garrison. The Florentines immediately sent envoys to him requesting the city as promised. The tyrant at first kindly requested them not to mind if there was a short delay while he settled the matter with the Rossi brothers. Then, when that was finished and the envoys pressed the matter, further difficulties appeared. He said that the king owed the Rossi brothers a debt, and that they

cum Ruffis fratribus componat,[68] exigui temporis moram ne gravate ferant postulat. Mox eo transacto, cum legati instarent, difficultates alias reperire; Ruffis fratribus debitam a rege pecuniam dicere, magnas insuper impensas ab iisdem factas, quas resarciri oporteat. Pro his omnibus summam promit[69] auri trecenta sexaginta millia. Qua in re licet improbitatem tyranni impudentissime versari cernebat florentinus populus, tamen, desiderio potiundae Lucae adductus, eam summam tradere paciscitur. In quo maxime admiretur quis huius populi mentem in utramque partem nimis proclivem; pro qua enim nuper offerentibus Germanis ac prope rogantibus parvam dare pecuniam recusarat, pro eadem paulo post intolerabilem auri summam recusanti ac prope deneganti tradere nitebatur.[70] Nam neque hoc ipsum pactum conventumque servavit tyrannus; sed alia ex aliis quaerens diffugia, turpi perfidia legatorum desideria frustrabatur. Venerat enim in eam spem, ut existimaret, Luca retenta, Etruriae civitatibus dominari posse. Hos illi animos faciebant latissimae per Galliam opes, quibus nemo eius saeculi tyrannus par fuit; frequentes praeterea adulatores, quibus dominatorum atria sunt referta; multi etiam tusci generis exules novarum rerum avidi concitabant. His accedebat facultas, quod ex parmensi in lucensem agrum brevis est transitus et Apennini fere dorso coniuncti fines, qua facile copias posset transmittere. Finitimos quin etiam Pisanos ob studia partium vetusque in Florentinos odium putabat causae non defuturos.

55   Haec meditantem frustrantemque animadvertens florentinus populus, legatis tandem mandavit, ut questi protestatique iniuriam discedant. Id cum fecissent legati, tyrannus, quasi lucrum arbitratus si omnia turbarentur, quas Lucae habebat copias repente in agrum florentinum praedatum misit. Ita rupto foedere bellum lucense ex integro nascitur. Florentini, etsi contentio magna propo-

had been put to great expenses, besides, which had to be reimbursed. He had promised a sum of 360,000 florins for all these costs. Although the Florentine People saw that the tyrant's wickedness was operating shamelessly in this matter, nevertheless, being gripped by their desire to take control of Lucca, they agreed to hand over the sum. The fickleness of the People in this matter may seem astonishing. They had refused to pay a small sum of money for Lucca when the Germans had offered and practically insisted on handing it over; a little later they were straining to pay an intolerable amount of gold to someone who was throwing up obstacles and close to denying their request for the same city. And in fact the tyrant did not observe this pact and agreement either, but sought one way out after another, eluding the legates' petitions with his shameful perfidy. For he had come to hope and believe that he could establish lordship over the cities of Tuscany if he held on to Lucca. He was given these ideas by the resources he disposed of throughout northern Italy, which no tyrant of the age could equal, and also by the crowds of flatterers who fill the courts of great lords; and numerous Tuscan exiles, who were eager for a coup, also incited him. Another factor was his capacity to send troops easily on the short journey from the territory of Parma to that of Lucca, whose borders are nearly adjacent along the spine of the Apennines. He also thought he could count on the neighboring Pisans, owing to their partisan loyalties and ancient hatred of the Florentines.

The Florentine People took note of his plans and his continuing attempts to delude them, and finally instructed their envoys to register a formal complaint protesting the injury and then depart. When they had done this, the tyrant, as though he stood to profit from universal disturbance, suddenly sent the troops he had in Lucca out to plunder Florentine territory. Thus, with the League broken, the war of Lucca began all over again. Although the conflict looked to be a great one and war was befalling them when

nebatur ac iam defessos novum excipiebat bellum, neque concide-
runt animis neque quicquam remiserunt pristinae dignitatis, sed
acrius vehementiusque se attollentes, non trepide nec turbulente,
sed maturo singula providebant consilio. Pecuniis enim comparan-
dis decemviros cum potestate publica, sex vero ad consilia belli gerendi praefecerunt. In primis quoque illud provisum, uti legati ad
Accium Vicecomitem ceterosque gallici belli⁷¹ socios mitterentur,
qui et arguerent Mastini perfidiam et opem illorum adversus eam
fraudem implorarent.

56   Societas quoque cum Perusinis et Senensibus renovata est, ve-
rentibus (id quod erat verisimile) ne Sacon, ob tradita Perusinis
auxilia, se Mastino coniungeret. Copias vero apud Catinum et Fucetium bipartito quasi in stationes distribuerunt, ne hostium equitatus, qui satis validus erat Lucae, in florentinum posset agrum
licenter discurrere. Inter haec Perusini, sociorum auxiliis freti,
agrum Arretinum magnis copiis intrarunt, cuncta igne ferroque
vastantes. Coniunxerant quoque se illis Arretinorum exules, multas magnasque clientelas in agro habentes. Hinc defectiones quaedam oppidorum fieri et in deterius labi res coeperunt.

57   Fregit tamen plurimum Arretinorum animos Tiferni amissio.
Huic urbi Rodulphus praeerat Tarlatus, eques arretinus, praesidiumque habebat non contemnendum. Verum eorum ipsorum qui
in praesidio erant corrupti pecunia quidam⁷² prodere hostibus urbem pacisciuntur. Huius arcani auctor deductorque fuit Nerius Fagiolanus, talium quidem rerum vel solertissimus artifex; quae ubi
satis composita sunt, accitis Perusinorum copiis, noctu ad Tiferni
portas accessit. Ibi a proditoribus qui pro moenibus excubabant
receptus, urbe potitus est, Rodulpho, post nocturnum proelium
quo frustra pellere hostem nixus erat, in arcem refugiente, quae et

they were already exhausted, the Florentines kept up their spirits and their old sense of self-worth, and, rising up more fiercely and energetically than ever, each one gave his considered opinion without timidity or turbulence. They put a civic board of ten men in charge of raising money, while six men were made responsible for military policy. Their principal decision was to send to Azzo Visconti and other allies of the Lombard war envoys who should both denounce Mastino's perfidy and appeal to the allies for aid against this act of fraud.[48]

The alliance with the Perugians and the Sienese was renewed, 56 since the Florentines feared (what was likely enough) that Saccone would join forces with Mastino in retaliation for the aid Florence had given to the Perugians. They divided their troops into two parts, stationing them at Montecatini and Fucecchio, to keep the enemy cavalry, which was quite strong at Lucca, from ranging at will into Florentine territory. Meanwhile the Perugians, relying on help from their allies, entered Aretine territory with large forces, devasting everything with fire and sword. The Aretine exiles, who had numerous powerful clients in that territory, also joined them. Hence certain revolts began in the towns, and matters began to take a turn for the worse.[49]

Yet what did the most to break the Aretines' spirits was the loss 57 of Città di Castello. The Aretine knight Ridolfo de' Tarlati was in charge of this city and he had a respectable garrison. But certain members of this garrison were bribed and agreed to betray the city to the enemy. The man behind the negotiations and the one who conducted them was Neri della Faggiuola, a crafty operator in such matters. Once the deal had been arranged, Perugian troops were summoned and he approached the gates of Città di Castello by night. Let in by the traitors who were standing guard behind the wall, he took control of the city. Ridolfo, after a nocturnal battle in which he fruitlessly tried to drive out the enemy, took refuge

ipsa mox una cum illo capitur. Per hunc modum Tifernum amissum est.

58   Sacon autem in castella quae sunt circa Ambram fluvium (ea namque rebellaverant), cum exercitu profectus, quaedam illorum expugnata receptaque subvertit; reliqua vero eiusdem regionis, Bucinum, Galatrone, Leolinum ac cetera his finitima Arretinorum castella, sese ob ancipitem belli metum Florentinis dedidere.

59   Haec eo sunt anno in Etruria atque Gallia gesta. Proximo dehinc anno Florentini[73] statim veris initio bellum Arretinis aperte indixerunt. Mox hinc Perusini, inde Florentini, magnis exercitibus agrum Arretinum ingressi, simulque circa urbem in unum coniuncti, crebra in portis ipsis commiserunt proelia ac late omnia vastaverunt.

60   Per hoc fere tempus rumor increbuit Mastinum ad octingentos equites per Flaminiam Sarsinatemque agrum Arretium mittere; et erant qui ad Forum Popilii iam pervenisse asseverarent. Eius rei causa copiae a Florentinis in Flaminiam missae, coniunctis Bononiensium auxiliis, ne qua Mastini equitatus transire posset observabant. Sed et Lucae qui erat hostium equitatus incursionibus nonnunquam factis in florentinum agrum turbabat sane accolas; ab illo et illata damna pleraque et accepta.

61   Cum itaque pluribus locis misceretur bellum, ac paene tota[74] Etruria fluctuaret, Mastinique potentia formidaretur, placuit in Galliam, si qua fieri posset, bellum transferre. Id unum maxime omnium salutare ab initio perspectum consultatumque in republica fuerat. Ceterum legati ad principes Galliae missi, cum singulos adiissent, neminem pellicere ad bellum contra Mastinum

in the citadel, which was also captured with him inside shortly thereafter. That is how Città di Castello was taken.

Saccone, however, set out with his army against the castles near   58
the river Ambra (for they too had rebelled) and levelled some of them which he had captured or which had given up. But the other castles of that region — Bucine, Galatrone, Sanleolino and other nearby Aretine strongholds — surrendered to the Florentines, fearing the uncertainties of war.[50]

Such were the deeds of that year in Tuscany and northern Italy.   59
The following year, as soon as spring began, the Florentines de-   1336
clared open war against the Aretines. Soon the Perugians from one side, the Florentines from another, entered Aretine territory with great armies, and joining together into one army near the city, they took part in frequent skirmishes before its very walls and inflicted widespread and thorough devastation.

Around this time the rumor spread that Mastino had sent as   60
many as eight hundred knights via the Romagna and the area of Sarsina, and some asserted that they had come as far as Forlimpopuli. For this reason the Florentines sent troops into the Romagna, where they were joined by Bolognese reinforcements who stood on guard to prevent any of Mastino's knights from getting through. But the enemy cavalry near Lucca, too, not infrequently made incursions into Florentine territory, and threw the inhabitants into turmoil, giving and receiving much damage.

Thus, since war was being stirred up in many places, and al-   61
most all of Tuscany was in a disturbed state, fearful of Mastino's power, it was decided to take the war into northern Italy if at all possible. This, the single most salutary course of action, had from the beginning been kept in view, and plans had been made for it in the state. But when the legates who were sent out to the princes of northern Italy approached them one by one, they were able to induce none of them to make war against Mastino — not because these princes loved him, but because they feared his power. At

potuerant, non quod amarent eum homines, sed quod eius potentiam formidarent. Demum ad Venetos conversa civitas, quos et finitimos tyranno et nonnihil laesos infensosque illius potentiae intelligebat, multis adhortationibus tandem obtinuit in societatem ut venirent belli. Ob eam societatem Florentinorum statim copiae quaedam ad ea loca transmissae, parique item numero a Venetis addito, in tarvisino primum agro bellum adversus tyrannum commoverunt.

62   Dum haec in Venetis geruntur, Ruffi fratres, de quibus Lucam Parmamque accepisse Mastinum diximus, reiecti ab eo et contra fidem exagitati, in oppido Pontremuli obsidebantur. Hi ad Florentinorum Venetorumque opem conversi in foedus recipiuntur. Ex his Petrus Ruffus, vir praestans in re militari, Florentiam veniens ostendit, si sibi copiae darentur, posse Lucae detrimenta inferri obsidionemque suorum simul dissolvi. Acceptis igitur octingentis Florentinorum equitibus magnoque peditatu addito Lucam petivit; nec longe a moenibus castrametatus, per singulos dies infestissima portis inferebat signa. Haec eo proposito fiebant, quo ii⁷⁵ qui in castris erant ad Pontremulum, Lucae auxilium ferre coacti, obsidionem dissolverent; quod tamen ipsum assequi non potuit, impeditus calliditate praefecti qui Lucae praeerat. Is enim, cum Ruffi propositum animadvertisset, cum omnibus fere copiis egressus, apud Cerulium consedit, qui locus florentinum versus agrum maxime spectat. Ex eo loco se cum de industria ostentaret commeatumque impediret, vi ipsa est assecutus, ut dux florentini exercitus omissa Luca retro duceret copias. In reducendo autem, quoniam sub ipso hoste transeundum erat, proelium committitur. Fossa erat iampridem bello castruciano facta a monte in paludem, aditum secans. Ad eam praemissi equites, fossam oppugnarunt ac demum, vi transgressi, praesidia hostium, quae ibi tutelae gratia fuerant, in fugam verterunt. Inde profligatos insecuti, neque ratione

length the city turned to the Venetians, who were neighbors of the tyrant and, it understood, had been harmed by him to some extent and were hostile to his power. With much persuasion the Venetians finally agreed to join them in a military alliance. In keeping with this alliance, Florentine troops were at once sent to that area, then an equal number were added by the Venetians, whereupon they together started a war against the tyrant, beginning with the territory of Treviso.[51]

While this was happening in the Veneto, Mastino, contrary to 62 his sworn word, drove out and persecuted the Rossi brothers (from whom, as we said, he had received Lucca and Parma) and was besieging them in the town of Pontremoli. They turned for aid to the Florentines and Venetians and were accepted into the league. Of these, Pietro Rossi, an outstanding military man, came to Florence and showed how, if they would give him troops, he could cause damage to Lucca and at the same time break the siege of Pontremoli. Thus, having received eight hundred Florentine cavalry and a great number of infantry in addition, he headed for Lucca. Camping not far from the walls, every day by the gates he would give signs of hostile action. This was done with the aim of forcing the men encamped around Pontremoli to abandon the siege and come to the aid of Lucca. But this plan failed owing to the wily governor of Lucca. When he realized what Rossi's plan was, he left Lucca with almost all his troops and stationed them at Cerruglio, a place overlooking Florentine territory. From this base he intentionally made a show of strength and interfered with the Florentine supply lines, and so through force he succeeded in making the Florentine commander abandon Lucca and retreat. While marching them back, however, since Pietro had to pass beneath the enemy, a battle broke out. There was a fosse, dug long before in the Castruccian war, cutting off the pass between the mountain and the swamp. The cavalry sent ahead attacked the fosse and at last crossed over it by force, putting to flight the enemy garrison

ulla neque consilio sed temere atque incaute, ad castra usque hostium delati sunt.

63　　Quorum periculum cum animadverteret Ruffus, receptui cani iussit, et post eos misit qui ex praecepto revocaret. Sed illi, victoria elati et proelio calentes, cum neque tubam neque monitorem exaudirent, circumventi repente ab hostibus, ita conciduntur, ut pauci eorum effusa retro fuga evaderent, reliquis aut captis aut interfectis. Vexillifer antesignanorum, qui princeps fuerat illius temeritatis, in portis paene castrorum hostium occiditur, vexilloque hostes potiti sunt. Qua victoria elati, confestim omnibus[76] copiis in reliquam Florentinorum aciem magno impetu magnoque clamore descenderunt. Ruffus interrito animo suos cohortatus, ruentis in se excipiebat hostis. Etsi primo quidem impetu, quoniam e monte in subiectos delati quasi procellam dabant, parumper mota acies retulerat pedem, mox tamen, aequato proelio, cum acriter pugnaretur, hostes superantur et in fugam vertuntur. Quos Ruffus insecutus, magnum eorum numerum occidit, complures etiam cepit, et in his Mastini praefectum qui dux fuerat copiarum. Post proelium, una nocte iisdem locis victores commorati, postea[77] Fucetium, inde Florentiam rediere.

64　　Nec multo post victoriam Ruffus poscentibus rebus in Venetos profectus, summam belli adversus Mastinum de sociorum sententia recepit gessitque cum summa constantia et moderatione. Prima eius militia ad Tarvisium fuit; quo in loco cum hostes varie perculisset, in patavinum inde agrum traductis copiis per palustria impeditaque loca improvisus advenit. Patavium per id tempus Mastinus tenebat, copiasque habebat in his locis[78] ingentis, quas tamen in Ruffi adventu sic intra munitiones continuit, ut pugnae fortu-

guarding it. Pursuing the fleeing troops rashly and thoughtlessly, they were carried up to the enemy camp.

When Rossi saw their peril, he ordered the retreat to be 63 sounded and sent men after them to recall them. But elated with victory and hot with battle, they paid no attention to the trumpet or the messenger. They were swiftly surrounded by the enemy and cut down, so that only a few of them escaped in the scattered flight backwards; the rest were either captured or killed. The standard bearer of the vanguard, who had been the leader in this rash attack, fell almost before the gates of the enemy encampment, and the enemy seized his standard. Elated by this victory, all the enemy troops immediately charged down upon the Florentine ranks with great ardor and noise. Rossi, unafraid, exhorted his men and bore the brunt of the onrushing foe. At the first onset, since the enemy blew down the mountain like a storm on the men below, the Florentine ranks were pushed back a little, but soon, as the battlefield grew more level, they fought back ferociously, overcoming the enemy and putting them to flight. Rossi pursued and killed a great number of them, capturing many others, among them Mastino's lieutenant who was in command of the troops. After the battle, the victors lingered a single night in the area, then returned to Florence via Fucecchio.

Not long after this victory Rossi set out for the Veneto where 64 affairs demanded his presence. By decree of the allies he took over supreme command of the war against Mastino and conducted that war with the greatest resolve and discipline. His first campaign was near Treviso, where he clashed with the enemy on various occasions. Then he brought his troops into the territory of Padua, arriving unexpectedly via swamps and rough terrain. At that time, Mastino controlled Padua and had huge forces in the area, which nevertheless kept behind their defenses when Rossi arrived, so that there was no opportunity to try the fortunes of battle; the enemy avoided any danger to themselves, hoping only to

nam experiri non pateretur, sperans a populationibus cohibendo et commeatus impediendo, citra ullum periculum sese hostem aversurum. Ruffus igitur detrectantibus pugnam hostibus magna difficultate per interrupta itinera cum exercitu profectus, ad Bogolentam posuit castra. Eum locum acri consilio ducis electum constat, quod fossam secus habet navigabilem per quam commeatus possit afferri, nec amplius septem passuum millibus Patavio abest, loco idoneo ad bellum inferendum. Ibi stativis vallo et fossa in antiquum morem communitis, nullam requiem permittebat hosti, saepe improviso impetu portas adusque discurrens, saepe signa inferre audens, saepe ingressum attentans; quibus rebus adeo mentem simul viresque tyranni fregit, ut qui paulo ante de occupanda Etruria cogitarat, tunc sollicitus esset de patrio solo retinendo.

65   Dum haec in Venetis geruntur, Arretini in dies magis premebantur, cum ad perusinum bellum, per se magnum, florentinum insuper bellum accessisset. Tiferno Burgoque amissis, crebra etiam castellorum[79] rebellione facta, cives Saconem adeunt, rogantque uti eum civitatis misereat: se quidem et durasse hactenus et durare paratos, modo spes aliqua et ratio belli gerandi ostendatur; sin desperata sint omnia, prospiciat aliquando urbi de se non improbe meritae et pacem si non bona, attamen aliqua conditione civitatis praestet.

66   Ea cum egissent cives, in suspicionem Saconi venerunt. Itaque, stipatus armatorum catervis, non cives iam minus quam hostes formidabat, et quasi desperatis rebus animum coeperat ad conditiones traducere. Cum Perusini et Florentini[80] per se quisque affectarent, ac in eo plane infida societas esset, Saconem plurimae ad Florentinos causae magis inclinabant. Primum, quod belli prin-

inhibit the Florentines from plundering and to block their supplies. With the enemy evading battle, Rossi set out with his army and with great difficulty via broken routes pitched camp at Bogolenta. The commander evidently chose the place wisely, as it was next to a navigable canal, by which supplies could be brought in, and was not more than seven miles from Padua. So it was a suitable base for making war. Fortifying his position there with earthwork and fosse in the ancient manner, he gave the enemy no rest, often ranging right up to the gates in surprise attacks, often daring to bring up his standards, often attempting entry. By these means he so shattered the confidence and forces of the tyrant that the man who shortly before had been planning to occupy Tuscany was now concerned how to retain control of his native soil.[52]

While this was happening in the Veneto, the Aretines were under increasing pressure each day, since to the Perugian war, itself a large one, had been added besides the war with Florence. With Borgo and Città di Castello lost, and a series of rebellions in the camps, the citizens went to Saccone and asked him to have mercy on the city: they had endured hitherto and were prepared to endure, so long as some hope or reason for waging war could be shown them; but if there were no hope, let him now at last make provision for a city which had not deserved badly of him, and grant it peace on some terms, if not on good terms.

Once the citizens had done this, Saccone began to regard them with suspicion. He now surrounded himself with troops of armed men, fearing the citizens no less than the enemy, and as his affairs began to appear desperate, he decided to come to terms. Since the Perugians and the Florentines were each contending in their particular interests, and their alliance in this matter was plainly mistrustful, Saccone was inclined to favor the Florentines for a number of reasons. First, because the roots of the war and the bitter hatred against him were all on the Perugian side. Then, too, most of his enemies had joined up with the Perugians, and he thought

cipia odiorumque acerbitates sibi cum Perusinis erant; deinde, quod plerique eius inimici se illis coniunxerant; quibus instiganti- bus vix arbitrabatur fore, ut ulla sibi conventa servarentur. Haec vero in Florentinis leviora omnia. Et accedebat illa quoque ratio in primis valida, quod ipse florentina matre ortus e familia nobili, permultos propinquitate Florentiae contingebat, quod plurimum videbatur ad securitatem eius attinere. His de causis, ad Florenti- nos magis inclinatus est. Ipsi vero, quia clandestinos tractatus ea de re habitos cum Sacone a Perusinis cognoverant, recipere condi- tiones festinarunt.

67   Summa vero conventorum huiusmodi fuit. Florentinus popu- lus[81] ius arbitriumque Arretii in decennium haberet; Sacon agna- tive omnes Saconis florentini cives in posterum forent; castella et praedia quae privatim habuissent, uti prius possederant, ita possi- derent. Praeter haec autem Saconi tradita quadraginta auri millia; insuper decem et septem millia Arretinis mutuata, quae conducto militi solverentur. Ita tyrannus improbus pecuniam militibus, quos ipse in cervices conduxerat civium, etiam post finitam tyrannidem a civibus ipsis exsolvendam providit. Quae vero ipse quasi pretium venditae patriae accipiebat, pro se retinuit.

68   Post foedus, duodecim ex primariis civibus Florentia missi ur- bem suscepere cum summa populi gratulatione. In Arretinis enim, quemadmodum et[82] in aliis Etruriae civitatibus, factiones erant duae, earumque adversatrix imperii fautrixque ecclesiae (quos Guelfos dicimus) fuit maior procul dubio ac potentior; multa[83] per saecula suo nomine rempublicam gubernavit. Declarant societates

it hardly likely that any agreements would be observed so long as they were present to incite violence. All of this was less of an issue with the Florentines. And there was the added consideration, of capital importance, that being himself born of a Florentine mother of noble family, he was connected with many people in Florence through this relationship, and this seemed highly relevant to his security. For these reasons he inclined more to the Florentines. The latter hastened to come to terms, as they knew that Saccone had had clandestine negotiations with the Perugians about the matter.

The terms, in summary form, were as follows. The Florentine 67 People was to have jurisdiction and authority over Arezzo for a decade; Saccone and all his male relatives were to be Florentine citizens in perpetuity; the castles and private possessions they had held previously they would continue to possess. In addition, Saccone was given 40,000 florins and 17,000 more were lent to the Aretines to pay for the soldiers they had hired. Thus a wicked tyrant, even after his tyranny was finished, found a way for money to be paid to his soldiers by the very citizens whose lives he had threatened with those same soldiers. And in fact he kept the money he had received for himself, as though it were his price for selling out his country.[53]

After the treaty, twelve leading citizens were sent from Florence 68 and took possession of the city, to the great joy of the populace. For among the Aretines, as also in other cities of Tuscany, there were two factions, and the faction of those opposed to the empire and favorable to the Church (whom we call Guelfs) was doubtless the larger and more powerful one; it governed the state for a long time in the Guelf name. This is proved by its ancient alliances with the Florentine People, beginning immediately after the death of Emperor Frederick [the Second] and lasting up to the time of the battle of Montaperti. In this battle (wherein the Guelf name was nearly wiped out in Tuscany) it is clear from public records

cum florentino populo antiquissimae sane, confestim post Federici imperatoris mortem initae, quae usque ad arbiensem pugnam duravere. In ipsa vero arbiensi pugna (in qua guelforum nomen in Etruria paene deletum est) constat publicis annalibus Arretinos cum Florentinis proelio interfuisse, ac plures fere caesos Arretinorum acervos quam ullius sociae civitatis. Caroli post haec nomen ab Arretinis statim receptum fuit et in partibus ita perseveratum, ut neque terror Corradini, neque hostium victoria et caedes amicorum, de moenibus prope conspecta, a fide partium dimoveret. Orta deinde post multos annos seditione inter nobilitatem et plebem, opera maxime Guillielmini praesulis, factio haec Guelforum Arretio pulsa se Florentinis coniunxit, communique robore iis[84] qui in urbe[85] remanserant intulerunt bellum. Quo tempore, commisso apud Campaldinum proelio, Guillielminus est interfectus. Post huius praesulis mortem, Tarlatum genus praepotens opibus gubernationem civitatis suscepit. Eo rempublicam tenente factio illa expulsa variis temporibus in urbem restituta est, nusquam tamen integra, sed alias alii, principibus solum ac maioris potentiae hominibus in exilio relictis.

69 Suscepta igitur a populo florentino urbe et exules omnes redierunt[86] et factio illa dudum pessumdata se confestim erexit, ac iam, dempto tyranni metu, liberis vocibus gratulabantur. Ut vero in constituenda republica priores populi ac vexillifer iustitiae creati sunt (quorum officiorum ne nomina quidem tyrannus esse in civitate passus fuerat), tanta repente laetitia est coorta, vix ut lacrimae prae gaudio tenerentur. Ita laetis tunc animis Arretini primum in florentini populi ius potestatemque venere.

70 At Perusini hoc Florentinorum factum gravissime ferentes, cum se delusos plane circumventosque putarent, legatos confestim Flo-

that the Aretines were present at the fight along with the Florentines, and suffered a greater number of casualties than any other allied city. Afterwards the Aretines immediately accepted the authority of Charles [I d'Anjou], and persevered as a member of his party with such spirit that neither fear of Conradin nor the victory of the enemy and the slaughter of friends, which they could almost see from their own walls, could budge them from their party loyalties. Then, many years later, internal strife arose between the nobility and the common people, and primarily through the efforts of Bishop Guglielmino, this Guelf faction was expelled from Arezzo and joined the Florentines. With their combined strength they made war against those who remained inside the city. That was the period when battle was joined at Campaldino and Guglielmino was killed. After the death of the bishop, the Tarlati family, which possessed extraordinary power and resources, took over the governance of the city. While that family ruled, the Guelf faction, which had been expelled at various times, was restored to the city, but never in its entirety: different men were restored at different times, and only the leaders and men of great power were left in exile.

Thus when the Florentine People took over the city, all the exiles returned, and the faction which for so long had been suppressed quickly rose again; and now, putting off its fear of the tyrant, celebrated with the voices of free men. And when in the course of establishing the republic the priors of the people and the standard-bearer of justice were created (offices whose very names the tyrant had not permitted in the city), such sudden joy arose that they could scarce restrain their tears for joy. Thus it was with happy hearts that the Aretines first came under the power and jurisdiction of the Florentine People.[54]

But the Perugians were gravely offended by this act of the Florentines, as they considered themselves to have been openly duped and circumvented, and they immediately sent men to Florence

rentiam misere qui et quererentur iniurias et bello parta secundum foedus reposcerent. Hi magistratum cum adiissent, potestate dicendi facta orationem huiusmodi[87] habuere.

71 'Adventus nostri causam, o Florentini, silentibus etiam nobis, palam esse omnibus arbitramur. Quis enim, qui modo pacta conventaque inter populos norit, non et a vobis contra foedus magnifice ventum et nos ferre non debere eam contumeliam intelligat? Nempe durum est contemni a socio, sceleratum destitui, prope sacrilegum oppugnari; quid ergo, spoliari simul et contumelia affici? Ita nuper foedus ictum est civitatibus, ut neque pax fieret ulla cum hoste nisi de sociorum voluntate, et cuncta bello parta forent communia. Haec iurata religiose ac tabulis literisque firmata, utrum tandem patiuntur vos sic Arretium suscepisse, vel testantur id a vobis fieri non potuisse, salva religione et fide? Nobis profecto haec eo gravior iniuria videtur, quo minus facti est ulla defensio; nam ex libidine contra foedus venire, id est socios pro nihilo ducere. Quod enim, quaesumus, diffugium aut quam defensionem quisquam vestrum assumat? Desiisse nos esse in armis? At nunc etiam sumus. Sero accessisse ad bellum? At prius quam vos inferre coepimus. Nullius momenti fuisse milites nostros? At nihil terribilius erat hosti. Profecisse parum? At plura et munitissima cepimus loca. Quae igitur contemnendi causa fuerit, cum nulla fuerit conquerendi?

72 'Atqui, si verum audire non piget, non tam de tyranno quam de nobis, Florentini, Arretium accepistis. Sacon, credo, vobis sponte dedit? Benivolentia se ipsum,[88] ut fit, utque tyrannorum est mos,

both to protest these injustices and to renew their demands for the profits of war as stipulated in the league. When these men had gained entry to the magistrate and had been given leave to speak, they delivered an oration along these lines:

"The reason for our coming, O Florentines, we believe is obvi- 71 ous to everyone, even before we begin to speak. For is there anyone privy to the pacts and agreements between our peoples who does not understand that you have contravened the treaty in a lordly way, and that we ought not to endure this insult? Surely it is a hard thing to be despised by an ally, a wicked thing to be deserted by him, and near sacrilege to be attacked by him. What then is it to be despoiled and treated insultingly by him? A treaty was lately agreed to by our cities that there should be no peace with the enemy except by consent of the allies, and that all profits from the war should be shared. This treaty, signed and sealed and affirmed with holy oaths — does it permit you to have taken Arezzo in this way? Or does it rather bear witness that you could not do this without violating religion and your word of honor? To us this injury seems the more grave the less defensible it is. For to violate a treaty arbitrarily is to treat allies as though they were worthless. What is your excuse, what is your defense? Please tell us, any of you! Did we fail to appear in arms? But we are still in arms! Did we arrive late to the war? But we began the war before you did! Were our troops of no account? But the enemy found nothing more frightening than they! Did they have little success? But we took numerous well-fortified places! What then could be the cause of your contempt, since you can have no cause for complaint?

"And indeed, though hearing the truth may displease you, Flor- 72 entines, it was less from the tyrant than from us that you took Arezzo. Am I to believe that Saccone handed it over of his own free will, that out of sheer benevolence, in the usual way, as is the custom with tyrants, he stripped himself of power and gave it to you? This, surely, is perfectly absurd. It is we, we! who forced the

potestate[89] exuit ⟨et⟩ vobis concessit? Nihil profecto dici potest
minus. Nos, nos, inquam, ad hoc invitum repugnantemque com-
pulimus tyrannum; nos hanc vim necessitatemque attulimus; a nobis circa urbem oppida illa adempta sunt; a nobis crebro incursu
noctu dieque vexatus, spem resistendi omnino amisit. Quis igitur
auctor est facti? Qui compulsus est, an qui compulit? Iste, credo,
nisi forte qui de navi iactat, causam sibi, non tempestati putemus
consignandam. Quod si auctores sumus, ut apparet, quanta iniuria
est nos his rebus, quarum ipsi causa sumus, spoliare pergere! Ve-
natores, medius fidius, etiam ii[90] quibus nulla inter se est societas,
si feram e silvis a se primo excitatam persequantur, eaque forte ab
aliis capiatur, reddi lex et mos gentium iubet: nihil enim indignius
visum est quam alieno labore parta retinere. Quid ergo vos et socii
et iurati, nonne indignissimum est, si ne in communionem quidem
praedae a nobis excitatae et persecutae nos admittatis?

73   "'At non vult hostis in tuas manus devenire." Ad hoc scilicet in[91]
societatem coivimus, ut voluntatem hostis spectaremus? Porro, ne
illud ipsum quod nunc facit vult, sed vi ipsa compellitur; necessitas enim omnia frangit. Quid autem minus convenit, quam voluntatem hostium attendere, sociorum negligere? Viri sapientes nulla
in re humana neque maiorem neque sanctiorem fidem quam in societatibus exegerunt; nam, si in socio fides violatur, quid iam in
vita stabile supersit? Itaque aliarum fere litium iudicia quodammodo privata sunt, nec aliud fere quam pecuniae damnum in illis
versatur; pro socio autem iudicium in caput transit. Nusquam
enim integrum hominem haberi leges voluerunt eum, qui non integra fide erga socios fuerit adinventus. A testimonio, a curia,[92] a
foro, a publicis honoribus, ab humana denique societate repellen-

tyrant, kicking and screaming, to this action; it is we who brought violence and necessity to bear; it is we who took the towns around the city; we who harried him day and night, taking away all his hope of resistance. So who then is responsible for his capitulation? Is it the one who was forced, or the one who did the forcing? The latter, I think, unless we are to believe that the cause of things being thrown overboard is the man who throws them and not the tempest. And if we are the ones responsible, as is clear, what an injustice it is to proceed to despoil us of the very things we are the cause of acquiring! Even hunters, for heaven's sake, men who have no formal alliance among themselves, if they are in pursuit of a wild animal and the animal happens to be flushed out of the woods by some of them but captured by others — even such men are commanded by law and custom to give it up, for nothing, apparently, is lower than to keep the fruits of another man's labor. Is it not then the lowest possible behavior for you, our sworn allies, not to share with us the prey we have flushed and pursued?

"'But the enemy did not want to fall into your hands,' [you argue.] So is this, if you please, the reason why we joined the alliance: to respect the will of the enemy? Besides, what he now does is *not* what he willed; he was compelled to it by force; it is necessity that breaks all things. And what is less fitting than to heed the will of an enemy and neglect that of an ally? Wise men have laid it down that there is no greater and holier trust in human affairs than the trust between allies, for if an ally violates his word, what stability would then be left in life? Judgements rendered in most other disputes are in a certain sense private, involving only monetary fines; but a judgement rendered on behalf of an ally is a capital affair. The law holds a man found to have acted towards his allies without full faith to be lacking in integrity forever after; it considers that such a man should be expelled and removed from bearing witness, from the court, from the marketplace, from public honors, and from all human society. In light of this, Florentines, you

73

dum illum amovendumque censuerunt. Quo magis est a vobis, Florentini, etiam nunc considerandum; non enim quid concupiscat animus, sed quid fas et iura sinant, spectare debetis.'

74   Legati quidem Perusinorum ita dixerunt. Florentinus vero magistratus, quoniam oratio quam decebat arrogantior visa fuerat, ne momento quidem temporis differre responsum statuit, ne intercapedo ipsa ulla ex parte minueret dignitatem. Quare ad legatos conversus, 'Audacem,' inquit, 'verborum copiam semper vobis, Perusini, adesse, et antea quidem sciebamus et nunc oratio vestra manifeste ostendit. Necesse autem fuerit in respondendo nostram parumper consuetudinem intermittere, vestram assumere; nam atrociter obiecta placide refelli non debent. Sed, antequam de iure foederis disputemus—quod violatum a vobis est, Perusini, non autem a nobis—refutanda videtur illa iactantia, qua vobis totum belli opus, quasi nos nulli aut nusquam fuerimus, tribuistis. Cuius id fuit immoderationis et de nobis et ad nos ista dicere, cuius praeterea vanitatis? An quid vobis sperare unquam licuit de Arretinis, si nos sedentes certamen vestrum, quasi de theatro quodam, spectassemus otiosi? Nempe quid vestrae quidve illorum possent vires, proelium inter vos initum patefecerat. Superatis, fractis atque fugatis vobis, cum Arretini victores circum moenia obstreperent vestra, opem tulimus indigentibus, qua servati estis. Audetis ergo vos solos confecisse bellum dicere, quibus nisi opitulati essemus, bello ipsi vos eratis confecti?

75   '"De nobis," inquit, "Arretium cepistis." O arrogantiam singularem! O verborum audaciam non ferendam! Nosne de vobis cepimus? Ipsi nulla pars belli eramus? Et quid mentes Arretinorum fregit? Quid desperationem resistendi attulit, nisi bellum a nobis illatum, cum vestrum ipsi per se longe contemnerent bellum?[93] Iactate in verbis quantum libet; nam id quidem perfacile est: levitas tamen verborum non mutat factorum gravitatem.

should even now give this matter more thought, and you ought to consider not only what your spirit desires, but what is permitted by the laws, human and divine."

Thus spoke the Perugian envoys. But the Florentine magistrate, 74 since the oration had seemed more arrogant than was fitting, decided not to put off his response by even a moment, lest the interval diminish in any degree his dignity. So turning to the envoys, he said, "You are ever bold and copious in your speech, Perugians, as we were aware before, and as your oration now makes manifest. In responding it will be necessary to lay aside our own custom of speaking awhile and adopt yours, for charges laid with ferocity should not be refuted with gentleness. But before we debate about the rights and wrongs of the treaty—which was violated by you, Perugians, not by us—it seems that we must refute that boast of yours, whereby you take credit for the whole war effort, as though none of us Florentines were ever there. What presumption, what vanity it is to say such things about us and to us! What hope would you ever have had against the Aretines if we had sat around at our leisure, as though in kind of theater, watching the two of you struggle? Indeed your relative strength was obvious from the initial battle between you. You were beaten, shattered and put to flight, and when the victorious Aretines were clamoring at your gates, we gave aid to you in your need and saved you. And now you dare say that you alone defeated the enemy, when it was you who would have been defeated without our help?

"'You have received Arezzo from our hands,' you say. What ex- 75 traordinary arrogance! What insufferable impudence! We received it from your hands? We ourselves had no part in the war? And what was it that broke the spirit of the Aretines? What made them despair of resisting, if not the war we made against them— since they had long held your war, by itself, in contempt? Make all the verbal boasts you like; that is easy enough; but empty verbosity does not alter solid facts.

76 'Venio nunc ad societatis fidem, quam a nobis violatam dicitis, cum id sit vestrum. Audete negare, si potestis, secretos cum Sacone de accipienda urbe tractatus habuisse; nuncios et literas ea de re clam ad eum misisse; voluisse accipere, si fieri potuisset. Quae cuius fidei sunt, Perusini? Cuius integritatis? Fides in societatibus nulla magis re quam voluntate et animo violatur; nam factum quidem perinde haberi solet, uti propositum fuerit agentis. Mens et voluntas pro scelere est, conatus fraudandi turpitudinem contrahit; qui cum fuerit in vobis, quid nunc obiicere audetis? Levius est a nobis factum, Perusini, quam a vobis attentatum, propterea quod vos eo tempore attentastis, cum integra erat societas, nos eo tempore fecimus, cum vestrum iam scelus et fraudandi conatus omne societatis vinculum iuraque dissolverat; nam perfido fides servanda non est. Quid enim facere nos oportuit, cum per fraudem vos conari adversus societatis fidem sentiremus? Nonne contra dolum et conatum vestrum nos[94] communire? Nonne fraudem anteveniendo excludere? Hoc nos fecimus a vobis edocti, qui per nos ipsos optima fide quieturi fueramus. Non potestis de eo facto a sociis iuste conqueri, quod vobis in socios licere statuistis. Si igitur viri sapientes nulla in re humana neque maiorem neque sanctiorem fidem quam in societatibus exegerunt; si nusquam integrum hominem haberi eum leges voluerunt, qui non integra fide erga socios fuerit adinventus; si ab humana denique societate repellendum amovendumque censuerunt, videte, quanta vos maneant, Perusini, qui tam gravi legum sapientumque censurae obnoxii reperiamini. Nam factum quidem nostrum legitimam habet defensionem, cum vos iam societatis iura fraude vestra sustulissetis; vester autem conatus, quo minus infamiam contraxerit, defendi non potest.

"I come now to the question of loyalty to allies, which you say 76
we have violated, although that is what you have done. Dare to
deny it, if you can, that you held secret negotiations with Saccone
about taking over the city; that you secretly sent messengers and
letters to him about the matter; that you would have taken it over
if you could have. What kind of loyalty is this, Perugians, what
kind of integrity? The worst violation of loyalty to allies is in will
and spirit, for actions are valued according to the purpose of the
actor. Ill will and intention stand proxy for crime, and attempts at
fraud bring disgrace. Since you had such intentions, why do you
dare blame us? What we did, Perugians, was less serious than
what you attempted, because you attempted it at a time when our
alliance was unsullied, but our action came at a time when your
wickedness and attempt at fraud had already dissolved the bonds
and rights of alliance; for one should not keep faith with the faith-
less. What ought we to have done when we learned that you were
attempting to commit fraud against the alliance? Should we not
have defended ourselves against your deceitful designs? Should we
not have taken steps to anticipate them? This we learned to do
from you; for our own part we intended to wait quietly in good
faith. You cannot justly complain of behavior in an ally which you
had decided to permit yourselves. If, then, wise men have laid it
down that there is no greater and holier trust in human affairs
than the trust between allies, if the law holds a man found to have
acted towards his allies without full faith to be lacking in integrity
forever after, if it considers that such a man should be expelled
and removed from all human society, consider what lies in store
for you, Perugians, when you are discovered to be liable to such
grave censure from the wise and from the law. What we did has a
legitimate defense, since you had already suspended the rights due
an ally by your act of fraud. But your designs cannot be defended
without infamy.

77   'Quanta igitur dementia est vestrummet crimen verbis augere!
Circumspicere vos oportuit, Perusini, et quid loqueremini et ad
quos magis attendere; nam impudentia ista verborum non turpitudinem occulit, sed acerbat. Quis enim ferat alteri obiectantem
quod ille ipse qui obiectat commisit? Perversa in[95] oratione vestra
impudentia fuit. Bellum vos confecisse solos dixistis, cum id sit
nostrum; fraudem a nobis commissam, cum id sit vestrum.

78   'At communionem saltem postulamus. Non habet eam vim le-
gatio vestra ut ista postulet, sed ut nos iurgio lacessat, ut contem-
nat, ut nullam in partem belli fuisse utiles redarguat. Ad haec,[96] ut
apparet, totum legationis vestrae propositum convertistis. Nam
qui ex iure postulant, neque maledictis neque contumelia potius
quam honestis verbis, praesertim ad civitatem loquentes, uti consuerunt.'

79   Cum dicendi finem magistratus fecisset, et qui assidebant cives
pro se quisque castigando mitigarent, lenioribus tandem verbis
tractari res coepta est, et utrinque iam rationes auditae. Denique,
inter has civitatum discordias quoniam diiudicari posse videbatur,
adhibita est mediocritas quaedam, ut Perusini Licinianum, Sabinum, Florianum, Anglare, oppida Arretinorum tenent, ac magistratum quinquennio Arretium mitterent, ad quem ex iudiciis pro-
vocatio esset. Et res quidem Arretii discordiaeque et bella in hunc
modum cecidere.[97]

80   Lucense iam negotium restabat magis porro difficile, nec in
Etruria solum, verum per Galliam quoque transpadanamque regionem varie implicatum. Principio igitur insequentis anni Mastinus, quoniam et captum Arretium et auctas in Etruria Florentino-

"How mad it is to augment your crime with words! You ought 77
to look about you, Perugians, and pay more attention to what you
are saying, and to whom, for the impudence of your words does
not conceal your disgrace, but exacerbates it. Who is going to
stand for someone who complains about actions in another that
he himself commits? The impudence in your oration was perverse.
You said that you alone won the war; but that was what we did.
You said that we had committed fraud; but that was what you did.

"However, let us at least share the spoils. You legation does not 78
have the purpose of requesting that, but rather of insulting us, de-
spising us, and maintaining that we were entirely useless in the
war. That was apparently the whole purpose of your legation. For
those who make requests with right on their side are accustomed
not to use curses or insults, but rather honorable words, especially
when addressing a sovereign city."

When the magistrate had finished speaking, the citizens pres- 79
ent each reprimanded himself, and softening their positions, they
began to treat the matter in more neutral terms, now that the arguments on both sides had been heard. Finally, it appeared that
the discords between the two cities could be adjudicated with a
certain amount of compromise. As a result, the Perugians took
control of the towns of Lucignano, Monte San Savino, Foiano,
and Anghiari, and were to send a magistrate to Arezzo for five
years, to whom appeal might be made in legal cases. In this way
the Aretine problem and its the discords and wars came to an
end.[55]

There remained the much more difficult business of Lucca, 80
with its various complications not only in Tuscany, but also
throughout Lombardy and the lands on the far side of the Po. So
at the beginning of the following year, Mastino, having learned of 1337
the capture of Arezzo and the increase in Florentine resources
throughout Tuscany, sent one of his commanders, a certain Azzo,
down to Lucca with a fresh force of cavalry. This force, added to

rum cognoverat opes, Accium quendam e suis ducibus cum novo equitatu Lucam dimisit. Is equitatus ad veterem additus, cum satis magnum numerum confecisset, movit hominum studia mentesque erexit. Itaque Florentini paratis confestim copiis, sociorum quoque auxiliaribus arcessitis, magno exercitu lucensem agrum ingressi, omnia ferro igneque popularunt. Hostis, impar tantae multitudini, signa conferre abnuit; oppida tantum et moenia tutabatur. Eam ob rem pugna nulla commissa eat, populationes modo latae actae.

81   In Gallia vero, cum in summa res esset spe, cuncta repente turbavit Germanorum seditio. Mastinus enim virtutem Ruffi metuens, grandi mercede a germanis equitibus qui sub Ruffo militabant redemerat, ut interfecto duce ad se transirent. Sed dum maturantur insidiae, res interea patefacta est. Itaque huius facinoris conscii ad mille germani equites, facto repente globo ac igne pluribus locis, ne quis persequi posset, per tabernacula iniecto, ad hostem transfugere. Erant in castris ante haec transfugia Florentinorum Venetorumque supra quinque millia equitum. Reliqua ergo multitudo refectis castris eodem in loco⁹⁸ perstitit; nec dux suo casu perterritus est, quo minus solita viveret utereturque fiducia.

82   Iam⁹⁹ ceteri Galliae principes, ruinam Mastini sperantes, in societatem coierant, et quantum nunquam¹⁰⁰ antea copiae mantuano in agro cogebantur Mediolanensium, Ferrarienaium, Mantuanorum. Ad hos Ruffus Marsilium fratrem cum duobus millibus quadringentis equitibus misit, ipse cum reliquis apud Bogolentam remansit in castris. Copiae sociorum, ubi coactae sunt, ex mantuano in veronensem transierunt agrum. Harum summa penes Lucinum Vicecomitem omnium sociorum concessu habebatur. Igitur Luci-

the existing cavalry, made quite a large number, and this was having an impact on men's designs and raising expectations. So the Florentines immediately marshalled their forces, calling also upon the allies for reinforcements, and invaded the territory of Lucca with a great army, devasting it thoroughly with fire and sword. The enemy, unequal to so large a host, refused to march out, but only guarded the towns and city walls. For this reason no battle was joined; there was only widespread pillage and destruction.

In northern Italy, where hopes were high, a sudden revolt by   81
the Germans threw everything into confusion. For Mastino, fearing Pietro Rossi's strength and ability, gave the German mercenaries fighting under the league's commander a large sum of money to kill him and come over to his own side. But while the conspiracy was being hatched, the matter was exposed. So the thousand or so German knights who were in on the deed quickly formed themselves into a body and fled to the enemy, setting fire to the tents in numerous places to inhibit pursuit. Before these desertions there were more than five thousand knights in the Florentine-Venetian camp. So the remains of this host rebuilt the encampment and stayed in the same place. Nor was their commander dismayed by this misadventure; he went on living and acting with his usual confidence.

Now the other princes of northern Italy, hoping for Mastino's   82
downfall, came together in an alliance and marshalled in Mantuan territory troops of the Milanese, Ferrarese and Mantuans as never before. Pietro Rossi sent his brother Marsilio to join them with 2400 cavalry, himself remaining encamped at Bogolenta with the rest. When the allied troops had been mustered, they passed from Mantuan into Veronese territory. By consent of all the allies high command was held by Luchino Visconti.[56] So Luchino advanced his troops on Verona and the propinquity of his soldiers caused the very seat and home of the tyrant to tremble. And at the same time, Charles, son of King John, coming from the other direction,

nus, Veronae admotis copiis, sedem ipsam ac domum tyranni propinquo milite quatiebat. Eodemque tempore Carolus Iohannis regis filius alia ex parte adveniens, Feltrum et Bellonam, Mastini urbes, invasit. Tertia Patavium castra premebant. Quibus circumventus malis tyrannus periculosum quidem verum tamen strenuum sumit consilium, Verona egreditur cum omnibus copiis. In his equitum fuerunt[101] ad tria millia, peditum multitudo ingens, ceterum urbana et inexercitata. Cum his ad hostem ferociter profectus, aciem in conspectu struxit potestatemque dimicandi fecit. Lucinus, etsi longe praestabat equitatu, tamen neque in aciem copias producere neque fortunam pugnae experiri voluit. Quae res hostium animos ferociamque adauxit; suorum vero ita fregit mentes, aliis alia suspicantibus, ut consilium sumerent discedendi.

83 Hoc incendio domi restincto, Mastinus, quasi secundam tempestatem nactus, in patavinum agrum copias traduxit, ac tribus passuum millibus infra Bogolentam ipso in flumine castra fecit, eo consilio ut commeatum impediret, simulque ut ceteras copias quae cum Marsilio aberant redire in castra prohiberet. Res erat iam[102] in angusto; nam et desperatum erat fortunam proelii tentare illa paucitate copiarum, et desperatum manere intercluso commeatu. Sed ingenium multa reparat invictum. Cum enim animadversum esset Mastini copias ex hoc eodem flumine, nec aliunde, aquandi facultatem habere, suis ipsum artibus Ruffus aggreditur. Herba est in his locis amaro nimium suco. Hanc milites iussu ducis quaesitam comportatamque in ripa fluvii conterebant et in aquam proiiciebant. Ea secundo cursu ad castra hostium delata, tetro horrendoque[103] sapore aquam inficiebat, ita ut nec hominibus nec equis utilis esset. Qua difficultate ad extremum victus hostis, irrito coepto abscedere coactus est.

invaded Feltre and Belluno, both cities belonging to Mastino. Padua was under pressure from a third camp. Surrounded by these evils, the tyrant took a dangerous but vigorous course. He marched out of Verona with all his troops. Among these were around three thousand knights and a huge mass of infantry, though the latter were city folk unused to battle. With these he set out fiercely towards the enemy, set up his battle line within sight of them, and offered battle. Although Luchino was far superior in cavalry, he had no wish to marshal his troops in battle formation or to try the fortunes of war. His unwillingness gave courage and ferocity to the enemy, but broke the confidence of his own troops, making them suspect each other, so that they decided to take their leave.[57]

With this fire put out at home, it was as though Mastino had found a favorable wind. He brought his troops into Paduan territory and made camp three miles below Bogolenta right on the river. His plan was to block supply lines and at the same time prevent the troops Marsilio had taken with him from returning to their camp. Affairs were now in a difficult position for the allies, for it was a desperate course to try the fortune of battle with so few troops, and it was a desperate course to stay there with their supplies cut off. But a mind that refuses to be conquered makes good many difficulties. When Pietro noticed that Mastino's troops drew their water from the same river and had no other source, he attacked the enemy with a ruse of his own. There grew in that place a herb with an exceedingly bitter juice. By Pietro's order the troops collected the herb, carried it to the river bank, crushed it and threw it in the water. The juice was carried downstream to the enemy camp, where it infected the water with a foul and horrible taste so that it could be used by neither man nor horse. The enemy was in the end overcome by this difficulty and was compelled to withdraw from his undertaking in failure.[58]

83

84   Ruffus post haec coniuncto fratre Patavio copias admovit. Patavi erat Albertus Mastini frater, natu quidem maior, sed nequaquam pari auctoritate. Hunc Patavini oderant cuncti, sed metus ut fit populum cohibebat. Stante igitur ad portas Ruffo omniaque tentante, tandem cives corripiunt arma domumque tyranni invadunt; Ruffum autem cum exercitu intra moenia admittunt. Auctor autem huius defectionis rerumque novarum fuit Ubertinus Carra, longe nobilitate et potentia princeps. Hic urbem tyranno primum dederat, coactus civili dissensione. Post multa atque gravia ab eo perpessus, hanc liberandi viam cogitarat. Praesidium omne tyranni a Patavinis oppressum est; ipse vero captus et Venetias missus.[104]

85   Verum hanc laetitiam felicitatemque victoriae haud multo post turbavit ipsius Ruffi obitus. Etenim compositis Patavi rebus Silicem oppidum expugnare adortus, cum in ipsa porta committeretur proelium ac vi perrumpere milites conarentur, oppidani vero contra pugnarent, Ruffus ex equo prosiliens, pedes ad primos suorum convolavit. Ibi suos adhortanti, manum etiam conserenti, cum undique tela volitarent, hasta supra femur transfigitur. Qua divulsa, cum hostem infestius irritatiusque urgeret, in fossam prosiluit ac per eam in oppidum transire perrexit. Hic madefactum vulnus exacerbatum est. Itaque paulo post relatus Patavium e vita migravit. Marsilius quoque, alter frater, morbo quem primo contraxerat et dolore germani, paucis post haec diebus moritur. Horum mors Florentinorum Venetorumque turbavit animos, magnique sunt illis ab utraque civitate honores impensi; nam eorum virtute maxima pars belli existimabatur[105] confecta.

86   Brixia ferme per hos ipsos dies a Mastino defecit; ea Mediolanensis potitus est. Proximo dehinc anno Venetorum Florentino-

After this, Pietro joined his brother and marched his troops on   84
Padua. Padua was ruled by Mastino's brother, Alberto, who was
older than he but by no means his equal in authority. All the
Paduans hated him, but fear as usual held the people back. So
with Pietro at the gates making all kinds of thrusts, the citizens finally took to arms and attacked the tyrant's house; they also let
Pietro and his army inside the city walls. The man responsible for
this defection and revolution was Ubertino da Carrara, by far the
city's leading man in nobility and power.[59] He had at first handed
the city over to the tyrant, being compelled to do so by civil discord. But after he had suffered many grave injuries from the tyrant, he conceived of this way of liberating his country. The tyrant's whole garrison was crushed by the Paduans, and the tyrant
himself was captured and sent to Venice.

But the joy and happiness of victory was soon spoiled by   85
Pietro's own death. Having settled affairs in Padua, he set out to
besiege the town of Monselice. When he had joined battle before
its very gates and his soldiers were trying to break in by force, the
townsmen started to put up a fight. So he jumped off his horse
and ran to the front of his forces. There he was urging on his
troops and also joining them in close combat, missiles flying everywhere, when he was struck above the thigh with a spear. Pulling it
out, he attacked the enemy harder and more ferociously than ever,
jumping into a ditch, through which he made his way inside the
town. But the wound was exacerbated by its soaking in the ditch.
Thus a little later he was carried to Padua and departed this life.[60]
His other brother, Marsilio, also died a few days later from a disease he had contracted earlier, and from grief at his brother's
death. Their deaths profoundly upset the Florentines and Venetians, and both cities paid them great honor, for it was held that
the war had mostly been won through their courage and ability.

It was around this time that Brescia rebelled from Mastino and   86
came under the control of the Milanese. The following year the   1338

rumque copiae in agrum veronensem traductae, non longe ab urbe castra fecerunt. Aliquot dies commorati, cum et castella quaedam munita cepissent ac hostium vires pluribus locis attrivissent, tandem maiori conatu Vicentiam obsederunt.

87   Mastinus, cum in deterius rem labi cerneret, capto fratre, amissis quatuor magnis urbibus multisque cum his oppidis, Vicentia finitima in periculo constituta, sibi iam ipsi diffidens, oratores de pace ad Venetos misit. Veneti autem et ipsi per se proclives erant ad pacem, et accedebat publice Mastini deprecatio, privatum autem multorum amicitiae. Itaque pax tandem illi a Venetis data est, ea conditione, ut Tarvisium tarvisinumque agrum Venetis dimitteret. Florentinis[106] vero id modo cautum, ut, si in pace venire ipsi vellent, Pisciam et Bugianum de hoste acciperent, ceteraque lucensis agri castella quae possidebant retinerent; exulibus vero Lucensium, qui cum Florentinis Venetisque in eo bello fuissent, in urbem Lucam redeundi ius foret. His arcane compositis, per legatos Florentiam missos et se pacem velle dixerunt et conditiones protulerunt; proinde, si pax Florentino[107] placeret, ei affore quae pacti essent; sin magis bellum, hoc etiam eorum arbitrio permitti.

88   Hoc Venetorum factum pergrave visum est florentino populo, sed ad curam deligendi necessitas ipsa vocabat. In eo consultationes variae frequentesque habitae. Remanere tyranno Lucam, quam nuper Florentino per fraudem ademisset, cuiusque gratia ipsi bellum suscepissent, turpissimum videbatur, ipsaque vicinitas nihil

Florentines and Venetians brought their troops into Veronese territory, making camp not far from the city. Having spent several days there, they took certain fortified castles and weakened the forces of enemy in numerous places. Then they finally launched a major campaign to besiege Vicenza.

Mastino, seeing his power slipping away, with his brother cap- 87 tured, four large cities with many of their towns lost, and neighboring Vicenza placed in peril, now lost his self-confidence and sent ambassadors to Venice to make peace. The Venetians for their part were inclined to peace, and Mastino's public entreaty and private friendships with many Venetians were further inducements. So the Venetians in the end gave him peace on condition that he should give up Treviso and its territory to them. For the Florentines the only assurances given were that, if they too wished to join the peace, they might receive Pescia and Buggiano from the enemy and keep the other castles they possessed in Lucchese territory; the Lucchese exiles who had fought alongside the Florentines and Venetians in the war would get the right to return to the city of Lucca. These conditions being secretly arranged, the Venetians sent envoys to Florence stating their own desire for peace and laying out the terms; if the Florentines wanted peace, they could have it on the these terms; if they preferred war, that too was their decision.[61]

This act on the part of the Venetians seemed a very serious 88 matter to the Florentine People, but necessity itself required them to be careful in their choices. Frequent consultations were held about the matter and various views expressed. It seemed shameful in the extreme for the tyrant to keep Lucca, the city he had recently taken from the Florentines through fraud, and on account of which they had undertaken the war; and his continued presence in the area was bound to be unsettling. On the other hand, if they prosecuted the war by themselves, they believed it would be a difficult and arduous affair, especially as they were worn out from

firmi habitura.[108] Contra vero, si bellum continuarent soli, arduum sane ac difficile, praesertim tot sumptibus defessis,[109] existimabant fore. Et invitabant Piscia Bugianumque, duo lucensis agri oppida, quae si reciperentur, infirmior tyrannus ad bellum videbatur futurus. Haec tandem vicit praevaluitque sententia; missisque ad Venetos legatis mandatum est pacem ut maxime improbarent ac dissuadere conarentur; quod si perstarent in sententia Veneti, conditiones quoad fieri posset augerent, pacem tandem oblatam reciperent. Legati fuerunt Franciscus Pactius, Alexius Rinutius, Iacobus Albertus. Ab his legatis nihil profectum est, obstinatis ad pacem Venetorum animis. Itaque pax est tandem iisdem quibus convenerat prius[110] conditionibus recepta.

89   Post haec liberae civium mentes non a bello tantum, sed etiam a suspicione belli conquieverunt,[111] nisi quod Mastinus per finem quasi eius anni Lucam venit. Eius quidem adventus etiam in pace formidabilis erat. Verum ille paucis diebus Lucae commoratus, nulla penitus innovata re, in Galliam rediit.

90   Proximo dehinc anno qui sub recentem fuit pacem nihil memoria dignum a civitate gestum comperio. Auguria tamen permulta et foeda futuras inde portendebant clades. Tacta est enim de coelo turris aedium publicarum; tacti sunt etiam muri urbis; porta quoque bononiensi via fulmine icta, et tres illic homines exanimati. Messes eo anno tenuissimae famem haud dubie minabantur. Ea solicitudo perpulit ad capita hominum dinoscenda, ut quanto importati opus foret cerneretur. Censu igitur habito, reperta sunt civium capita intra urbem degentium nonaginta millia.

91   Sequitur annus trecentesimus quadragesimus supra mille. Hic annus insignis fuit multarum rerum novitatibus. Principio cometes in coelo visa hominum mentes superioris anni auguriis pavidas magis conterruit. Nec vanum id praesagium fuit. Secuta enim mox

so many expenses. And Pescia and Buggiano were real inducements, two towns in Lucchese territory; with them under Florentine control, the tyrant's ability to make war would be weakened.
The latter view finally prevailed, and they sent envoys to Venice
with instructions to condemn the peace in the strongest terms and
to try to change the Venetians' minds; but if the latter should persist in their decision, they should improve the terms as much as
possible and finally accept the offered peace. The envoys were
Francesco de' Pazzi, Alessio de' Rinucci, and Jacopo degli Alberti.
These envoys got nothing, as the minds of the Venetians were
made up with regard to the peace. So the peace was finally accepted on the same terms which had been agreed upon earlier.

Afterwards, the minds of the citizens were put to rest, freed not   89
only from war, but from the suspicion of war. Except that Mastino
came to Lucca around the end of that year. His coming, indeed,
was something to fear even in time of peace. But after spending a
few days in Lucca, he took no new steps and returned to northern
Italy.

In the year following the peace, I find nothing worthy of record   90
that the city did. Yet there were numerous foul auguries portend-   *1339*
ing future disasters. The tower of the Palazzo Vecchio was struck
by lightning, as also were the walls of the city and the gate on the
road to Bologna,[62] and three men died from these bolts. The harvests that year were extremely meager, a clear sign of famine to
come. Concern for this drove the city to count its population in
order to find out how much they would have to import. After
holding a census, it was discovered that the number of citizens living inside the city was 90,000.[63]

The year 1340 followed. This year was notable for the number   91
of revolutionary changes it saw. First a comet was seen in the sky,   *1340*
which terrified men the more as they were already fearful from the
auguries of the previous year. And it was no vain portent. For a
pestilence followed not just in the city, but throughout the region,

pestis non per urbem modo, verum etiam per agrum, foeda strage magnam vim hominum absumpsit, nec adolescentes tantum, sed etiam provectos aetate, et aliquot in republica insignes. Sedecim millia urbanae multitudinis extincta per eam pestem[112] tradunt.

92   Vergente iam in hiemem anno, cum ea pestis desenuisset,[113] novae res inter cives coortae maiorem in modum quassarunt civitatem. Caput vero seditionum hinc fluxit. Magni quidam e plebe homines, nec ii[114] quidem multo admodum numero, ceterum plus aequo sibi arrogantes, rempublicam pro arbitrio gubernabant; impositoque ad biennium peregrino magistratu, homine crudeli et cuncta pro libidine eorum[115] ministrante, omnibus nimirum erant terrori. Affecti ab hoc iniuriis multi, sed insignes ea tempestate familiae duae, Bardi Frescobaldique. Qua indignatione conciti, principes earum familiarum coniurarunt, ut raptis subito armis magistratum eiusque fautores adorirentur. Cum patrandi dies adesset, res ad priores delata est. Itaque populus confestim, quasi nobilitas adversus eum insurgeret, ad arma vocatur. Contra vero ea pars nobilitatis cui periculum parabatur, raptis et ipsa armis, trans Arnum loca tenebat, pontesque stationibus positis tutabatur, sperans, si auxilia supervenirent externa, facile inde in reliquam urbem evadere posse. Ea formido movit populum, ut eorum spem cogitataque praeverteret. Itaque insurgente trans Arnum plebe, cis Arnum quoque magna manu per infimum pontem[116] irrumpente, impetus fit in coniuratos. Ex hoc illi paulatim cedere ac pedem referre coeperunt, circaque aedes proprias magis conglobari quoad, amissa tandem spe, nocte proxima urbe excesserunt.

93   Post haec populus arma deposuit ac iudicio acta res. Postulati enim de vi publica, cum nemo compareret, absentes damnati sunt,

which carried off a great many men with its foul slaughter, not just the young but even those of more advanced years, including several distinguished statesmen. Sixteen thousand of the urban multitude were killed by this pestilence, it is said.[64]

As winter came on and the pestilence died away, a revolution 92 among the citizens arose which greatly shook the city. The source of this sedition was as follows. Certain great men from the commons, not a large number but laying claim to more than their rightful share of power, were governing the state arbitrarily. Having imposed a foreign magistrate for a two-year period, a cruel man who administered everything to their liking,[65] they naturally terrorized everyone. The man treated many men unjustly, but two famous families of the time in particular: the Bardi and Frescobaldi. Incensed by this treatment, the leaders of these families conspired to take up arms suddenly and attack the magistrate and his supporters. When the day came for the attack to be carried out, the plot was reported to the priors. So the people were called to arms, as though the nobility were rising up against them. Against them the part of the nobility who felt themselves threatened seized arms and held the Oltrarno district, guarding the bridges with pickets. Their hope was that, if help arrived from abroad, they could easily invade the rest of the city from that district. Fear of this drove the people to forestall the nobles' hopes and plans. Thus the plebs of the Oltrarno rose up, and a large band from this side of the Arno, too, broke through by the lowest bridge and attacked the conspirators. At this, the conspirators began little by little to give way and retreat, mostly gathering around their own houses, until they lost hope and left the city on the following night.

After this the people put down their arms and turned to the 93 courts. Arraigned for criminal violence against the public, none of the noblemen appeared, and they were condemned in absentia; and their houses were demolished, greatly disfiguring the city.

aedesque illorum magna urbis deformitate subversae. Denique eo usque processum est severitatis, ut vel diligens opera dedita sit, ne qua sociorum amicorumve civitas profugos reciperet. Quod malo consilio factum haud multo post non contemnendum reipublicae attulit detrimentum. Exclusi siquidem ac repulsi a civitatibus amicorum, contra voluntatem propositumque animi, multa Deum hominesque testati, tandem coacti sunt sese ad Pisanos conferre; quae res secutis mox certaminibus multum obfuit civitati. Cives enim sic odendi sunt, ut tamen cives illos esse meminerimus.

94   Turbatam domi rempublicam externum mox excepit bellum. Parmam enim per hoc tempus Accius quidam parmensis e suprema et ipse nobilitate a Mastini dominatu avertit, auxilio fretus maxime principum mantuanorum. Itaque et bellum confestim inter Veronensem Mantuanumque renovatum est, et quia accessus ad urbem Lucam per agrum parmensem Mastino fuerat, praecisa iam ea facilitate,[117] apparebat Lucam ab eo teneri[118] non posse. Ea res Florentinos Pisanosque simul erexit studio Lucae potiundi. Duae erant conficiendi viae: una belli; altera pactionis. Bellum quo minus Florentini susciperent, obstabat novae pacis auctoritas; et simul erat metus, ne ille indignatione ex bello concepta ad Pisanos inclinaret. Itaque, ut minus gloriosa, sic magis certa visa est pactionis via. Quare viginti viri ad hoc ipsum cum potestate publica creati hanc viam secuti sunt. Sagax vero tyranni mens cum civitatum desideria odorasset, Luca venali hastae subiecta, licitationem augebat. Primum igitur certamen de pretio fuit; de quo ita contendebatur, ut appareret qui pecunia superati forent, eos ad arma esse ituros. Tandem, cum plus offerrent Florentini, tyrannus, velut libra ad pondus, inclinavit. Summa licitationis fuit CCL millium. At

Finally, the People's severity went so far as to take pains that no allied or friendly city should accept them as refugees. This piece of bad advice soon brought no inconsiderable damage to the state. For the men who were shut out and expelled from friendly cities were at last, against their will and intention, and after much calling of God and men to witness, compelled to betake themselves to the Pisans, a circumstance which soon proved a great obstacle to the city in the struggles that followed. We should remember that citizens, however odious, are still to be treated as citizens.[66]

A foreign war next befell the republic while it was in this state 94 of domestic turbulence. A certain Azzo of Parma, who was himself from the high nobility, at this time wrenched Parma from Mastino's lordship, relying most of all on help from the princes of Mantua. Thus war was immediately renewed between Verona and Mantua, and since Mastino's access to Lucca was via the territory of Parma, and that access was now cut off, it appeared that Mastino would not be able to hold on to Lucca. This circumstance aroused simultaneously the desire of both the Florentines and the Pisans to take control of Lucca. There were two ways of compassing that end: the way of war and the way of diplomatic agreement. The authority of the new peace treaty stood in the way of the Florentines' choosing war; and at the same time it was feared that Mastino would be angered by a war and would take the side of the Pisans. Thus the less glorious but certainly more secure path of diplomacy was approved. For this purpose a board of twenty men were created to pursue that avenue. But when the crafty mind of the tyrant sniffed out the desires of the two cities, he put Lucca up to auction, and so raised the bidding. The first quarrel was over price, about which there was so much contention that it appeared the losing side would take to arms. Finally, when the Florentines offered more, the tyrant inclined their way, as though weight had been put on a scale. The sum bid was 250,000 florins. But the Pisans, as soon as they realized that the matter was going the Flor-

Pisani, simul ac rem ad Florentinos inclinare senserunt, in arma vertuntur. Urebat enim propinquus Florentinorum metus; et faciebat animos quod Lucinus Vicecomes (is enim Accio nuper defuncto in principatu successerat) ceterique per Galliam Mastini hostes magna ultro pollicebantur auxilia. Itaque Mediolanensium, Mantuanorum, Parmensium, Patavinorum auxiliaribus acceptis, ipsi domestico equitatu peditatuque affatim addito Lucam circumsedere.

95   Id postquam a Florentinis intellectum est, nec erat iam dubium quin ea res ad arma spectaret, suas et ipsi copias expediunt, sociorum amicorumque auxilia rogant. Profecti cum omnibus copiis, ad Fucetium constitere. Inde missis ad Pisanos nunciis qui iuberent Luca absistere, cum illi nihilominus perstarent ac prope inexpugnabiliter castra communissent, consilium cepere pisanum agrum pervadendi. Itaque Arnum transgressi Pisas duxerunt, ac omnia circum urbem longe lateque popularunt; loca etiam quaedam munita ceperunt. Sed neque terror urbis neque vastatio agri neque castellorum expugnatio Pisanorum obstinatam mentem infringere valuit, quin perstantes in obsidione durarent. Itaque, cum nihil per eam viam se profecturos Florentini viderent, et imbres prope continui per hos ipsos dies quasi dedita opera turbarent, retro ad Fucetium duxerunt.

96   Mastinus inter haec per legatos postulabat, uti ne iam ultra differret Florentinus Lucam accipere, pecuniam solvere. Ea res agitata ex integro est, variantibus sententiis civium. Neque enim dubium erat quin honeste resilire a pactione liceret, urbe obsessa et castellis a Pisanis quibusdam captis. Itaque, illud ipsum iam libere in

entines' way, turned to arms. For their fear of having Florentines nearby was inflamed, and they were given courage by the promise of Luchino Visconti (who had now succeeded to the rulership following the death of Azzo) and the other enemies of Mastino in northern Italy to provide large reinforcements. So as soon as they had received reinforcements from Milan, Mantua, Parma and Padua and added their own ample supply of cavalry and infantry, they invested Lucca.

Once the Florentines learned of this, and there was no doubt   95 that the business was pointing to war, they, too, marshalled their troops and called for reinforcements from their allies and friends. Setting out with all their forces they came to a halt in Fucecchio. From there they sent out heralds to the Pisans, ordering them to leave Lucca. When the latter nonetheless refused to budge (and they had fortified their camp to make it almost impregnable), it was decided to invade Pisan territory. So they crossed the Arno and marched to Pisa, devastating the whole area far and wide around the city; they also took some fortified positions. But neither terror for their city nor devastation of their territory nor capture of their castles was able to shake the Pisans' obstinate intention to persist in the siege. Thus, when the Florentines saw that there was no profit in this course of action, and almost continuous rain throughout that time, as though on purpose, disrupted their operations, they marched back to Fucecchio.

Meanwhile Mastino was demanding through his envoys that   96 the Florentines not put off any longer taking possession of Lucca and paying the money. This demand led to renewed discussion, and a variety of opinions were expressed by the citizenry. There was no doubt that they could back out of the agreement honorably, given that the city was besieged and certain castles had been captured by the Pisans. So there was unrestricted debate on the issue whether they should take possession of Lucca, even besieged as it was, or abandon the whole enterprise. Finally the view that

consultationem veniebat suscipienda ne foret Luca et[119] sic obsessa, an totum huiusmodi coeptum relinquendum. Vicit tandem ea pars quae ad dignitatem potior videbatur, quasi turpe esset coeptum omittere. Illud modo provisum assentiente tyranno, ut ob praesentes difficultates septuaginta millibus de priori summa detractis, Luca[120] uti tunc erat, ita reciperetur. Horum gratia obsides dati, adolescentes primarii, Ferrariae mansuri donec promissa complerentur. Solutionibus vero taxata intervallis tempora.

97 His conventis sollemniter firmatisque, quod reliquum erat ad suspiciendam urbem ire placuit. Profecti cum omnibus copiis, in colle qui Lucae imminet castra fecerunt. Pisani ante Florentinorum adventum trina circum Lucam muniverant castra; tunc autem ob praesentiam hostis se contrahentes, in una magis parte continebant. Ea res facultatem nostris praebuit urbis recipiendae. Quare delectis e toto exercitu equitibus trecentis, quingentis vero peditibus, dedito inter se signo, unum sub tempus et a Luca et a Florentinorum castris ad munitiones Pisanorum impetum fecerunt; hisque ab ea parte disiectis, Lucam intrarunt. Cum his[121] copiis legati tres ad recipiendam profecti: Iohannes Bernardini filius Medix, Naddus[122] Oricella et Ricciardus Riccius. Hi, pecunia (sic enim convenerat) Mastini militibus qui in praesidio erant[123] persoluta, urbem arcemque susceperunt.

98 Recepta igitur Luca ingenti laetitia et gratulatione, de tutanda iam cogitabatur. Praesidium erat validum; urbs munitissima rerum suppeditabat copia; itaque vel lenta expectatione perfringere licebat Pisanorum conatus, qui et duobus amplius mensibus steterant

seemed more honorable triumphed, as though to abandon an enterprise were shameful. The only provisos, agreed to by the tyrant, were that 70,000 florins should be knocked off the earlier price in view of the present difficulties, and that Lucca should be taken "as is." As security they were to hand over some noble youths, to remain as hostages in Ferrara until the promised sum was paid; for the payments were to be made in installments.[67]

Once the agreement was solemnly signed and sealed, it was decided to proceed with what remained: taking possession of the city. Setting out with all their troops, they pitched camp on a hill overlooking Lucca. Before the Florentines arrived the Pisans had constructed triple fortified camps around the city, but at that time, owing to the presence of the enemy, they drew together and kept mostly to one part of the fortifications. This situation afforded our troops the chance to take possession of the city. So three hundred knights and five hundred infantry were picked from the whole army, and when the signal was given they attacked the Pisan fortifications simultaneously from Lucca and from the Florentine camp. Once the defenses in that area were thrown down, they entered Lucca. With these troops were three envoys[68] sent to take possession of the city: Giovanni di Bernardino de' Medici, Naldo Rucellai, and Ricciardo de' Ricci. These men, as agreed, paid the money to Mastino's soldiers who were in the garrison and took control of the city and the citadel.[69]

Having taken possession of Lucca with great happiness and rejoicing, they now turned their thoughts to defending it. The garrison was strong, the city was well-fortified and well-supplied, so it was quite possible to break the Pisan siege by waiting it out. The Pisans had already been besieging it for more than two months, and their spirits were low and shattered by the Florentine takeover of the city. But a rash and arrogant counsel won the day, for they considered themselves to have done nothing unless they had expelled the enemy by force and fighting. Thus on the eighth day af-

97

98

1341

in obsidione et, quoniam recepta iam a Florentinis erat, fractis debilitatisque iacebant animis. Sed vicit superbum praecepsque consilium, nil actum existimantibus, nisi hostis vi et manu pelleretur. Quare, octavo post receptionem die, e colle quo prius constiterant descendentes, ad fluvium Auserim fecerunt castra, procul ab hoste non amplius mille passibus; inde postridie prima luce copias producunt, potestatemque pugnandi hostibus faciunt. Pisani, cum sibi pugnandum viderent, partem valli ad Florentinos versam sustulerunt fossasque complanarunt; mox productis copiis aciem struxere. Triplici subsidio Pisanorum acies stetit. Primum antesignani equites ad octingentos delecti; hos sagittarii utrinque cingebant; post hos signa stabant cum omni robore virorum. Tertium fuit expeditum agmen, cui reprimere obsessos, si forte ex urbe in castra eruptionem facere conarentur, mandatum erat. Florentinorum vero duo tantum fuerunt agmina. Unum antesignanorum, in quo fortissimi e toto exercitu delecti equites ad mille ducentos. Hos tria sagittariorum millia cinxerunt. Post hos signa cum omni robore equitum peditumque affatim structa.

99 Ut igitur occanuerunt classica, terribili inter se congressu[124] conflixerunt antesignanorum acies, dureque et atrociter aliquandiu pugnarunt. Tandem superantibus Florentinis, Pisanorum antesignani terga verterunt seque ad maiorem aciem ubi signa stabant receperunt. In eam quoque velut procella quaedam secuti victores, primo statim impetu ita turbarunt, ut et signa prosternerent et ducem exercitus cum aliquot proceribus caperent. In his fuit Arrigus Castruci filius et supremi quidam Pisanorum, exules quoque Florentinorum aliqui. Victoria haud dubie parta erat, si alterum agmen prosecutum fuisset, sed stetit immobile, nec post suos incessit. Itaque, quo magis retulerat pedem hostis,[125] eo plus a suis

ter taking possession of the city they came down from the hill on which they had halted earlier and pitched camp by the river Serchio, not more than a mile from the enemy. From there at dawn on the following day they sent out their troops and challenged the enemy to battle. The Pisans, realizing that they had to fight, removed the part of the earthwork facing the Florentines, and levelled the fosse; then, bringing out their troops, they set up their order of battle. The Pisan line had three ranks. The first consisted of an elite striking force of eight hundred knights flanked by archers on both sides; behind them stood the standards and the main body of men. The third line was lightly armed, and was instructed to hold back the besieged if any of them should try to make a sally from the city into the camp. The Florentines had only two ranks: an elite striking force consisting of twelve hundred of the bravest and strongest knights in the whole army. These were flanked by three thousand archers. Behind them were the standards with the main body of horse and foot arrayed in ample numbers.

So as the trumpets sounded, the front ranks of both armies 99 came together with a terrifying clash; the fighting was long, hard, and bitter. Finally the Florentines got the better of them and the Pisan elite turned tail, joining the main body of troops with the standards. The victorious Florentines stormed after them and with their first attack threw their ranks into such confusion that their standards were knocked down and the commander of their army captured along with several other leaders. Among them was Arrigo, son of Castruccio, certain high-ranking Pisans, and some of the Florentine exiles as well. They would undoubtedly have had a victory if the other line had followed, but it stood immobile and did not march after its own troops. Thus, the further the enemy retreated, the more the front rank of the Florentines, separated from the main body, was outnumbered. So, pushed back to their last rank, the Pisans formed a dense mass, and by fighting the sin-

disiuncta Florentinorum prima acies, impar tantae molis fuit. Quare conglobati ad extremum agmen Pisani, toto simul exercitu adversus unam aciem dimicantes, illam profligarunt. Alterum vero Florentinorum agmen nec se pugnae admiscuit nec quemquam amisit, sed fuga protinus arrepta Pisciam aufugit. Ex prima vero acie plurimi caesi captique sunt. Fuerunt etiam qui munitiones trangressi Lucam refugerunt. Captivi vero Pisanorum omnes servati, praeter Iohannem Vicecomitem pisani exercitus ducem, qui ad signa captus ac inde ad maius Florentinorum agmen traductus, in ipsa fuga Pisciam tractus est.

100 Florentiae confestim delatus rumor multo quam fuerant atrociora vulgarat; caesum exercitum omnem, deletas funditus copias, signa ab hostibus capta murmur fuit. Sed ubi salva esse signa ac supra duas exercitus partes incolumes esse auditum est, resumptis rursum animis, ad studium reparandarum virium convertuntur. In primis, ut durioribus fere in rebus fieri consuevit, ad Robertum regem respicere, et aliquem ex regio genere cum auxilio postulare. Cum ea peterentur, ultro rex ipse Lucam per legatos de Florentinis repetiit, sua dudum cum esset, a Fagiolano per vim occupatam ostendens. Nec latuit florentinum populum id eo consilio a rege fieri, quo mittendi subsidii onus averteretur. Itaque suis illum vaframentis aggressi, dedere se illi Lucam responderunt. Eam tamen ob rem non ultra motus est rex, quam ut legatos mitteret qui ex auctoritate regia agerent cum Pisanis, ut Lucam, suam utique veterem urbem et nunc a Florentinis restitutam, oppugnare desisterent. Sed vana regis postulatio vanioribus item verbis delusa est a Pisanis. Nullo enim alio responso dato quam se de ea re legatos ad regem missuros, obsidionem pertinacius quam ante sunt persecuti.

gle Florentine rank simultaneously with their whole army, they put them to flight. The other Florentine rank did not join the battle or lose anyone, but immediately fled and took refuge in Pescia. Many from the front line were killed and captured. There were also some who crossed the defenses and took refuge in Lucca. The Pisans saved all of their men who had been taken captive with the exception of Giovanni Visconti, their commander. He had been captured by the standards and, having been brought back to the main Florentine line, he was dragged off to Pescia in the Florentine flight.[70]

Reported immediately in Florence, the rumor spread of a disaster far worse than the actual battle: it was whispered that the whole army had been slaughtered; the troops completely wiped out; the standards taken by the enemy. But when it was learned that the standards had been saved and more than two thirds of the army was safe, people recovered their spirits and turned their attention to rebuilding their strength. First of all, as usual when they were in a tight spot, they looked to King Robert and requested a royal scion to come to their aid. When this request had been lodged, the king himself through his envoys countered by asking the Florentines for Lucca, which, he explained, had long been his, though Uguccione della Faggiuola had occupied it by force. The Florentine People were well aware that the king had made this request with the purpose of evading the burden of sending aid. So, using his same wiles, they replied that they would give Lucca up to him. But the king's only response was to send out envoys under royal authority to plead with the Pisans to stop laying siege to Lucca, a city that in earlier times had been absolutely his and that had now been restored to him by the Florentines. But this empty demand of the king was mocked by still emptier words from the Pisans. For it elicited no response except that the Pisans sent envoys of their own to negotiate the matter, while they prosecuted the siege more obstinately than before.[71]

100

101   Per idem tempus suspicio ingens fuit apud Arretinos, ne Sacon, rebus adversis florentini populi elatus, tyrannidem rursus invaderet. Nam affectare quidem illum nemo dubitabat, quoniam ante regnare consuesset; rediisse vero adversarios in urbem et ante oculos versari suos, nonnunquam etiam verbis insectari, anxie ferre putabatur. Crescente igitur suspicione cives praesidem adeunt, periculum ostendunt. Trahitur in sententiam praes et arma capere iubet. Illi correptis armis Saconem circumsistunt. Capiuntur multi praeterea diversae factionis; multi ob eas suspiciones ablegantur.

102   Capitur etiam Lucae Tarlatus Saconis frater. Is enim nuper cum aliqua manu equitum peditumque in expeditionem florentini populi profectus, commisso proelio, inter antesignanos egregie dimicaverat; qui, postquam a Pisanis victores ipsi, ut diximus, victi sunt, per medios hostium cuneos sibi via gladio facta, Lucam aufugit, ibique cum ceteris obsessus[126] remansit. Hic, quia expers omnis culpae credebatur, et quia in proelio ipso et obsidione egregia virtute erat cognitus, honestiori genere captivitatis sine carcere asservabatur. Itaque non multo post, dum una cum Iohanne Medice praefecto praesidii extra Lucae portam equitaret, concito repente equo, ad Pisanos transfugit. Ob eas res Sacon et agnati qui cum illo capti erant, Florentiam ducti, carceri mancipantur; bellumque his de causis in Arretinis suscitatum est, frequentibus illorum castellis rebellantibus. Ad id bellum Ricciardus Cancellarius eques pistoriensis dux missus, armata Arretinorum multitudine. Bibienam ceteraque Saconis castella infesto milite populatus est, domosque eius familiae intra urbem insigni magnificentia aedificatas evertit.

At the same time great suspicion arose among the Aretines that   101
Saccone, encouraged by the misfortunes of the Florentine People,
might reestablish his tyranny. No one doubted that he longed for
it, as he had grown used to ruling before; he was thought to be an-
guished at the return of his enemies to the city before his very
eyes, enemies who would sometimes even insult him. So as suspicion grew, the citizens went before the rector[72] and explained the
danger. The rector was brought over to their view, and he ordered
them to take up arms. Seizing arms, they surrounded Saccone.
Many Ghibellines were also taken, and many were banished owing
to these suspicions.

At Lucca, Tarlato, Saccone's brother, was also being held. He   102
had lately joined the campaign of the Florentine People with a
force of horse and foot, had taken part in the battle, and had distinguished himself fighting in the front rank. After the victors
themselves had been vanquished by the Pisans in the way we have
described, he cut a path for himself with his sword through the
enemy shields and took refuge in Lucca, remaining under seige
there with the rest. Because he was believed to be free of all guilt
and had been recognized for his exceptional gallantry in the battle
and the siege, he was kept in honorable captivity and not put in
prison. So soon thereafter, when he was out riding before the gate
of Lucca with Giovanni de' Medici, the captain of the garrison, he
suddenly spurred his horse and deserted to the Pisans. Thanks to
this, Saccone and the relatives who had been taken with him were
brought to Florence and thrown into prison; and on this account
civil war was revived in Aretine territory, and their densely
populated castles were in a state of rebellion. Ricciardo Cancellieri,
a knight from Pistoia, was sent as the Florentine military commander, and the populace of Arezzo was armed. Bibbiena and
other castles belonging to Saccone were devastated by military
forces, and the homes of his family inside the city, constructed
with exceptional magnificence, were torn down.[73]

103   Dum haec in Arretinis geruntur, Florentini in Lucam versi, de ulciscenda clade servandaque urbe cogitabant. Cum ergo urgerent obsidionem Pisani, auxiliaque ab rege sperata nequaquam esse ventura appareret, Florentini hoc regis factum gravissime indignabantur et circumspiciebant oculis, si quem asciscere possent in belli societatem.

104   Forte per id tempus Ludovicus, qui romani imperatoris nomen insigniaque invaserat, transmissis Alpibus, redierat Tridentum. Ad hunc, Mastino auctore adhortatoreque, Florentini legatos miserunt. Is singulari in Pisanos erat odio ob superiorem defectionem, et coire foedus cum Florentinis cupiebat. Erat quoque Roberti regis pontificisque romani manifestissimus hostis; sed tamen civitas indignatione accensa nihil non factura putabatur. Huius rei in dies[127] subcrescens fama multos conterruit, quasi turbatis rebus Florentini per Ludovici favorem a Roberto et pontifice dissidentes, bello tandem adversus illos implicarentur.

105   Societates Florentinorum permultae ac maximae in Roberti regno et Galliarum partibus integra ad eam diem fide negotiabantur. Apud has magna pecuniarum vis, cum iampridem variis ex causis fuisset, unum sub tempus ob natum hinc metum, repetentibus cunctis, fidem abrumpere coactae sunt cum incredibili damno civitatis. Nec tamen coivit cum Ludovico Florentinus. Etsi enim res peropportuna videbatur, vicit tamen ad extremum partium respectus, ac per se potius conari statuit. Quamobrem duo millia equitum mercede conducta; ex Bononiensibus vero ac Ferrariensibus sexcentos, a Mastino quingentos coegere. Ad hoc domestico equitatu peditatuque addito, magnum exercitum compararunt. Copiis

While this was going on in Arezzo, the Florentines turned to   103
Lucca and gave their attention to avenging the defeat and saving
the city. Since the Pisans were pressing ahead with the siege, and it
was evident that the hoped-for royal reinforcements were not going to come, the Florentines became outraged at the king's behavior and looked about to see whether they could forge another military alliance.

At this time Ludwig, who had usurped the name and insignia   104
of the Roman emperor, chanced to have crossed the Alps and returned to Trent. At Mastino's urging and advice, the Florentines
sent envoys to him. He nurtured a deep hatred for the Pisans owing to their earlier desertion of his cause, and was eager to join a
league with the Florentines. He was also an undisguised enemy of
King Robert and the Roman pontiff, but the city, boiling with indignation, was ready to do anything. The story of this alliance,
spreading day by day, terrified many, who believed that the Florentines, with their affairs in an uproar, were becoming alienated from
Robert and the pope thanks to Ludwig's favor, and would in the
end become involved in a war against them.

The Florentines had a great many large businesses operating in   105
Robert's kingdom and in France. Up to that day, they had enjoyed
full credit. For a long time they had been holding large sums of
money for various reasons, and thanks to the fear that had arisen
[of an alliance between the emperor and the Florentines], all their
depositors wanted their money back at the same time. They were
thus forced to default, with an incredible monetary loss to the city.
Yet the Florentines had not joined Ludwig. For although the alliance offered great advantages, in the end regard for party alliances
won out, and they decided to campaign by themselves. On this account they hired two thousand knights; and they mustered six
hundred from the Bolognese and Ferrarese and five hundred from
Mastino. To this force they added their own horse and foot, assembling a great army. They put Malatesta of Rimini, the most

autem ducendis belloque administrando praefectus est Malatesta ariminensis, vir per eam tempestatem in primis clarus.

106   Quarto Nonas octobris accepta clades proelii fuerat. Legationibus mittendis apparatibusque faciendis cum hiems intervenisset, necessario in futurum ver expeditio est dilata. Id ubi venit, Florentia moventes, per Nebulam fluvium ad hostem duxerunt; cumque in conspectum venissent, castra in colle supereminenti fecerunt, procul ab hoste quinque millibus passuum. Pisanis fortunam pugnae nequaquam experiri[128] propositum erat, seque intra munitiones continebant. Itaque, scrutandis sagaciter locis tentandisque hostium animis aliquot diebus consumptis, tandem, in plana descendentes loca, aciem castris hostium admoverunt, conati si qua pellicere ad proelium possent. Cum vero a Pisanis nemo prodiret, satis ad speciem actum existimantes, perrumpere in urbem aggrediuntur, commeatumque ad id paratum importare. Munitiones et fossae ab hostibus de industria factae impediebant omnia, ut etiam sine repugnantia transeundum si esset, difficillima tamen et anxia foret transitio; hoste vero custodiente armato traducere impedimenta impossibile videbatur.

107   Quare ad dexteram flectentes, per Auserim fluvium transire contenderunt. His quoque locis difficultates oriebantur. Duo erant pontes in Auseri quibus ad urbem iri posset; horum utrumque hostis tenebat munimentisque comprehenderat. Florentini ergo inter utrumque pontem delecto loco, maxime contra urbem castra fecere, eo consilio ut postridie structi paratique vado traiicerent. Id eo facilius erat, quod amnis ibi scissus in brachia insulam facit, nec integer uno alveo, sed imminutus distractusque procurrit. Hac igi-

distinguished soldier of the time, in charge of leading the troops and managing the war.[74]

The Florentines' defeat in battle had taken place on the fourth of November. Since winter interrupted the sending of envoys and preparations for war, the campaign was necessarily put off to the next spring. When that season came, they left Florence and marched along the river Nievole to the enemy; and when they came in sight of them, they pitched camp high on a hill overlooking the city, about five miles distant from the foe. The Pisans had no intention whatever of trying the fortune of battle and kept behind their defenses. So the Florentines spent several days keenly reconnoitring the area and testing the courage of the enemy. Finally they came down onto the plain and moved their battle-line up to the enemy camp with the aim of drawing them into a fight. But when no one came out of the Pisan camp, the Florentines reckoned they had done enough for appearances' sake, and set about breaking into the city and bringing in the supplies they had prepared for its relief. But the defenses and trenches blocked any attempt, having been intentionally constructed so that crossing them would be difficult and dangerous even without opposition; and to bring baggage through them with an armed host standing guard seemed perfectly impossible.

So they moved off to the north and tried to cross the Nievole. Here too difficulties arose. There were two bridges over the Nievole on roads leading up to the city; the enemy held both of them and had ringed them with defenses. The Florentines therefore chose a place between the two bridges, directly opposite the city, and there pitched camp. Their plan was to cross by a ford on the day following in full battle array. This was all the easier in that the river at that point broke in two, forming an island between its branches, so that it ran, not in one deep bed, but through shallows and multiple channels. So with this hope they quietly awaited the light, making ready the bundles and provisions which were to be

106

1342

107

tur spe quiescentes lucem expectarunt, sarcinasque et commeatum expedierunt,[129] quae in urbem traducerentur. Ea nocte imbres assidui cadentes flumen sic auxerunt, ut transeundi vado nulla esset facultas. Quamobrem quatriduo iisdem in locis retenti, spatium dedere hostibus adversam sibi ripam muniendi. Itaque redeunte postea serena luce alveoque decrescente, munitionibus et concursu hostium impediti, frustra transire conati sunt, desperatoque demum transitu, abscedere compelluntur. Post haec in agrum pisanum transgressae copiae foeda populatione cuncta vastarunt. Sed Pisani nihilo ob eam rem commoti in obsidione perstiterunt, certa iam fiducia urbis potiundi.

108   Dum haec in Pisanis geruntur, Arretinorum exules contracta in unum multitudine paulo ante lucem ad urbem venerunt. Ibi locum nacti custodibus vacuum, qua fluvius[130] secans moenia in agrum exit, urbem subito intrarunt. Fuerunt autem hominum ad tria millia. Cum urbem pervadere coepissent, exciti eo tumultu cives arma corripiunt, seseque cohortantes[131] impetum faciunt. Proelium fuit atrox, multaeque utrinque caedes; sed tandem superati exules, per ea ipsa quibus paulo prius intraverant loca praecipites aguntur. Capta sunt de exulibus vexilla sex; praeterea intercepti complures, de quibus supplicium est postea sumptum. Ceciderunt autem illo proelio[132] Arretinorum insignes viri duo, quorum virtute ea nocte urbs plurimum defensa fuerat: Lucius Guasco et Cincius Branca. Hi cum adversum exules fortiter dimicarent, interfecti sunt; praeterea optimus quisque et fortissimus civium vulneratus. Ob eius noctis periculum, omnes ghibellinae factionis homines qui reliqui erant in urbe expelluntur.

109   At hi qui Lucae praeerant[133] Florentini, cum neque ad se deferri commeatum posse, neque moveri Pisanos ob vastationem agri viderent, necessitate coacti, deditionem facere constituunt. Quare

taken into the city. That night, heavy rains fell which swelled the river, making it impossible to ford. On this account they clung to their position for four days, giving the enemy time to fortify the opposite bank. Thus by the time clear skies returned and the depth of the river fell, they were blocked by defense-works and the arrival of enemy troops. In vain they tried to cross. At length they despaired of crossing and were forced to leave. After this, the troops passed into Pisan territory and created foul devastation everywhere. But this failed to dislodge the Pisans, and the latter stuck to their siege, sure now in their confidence that the city would be theirs.[75]

While this was going on the Pisan front, the Aretine exiles, 108 gathering together in a single multitude, came to that city before dawn. There they found an unguarded place where a stream cuts through the walls and exits into the countryside, and in this way they suddenly entered the city. They numbered about three thousand men. When they had begun to spread out through the city, the citizens were awakened by the uproar, seized arms, and exhorting one another, attacked the invaders. The battle was ferocious with many casualties on both sides, but in the end the exiles were beaten and were driven headlong out through the very places they had entered shortly before. Six standards were taken from the exiles; and a great number of them were captured and executed. There fell also in this battle two distinguished Aretines to whose courage the city's defense owed much that night: Lucio de' Guaschi and Cencio Branca. These men were killed fighting bravely against the exiles; and the best and bravest citizens were all wounded. Owing to the peril of that night, all members of the Ghibelline faction left in the city were expelled.

But the Florentines ruling in Lucca, seeing that provisions 109 could not be brought to them, nor could the Pisans be dislodged by devastating their territory, were compelled by necessity and decided to surrender. So it was agreed that the garrison might with-

pacti ut incolume praesidium abducere liceret, urbem reliquerunt Pisanis nono fere mense postquam fuerat recepta. Nullo unquam bello magis dehonestatum est florentini populi nomen.

110   Et traxit mox ignominia foris accepta aliud domi dedecus maius. Quasi enim ira quaedam caelitus premeret, tyrannus (quod nunquam ante fuerat) civitati impositus, libertate sublata, in civium sanguinem desaevivit. Nam amissa Luca cives male concordes atque (ut rebus fit adversis) superiora errata alii aliis obiectantes, spreta belli cura, simultatibus odiisque secum ipsi pugnabant. Viginti viros, quibus auctoribus empta nuper Luca bellumque erat susceptum, populus sic oderat, ut ne nomen quidem sine execratione sustineret audire. Horum existimatio non publice modo, verum etiam privatim per vicos et compita lacerabatur.[134] Malatestae quoque ducis, qui bello praefuerat gerendo, quia parum successerat, non satis nomen erat acceptum. Ita fato quodam impellente alter qui rebus praeesset quaerebatur.

111   Gualterius erat gallus, claro natus genere, quem nudo inanique titulo Athenarum Ducem vocitabant. Hunc, nuper fervente bello cum Neapoli applicuisset, cognito Florentinorum conatu, amor cepit in expeditionem veniendi. Fuerat enim per tempora castruciani belli Florentiae commoratus cum Carolo Roberti regis filio, moresque civitatis et homines norat. Quare invitatus a florentinis civibus, alacri se animo ad iter paravit, pervenitque ad exercitum cum parva equitum manu ea ipsa die, qua Malatesta dux, e colle quo castra fecerat descendens, structas copias hostium castris admovit.

draw unmolested, leaving the city to the Pisans about nine months after they had taken possession of it. No war ever did more to bring the Florentine name into dishonor.

And the ignominy suffered abroad drew after it another, still greater disgrace at home. As though heaven's wrath sought to crush her, a tyrant was imposed on the city—something that had never happened before—who took away her liberty and lusted for the blood of her citizens. For with the loss of Lucca the citizens were at odds with each other, and (as always happens when things go wrong) they each blamed the other for the errors of the war. Spurning their military responsibilities, they fought one another, breeding feuds and hatreds. The board of twenty men who had been responsible for buying Lucca and undertaking the war were so hated by the People that it could not bear even to hear their names without cursing them. Their reputations were torn to shreds not only in public, but in private as well, in the streets and alleys. The name of Malatesta, who had been their commander in the campaign, was also unpopular owing to his ill success. And so, as though fate were driving them to it, they began to seek another man to take charge of their affairs.[76]

Walter was a Frenchman born of noble stock, whom they used to call by the unadorned and empty title, "Duke of Athens."[77] He had come to Naples not long ago when war was brewing, and learning of the Florentines' enterprise, he was seized with a desire to join the campaign. During the period of the Castruccian war he had lived in Florence with Charles, son of King Robert, and had come to know the ways of the city and its people. Thus, when invited by the citizens of Florence he readied himself for the journey with alacrity, and joined the army with a small force of cavalry. This was on the very day when Malatesta, the commander, came down from the hill where he had encamped and advanced in formation on the enemy camps. Walter earned no small commenda-

110

111

In exercitu autem vigilando et impigre res obeundo, commendationem sibi non exiguam comparavit.

112   Ita et nobilitatis favore et virtutis opinione sublevatus in hac difficultate temporum et discordia civium, quasi idoneus rebus sanandis, cum potestate legitima praeficitur urbi ac belli cura sibi demandatur. Domi igitur militiaeque potestatem nactus, volvere multa secum et cogitare coepit, quemadmodum pro arbitrio dominari posset. Vir enim gallus et Galliarum moribus assuetus, ubi plebs paene servorum habetur loco, nomina artium artificumque ridebat; multitudinis arbitrio regi civitatem ridiculum existimabat. Faciebat vero animos discordia civium plenaeque odiorum mentes. Primo nobilitatem duris legibus obnoxiam, iniquo animo constituta ferentem, suam fore totam arbitrabatur, propterea quod quae pars civitatis premitur, ea semper novas res consuevit optare. Tenues vero et opifices ac totam illam civitatis turbam nullum negotium putabat ad se traducere; nullam enim iis[135] neque dignitatis neque libertatis curam intelligebat esse.

113   Restabat medius populus. In eo difficultas omnis versabatur. Igitur in hunc audendum putans, homines proximo lucensi negotio versatos atque ob id recenti infamia flagrantes arripi iubet. Ex his Iohannem Medicem florentinum equitem securi percuti iubet. Naddo autem Oricellae et Ricciardo Riccio, qui item Lucae cum potestate publica fuerant, eidem supplicio destinatis, summis civium precibus vitam largitus est, grandiori tamen pecunia multatis. Obiectum est alteri, quod pecunias a Pisanis accepisset; utrique, quod rempublicam in quaestura fraudasset. Post haec, Guilielmum Altovitam capit, extremoque supplicio afficit. Causa adscripta quod, dum Arretio praefuit, multa ob pecuniam nefaria commisisset.

tion for himself in the army thanks to his vigilance and energy in taking on tasks.

Thus, in this difficult and fractious period he was raised up by 112 the favor of the nobility and by his own reputation for courage and ability. Considered the right man to cure the city's ills, he was legitimately put in charge of the city and the responsibility for military affairs was also entrusted to him. Having acquired power in domestic and military affairs, he began to scheme and plot how he might acquire untrammeled lordship over the city. Being a Frenchmen and used to the ways of France, where the common people are considered to be almost slaves, he laughed at the authority of the guilds and guildsmen, and thought it absurd that the will of the multitude should rule a city.[78] He was encouraged by Florence's civic discords and animosities. First, he thought that the nobility would be completely on his side, subject as they were to harsh laws and discontented with their legal position;[79] any oppressed element in a city will always be ripe for revolution. He thought it would be no trouble to bring over to his side the poor, the workers, and that whole rabble; for he knew they had no interest in honor or liberty.

There remained the middle classes. His whole difficulty lay 113 with them. So, thinking to act boldly against them, he arrested the men involved in the late war for Lucca, who on that account were in desperate disgrace. Of these he ordered Giovanni de' Medici, the Florentine knight, to be beheaded. He planned the same punishment for Naldo Rucellai and Ricciardo de' Ricci, who had also served as governors of Lucca, but then spared them at the city's entreaty; nevertheless, they were fined large sums of money. One of them was charged with taking money from the Pisans, and both were accused of defrauding the state in matters of finance. After this, he arrested Guglielmo Altoviti and executed him. The cause alleged was that he had been bribed to commit numerous misdeeds while governor of Arezzo.

114   Hanc eius sive crudelitatem sive saevitiam in civibus puniendis multitudo usque adeo laetis excipiebat animis, ut palam gratularetur. Hunc virum fortem, hunc interritum[136] praedicabat; ceteros magistratus potentiorum satellites carnificesque venisse; hunc unum repertum qui in potentiores ipsos animadvertere non formidarat. His vocibus ubique nomen eius celebrabat tollebatque multitudo; ac, si quando per urbem incederet, laudibus acclamationibusque prosequebatur. Accedebat nobilitatis favor, ut verbis occultior, sic ad agendum efficacior. Optimates etiam quidam vel metu publico vel privata familiaritate sese illi addixerant; et iam suadebant multi totius civitatis frena capessere. Ipse quoque in spem elatus, non dubitabat cupiditatem animi prae se ferre. Modus tantum facinori quaerebatur.

115   Priores qui tunc erant, viri integri libertatisque tenaces, varie per illius fautores tentati, non modo non concedebant, sed etiam repugnabant aperte. Quare alia ingrediendum ratus, in concionem populum vocat. Hoc facit per praeconem, cum iam advesperasceret. Concio in crastinum erat futura; neutrum erat obscurum, nec quid ille vellet nec quid multitudo sentiret. Itaque priores curis anxii per noctem ad eum conveniunt; queruntur palam de vocatione populi; ostendunt se inconsultis nihil tale factum oportuisse. Ille contra verba dat: populum quae velit declarare posse; aliter non libertatem populi sed servitutem esse. Tandem ita deciditur, ut proxima concione imperium sibi priores in annum decernant, iisdem exceptionibus quibus Carolo Roberti regis filio fuerat ante concessum. His compositis, ad multam noctem priores discedunt.

This cruelty or savagery of his in punishing citizens was re-   114
ceived by the multitude with such happy hearts that they openly
rejoiced. They described him as "that brave fellow", "that fearless
man"; the other magistrates (they said) turned into pawns and ex-
ecutioners of the powerful; they found him to be the only one who
was unafraid to punish even the powerful themselves. The multitude celebrated and extolled his name everywhere, and whenever
he passed through the city he was accompanied by shouts of praise
and acclaim. The nobility also accorded him their favor, which was
less noisy but more effective. For certain of the optimates attached
themselves to him, either through fear of the public or because of
private relationships; and many of them were now urging him to
take the reins of the city completely into his hands. He too was
elated by his hopes and did not disguise his desires. The only
thing lacking was a means to carry out the deed.

The priors of that time were men of integrity and tenacious of   115
liberty; and though variously tempted by his supporters, they not
only did not yield, but even openly fought against him. So, reckoning he should enter the public palace by another route, he summoned the people to an assembly. He did this through a herald at
sundown. The assembly was to be held the following day, and
there was no doubt what he wanted and what the multitude
thought. So the priors grew anxious and came to him during the
night; they registered frank complaints about his summoning of
the people; they explained that he should have done no such thing
without consulting them. He replied that the people should be
able to declare their wishes; otherwise they had no liberty, only
servitude. Finally it was decided that in the assembly the following
day the priors would declare him empowered for one year under
the same limits and exceptions that had earlier been conceded to
Charles, the son of King Robert. Having made these arrangements, the priors departed late into the night.[80]

116   Postridie orto sole concio aderat frequens. Gualterium in concionem venientem multi e nobilitate comitati sunt; quidam etiam populares illius fautores circumstabant; arma vestes contegebant. Ubi in concionem ventum est, priores pro rostris sedentes medium exceperunt; assurgensque unus e prioribus concionari coepit; ea rogaturus populum quae per noctem convenissent. Vix principia orationis ingresso, cerdones et opifices ac tota illa civitatis fex ab extrema concionis parti acclamare coepit ac dominum sine ulla exceptione esse iubere. Suscipitur a fautoribus eius clamor, ac secunda per comitium aura discurrit. Ita, concione tota acclamante, priores decepti ac metu perculsi conticuerunt, ultra repugnare non ausi. Gualterium autem principes nobilitatis sublatum manibus palatio intulerunt in sedeque constituerunt.

117   Factus per hunc modum dominus, et quid post haec gesserit et quamdiu regnarit est a nobis explicandum. Res enim digna est literis annotetur vel pro admonitu civium vel pro castigatione regnantium. Apparebit enim civibus nihil magis formidandum esse quam servitutem; dominantibus vero nihil magis ad ruinam tendere quam immoderatam incivilemque superbiam.

118   Parto igitur ut voluerat dominatu, de servando iam illo cura supererat. Huius autem gratia, et foris et domi multa duxit providendum. Itaque, statim per legatos Arretii et Pistorii concionibus advocatis, imperium a populis earum civitatum suscepit, non iam florentini populi nomine, sed sui ipsius. Id astuto admodum consilio factum, quo sibi benevolentia aliqua devinciret civitates: existimavit enim velut beneficium se conferre, si quae dudum Florentinis subessent, eas aequa conditione cum Florentinis redderet, nec [ipse] per alios sed per se ipse voluntariis dominaretur.

The following day the sun rose on a crowded assembly. Walter   116
arrived at the assembly accompanied by many nobles; certain of
his popular supporters also surrounded him; and he concealed
arms beneath his clothing. On his arrival the priors seated him in
the middle of the ringhiera,[81] and one of the priors arose to open
the assembly, with the intention of asking the people to approve
what had been agreed to during the night. He had scarcely begun
when the artisans and workmen and the whole rabble of the city
from a distant corner of the piazza began shouting and commanding that Walter be made their lord unconditionally. The cry was
taken up by his supporters and spread throughout the assembly as
by a favorable wind. Thus, with the whole assembly shouting at
once, the priors fell silent, deceived and stricken with fear, not daring to fight on any longer. The leaders of the nobility raised Walter up with their hands and carried him into the palace, placing
him in the seat of power.[82]

That was how he became the lord of Florence. We must now   117
explain what he did after this and for how long he reigned. The
subject is worth putting on record both as a warning to citizens
and as a reproof to rulers. For it will become clear that citizens
should fear nothing more than servitude, and lords will learn that
nothing is more ruinous than immoderate and uncivil arrogance.

Having, then, acquired lordship as he wished, Walter's next   118
concern was preserving it. On this account he made numerous
provisions both abroad and at home. Accordingly, by means of envoys he at once summoned assemblies in Arezzo and Pistoia, and
was granted power by the peoples of those cities, not in the name
of the Florentine People, but in his own name. It was an extremely
astute idea he had to bind those cities to himself by an act of good
will, for he reckoned he would be taken as conferring a benefit if
he put those cities, long subject to Florentines, on equal terms
with Florence; they would voluntarily accept his personal rule, and
he would not have to rule them through others.

119   Post haec bellum tollere adortus, de pace cum Pisanis egit, firmavitque nulla neque honoris neque dignitatis cura. Conditiones huiusmodi fuerunt: ut Pisani Lucam quindecim annis retinerent; arcem custodirent; post id tempus liberam dimitterent; exules Lucensium omnes ab exilio revocarent; bona restituerent; captivos Florentinorum sociorumve sine pretio dimitterent; castella florentinus populus quae lucensis agri tenuisset retineret; penderet insuper Pisanus in annos singulos auri novem millia. Florentinus vero exulibus, quicumque Pisanis in eo bello favissent, reditum in urbem permitteret, bona restitui iuberet; Saconem et agnatos qui captivi tenebantur dimitteret; pacem his ac ceteris qui vel Arretio vel Florentiae bellum intulissent daret; Lucae durante eo tempore magistratum imponeret. Hoc extremum nonnihil videbatur, sed erat parum: nam cum Pisani arcem praesidio urbemque tenerent, domini ac moderatores omnium essent; nudum magistratus nomen ac titulo dumtaxat speciosum habebatur. Ex hac pace nobilitatis ea pars, quae per seditionem pulsa nuper fuerat, in urbem rediit, et quidem summa dominatoris gratia, quasi eius beneficio restituta. Sacon vero et agnati carcere exempti Bibienam ac cetera eorum castella circa Arretium tenuere.

120   Cum de pisano providisset bello, aliis rursus curis intentus, Gallos omnes qui erant per Italiam evocavit; frequentes etiam domo, fama illius potentiae exciti advenerunt. Ex his confecit equites circiter octingentos, quos circa se custodes habere constituit. Societatem post haec et amicitiam cum Pisanis inivit, magis, ut

After this, he took steps to end the war and negotiated a peace 119
with the Pisans, confirming it without the least concern for honor
or dignity. The terms were as follows: the Pisans should retain
control of Lucca for fifteen years; they should maintain a guard in
the citadel; after that time they should allow the city to go free; all
the Lucchese exiles should be recalled from exile and their property should be restored; the Pisans should release Florentines or
allied prisoners without a ransom; the Florentine People should
retain the castles they held in Lucchese territory; the Pisans
should pay them 9000 florins every year. The Florentines would
allow their exiles, and whoever had favored Pisa in the late war, to
return to the city; they should command that the exiles' goods be
restored; they were to release Saccone and his relatives who were
being held captive; they should accord peace to them and to others
who had made war against Arezzo or Florence; and they should
appoint the magistrate in Lucca during that period. This last condition seemed a considerable concession, but it was in fact a small
one, for since the Pisans kept control of the city and the citadel,
they could rule and control everything; the magistrate was regarded as a magistrate in name only, a mere title for appearances'
sake. In accordance with this peace, the part of the nobility which
had been expelled during the uprising returned to the city. They
were highly grateful to the city's lord, as though they had been restored through his favor. Saccone and his relatives, having been released from prison, kept control of Bibbiena and their other castles near Arezzo.

When he had settled the Pisan war, he again turned his atten- 120
tion to other concerns. He summoned all the Frenchmen in Italy,
and they came in droves to his house, drawn by the fame of his
power. Eight hundred of them he made knights and set them up
as his personal guard. Then he entered into an alliance and friendship with the Pisans, a move directed, it appeared, more against

apparebat, contra cives quam contra externos hostes. In hanc societatem duo millia equitum descripta.

121   Haec foris provisa non incaute; domi vero omnia perverse; quaedam etiam leviter et stulte. Priores (qui summus in civitate esse consueverat[137] magistratus) non sustulit ille quidem, quod ipsum fuit tolerabilius, sed omni auctoritate spoliatos, parvo admodum ministerio relicto, quasi spectaculum quoddam acerbum miserabileque in oculis civium dereliquit; cumque Carolus Roberti regis filius qui ante hunc civitatis imperium obtinuerat, vir tanto genere tantaque expectatione dignitatis, numquam ab honore aedium publicarum priores dimovisset, sed ipse alibi inhabitasset, hic, longe dispar ac dissimilis, priores aedibus suis expulit, ipse incubuit. Vexilliferos ac societates funditus sustulit; arma civibus ademit; honores ac magistratus irritavit omnes, nisi qui ab eo essent concessi. In civium autem favore ita variavit, ut modo nobilitatem, modo populum videretur praeferre; saepe his reiectis ad plebem magis inclinare. Et sane multitudini plura indulsit quam alii cuiquam parti civitatis. Pecunias omnes publicas cupidissime in se unum convertit: quarum etiam gratia, portoria auxit et nova excogitavit vectigalia, et tributa insuper imposuit crebra. Consignationes a populo factas iisdem ex pecuniis irritas duxit. Obsides Mastino datos, pro quibus solvendum fuit, neglexit, cum summa querela propinquorum summoque dedecore civitatis. Accipiendis computandisque pecuniis publicis, de fide civium diffisus, peregrinos imposuit homines. Arcem inde facere aggressus, proximas

Florentine citizens than against external enemies. Two thousand knights were enlisted for the purposes of this alliance.[83]

Walter's foreign policies were not imprudent, but everything he did domestically was wrong-headed, and some of his actions were also frivolous and stupid. Because it was the more tolerable policy, he did not do away with the priors, who by custom were the highest magistracy in the city, but he stripped them of all authority, leaving them greatly reduced duties as a kind of spectacle of bitterness and misery, abandoned before the eyes of the citizens. Whereas Charles, the son of King Robert, who had previously held power in the city, a man of high descent and the utmost dignity, had never dishonored the priors by removing them from the Palazzo Vecchio, but himself dwelt elsewhere, Walter, a far different and inferior man, expelled the priors from their dwelling and roosted in it himself. He entirely abolished the standard-bearers and militia companies; disarmed the citizenry; and nullified all honors and magistracies except those he had distributed himself. He seemed variable in his marks of favor towards citizens, so that now he appeared to prefer the nobility, now the people; and often he rejected both, favoring the lowest classes instead. Indeed, he was much more indulgent towards the multitude than towards any other part of the city. With the utmost greed he turned all public monies to his private purposes alone, and to this end increased the gabelles, concocted new kinds of rents and imposed direct taxes with greater frequency. The appropriations the people made from these monies he treated as null and void. He abandoned the hostages given to Mastino for whom he was supposed to be paying, giving rise to loud complaints from their relatives and causing great dishonor to the city. He would not trust the citizens to collect and account for public funds, but brought in foreigners. He then began to construct a citadel, putting towers on the buildings next to the palace and adding crenellations. He added a great gate to the palace itself and iron gratings on the windows; he enlarged

121

palatio aedes turresque adiunxit crepidasque effecit. Palatio ipsi propylaea, fenestris ferreos cancellos apposuit; plateam dilatavit, portas urbis turresque desuper communivit. Alias[138] iuxta singulas populi ad usum portulas struxit. Delationes civium ita morose suscepit, ut saepius eos qui deferrent, ne pervestigata quidem re neve perquisita, talione multaret. Interdum vero ob maledictum ad crudelitatem irritatus est. Civi paulo ante prioratu egresso, quod mediocriter questus de republica fuisset, funditus linguam iussit evelli. In exilium actum, quod de se male loqui suspicabatur, per simulationem veniae revocatum, supplicio crudeli indignoque occidit.

122   Cum intolerabilis videretur, ac in dies magis crescerent mala, superante iam odio metum, variae primo querelae, civium mox coniurationes sunt consecutae, et quidem plures uno tempore, ignorantibus aliis alias. Consilium invadendi varium fuit. Fuerunt qui in palatio ipso vi irrumpendum necandumque putarent; fuerunt qui dum per urbem incederet, quod ille frequenter ab initio faciebat. Sed inerat his[139] rebus difficultas, quod suspicio ex conscientia malefactorum coorta cautum magis diffidentemque in dies reddebat. Quare et intra palatium firmo stabat praesidio, et foris nec temere nec sine ingenti comitatu versabatur.

123   His difficultatibus res protracta est, nec prius confecta quam patefacta. Senensis erat quidam vir militiae cognitus, et ob id a studio nobilitatis nequaquam abhorrens. Is igitur cum forte ascitus esset, commotus primo aspectu, rem totam ad Franciscum Brunelletium[140] equitem florentinum (cuius familiaritate plurimum utebatur) detulit. Ille re subita perculsus, cum esset totius coniuratio-

the piazza and fortified the gates and towers of the city in addition. He constructed small gates near the large ones for the use of the people. He received denunciations from the people with such an ill spirit that he very often exacted compensation from those who brought them without investigation or inquiry. From time to time criticism provoked him to cruelty. In the case of one citizen who had just left the priorate and had ventured some mild expression of dissatisfaction relating to public affairs, he had his tongue pulled out. A man sent into exile on suspicion of having criticized him was recalled under pretence of pardon and was put to death, a cruel and undeserved punishment.[84]

As the man seemed intolerable and his evil acts grew worse every day, fear gave way to hatred, and complaints, then conspiracies followed. Indeed there were many conspiracies at the same time, each ignorant of the rest. There were various ideas about how to attack him. Some thought they should force their way in and cut him down in the palace itself; while others thought he should be attacked while he walked through the streets, which at the beginning of his reign he had often done. But the difficulty with these plans was that he had now become suspicious, being conscious of his misdeeds, and he became more cautious and mistrustful each day. On this account he also stayed inside the palace with a strong guard and did not venture outside rashly, or without a large retinue.[85]

Owing to these difficulties the scheme began to drag out, and was detected as soon as it was plotted. There was a certain Sienese man, knowledgeable in war, who on that account enjoyed a certain good will among the nobility. It so happened that he was admitted to their counsels, and shaken at first sight, revealed everything to his great friend Francesco Brunelleschi, a Florentine knight. The latter, being entirely ignorant of the conspiracy, was for his part struck by what was afoot, and revealed to the tyrant what he had heard from the Sienese. The informer was swiftly sent for and

122

1343

123

nis ignarus, tyranno quid ex Senensi audisset patefecit. Index subito arcessitus duos nominavit, quibus statim correptis, cum tormenta adhiberentur, capita ipsa ac principes coniurationis extorsit. Magnitudo multitudoque civium tyranni animum conterruit. Itaque parumper primo cunctatus, tandem ex illo numero Antonium Adimarem Baldinacci filium, virum et genere et potentia clarum, per apparitorem ad se vocat. Paruit illi vocanti, sive ignoratione periculi sive fiducia multitudinis coniuratorum. Quo deprehenso atque convicto, cum alios quoque complures versari in ea coniuratione tyrannus comperisset, bifariam fluctuare coepit, ardens quidem animo supplicium sumere, metuens vero multitudinem civium, quos esse conscios affinesque eius rei deprehenderat. His curis anxius consilium capit ante omnia militum praesidia ex finitimis oppidis in urbem vocare. Ea intercapedo fuit dierum sex.

124   Quae cum iam convenissent, tempus esse ratus ea quae cogitaverat patrandi, egregium quemque civem ad se vocat. Numerus vocatorum fuit circiter trecentos. Causa vero praetenditur, ut de coniuratione ad consilium referat. Ceterum id agebatur, ut cum ii[141] convenissent, in palatio ipso opprimerentur; reliqua inde iam secure transigeret. Fuerunt in numero vocatorum plerique ex coniuratis, qui forte uti[142] fit ex conscientia periculum suspicantes[143] metumque apud alios de industria augentes, in eam formidinem adduxerunt, ut nemo vocanti pareret, nemo in consilium iret.

125   Ex hoc iam civitas aperte rebellis, qui coniuraverant sese ultro nudantibus, una omnium mente in tyrannum surrexit. Tunc demum compertum est tres in civitate coniurationes iampridem adversus tyrannum initas viguisse; nec erat ferme ulla paulo amplior

named two persons, who were immediately seized. Under torture he extracted from them the essential features of the plot and the names of the ringleaders. The greatness and numbers of the citizens involved terrified the tyrant. So after some initial delay, he finally sent his bailiff to summon before him Antonio di Baldinaccio Adimari, a man famous for his power and lineage. The man answered the summons either through ignorance of his peril or trusting in the great number of the conspirators. Adimari was arrested and convicted, but having learned of the great number of other men involved in the conspiracy, Walter began to hem and haw. He was eager to carry out the punishment, but feared the great number of citizens who, as he had discovered, were privy to and implicated in the plot. In his anxiety he undertook first of all to summon to the city the garrisons of the neighboring towns. He gave them six days to appear.

When they had arrived, he reckoned the time had come to   124
carry out his plans, and he called all the distinguished citizens before him. The number of those summoned was about three hundred. The pretext given was that he wished to take counsel about the conspiracy.[86] But he was in fact doing this so as to crush them in the palace itself when they came; after that, he could carry out the rest of his plans in security. Among those summoned were many conspirators who, probably owing to their knowledge of the plot, suspected the danger they were in, and purposely spread their fear to the others, so that no one obeyed the summons and no one came to give counsel.

After this act of defiance the city became openly rebellious, and   125
those involved in conspiracies revealed themselves voluntarily, rising up with one accord against the tyrant. At that point it was discovered that there were three separate conspiracies against the tyrant that had long been active in the city, and that practically every family of any importance, whether from the nobility or the common people, was involved in some conspiracy. The people then

familia ex nobilitate aut plebe quae expers esset coniurationis. Armis igitur populariter sumptis, cum arcem circumstetissent, obsidere ex composito perrexerunt. Contra vero tyrannus tela desuper iacere ac repugnare, et arcere populi impetum. Quae postquam incassum agitare videt, quo multitudinis placaretur ira, concedere animo ac ultro submittere statuit. Itaque postridie orto sole Antonium Adimarem equestribus donatum insignibus dimisit. Idem fecit de ceteris, quos in captivis habebat. Prioribus vero (eos namque ab initio tumultus in palatium traxerat) contra consuetudinem suam[144] honorem exhibuit, et vexilla quaedam populi, quasi libertatis ultro ab se permissae indicia, ex summa arce protulit.

126   Sed ob eas res nihilo magis pacata civitas est. Urebat enim mentes ulciscendi libido, eorum praesertim quorum ille propinquos agnatosque necarat, nec sine sanguine tyranni expiari posse caedem suorum arbitrabantur. Ut tamen multitudo, quae sine ullo publico decreto, sine ullo duce legitimo in armis erat, modum aliquem formamque susciperet, principibus vocantibus, concio populi convenit ad Reparatae aedem. Ibi per suffragia quatuordecim viri cum imperio delecti sunt ad rempublicam conformandam ordinandamque civitatem. Additus est iis[145] Angelus Acciaiolus praesul, vir summo consilio summaque auctoritate, qui fere princeps fuerat libertatis recuperandae.

127   Obsidio inter haec et oppugnatio neque die neque noctu intermittebatur. Sed erat cum tyranno manus valida militum ferme trecentorum; locus vero egregie munitus. Verum haec talia erant, ut procrastinationem tantum periculi, non autem spem ullam salutis viderentur afferre. Quare, modo colloquia civium poscere, modo fidem implorare, supplicare denique et obtestari obsessi pergebant. Quin etiam, quo piaculo aliquo deleniretur ira, tyranni satellites

took to arms, surrounded the citadel and started to besiege it in an orderly way. In response the tyrant threw down missiles from above and fought back, warding off the attack of the people. Soon he saw that this was useless, and decided to make concessions and voluntary gestures of submission to placate the multitude's anger. So the following day at sunrise he knighted Antonio Adimari and let him go. He also released others he was holding captive. In violation of his usual practice he showed honor to the priors (whom he had brought inside the palace at the beginning of the tumult), and he flew from the top of the citadel certain standards of the People, as signs of the liberty he was now willing to allow.

But this did nothing to pacify the city. The desire for revenge 126 burned in the citizens' minds, especially in those whose relatives and associates had been killed, and they reckoned they could not expiate the slaughter of their own without spilling the blood of the tyrant. So that the multitude, which had taken to arms with no public decree or legitimate leader, might take on some measure and form, its leaders called for a council of the people to be convened in the church of Santa Reparata.[87] There a board of Fourteen was elected with powers to reform the state and set the city in order. Angelo Acciaiuoli, the bishop, was added to their number, a man of great wisdom and authority, who had effectively been their leader in the recovery of liberty.

Meanwhile, the siege went on day and night. The tyrant had 127 with him a strong force of about three hundred soldiers, and the place was well fortified. But these advantages were such that it seemed the danger could only be delayed; they would not afford any hope of salvation. So the besieged proceeded, now to ask for parleys with the citizens, now to beg for a safe conduct, and finally were reduced to supplications and solemn vows. Furthermore, to soothe the people's anger with some act of atonement, they shoved outside the gates the tyrant's satellites who in former times had run riot tormenting the people, and whom they now heard the

quondam in civium suppliciis[146] debacchatos, quos ad vindictam deposci sentiebant, per vim porta detrusos gladiis ardentis populi obiecerunt; qui, illico membratim discerpti,[147] fructum crudelitatis suae dignissimum reportarunt.

128 Ex hoc iam restincta parumper civium ira, praesul et quatuordecim viri colloquia magis iniverunt. Denique mitiori consilio tyranno et cum illo obsessis vita permissa est, arcem dedenti ac omni potestate, quam iussu populi habuisset, sponte se abdicanti. Eam abdicationem, quo vitium abesset, extra territorium quoque fieri placuit. Ita arce praesuli quatuordecimque viris tradita, tyrannus sese in eorum manus permisit. Custoditus posthac biduo in ipsa arce, ne a populo violaretur, tandem noctu[148] urbe emissus. In Casentinatem iter primum fuit. Ibi abdicatione iterum facta, abiit decimo fere mense postquam regnare inceperat.

129 Dum haec Florentiae geruntur, Arretini, cognita obsidione tyranni, arma et ipsi corripuerunt.[149] Tres erant Arretii arces: una ad florentinam portam, duae in summa urbis parte. Earum primo statim impetu duas expugnarunt. Restabat tertia arx, et ea munitissima, quam omni conatu oppugnare dum pergunt, Sacon, dudum Arretinorum tyrannus, magna multitudine superveniens, contra ipsam arcem extra urbem consedit. Hinc iniecta civibus formido est, ne arx Saconi dederetur. Ob haec intermissa oppugnatio est, et per colloquium res tentata.

130 Praefectus erat arcis Guelfus Bondelmontes. Is, cum a civibus intra urbem, extra vero a Sacone obsideretur, et ruina tyranni, cuius nomine praesidebat, spem omnem abstulisset, vocatis in col-

people calling for so that they might take their revenge. Thrown on the swords of the inflamed people, these men were instantly torn limb from limb, earning a most fitting reward for their acts of cruelty.

After this act the citizens' anger abated somewhat, and the 128 bishop and the Fourteen entered into a parley. In the end it seemed the milder course to allow the tyrant and the men besieged with him to escape with their lives if he surrendered the citadel and voluntarily gave up all power the people's command had given him. To avoid any legal defect, it was decided that the abdication should be made outside of Florentine territory.[88] Thus the citadel was handed over to the bishop and the Fourteen, and the tyrant released himself into their custody. He was guarded inside the palace itself for a space of two days to save him from the people's violence, and finally was taken out by night. They journeyed first into the Casentino. There he again repeated his act of abdication, and took his departure, about ten months after the beginning of his reign.

While this was happening in Florence, the Aretines, learning 129 that the tyrant was under siege, themselves seized arms. There were three strongholds in Arezzo: one by the Florentine gate, two in the highest part of the city. They immediately captured the last two in their first attack. There remained the third stronghold, the best fortified one. While they were proceeding to besiege it, Saccone, the erstwhile Aretine tyrant, appeared with a large following and laid siege the same citadel from outside the city. Hence the fear arose among the citizens that the stronghold would be surrendered to Saccone. So they interrupted the siege and sought to hold a parley.

The commander of the stronghold was Guelfo Buondelmonte. 130 Seeing himself besieged by the citizens within and Saccone outside the city, and aware of the tyrant's fall in whose name he commanded, he lost all hope. Summoning the citizens to a parley, he

loquium civibus, 'Non ignoro', inquit, 'Arretini, vix mea referre vobisne an Saconi arcem dimittam. Ceterum, ut ad vos magis incliner, duae res faciunt: primum, quod nostra familia guelfarum partium semper praecipua fuit, qua in re vos mecum convenitis, Sacon dissentit; altera, quod aequiore hominum laude me fore puto, si videbor libertati potius vestrae quam Saconis tyrannidi gratificari voluisse.'

131   Ita civibus arcem tradit. Eodem fere modo Pistorienses et Volaterrani, qui et ipsi in potestatem fuerant tyranni, per illius ruinam libertatem consecuti sunt.[150]

said, "I have no idea, Aretines, whether it is to my advantage to surrender the stronghold to you or to Saccone. But I am inclined to favor you for two reasons: first, because our family has always been prominent in the Guelf party, and in that respect you are on my side, whereas Saccone is not. Secondly, I think I shall enjoy fairer praise from mankind if I shall appear to have voluntarily favored your liberty rather than Saccone's tyranny."

Thus he turned the citadel over to the citizens. In the same way 131 the Pistoiesi and the Volterrans, who had also themselves been in the power of the tyrant, recovered their liberty through his downfall.[89]

LIBER SEPTIMUS

1   Liberi iam populi civitatisque in suum arbitrium assertae fundamenta rursus reipublicae, novasque subinde res, et primo communicatam nobilitati gubernandi curam, mox ademptam, ac divisam novo more urbem, ceteraque memoratu digna prosequemur.

2   Pulso tyranno libertateque recepta, civitas quidem sui iuris facta, ceterum multis ac magnis praesidiis auctoque dudum imperio spoliata remansit, Arretinis, Pistoriensibus, Volaterranis per eandem tyranni ruinam et ipsis quoque sese in libertatem pristinam vindicantibus. Foris igitur unum sub tempus cuncta perdita profligataque iam erant quae dudum multorum annorum labore plurimisque contentionibus fuerant acquisita. Intus vero inordinata omnia. Nulli magistratus in urbe, nulla subsellia. Quatuordecim tantum viri, quos sibi per tumultum civitas creaverat, una cum praesule auctoritatem publicam tuebantur. In hos cura reipublicae et omnium[1] consilia recidebant.

3   Ad constituendum igitur civitatis statum ante omnia intendentibus, quaedam ab his veterum identidem confirmata, permulta etiam novo more constituta fuere. Vetus illud retentum, ut priores summi magistratus nomen in civitate foret, quod ne tyrannus quidem omnino substulerat. Illud autem novum ac maximi in republica momenti, quod contra superioris temporis exempla nobilitatem ad hunc ipsum ceterosque reipublicae magistratus recipiendam esse statuerunt. Causae vero huius consilii duae potissimum ferebantur. Una concordiae civilis respectus. Ita demum enim

BOOK VII

We shall now go on to describe how, once the city had asserted its claim to self-rule, a free people founded the state anew. We shall describe the revolutionary changes that followed: first, how the responsibility for governing was shared with the nobility, then taken away from them; and how the city was divided in a new way; and other matters worthy of memory.

The tyrant had been expelled, liberty restored, and the city had come under its own jurisdiction, but it remained bereft of many important protections and of its empire, enlarged over so long a period. For the Aretines, Pistoiesi and Volterrans, thanks to the fall of the tyrant, had also themselves laid claim to their ancient liberty. Abroad, therefore, everything was now lost and squandered in a moment that had been acquired with the labor of many long years and innumerable struggles. Inside the city, everything was in a state of disorder. There were no magistrates in the city, and the courts were empty. Only the Fourteen, a board the city had created in the midst of tumult, together with the bishop, upheld public authority. Upon them had fallen responsibility for the republic and the mechanisms for collective decision-making.

Since their main priority was establishing the city's political system, they confirmed again certain ancient practices, and also instituted many new ones. They kept the old practice whereby the name for the highest magistracy in the city was the Priorate — something that not even the tyrant had done away with entirely. What was new, and of the greatest import to the republic, was their decision, against the example of earlier times, to accept the nobility into this and other magistracies of the republic. There were two principal reasons for this decision. One was concern for civic harmony. It was believed that the state would be tranquil and

quietis pacatisque civium animis tranquillam fore rempublicam credidere, si nulla in ea pars honore exclusa, praesentem civitatis statum odisse per suam iniuriam cogeretur. Altera praesens meritum, quod in pellendo tyranno haud segnem nobilitas operam civitati navarat. Id autem eo fuerat gratius, quod a tyranno ipso permulta ei generi hominum indulta videbantur, cuius porro beneficiis amorem patriae libertatemque praetulisse maximum sinceri in rem publicam animi fuerat argumentum. His ergo rationibus ad communionem reipublicae gubernandae recepta nobilitas est.

4   Ceterum ex eo facto permagna rerum mutatio sequebatur, antiqua gubernandi forma omnino convulsa. Duo siquidem maxima libertatis praesidia, quibus ante respublica steterat, necessario tollebantur; iustitiae constituta et populi societates.[2] Nam et constituta iustitiae contra vim nobilitatis reperta ostendimus, et societates[3] populi, quo grandioribus familiis resistere imbecilli homines possent, et ab initio sapienter excogitatae et postea salubriter conservatae in republica fuerant. Tunc autem, exaequato penitus civitatis corpore,[4] ac velut uno per concordiam facto, contentionibus antiquatis, praesidia quoque antiquabantur. Prioribus octo viri in consilium attributi, et hi quoque mixti ex nobilitate et plebe, cum antea duodecim e plebe dumtaxat esse consuessent. Illud quoque novum, quod urbem primo in sex divisam tribus, hi quadrifariam partiti sunt. Pro sexta enim parte tribus unaquaeque honores in republica suscipiebat, atque ex eo fiebat, ut quae tribus populosissima esset, ex ea homines minus honorarentur. Quadrifariam igitur partiri placuit, habitaque est ratio, quantum fieri potuit, ut par multitudo in singulis comprehenderetur; evenitque, ut

the spirits of its citizens quiet and peaceable if no part of the city were excluded from honors and thus driven to hate the present regime because of injustices to itself. The other reason was manifest merit, since the nobility had actively devoted its energies to expelling the tyrant. Their actions won still more approval in that the tyrant had granted many favors to their class, but they had preferred liberty and love of country to his acts of beneficence, which was a great proof of the sincerity of their public spirit. So for these reasons the nobility were allowed to share in the governance of the state.[1]

However, from this act a great political change ensued, and the ancient constitution was turned upside down. The two greatest safeguards of liberty which had hitherto preserved the republic — the Ordinances of Justice and the popular militia companies — were necessarily removed. For the Ordinances of Justice, as we showed,[2] were devised against the violence of the nobility, and the popular militia companies were designed to enable the weak to resist the great families. The latter had been wisely framed in the beginning and afterwards preserved in the state with salutary effect. But at this time, the body politic had been entirely equalized and through concord made as one; so with the sources of contention having lapsed, the safeguards against it lapsed as well.[3] The priors were given an advisory board of eight men, also consisting of both nobles and commoners, whereas before, their advisors had customarily been twelve men drawn from the common people only. Another innovation was the division of the city into quarters, whereas before it had been divided in sixths or *sestieri*. The population of each sestiere received one-sixth of the public honors, with the result that the men in the most populous sestieri enjoyed fewer honors.[4] They decided to divide the city into quarters in such a way that, as far as possible, the population of each *quartiere* should be equal to the others. As a result, the population

4

287

transarnina tribus quae pro sexta quondam honores capiebat, ex hac nova divisione pro quarta susciperet.

5   His constitutis nomina civium in suffragium missa, ex quibus postea magistratus sortirentur. Suffragio tandem perfecto nominibusque inclusis, priores sortiti sunt duodecim, quatuor ex nobilitate, octo ex plebe. Inierunt autem magistratum Kalendis septembribus, et in aedes publicas, ut mos ante tyrannidem fuerat, cum apparitoribus reducti, rempublicam tractare gubernareque coeperunt.

6   Haec igitur a quatuordecim viris acta et constituta sunt; quae, etsi bonis rationibus excogitata videbantur, tamen diuturnitatem minimam habuere. Vixdum enim magistratu inito, res insolita primo commovit animos; nec iam tunc communio grata erat et in futurum metuebatur magis. Homines enim nobiles, magnarum principes familiarum, qui sine ulla potestate publica ipsi per se formidabiles erant, si magistratum insuper nacti forent, intolerabiles videbantur, nec temperaturos ab iniuriis extimabant. Haec praetexebatur causa, et erat sane nonnulla.

7   Ceterum invidia atque contentio, consueti dudum civitatis morbi, una cum libertate in urbem redierant. Odio et certamine res tota gerebatur. Igitur de his murmur primo apud populares exortum; mox de industria in plebem diffusum. Quid enim laetata sit plebs deiectione[5] tyranni, si multi pro uno cervicibus suis imminere debebant? Nisi forte moderaturos in magistratu eos homines

of the Oltrarno district, which formerly used to get a sixth of the honors, now after the new division received a fourth.[5]

With the city's constitution established in this way, the names 5 of the citizens were put to a vote; from those so elected the magistrates would afterwards be chosen by lot. When the election was over and the names put in bags, twelve priors were drawn, four from the nobility and eight from the common people. Their magistracy was inaugurated on the first of September, and they were conducted into the Palazzo Vecchio with their attendents, as had been the custom before the tyranny, and began to govern and handle affairs of state.

This, then, is what the Fourteen did and established. Although 6 they seemed to have good reasons for designing the constitution as they did, it did not last very long. For scarcely had the new priors been installed when the people were stirred up by this unaccustomed state of affairs; by that time the sharing of offices with the nobility was no longer in favor and was a cause of fear for the future. For it seemed likely that noblemen, leaders of great families, who were already formidable by themselves without any public power, would become intolerable if they acquired a magistracy as well, and people reckoned that they would not restrain themselves from acts of injustice. This reason was advanced as a pretext, and there was something to it.

In any event, envy and contention, the usual civic diseases, had 7 returned to the city together with liberty. Everything was done out of hatred and a spirit of contention. Thus a murmur about the noble magistrates first arose among the popular party, and soon, on purpose, was spread among the common people: Why indeed should the common people rejoice at the downfall of the tyrant, if many lords must now threaten their necks in place of one? Did they think that these men were going to be even-handed in the conduct of public office, whose violence and arrogance they had experienced in private life, who in earlier times could not be re-

putent, quorum vim ac superbiam in privata experti sunt vita, qui tot iampridem legibus totque praesidiis a violentia coerceri non possint. His dictis erecta plebs, minime quietura videbatur, nec liberae modo, sed interdum effrenes etiam voces audiebantur, societatem hanc quasi perniciosam exitioque tandem reipublicae futuram detestantes.

8 Quibus tandem permotus, praesul (erat enim ipse ex familia insigni quidem et ornatissima, ceterum populares in republica secuta partes), quasi rem emendaturus, collegas vocavit, egitque cum his, ut, cognita voluntate populi communionem improbantis, rem potius ipsi corrigere, quam vim multitudinis experiri[6] malint; si sponte se arbitrio submittant, multa retenturi; sin contumaciter resistant (ut sunt multitudinis animi), omnia perdituri.

9 Haec monentem praesulem ac frustra suadentem nobilitatis principes longe respuerunt, nec rem modo ipsam, verum etiam suasorem indignabantur. Nimirum enim id agere plebem, ab eo concitatam inquieti spiritus homine atque infidi, qui modo in intimum tyranni sinum adulando irrepserit, eundemque mox pessima suadendo ad ruinam impulerit. Nunc vero non absimilem ludum quaerere, quo cives inter sese confligant atque collidant,[7] nempe cui una sit ars, tamquam puerili in ludo, quosdam extollere, eosdemque rursus deprimere. Quantum ad se attinet, libertatem patriae defendisse, propriam vero libertatem suam nequaquam neglecturos esse, visurosque aliquando quinam sint qui se non tantum innocuos, verum etiam bene de republica merentes, a dignitate excludere pergant. 'An vero Simifonte Fighinoque profectis hominibus, quondam populi florentini hostibus, honores in republica tradentur, nobis autem vetustis ac veris florentinis civibus,

strained from violence by a mass of laws and safeguards? Excited
by such talk, it seemed the plebs was not going to stay quiet, and
not just unrestrained but sometimes unruly voices were being
heard, expressing detestation of the present alliance [between
commoners and nobles] as pernicious and potentially destructive
to the republic.

Finally, these voices had their effect on the bishop (who was 8
himself from a distinguished and celebrated family, but one which
adhered to the popular party in the state). As though to correct
the situation, he summoned his colleagues[6] and urged them, now
that they had learned the will of the people—who were condemning the power-sharing arrangement—to rectify the situation themselves rather than experience mob violence.[7] If they submitted
themselves voluntarily to its judgment, much might be salvaged,
but if they defied the multitude, its nature was such that all would
be lost.

The leaders of the nobility rejected the bishop's advice and 9
counsel, and were incensed, not just at what was being advocated,
but also at the advocate. Plainly, the commoners were acting the
way they were because of the incitement of this man, an untrust-
worthy and unquiet spirit, who had slithered his way into the tyrant's bosom by flattery, and then, by giving him bad counsel, had
driven him to ruin. Now he was trying to play the same game, setting citizens at variance, making them quarrel with each other, this
doubtless being his one talent, raising up certain people, then
pushing them down again, as in a childish game. As for themselves, they had defended the liberty of their country, but they
were by no means going to neglect their own liberty; and at some
point they were going to identify the persons who were trying to
exclude from office men who were not only harmless, but well-deserving of the republic. "Shall civic honors be given to these men
who came from Simifonte and Figline, former enemies of the Florentine People, but denied to us, old and true Florentine citizens,

per quos illi dudum victi sunt, honores in republica negabuntur, et
advenae ac subacti dominabuntur? Nos cives victoresque illorum
illis ipsis quos vicimus in propria patria serviemus? Et quis tantam
iniquitatem ac repugnantiam rerum non modo perferre, sed audire
sustineat?'

10   Cum praesul haec et huiusmodi vociferantes haud molliter refu-
taret, eaque ex re iurgia contentionesque exorta essent, ita ut a
proximis exciperentur, it confestim per urbem rumor, invaditque
arma plebs, et ad publicas aedes decurrens, eos qui ex nobilitate in
magistratu fuerant, vi et armis detractos, in privatam redegit formam, ac in proprias aedes exauctoratos redire iussit. Nobilitas autem, ob eam iniuriam erecta, sumpsit quidem arma. Non tamen in
unum convenit; nec decertare ea die contra vim populi ausa est,
sed domi consistens, unaquaeque familiarum aedes suas tutabatur,
adventabatque his multitudo hominum ex agro permagna, ut
cuiusque clientelae amicitiaeque erant, auxilio futura.

11   Cum igitur tota civitas in armis esset ac proelium exinde futurum appareret, ac permagna undique auxilia nobilitati ventura dicerentur, antevenire populus constituit. Itaque postera mox die
primo cis Arnum familias aggressus arma intulit. Diversis in urbe
locis nobilitas habitabat; eo facilius fuit singulas invadendo pervincere. Quamquam enim domos turresque suas quaeque gens com-
munierat ac fortiter adversus impetum populi repugnabat, tamen,
ubi multitudo paene innumera undique cingebat, telaque et faces
mittebantur, impar tanto certamini unaquaeque familia brevi supe-
rabatur. Non tamen caedes facta est nobilitatis; sed ut sese populi
arbitrio permiserint, incolumes servabantur.

12   Expugnatis cis Arnum familiis et in potestatem redactis, trans
Arnum eodem modo invadere placuit. Ibi contentio longe maior

by whom these men were once vanquished? Shall immigrants and subjects be made lords? Shall we citizens, their conquerors, be enslaved by those we conquered in our own country? Who could bear to hear, let alone propose, such an unjust and contradictory thing?"

The bishop contradicted in no mild terms the men who were 10 shouting this and similar things. Such oaths and quarrelling ensued that they were heard by persons close by, and the rumor of it spread immediately through the city. The common people took to arms and ran to the Palazzo Vecchio. There by armed violence they seized the noble members of the magistracy and reduced them to private citizens, ordering them to return to their private dwellings, stripped of authority. The nobility was roused by this act of injustice and seized arms. They did not assemble, however, nor did they dare that day to fight against the people's violence. Instead, they remained in their homes, and each family guarded its own dwellings. And an enormous multitude of men from the countryside, their clients and friends, arrived to help them.

With the whole city in arms and large reinforcements coming 11 in from everywhere to help the nobility, the people decided to anticipate the battle that was plainly looming. Thus on the following day they first marched out and attacked the noble families on this side of the Arno. The nobility lived in various places in the city, so it was easier to beat them by attacking them individually. Although each clan fortified its own dwellings and towers and fought back bravely against the people's attack, nevertheless, being surrounded on all sides by a nearly infinite multitude launching spears and fiery arrows at them, individual families proved unequal to so great a contest and were quickly overcome. However, the nobility was not slaughtered, but were kept unharmed, as they had surrendered themselves to judgement by the people.

With the families on this side of the Arno defeated and under 12 control, it was decided to invade the Oltrarno in a similar fashion.

fuit, quod et robustissimae nobilitatis familiae trans Arnum habitabant, ac singulorum capita pontium aedibus turribusque comprehenderant, ut eo pervadere multitudo non posset. Haec difficultas aliquandiu impetum populi remorata est. Tandem vero ad infimum pontem (ibi namque nobilitas imbecillior erat) impetu facto, cum a plebe quoque quae trans Arnum incolit, raptis armis procurreretur, ac ex utraque simul parte multitudo populi nobilitatem invaderet, deserto qui pro ponte stabant praesidio, aufugerunt, populoque transitum liberum permiserunt. Transgressa igitur per infimum pontem multitudo, cum proximas familias in potestatem redegisset, mox inde in cetera pontium capita vim intulit. Idem ad Trinitatis, idem ad Veterem Pontem factum, et utroque in loco proelia conserta.

13   Vehementissime tamen omnium ad superiorem pontem decertatum propter egregiam[8] quae circa id erat loci nobilitatis potentiam. Et adiuvabatur natura ac[9] situ, quod ex altera flumen, ex altera mons domos muniebat. Viam, quae unica ad eos ferebat, impedimentis iactis et domorum altitudine facile tutabantur. Hic igitur aliquandiu constitit populi impetus, nec prius perrumpere potuit quam multitudinis pars sub vexillis missa e diversa protinus regione, ascenso monte, desuper arma coepit inferre. Tunc fractae vires dissipataeque sunt, et simul a superiore quoque ponte, cessante praesidio, penetratum. Aedes propter contumaciorem resistentiam in his locis a multitudine infima[10] direptae; frequentes etiam incendio conflagrarunt; hominibus tamen ipsis, postquam in potestatem populi se dedidere, humaniter parsum. Non enim odio neque maleficio certabatur, sed de potentia, de auctoritate, de praestantia in republica omnis erat contentio.

14   Victa nobilitate, populus, cum in arbitrium potestatemque suam haud ambiguo rem publicam redegisset, conformare[11] iam

There the fighting was much greater because the strongest noble families lived in that district and had encircled all the bridgeheads with their houses and towers so that the multitude could not cross over. This difficulty delayed for some time the people's assault. But finally they assaulted the lowest bridge, where the nobility was weakest. When the commoners who lived in Oltrarno seized arms and rushed up, and the nobility found themselves attacked simultaneously on both sides, they abandoned their fortifications at the bridgehead and fled, allowing the people free passage. So the multitude crossed over by the lowest bridge and, having reduced the nearby families, they attacked the rest of the bridgeheads. In due course they captured the Ponte San Trinita and the Ponte Vecchio after pitched battles in both places.

The bitterest fighting of all was at the highest bridge,[8] owing to 13 the extraordinary power the nobility disposed of in that place. The nature of the situation helped them, too, because their dwellings were guarded on one side by the river and on the other by a hill. On the one street which led up to their houses they had set up barricades, and the height of the houses also made them easily defensible. So the people's advance was stopped here for some time, and they were unable to break through until part of the multitude was sent around under the standards to the opposite side of the city, climbed the hill, and began to attack from above. Then the nobility's forces became divided and scattered as the garrison on the higher bridge gave way and the people there simultaneously broke through. Because of the more defiant resistance in this place the lower classes sacked the nobles' houses and set fire to many of them, yet the persons of the nobility, after they had surrendered themselves into the power of the people, were humanely spared. For they had not fought out of hatred or malice, but their whole struggle was for power, authority and preeminence in the state.

Having defeated the nobility, the People had unambiguously 14 brought the state under their own power and direction. Now they

inde civitatis statum suo arbitratu perrexit. Itaque et constituta iustitiae in antiquam formam restituit, et societates populi renovavit, numero tamen earum mutato pro nova partitione urbis, ut quaternae singulis tribubus inessent. Ita sedecim tunc primum societates populi factae, cum antea viginti, mox decem et novem fuissent. Duodecim viri, ut ante, in consilium prioribus attributi, omnes e plebe. Suffragia quoque magistratuum ex integro refecta, quibus in triennium sortirentur, eaque delectu habito diligenti, ut ex magna multitudine pauci obtinerent. Ad minuendam vero nobilitatis potentiam, permulti ex eo numero ad plebem volentes id flagitantesque traducti. Datum id pro summo beneficio illis, quorum aut vita modestior fuerat aut potentiae parum.

15 His peractis, cum tranquilla domi iam omnia viderentur, foris identidem cura suscepta. Illud in primis provisum, ut Arretinis, qui per tyranni ruinam libertatem sibi arripuerant, suspicio omnis tolleretur, ne quid ea formido turbationis induceret. Decreto igitur publice facto, ius omne quod florentinus populus in urbe Arretio habuisset, sponte remissum est, missique legati qui Arretinis gratularentur pro libertate de tyranno recepta et florentini decretum populi de remissione iuris deferrent. Ii,[12] cum Arretium venissent, in contione populi mandata exposuerunt, decretumque publicum ex scripto recitarunt. Arretini vero haec audientes laetati sunt, et omissa suspicione, fidem florentini populi maiorem in modum complexi, in amicitia perseverarunt. Nec multo post inita societas est, in qua Perusini et Senenses et Arretini cum Florentinis fuere.

16 His ab ea parte Etruriae constitutis, in Pisanos inde versi animi; fuerat enim cum his bellum. Ex quo, etsi pax recepta post-

turned to reforming the constitution of the city to their own liking. Thus they restored the Ordinances of Justice in their ancient form, and reinstituted the popular militia companies, though adjusting their number in accordance with the new partition of the city, so that each quarter had four companies. So now for the first time there were sixteen militia companies, whereas before there had been twenty and after that nineteen. As before, a board of Twelve Men, all commoners, was set up to advise the priors.[9] The selection of magistrates was also entirely redone. They were chosen for a three-year period, and the selection was done so exactingly that only a few were taken out of so vast a multitude.[10] To reduce the power of the nobility, many of their number—with their consent and indeed at their insistence—were transferred to the common people. This transfer was granted as the highest of favors to those of them who lived modestly or had little power.[11]

With these reforms, domestic affairs now seemed wholly tranquil, so the people turned their attention abroad. Their first action was to reduce tensions with the Aretines, who had seized liberty for themselves after the fall of the tyrant. So to prevent any uprising there, they issued a public decree, voluntarily renouncing all jurisdiction held by the Florentine People in the city of Arezzo. Envoys were sent out to congratulate the Aretines on the recovery of their liberty from the tyrant and to deliver the decree of the Florentine People renouncing jurisdiction there. When they had arrived in Arezzo they explained their mandate in a popular assembly and read out the public decree from the document. The Aretines rejoiced to hear it and, dropping their suspicions, embraced with renewed fervor their allegiance to the Florentine People and resolved to continue friendly relations with them. Soon thereafter an alliance was formed between the Florentines and the Perugians, Sienese, and Aretines.

With their affairs in this part of Tuscany settled, the people 16 then turned their minds to the Pisans, with whom they had been

modum erat, tamen, quia tyranno auctore gesta res fuerat, non obligasse populum videbatur. Rursus igitur fieri placuit. Per eam pacem Luca Pisanis concessa; castella modo lucensis agri, quae tunc Florentinus possideret, retenta.

17   Haec eo anno quo tyrannus pulsus est domi forisque gesta. Principio insequentis anni multitudo hominum ex Arretino florentinoque collecta agro Pactios oppressit. Id erat genus nobile castella in agro Arretino possidens; ceterum, praeter quam quod diversarum partium, viciniae[13] insuper invisum atque grave ob rapinarum crebritatem.

18   Eodem anno contra nobilitatem exasperatae leges, atque illo insuper incommodo affecta, ut qui ex nobilitate apud quemquam regum tyrannorumve degerent, continuo domum remearent, exilium publicationemque bonorum, nisi legi parerent, subituri. Ob eam legem complures liberalitatem principum relinquere coacti, domum rediere. Eius legis ferendae non malevolentia modo causa fuit, verum etiam suspicio, ne maiori gratia apud reges principesque inita, aliquid per favorem illorum aliquando molirentur.

19   Per idem fere tempus in eos cives, qui per tyranni ruinam arces castellaque quibus praefecti erant dedissent, poena constituta est, et magistratibus mandata cura uti diligentius inquirerent. Eam ob legem frequentes damnati, praesertim nobilium, quibus plurimum arces crediderat tyrannus.

20   Per haec ipsa tempora florentini cives qui in Gallia negotiabantur nuntiarunt Gualterum nuper tyrannide pulsum, in Galliam ad

at war. Even though peace had subsequently been made, it had been made under the authority of the tyrant, and so did not appear to be binding on the People. So they decided to renegotiate it. By the terms of this new peace Lucca was ceded to the Pisans, while the Florentines retained the castles they currently possessed in Lucchese territory.[12]

Such were the deeds at home and abroad in the year the tyrant was expelled. At the beginning of the following year, a large body of men assembled from Aretine and Florentine territory to crush the Pazzi family. The latter was a noble clan possessing castles in Aretine territory who, aside from being Ghibellines, were a hateful burden upon their neighbors owing to their frequent acts of plunder and rapine.[13]   17 1344

In the same year the laws against the nobility were made harsher, and a further restriction was laid upon them: that those noblemen dwelling in the court of any king or tyrant should immediately return home, and that they would face exile and confiscation of their goods if they failed to comply. Thanks to this law, numerous noblemen were compelled to abandon the liberality of princes and return home. The reason for passing this law was not merely ill-will, but also the fear that, having acquired favor with kings and princes, the nobility would at some point use that favor to conspire against the state.   18

Around the same time penalties were levelled against those citizens who after the tyrant's downfall had surrendered the castles they commanded. The magistrates were instructed to make diligent inquiries into the matter. Thanks to this law there were numerous condemnations, especially of nobles, to whom the tyrant had mostly entrusted these strongholds.[14]   19

Meanwhile, Florentine merchants in France notified the city that the former tyrant Walter had gone to the king in France and lodged serious complaints against Florence; using his own influence and that of his friends, he had tried to acquire rights over the   20

regem profectum, querelas gravissimas contra civitatem posuisse ac
per se amicosque apud regem niti, ut ius in corpora bonaque florentinorum civium qui per Galliam forent sibi permitteretur; esse
vero periculum ingens, ne corpora in cruciatus, bona in praedam
illi dedantur; iamque ob eam suspicionem plerasque societates ins-
titoresque earum conterritos ad fugam respicere.

21   Eo quidem nuncio commota civitas, incendente insuper vetere
odio, privilegium tulit in tyrannum, praemio ingenti constituto, si
quis eum necaret; et per contumeliam effigies illius apud aedes publicas cum insignibus vitiorum notis depicta. Oratores quoque ea
de causa ad regem missi, ne forte, re temere credita, aliquid, ut fit,
per gratiam tyranno condonaret.

22   Nec multo post legati regis Florentiam venerunt, satisfieri
tyranno postulantes. Petebant vero permagnum auri pondus ob
compensationem damnorum quae a furente multitudine sibi praedicabat[14] illata. His amplissimo consilio cum mandata regis exposuissent, responsum humaniter est, pro regis qui mittebat reverentia. Ceterum ipsius tyranni scelera, sordes, periuria, ceteraque
improbissimi[15] hominis flagitia sic patefacta, ut legati ipsi obmu-
tescere tantam ob malignitatem cogerentur. Ad extremum abdica-
tiones prolatae, quas ille non Florentiae modo, sed etiam Puppi,
tam procul ab urbe, libero in loco, metu omni cessante, sua sponte
fecisset. Nec se tamen admirari, quod ille contra confessiones ac
iusiurandum suum nunc veniat; desisse enim iampridem hoc admirari, cum ille, calcata religione et fide populo data, per fas et ne-
fas omnia fecerit ad quae libido animi cupiditasque impulerit; nullum pudorem hominum, nullum Dei metum unquam habuisse;
debere praestantissimum regem non modo aures scelerato homini

persons and goods of Florentine citizens in France. There was, they said, a great danger that he would be given their bodies to torture and their goods to plunder; and already numerous merchant companies and their employees were in terror of this threat and were contemplating flight.

The city was alarmed by this news, and their old hatred burst   21
into flame with still greater vigor. They passed a bill of attainder against the tyrant, establishing a large reward for anyone who killed him; and, as a further insult, they ordered his image to be painted on public buildings with a description of his notorious vices. Ambassadors were also sent for this purpose to the king, to prevent him giving rash credence to the tyrant's charges and thus condoning the latter's acts through his customary grace and favor.

Soon thereafter the king's representatives came to Florence de-   22
manding satisfaction on the tyrant's behalf. Indeed, they sought an enormous sum of gold in compensation for the damages he claimed to have suffered at the hands of the furious mob. When they had presented their mandate before a very large council,[15] they received a friendly response out of reverence for the king who had sent them. But when the tyrant's wicked deeds, his baseness, perjuries and the other crimes of this most unscrupulous of men were laid bare, the legates themselves were forced into silence in the face of so much malignity. In the end, his acts of abdication were produced, not only the one he had made in Florence, but also the one he had made in far-off Poppi, of his own free will and not under duress. Still, the Florentines were not surprised that he was contravening his own oaths and admissions of guilt; they had indeed ceased being surprised long ago, when that man had trodden under foot conscience and the promises he had made to the People, and without respect for the moral law had done whatever his lust and cupidity had driven him to do; he had never shown the least shame before men or fear before God. So excellent a king should not only not give audience to this rascal, he should also go

non praebere, verum etiam illius nequitiam ultro compescere. In hunc fere modum illis[16] responsum est, et honor de industria maior habitus[17] legatis, quo regis animus per obsequium teneretur.[18]

23   Eodem anno maximum est reipublicae fundamentum parvo ex principio iaci coeptum. Civibus respublica debebat auri pondo circiter septuaginta millia, dudum mutuo sumpta ob Lucae redemptionem. Ea igitur summa cum ob angustiam aerarii dissolvi non posset, ac iniquum videretur suo fraudari cives qui fidem publicam secuti mutuo dederant, media quaedam inter has difficultates reperta[19] est via. Nominibus enim eorum quibus debebatur tributim descriptis, annui redditus e publico constituti sunt, quina singulis centenis. Quantitates vero ipsas in unum coacervatas a similitudine cumulandi vulgo 'montem' vocavere; idque postea in civitate servatum, quotiens respublica indiget, cives tributa persolvunt; solutorum vero pensiones annuas percipiunt. Hi montes cumulationesque pecuniarum bellis quidem crescunt; pace minuuntur, propterea quod abundante republica dissolutio fit crebra atque peremptio. Quantitatum vero descriptarum et venditio est civibus inter se et permutatio atque (ut in ceteris mercimoniis) pro tempore, pro spe, pro commodo minuitur earum pretium atque augescit. In emptorem eadem commoda quae solutor ipse percepturus erat transferuntur. Ea res facit, uti cives ad crebras tributorum solutiones perdurent, non pereunte omnino quod solutum est, sed utilitatem, si non magnam, attamen aliquam afferente.

24   Principio insequentis anni crescente in potentiores odio, leges duae[20] ad populum latae sunt: una in clericos iniqua, per quam omnibus eorum privilegiis derogabatur; altera in cives ingrata, per

further and put a stop to the man's wickedness. This was, approximately, the response given to the king's representatives, and greater honor was intentionally shown them in order to retain the king's good will through deference.

In the same year, a great foundation-stone of the republic was 23 laid, starting from small beginnings. The state owed its citizens about 70,000 florins which it had borrowed to buy back Lucca. The sum could not be paid because of the empty treasury, but it seemed iniquitous to defraud of their due citizens who had given a loan on public security. So a middle course was found between the extremes of fraud and bankruptcy. The names of those to whom payment was owed were written down by *gonfaloni*, and an annual return of five per cent from the public fisc was established. The amounts consolidated into one sum were called "the mountain" or *monte* in the vulgar tongue[16] from its similarity to a mound, and the practice was maintained afterwards in the city.[17] Whenever the state needed funds, the citizens paid a contribution and received annual pensions in repayment thereof. These 'mountains' or consolidated funds grow in time of war and decrease in peacetime, since when the state is wealthy it makes more frequent payments and liquidations. The citizens can buy and exchange Monte credits among themselves, and (as in the case of other commodities) their price increases or decreases in relation to time, investor confidence and yield. The same yield is transferred to the buyer which the seller himself is supposed to receive. This device allow citizens to endure frequent tax assessments, since they don't lose everything they pay, but derive some benefit from it, even if it is not a great benefit.[18]

At the beginning of the following year, as hatred towards the 24 powerful grew, two laws were passed in the popular assembly: an 1345 unjust one against clerics, whereby they were stripped of all their privileges, and an ungrateful one against citizens, whereby grants and prerogatives that had hitherto been bestowed by the people

quam dona ac munera hactenus quibuscumque meritis a populo tradita in irritum vocabantur. Fuisse tunc civitatem in arbitrio multitudinis imperitae decreta ipsa ostendunt. Quid enim hac postrema lege (si modo illa lex nominanda est quae dedecus et infamiam reipublicae parit) iniquius ac vilius excogitare quisquam potest? Defectionem fidei, quae etiam uni privato turpissima est, populo toti[21] impingere. Nihil unquam in republica utile existimandum est quod sit contra dignitatem. Dignitas porro et inconstantiam et ingratitudinem longe repellit. Per eam legem multi, quorum maiores virtutis gratia a populo donati fuerant, munera ipsa et dona relinquere magna cum hominum querela coacti sunt.

25   Eodem anno privata ex re permagna non in singulos modo, sed etiam universae civitati incommoda pervenerunt. Bardorum erat familia omnium locupletissima, permagnas multis in locis societates habens. Haec summa et indubitata fide cum apud cives exterosque ad eam usque diem fuisset, ac multorum ut fit pecunias in manibus[22] haberet, repente inopinatoque decoxit. Causa vero huius fuit quod, surgentibus tunc maxime inter Francorum Anglorumque reges bellis, quidam eius societatis magistri[23] in Britannia degentes, credita regi Anglorum intolerabili pecunia, eo rem adduxere, ut necessarium fuerit fidem societatis abrumpere. Fracta igitur societate, creditores cum reliquias persequerentur,[24] compertum est auri supra quinquies centena millia privatis nominibus societatem debere; mutuo autem regi data circiter septies centena millia, in quibus et propriam societatis pecuniam et eorum qui societati crediderant absumptam constabat. Ea res inopinata et gravis, cum multorum patrimonia afflixisset, traxit post se ruinam minorum societatum, cum ob varia damna quibus singulae implicatae erant, tum quod, ortis apud omnes suspicionibus, ad reposcenda sua[25] quisque credita properabat. Decoquentibus itaque permultis, inaestimabilem iacturam civitas subivit, fidesque angusta in foro omnia perturbabat.

for merit of any kind were revoked. These decrees showed that the city was then controlled by the ignorant multitude. For what more unjust and base law than this latter measure can be imagined — if something that brought so much shame and infamy upon the city can be called a law? The whole city was forced to break faith, something that is extremely shameful even for a single private person. Something that violates the honor of the state should never be reckoned useful. By this law many men were compelled to give up prerogatives and grants that had been bestowed by the People on their ancestors as rewards for virtue, and this caused widespread complaint.[19]

In the same year a private business disaster caused great harm   25 not only to individuals but also to the whole city. The Bardi were the richest of all families, having large business partnerships in many locations. Up to that moment they had enjoyed the highest confidence among citizens and foreigners, and as usual they were holding in their hands monies on behalf of many people. Suddenly, without warning, they failed. The reason for the failure was the wars that had arisen at that time between the French and English kings.[20] Certain managers of the partnership that was based in Britain, having lent an unsustainable amount of money to the king of England, brought matters to the point where it was necessary for them to declare insolvency. So when the partnership failed, its creditors began to go after its assets, and it was discovered that the partnership owed 500,000 florins to private individuals and had lent the king about 700,000 florins, debts that clearly exhausted the resources of the partnership itself and its backers. This serious and unexpected event placed many persons in financial distress and caused the ruin of smaller companies, both because of associated losses and because everybody panicked and ran to withdraw their deposits. Thus there were a large number of bankruptcies, causing inestimable losses to the city, and the lack of credit disturbed everything in the marketplace.

26   Sollicita ob eam rem civitate, lupus medio die Porta Collina ingressus, per urbem decucurrit. Peragrata maxima trans Arnum parte, cum clamor venantium more illum prosequeretur, tandem egressus alia porta, via pisana oppressus est. Eadem quoque die signa populi ad publicas aedes supra portam sculpta sponte sua cecidere. His auguriis multorum animi in timorem versi.

27   Nec multo post a Gallia nuntiatum est regem civitatis causam contra iustitiam aequitatemque improbasse, praedicto tamen tempore, ut qui civis florentinus quaeque civis florentini bona post dies sexaginta in regno reperirentur, in eos eaque ius ac potestas tyranno foret. Ob eam rem incommoda magis accepta sunt quam damna, quod spatium habuerant se suaque colligendi.[26]

28   Altero dehinc anno, primo statim vere, sollicitam habuit civitatem sterilitatis formido, nec id verna tantum intemperie coeli, quantum superioribus imbribus, quae circa sementem omnia diluerant. Itaque segetes perpaucae in agris, et illae ipsae squalidae arentesque cernebantur. Et augebat metum, quod non unam aut alteram Italiae partem, sed totas omnino regiones eadem premebat calamitas. Ex hoc metu caritas primo coorta, eaque ipsa in dies augescens. Tandem, ubi ad messis tempora ventum est, tunc re iam ipsa defectum arguente, cum nil fere ex agris reportaretur, circumspicere sese homines ac futurum horrere, parvosque iam inde natos et imbecillem turbam miserescere.

29   Cum ergo fames haud dubie immineret, sollers plane ad hoc civitas, in Africa et Sardinia et Sicilia aliisque locis permultis magna vi frumenti comparata, mari simul terraque importandum curavit. Nec eo tamen modo evitari potuit, quin difficultates permaximae

While this disaster was afflicting the city, a wolf entered the   26
Porta Collina at midday and ran freely through the city. Traversing
the greatest part of the Oltrarno district, it was pursued with
hunting cries until at last it went out another gate and was killed
on the Via Pisana.[21] On the same day, the arms of the People,
carved above the portal of the Palazzo Vecchio, fell down of their
own accord. These auguries plunged many into a state of fear.

Shortly thereafter the news arrived from France that the king,   27
against all justice and equity, had rejected the city's case [against
Walter of Brienne], and that on a fixed date sixty days from now
all Florentine citizens and all goods of Florentine citizens would
be subject to the jurisdiction and power of the tyrant. This decision caused more inconvenience than loss, since they were given a
period of time to withdraw themselves and their goods.[22]

The following year, at the beginning of spring, the city became   28
concerned about famine, not so much because of the bad weather   *1346*
in the springtime than because of the rains that had preceded it,
which had brought floods everywhere during the sowing. On this
account there were very few crops to be seen in the fields, and
those were rough and parched. The fear of famine was augmented
in that the same calamity threatened not just one or another part,
but every region of Italy. Famine itself, growing every day, followed
in the train of fear. Finally, when the harvest-time came, the real-
ity of the famine was demonstrated, as practically nothing was
brought in from the fields. People began to look at one another in
horror for the future, pitying their new-born children and the im-
poverished multitude.

So, as there was now no doubt about the threat of famine, the   29
city showed its resourcefulness, gathering large supplies of grain in
Africa, Sardinia, Sicily and many other places and seeing to their
importation simultaneously by land and sea. But these steps were
not enough to avoid the enormous difficulties they faced that year.
For throngs of women and children from the countryside came

eo anno subirentur. Turba enim ex agro in urbem mendicatura longis agminibus mulierum puerorumque advenerat. Ex finitimis etiam civitatibus quae minus ad hoc providae fuerant multitudo concurrerat, ut infinitus prope numerus hominum esset alendus. Magnumque in his civitatis meritum humanitasque eluxit; non modo enim non reiectus est quisquam advenarum peregrinorumque, sed etiam si tenuis foret, liberalitate gratuita per tantam rei frumentariae inopiam sustentatus, ut prope collatum a civitate beneficium in genus humanum videretur. Multa insuper eo anno tenuioribus indulta, et illud in primis, quod creditorum acerbitas repressa est, lege lata, ne quis nisi certa forma pro aere alieno conveniri posset. Satis enim premi caritate ipsa multitudinem existimavit civitas. Et accedebant ad caritatem morbi, qui multitudinem convenam et urbis insuetam consecuti, urbanam quoque apprehenderant turbam, ut et commiserendum et succurrendum esset.

30 Fame ac morbo laborantem civitatem nova insuper cura sollicitam reddidit. Carolus enim Iohannis regis filius electus ad imperium ferebatur. Ob eam rem formido iniecta est civitati, nec immerito quidem. Veniebat enim in mentem et cum Herrico huius[27] avo, qui castra ad portas ipsas florentinae urbis habuerat, et cum Iohanne patre bella prope[28] continuata serie gesta fuisse, multisque illorum coeptis per Italiam ab hac civitate obviatum; denique hunc ipsum Carolum adolescentem non expertem fuisse belli, cum et Lucae et per Galliam rudimenta ipsa iuventae adversus hunc populum suo etiam detrimento posuerit. Quibus de causis residere odia infensionesque credebantur. Ceterum harum rerum querela et consternatio erat; nulla tamen remedia tunc adhiberi poterant, prementibus iis de quibus supra diximus incommodis.

into the city in long lines to beg. They were joined by multitudes from the nearby cities which had been less provident in this respect, so that there was almost an infinite number of people to feed. Amid these challenges the city's great merit and humanity shone forth. For not only was not a single immigrant or foreigner turned away, but even the poor, with gratuitous liberality, were sustained throughout this great dearth of provisions, so that Florence seemed almost to have conferred a benefit on the human race. In this year, moreover, many allowances were made on behalf of the poor, and principally this: that the harshness of creditors was kept in check. A law was passed prohibiting suitors to collect debt except under particular conditions; the city felt that the multitude was oppressed enough already by the famine. And in addition to the famine there were the diseases which broke out among the throng of immigrants unused to the city, then spread among the urban masses, so that mercy and succor were needful.[23]

Already struggling with famine and disease, the city now grew   30
anxious about a fresh cause for worry besides. News came that Charles, son of King John, had been elected to rule the empire.[24] This event alarmed the city, and it was right to be alarmed. For the citizens remembered that they had fought a nearly continuous series of wars against Charles' grandfather Henry, who had pitched his camp before the very gates of Florence, as well as against his father John, and that their city had made itself an obstacle to numerous imperial undertakings throughout Italy. They remembered, too, that this same Charles, while still an adolescent untried in war, had, to his loss, had his first youthful experiences at Lucca and in the Lombard campaigns in opposition to this People. For these reasons, it was believed that he would harbor hatred and hostility towards them. But although these considerations caused complaint and consternation, the people were unable to apply any remedies at that time, pressed as they were by the other misfortunes we have already mentioned.

31   Eo anno Minias oppidum[29] in potestatem florentini populi pervenit, dedentibus oppidanis, ob intestinas seditiones et nobilitatis
iniurias fatigatis.

32   Altero dehinc anno, priusquam segetes maturescerent, eaedem
quae superiori tempore difficultates rei frumentariae populum tenuere. Maturis deinde frugibus atque collectis, difficultates illae
pristinae cessavere. Variis tamen morborum generibus laboraba-
tur,[30] et pestilentiae, qua postmodum vastata Italia est, signa quaedam horrenda tunc primum apparuerunt. Ea clades biennio fere
ante (quantum haberi notitia poterat) in Orientis partibus coorta;
mox inde per populos pestilenti contagio evagata, alia subinde appetendo loca, regiones cumulatis funeribus inanierat. Febris erat
sopifera et inguinis tumor. Id quasi venenum quoddam robustissi-
mos iuvenes, alioquin sanos, repente invadens, paucissimis interdum enecabat horis. Contagia omnium exitiosa erant. Ea igitur
tunc civitatem ingressa imbecilliora primum corpora puerorum
puellarumque conficere coepit; inde ad firmiora transgrediens, per
omnem sexum aetatemque vagata est.

33   Eodem anno Ludovicus Roberti regis nepos domo profugus,
parvo admodum comitatu in agrum florentinum pervenit. Fugie-
bat autem Hungariae regem magno cum exercitu Apuliam ingressum, necem fratris nuper interfecti persequentem, ac regnum
quasi haereditarium sibi vindicantem.[31] Pro quarum cognitione rerum paulo altius repetendum est, ut[32] familia civitati nostrae ami-
cissima eiusque casus progressusque non ignorarentur.[33]

34   Carolo, qui primus eius familiae regnum Siciliae obtinuit, filius
unicus superstes fuit, ex eoque numerosa nepotum series. Sed

In that year the town of San Miniato came into the power of   31
the Florentine People. It was surrendered to them by the townsmen, who were exhausted by intestine strife and the nobility's acts
of injustice.

The next year, up until harvest-time, the People were preoccu-   32
pied with the same difficulties of provisioning as before; but once   1347
the crops ripened and were harvested, these earlier difficulties
ceased. Yet they were still suffering from diseases of various kinds,
and certain horrid signs of the pestilence which afterwards devastated Italy then became manifest for the first time.[25] As far as one
can tell, this disaster had arisen two years earlier in parts of the
East, then soon spread with epidemic virulence from populace to
populace, seeking out one place after another, emptying whole regions with piles of corpses. It caused a sleep-inducing fever and a
swelling in the groin. Like a kind of poison it suddenly attacked
the most robust young men, otherwise healthy, and killed them in
a few hours. It was the most destructive of all epidemics; and it
was this epidemic that entered the city at that time. It began by
first consuming the weaker bodies of boys and girls, then passed
on to the stronger, spreading through both sexes and persons of
every age.[26]

In the same year, Luigi, grandson of King Robert,[27] fled from   33
his home and arrived in Florentine territory with a small retinue.
He was fleeing from the King of Hungary,[28] who had entered
Apulia with a great army; the latter was seeking to avenge the recent killing of his brother and was laying claim to the Kingdom as
though it were his inheritance. But to understand these matters,
we must go back a little earlier and familiarize ourselves with the
fortunes and progress of a family that has been a true friend of
our city.

Charles, the first of his family to hold the Kingdom of Sicily,[29]   34
left one son but had a long series of grandchildren from this one
son. Charles' son was defeated in a naval battle not far from Na-

filius ipse navali proelio non procul Neapoli superatus, in Arrago-
nia captivus aliquandiu fuit, ut supra a[34] nobis est quodam loco
narratum. Morienti deinde Carolo, quoniam filius in captivitate
tenebatur, nepotum maximus in regno successit, Carolus et ipse
nomine. Hic igitur adolescens statim post mortem avi regium nomen obtinuit. Reverso deinde[35] a captivitate patre ac regio nomine
suscepto, filius in Pannonias missus, regnum illic obtinuit ex hae-
reditate materna. Ita partito quodammodo honore filius apud Pannonias, pater in Italia regnavit.

35   Mortuo deinde post aliquot annos patre, Robertus secundo natus loco in regno Siciliae successit, etsi non deerant permulti qui
Pannoniis evocandum legitimum successorem existimarent. Et
suberant iam tunc querelae et incusationes, sed Robertum, per
omnem aetatem in Italia commoratum, egregia insuper indole, favor populorum complectebatur; fratris vero filios, veluti longinqui-
tate alienatos, vix iam agnoscebant[36] populi, et quia latissime in
Pannoniis dominabantur, satis superque regni possidere existimabant. Robertus filium habuit Carolum, quem per castruciani belli
tempora cum ingentibus copiis Florentiam venisse ostendimus.
Sed hic vivente adhuc patre defunctus absque virili sobole, filias
reliquit duas, quae parvulae admodum ac paene infantes apud Robertum avum educabantur. Ex Carolo Hungariae rege alius item
Carolus est exortus. Huic filii duo superstites fuere, Ludovicus et
Andreas, quem adolescentem adhuc Robertus, quasi bonam fidem
recognoscens, Iohannae nepti maritum dederat, ac una cum illa regnare in Apulia testamento iusserat. Traductus igitur in Italiam
adolescens et Iohannae coniunctus, cum non[37] satis bene inter eos
conveniret, nec deessent qui reginam contra maritum incitarent,
eo usque simultates occultaque odia processere, ut vocatus per
noctem adolescens, quasi magnum aliquid urgensque instaret, per
fautores reginae, laqueo repente iniecto, suspendio necaretur. Con-

ples and was taken captive for a time in Aragon, as we have narrated above.[30] When Charles died, his oldest grandchild succeeded to the kingdom, since Charles' son was being held in captivity. The grandchild's name was also Charles, and it was this youth who received the royal title immediately after his grandfather's death. Then his father returned from captivity, and taking the royal title sent his son to Hungary, where he took that kingdom by inheritance from his mother.[31] Thus, having shared the honors, as it were, the son ruled in Hungary, the father in Italy.

Then, when the father died a few years later, his second son, Robert, succeeded to the Kingdom of Sicily,[32] although there were not lacking persons who thought that the legitimate successor should be summoned from Hungary. Thereupon followed protests and accusations, but Robert, who had spent his entire life in Italy and was remarkably gifted as well, won the hearts of his people. His brother's sons, on the other hand, as though made foreign by distance, were hardly recognized by the people, who reckoned that, with their vast lordship in Hungary, they possessed kingdom enough and more. Robert had a son, Charles, who (as we showed) came to Florence with great forces during the time of the Castruccian war.[33] But he died without male issue while his father was still alive, leaving behind two daughters who were brought up by their grandfather Robert. They were still little girls, almost babies. Yet another Charles was born to Charles, king of Hungary. This Charles was survived by two sons, Louis and Andreas.[34] As a sign of good faith King Robert gave his granddaughter Johanna in marriage to Andreas, and ordered in his will that he should reign in Apulia with her. The youth was thus brought to Italy and married to Johanna, but they did not get along very well, and there was no lack of people to incite her against her husband. The feuds and hatreds proceeded to the point where the youth, summoned by night on the pretext of some great and urgent crisis, was garrotted and strung up by supporters of the queen. It was believed that the

35

sciam fuisse reginam tam atrocis facinoris creditum est; et auxit infamiam alter subinde coniunx ab illa susceptus.

36   Ea foeditas Ludovicum Hungariae regem permovit, ut cum exercitu in Italiam veniens et fratris necem indignam et regnum quasi debitum sibi vindicaret. Regina metu extorris in narbonensem aufugit provinciam. Nec multo post eam secutus novus coniunx (erat enim ipse quoque patruelis), parvo comitatu in agrum florentinum advenerat. Civitas, quoniam domesticae illius familiae erant discordiae ac res atrocissima agebatur, neutrae parti favere constituit. Itaque nec venire in urbem cupientem permisit, nec ullo auxilii genere, postulantem licet, prosecuta est.

37   Proximo dehinc anno pestis iampridem ingressa urbem[38] ita desaevivit, ut supra fidem videatur eius stragem referre. Sexaginta amplius hominum millia defuncta morbo intra urbem constat, et insignes viros, quorum consilio respublica nitebatur, ferme omnes sublatos. In agro autem exinanita cuncta ac paene deserta. Ob eam calamitatem, nihil publice geri eo anno potuit. Tantum adversus latrones, qui per Apennini iugum itinera infestabant, copiae quaedam missae.

38   Sequenti etiam anno parum aut nihil gestum, consternata adhuc civitate superiori pestilentia. Collenses tantum et Geminianenses domesticis seditionibus laborantes in potestatem florentini populi redierunt. Et circa Apenninum aliquot castella de Ubaldinis capta, quibus latrocinia exercebantur.

39   Altero dehinc anno (is erat annus quinquagesimus supra millesimum trecentesimum) nova sunt ac magna rerum certamina civitati exorta. Johannes erat Vicecomes Mediolanensium praesul. Is suscepta a suis dominatione[39] late per Galliam imperabat, et ad ve-

queen had been party to this atrocious crime, and her infamy increased when she immediately took another husband.[35]

It was this foul and shameful situation that caused Louis of 36 Hungary to come with his army to Italy to avenge the undeserved death of his brother and lay claim to the Kingdom as his due. The queen, driven into exile by fear, took refuge in the province of Narbonne. Shortly thereafter, her new husband, who was also her cousin, entered Florentine territory with a small retinue.[36] Since the matter involved a dreadful crime and internal family quarrels, the city decided to favor neither party. So it did not give its permission to the husband, who wanted to enter the city, nor did it provide him with any kind of aid, despite his requests.[37]

By the next year, the plague had long since entered the city and 37 ravaged it to such an extent that the tale of its slaughter seems be- 1348 yond belief. It is evident that more than 70,000 people inside the city died of the disease, and nearly all the distinguished men on whom the city relied were wiped out. The countryside was entirely emptied out and practically deserted. Thanks to this calamity, no public business could be conducted this year. The only action was to send some troops out against robbers infesting the roads that crossed the Apennine passes.[38]

In the following year, too, little or nothing was done, as the city 38 was still in shock from the plague. The peoples of Colle Val d'Elsa 1349 and San Gimignano, wracked by domestic turmoils, returned to the power of the Florentine People. And in the Apennines several castles of the Ubaldini were taken which had been centers of brigandage.[39]

The next year — it was now the year 1350 — a new and great 39 challenge arose for the city. The archbishop of Milan, Giovanni 1350 Visconti, had received the lordship of the city from his relations, and was exercising vast power throughout Lombardy, having himself increased greatly the old power that had belonged to his family.[40] In so doing he had become the most powerful of all the ty-

terem suorum potentiam maxima et ipse addiderat incrementa. Ex
quo egregie potens tyrannorum omnium factus, cum iam antea
formidabilis esset, tum auxit timorem Bononia, per hoc ipsum
tempus dominio eius adiuncta, civitas magna atque finitima, ut
eam possidens, tam ingens potentia minime quietura videretur.

40   Adversus hunc igitur nascentem morbum remedia quaerens civitas non subito nec impotenti et temerario impetu, sed maturitate
consilii et prudentia vestigabat. Graviter ferre pontificem romanum Bononiae occupationem non ambiguum erat. Formidari
etiam mediolanensis robur a Mastino ceterisque finitimis tyrannis
aestimabatur. Cum his omnibus si societas iniretur, accedentibus
Etruriae civitatibus quae erant in foedere, satis superque virium
fore ad comprimendam Mediolanensis potentiam iudicabant.
Data his omnibus occulte opera est a civitate. Denique civitatis
consilio et opera factum est, ut et[40] legatus a pontifice missus et
tyrannorum civitatumque oratores huius rei gratia[41] in unum coirent. Conventus congressusque omnium Arretii fuit. In re agi-
tanda tractandaque Perusini, quoniam longius aberant a suspicione periculi, minus eam societatem appetere comperti sunt, etsi
id non aperte, ne discrepare a sociorum voluntate viderentur, sed
per singula rerum tractandarum capitula difficultatem reperientes
disceptantesque ac demum allegantes, rem in longum protrahe-
bant.

41   Inter hanc moram nuntius de Mastini morte supervenit. Eaque
de causa conventus re infecta[42] dimissus, cum iam deprehensa Perusinorum mente vel praeter eos statuissent ceteri societatem
coire. Hoc igitur quasi fortunae beneficium coeptis suis faventis
accipiens, praesul (senserat enim conventus Arretii factos et contra

rants. He had been formidable already before, but the addition of Bologna to his dominions around this time increased the Florentines' alarm. It seemed that so great a power, now in possession of this large neighboring city, was hardly going to refrain from aggression.

So the city began to investigate remedies against this nascent 40 disease—not precipitately or with rash and impotent force, but with prudence and after mature counsel. There was no doubt that the pope was gravely distressed by the occupation of Bologna. It was reckoned, too, that Milanese strength was feared by Mastino and the other nearby tyrants. They concluded that, if they formed an alliance with all these powers, adding to them the Tuscan cities belonging to their federation, they would have more than enough strength to subdue the power of Milan. The city secretly took steps to compass these ends. Finally, through the city's advice and activity, a meeting was arranged to discuss the matter with the papal legate and the ambassadors of the tyrants and the cities. The conference of all the allies was held in Arezzo. In the course of the negotiations the Perugians were found to be less eager for the alliance, owing to their greater distance from the danger. They made no open opposition to it, lest they should seem to deviate from the will of the allies, but they discovered difficulties with every single clause of the negotiation, making demurrals and counter-proposals, thus dragging the matter out.

During this delay, news arrived of Mastino's death. As a result, 41 the conference broke up with its business unfinished, although, 1351 having learned the intentions of the Perugians, the other parties had already decided to enter the alliance even without them. The archbishop took this as Fortune favoring his designs, for he knew about the meetings in Arezzo and understood that they had been set on foot against himself. Immediately he planned still greater designs. Rapidly and with clever foresight he won over to his friendship and protection all the Ghibellines in Tuscany and the

se parari[43] illa intelligebat) maiora statim animo concepit. Itaque dedita confestim sagaci opera, per Etruriam ac Flaminiam cunctos diversae factionis homines in suam amicitiam tutelamque pellexit. Ne quid vero sibi a tergo relinqueretur, Mastini filium, qui mortuo patri in dominatu successerat, multis magnisque pollicitationibus delinitum, non modo avertit a proposito paterno, verum etiam foedere sibi insuper amicitiaque coniunxit. Quo facto ceteri quoque per Galliam tyranni in eius amicitiam concessere. Inter haec propositum dissimulans, de florentino populo amicissime loquebatur, scribebatque nonnumquam, quo suspicionem auferret. Bononiae copiis quas ea[44] in urbe habebat, Bernabovem praefecerat nepotem, viderique cupiebat mentem suam ad alia spectare.

42   Quin etiam, ut alibi implicaretur bello, exercitum[45] ad Imolam misso, obsideri eam urbem iussit. Affuerunt in obsidione Bononienses magno quidem numero, iussi hoc agere, ne relicti domi per absentiam copiarum aliquid molirentur. Affuerunt etiam Faventini et Forolivienses, quorum tyranni, partim ob inimicitias romani pontificis, partim simili studio partium, sese Mediolanensi coniunxerant. Praeter hos, copias suas adduxerat Bernabos equitum ad tria,[46] peditum vero mercede conductorum ad quatuor millia. Hac multitudine copiarum fretus, Imolam primo statim adventu expugnare aggressus est. Quod cum minus succederet, eam undequaque praesidiis cinxit. Vi autem expugnare non amplius[47] tentavit, expertus aliquotiens frustra conari se adversus urbem munitam fossis atque ab his qui erant intus egregie defensam.

43   Florentinis vero haec intuentibus in dies magis crescebat formido, praesertim cum Pisanos Mediolanensi adhaesisse rumor vulgasset. Et dubitabatur de Pratensium Pistoriensiumque fide, quorum[48] oppida et finitima urbi et opportunissima bello infe-

Romagna. And lest he should be threatened from the rear, he mollified with many great promises Mastino's son, who had succeeded to his father's dominions after the latter's death. Not only did Visconti alienate the son from his father's purpose, but he even attached the man to himself in friendship and alliance. Whereupon the rest of the north Italian tyrants also yielded to his overtures of friendship. Meanwhile, disguising his aim, he began to speak in a most friendly way about the Florentine People, and used to write from time to time so as to allay suspicion. He put his nephew Bernabò in charge of his troops in Bologna, and wanted it to seem as though his thoughts were trained on other objectives.

And indeed, in order to become involved in a war elsewhere, he 42 sent his army to Imola with orders to besiege that town. A large number of Bolognese were present at the siege; they were ordered to take part in case, being left behind, they should engage in some plot in the absence of the troops. Men from Faenza and Forlì were also present, as their tyrants, partly from enmity towards the pope, partly from party loyalty, had joined the Milanese. In addition, Bernabò brought his three thousand horse and four thousand mercenary infantry. Relying on this mass of troops, he began to attack Imola the moment he arrived. When this attack was less than successful, he surrounded the city with fortifications on all sides. No longer did he try to take the city by force, having learned after several attempts that it was vain to attack a city fortified by a moat and bravely defended by those inside.

When the Florentines saw what was happening they became 43 increasingly alarmed, especially since the rumor had been going around that the Pisans were siding with the Milanese. There were also doubts about the loyalty of the Pratesi and the Pistoiesi, whose towns were nearby and extremely suitable as bases for making war. If the adversary should get control of either one of them, it was reckoned that liberty would be done for. Their internal dis-

rendo plurimum erant. Eorum si alterutro potiretur adversarius tam potens, actum de libertate existimabatur. Suspiciosiorem vero rem faciebant eorum discordiae, per quas facile subrepere adversarius posset. Ad haec igitur ante omnia conversae mentes, neque negligendum neque differendum statuere. Itaque multitudine confestim armata missisque repente copiis, ad ipsa Prati moenia, non tam hostili quam inopinato terrore, posuerunt castra. Pratenses subita re trepidi, utpote qui nec rationem huius facti neque consilium nossent, sumpserunt raptim arma et ad eam partem oppidi qua castra erant concurrerunt.[49] Ibi, cum Florentinos in armis cernerent, nihil hostiliter molientes neque laedentes quemquam, sed illud modo postulantes, ut ad tollendas suspiciones custodia eius oppidi florentino populo traderetur, pro communi utilitate quieteque eam habituro, etsi dura vox plerisque videbatur, tamen, quando tantae copiae ad portas starent, ipsi vero imparati omnino essent, incerti primum consilii aliquandiu stetere, neque concedere postulata neque negare audentes.

44 Inter haec florentini cives qui in armis erant, ut quisque notum amicumque Prati habebat, compellando benigne exhortandoque in sententiam trahere conabantur, monentes, quoniam desiderium florentini populi conspiciant, parere voluntati quam vim experiri malint; multa quae interdum aspera primo videantur, prospera tamen ad extremum reperiri;[50] id esse consilium florentini populi, ut non minus de Pratensium quam de sua propria salute cogitetur. His tandem vocibus ac virorum reverentia et praesenti necessitate compulsi, Pratenses portas aperuere et Florentinorum praesidium intra moenia recepere.

45 Et res quidem pratensis in hunc modum composita, suspicionem[51] ab ea parte sustulerat. Restabant Pistorienses. Ea quo am-

cords, which might easily allow their adversary to slither his way in, made the situation even more fraught with danger. So the Florentines made this situation their first priority, and decided that the problem could neither be neglected nor put off. Hastily they armed the urban masses and sent troops suddenly to pitch camp by the very walls of Prato, frightening the Pratesi more by their unexpected arrival than by their hostile intent. The Pratesi, knowing neither the reason nor the purpose of this act, in panic seized arms quickly and ran to the part of the city opposite the encampment. There they saw the Florentines in arms, not taking any hostile actions nor harming anyone, but just asking, in order to remove any suspicion, that guardianship of the city be handed over to the Florentine People, who would hold it for the sake of peace and the common good. To many this seemed rough language, yet with so many troops on their doorstep and themselves entirely unprepared, they at first remained undecided for some time, daring neither to allow nor deny the Florentine demands.

44 Meanwhile, the Florentine citizens in the army, each of whom had some acquaintance or friend in Prato, tried to convince the Pratesi through kindly pressure and exhortation. They advised them, in view of the Florentine People's desires, to accede to its wishes rather than experience its warlike strength; many things which seem hard in the short run turned out prosperously in the end; the aim of the Florentine People was to plan for the safety of the Pratese people no less than for their own. Convinced at last by these assurances, their respect for the men who made them, and by present necessity, the Pratesi opened their gates and accepted a Florentine garrison inside their walls.[41]

45 Having settled the situation in Prato in this way and removed the threat from that direction, there remained the Pistoiesi. That city being larger, it seemed advisable to treat it with greater care. But factional strife had recently arisen in the city which had driven one party of citizens into exile, and this provided a suitable open-

plior erat civitas, eo cautiori studio tractanda videbatur. Sed obtulit occasionem idoneam seditio, quae recens in ea civitate coorta
partem civium egerat extorrem. Itaque per speciem officii praesidium eo mittere Florentini postularunt. Pistorienses vero non dis-
simili figmento id recipere annuerunt, sed nec ita multum, ut sibi
formidandum esset, et eos ipsos quos receperant sacramento obli-
garunt. Quare per eam quidem viam nihil profectum videbatur, et
suberat formido mentibus[52] infixa. Qua intenti priores civitatis,
dum ipsi per sese absque populi scitu providere festinant, inhones-
tum tandem[53] consilium susceperunt. Re enim cum exulibus Pistoriensium arcane composita, subitarias cum illis miserunt copias.
Hi noctu progressi, nullo penitus suspicante, primo statim adventu scalis moenia conscenderunt, et quosdam in urbem dimiserunt. Ipsi vero[54] de muris clamorem tollentes, sperabant milites,
qui praesidii causa missi fuerant, una secum rem aggressuros. Etenim praemiserat magistratus ad[55] eos Petrum quendam,[56] condu-
cendis militibus scribam, et ob id plerisque eorum familiarem qui
rem ediceret. Sed is sive metu sive negligentia per viam desederat.
Itaque milites, totius rei ignari, ut primum clamor e muris sublatus est, integra fide cum Pistoriensibus concurrerunt, factoque
confestim globo ingressores deturbarunt. Ita pulsi e muris qui cum
exulibus ascenderant,[57] quot eorum se in urbem dimiserant, aut
capti aut interfecti sunt.

46   Crediderant primo Pistorienses exulum modo suorum fuisse
conatum, qui error audaciam eorum plurimum iuvit. Sed postquam ex captivis adesse florentini populi copias intellexere, atque
orta subinde lux vexilla patefecit, maiorem sibi imminere periculi

ing. Hence under the guise of offering help, the Florentines asked if they might send a garrison there. The Pistoiesi, employing a similar disguise, agreed to receive one, but not so large a force as to cause fear, and they bound those who were sent them with a loyalty oath. Thus it appeared that nothing had been accomplished by that course of action, and the Florentines remained apprehensive. The priors, preoccupied by this fear, hastened to take preemptive action on their own, without the knowledge of the people, and in the end followed dishonorable counsel. They plotted secretly with the Pistoiese exiles and sent out some makeshift forces with them. Setting out by night without arousing anyone's suspicion, these men immediately swarmed up ladders as soon as they arrived, and some of them climbed down into the city. The others raised a clamor from the walls, hoping that the soldiers who had been sent to garrison the city would join their attack. And indeed, the priors had sent in advance to the garrison the notary in charge of hiring soldiers, a certain Piero,[12] who was on that account known to most of them, so as to inform them of the plot. But he, whether through fear or negligence, had loitered on the way, and so the soldiers were ignorant of the whole affair. Thus, when the cry first went up from the walls, they loyally ran out alongside the Pistoiesi, quickly formed themselves into a single mass, and expelled the intruders. Those who had climbed up the walls with the exiles were cast down, and all those who had managed to get inside the city were either captured or killed.

At first the Pistoiesi believed that the attempt had been made   46 by their exiles acting alone, and this mistake had contributed to their boldness of action. But when they learnt from the captives that troops of the Florentine People had been present, and the morning light revealed their standards, the Pistoiesi realized that the danger threatening them was a much greater one, and they prepared themselves for a fight, rising up fiercely to protect their city. When the news of the attempt made its way shortly thereaf-

molem sentientes, ad certamen se compararunt et ad tutelam urbis acrius surrexere. Haec paulo post Florentiae vulgata optimum quemque et gravissimum commoverunt, lacerabaturque circulis et conventibus magistratus coeptum, utpote foedum atque nefarium. Ignaviam vero et imperitiam omnes detestabantur: iam vero non adauctam modo suspicionem, sed certum in periculum rem coniectam existimabant, putantibus cunctis Pistorienses tanta fraude iniuriaque compulsos, ad tyrannum eiusque propinquas opes se haud dubie conversuros. Cum vero quid agendum foret consultaretur, etsi coeptum improbabant omnes maxime, tamen quid potissimum ut in malis sequendum foret dubitabant. Denique coacto civium consilio,[58] cum de hoc ipso consultaretur, assurgens quidam ex senioribus, in hunc fere modum orationem habuit:

47   'Si res integra nobis foret, o praesides, nec attentata prius neque detecta, non difficile mihi videretur consilium explicare; quippe suspicionem libertatis alterius occupandae finitimis inferre, et omnem incertum atque iniustum motum, nostris rationibus inimicum censerem. Nunc autem eo difficilior consultatio est, quod perperam ac[59] paene contra naturam agitur. Quippe ceteri quidem omnes ante rem consultare solent; vos autem (quod bona venia dictum sit) post rem actam consilium postulatis. Atqui bono quidem animo factum a vobis, praesides, existimare debemus qualecumque tandem est[60] factum; nota est enim integritas vestra et fides et animus in republica sincerus et rectus. Verumtamen res gerendae, praesertim magnae et non ad privati alicuius sed ad totius civitatis discrimen pertinentes, non propositum solummodo bonum, sed considerationem maximam et circumspectam multorum deliberationem efflagitant. Nam ea quae multorum sunt, a paucis determinari nec honestum est, nec illis ipsis qui determinant tutum. Populus enim, nisi suarum rerum auctor ipse sit, quaecumque non recte ceciderunt exagitare solet ac poenas non-

ter to Florence, it distressed all the best and gravest men, and the priors' undertaking was sharply criticized in informal gatherings and meetings as a foul and wicked act. People felt abhorrence for their base and ignorant behavior, for now, they reckoned, the plot had not only increased tensions, but placed themselves in certain danger. Everyone thought that the Pistoiesi would undoubtedly be compelled by this deceitful and unjust act to have recourse to the tyrant and the resources he had nearby.[43] But when they took counsel about what should be done, although there was universal condemnation of the priors' enterprise, there was still considerable doubt what course to follow in this evil state of affairs. Finally, citizens were summoned to give advice, and when the matter came up for discussion, one of the older men arose and delivered an oration something like this:

"If it were possible to start over, O priors, and your enterprise 47 was not already compromised and exposed to view, I think it would not be hard to offer counsel. Indeed, I should think that causing one's neighbors to suspect that one has designs on their liberty, and every dubious and unjust activity, is hostile to our way of thinking. As it is, however, giving advice is more difficult because the problem has been dealt with wrongly and almost unnaturally. Everyone else takes counsel before acting, but you (begging your pardon) are asking for counsel after having acted. Yet we are obliged to believe that you acted from good motives, priors, whatever the outcome of your actions; your integrity, loyalty and sincere habit of rectitude towards the republic are not in question. But the conduct of affairs, especially great affairs affecting the fate, not of some private citizen, but of the whole city, requires not just good motives but the widest consultation and careful deliberation on the part of many persons. For it is not honorable for a few to take decisions which affect many, nor is it safe for the decision-makers. When a people is not responsible for its own affairs, it will find fault whenever things go wrong, and will sometimes de-

numquam imperiose exigere. Sed facta quidem, ne facta sint, fieri
non potest. Itaque haec omittamus conqueri, et quid remedii sit in
hisce malis potius meditemur.

48 'Dico igitur non esse pistoriense coeptum a nobis deserendum,
non quia id probem—nec enim si res integra foret, idem consulerem[61]—sed quia, cum semel coeptum fuerit, periculosum nimis
foret, si in hac suspicione Pistorienses dimitterentur. Longe autem
minus dubitandum esset de Pistoriensium voluntate, si lacessiti
non fuissent a nobis, qui, praeter quam occupare nocturna fraude
illorum urbem, exules insuper, inimicos eorum qui rempublicam
gubernant, armatos reducere in ipsorum cervices studuimus. Haec
autem qualia sint de nobis ipsis coniecturam facite. Neque enim,
cum ipsi tam[62] caram[63] habeamus libertatem nostram, cum pro illa
pericula omnia, mortem etiam, si expediat, oppetendam praedice-
mus, non eundem sensum esse ceteris hominibus existimandum
est. Nonnullis[64] forsan eius rei facultatem deesse, at enim voluntatem omnibus eandem esse putandum est. Reductionem vero exulum nostrorum[65] quibus nos, quaeso, indignationibus perferremus,
si non pactione consensuque nostro, sed armatos et per vim im-
provisam quis eos reduceret contra cervices nostras?

49 'Haec igitur omnia pensantes, inimicissimo erga nos esse animo
Pistorienses existimare debemus, ac potestatem omnem praeripere
nocendi. Illud[66] ostendatur verbis non esse propositi nostri libertatem eorum auferre, sed pro incolumitate sua ac nostra praesidium
in urbe ipsorum quoddam habere, quo et ipsi tranquillius degant,
nos vero securius, et suspicio de mentibus florentini populi auferatur. Quod si recipere nolint, non esse nos sic habituros, ut cum
hac suspicione nos et ipsi relinquamur.[67] Denique ostendatur illis
esse in eorum arbitrio, utrum hostem florentinum populum an

mand punishment in an arbitrary fashion. But what's done is done. So let us not complain, but let us rather consider how to remedy this evil state of affairs.

"My view, then, is that the Pistoiese enterprise should not be 48 abandoned, not because I approve of it—and I should not advise it if we could start over—but because it would be too dangerous to leave the Pistoiesi to their suspicions now that we have undertaken it. We should be in far less doubt about the good will of the Pistoiesi if we had not injured them, not only by trying to seize their city in an act of nocturnal trickery, but also by attempting to impose rulers on them, armed exiles hostile to their regime. The effects of these actions you can guess from your own sentiments. When we ourselves hold liberty so dear that we declare we would face all dangers, even death, to secure it, we should not imagine that this same sentiment is lacking in the rest of mankind. Some may lack the capacity for freedom, but we must believe that everyone shares the will to be free. Think how indignant we would be at the return of our exiles if someone should arm them and by force, without warning, impose them as rulers over our heads without our agreement or consent.

"Weighing all these circumstances, therefore, we should reckon 49 that the Pistoiesi will be extremely hostile towards us and we must strip them of any power to harm us. We should make it plain to them verbally that it is not our intention to take away their liberty, but to maintain a kind of garrison in their city for our mutual protection, so that they can dwell in greater tranquillity and we in greater safety, and so that suspicion about the intentions of the Florentine People may be removed. If they will not accept a garrison, we should tell them that it is unacceptable to us, for our part, to be left in a state of suspicion. Finally we should make it clear to them that it is their decision whether they prefer to have the Florentine People as their enemy or as a well-disposed friend. Such discussions should not slow down any of our preparations for

propitium et amicum habere malint. Nec ob ea verba retardentur quaecumque ad obsidendas expugnandasque urbes sunt comparanda. Rogentur auxilia socii; copiae omnes ad[68] Pistorium cogantur; iuventus nostra sub vexillis egrediatur; ostententur machinae; tormenta convehantur, ut non levi conatu, sed praesenti obstinatoque animo cuncta facere videamur. Aut enim verbis apparatuque nostro flectentur Pistorienses aut, si pertinaces protervique esse pergent, malo domiti frangentur. Dixi quae mihi optima factu in hoc tempore videantur. Deum rogo vestris in mentibus ponere quae salutaria maxime sint futura.'

50 Hanc sententiam ad extremum secuta civitas, statuit ab incepto haudquaquam desistere, sed extrema cuncta experiri, quo Pistorium in potestatem venire cogeretur. Hac itaque[69] mente undique copias contrahere ac maiore vi urgere Pistorium perrexere, ut essent intra triduum in castris armatorum supra quindecim millia. Hac multitudine urbem circumdantes, vallo et fossa illam cinxere, ut nemo ingredi egredive posset. Pistorienses contra vi summa obnixi ius libertatemque tueri contendebant, neque noctu neque interdiu[70] laboribus absistentes. Milites autem florentini populi qui intus fuerant incolumes dimiserunt; neque enim nocte illa, qua tentata invasio est, inutiles fuerant Pistoriensibus, nec postea quicquam contra fidem egerant, sed arma tenentes, cum honestate quierant, nec faventes cuiquam neque[71] molesti.

51 Et Pistorium quidem in hunc modum obsidebatur. Hostilis tamen oppugnatio deerat; colloquia vero prope quotidiana fiebant obsessos inter et obsidentes, his, ut acciperent praesidium in urbem ad tollendas suspiciones, illis, nec iustam nec aequam postulationem nullamque esse causam cur suspicari de se debuerint,

siege warfare. Let the allies be asked for aid; let all our forces be mustered near Pistoia; let our young men march out under their banners; let us display our engines of war; let the catapults be wheeled out, so that we may seem to be undertaking a resolute, steadfast action, not some harebrained scheme. Either the Pistoiesi will be swayed by our words and our preparations for war, or, if they continue in their shameless pertinacity, they will be mastered and crushed to their harm. I have said what I believe to be the best course at this moment; I pray God that He may put into your minds what will be the most salutary decision."

In the end the city followed this counsel, and decided it should by no means desist from the enterprise, but try every last means to subdue Pistoia. So with this intention, they collected forces from all over and tried with yet greater energy to put pressure on Pistoia. As a result, within three days over fifteen thousand men joined the camps. Surrounding the city with these forces, they ringed it with trenches and earthworks so that no one could go in or leave. The Pistoiesi in return tried to protect their rights and liberty with all their strength, working night and day. They released unharmed the soldiers of the Florentine People who were inside. The latter had been of some use to the Pistoiesi on the night of the attack and had afterwards done nothing to violate their trust, and though armed, had honorably remained quiescent, neither favoring nor harming anyone.

Thus was Pistoia placed under siege. Yet there was no hostile encounter, but almost daily there were parleys between the besieged and the besiegers. The Florentines argued that the Pistoiesi should receive a garrison in their city to remove any suspicions, while the Pistoiesi maintained that this demand was neither just nor fair and that there was no reason why they ought to be held suspect. But since nothing was accomplished in this way and it appeared that time was being wasted fruitlessly, and since the parleys themselves, being conducted with a little too much freedom of ex-

contendentibus. Sed cum per eum modum nihil proficeretur ac teri frustra tempus appareret, et colloquia ipsa interdum liberius agitata contentionem certamenque accenderent, ad vim converti res coepit, et quasi iusto cum hoste bellum et oppugnatio parabatur. Ea de causa vineas agere turresque ligneas excitari atque cetera convehi ad oppugnandas urbes opportuna, cum aspicerent Pistoriensium ii qui amicitiores[72] florentini populi per omnem vitam fuerant, veriti ne oppugnatione adhibita reliqui Pistoriensium ad opes tyranni convertantur, ac suarum partium eversio sequatur, praestare tandem statuerunt praesidium florentini populi in urbem recipere. Horum sententiam (erat enim haec maxima pars) ceteri quoque tandem secuti sunt. Per hunc modum res male coepta bonum tandem exitum habuit.

52   Pistorio Pratoque receptis, Florentini, minus iam suspiciose degentes, conquierunt. Neque enim hostile quicquam adversus se moveri intuebantur, neque causas ullas belli iustas subesse. Sublata quoque facultate propinqui alicuius oppidi potiundi, magna ex parte obviatum periculo existimabant. Et augebat fidem caritas ficta, quod praesul ac sui qui Bononiae praeerant[73] honorificentissime de florentino populo loquebantur; et quotiens quid incidebat, promptus in primis erat favor, ut nihil minus diceres quam aliquid adversi cogitare, contentumque vicinitate, satis bene secum agi, si dominatus Bononiae sibi nequaquam turbaretur. His de causis Florentini neque militem parare neque ducem pergebant, ne ipsi non parum confidere praesenti quiete viderentur, eoque ipso quod augerent copias, aliquid suspicionis illi afferrent. Enimvero[74] parandi augendique copias praesuli magna suberat facultas. Nam et imolense bellum superstes videbatur, et per Galliam suspiciones

pression, from time to time kindled contention and rivalry, the parties began to resort to violent means, and readied themselves for war and assault as though fighting a real enemy. Hence when those Pistoiesi who had been lifelong friends of the Florentine People saw siege engines and wooden towers being constructed and other materiel useful for attacking cities being hauled up, they grew fearful that the rest of the Pistoiesi would have recourse to the tyrant's resources when the attack began, leading to the overthrow of their own party. So finally they decided it would be better to receive the garrison of the Florentine People inside the city. In the end the rest, too, accepted the decision of the pro-Florentine party, which was in fact the largest party. Thus an enterprise which began badly in the end turned out well.[44]

Having taken control of Pistoia and Prato, the Florentines' suspicions subsided and they relaxed. They could see no hostile plans afoot and were aware of no just reasons for a war. Once they had removed the possibility that someone might get control over a nearby town, they reckoned they had in large part checked the danger. A pretense of affection increased their confidence, for the archbishop and his authorities in Bologna were in the habit of speaking of the Florentine People with the highest respect; and whenever some incident occurred they were immediately ready with an act of goodwill. You would have thought that the man had no designs whatsoever against Florence, but was content to be her neighbor and was satisfied to remain unmolested in his lordship over Bologna. Hence the Florentines did not make military preparations or appoint a captain lest they should appear to lack confidence in the current state of peace and themselves arouse suspicion by the very act of increasing their forces. On the other hand, the archbishop had an excellent opportunity to mobilize and enlarge his forces. For the war with Imola still continued and it was not hard to find cover in the existing tensions throughout Lombardy, while his new lordship in Bologna was highly suspicious of

metusque praetexere non difficile erat, et nova Bononiae dominatio contra cives ipsos suspiciosissima, citra ullum florentini populi
respectum, robur et arma flagitare videbatur. His rationibus effectum est, ut civitas inter spem et[75] metum dubia perstaret inermis,
adversarius vero armaretur.

53   Cum satis paratus esset mediolanensis praesul, cives bononienses, primarios in ea civitate homines, quasi coniurationis reos capi
iubet. Ab his, uti voluit, tormentis extorquet sese de dominatu
eius repellendo liberandaque civitate cum florentino populo consilium iniisse. Hinc arrepta belli occasio est. Quid enim minus deest
tyrannis quam falsas pro veris causas effingere?

54   Hanc igitur ille praetexens causam, cum bellum movere statuisset, diversae factionis homines, quos per Etruriam sibi coniunxisse
supra diximus, ad se in Galliam vocat. Ivere frequentes quasi salu-
tandi officio; quorum vero profectio suspiciosior erat, ii[76] legatos
misere. Eos ergo in unum convocatos adversus florentinum populum incendit; damna quae singuli per superiora tempora perpessi
sunt[77] commemorat;[78] venisse tempus affirmat, si modo viri esse
velint, florentinum populum opprimendi ac diversae factionis nomen penitus extinguendi; se enim, si operam illi suam polliceant-
tur, exercitum magna multitudine florentinum in agrum mittere
urbemque urgere statuisse; providendum ab illis esse, cum exercitus illis in locis fuerit, quisque res novas, ut a suis oppidis unum
sub tempus, quanto maxime valet, impetu moliatur; ita subito cir-
cumventum undique[79] florentinum populum resistere non posse.
Huius dicta—erant enim vero similia propter summam dicentis
auctoritatem ac potentiam—omnes qui aderant laetis animis exceperunt; operam suam strenue polliciti, cohortati etiam, ne tam
certae spei deesse vellet. Re itaque in hunc modum composita discedunt, quae opus ad bellum sunt tacite parant adventumque copiarum praestolantur.

its own citizens, a situation which appeared to require armed strength, without reference to any considerations regarding the Florentine People. Thus it came about that, caught between hope and fear, the city remained unarmed, while its adversary armed himself.

Once all was ready, the archbishop of Milan ordered the leading 53 citizens of Bologna to be arrested as though they were guilty of a conspiracy. He extracted from them under torture, as he had intended, a confession that they had held discussions with the Florentine People about throwing off his lordship and freeing the city. This became his pretext for war. Is there anything more common than for tyrants to invent false reasons in place of true ones?

So, alleging this as his reason, once he had decided to start the 54 war, he summoned to himself in Lombardy the Tuscan Ghibellines he had attached to his cause, as described above. Crowds of them came as though to pay their respects, while those whose coming would arouse more suspicion were sent as envoys. Assembling them all together, he set them ablaze against the Florentine People. He recounted the losses each of them had suffered in times past, and declared that, if only they would act like men, the time had come for crushing the Florentine People and for stamping out entirely the Guelf name. If they would promise him their aid, he had resolved to send a mighty host into Florentine territory and beset the city. For their part they should each do their best, once the army was in place, to see that revolts broke out simultaneously in their several towns, so that, surrounded suddenly on all sides, the Florentine People would not be able to resist. All those present took in his words with great joy, and the great authority and power of the speaker made them plausible. They promised him their active assistance, even exhorting him to persevere in a project so sure of success. Having made these arrangements, the Tuscan Ghibellines departed to make secret preparations for war and to await the coming of the troops.

55   Praesul omnibus copiis Iohannem praefecerat Vicecomitem, cui
Olegiano fuit cognomentum, et quae fieri vellet secreto mandave-
rat. Hic igitur copiis undique in agrum bononiensem contractis,
cum omnes in unum convenissent, inde repente movens nemine
penitus suspicante ad iugum Apennini duxit, qua bononiensem
agrum pistoriensemque disterminat. Ibi nocte una commoratus,
altera mox luce circa Pistorium descendit, nec longe ab ea urbe posuit castra. Florentini, subita re paene attoniti, quo se verterent ad
primum statim nuntium nesciebant; et trepidabatur ubique, et (ut
in gravibus repentinisque periculis accidere solet) subesse aliquid
arcanae fraudis timebatur. Missi tamen raptim equites quingenti et
pedites trecenti Pistorium intrarunt. Hi praesidio quod prius in ea
urbe fuerat adiuncti, amicis quidem animos fecerunt ad urbem de-
fendendam et simul, si qui res novas cuperent, eos adventu suo
compressere.

56   Legati etiam inter primum statim tumultum ad Olegianum
missi, qui causas sciscitarentur hostilis adventus, et quid sibi vellet
flagitarent. His in castra profectis, cum mandata exposuissent, nihil aliud dux hostium respondit, quam consuesse praesulem mediolanensem amicis vicinisque suis qui iniuriis premerentur subvenire; audisse vero multos per Etruriam a Florentinis premi et
indigne iniuriis affici; venisse ergo ut his opituletur; proinde aut
accipiendum praesulem arbitrum cognitoremque iuris et querelarum aut vim eius experiundam. Eo responso accepto legati, non
disceptandum verbis rati cum eo qui non rationem sed arma inferret, e vestigio abscessere.

The archbishop placed Giovanni Visconti, called Giovanni da   55
Oleggio,[45] in command of the troops and gave him secret instructions about what he wished to be done. Thus Giovanni collected
troops from all over Bolognese territory, and when they had come
together, he set out from thence, with no one having the least
suspicion, and marched to the Apennine pass which separated
Bolognese from Pistoiese territory. Stopping there for a night, he
descended into the countryside near Pistoia the following morning
and pitched camp not far from that city. The Florentines were almost stunned by this sudden move, and on first hearing the news
knew not where to turn. There was general panic, and (as usually
happens in the case of sudden and grave dangers) they feared that
some secret act of treachery was afoot. Nevertheless, they quickly
sent out five hundred horse and three hundred foot, who entered
Pistoia. This force joined the garrison already in the city and encouraged their friends there to defend the city; at the same time,
their arrival spoiled any appetite for a coup on the part of their enemies.

In the midst of that first uproar, too, they immediately sent en-   56
voys to Giovanni to find out the reasons for his invasion and to
ask what he wanted. When these men arrived in his camp and
had explained their commission, the enemy commander made no
other response except that the Archbishop of Milan was accustomed to help his friends and neighbors who were suffering injuries; that he had heard there were many in Tuscany whom the
Florentines were oppressing and subjecting to undue injury; and
that he had come, therefore, to help them; wherefore they would
have to accept the archbishop as judge and inquisitor with respect
to these complaints or experience the power of his arms. Having
received this response, the envoys decided not to bandy words
with a man bearing arms rather than arguments, and straightway
took their leave.

57   Erat hosti permagna spes urbe Pistorio potiundi, ducto maxime
ea ratione, quod recenti Florentinorum iniuria Pistoriensium animos infensos plane exulceratosque putabat. Itaque, cum iam omnes convenissent copiae, sub ipsa moenia profectus, recipi in urbem postulavit. Id vero cum longe aspernarentur qui intus erant,
obsidere oppugnareque perrexit.

58   Per hoc ipsum tempus multis per finitimas regiones locis tumultus sunt concitati. Nam et Sacon a Bibiena, Arretinorum oppido, subito confestim insultu regionem terrore cladeque involvit;
et Pactii Ubertinique ab eorum castellis omnia per superiorem
Arnum loca repentinis incursionibus infestarunt; et Ubaldini per
mugellanum ruentes agrum Florentiolam et alia quaedam castella
improviso ceperunt, indeque auctis copiis late praedabantur. Quae
uno tempore nuntiata, cuncta horrore trepidationeque repleverant.

59   Olegianus, aliquot dies circa Pistorium commoratus, cum pers-
piceret constanter a Pistoriensibus resisti, et motum intra urbem
nullum[80] oriri, nolens in eo uno tempus terere, ab oppugnatione
destitit, ac Florentiam versus recta via per agrum pratensem exercitum duxit, habens equitum supra decem, peditum vero mercede
conductorum supra sex millia; praeter hos auxiliarium voluntario-
rumque multitudo ingens sequebatur. Cum his copiis haud procul
ab urbe castra fecit super[81] Bisentium amnem. Commeatum exercitui praedae rapinaeque primo adventu suppeditabant egregie.
Longa enim pace bonis omnibus refertas domos et pecoris magnam vim nacti, ab his facile educabantur. Agmina vero armatorum saepe ad portas usque discurrentia magno tumultu infestabant.

60   His in locis cum aliquot dies perstitissent, et commeatus profli-
gate abusos[82] iam deficere viderentur,[83] simulavit hostis se trans

The enemy had great hopes of getting control of Pistoia, count- 57
ing on that city's recent injuries at the hands of the Florentines to
have inflamed their hearts against the Arno city. Thus when all his
forces were assembled he came up right below the walls of the city
and demanded to be allowed entry. But when those inside spurned
this demand, he set about besieging and attacking the city.

Around this same time tumults were stirred up in many places 58
throughout the neighboring regions. Saccone immediately leapt
out of Bibbiena, the town of the Aretines, and roiled that region
with terror and destruction. The Pazzi and the Ubertini from
their castles made lightning strikes everywhere in the upper Arno
valley. And the Ubaldini dashed through the Mugello, unexpectedly seizing Firenzuola and certain other castles; from there they
enlarged their forces and plundered far and wide. All of this was
reported at one and the same time, filling everyone with fear and
horror.

Giovanni da Oleggio spent several days near Pistoia. Having 59
observed the unwavering resistance of the Pistoiesi and the absence of any rising in the city, he abandoned the siege, not wishing
to waste time in that one place. Turning in the direction of Florence, he led his army straight there through the Pratese countryside. He had over ten thousand horse and six thousand hired infantry, and in addition to these forces a huge host of auxiliaries
and volunteers followed him. With these forces he pitched camp
on the river Bisenzio. When he first arrived, plunder and rapine
supplied his army admirably. Thanks to the long peace, the farms
were full of every good thing and abundant cattle, and his troops
easily found and carried these off. Columns of armed men often
ranged right up to the gates, causing great confusion with their
attacks.

When they had remained in this area for several days, and the 60
victuals they had so profligately consumed seemed already to be
giving out, the enemy pretended it was his intention to march past

urbem ducere in animo habere; et iactabant in castris ad Salvianum templum vexilla posituros. Id cum ex captivis transfugisque cognitum esset, permoti eo terrore Florentini, fossam a moenibus urbis ad proximum inde collem, parum citra viam bononiensem, subito perficiendam[84] opere curaverunt; eamque fossam crebra statione militum ac magna sagittariorum manu die noctuque custodiebant. Faesulana vero in arce summa praesidium munierunt, quo transitus hostium impediretur.

61   Inter haec Olegianus, sive deterritus munimentis, sive quod ab initio ita constituisset, omissa transeundi cura, retro profectus, ad Marinam fluvium castra fecit. Ibi Calentiano aliisque munitis quibusdam locis expugnatis, cum praedae aliquantum ex eo redegisset, per ipsum fluvium profectus, arctis difficillimisque saltibus praemisso pedite occupatis, nullo impediente, in agrum mugellanum transmisit. His rursus in locis Barbarinum et alia quaedam castella non satis contra vim hostium munita dedentibus sese incolis suscepit; a quibus commeatu abunde refectus cum esset, Scarpariae copias admovit. Placuerat enim iampridem hostibus ea belli sedes, quod ad Bononiam versa Apenninique arcibus finitima, opportunitates ad bellum quamplures[85] habitura videbatur. Itaque id oppidum in potestatem[86] redigere omnino constituerant, volentes belli totius sedem in eo oppido constituere.

62   Florentini quoque, statim atque in agrum mugellanum transisse hostem intellexere, hoc idem coniectura suspicati, valido confestim praesidio delectorum militum Scarpariam firmarunt; qui oppidanis coniuncti, purgatis fossis valloque refecto (neque enim totum moenibus cingebatur oppidum), alacribus animis obsidionem expectabant. Hostes igitur magno tumultu copiis admotis, cum nihil trepide neque temere agi ab iis qui intus erant conspexissent, sed constanti animo sagacique consilio obviam iri, accuratiore oppu-

the city, and they boasted in the camps that they would plant their standards by the church of San Salvi. Thanks to captives and deserters this became known to the Florentines, who in terror set to work to finish a moat leading from the city walls to the next hill,[46] just below the Via Bolognese. This moat they guarded day and night with frequent pickets and a large force of archers. They reinforced the garrison at the top of the citadel of Fiesole to block the passage of the enemy.

Meanwhile Giovanni da Oleggio, either deterred by the defenses or because it had been his original plan, abandoned his effort to bypass the city and turned back, pitching camp by the river Marina. There he captured Calenzano and certain other fortified places, and when he had collected some plunder from there, he set out along the river, sending ahead infantry to occupy the difficult and narrow passes. With no one to block his way, he passed into the Mugello. Here, once again, he captured Barberino and some other castles that, being poorly fortified, surrendered to him; and once he had restored his strength from their abundant provisions, he marched on to Scarperia. This town had long found favor with enemies as a base for war. Looking out towards Bologna and situated near the citadels of the Apennines, it seemed to offer numerous advantages for hostile action. So they decided to bring the town completely under their control, with the aim of making it their base for the whole war.

The Florentines, too, as soon as they learned that the enemy had passed into the Mugello, suspected that this was precisely their purpose, and they at once sent a strong garrison of picked soldiers to strengthen Scarperia. These men joined forces with the townsmen, cleaned out the moats and restored the earthwork (for the town was not completely ringed with walls) and with ardent spirits awaited the siege. Having noisily advanced their forces, the enemy observed the absence of fear and disorder among those inside and took note of their steadiness and foresight. Reckoning

gnatione opus fore arbitrati, circa illud consederunt, et machinas
atque tormenta ceteraque oppugnandarum urbium instrumenta
parare adorsi sunt. Contra vero obsessi, permagnum sibi certamen
impendere cernentes, omnia quae auxilio consuerunt esse, iam
inde prospicere atque meditari severa nimium disciplina coeperunt.[87]

63   Dum haec ad Scarpariam geruntur, Sacon, diversarum partium
hominibus sibi coniunctis, cum duobus millibus peditum et quadringentis equitibus per agrum Arretinum evadens, circa Ambram
fluvium duxit, cogitans inde maiori coacta manu Varicum ceteraque superioris Arni oppida e regione diversa urgere. Adversus
hanc tumultariam manum excitatis superioris Arni populis, atque
capere arma iussis, magna confestim peditum manus apud Varicum convenit; et accesserunt insuper equites Florentia missi circiter trecentos. Coniunxerunt se quoque his[88] copiis Arretinorum
equites peditesque, qui vestigia hostium[89] secuti, audita manu
quae Varici parabatur, et ipsi eo profecti sese illis coniunxerunt.
His[90] copiis omnibus praefectus est Albertaccius Ricasolanus, qui
cum multitudine abundaret (erat enim concursus ad eum vehementer factus), non expectare adventum hostis, sed ultro ad ipsum
ducere constituit.

64   Sacon per id tempus circum Ambram castellum positis castris
(est enim eiusdem cum fluvio nominis), adigere id in potestatem
nitebatur. Cui cum nostri contra quam ille aestimarat[91] numero et
structura superiores apparuissent, veritus Sacon ne primo statim
adventu pugnare cogeretur, undique in unum suos contrahi con-
globarique iussit; structaque de superiori loco acie nullum a suis
motum fieri permittebat, sed consistentes loco, expectare invaden-
tes atque ulcisci. Ricasolanus autem, cum videret hostes in colle
sese continere, anceps parumper stetit: adorireturne eos, iniquo licet loco stantes, an potius differret? Et placebat multis eos statim

that they would need to undertake a formal siege, they surrounded the town and set about preparing siege engines, catapults, and other devices for besieging towns. The besieged, on the other hand, seeing the great fight that was facing them, from that point on began with the utmost discipline to plan and make every provision that is usually helpful.[47]

While this was happening at Scarperia, Saccone attached to 63 himself the men of the Ghibelline party and made his way through Aretine territory with two thousand foot and four hundred horse. He marched them into the valley of the Ambra, thinking that he might assemble larger forces there and attack Montevarchi and other towns of the upper Arno from the opposite direction. The peoples of the upper Arno were stirred up against this marauding force and, bidden to take to arms, they assembled a large force of infantry at Montevarchi. About three hundred cavalry sent from Florence also came. The cavalry and infantry of the Aretines joined these forces as well, following in the footsteps of the enemy: for hearing of the troops being readied at Montevarchi, they themselves set out for that place and joined them. Albertaccio Ricasoli commanded all these forces. Since he had plenty of troops (for a spirited throng had joined him), he decided not to await the arrival of the enemy but to march out and meet him.

Meanwhile Saccone had pitched camp near Castello dell'Ambra 64 (it has the same name as the river) and tried to subdue it. But when our forces appeared in greater numbers and better order than he had counted on, Saccone grew fearful that he would have to fight them immediately. So he pulled his men all together in a single body and set up his battle line on high ground, with instructions to keep still, remain in position, and wait before taking vengeance on the attackers. Ricasoli, when he saw the enemy keeping to their hill, stopped awhile indecisively: should he attack them on unfavorable ground, or should he delay? Many wanted to attack immediately. But to the commander to whom the host

invadere. At enim duci, cuius fidei multitudo commissa erat, periculosum videbatur subitarium militem (erat enim collectitius vixdum inter se notus) exercitato hosti loco iniquo obiicere; et simul inclinarat iam sol, nec multum supererat diei. Itaque, cum ad pugnam provocasset ac manifestum esset hostem illam detrectare, contentus minas eorum iactantiamque primo statim adventu suo repressisse, delecto castris idoneo loco, non procul ab hoste consedit.

65   Eius noctis, cum iam media pars transacta esset, hostes desertis silentio castris abiere. Quod cum prima statim luce palam esset, indignationes quaerelaeque ortae sunt, praesertim apud eos quibus e vestigio placuerat invasisse. Quamobrem, ne insectari quidem vestigia voluere. Arretini post fugam hostium confestim domum versus iter arripuere, veriti ne Sacon aliquid cladis rediens inferret. Ceteram vero dux multitudinem Agnanum duxit. Receperant enim se per noctem in id castellum equites hostium circiter ducentos, Bustacium Ubertinum secuti, ipsius loci dominatorem. Nostri ergo hortante duce, primo statim adventu castellum expugnare adorti, cum planiorem iam eius partem cepissent, eruptione hostium paulo post deturbati atque expulsi, et damna quaedam alia susceperunt, et signa militaria tria amiserunt. Ea veluti ignominia tacti irritatique, cum rursus maiore vi adoriri statuissent, et appareret victoriam fore in manibus, non tamen incruentam, nec sine multorum certissima clade, colloquia peropportune inducta sunt; pactique tandem hostes ut sibi incolumibus abire liceret, Agnanum dedidere.

66   Per hoc ipsum tempus praesul, oratoribus ad Pisanos missis, ut bellum adversus[92] Florentinos susciperent, flagitabat. Etsi enim pax erat civitatibus, tamen, quia audiverat pervetustas utrique po-

had been entrusted it seemed a dangerous thing to throw a makeshift army (a motley force that scarcely yet knew one another) into
battle on unfavorable ground against a trained enemy; and at the
same time, the sun was going down and little was left of the day.
Thus, after he had challenged them to battle, and the enemy had
manifestly refused it, he satisfied himself with having squelched
the threats and boasting that had greeted his first arrival.
Choosing a suitable place, he encamped not far from the enemy.

In the middle of the night, the enemy silently deserted their 65
camp and left. When this became evident at first light, anger and
complaints immediately arose, especially among those who had
wanted to attack immediately. On this account they refused even
to pursue the enemy. The Aretines took to the road immediately
after the enemy's flight, fearing that Saccone would inflict some disaster on his way back. The captain led the rest of the host to
Agnano. For two hundred of the enemy cavalry had taken refuge
for the night in that castle, the followers of Bustaccio Ubertini, the
lord of that place. At the urging of their captain, our forces began
to attack the castle as soon as they arrived. They had already taken
its lower reaches when, soon thereafter, they were thrown into
confusion and repelled by an enemy sally. They sustained some
damage and lost three military standards. Stung by this ignominious failure, they decided to attack again in greater force. They saw
that victory would be within their grasp, but that it would be a
bloody one and would most certainly cost the lives of many men.
So a parley was arranged in a timely fashion, and in the end the
enemy agreed to surrender Agnano on condition that he be allowed to leave unharmed.[48]

Meanwhile the archbishop had sent ambassadors to the Pisans 66
to demand that they start a war against the Florentines. Although
there was a peace treaty between the cities, nevertheless, since he
had heard that ancient enmities existed between the two peoples
and that their loyalties belonged to opposing parties, he persuaded

pulo inimicitias fuisse studiaque partium omnino diversa, persua-
serat ipse sibi perfacile eos, tali praesertim opportunitate oblata,
ad capessendum bellum impellere posse. Hac igitur fiducia, legatis
ad Pisanos missis, refricandis vetustis Florentinorum iniuriis, multaque pollicendo ostentandoque et studia partium incendendo, ad
suscipiendum bellum cohortatus est. Pollicebatur autem Bernabovem nepotem cum maximo novoque equitatu se ad Pisanos missu-
rum, qui illis coniunctus, alia ex parte novo exercitu Florentinos
adoriretur. Haec facunda oratione ab oratoribus explicata audientes illexerant, praesertim cum inevitabilem ruinam florentini populi certamque existimarent perniciem haud dubie secuturam.

67   In Pisanis tunc maxime Gambacurtae pollebant, familia opulenta atque otii appetens et a studio florentini populi nequaquam
abhorrens. Hi ergo verissimam rationem secuti, intelligebant ea
quae postulabantur non minus Pisanorum libertati quam Florentinorum periculum afferre; praesulem enim dominatum quaerere
idque unum meditari; nec si Florentiae compos fiat, Pisis tempera-
turum. Monentes igitur privatim singulos, ne Florentinorum odio
libertatem propriam abiicere velint, reiicendi postulata auctores
fuere. Itaque tandem legatis id modo responsum est: Pisanum populum de rebus postulatis legatos ad praesulem mittere consti-
tuisse, coramque responsuros esse.

68   Nec multo post legati ab his profecti, cum ad praesulem pervenissent, allegata Florentinorum pace quasi deliberabundi subsiste-
bant, neque negantes postulata neque plane recipientes. Quam lu-
dificationem cum animadverteret praesul, intelligeretque non ex

himself that the Pisans could be easily driven to start a war, especially given such a fine opportunity for success. So he confidently sent envoys to the Pisans to rub raw the old injuries inflicted by the Florentines, and by promising and revealing much, and by inflaming partisan feeling, he exhorted them to undertake a war. He promised he would send them his nephew Bernabò with a large, fresh force of cavalry. He would join their own forces and attack Florence from the other direction with another army. This proposal, explained by the ambassadors with great eloquence, enticed those who heard it, especially as they reckoned that the inevitable ruin of the Florentine People and their certain destruction would surely follow.

The Gambacurta were a highly influential clan in Pisa at that   67
time; they were rich, peace-loving and by no means ill-disposed towards the Florentine People. Hence they followed the truest reasoning, understanding that what was being asked would endanger the liberty of the Pisans no less than that of the Florentines. They recognized that the archbishop was seeking absolute rule and that this alone was in his thoughts; that if he were put in control of Florence, he would not restrain himself from taking Pisa. So they privately advised individual Pisans not to throw away their own liberty out of hatred for the Florentines, and in this way they were responsible for rejecting the request. Thus in the end this simple answer was made to the envoys: that the Pisan people had decided to send envoys to the archbishop concerning his proposals, and that they would respond to him in person.

Shortly thereafter envoys set out from Pisa and came to the   68
archbishop. Citing the peace treaty with the Florentines, as though their process of deliberation had ground to a halt, they would neither say no to his proposals nor openly accept them. The archbishop understood their game, and realized that it was not being played in accordance with the will of Pisan people, but was the work of a few men only. Immediately he sent his ambassa-

populi pisani, sed ex paucorum voluntate id agi, confestim oratores suos maiori apparatu Pisas remisit, iubens ut contionem populi
flagitarent et in ea multitudinem alloquerentur. Oratores igitur
praesulis reversi Pisas, cum sibi a magistratu contio data esset, ingressi ad multitudinem, verba fecerunt, maxima pollicentes auxilia
ac victoriam in manibus esse praedicantes,[93] modo ipsimet sibi nolint deesse. Multitudo autem Pisanorum haec libenter audivit ob
Florentinorum odium et annuere postulatis cupiens erat; reverentia modo gubernatorum eos morabatur.

69   Tunc magistratus ad legatos conversus, 'Laudastis', inquit, 'o legati, veterem contionandi morem, et recte quidem. Nam quid lau-
dabilius quam populum ipsum sua ipsius et scire et agere? Ceterum illud[94] quoque laudetis oportet secundum eundem morem,
ut libera deliberandi ratio sit, nec ob alicuius praesentiam quae
quisque sentit dicere cunctetur. Quamobrem rectum fuerit vos
contione excedere.'

70   Id cum fecissent legati (neque enim repugnare honestum erat),
magistratus, quae dicenda videbantur ex integro praefatus, ad populum retulit de legatorum postulatis. Tunc Francischinus Gambacurta, princeps eius familiae, assurgens in hunc modum verba
fecisse dicitur:

71   'Cum praesule mediolanensi[95] tanta mihi privatim amicitia est,
ut non existimem alicui Pisanorum esse maiorem. Nam et vetus-
tam cum illo familiaritatem habeo, iam inde a parentibus coeptam,
ac multis quidem illius beneficiis, nonnullis etiam meis obsequiis,
continuo studio adauctam. Sed haec privatim mihi tuenda censeo.
Publice autem dum consulitur, caritas patriae me vindicat sibi, cui
pietatem debitam negare non possum. Quare mihi veniam ille da-

dors back to Pisa with still greater pomp, ordering them to ask for an assembly of the people so that they might address the multitude. Hence the archbishop's ambassadors came back to Pisa and were granted an assembly by the government. Coming before the multitude, they made a speech promising them the utmost aid and declaring that victory was within their grasp so long as they themselves were equal to the task. Thanks to their hatred of the Florentines, the Pisan multitude heard these words gladly and wanted to approve the proposals, but only held back out of respect for their magistrates.

Then the magistrate turned to the envoys and said, "O envoys,   69
you have praised the ancient custom of assembly, and rightly so. Indeed, what is more laudable than for the people itself to know and act on its own affairs? But you also ought to praise the practice, which accords with the same ancient custom, of free deliberation. No one should hesitate to say what he thinks because of anyone's presence. So the correct thing will be for you to leave the assembly."

When the envoys had done this (for to refuse would have been   70
dishonorable), the magistrate repeated by way of preamble what appeared to have been said, and referred the envoys' proposals to the people for discussion. At that point Franceschino Gambacurta, the head of that family, arose and is said to have spoken in the following way:

"My friendly relations as a private citizen with the archbishop   71
of Milan are closer than those of any other Pisan, I believe. I have been on familiar terms with him from of old, a familiarity initiated by my ancestors, and my devotion has been enlarged continually by many benefits conferred by him, and by no few services rendered on my own part. But I believe that I should maintain this friendship as a private citizen. While giving advice on public affairs, love of country makes its claims on me, and I cannot deny

bit, si patriae saluti magis consultum esse velim quam illius sive potentiae sive cupiditati.

72 'Adversum Florentinos suscipere nos bellum postulat et magnas copias magnaque auxilia nobis pollicetur; ruinam vero florentini populi certissimam nobis repromittit. Urget denique et instat per oratores suos, ut haec ceu nobis commodissima suscipiamus et insurgamus ad bellum inferendum. Mihi vero in ista consultatione illud maxime cavendum videtur, ne nimio Florentinorum odio turpe ac damnosum nobis consilium assumamus. Numquam enim recte consulit qui odio consulit. Honor sane atque utilitas libero animo in consultantibus quaeri debent. Ad haec duo prudentes viri consilia sua dirigunt universa. Haec igitur qualia sint in hac re proposita considerare non[96] pigeat.

73 'Pacem et foedera esse nobis cum florentino populo sciunt omnes, nec posse adversus illos a nobis bellum moveri, nisi contra fidem, contra promissiones, contra iusiurandum quod de pace servanda praestitimus[97] veniatur. Quae igitur tanta utilitas ex hoc foedifragio provenire nobis posset, ut non praestabilius sit conventa servare quam turpiter et ignominiose fidem fregisse? In gubernanda republica honoris curam magis habendam esse quam utilitatis omnes fatentur. Ut enim magna est civitatis dignitas magnaque maiestas, ita et fidem et gravitatem inesse maximam decet. Itaque multa in privatis hominibus toleramus et inconstantiae avaritiaeque ac sordidis quaestibus veniam impartimur, quae in civitate nullo modo forent toleranda. Splendor enim et fides et gravitas in civitatibus elucere debent. Nam unius aut alterius aut paucorum quorundam improbitas hominum forsan vitari nequit. Ut vero totus populus deliberatione publica deiceret[98] ac fidem promissaque consulto infringat, nimis foret detestandum. Contra honorem igitur ac dignitatem[99] civitatis nostrae hanc postulatio-

it due reverence. He will forgive me if I consult the welfare of my country before his power and wishes.

"He is asking us to start a war against the Florentines and 72 promising us large forces and ample aid; he guarantees us that the fall of the Florentine People will be most certain. Through his ambassadors he urges and insists that we do this as a course of action most advantageous to ourselves; that we rise up and make war. But in my view, we should be extremely cautious in this discussion and not accept dishonorable and dangerous counsel out of an excess of hatred for the Florentines. The man who gives counsel out of hatred never gives good counsel. Surely honor and utility should be sought when giving counsel in a spirit of freedom. Prudent men direct all of their advice to these two aims. Let us not draw back from considering the kind of honor and utility to be found in this proposal.

"Everyone knows we have a peace treaty with the Florentine 73 People, and we cannot launch a war against them without contravening our good faith, our promises and the oaths we have taken to preserve the peace. What utility can come from this treaty-breaking? Is it so great that it would not be finer to preserve our covenants rather than dishonorably and shamefully violate our good faith? Everyone admits that in governing a republic one must have more regard for honor than utility. When the rank and majesty of a city are great, it is fitting that it manifest the greatest good faith and steadfastness. Thus we tolerate many things in private individuals and pardon inconstancy, avarice and sordid profits that would by no means be tolerable in a city. In cities, indeed, glory, good faith and authority ought to shine forth. Wickedness cannot perhaps be avoided in one or two or a few men. But that an entire people, after public debate, should act basely and deliberately break its good faith and promises, is utterly abhorrent. Clearly, this demand is contrary to the honor and rank of our city,

nem esse constat; quam etsi magnae utilitates sequerentur,[100] tamen concedere nullo modo debemus.

74   'Quid vero, si nullam inesse utilitatem apparet? Quid, si insuper maximi damni periculum? An capiemus id consilium, quod sit turpe simul ac damnosum? An est quisquam vestrum[101] usque adeo hebes, ut non intelligat, bello a nobis suscepto, necessarium fore ut vel vincat praesul vel non vincat? Atqui, si non vincat, duriores infestioresque habebimus Florentinos, qui cum sint vicini perpetuo futuri, nunquam acerba vicinitate carebimus. Sin autem vincat, potentissimam vicinitatem praesulis recipiemus. Equidem potentissimum ac late dominantem videre praesulem velim, dum tamen procul a civitate nostra. Licet enim amicissimus sit ac propensissima benevolentia erga populum pisanum affectus, nunquam tamen eum[102] pluris facere nos existimabo quam mediolanenses cives suos, quibus tamen dominatur — adeo cupiditas imperandi cuique celso animo indita est! Nos libertatem a patribus nostris relictam tueri debemus, ac finitimos optare potius aequos ac pares nobis quam praepotentes ac formidabiles habere,[103] qui, si modo velint, possint libertatem auferre. "At subici Florentinos optabile nobis est!" Fateor, modo sine iactura libertatis nostrae id fieri possit. Quod si periculum subiectionis eorum subiectio nobis affert, potius stent quam eorum ruina civitatem quoque nostram secum in ruinam[104] trahat. Castrucius lucensis, vir magni animi sed nequaquam pari potentia cum praesule nec pari dignitate, patrocinium opprimendi florentini populi cum sibi assumpsisset, quis non gaudebat? Quis non laetabatur? Atqui laetitia illa quantum maerorem nobis ad extremum attulerit scimus! Non enim prius nocuit Florentinis Castrucius, quam Pisanos iugo servitutis oppressit. Ita, dum aliis nocere voluerunt Pisani, sibi ipsis tyrannidem superinduxere.

and we should in no way allow it, even if great utility were to follow therefrom.

"But what if it is evident that there is *no* utility in this demand? 74 What if there is a danger of great loss besides? Should we seize on this plan, which is so shameful and damaging? Is there anyone among you so dim as not to understand that, if we undertake this war, the archbishop necessarily is either going to win or lose? If he loses, the Florentines are going to be harsher and more hostile, and since they are going to be our neighbors forever, our neighborly relations will never lack bitterness. But if he wins, we shall have an extremely powerful archbishop as our neighbor. For my part, I should like to see the archbishop exercise great power and broad dominion—so long as it is far from our own city! For although he is extremely friendly and shows great good will towards the Pisan people, I don't think he will ever place a higher value on us than he does on his own Milanese citizens, over whom he nevertheless exercises lordship   such is the yearning for command instilled in every high-minded man! But we ought to guard the liberty left us by our forefathers and desire to have neighbors that are equals and peers rather than overwhelmingly strong and formidable men who can take away our liberty whenever they wish. 'But it would be so desirable to subdue the Florentines!'—I admit it, but only if it could be done without throwing away our own liberty. But if their subjection entails the danger of our own, let them remain as they are; let us not allow their ruin to bring ruin on us as well. Who was there who was not glad, who did not rejoice, when Castruccio of Lucca—a great man, but by no means equal in power or rank to the archbishop—made himself the advocate of crushing the Florentine People? Yet we know how much grief that joy brought us in the end! For no sooner did Castruccio harm the Florentines than he laid the yoke of servitude upon the Pisans. Thus the Pisans, wishing to harm others, brought down tyranny on themselves.

75 'Hoc ergo[105] cavendum nobis censeo, praesertim cum potentia Castrucii cum praesulis potentia nullo sit modo comparanda, nec dominandi consuetudo atque natura. His ergo[106] rationibus pacem cum Florentinis servandam puto, ac praesuli hoc ipsum pro excusatione allegandum, quod salva fide ac promissionibus nostris contra Florentinos bellum suscipere non valemus.'

76 [Haec oratio graviores pisanorum in sententiam traxit et certatim optimus quisque surrexit ad haec ipsa consulenda.][107] Secundum hanc orationem magistratus populum rogavit vellentne iuberent pacem cum Florentinis rite factam servatamque contra iusiurandum fidemque publicam rumpere. Tunc optimus quisque, quod facillimum erat, pro honestate, contra dedecus et infamiam populi, suffragium tulit. Ita[108] qui contra sentiebant, pudore deterriti concessere; decretumque fit e dignitate pisani populi non videri pacem cum Florentinis initam nulla interveniente iniuria perfringere. Per hunc modum pisana spes mediolanensem praesulem fefellit; quam ille quasi certam ab initio complexus, eius maxime fiducia etruscum susceperat bellum.

77 Hostes inter haec castris, ut diximus, ad Scarpariam positis, omni apparatu oppidum oppugnabant. Machinis enim et tormentis circa dispositis muros diruere, tabulata deiicere, propugnacula refringere, assiduo opere non cessabant. Grandibus insuper saxis rotatu tormentorum in oppidum cadentibus tecta parietesque infringebantur, frequentesque sub eorum casu obsessi peribant. Crebro etiam per noctem scalis, die vero subitanea et improvisa vi oppidum aggressi, nullum requietis spatium dabant obsessis. Sed erat praefectorum ac militum qui se oppido incluserant admiranda sollertia. Muros enim ac propugnacula ubicumque machinae deiecis-

"My view, then, is that we should beware of this counsel, espe-   75
cially as neither Castruccio's power nor his lordly ways and nature
were in any way comparable to the archbishop's. For these reasons
I think we should preserve peace with the Florentines, and allege
this as our excuse to the archbishop: in order to preserve our good
faith and promises, we have no power to start a war against the
Florentines."

This oration convinced the graver sort among the Pisans, and all the   76
best men competed to get up and give the same advice.[49] After this oration the magistrate asked the people whether they wanted to decree that the peace duly made and kept with the Florentines
should be broken against the oaths and good faith of the public.
This then made it easy for all the best men to give their vote in favor of the honor and against the dishonor and infamy of the People. Thus those who held the opposite view gave in, deterred by
shame, and a decree was passed: that it was inconsistent with the
dignity of the Pisan People to break their peace treaty with the
Florentines without any antecedent injury. In this way the archbishop was deceived in the hope he had of the Pisans; and indeed
from the beginning he had embraced this hope as a certainty and
had undertaken the Tuscan war chiefly in reliance upon it.[50]

Meanwhile, the enemy was encamped at Scarperia, as we said,   77
and was attacking the town with every instrument of war. De-
ploying machines and catapults all around, they ceaselessly and
with great energy demolished walls, knocked down wooden defenses, and shattered ramparts. Catapults hurled huge rocks which
crashed down on the town, breaking roofs and walls, and many
were the besieged who perished in the collapsing buildings. Frequent, too, were the ladder attacks they made by night and the
surprise attacks by day; the besieged were not given a moment's
rest. But the authorities[51] and soldiers shut inside showed admira-
ble resourcefulness. Whenever machines had knocked down walls
and ramparts, they tirelessly repaired them with great effort; they

sent, magnis laboribus impigre reparantes ac munera vigiliarum assidue obeuntes, et quotiens manu opus erat, certatim se periculis obiectantes, provocantes etiam saepe hostem, permagnam sunt in ea obsidione gloriam consecuti.

78   Florentiae vero per hoc tempus omnia circumspecte simul impigreque agebantur; militem conducere quam maximo numero; domesticorum acrem delectum habere; socios in amicitia continere, hortari agere, bonam spem afferre; magno et invicto animo rebus incumbere. Iam mercede conductorum effecerant equitum germanorum circiter duo millia quingentos. Venerant insuper Senensium equites ducenti; Perusinorum vero sexcenti expectabantur. Ad hos si domesticus equitatus peditatusque, qui passim affluebat, adderetur, sufficientem exercitum videbantur habituri. Mittere vero has copias adversus hostem decreverant obsessisque auxilium praesentes afferre.

79   Hoc propositum florentini populi totamque huiusce rei spem conatumque turbavit paulo post equitum perusinorum adversus casus. Illi enim cum expectarentur vehementer ac in itinere iam essent, Sacon adventu eorum cognito cum duobus millibus peditum et quingentis equitibus obviam profectus, apud vicum qui dicitur Ulmus duobus passuum millibus ab Arretio nocte una commoratus, primam sub lucem invasit. Et proelium satis acre primo statim congressu initum est. Nam perusinorum equitum pars iam equos conscenderat, iter ingressura. Haec itaque pars impetum Saconis fortiter excepit, et ceteris arma capiendi prosiliendique in equos spatium dedit, ut iam Perusini haud dubie equitatu pares futuri viderentur. Sed postquam pedes superiore de colle, ubi Sacon eum collocaverat supervenit, equitatumque Perusinorum in medio nactus adoriri coepit, fracti confestim illi atque profligati, multa caede opprimuntur. Qui vero a caede superfuerunt, capiuntur fere omnes.

constantly took on guard duties, and whenever a force was needed they competed to throw themselves into harm's way, often even provoking the enemy; and they achieved immense glory in that siege.

At the same time, everything in Florence was being done with 78
prudence and energy. The largest possible number of soldiers was hired; a keen levy of local men was raised; friendly relations with allies were kept up; the latter were encouraged and exhorted to act; and the Florentines set about their affairs with an unconquerable spirit. Already they had hired 2,500 German cavalry. In addition, two hundred knights came from the Sienese, and six hundred Perugian calvary were expected to arrive. When the domestic foot and horse, which streamed in from everywhere, were added to these forces, the Florentines reckoned that they would have enough of an army. Indeed, they had resolved to send these forces out against the enemy and to bring prompt help to the besieged.

But shortly thereafter, a misfortune suffered by the Perugian 79
knights threw into confusion all the hopes and plans and efforts of the Florentine People. These knights, so eagerly awaited, were already on the road when Saccone learned of their coming. Setting out to meet them with two thousand foot and five hundred horse, he spent a single night at the village of Ulmo two miles from Arezzo, then attacked at dawn. And from the first clash a bitter battle began. Part of the Perugian cavalry had already mounted their horses to begin their journey, and it was this part that bravely withstood Saccone's attack, giving time for the rest to seize their arms and leap onto their horses. At this point it seemed that the Perugians would certainly be evenly matched with Saccone's cavalry. But once his infantry came down from the nearby hill where Saccone had positioned them and, getting into the middle of the Perugian cavalry, began to attack, the Perugians at once were shattered and put to flight, and a great many were slaughtered. Practically all of those who escaped the slaughter were taken captive.

80   Arretini sensere quidem pugnam ac primum egressi urbe,[109] opem ferre Perusinorum equitibus properabant. Mox vero, cum intellexissent Saconem cum copiis adesse (qui et tyrannidem Arretii quondam habuerat et extabat adhuc in urbe Gebellinorum factio qua ille nitebatur, exclusa quidem a reipublicae gubernatione, ceterum non satis extincta), veriti ne forte ob Saconis praesentiam motus aliquis intra urbem oriretur, e vestigio domum reversi, clausis portis in potestate urbem continere studuerunt. Eam ob rem Saconi captivos equites abducendi plurimo cum otio facultas fuit.

81   Haec Saconis victoria equitumque profligatio spem consiliumque florentini populi mutari coegit. Neque enim deficiente ea equitatus parte satis copiarum restare visum est, quae castra castris auderent conferre. Supererat igitur de his qui obsidebantur formido et quidem anxia. Nam illi, quamdiu spes fuerat copiarum adventus, supra vires proprias contra vim hostium restiterant; verum, ubi rem trahi in longum frustrarique spem[110] auxilii conspexerunt,[111] labante iam animorum vigore, minus alacriter tantam certaminis molem tolerabant, praesertim cum in dies labor ad pauciores recideret, frequentibus vulneratis, quibusdam etiam peremptis, non paucis insuper ob nimium vigiliarum operumque laborem in varios morbos languoresque transvectis. Hae vero difficultates obsessorum nequaquam Florentiae ignorabantur. Lixae enim atque calones, per noctem dimissi, latenter sese hostibus admiscentes, mandata et literas deferebant. Ex quo cuncta scientibus metus insidebat animis ne illi, labore nimio fatiscentes, ab hoste pertinaci tandem opprimerentur.

82   In ea cura cum esset civitas aliusque alium respiceret, primus omnium ausus est profiteri Iohannes Vicedomini e nobilitate flo-

The Aretines of course heard the noise of battle and at first 80
marched out of the city, hastening to help the Perugian knights.
But soon they learned that Saccone had come with his troops—
the same Saccone who had formerly been tyrant of Arezzo. Since
the Ghibelline faction which supported him was still in the city—
excluded, to be sure, from the goverment but not completely ex-
tinct—the Aretines grew fearful that, thanks to Saccone's presence, some coup might arise inside the city. So they immediately
returned home and shut the gates in their zeal to keep the city under their control. On this account Saccone had plenty of time to
carry off the knights he had taken captive.[52]

Saccone's victory and the rout of the Perugian knights forced 81
the Florentine People to change its expectations and plans. With
the loss of that portion of their cavalry, it appeared that the rest
were insufficiently strong to challenge the enemy encampment. So
the besieged were left in a state of anxious fear. As long as they
had some hope that fresh forces would arrive, they made superhu-
man efforts to resist the enemy attacks. But once the affair began
to drag out and they saw their hope of reinforcements dashed,
their spirits began to fall and they bore the burden of resistance
with less enthusiasm, especially as the effort fell every day on fewer
men. Many were wounded, and some perished; not a few of the
latter were carried off by diseases and exhaustion incurred from
excessive labor and lack of sleep. The difficult position of the besieged was well known in Florence, as sutlers and orderlies, sent
out by night, had slipped through the enemy camp bearing instructions and letters. Hence those who knew all this began to
fear lest the besieged would collapse from their extraordinary labors and in the end be crushed by the tenacity of their enemy.

The city was troubled and everyone was looking around at ev- 82
eryone else when Giovanni Visdomini, a Florentine noble of high
spirit and experienced in war, first dared to volunteer. With thirty
picked soldiers he set out by night towards the enemy and made

rentina, celsi vir animi et bellorum gnarus; trigintaque delectis militibus nocte profectus ad hostes, per media illorum castra incolumibus suis omnibus Scarpariam ingressus est, receptusque ingenti
laetitia, spem atque animos confirmavit obsessis. Sed quae adhuc[112] facta erant non satis videbantur, quaerebanturque alii virtutis aemuli qui ad obsessos pervaderent. Quod etsi multi cuperent,
absterrebantur tamen hostium diligentia. Neque enim iam fallere
erat, sed vi et pugna opus fore credebatur.

83   Detrectantibus ergo ceteris, profiteri ausus est Iohannes Medix,
iam tum inde clara vir fama. Hic igitur dedecus sibi ducens si quibusdam suorum civium inclusis et in periculo constitutis, ipse liber atque[113] expers periculi in oculis hominum vagaretur nec
patriae indigenti debitam solveret pietatem, centum delectos milites sub vexillis[114] ducens, diverso ab hoste itinere ad Apenninum
pervenit. Inde structus atque paratus, intempesta nocte descendens e diversa maxime regione qua minus hosti suspicionis erat,
castra ingressus, cum primo statim adventu clamor et concursus
hostium factus esset, tamen nihilo deterritus, cum globo suorum
destrictis gladiis obvios caedente, pectore atque armis sibi viam
aperuit, celeriterque praetervectus, ad obsessos pervenit, octoginta
secum habens milites; nam viginti ex omni numero vel amissi vel
exclusi in via remanserant.

84   Horum adventu recreati sunt qui obsidebantur; hostes vero,
cum ingressum novorum militum conspexissent, indignatione per-
citi, non ultra differre expugnationem statuere. Et instrumenta
quidem machinaeque abunde aderant, ligneae turres cratesque et
valli et harpagones et huius generis permulta; scalarum praeterea
numerus ingens. Quamobrem armati omnes intolerandis prope
clamoribus succedentes, scalas atque alia pervincendi instrumen-

his way unharmed right through the middle of the enemy camp and into Scarperia. He was received with great joy, and strengthened the hope and spirits of the besieged. But this did not yet seem enough, so other volunteers were sought to rival Visdomini's courage and break through to the besieged. Many wanted to volunteer but were deterred by the enemy's precautions, for it was believed that deception would no longer work, and one would need to fight one's way in.

Thus, while others were hanging back, Giovanni de' Medici, a 83 man thereafter famous, dared to volunteer. He believed it would be dishonorable for himself to wander about, safe and free, not rendering due service to his country in its time of need, when some of his fellow-citizens were trapped and in danger. Leading a hundred picked soldiers under battle-standards he came through the Apennines by a route different from that used by the enemy. Then he drew up his men in battle formation and in the dead of night came down from the opposite side of the city, where the enemy least expected it, and entered their camp. Immediately the enemy began shouting and running around, but undeterred, his band of men drew their swords, slaughtering those in their path, and by force of arms opened a way for themselves. Charging swiftly past the camp, he arrived at the besieged town, having with him a force of eighty soldiers; for twenty of the total number were either lost or shut out and remained in the road.

The arrival of these men refreshed the spirits of the besieged, 84 but the enemy, seeing the arrival of fresh troops, was moved to anger and decided not to put off the attack any longer. The enemy had a large supply of war-machines, wooden towers, fascines, stakes and grappling hooks and things of this kind, and a huge number of ladders besides. So they all armed themselves and fell upon the town, shouting almost unbearably, carrying ladders and other instruments of conquest. The besieged awaited their arrival with remarkable silence, as they had been instructed, until the en-

ta[115] intulere. Obsessi vero, uti praeceptum erat, mirabili silentio adventum eorum expectarunt, donec fossas transgressi successerunt moenibus, ut miraretur quidem hostis neminem repugnare. Sed cum ad moenia successissent scalaeque ponerentur, tunc signo dato, tanta vis telorum saxorumque repente super ingesta est ab obsessis, ut praecipites agerentur hostes, scalisque relictis extra fossas eiicerentur, multis occisis, pluribus etiam vulneratis atque oppressis.

85   Constituerat dux iam inde ab initio plura agmina, ut quieti fatigatis et integri succederent fessis, sperans per hoc obsessos, etsi non alia vi, tamen laboris assiduitate obruere. Itaque, ut primum agmen repulsum est, secundum pugnae successit. Sed tanta fuit obsessorum virtus, ut pari vigore animi parique alacritate adversus primos ultimosque resisterent. Ita saepe mutatis agminibus, cum a solis ortu ad meridiem usque pugnatum esset, nec quicquam se proficere dux videret, receptui cani iussit.

86   Aliud deinde certamen paucis post diebus ad cuniculos fuit. Hostes enim iampridem cuniculum agebant, summa quidem spe muri evertendi. Cum iam appropinquare moenibus verisimile esset, solliciti qui obsidebantur de murorum ruina, praefodere ante moenia ex illa parte et praevenire statuerunt, profundiorem agentes fossam,[116] quo cuniculus hostium nudaretur. Id cum studiose facerent, et ab hostibus prohiberentur, praesidio armatorum opposito se tutabantur. Biduo per hunc modum res acta certamen animorum utrinque incendit, aliis perficere destinatum opus, aliis prohibere nitentibus.

87   Tertia demum luce hostes[117] ligneam turrim primas ad fossas erexere, in qua pugnatores collocati, non sagittis modo et tragulis

emy had crossed the moat and came under the walls. The enemy were surprised that no one fought back, but when they came under the walls and put their ladders in position, a signal was then given, and a hail of spears and rocks was suddenly launched upon them from above by the besieged, so that the enemy ran away, leaving their ladders behind, and were forced outside the moat, leaving many dead and a great number wounded and trampled underfoot.

From the outset the enemy commander had set up numerous 85 battle-lines, so that fresh and rested troops might succeed tired and exhausted ones. By this means, he hoped, the besieged might collapse from the unending expense of effort if not from other, violent means. Thus when the first line was thrown back, it was succeeded in battle by the second. But such was the courage of the besieged that they resisted the first and last battle-lines with equal strength and equal keenness of spirit. So line succeeded line, but when the enemy commander saw the battle continue from dawn to mid-day without any progress being made, he ordered the retreat to be sounded.

Then, a few days later, another battle was fought around some 86 tunnels. The enemy had long been digging a tunnel with high hopes of undermining the wall. When it seemed likely that the tunnel was getting close to the walls, the defenders of the town became concerned that the walls would fall down, and decided to go out in front of the walls on that side and dig a trench, deepening the moat so as to uncover the enemy tunnel. While they were intent on doing this, the enemy tried to stop them, so they protected themselves with an armed guard between themselves and the enemy. The affair went on in this way for two days, igniting a contest of wills on both sides, one side trying to finish the job, the other trying to prevent them from doing so.

On the third day the enemy erected a wooden tower by the first 87 fosse and placed fighters in it who not only attacked with arrows

sed lapidibus etiam fodientes infestabant. Opus enim fiebat medium inter moenia oppidi ac turrim hostium, impedito quidem ad[118] congressum loco, sed omnifariam telis exposito. Post longum certamen obsessi incredibili virtute operarios protegentes ut compleretur opus, pervicere, cuniculumque infra[119] repertum iniecto igne cremaverunt; eademque alacritate et secundo victoriae cursu progressi, ligneam turrim, quam hostes ad impediendum opus effecerant, nudatam defensoribus incenderunt.

88 Postera vero die[120] hostes, quasi infamia superioris proelii tacti, prima luce armato exercitu et in agmina diviso, cum partes suas cuique dux attribuisset, ex composito vadentes, maiori quam antea conatu expugnare rursus oppidum aggressi sunt; ac primo statim impetu, fasces et stipulam et materiam deferentes, primas complevere fossas. Inde eas transgressi, cum ad secundas pervenissent, complere quoque illas ac transire nitebantur. Obsessi autem ab initio ex vallo et moenibus repugnabant, sed cum magis magisque premerentur et compleri fossas cernerent, eruptionem facere cominusque ferire ac pedem pedi conferre non dubitarunt. Itaque repente egressi oppido, proelium commisere, ostendentes non tam moenibus quam armis et virtute sua confidere. Ea res ita hostes fregit, ut receptui canerent, et omissa per vim expugnandi spe, ad dolum et fraudem converterentur.

89 Quiescentes igitur per diem, nocte intempesta trecentos delectos milites scalis moenia invadere ab ea parte oppidi qua luna obumbrabat iusserunt. Cetera vero multitudo cum facibus et telis omnique expugnandarum urbium apparatu e diversa maxime regione summis clamoribus impetum fecit, volens totas obsessorum mentes in se conversas ab aliis oppidi partibus per tumultum ab-

and darts but also hurled rocks. The work was being done between the walls of the town and the enemy tower, a confined space
for an encounter but exposed to every kind of missile. After a long
struggle the besieged, with incredible courage, succeeded in protecting their workers so that they completed the job, and when the
tunnel below was uncovered, they threw fire inside and burnt it
down. Then with the same keenness and propelled by their success, they stripped of its defenders and set on fire the wooden
tower the enemy had built to stop the digging.

The following day, the enemy, as though stung by the shame 88
of the previous battle, armed the host at first light and divided it
into ranks. The commander assigned a task to each rank, and
they marched ahead as agreed, attacking the town again with yet
greater energy than before. In the first onrush they carried bundles
of sticks, stubble and wood and filled up the first fosses. Then
having crossed them, they came to the second line of fosses and
tried to fill them too and cross over. At first the besieged fought
back from behind their walls and earthwork, but as the enemy attacked harder and harder and they saw the fosses being filled up,
without hesitation they made a sally and fought hand-to-hand and
foot-to-foot. Bursting forth rapidly from the town, they joined
battle, showing that they trusted not so much their walls as their
arms and courage. This attack shattered the enemy so that they
sounded the retreat; and having set aside their hope of capturing
the town by violence, they turned to deceit and trickery.

Thus, after resting for a day, they commanded three hundred 89
picked soldiers to scale the walls in the middle of the night on the
side of the town that lay enshadowed by the moon. The rest of the
host with torches and spears and every device for capturing cities
attacked on the opposite side with loud cries, aiming to divert the
whole attention of the besieged from the other parts of the town
by means of this uproar. But the besieged, though eagerly embrac-
ing their nightly rest, when roused by the sentinels ran each to his

ducere. Obsessi vero, etsi nocturnam quietem avide complectebantur, tamen a vigilibus excitati, cum ad sua quique loca, ut constitutum erat, cucurrissent, haud difficulter suspicati sunt hostilem dolum. Quamobrem, ubi aperta erat vis, aperte repugnarunt; aliis vero locis silentio consistentes, si quid repente emergeret intenti erant. Fervescente certamine, cum in id versos omnes existimarent, qui per umbram latuerant, transgressi silentio fossas, scalas moenibus admoverunt. Cum iam plane conscenderent, repente clamor de superiori loco attollitur, saxaque et robora quaedam ad id comparata[121] superfunduntur, quibus elisi hostes atque deiecti, fractis etiam plerisque scalis, praecipites dati sunt. Ubi vero patuit dolus, pugnam hostes dimisere. Obsessi autem[122] (iam enim albescebat dies) egressi oppido, machinas et omnia instrumenta quae per noctem admoverant igne cremaverunt.[123]

90   Olegianus igitur omnia expertus, cum nihil se profecisse appareret, frigoraque iam illis in locis equitibus molesta pabulique penuria instarent, dissolvere obsidionem statuit. Quare biduo post de tertia vigilia movens cum impedimentis omnibus, superato Apennini proximo iugo, Bononiam versus remeavit.

91   Florentinus vero populus illorum qui obsessi fuerant virtutem liberalitate gratissima prosecutus est. Militibus cunctis qui in oppido fuerant duplicata stipendia; oppidanis autem vacatio munerum tributorumque in decennium data. Iohannem autem et Silvestrem Medices, quod eximia virtute fuissent, equestri militia insigniri honestarique decrevit, quingentis in singulos pondo auri pecuniae publicae decretis; his pro equestri ornatu, centum vero et quinquaginta in epuli apparatum. Traducti etiam quidam ad populum e nobilitate ex Donatis Ruffisque et Vicedominis, qui in ea obsidione rem strenue gesserant.

assigned place, guessing with ease the enemy's trick. Accordingly they fought back openly where the violence was open, while in other places they kept silent and stayed on the lookout for a surprise attack. As the struggle grew hotter, the men hidden in the shadows reckoned that all the defenders were preoccupied, so they crossed the fosses in silence and placed ladders on the walls. When it was plain that they were swarming up, a shout was suddenly raised from a higher vantage, and rocks and specially-prepared logs were thrown down which knocked down the enemy and even shattered many of the ladders, so that they took to their heels. Their trick exposed, the enemy abandoned the fight. The besieged, however—for dawn was now breaking—came out of the town and burned the machines and all the tools which had been brought there during the night.

Thus, having tried everything without profit, and with the cold 90 weather that knights dislike now coming on in that place and the lack of pasture, Giovanni da Oleggio finally decided to abandon the siege. So two days later during the third watch he moved off with all his baggage, crossed the next ridge of the Apennines and headed toward Bologna.[53]

The Florentine People rewarded the courage of the besieged 91 with the liberality of extreme gratitude. All the soldiers who had been in the town had their pay doubled, and the townsmen were given immunity from taxes and services for a period of ten years. The People decreed that Giovanni and Salvestro de' Medici should be decorated with the insignia of knighthood in token of their exceptional valor, and each man was given five hundred florins by public decree. The latter sum was to pay for their knightly equipage, while one hundred and fifty went for a public feast. Certain members of the Donati, Rossi and Visdomini clans who had performed strenuous deeds in that siege were transferred from the nobility to the People.[54]

92   Eodem anno in Arretinis motus rerum novarum gravis in extremum paene discrimen civitatem adduxit. Brandaliae gens nobilis
erat magnis opibus clientelisque. Eius familiae principes,[124] quamquam honore et gratia apud cives pollerent, tamen offensi legibus
quae grandiores familias a republicae gubernatione secludunt, infensi etiam popularibus quibusdam, qui plus nimio posse in civitate videbantur, de invadenda republica consilium iniere. Spem
vero faciebat mediolanensis praesul, cuius potentia ubique per
Etruriam implicata atque diffusa omnibus inde casibus imminebat.
Arretini per id tempus in societate Florentinorum erant, ex quo
facilius visum est, si quid inde turbaretur, tyranni favorem prome-
reri.[125]

93   Hac igitur Brandaliae ducti spe quosdam e civibus praesentem
reipublicae statum indignantes in societatem facinoris adscivere,
celatimque paratis externorum auxiliis rem perficere maturabant.
Expectabatur vero facultas perficiendi talis. Florentini dudum Arretii dominatu, ut supra ostendimus, potiti, arcem in summa urbis parte facere coeperunt, quam complevit deinde atque absolvit
Gualterus Athenarum dux, cum Florentinis simul Arretinisque
dominatus est. Pulso deinde tyranno libertateque recepta Arretini
arcem nacti, eam non everterunt, metu contrariae factionis, sed illam servantes, fidos ad custodiam cives deligebant. Est autem in ea
turris portam urbis complexa, quae ingressum tradere externis potest. Expectabant igitur coniurati, ut aliqui[126] ex consciis praefecturam arcis sortirentur.

94   Quod ubi tandem evenit—Corbici enim fratres, duo ex eorum
(ut ita dixerim) sinu, arcem susceperant—multitudinem domi

In the same year a serious revolutionary uprising among the   92
Aretines almost brought the city to the point of crisis. The de'
Brandagli were a noble clan with great wealth and a large following. The heads of this family, although disposing of great honor
and influence among the citizenry, nevertheless had taken offense
at the laws which excluded the greater families from governance of
the state, and they were also hostile towards certain members of
the popular party who appeared to possess excessive power in the
city. So they made up their minds to take over the state. They
were given hope by the archbishop of Milan, whose power spread
and entwined everywhere in Tuscany and loomed behind every
unfortunate thing that happened. The Aretines at this time were
allied with Florence, and this circumstance made it appear quite
easy to win the tyrant's favor should there be a disturbance in
Arezzo.

Thus the de' Brandagli, encouraged by this hope, made associ-   93
ates in their crime certain citizens who were angry about the current state of affairs in the republic. In secret they prepared reinforcements from outside and set about ripening and perfecting
their plot. The opportunity they were waiting for to complete it
was as follows. The Florentines, in the period when they had exercised lordship in Arezzo, as described above,[55] had begun to build
a citadel in the highest part of the city, a citadel later manned and
completed by Walter, duke of Athens, when he was lord of Florence and Arezzo. Then, after the expulsion of the tyrant and the
recovery of their liberty, the Aretines had taken the citadel but not
destroyed it. Fearing the Ghibelline faction, they preserved it and
chose trustworthy citizens to guard it. In this citadel is a tower
commanding the gate of the city, which can betray the portal to
outsiders. So the conspirators were waiting for one of their number to be chosen by lot as commander of the citadel.

When this at length occurred—after the Corbizzi brothers,   94
two men after their own hearts, took charge of the citadel—the

comparantes multaque molientes[127] latere nequiverunt.[128] Vocatus ergo[129] unus eorum[130] a magistratu, cum facinus longe infitiaretur,[131] coniectura⟨m⟩ etiam dilueret, in ambiguum rem protraxit;[132] nec prius accusatoribus fides praestita quam externorum auxilia per noctem adventare cognitum est. Tunc demum arma populariter sumpta et ad aedes coniuratorum concursum. Sed erant aedes egregiae, simulque armatorum manus iam pridem parata populi impetum arcebat. Cum ergo intra urbem coniuratos, extra vero hostes adesse non ambiguum esset, ancipites primo hosne vel illos adorirentur, tandem (quod periculosius videbatur) excludere hostem properarunt. Itaque manu quadam populi circa aedes coniuratorum relicta, primores civium ad arcem profecti, compellantes praefectos verbis absterrere a tam nefario coepto conati sunt. Postquam vero nihil sincerum respondebatur, effracta proxima muri parte, iuventutem armatam eduxere.[133] Quae ante portam ipsam consistens, decisis undique arboribus itineribusque praeclusis, suburbanis etiam aedificiis (erant enim extra eam portam frequentia) occupatis, structaque subinde acie, prohibere hostem ab ingressu constituere. Hostes vero, quamquam peditatu equitatuque abundabant (erant enim peditum supra tria millia, equites vero sexcenti), tamen, ubi detectam coniurationem intellexere, in manus cum Arretinis venire non ausi, frustra eos revocantibus qui pro arce stabant, abiere.

95   Abacto per hunc modum externorum periculo, in urbem reversi cives, intestina curare aggrediuntur. Aedes coniuratorum non so-

conspirators were unable to conceal their plot, as they were collecting a crowd of men inside the city and were engaged in numerous machinations. Thus one of the brothers was summoned before the magistrate, and while he was denying the crime roundly and explaining away the insinuation, he caused delay by keeping the matter in a state of uncertainty. His accusers were not believed until it was learned that outside aid had arrived in the course of the night. Only then did the people seize arms and run to the dwellings of the conspirators. But these were imposing edifices, and at the same time their armed defenders, long since in a state of readiness, warded off the people's attack. Since there was now no question that conspirators were inside the city and enemies outside, the people were at first in doubt whether to attack the former or the latter; but in the end they hurried away to shut out the outsiders, who seemed the more perilous threat. So leaving a band of popolani near the conspirators' dwellings, the principal citizens set out for the citadel where, rebuking its commanders, they tried verbally to deter them from so wicked an enterprise. Receiving a disingenuous response, the part of the wall that was nearest was knocked down, and the young men in arms were marched out. Forming up outside the gate, they cut down trees on every side and blocked the roads, and also took possession of the suburban buildings (of which there were a great many outside that gate); then, drawn up in battle formation, they resolved to prevent the foe from entering. But though plentifully supplied with infantry and cavalry (they had more than three thousand infantry and six hundred knights), nevertheless, once they learned that the conspiracy had been detected, the enemy did not dare to come to blows with the Aretines but went away, with the young men standing before the citadel calling upon them vainly to come back.

Having driven off in this way the danger presented by the outsiders, the citizens turned back to the city and set out to remedy their internal problems. The dwellings of the conspirators were 95

lum egregiae, verum etiam multitudine armatorum affatim structae, vim populi facile sustinebant. Turris quoque ad arcem strenue defendebatur. Triduo in his locis pugnatum. Tandem cognatis amicisque intercedentibus pactione res composita est, ut coniuratis urbe excedere tuto liceret; qui e vestigio Mediolanum ad praesulem abeuntes, et apud illum in honore habiti, fidem ambigentibus fecere nutu illius cuncta transacta administrataque fuisse. Haec itaque Arretii proditio incassum tentata, haudquaquam eum est finem quem hostis optaverat consecuta. Diversum tamen paulo post evenit in finitimo loco.

96   Burgum est oppidum in finibus Arretinorum pernobile, secus Tiberim amnem. Id Perusini per superiora susceptum bella in potestate continebant, arcesque in eo habebant duas, neque contemnendum in utraque praesidium. Sacon igitur, cum id oppidum, si qua posset, capere statuisset, omniaque sagaciter scrutaretur, tandem profectus cum equitum peditumque copiis, nemine penitus suspicante, intempesta nocte ad ea loca pervenit, proculque ab oppido consistens, milites paucos praemisit scalas ferentes, huius artificii gnaros. Tempus erat procellosum et subobscurum, ventorumque violentia custodes ipsos in aediculam turris incluserat. Haec omnia usque adeo Saconis coeptum adiuvarunt, ut prius scalis[134] capta sit turris portae supereminens quam a custodibus quicquam sentiretur. Tunc demum strictis gladiis in custodes ruentes, cum eos terrore[135] mortis silere compulissent, acceptis per silentium commilitonibus, ubi satis multos conscendisse[136] visum est, Saconi id praestolanti significarunt. Ille vero cum reliquis statim copiis adveniens, portam refregit, sublatusque clamor repentino metu oppidanos involvit. Erant in eo oppido factiones

not only imposing, but were also amply defended by a host of armed men, and so easily resisted the power of the people. The tower by the citadel was also strenuously defended. The fight in these places went on for three days. Finally, friends and relatives intervened, and an agreement was reached whereby the conspirators were allowed to leave the city in safety. These men went off immediately to the archbishop in Milan, who received them with honor, leaving no doubt that he was behind everything that had happened. Thus the attempted betrayal of Arezzo failed, and had an ending quite different from the one hoped for by the enemy. Nevertheless, a different outcome transpired shortly thereafter in the neighboring area.[56]

Borgo is a very fine town bordering on Aretine territory along the river Tiber.[57] It had been captured by the Perugians in earlier wars and was controlled by them, and they had two citadels in it, each with a considerable garrison. Thus when Saccone had decided to capture the town if he could, he shrewdly assessed the whole situation and finally set out with his cavalry and infantry. Without arousing anyone's suspicion, he arrived near the place in the dead of night, and halting some distance from the town, he sent on ahead a few soldiers who were in on the ruse, bearing ladders. The weather was stormy and dark, and the violence of the winds kept the guards themselves inside the chamber of the tower. All this was so helpful to Saccone's enterprise that the tower overlooking the gate was captured by ladders before the guards had heard anything. Only then did they rush the guards, swords in hand, forcing them keep quiet by threatening to kill them. Then they silently let in their fellow soldiers, and when it seemed enough of them had climbed up, they signalled the fact to Saccone, who was waiting for this to happen. He then came up with the rest of his troops and broke down the gate. A cry went up, sending a shock wave of fear through the townsmen. There were two factions in this as in other towns of Tuscany. When the

96

duae,[137] ut fere ceteris Etruriae locis esse consuerunt. Earum altera studio partium Saconi conveniens, ubi illum adesse portamque tenere cognovit, in favorem eius non invita concessit. Altera vero perculsa metu, cum arma cepisset cucurrissetque in forum, conspecto alterius factionis animo et ipsa dilabitur, maiorem vim adesse putans quam cui resisti quiret. Non tamen in ea saevitum est, nec detrimenti quicquam a Sacone illatum, sed absque ulla oppidanorum clade oppido potitus est.

97   Restabant arces, in quibus Perusinorum erant praesidia. Eas cum frustra expugnare tentasset, quod reliquum erat, Sacon, extra oppidum ductis copiis, vallo et fossa illas cingere instituit, ne qua auxilii superesset spes; simulque ad amicos scribens, equitatum adauxit.

98   Perusini occupatione eius oppidi audita confestim miserant Tifernum copias et Florentinorum auxilia rogarant, sperantes si in unum omnes convenissent copiae, satis superque fore virium ad hostes opprimendos oppidumque recuperandum. Cum igitur undique cogerentur auxilia ac summa expectatione res esset, praefecti arcium, sive non intellecto suorum apparatu, sive ob circumvallationem amissa spe, arces Saconi dedidere. Itaque, cum paulo post venissent Perusinorum auxilia, proficere nihil potuerunt. In adventu hostilium copiarum Sacon intra oppidum suos continuit.

99   Post haec proelium fuit equestre non longe a Tiferno. Nam Sacon, post recessum copiarum ad Tifernum cum equitibus discurrens, cum in se equitatum hostium concisset, simulata fuga in insidias traxit. Ibi cum repente invaderentur, proelium atrox committitur et egregie ab utraque parte certatur. Pugna fuit insignis et acer absque ullo pedite; et ceciderunt ab utraque parte optimi

faction sympathetic to Saccone found out that he was at the gate, they willingly yielded in his favor. The other faction was struck with fear, and when they had seized arms and had run into the marketplace, they read the other faction's minds and they too collapsed, believing that the forces he had deployed were irresistible. Nevertheless, Saccone did not commit acts of cruelty against that faction or harm it in any way, but took control of the town without the townsmen suffering any calamity.

There remained the two citadels garrisoned by the Perugians. 97 After trying in vain to capture them, Saccone had no choice but to bring his troops outside the town and ring it with fosses and earthworks, to take away any hope of relief. At the same time, he wrote to his friends and increased his mounted forces.

When the Perugians heard about the occupation of the town 98 they immediately sent troops to Città di Castello and requested help from the Florentines, hoping that their combined forces would be more than sufficient to crush the enemy and recover the town. So while the Perugians were assembling reinforcements and expectations were high, whether because they were ignorant of the preparations for war on the part of their fellow Perugians, or because their being surrounded had caused them to lose hope, the commanders of the citadels surrendered them to Saccone. Thus, when the Perugian reinforcements arrived shortly thereafter, there was nothing they could do. Saccone kept his own forces inside the town when the hostile troops arrived.[58]

Next there was a cavalry battle not far from Città di Castello. 99 For Saccone, after the Perugian troops had withdrawn, went marauding with his knights in the direction of that city, and when the cavalry of his enemies headed off in pursuit, he led them into a trap by pretending to flee. Near Città di Castello he suddenly attacked, and a bitter battle commenced, fought with distinction on both sides. In the absence of infantry, the battle was bitter and glorious and around sixty of the best knights fell on both sides.[59] *But*

equitum circiter sexaginta. Sed cum pertinaciter utrinque dimica-
retur tempusque pugna longius suscepisset, succedentibus continuo Perusinorum auxiliis pugnamque ex integro capessentibus,
Sacon ad extremum cedere coactus est.[138]

100   Per idem tempus Anglare oppidum ad Saconem defecit. Tenuerant vero illud Perusini iampridem ex eo bello, quod adversum
Arretinos gessere.

101   Eodem anno renovata societas est inter civitates Etruriae, quae
bellum adversus[139] Mediolanensem exceperant. Fuerunt autem hae
Florentini et Arretini et Perusini et Senenses; apparatusque subinde per hiemem facti, quibus aestate proxima uterentur. Multa
quoque per eam hiemem Florentiae constituta, quo pecuniae ad
bellum suppeditarent. Illud vero inter cetera non probandum, ut
qui florentinum per agrum militare debebant, pecunia reipublicae
soluta qua peregrini externique conducerentur milites, vacationem
militiae haberent. Hoc profecto nil aliud fuit quam propriam
domesticamque multitudinem imbellem efficere, ut alios suarum
fortunarum inspiciat defensores, ipsa vero nec defendere sese nec
pugnare pro patria sciat. Haec et huiusmodi permulta rerum publicarum a gubernatoribus imperitis[140] committuntur, quae parvis
ab initio erratis permagna deinde pariunt detrimenta.

102   Eodem anno Florentinorum sociorumque legati in Galliam
missi, qui pontificem romanum tunc Avinione residentem contra
Mediolanensem incenderent. Causae quidem indignationis oppor-
tunae suberant pro Bononia occupata, cuius gratia processus quidam adversus[141] illum coepti a pontifice ferebantur. Quibus de
causis magna spes suberat opes atque vires romanae sedis ad bellum coniungere. Ierunt[142] igitur oratores cum magna spe civitatis
mirabilia quaedam a pontifice expectantes; quae spes quam fefelle-
rit postea dicemus.

after a stubborn struggle on both sides, when the fighting had gone on for quite a long time, Perugian reinforcements continued to arrive, forcing a new start to the battle. So in the end, Saccone was compelled to give way.[60]

Around the same time the town of Anghiari defected to Saccone. It had been held by the Perugians for some time, since the war they had waged against the Aretines. 100

In the same year there was renewed between the cities of Tuscany the league that had undertaken the war against the Milanese. The allied peoples were the Florentines, Aretines, Perugians and Sienese; and armaments were made ready throughout the winter for use the next summer. Many decisions were also taken that winter about raising funds for war. Among other blameworthy decisions, those with military obligations in Florentine territory were allowed exemption from military service if they paid money to the state for hiring foreign and outside soldiers. The only sure effect of this was to render the city's own population unwarlike, so that the citizens would look to others to defend their own fortunes, and would not know how to defend themselves or fight for their country. These and many similar mistakes of statecraft are committed by governors who lack experience, and though small in the beginning, such errors later give birth to massive harms. 101

In the same year, envoys of the Florentines and their allies were sent to France to stir up the Roman pontiff, then resident at Avignon, against the archbishop of Milan. There were latent grounds for anger owing to the latter's occupation of Bologna, thanks to which, it was reported, the pontiff had initiated certain legal processes. For this reason there was great hope that the resources and power of the Roman see might join them in the war. Ambassadors therefore went, expecting marvelous things from the pontiff, bearing along with them the city's high hopes. How this hope was deceived we shall afterwards explain.[61] 102

103   Inter haec Scarparia, oppidum tanto labore nuper defensum, improviso paene casu amissum est. Florentini enim, post solutam obsidionem hostiumque recessum, moenia perficere ab ea qua deerant parte curabant. Erat itaque oppidum operariorum plenum; milites vero in praesidio nequaquam multi, et hi ipsi gravissimas adversus oppidanos inimicitias contraxerant, vulneraque et rixae per eos dies inciderant; quibus accensi animi et ad vindictam exitiumque parati, suspectos inter se utrosque reddiderant. Haec hostes sagaciter odorati, docti etiam a speculatoribus quibusdam, qui per operariorum speciem fuerant in oppido versati, novum inter ac vetustum aggerem facilem esse aditum, cum peditibus quingentis, equitibus vero circiter centum, de proximis hostium castellis profecti, ad Scarpariam duxere; positisque subsidiis non longe ab oppido, delectos milites ducentos quinquaginta, et cum his ducem quendam itineris locorumque gnarum praemiserunt, qui oppidum occuparent. Hi per aggerem ipsum nullo negotio ingressi, dum audacius feruntur, neque signum dare suis qui in subsidiis relicti erant, neque stationem qua ingressi fuerant ponere memores, sed in forum vadentes, clamorem sustulere. Tenebrae erant densissimae, et milites qui in tutela oppidi erant positi[143] suam in perniciem arma sumpta ab oppidanis, oppidani vero hoc ipsum a militibus suspicabantur factum. Is error aliquandiu eos continuit.

104   Tandem vero, cum hostes versari medio foro cognitum esset, tunc deposito suorum metu ad communem salutem omnes convertuntur; factoque confestim globo, strictis gladiis in hostes ruentes, primo statim impetu in fugam vertere, paucis interfectis, non-

Meanwhile, the town of Scarperia, which had been defended 103
with such effort, was nearly lost through an unlooked-for misfortune. After the lifting of the siege and the departure of the enemy,
the Florentines had taken care to finish the wall on the side where
it was incomplete. So the town was full of workmen, but there
were not many soldiers in the garrison, and the latter had formed
an intense hostility towards the townsmen. Blows and fights occurred during those days which inflamed tempers and made men
ready to kill and take revenge, and made both groups suspicious of
each other. The enemy shrewdly sniffed out the situation, and
learned also from certain spies who had gone around town disguised as workers that there was an easy way to get in between the
old and new earthwork. So the enemy set out with five hundred
infantry and about a hundred knights from nearby castles and
marched to Scarperia. Positioning reinforcements not far from the
town, they sent ahead 250 picked soldiers, accompanied by a guide
who knew the route and the terrain. These men were to take over
the town. The entered via the earthwork without difficulty and,
carried away by their own audacity, they forgot to give the signal to the reinforcements that had been left behind and forgot to
place pickets where they had entered. Making their way into the
town square, they raised a shout. The night was extremely dark,
and the soldiers guarding the town suspected that the townsmen
had taken up arms to destroy them, while the townsmen believed
the same thing of the soldiers. This error hindered them for some
time.

Finally, however, it became known that the enemy was loose in 104
the middle of the town square, and at that point everyone laid
aside their mutual suspicions and together turned to securing their
common safety. Immediately forming themselves into a body, they
rushed on the enemy with drawn swords and turned them to flight
with their first attack, killing a few and capturing some others.
The rest hunted for the place where they had entered shortly be-

nullis etiam captis. Reliqui locum ipsum quo paulo ante ingressi fuerant repetentes ac se praecipites dantes evasere. Per hunc modum Scarparia manifesto ex periculo ac paene ex hostium faucibus divina potius quam humana ope servata est atque erepta. Qui in subsidiis[144] erant, cum diu signum expectassent, non prius sensere ingressum[145] suorum, quam ipsi idem fugati narraverunt captum a se primo oppidum, mox inde amissum. Ita indignationum irarumque pleni, alteros alteri incusantes, priusquam plane dilucesceret abiere.

105   Eadem hieme Sacon, equites habens circiter mille, peditum vero ad quattuor millia, perusinum ingressus agrum, non solum praedas abegit ab ipso prope[146] urbis conspectu, verum etiam castella quaedam Perusinorum expugnavit atque incendit. Inde, cum per agrum cortonensem onustus praeda rediret, sua praesentia effecit ut Cortonenses, qui prius ambiguo favore habiti fuerant, ad Mediolanensem omnino cohaerescerent, eiusque in bello sectarentur partes.

106   Per idem tempus Florentinorum sociorumque legati nuper in Galliam missi, cum ad pontificem pervenissent, magno in honore suscepti ac benigne auditi, etsi speciosa reddebantur verba, tamen rem atque effectum languidiorem opinione reppererunt. Causa vero huius erat hostis sollertia atque largitio, qui obeundo[147] impigre largiendoque magnifice, et principes Galliae et patrum magnam partem in favorem sui converterat. Per hos delenitus pontifex, non multum videbatur ab illius amicitia distare. Haec domi per literas oratorum cognita fecerunt, ut aliam subinde spem civitates respicerent.

107   Carolus erat ad imperium delectus. Is, quia dudum adolescens sub patre cisalpinam per Galliam longo tempore militarat varieque

fore and escaped by running away. In this way was Scarperia delivered from danger and snatched almost from the jaws of the enemy: thanks more to divine than to human assistance. The reinforcements who had been waiting so long for a signal only learned that the town had been entered by their troops at the point when the fugitives themselves told them how the town had first been captured, then lost soon thereafter. They were filled with anger and fury, each group blaming the others, and went off just before dawn.[62]

That same winter Saccone, taking about a thousand knights and four thousand infantry, entered Perugian territory and not only made off with plunder practically within sight of the city, but also captured and burned some of the Perugians' castles. Then, returning through the territory of Cortona, loaded with plunder, his presence caused the Cortonesi, previously neutral, to commit themselves completely to the archbishop of Milan and to follow his party in the war.[63]

Around the same time, the envoys of the Florentines and their allies that had recently been sent to France reached the pontiff and were received with great honor and listened to with good will. Nevertheless, although seemly words were spoken, they found less enthusiasm for carrying out their enterprise than they had expected. The reason for this was the enemy's cleverness and largesse. By tireless visitations and by handing out magnificent presents, he had turned the princes of France and a large section of the prelacy[64] in his favor. These men had softened the pope's anger, and he now seemed near to forming a friendship with archbishop. This situation was reported in the ambassadors' letters home, so that the allied cities thereafter looked for hope in other quarters.

Charles[65] had been elected to the empire. It was believed that he was hostile to the Visconti because for a long time in his youth he had seen military service under his father in Northern Italy and had undergone various reverses in that land and had suffered in-

105

106

107

iactatus in his fuerat locis, laesus iam tunc a Vicecomitum familia,
ob eamque rem hosti credebatur infensus. Consilium itaque initum est a civitatibus hunc in Italiam arcessendi. Arcane tentata res
usque adeo non ingrata Carolo fuit, ut eius rei[148] gratia quendam e
familiaribus amicisque Florentiam mitteret, qui celatim gubernatores reipublicae alloqueretur pactaque componeret. Quae quidem
res ut spem afferebat magnam, sic etiam difficultates habere pluri-
mas videbatur. Itaque nec effectum sortita est.

108   Per extremum eius anni Vertinae castellum a Florentinis obsessum est. Occupaverat autem illud non hostis, sed exulum florentinorum manus ex huiusmodi initio. Ricasolani erant familia nobilis
divitiis virisque opulenta. Ceterum gentiles agnatique eius familiae
discordiis factionibusque inter se conflictabantur, certaminibusque
ut fit coortis, dum alteri praevenire anticipareque communia pro-
perant iura, de vi publica accusati damnatique eorum aliqui exula-
rant. Hi ergo exilium indigne ferentes, Vertinas, antiquam eius
gentis arcem, cum manu familiarium[149] clientiumque occupantes,
spoliatis proximis vicis, magnam vim frumenti eo congesserunt,
castellumque ipsum natura munitum etiam manu atque opere
magis munierunt; et iactabant, ni revocarentur ab exilio, quod
indigne subiissent, mediolanensi praesuli se cohaesuros. Magis
contemnendas eorum minas faciebat, quod locus ab hoste remotis-
simus erat. Non tamen ferendam illorum contumeliam rata civitas, missis eo copiis, duobus castris Vertinas obsedit. Expugnare
deinde adortos milites, cum omnia parata essent, continui prohi-
buerunt imbres; dilataque rursus atque iterum die, ita pluviae ob-
stiterunt, ut coniurasse nubes in obsessorum defensionem viderentur. Ea de causa intermissa expugnatio est, machinisque modo et
telis exules lacessiti.

jury at the hands of the Visconti family. So the [allied] cities [of Tuscany] made plans to summon him to Italy. Secret approaches were made, which were so far from being unwelcome to Charles that on this very account he sent some of his friends and family to Florence, who were to speak confidentially to governors of the republic and come to an agreement. The business raised great hopes, but also seemed to be attended by numerous difficulties, so nothing came of it.

At the end of the year the Florentines besieged the castle of 108 Vertine.[66] It had been occupied, not by the enemy, but by a band of Florentine exiles, for the following reason. The Ricasoli were a noble family abounding with men and riches. But there were numerous discords and factions among the male members of the clan, and, as usual, fighting broke out. When one faction rushed to preempt the other in taking possession of their common rights, they were prosecuted and condemned by the public power, and some of them were exiled. These men were enraged by their exile and therefore occupied, with a band of family members and clients, an old citadel of their clan, Vertine. Having raided the nearby settlements and collected a large supply of grain, they strengthened this naturally-fortified castle with their band of men and with defense-works; and they boasted that if they were not recalled from undeserved exile they would side with the archbishop of Milan. Their threats were largely treated with contempt as the place was extremely remote from the enemy. Nevertheless, the city decided it should not suffer this affront of theirs, and sent troops there who encamped in two places to besiege the castle. When the soldiers had everything ready to begin the siege, they were prevented from doing so by continuous rains, and as day succeeded day the rainfall kept blocking them, so it seemed that the clouds were conspiring to defend the besieged. For this reason the siege was broken off, and the exiles were assailed with spears and catapults only.[67]

109   Principio insequentis anni Ruffus, mugellani praefectus agri, contracta grandi peditum manu, iumentis etiam compluribus ad frumentum importandum coactis, Losolae castello de Ubaldinis dudum recepto, quod in Apennino situm ab hostibus premi coarctarique nunciabatur et iam commeatus deerant, succurrere statuit. Ea siquidem cura paulo ante publice sibi fuerat commissa.[150] Profectus igitur cum peditum copiis atque impedimentis cumque equitibus quadringentis per loca montana saltusque difficiles, cum neque explorato neque callide iter faceret, neque clam hostibus rem molitus esset, in insidias praecipitatur, et undique circumventus, impedimenta omnia partemque non exiguam copiarum amisit. Qui a clade superfuerunt,[151] dissipati varie atque palantes, non nisi effusa fuga evaserunt. Eam vero notam ob imperitiam ducis acceptam quo deleret florentinus populus, paratis iterum copiis duceque mutato, praemissis qui arces atque aditus qua praetereundum erat occuparent, non solum frumenta intulit nullo prohibente, sed etiam praesidium quoddam hostium contra id castellum munitum expugnavit. Inde omnibus quae usui erant intra castellum devectis, reliquis vero simul cum praesidio crematis, cum satis pro dignitate reipublicae factum dux existimaret, iisdem quibus profectus erat itineribus copias reduxit.

110   Per idem tempus Clemens pontifex romanus, ab oratoribus Florentinorum ceterarumque Etruriae civitatum quae erant in foedere assidua prope flagitatione pulsatus, tria demum eis[152] proposuit; societatem romanae ecclesiae; transitum in[153] Italiam Caroli ad imperium delecti; pacem cum praesule mediolanensi; horum trium quod mallent oratores eligerent; sese eorum voluntatem electionemque secuturum. Legati vero inter se cogitata re, tandem

At the beginning of the following year, Rosso,[68] the military 109
captain of the Mugello, having collected a large force of infantry 1352
and also many pack animals to carry grain, undertook to bring
succor to the castle of Lozzole in the Apennines. It had been captured some time ago from the Ubaldini and according to information received it was being hard pressed by the enemy and lacked
supplies of food. *Rosso had been publicly charged with this task a short
while before.*[69] So he set out with his infantry forces and baggage as
well as four hundred cavalry through difficult mountain passes.
Having failed to reconnoiter the way thoroughly or keep his plans
secret from the enemy, he fell into a trap, was surrounded, and lost
all his baggage and no small part of his forces. Those who survived
the disaster were scattered and wandered aimlessly, escaping only
through flight. To wipe out this stain caused by the inexperience
of a captain, the Florentine People once again readied troops and,
having changed captains, sent them out to take control of the citadels and the approaches they would have to pass through. Not
only did the new captain transport the supplies without opposition, but he also captured the fort the enemy had built opposite
the castle. Bringing everything useful inside the castle, they burned
the rest, and the enemy fort at the same time. Then, reckoning
he had done enough for the honor of the republic, the captain
marched his troops back the same way he had come.[70]

Meanwhile, Pope Clement,[71] responding to almost continuous 110
pressure from the ambassadors of Florence and the other allied
cities in Tuscany, made three proposals to them: an alliance with
the Roman Church; an expedition to Italy on the part of Charles,
the emperor-elect; and peace with the archbishop of Milan. The
ambassadors should choose which of these three proposals they
preferred, and he would follow their desire and choice. But the legates, after giving the matter thought amongst themselves, in the
end thought it would be better to refer the whole matter to the decision of the pope. This done, the pope made his choice, saying

praestare existimarunt ad arbitrium[154] eius totum referre. Quod cum fecissent, suscepta optione pontifex mitissimam innocentissimamque partem sibi placere dixit; esse vero eam, pacem dare; neque enim aliud romanum pontificem, si optio illi detur, eligere decere;[155] itaque daturum se operam, uti pax probabilis habeatur. Neque multo post, quasi facultatem nactus absque civitatum querela hostem sibi conciliandi, publico in auditorio coram omni multitudine censuras in praesulem mediolanensem latas remisit, illumque ad gratiam recepit; ne restituta quidem Bononia, sed in duodecim annos gubernatione eius civitatis illi concessa. Pro quibus quidem rebus permagnam vim pecuniae censuum nomine ab hoste suscepit. De pace autem, quasi illa tractatum exigeret longiorem, dilata res est. Indutiae modo ad annum ex auctoritate pontificis indictae, ut per hoc medium tempus tractandi maturius agitandique facultate affutura.

III In hoc pontificis facto, multa simul oratores nostros offendebant. Maxime tamen omnium indignabantur approperatam in eorum oculis reconciliationem hostis; pacis vero negotium dilatum atque posthabitum, cum percommodum fuisset non prius illud quam hoc expediri. Deinde vicinum sibi pergravem atque infestum auctoritate pontificis[156] datum confirmatumque dolebant. Augebat insuper dolorem adversariorum laetitia, qui quasi illis repugnantibus omnia consecuti, exultare gaudio triumphareque videbantur. Itaque, ne indutiae quidem a legatis comprobatae sunt, sed cuncta civitatum[157] suarum arbitrio integra reliquere.

112 Haec ab oratoribus per literas nuntiata civitates permoverunt, ut nullo pontificis respectu ad spem Caroli adventus converterentur; cumque satis tractata res esset, conditiones acceptae sunt.

that he would like to follow the gentlest and most blameless course, namely to make peace. It would not (he said) be fitting for the Roman pontiff to choose otherwise, if he were given the choice, and so he would take pains to make an acceptable peace. Shortly thereafter, as though seizing the chance to reconcile an enemy to himself without complaint from the [Tuscan] cities,[72] in public concistory before the whole crowd he lifted the censures he had placed upon the archbishop[73] and received him back into his favor. He did not even get Bologna back, but allowed the archbishop to be governor of that city for twelve years. In return he received from the enemy a large sum of money under the name of a "census." Yet he was dilatory in making the peace treaty, as though it were something requiring long negotiation. He would only declare a one-year truce on papal authority, so that in the meantime he would be able to negotiate and discuss the matter in good time.

Many things at once in this pontifical act gave offense to our ambassadors. But what made them angriest was his hasty reconciliation, before their very eyes, with the archbishop, coupled with his delay and disregard when it came to negotiating the peace. In their view it would have been most advantageous to settle the latter business before proceeding to the former. They were furthermore aggrieved that a man so hostile and threatening towards themselves was being made and confirmed as their neighbor by pontifical authority. The happiness of their adversaries further increased their pain, for in spite of their resistance the enemy had achieved his every aim and seemed to be triumphant and exulting with joy. So the envoys refused to ratify even the truce, but left the whole settlement to be decided by the [allied] cities [of Tuscany].[74]

When the ambassadors communicated these terms by letter to the cities, the latter were deeply upset, so that, ignoring the pontiff, they were again driven to hope for Charles' coming; and after some negotiation they accepted his terms. These were,

Fuerunt autem, ut summatim dixerim, eiuscemodi. Ille in Italiam venire contra Mediolanensem; hi pecunias praebere eique ut romano principi favere promiserunt. Ita nova spes expectatioque mentes erexit.

113   Vertinae castellum iam pridem obsessum per hoc ipsum tempus pactione receptum est et ad solum eversum. Semel enim id acriter oppugnatum, quamquam egregie defendissent exules, tamen postea deterriti magnitudine apparatus, incolumes abire suaque asportare pacti, castellum dedidere. Egressi sunt autem cum Ricasolanis exulibus milites centum quinquaginta octo; datumque his spatium est ad sua deportanda. Id cum factum esset, dirutae arces atque muri.

114   Eadem aestate Florentinorum sociorumque copiae in agrum Arretinum profectae Pinnam et Gaennem et alia quaedam exulum castella populati sunt. Inde Bibienam profecti, cum omnia vastare pergerent, Sacon, parva manu occurrens, damna quaedam prima die[158] intulit. Altera vero die, dum castra moverentur, re per exploratores cognita Sacon collem quendam medium occupavit, praetereuntique[159] exercitui supra verticem conspectus in se omnes convertit. Itaque rapta in eum signa sunt, ac proelium acriter incoeptum. Sacon, praeter virtutem militum suorum[160] natura etiam loci plurimum iuvabatur, ut parva ipse manu videretur permagnas licet copias impediturus. At pars quaedam exercitus circumdato celeriter colle per loca prope invia verticem occupavit. Inde magno clamore in terga hostium ruens, invadere acriter coepit; et simul qui ab radice montis pugnabant, sursum versus annixi proeliabantur. Ita in medio constituti hostes, a fronte simul et a tergo caesi,

briefly, as follows: he was to come to Italy and oppose the archbishop; the cities were to provide the money, and promised to support him as Roman Emperor.[75] This new hope and expectation
raised spirits.[76]

The castle of Vertine, long under siege, surrendered at this time   113
through a negotiated agreement and was razed to the ground. It
had been attacked ferociously on a single occasion, and though the
exiles had defended it admirably, they were afterwards discouraged
by the great size of the Florentine war machine and agreed to surrender the castle on condition that they might leave unharmed
and take away their goods. One hundred and fifty-eight knights
came out with the Ricasoli exiles, and they were given time to
carry away their property. This done, the citadel and walls were
knocked down.[77]

The same summer the troops of the Florentines and their allies   114
went into Aretine territory and ravaged Penna, Gaenna and some
other castles of the exiles. Then they went to Bibbiena, continuing
to devastate everything in their path. Saccone came out to meet
them with a small force, and inflicted some damage on them the
first day. But the next day, learning from his spies that the allies
were moving their camp, Saccone occupied a hill in their path.
When the passing army saw him on the summit they all turned
towards him and, wrenching their standards quickly round in his
direction, a fierce battle began. Saccone was aided by the courage
of his soldiers but also, much more, by his situation, for it seemed
he would be able to block even quite large forces with his small
band. But part of the Florentine army quickly circled the hill, and
by nearly impassable routes took control of the summit. Then
with a great cry they rushed down upon the enemy from behind
and began to attack ferociously, while at the same time those who
were fighting at the bottom of the mountain surged upwards and
joined the battle. Placed thus in the middle and struck simultaneously in front and from behind, the enemy was in the end com-

fugam tandem arripere coacti sunt, multis interfectis, pluribus captis. Florentini vero post haec liberius populatione peracta, cum satietas tandem eos haberet, abscessere.

115   Per idem tempus equites hostium circiter duo millia, pedites totidem, ducentibus[161] Nolfo feretrano et Ugucio[162] cortonensi, perusinum agrum tumultuosius ingressi, Bettonam oppidum per proditionem occuparunt. Ea occupatio cum periculosa videretur et iam circumstantia castella ad eorum favorem inclinarent, commoti sociorum periculis, Florentini octingentorum equitum subsidium Perusinis miserunt. Id bellum prosperrimo eventu gestum est a Perusinis. Nam, cum hostium duces parte copiarum ad Bettonam retenta, ceteram multitudinem in cortonensem agrum remisissent, obsessi tandem sunt a Perusinis et ad extremam difficultatem rerum omnium redacti,[163] frustraque expectato suorum auxilio, cum tandem nemo succurrere posset, desperatis ad extremum rebus, duces ipsi per noctem incogniti aufugerunt, suos pariter hostesque latentes. Milites autem relicti, confestim[164] incolumes abire pacti, oppidum dedidere.

116   Per extremum eius anni equites hostium ad mille sexcentos, per speciem finiti stipendii in agrum Arretinum profecti, apud Classam[165] fluvium consederunt. Simulabant vero amicitiam, neque pecoribus neque hominibus molesti, ementes necessaria, non rapientes. Et sermonem dederant finitis cum hoste stipendiis, ad alia sese loca properare. Eo praetextu aliquot dies commorati, cum tandem[166] metu agricolarum pastorumque penitus adempto, iumenta atque viri liberius vagarentur, ex composito irruentes, ma-

pelled to flee, with many killed and even more captured. Thereafter the Florentines were quite free to engage in devastation, and when they had finally had their fill, they departed.[78]

Meanwhile about two thousand enemy cavalry and an equal 115 number of infantry under the leadership of Nolfo da Montefeltro and Uguccione da Cortona entered Perugian territory with great uproar and seized the town of Bettona thanks to an act of treachery. As this seizure seemed perilous and the neighboring castles were inclined to favor the enemy, the Florentines were sympathetic to their allies' troubles. So they sent eight hundred cavalry as reinforcements to the Perugians. The Perugians brought this war to a highly successful outcome. The enemy commanders had kept part of their forces at Bettona and sent the rest of the host back to Cortonese territory. In the end, when they were besieged by the Perugians and reduced to a condition of extreme difficulty in all things, they awaited aid from their own forces in vain, and finally, when no one came to help them, they despaired. The commanders themselves fled incognito under cover of darkness, hiding from their own forces as well as from those of their enemies. The soldiers who had been left behind immediately negotiated a surrender which allowed them to leave unmolested.[79]

At the end of that year, around sixteen hundred enemy knights 116 set out for Aretine territory, and, under the pretense that their contracts were at an end,[80] they settled by the stream of Chiassa. Pretending to be friendly, they did no damage to man or beast, paying for what they needed rather than seizing it. They gave out that they had finished their contract with the enemy and were in haste to move on to other places. On this pretext they stopped for several days until they had thoroughly lulled the suspicions of the farmers and herdsmen and they and their pack animals were able to move about freely. At that point, by previous agreement they attacked suddenly and made off with a large amount of booty and captives of every kind. Fortifying a nearby hill overlooking the

gnas praedas multosque omnis generis captivos abegerunt; munitoque proximo super amnem colle, in eo stativa habuere; gravis profecto vicinitas, et omnia igne ferroque permiscens. Arretini neque equitatu per id tempus abundabant, neque Florentinorum aut Perusinorum qui erant in foedere satis confidebant equitatum recipere; suspicione quadam et cura libertatis, quam non multis prius annis receptam meminissent, suo se magis robore tutari pergebant. Hostes igitur, diutius iisdem[167] in locis commorati, magnas per Arretinum agrum intulerunt clades.

117   Nec multo post Sacon his[168] copiis acceptis additoque proprio atque domestico milite, cum satis magnas copias confecisset, florentinum agrum ingressus, Ancisam usque populabundus pervenit. Mox inde regressus, Fighini constitit, cunctis incendio foedatis. Cum inde se postera die proripuisset, Tartaglese vi cepit atque evertit. Inde Varicum praetergressus, magna cum praeda longoque captivorum agmine in agrum Arretinum remeavit.

118   Per hoc ipsum tempus Barga oppido sociorum a vicinis hostibus obsesso, Florentini eo copias miserant; quarum adventu hostes profligati, praesidia etiam quae circumstruxerant amisere.

119   Nec multo post de pace per Mediolanensem agi coeptum. Cum enim cerneret se ab adulatoribus deceptum, Pisanosque spei suae defuisse, ac validiorem etruscam rem quam ipse futuram existimasset, labescente iam feroci animo, ferebatur ad pacem. Mota igitur illius iussu pacis mentio est per Franceschinum Gambacurtam pisanum. Nec Florentini rem aspernati; quippe non ab his inferebatur sed repellebatur bellum, ac se destitutos a spe pontificis Ca-

stream, they pitched camp there, making the vicinity a grave threat and involving everything in fire and the sword. The Aretines were not well supplied with cavalry at that time, and were too suspicious to accept mounted reinforcements from the Florentines or Perugians with whom they were allied; out of concern for their own liberty, which they remembered recovering not many years before, they proceeded to protect themselves using their own forces. Thus the enemy spent some time in that area, causing great destruction throughout Aretine territory.[81]

Soon thereafter Saccone took over these troops and added his own domestic soldiery; and having put together a rather large force he invaded Florentine territory and ravaged it all the way down to Incisa. Then he turned back and stopped at Figline, ruining everything and setting it on fire. Then, the next day, he swooped down on the lands of the Tartaglia family, seizing and destroying them. Then he bypassed Montevarchi and returned to Aretine territory with vast plunder and a long line of prisoners.

During this time Barga, a town belonging to the allies, was besieged by nearby enemies. The Florentines sent troops there, and upon their arrival the foe was put to flight, losing also the forts he had built around the town.[82]

Soon thereafter the archbishop of Milan entered into peace negotiations. For seeing that he had been deceived by flatterers, that the Pisans would not meet his hopes, and that Tuscan resistance was stronger than he had reckoned it would be, his ferocious spirit began to slacken and he was brought to make peace. At the archbishop's request, Franceschino Gambacurta of Pisa broached the subject of a peace. The Florentines in their turn were not deaf to the suggestion, as their part in the war had been defensive, not offensive, and they had themselves been disappointed by the pope and Charles of Luxembourg. For these reasons peace was welcomed on both sides, and envoys were sent to Sarzana, where a meeting was held, and after long discussions the peace was finally

rolique videbant. His igitur rationibus placente iam utrisque[169] pace, legatis Serazanam missis conventuque habito, post longas disceptationes, tandem recepta pax est, his fere conditionibus: Pax esto Florentinis sociisque eorum cum praesule mediolanensi eiusque cohaerentibus ac sectatoribus; praesul exercitus omnes praesidiaque ex Etruria deducet, nec posthac alicui ex civitatibus Etruriae bellum inferet; castella et arces, quaecumque ceperat in agro pistoriensi, dimittet; Burgum sui iuris esse sinet, praesidiumque ex eo deducet; Pisani Lucensesque medii sint; si adversus Pisanos vel Lucenses Florentini intulerint bellum,[170] liceat praesuli opem ferre; idem ius esto florentino populo, si praesul Pisanis aut Lucensibus inferat bellum; Florentini et Arretini et Perusini exules reducant, quot huius belli causa extorres patria sint;[171] si quis exul alia de causa quam huius belli exularit,[172] nemo reducat, ni[173] nominatim de eo sit actum;[174] Sacon agnatique patrimonia sua ab Arretinis recipiant; ipsi tamen urbem Arretium introire[175] non possint neve propius ad urbem accedere millibus passuum quatuor. Multa praeterea eiusmodi cauta circa exules cuiusque civitatis eorumque reductiones et bona. Pax deinde publice indicta est, et arma ubique deposita.[176]

agreed to on the following terms. The Florentines and their allies were to be at peace with the archbishop of Milan and his adherents and followers; the archbishop was to withdraw all his armies and garrisons from Tuscany and should henceforth not make war against any Tuscan city; he should release all the castles and strongholds he had taken in Pistoiese territory; he should allow Borgo to be independent, and remove his garrison from it; the Pisans and Lucchesi should remain neutral; if the Florentines should make war on the Pisans and Lucchesi, the archbishop would be permitted to help them; and the Florentine People should have the same right if the archbishop should attack the Pisans or Lucchesi. The Florentines, Aretines and Perugians should restore their exiles, all those banished on account of the war; and if some exile had been banished for reasons unconnected with the present war, he should not be restored unless explicitly named in the treaty; Saccone and his male relatives should get back their patrimonies from the Aretines; but they could not enter the city of Arezzo or approach within four miles of that city. There were many other stipulations besides relating to exiles of individual cities and to the restoration of their persons and property. Then the peace was publicly proclaimed and each side laid down its arms.[83]

LIBER OCTAVUS

1   Altero dehinc anno qui fuit statim sub recentem pacem, nulla fere prius acta res[1] quam de fraude scribarum cognitum. Cum enim sordidus quisque improbusque quasi in pace nominatus ad beneficium reductionis irreperet, querela primo et admiratio fuit, mox et pervestigatio; compertumque tandem est scribarum fraude quosdam insuper adscriptos quotidieque adscribi. Itaque corruptelae auctoribus supplicio affectis, reductio castigata est ac debito[2] modo repressa. Militibus mercede conductis qui in eo bello militaverant stipendia ex fide persoluta sunt a civitate, et quoniam respublica eorum opera non indigeret, plerique dimissi. Secuta deinde quies ex pace aliquot menses hominum curas exemit. Intenti omnes rebus gerendis et longum sperantes otium, belli cogitationem omnino reliquerant.

2   Cum haec esset conditio rerum, tandem ex re quam minime quisquam suspicabatur, metus primo, mox et tumultus est maiorem in modum civitati coortus. Causam vero huius turbationis hinc fluxisse apparet. Morialis erat gallus vir diuturna militia per Italiam notus. Is, cum forte per id tempus quies a bellis esset, sollicitata Gallorum Germanorumque multitudine quae stipendia facere per Italiam consuerat, permagna quaedam ac memoranda non defore illis praemia suasit, si in unam latrocinii praedarumque societatem coirent; praevalidis quippe virorum robore armorumque futuris nullam civitatum[3] Italiae tantarum virium esse, ut sibi resistere pervadentibus queat; quamobrem vel pecunia se redimere

BOOK VIII

The next year, just after the recent peace, there was almost no 1
public activity before the fraud trial of the notaries. Every low and 1353
wicked fellow had been trying to worm his way in to benefit from
the restoration as though he had been named in the peace. At first
this caused surprise and complaint; then an investigation was
made; and in the end it was discovered that, owing to fraud on
the part of notaries, certain persons had been added to the list
and were continuing to be added daily.[1] So those responsible for
this corruption were punished, and the list of those restored was
amended and put back into proper order. The city paid off the
mercenaries who had fought in the late war as agreed, and since
the state did not need their help, most of them were dismissed. A
period of quiet then ensued following the peace treaty, which banished men's cares for several months. Everyone concentrated on his
own affairs and hoped for a long period of tranquillity, putting
aside entirely any thoughts about war.[2]

Such was the state of affairs when at last, from a quarter no one 2
expected, greater alarm than ever, followed by uproar, arose in the
city. The disturbance seems to have issued from the following
source. Moriale was a Frenchman known throughout Italy owing
to his long military career.[3] As there happened to be at this time a
respite from the wars, this man stirred up a host of Frenchmen
and Germans who were used to earning stipends [for military ser-
vice] throughout Italy, and persuaded them that there would be
enormous and memorable rewards for them if they banded together into a single company for robbery and plunder. No city in
Italy would have enough men to resist their attack, given the overwhelming strength they would have in men and arms. Hence they
would force the cities to pay them off with money, or they would

compulsuros civitates vel agros singularum regionesque populando praedam inaestimabilem consecuturos. His rationibus allectos, magnam manum coegit.

3 Prima conventus sedes in agro piceno fuit et confluebat quotidie turba facinorosorum hominum rapto vivere cupientium, nec externi modo, verum etiam italici generis. Haec manus omnia circum loca rapinis late coepit involvere, et alia subinde loca tamquam incendium quoddam apprehendere. Iamque ex agro piceno exire ac in Umbriam Etruriamque vim transferre cogitabant. Ob hunc metum in dies crescentem, Florentini militem scribere ac Perusinos et Senenses novo foedere sibi coniungere perrexerunt, ut, simul in unum[4] collatis viribus, pari concursu sese mutuo tutarentur. Hostes autem (sive illi latrones sive milites fuerint appellandi), cum in Picentibus satis debacchati fuissent, Apenninum transgressi in Fulginates primo, inde in Perusinos transierunt. Perusini vero,[5] quamquam auxilia non deerant ob foedus renovatum, tamen tantam molem belli contra se ruere videntes, statim cohorruerunt. Erant enim hostium copiae supra octo millia equitum, peditum vero armatorum supra quatuor millia; praeterea lixarum et calonum et huiusmodi hominum qui castra sectari consuerunt innumerabilis multitudo. Quare, ne eorum ager suprema clade afficeretur, Perusini, tradita pecunia commeatuque, ne sibi[6] laedant, paciscuntur.

4 Hostes de perusino in senensem, mox inde in florentinum agrum transgressi, infesto agmine usque ad Cassianum vicum octo[7] millibus passuum ab urbe devenere. Ibi cum vastarent omnia, tandem iisdem muneribus placati, in arretinum et tifernatem transiverunt agrum. In hoc demum loco praedam pecuniasque inter se partiti (erat enim iam autumni extremum), alias subinde res moliri in futurum[8] parabant.

acquire inestimable plunder by pillaging the territories and environs of each city. He brought together a large force of men who were lured by these arguments.

The first base of this company was in the Marche, and there 3 streamed in daily a mob of men who wanted to live by pillage—and not only foreigners, but Italians too. This gang began to ravage widely all the lands close by, and their depredations soon spread like fire to other places as well. Next they planned to leave the Marche and move their violent activities into Umbria and Tuscany. Their alarm increasing daily, the Florentines began to sign up soldiers and to join together with the Perugians and Sienese in a new confederation. The enemy (whether you would call them robbers or soldiers), once they had had their fill of savage violence in the Marche, crossed the Apennines and passed first into the lands of Foligno, then into Perugian territory. But the Perugians, though not lacking for help thanks to the renewal of the treaty, nevertheless, seeing the great boulder of war hurtling down upon them, were instantly struck with horror. For the enemy had forces in excess of eight thousand cavalry and four thousand armored infantry, and in addition an innumerable multitude of sutlers and orderlies and the usual camp-followers. So to prevent their territory suffering the worst of disasters, the Perugians handed over money and provisions and came to terms so as to prevent harm to themselves.

The enemy then passed from Perugian into Sienese lands, and 4 from there into Florentine territory. They came marauding down as far as San Casciano, eight miles from the city. There, after causing universal devastation, they were finally placated with the same tribute, whereupon they passed into the territory of Arezzo and Città di Castello. There they divided the plunder and money among themselves (for it was now the end of autumn) and made preparations to mount similar enterprises in the future.[4]

5   Eodem anno Carolus, aliquanto prius ad imperium delectus, in Italiam venit, sollicitatus maxime ab inimicis praesulis mediolanensis, qui multi ac potentes in unam coierant voluntatem illius fastigii deprimendi. Qua de re, quo clarior sit notitia, superius aliquanto repetere libet.

6   Post pacem cum Florentinis ceterisque civitatibus Etruriae initam, Genuenses, acri diutinoque Venetorum Catalanorumque bello conflictati, tandem ad praesulem mediolanensem confugientes, dominationem suae civitatis illi tradiderant.[9] Haec susceptio Genuae traxerat secum adversus praesulem Venetorum bellum, coierantque[10] una cum Venetis Patavinus ac Veronensis et Ferrariensis ceterique praesulis veteres inimici. Hi ergo, sollicitato Caroli adventu, ut transiret in Italiam auctores fuere, rati per illius adventum invidiosam ac supra modum auctam praesulis potentiam esse labituram. Sed cum iam Italiam ingressus esset Carolus ac Patavi constitisset, paucis post diebus praesul moritur, nepotesque eius ex fratre in dominatu successere. Haec praesulis subita ac paene repentina mors spem Caroli adauxit. Itaque ex urbe Patavio Mantuam petens, si qua res innovaretur, observabat. Sed cum videret stabilitatem rerum et concordiam in successoribus, nullumque protinus motum per civitates oriri, ad pacem animum traducere coepit; factisque indutiis quibusdam inter Mediolanenses ac eorum hostes, ipse iam quasi amicus pacatusque Mediolanum adivit, peractisque solemnibus Etruriam petiit. Pisas cum ingressus esset, revolutiones rerum maximae sunt consecutae, et gubernatores reipublicae qui recipiendi auctores fuerant, ab eo ipso qui receptus erat[11] oppressi.

7   Ad Carolum Pisis degentem Florentini et Senenses et Arretini (quae civitates tunc[12] inter se confoederatae erant) oratores simul misere. Erat autem consilium, ut, quemadmodum decet socios, ea-

In the same year Charles,[5] having been elected to the Empire, came to Italy. He had been incited to do so chiefly by enemies of the archbishop of Milan, who, being numerous and powerful, had united together with the aim of checking that prelate's arrogance. To explain this with greater clarity, we must trace the story back a bit.[6]

After making peace with the Florentines and the other cities of Tuscany, the Genoese, buffeted by a long and bitter war with the Venetians and Catalans, finally took refuge with the archbishop of Milan, handing him the lordship over their city. Accepting Genoa brought the Venetian war down upon the archbishop, and the Paduan, Veronese, Ferrarese and other ancient enemies of that prelate united with the Venetians against him. It was they who were responsible for inciting Charles to come to Italy, reckoning that his advent would shake to its foundations the hateful hypertrophy of the archbishop's power. But Charles no sooner had entered Italy and come to a halt in Padua, when a few days later the archbishop died.[7] His brother's sons succeeded to his dominions. The prelate's sudden and unexpected death raised Charles' hopes. So he set out from the city of Padua for Mantua to keep watch for signs of an uprising. But when he saw that conditions were stable, that there was harmony among the archbishop's successors and that there were no immediate uprisings in the [Lombard] cities, he began to turn his thoughts to peace. Making an armistice between the Milanese and their enemies, he himself now went to Milan in the character of a friend and peacemaker. When the solemnities had been enacted, he then went to Tuscany. He entered Pisa, giving rise to a complete change of regime, and the rulers of the state who had been responsible for receiving him were themselves overthrown by the man they had received.[8]

The Florentines, Sienese and Aretines, whose cities were leagued together at that time, sent ambassadors simultaneously to Charles during his sojourn in Pisa. It was the plan for all of them

5

1354

6

7

dem cuncti et sentirent et loquerentur. Quod tamen servatum non est; nam Senenses quidem in rebus agitandis longe se magis Carolo permittere visi sunt. Nec id sane mirum. Nam neque exules habebant quos formidarent, ut Arretini, neque ab imperatorio nomine abhorrebant, ut Florentini. Quibus ex rebus factum est, ut multo magis sese Carolo vindicarent ac illius adventum Senas praestolarentur.

8   Per eosdem dies Volaterrani et Miniatenses, absque ullo florentini populi scitu, sese ac urbes suas Carolo tradidere. Florentini et Arretini solum in uno eodemque proposito perseverarunt; agitataque res est de Arretinis non mediocri contentione atque certamine. Exules enim Arretinorum primo statim Caroli adventu ad illum concurrerant ac restitui in patriam flagitabant. Inter hos eminebat Sacon, quondam Arretinorum tyrannus, et Nerius Fagiolanus, nepos illius qui Pisis dudum Lucaeque dominatus fuerat. Adversus horum postulata querelasque fortiter resistebatur ab Arretinorum legatis.

9   Denique, cum seriosius dicendi facultas data esset, in hunc modum orationem habuere: 'Utrum iniustius an impudentius postulent Arretini exules in patriam restitui, difficilis sane[13] comparatio foret. Utrumque certe tale est ut excellere magnitudo ac superare alterum videatur. Iniustissima quippe postulatio est quae contra fas et iura contendit; impudentissima vero, si apud eum qui maxime offensus est quive poenam infligere ob errata debet, praemium, quasi recte feceris, postuletur. Atque[14] nobis ante omnia refellendum est illud, quod isti tamquam fundamentum atque[15] columen rerum suarum ubique iactant, se propterea quod partes imperii tenuerunt[16] fuisse eiectos. Haec videlicet praestigia⟨e⟩

to express identical views, as befits allies. But this plan was not followed, for in the course of the negotiations the Sienese seemed to
be deferring more to Charles. This was no surprise. Unlike the
Aretines they had no exiles to fear, and unlike the Florentines they
had no horror of the imperial name. Hence it came about that
they had a much greater claim upon Charles and eagerly awaited
his arrival in Siena.

In these same days the inhabitants of Volterra and San 8
Miniato, without giving any notice to the Florentine People,
handed themselves and their cities over to Charles. The Florentines and Aretines alone kept to one and the same goal, and in the
case of the Aretines the matter aroused no small quarrels and division. For the Aretine exiles, immediately upon Charles' arrival,
had rushed to him and demanded to be restored to their country. Chief among them was Saccone, the quondam tyrant of the
Aretines, and Neri della Faggiuola, grandson of the man who had
once been lord of Pisa and Lucca.[9] The Aretine envoys put up
strong resistance to the demands and remonstrances of these
men.[10]

Finally, when the opportunity arose to address the subject in a 9
more formal way, they gave an oration along these lines: "It would
certainly be a difficult matter to decide whether the Aretine exiles'
demand to be restored to their country was more remarkable for
its injustice or for its impudence. Certainly both its injustice and
its impudence are such that each seems to exceed and overtop the
other in scale. A demand contrary to all that is holy and right
seems the height of injustice, but it is the utmost impudence to
demand a reward, as though one has acted correctly, for a man
who has committed the greatest wrongs and who ought to be punished for his moral errors. What we must principally rebut is the
boast these man make as the foundation and principal support of
their case: that they were expelled because they took the side of

sunt, o princeps, et verba praesentiae tuae accommodata; ceterum veritas est longe diversa.

10   'Non enim studia partium, sed sua illos flagitia praecipites egere. Cum enim Sacon—non principem civitatis, sed dominum ageret—libertatem[17] patriae abstulisset, iura legesque conculcasset, cuncta ad sui unius nutum libidinemque revocasset—cives alios pelleret, alios necaret—cum haec omnia faceret ac moliretur, non tamen prius ab illis labefactari status illius est coeptus, quam a suarum partium hominibus. Nega, si potes, Sacon, non a Nerio Fagiolano, qui nunc reconciliatus tecum petit, ruinae tuae initia processisse! Nam quis alter Burgi et Tiferni ceterorumque oppido-rum rebellandi auctor fuit? Quid ubertinum genus, et ipsum tua-rum partium? An non stante tecum populo Arretino ac bellum acerrimum pro te patiente, Ubertini contra te arma tulere, hosti-bus tuis[18] se coniunxere, magnam agri partem et complura oppida in tuam perniciem convertere? Qua fronte igitur te ob studia par-tium eiectum praedicas, cum illi ipsi qui eiecerunt, tuarum par-tium esse probentur?

11   'Quaeris: num recte fecerint? Laudare non possumus; nemo enim civis quod contra patriam veniret laudandus est. Sed habe-bant illi quidem excusationem, quod tu patria eos pepuleras. Nec studia partium inter vos agebantur, in quibus consentiebatis, sed potentia et dominatio, in qua longe diffidebatis. Cives te, Sacon, tui, quos tu diversarum partium esse dicis, usque ad extremam ob-sidionem pertulere; bella tuis iniuriis concitata patienter perpessa sunt; patrimonia, pecunias, corpora denique sua pro te tutando protegendoque opposuere. Tu quid illis pro eiuscemodi meritis

the Empire. These are tricks, O Emperor, words suited to your presence, but the truth is far different.

"It was not partisanship, but their own crimes that drove these 10 men out. For it was after Saccone — acting not as leader but as lord of our city — had taken away his country's liberty, trodden her rights and laws underfoot, and reduced every decision to his own will and pleasure, expelling some citizens, killing others — it was not until he had done and plotted all this that his position began to slip, thanks to the actions of his own partisans. Deny it, if you can, Saccone, that the beginnings of your downfall were put in train by Neri della Faggiuola, who is now reconciled with you and joins you in your petition. Who else was responsible for the rebellion of Borgo and Città di Castello and the other towns? What about the Ubertini, your fellow Ghibellines? When the Aretine people stood by you and suffered a bitter war on your behalf, did not the Ubertini take up arms against you, ally themselves with your enemies, and bring a large part of our territory and numerous towns to aim at your destruction? How dare you claim you were expelled because of your partisanship, when those who expelled you are demonstrably members of your own party!

"You will say: 'But surely they did not do what was right?' We 11 are not praising them; no citizen should be praised for opposing his country. But they certainly had the excuse that you had expelled them from their country. The struggle between you was not over partisan matters, on which you agreed, but over power and lordship, about which your showed a high degree of mutual mistrust. Your citizens, Saccone, whom you say belonged to the opposite party, stuck with you to the very end of the siege; they patiently bore up under wars provoked by your own wrongdoing; they exposed to danger their patrimonies, wealth, and even their own bodies to safeguard and protect you. And how have you rewarded them for these meritorious acts? By the immortal God, the misery of that time shames me even now! You took money to

reddidisti? O Deus immortalis! Pudet etiam nunc illius miseriae temporis! Pecunia suscepta urbem et patriam aliis tradidisti; servitutis turpissimum iugum civibus tuis de te bene meritis imposuisti; imperii iura maiestatemque pro turpi mercede minuisti. Audes apud imperatorem romanum postulare ut patriae praeficiaris, cum tu dudum praefectus iura[19] romani imperii, quantum in te fuit, in illa sustuleris, et commissam tibi patriam[20] alteri subieceris? Quibus oculis, quaeso, aspicere te possent cives in patria restitutum? Num sine gemitu et cordis amaritudine visuros te illos existimas, cum civitatem illam, quondam Etruriae caput, tu unus civis inventus sis, qui pecunia accepta alteri dederis in servitutem? Tu ipse, si sapis, in eam urbem redire vis,[21] in qua non vir, non mulier, non puer denique quisquam, te sine execratione sit praeteriturus?

12   'Enimvero, non Sacon petit solum in patriam restitui, sed et alii exules, qui in eadem causa cum Sacone non sunt. An putas, imperator, horum contentiones atque certamina in unis atque eisdem moenibus posse consistere? Oderunt se mutuo atque alter alterius exitium quaerit. Simul atque unis moenibus includerentur, facibus et incendiis omnia conflagrarent. Nemo est eorum qui aequo iure cum ceteris vivere sciat; per superbiam atque insolentiam dominatum affectant. Denique cives qui nunc in patria degunt, illam in servitutem ab istis impulsam et a Sacone traditam, in suum ius libertatemque restituerunt; nec reditum istorum ferre possunt, nec se tutos existimant, si isti revertantur.

13   'Quare videndum est tibi, imperator, utrum praestet illos qui bene meriti de patria sunt in ea sinere, vel istis reductis illos expellere; nam utrique simul esse non possunt. Illud certe[22] plurimum considerare debet maiestas tua: quodcumque de hoc statueris,

betray your city and country to others. You laid the horrible shame of servitude on the necks of your fellow citizens who had deserved so well of you. You reduced the rights and majesty of the Empire in return for filthy gain. You dare to ask the Roman Emperor to place you in charge of your country, when so long as you *were* in charge of it you subverted the rights of the Roman Empire as much as you could, and subjected to another the country that had been entrusted to you? How, pray, will our citizens regard you should you be restored to your country? Do you think they can look upon you without groans and bitterness of heart, now that you have been found out as the one citizen who in return for money would betray that city, once the head of Tuscany, into servitude? If you were wise, would you yourself want to return to a city in which there is no man, woman or child who can pass you on the street without cursing you?

"But indeed, not only Saccone asks to be restored to his coun-   12
try, but also the other exiles who do not join Saccone in his plea. Do you think, O Emperor, that the quarrels and struggles of these men can coexist within one and the same set of walls? They hate each other and seek each other's ruin. If they are shut up inside the same walls, they will put the whole city to the torch. There is not one of them who knows how to live on equal terms with the rest; their insolence and pride makes them thirst for lordship. Lastly, these men have driven their country into servitude and Saccone has betrayed it; the citizens who now dwell there have restored its rights and liberty. The latter cannot endure that these men should return, nor will they reckon themselves safe if they come back.

"So you should consider, O Emperor, whether it is better to al-   13
low men well-deserving of their country to remain in it, or to expel good citizens and restore such men as these; for both of them cannot exist there simultaneously. Above all, Your Majesty should certainly consider this: that whatever you decide, you will be set-

exemplum fore ceteris quoque civitatibus et gentibus, utrum a te probentur occupatores venditoresque suarum patriarum, an improbentur.'[23]

14   Carolus, cum haec audisset, improbare causam exulum visus est. Non tamen aperte postulata reiecit, sed differendo ac procrastinando in irritum duxit. Florentinorum vero legati post multorum dierum disceptationem, tandem pecuniam dare pacti, cuncta quae postulabant consecuti sunt. His peractis, Carolus, Pisis movens, in Volaterranos primo, mox in Miniatenses transiit. Utroque in oppido benigne receptus, paucisque diebus in his locis commoratus, tandem Senas pervenit. Urbem illam ingresso,[24] tumultus quidam consecuti sunt. Denique ut Pisis nuper, ita et Senis: qui rempublicam ad eam diem gubernarant[25] depulsis, ipse civitates in suam propriam curam administrationemque reduxit. Ad hunc Senis existentem Florentini pecuniis ex fide missis, contra spem ac vota inimicorum praecipua benevolentia in sinum eius irrepsere, ut nemini uni populo per Italiam magis fidere videretur; non enim antiqua partium levitate, sed praesenti commodo res existimabat. Itaque plus ab hac una civitate per amicitiam adiutus est quam a ceteris simul omnibus italici generis. Quod si inimicitia, ut avus quondam eius, certare voluisset, permagnae difficultates erant illi subeundae. Nunc autem et militibus et pecunia a civitate adiutus, nemine penitus repugnante Romam pervenit, solemnibusque peractis tranquillissime coronatus est.

15   Haec facta sunt in principio anni subsequentis, qui fuit annus quinquagesimus quintus supra mille trecentos. Mox repetitis Senis, cum in ea urbe paucos dies resedisset, Florentinis sociisque cuncta indulsit quae ad amplitudinem honoremque eorum pertinere videbantur, absque ullo partium respectu. In Arretinos

ting an example also to other cities and nations, and showing whether you approve or disapprove of men who seize and sell their own countries."

Upon hearing this, Charles seemed to express disapproval of 14 the exiles' case, yet he did not reject it openly, but caused it to fail through delay and procrastination. The Florentine legates, after a dispute lasting many days, finally agreed to pay money, and were granted all their requests. This done, Charles left Pisa and passed first to Volterran territory, then to San Miniato. In both cities he was warmly received, and having remained a few days in these places, he at length came to Siena. A uprising followed upon his entry into that city. Finally, there took place in Siena what had recently happened in Pisa: the previous regime was expelled, and Charles himself brought these cities under his own supervision. While he was at Siena the Florentines sent him the money as agreed, and against the hope and wishes of its enemies our city insinuated its way into Charles' bosom, enjoying his particular good will. Our people seemed to enjoy his unique trust among all the cities of Italy, for he was a man who reckoned matters, not in accordance with the old partisan nonsense, but by present needs. So he received more friendly help from this one city than from all the other peoples of Italy combined. If he had wished to fight her as a enemy like his grandfather before him, he would have experienced great difficulties; but as it was, the city helped him with soldiers and money, and he arrived in Rome without opposition, where, having completed the ceremonial, he was crowned in the greatest tranquillity.[11]

This occurred at the beginning of the following year, which was 15 the year 1355. Then he returned to Siena, taking up residence in 1355 that city again for a few days. There he granted the Florentines and their allies every favor which might redound to their greatness and honor, without any respect for parties. Towards the Aretines he used the same indulgence, although not without the strongest

quoque eadem indulgentia fuit, quamquam adversantibus maxime
exulibus, qui primo illius adventu pleni spe ad eum cucurrerant.
Ex Senis Pisas, inde per Ligures transmisso Apennino, in Galliam
trans Alpisque abivit.

16   Eodem anno Cassianus vicus muro cinctus est et in oppidi
formam redactus, iampridem admonitis hominibus opportunitate
loci castris hostilibus idonei, in quo dudum Herricus imperator
stativa, et nuper latrones in societatem coacti sedem belli habuissent. Quo igitur ea opportunitas adimeretur hostibus, communire
locum placuit; idque factum est validis moenibus, quo tutus adversum oppugnationes foret. Rumor quippe iam increbuerat latrones
convenas,[26] superioris temporis exemplo ad vexandos Etruriae populos incredibili multitudine coire; eoque metu anxiae civitates
foedera inter se renovarant.

17   Per haec ipsa tempora Sacon, dudum Arretinorum tyrannus,
in oppido Bibiena moritur, aetate quidem admodum senex (erat
enim supra octogenarium), sed corpore ita robusto, ut usque ad
extremos ferme annos arma induere ac nocturnos diurnosque militiae labores suscipere ac proeliis periculisque interesse nunquam
destiterit. Hic aetate sua multa gessit ac varie iactatus est; dux
bello quidem satis bonus, nisi quod audacia nimia parum cautus,
et ob id nonnunquam detrimenta perpessus; ad civilem vero toga-
tamque vitam nequaquam aptus. Arretini mortem eius laetis animis complexi (erat enim terrori dum vixit), delere familiae reliquias constituerunt. Itaque haud multo post eius mortem, emissa
iuventute, castella illius urbi propinqua circumdantes,[27] positis validis praesidiis, lenta obsidione expugnare adorti sunt. Ita bellum
in Arretinis ex integro renascitur.

18   Altero dehinc anno Fighinum moenibus cinctum est. Fuerat
enim ante oppidum nobile, sed paulo supra eum locum in monti-

opposition from the exiles, who upon his first arrival had rushed to him, full of hope. From Siena he went to Pisa, and from thence, crossing the Apennines, into Liguria; then he went into Lombardy and across the Alps.[12]

In the same year the village of San Casciano was ringed with a wall and refashioned as a fortified town. Men had been warning for a long time about the suitability of the place as a base for enemies. It was there that the Emperor Henry long ago had pitched camp, and in recent times companies of marauders had held it as a staging-ground for war. So to take away its usefulness to enemies, it was decided to fortify it, and this was accomplished by means of strong walls to safeguard it against attacks.[13] The rumor was in fact spreading that the marauders had met together and on the model of the previous occasion were gathering together an incredible host of men to harass the peoples of Tuscany. Alarmed, the cities renewed their league with each other.[14]

Around this time, Saccone, the former tyrant of Arezzo, died in the town of Bibbiena. He was quite advanced in years—over eighty in fact—but so robust that almost to the very end he never stopped donning armor, taking on military tasks by day and night, and involving himself in battles and perils. He performed many deeds in his life with variable fortune; he was a rather good captain in war, aside from his excessive audacity and lack of caution, which sometimes worked to his disadvantage. But he was totally unsuited to civic life.[15] The Aretines welcomed his death with happy hearts (for he was a source of terror to them while he lived), and they decided to extirpate the remains of his family. So shortly after his death, they sent out their young men and surrounded his castles near the city. Posting strong garrisons, they began slowly to lay siege to them. Thus war began afresh in Aretine territory.

The next year Figline was ringed with walls. It had earlier been an important town, sited in the mountains a little above its present location, because, as we showed,[16] it had been destroyed by the

16

17
1356

18
1357

bus situm, quod a Florentinis eversum ostendimus et oppidanos Florentiam traductos in partemque civitatis receptos. Medio autem desolationis tempore, vicus in via publica diversoriis mercatibusque rusticorum increverat, quod post moenibus cinctum antiqui nomen oppidi retinuit. Auxilia quoque missa quaedam Foroliviensibus, quo diutius hisce in locis latronum copiae detinerentur.

19   Haec foris. Domi autem non mediocris per hunc annum turbatio exorta est huiuscemodi ex causa. Vetusta fuerant civitati partium studia, de quarum origine atque progressu in primo huius operis libro mentionem fecimus. Ea, post illorum qui cum Carolo militaverant reditum, aliquandiu acriter servata, tandem procedente tempore, ut fit, minus custodita, quodammodo exoleverant, ut iam permulti, quorum maiores gebellinarum partium fuisse dicerentur, ad rempublicam gerendam irreperent, lege nil tale licere illis permittente. Insurgentes igitur quidam civium et antiquam observantiam prolabi querentes, auctores fuere novae legis ferendae, ut quorum maiores aut gebellinarum partium aut non sui corporis fuissent, hi a republica gerenda prohiberentur, poena constituta adversus eos qui huiusmodi conditionis cum essent, magistratum aliquem reipublicae, etiam ultro sibi delatum, suscepissent. Id vero, quia difficile probatu erat, ut septem testium fides pro vera probatione haberetur, constitutum est. Hinc cives alii aliunde vexari sunt coepti. Duces enim partium hanc maxime[28] curam sibi incumbere arbitrantes, deferabant illorum nomina condemnarique faciebant. Verum haec auctoritas ducum, ab initio non immoderate habita, prolabi confestim ac modum transcendere

Florentines and its inhabitants transferred to Florence and settled in a part of the city. In the meantime, while it lay desolate, a village grew up by the public road as a stopping-place and market for the country people. After it was girt with walls it kept the name of the old town. A certain amount of help was also sent to the citizens of Forlì, so that the marauding troops would be detained a little longer in that area.[17]

These were the events that took place abroad. At home, a considerable disturbance arose during that year for the following reason. Of old there had been partisan divisions in the city, whose origin and progress we discussed in the first book of this work.[18] For some time after the return of those who fought with Charles[19] these divisions remained bitter, but in the end, with the passage of time, they were gradually abandoned and forgotten. As a result, a large number of men whose ancestors were said to have been Ghibellines insinuated themselves into the regime, despite the legal prohibitions against them. Certain citizens rose up and complained about the lapse of the old practice, and the latter were responsible for passing a new law, to this effect: All those whose ancestors were Ghibellines or did not belong to their own corporation[20] were prohibited from holding office; and a penalty was laid down against men of this description who had accepted a magistracy of state, even if they had been offered it spontaneously. As this was difficult to prove, it was established that a genuine proof would require the evidence of seven witnesses. In this way citizens began to be harassed, one from one side, another from another. The leaders of the Guelf Party reckoned that this responsibility fell chiefly on themselves, and passed along the names of the Ghibellines, causing them to be condemned. But this authority of the party leaders, though in the beginning it was exercised not without moderation, was quickly corrupted and began to transgress all bounds, so that not only those who deserved it were threatened, but even those who did not. As the number of sus-

coepit, nec merentes modo, verum etiam immerentes in periculum vocari; crescenteque in dies suspectorum numero, metus universos pervaserat, faciesque civitatis ex tranquilla et laeta, trepida et anxia erat effecta. Querelae magis in fronte quam in verbis erant; terror enim ac periculum sui linguas praecluserat, propterea quod non probantes ea quae fiebant, quasi suspecti partibus ac diversa sentientes, periculum subibant.

20   Haec maxime commoverunt homines ad rem corripiendam. Quare principio insequentis anni huic turbationi occursum est, lege lata ut ad priorem numerum ducum insuper duo plebei adiungerentur. Deprehensum enim fuerat per nobilitatem maxime in eo magistratu saeviri. Itaque, ad frenandam moderandamque eam rem, plebei duo sunt additi, sine quorum interventu nihil decerni posset; et sortitiones refectae ex minus implacabili genere hominum.

21   Eodem anno ad tutelam florentinorum civium rerumque eorum quindecim naves mari conductae ex provincia narbonensi. Cives enim florentini qui Pisis negotiari consueverant, variis Pisanorum iniuriis vexati, cum neque immunitas eis[29] servaretur, neque in aliis grate humaneque tractarentur, tandem Pisis relictis Talamone se transtulerunt. Eo in loco statim celebritas consecuta est et emporium factum; navesque mercibus onustae eo undique veniebant; inde a mercatoribus susceptae, terrestri itinere deferebantur. Itaque Pisani, per hunc modum destituti, quo Talamonis portum incommodarent, praedari navigantes et impedire coeperunt. Adversus hanc Pisanorum iniuriam conductae Provincialium naves, non modo Talamonis portum navesque eo navigantes tutatae sunt, ve-

pects grew each day, fear became universal and pervasive, and the feeling in the city changed from one of peace and happiness to one of alarm and anxiety. The dissatisfaction was shown more in expressions than in words, for terror and threats to one's personal safety stopped tongues, given that those who did not approve of what was being done incurred danger as persons whose party loyalty was in question and whose views were incorrect.[21]

These fears strongly motived people to find fault with the situation. Thus, at the beginning of the following year, they dealt with the disturbances by passing a law that added two commoners over and above the previous number of Guelf Party leaders. For it was recognized that the outrageous behavior of this magistracy was primarily engineered by the nobility. So to rein in and bring the situation under control the two commoners were added, without whose participation nothing could be decided, and the methods of sortition were reformed so as to choose men of a less implacable kind. 20 1358

In the same year, fifteen galleys were hired from Provence to protect Florentine citizens and their goods. For Florentine citizens who had been used to conducting their business in Pisa had been harassed by various unjust acts at the hands of the Pisans. Since their immunities were not being observed and they were not being treated with kindness and gratitude in other respects, they finally left Pisa and betook themselves to Talamone. This place at once became a crowded and famous center of trade; ships loaded with goods came there from every direction, whence merchants conveyed the goods by land. Thus the Pisans, being in this way deserted, began to prey upon and block those coming by sea so as to render the port of Talamone less convenient. It was against this unjust act of the Pisans that the Provençal ships were hired. Not only did they protect the port of Talamone and the ships sailing there, but they also advanced in the direction of Pisa to show that 21

rum etiam circa Pisas profectae ostenderunt Florentinos ne mari quidem Pisanorum contumelias esse laturos.

22 Per haec ipsa tempora sollicitam civitatem habebat[30] Germanorum terror, qui in Etruriam transituri dicebantur. Haec gens eandem habuit conventus occasionem quam prius habuerat Morialis manus; varieque per Italiam vagata, in Apulia Calabriaque aliquandiu desedit, indeque tandem emersa in picenum gallicumque agrum, mox subinde in Mediolanensium fines progressa, magnos ubique terrores ac rerum novationes pepererat. Ex Gallia tandem in agrum bononiensem reiecta, cum transitum in Etruriam minaretur, commota ob eum timorem civitas, Apennini aditus magnis copiis magnaque sagittariorum multitudine tuendos curavit.

23 Germani, ex bononiensi in faventinum agrum transgressi, cum ubique custoditos Apennini aditus sentirent (et sunt loca montana[31] et aspera et difficilia transitu), legatos florentini populi alloquuntur. Dicunt se cogitatum ac rectum iter deserere velle, nec si possint quidem, tamen invita civitate transituros esse; cogitasse vero in Arretinos ducere per Amonam fluvium et casentinatem agrum; quo quidem itinere angulus modo[32] florentini agri, et hic ipse montanus sterilisque, attingatur. Haec postulata Germanorum civitas demum per legatos certior facta concessit, quo certamen contentioque abesset.

24 Itaque per Amonam fluvium vadentes Germani, ad Apenninum duxere, et una quidem nocte sub ipso iugo constiterunt, quietem sibi equisque sumentes. Postridie vero prima luce bifariam partiti copias, partem exercitus praemisere, reliquam in subsidiis retinue-

the Florentines were not going to put up with Pisan insults, even at sea.[22]

Around this same time, the Germans, who were said to be 22 passing into Tuscany, gave the city cause for terror and alarm. This race of men had the same reasons for forming a company as Moriale's band had earlier. After wandering in various places throughout Italy they settled for a while in Apulia and Calabria, and from thence in due course turned up in the Marche and Lombardy, marching straight away to the borders of the Milanese, causing great terror and political unrest. Finally, they were repulsed from Lombardy back into Bolognese territory and were threatening to pass into Tuscany. Alarmed, our city took steps to guard the Apennine passes with numerous troops and a host of archers.

The Germans passed from Bolognese territory into the lands of 23 Faenza, where, hearing that the Apennine passes were guarded on all sides (this being a mountainous region, rough and difficult of passage), they had a parley with representatives of the Florentine People. They said they wanted to give up on the direct route they had thought to take—and indeed they could not pass without the city's permission—but they had been thinking of marching towards Arezzo by the Valdilamone and the Casentino; this route would cross just a corner of Florentine territory, and a mountainous, barren corner at that. The city, informed by its envoys of this request on the part of the Germans, granted it in order to avoid hostilities.

So the Germans made their way along the river Lamone, 24 marching towards the Apennines; they stopped below the pass for a night to rest themselves and their horses.[23] On the following day, at dawn, they divided their troops into two parts, sending one part ahead and keeping the rest in reserve. The advance party, having begun its journey immediately at first light, crossed in safety, while the rest (including their leader, Corrado di Lando[24]) followed a lit-

runt. Quae praemissa fuerat multitudo, statim prima luce iter ingressa, tuto pertransiit: reliqua vero pars (in qua fuit Corradus
Lindo eorum dux) post aliquanto secuta est. Interea montani accolae, Germanorum iniuriis per noctem vexati, convenerant plerique et tumulos viae imminentes occuparant.[33] Sunt vero saltus difficillimi atque asperrimi, profundaeque et arctae convallium
viae. In his locis Germanos nacti accolae, invadere coeperunt:
primo pauci ac rari, mox vero plures concurrere. Ab his Germani a
fronte reiecti cum in itinere ipso substitissent,[34] ac postremi nihilominus sequerentur, conglobatio facta est in via difficili atque
arcta, et hinc ripas fluvii praealtas,[35] illinc montes arduos habente.
Montani desuper volventes saxa ingentia et in praeceps dantes,
Germanos in subiecta conglobatos valle sic obruebant, ut equi vi-
rique simul opprimerentur; nec arma, nec virtus ulla proderant
Germanis.

25   Quod tamen unicum videbatur remedium, pars quaedam ex
equis descendere a duce iussa (erant autem hi plurimum sagittarii), clamore minaci ac telorum iactu montanos reicere conabantur.[36] Sed illi, de superioribus irruentes locis, post levem pugnam
facile sagittarios dissiparunt; moxque cominus ferire equitatum
ausi, cum equorum nullus esset usus loco iniquissimo ac impeditissimo, miserabiliter opprimebant, et a tergo iam alia detecta manus arcta quaedam obsederat ac pedem referendi facultatem abstulerat. In his difficultatibus constituti Germani, ut quisque poterat,
saluti consulebat suae. Evasionis unica erat via; prosilientes equis
arma abiicere, levesque et inermes sese per quaeque confragosa dimittere. Sed et hi postmodum per silvas deprehensi a montanis,
qui instar imbris undique pluebant, occidebantur. Nec viri modo,

tle later. In the meantime the inhabitants of the mountains, having been ill-used by the Germans during the night, had come together in great numbers and had taken up position on hills overlooking the road. The climb was rough and difficult in the extreme, and the road wound through deep glens. It was there that the inhabitants came upon the Germans and began to attack them; at first there were only a few scattered attackers, but soon they began to assemble in greater numbers. They threw back the Germans who were in the lead, and while these were stopped in their tracks, the Germans in the rear continued to advance, thus creating a disordered mass on this difficult, narrow road, bordered on one side by a steep river bank and on the other by high mountains. Then the mountain men began rolling great rocks upon them from the heights, which crashed down on the Germans massed together in the valley below, and man and horse were crushed together; nor were they able to perform any feat of arms or valor.

There seemed to be only one remedy. Di Lando ordered part of 25 his men to dismount (most of these being archers) who then tried to repulse the mountain men with menacing shouts and crossbow shots. But the latter poured down from their elevated positions and easily scattered the crossbowmen after a short battle. Then they dared to fight hand-to-hand with the cavalry, and since horses were useless in that uneven and impassible ground, they crushed the wretches. Another band of mountain men now disclosed itself in the rear; it blocked the narrow pass, making retreat impossible. Being placed in this parlous state, the Germans each began to look to his own safety, insofar as they could. The only way of escape was flight, so leaping off their horses and throwing away their arms, they scattered in their unarmed and unburdened condition by whatever rough route they could find. But even these men, running like rain down the cliffs, were later captured by the mountain men in the woods and killed. Not only the men of the mountains, but even their women took captives, many of whom voluntarily

verum etiam feminae montanorum multos sese ultro dedentes, salutem vitamque precantes, captivos suscepere; pecuniasque et ar-
gentum nactae, mulieres nonnullae ditatae sunt. Equi et arma et
vestis[37] et omnia male parta quondam atque direpta, in praedam
montanis devenere. Corradus Lindo exercitus dux, cum nullam
diffugii videret viam, sese montanorum in manus ultro permisit,
ingentia pollicitus praemia, si vita servaretur; quod et illi contigit.
Et haec quidem exercitus pars omnino profligata atque deleta est.

26   Cetera vero pars quae primo incesserat, iugum Apennini transgressa, cum iam in subiectas descenderet valles, audita reliqui exercitus clade, pavida et sui diffidens, citato agmine ad Decumanum
se recepit, qui est vicus florentini agri. Ibi munitis castris ac legatis
florentinis qui transeundi auctores fuerant infesto minacique clamore penes se retentis, illorum auxilio peropportune utebantur.
Convenerant enim illorum quoque locorum accolae magna multitudine, hanc quoque partem exercitus deletura; vixque iussu auc-
toritateque legatorum ab invadendo poterant coerceri. Denique,
nisi adfuissent legati, non minus haec pars cis Apennini iugum
quam illa trans iugum fuisset oppressa. Sed legati, partim metu
sui, utpote qui essent in eorum manibus, partim verecundia pro-
missorum adducti, manifestissimis certissimisque ex periculis eos
servavere.

27   Iter illorum a Decumano ad Viculum mugellani agri. Inde alio
quam prius itinere ad iugum Apennini redeuntes, eo transmisso,
in imolensem agrum descenderunt, irati quidem florentino populo, neque tam beneficii memores quo[38] servati fuerant, quam

surrendered, begging for their lives; and some of the women acquired money and silver and became rich. Horses and arms and clothing and all the Germans' ill-gotten gains ended up as plunder for the mountain dwellers. Corrado di Lando, the leader of the army, seeing no way of escape, gave himself up voluntarily into the hands of the mountain men, promising huge rewards if his life were spared; which it was. So this part of the army, at least, was put to flight and completely destroyed.

But the other part which had set out earlier, having crossed the 26 Apennine pass, was coming down into the valleys below when it heard of the disaster to the rest of the army. Fearful and losing its self-confidence, it galloped off to take refuge at Dicomano, a village in Florentine territory. There the Germans set up a fortified camp and held in their keeping the Florentine envoys who had authorized their crossing; the latter, after many loud and hostile threats, were employed to help them in a most advantageous way. For the inhabitants of this area, too, had come together in a great host with the aim of destroying the other part of the army as well, and the command and authority of the envoys was barely sufficient to restrain them from attacking. In the end, if it had not been for the envoys' presence, the part of the army on the near side of the Apennines would have been crushed just like that on the far side. But the envoys, partly out of fear for their own safety (for they were in the hands of the Germans) and partly out of shame for the promises they had made, saved the Germans from a most manifest and certain danger.

Then they set out from Dicomano to Vicchio in the Mugello, 27 and from there crossed over the Apennines again by another route different from the earlier one, coming down in the territory of Imola. They were very angry indeed with the Florentine People, being mindful less of the favor they had received in being saved than of their anger at the inhabitants who had wanted to destroy them. Thus, no sooner had they come safely to a halt than they

infensi quod se accolae delere concupissent. Itaque vix in tuto constiterant, cum minas querelis permixtas coeperunt contra Florentinos effundere, ac ceteri quoque profligationem exercitus dolo Florentinorum machinatam praedicare. In quo mentiebantur; neque enim loca trans iugum in quibus deleti fuerant Germani, neque homines qui deleverant, Florentinorum erant; et suopte ingenio permoti accolae ob iniurias quoque prius acceptas eos invaserant.

28   Nec multo post Corradus Lindo servatus ad eos rediit. Vulnere quidem adhuc laborans, ceterum incenso ad vindictam animo, reparare coepit statim copias ac maiora quaedam in dies moliri.

29   Bellum per hoc tempus gravissimum gerebatur inter Perusinos[39] et Senenses, mutuaeque utrinque clades fuerant illatae. Sumpserat vero initium ob Cortonae obsidionem; quam urbem in fide amicitiaque Senensium requiescentem Perusini persequebantur. Cum igitur bellando utrique defessi iam essent, missis ad eos legatis, monendo ac[40] suadendo, tandem arbitrio suscepto, Florentini pacem inter eos pronunciarunt. Qua mox palam facta, ita se utraque civitas invitam renitentemque adversus conditiones pacis ostendit, ut oratores confestim Florentiam mitterent pro rebus irritandis. Sed constans plane in eo civitas fuit; utque paci maneretur obtinuit.

30   Ob eam pacem Germani[41] qui apud Senenses Perusinosque militabant, ad tria millia equitum, sese Lindoni priorique exercitui coniunxerunt. Eo supplemento elati, ex agro gallico, ubi diutius fuerant commorati, transire in Etruriam constituerunt, nec per Apennini montis iuga, ut prius, sed patentiori itinere per cesenatem ariminensemque vadentes agrum, in Picentes primo, mox inde

began to issue threats mixed with complaints against the Florentines, and otherwise to announce that the utter defeat of their
army had been engineered through Florentine trickery. In this respect they were lying, for neither the lands across the Apennine
passes where the Germans had been crushed nor the people who
had crushed them belonged to Florentines; the local inhabitants
had been galvanized into action by their own natural wits and had
attacked them because of the injuries they had received.

Shortly thereafter Corrado di Lando returned to them in safety. 28
He was still suffering from a wound, but in his heart he was burning for revenge. He began at once to make his forces ready again
and with each passing day set afoot still more ambitious plans.[25]

A war of great severity was being waged at this time between 29
the Perugians and the Sienese, and each side had inflicted disasters
on the other. The war had its origin in the siege of Cortona, a city
the Perugians were harassing because of its loyalty and friendship
towards the Sienese. As both sides had now grown tired of making war, the Florentines sent envoys to them, thanks to whose ad-
monition and persuasion the warring parties accepted arbitration,
and peace between them was declared. When this was made public, both cities showed themselves so resistant to the terms of the
peace that they immediately sent ambassadors to Florence to nul-
lify them. But our city stood absolutely firm in its purpose and
succeeded in preserving the peace.[26]

Thanks to this peace the Germans who had been fighting in 30
Sienese and Perugian service, about three thousand knights, joined 1359
up with di Lando and his existing army. Emboldened by this addition to their forces, they decided to leave Lombardy, where they
had dwelt for some time, and to pass into Tuscany. They came,
however, not by the Apennine passes, as before, but by a more
open route through the territory of Cesena and Rimini, passing
thence to the Marche and afterwards into the lands of Foligno and
Perugia. The Perugians, seeing the great boulder of war rushing

in Fulginates et Perusinos transierunt. Perusini, tantam belli molem contra se ruere cernentes, legatis ad illos missis, pecunia vexationem suam redemerunt. Itaque pacate per agrum perusinum vadentes, Florentiae propinquabant. Erat vero[42] multitudo ingens, famaque eorum terribilis, multaque ab iis[43] oppida vi capta, multaeque funditus eversae regiones ferebantur. Senenses et Pisani simul atque de concordia Perusinorum audiverunt, et ipsi eandem viam secuti, pecuniam tradere et commeatu insuper iuvare paciscuntur.

31   Ob haec maiorem in modum elati Germani, contra Florentinos minacius loquebantur, et hanc unam se petere urbem tam longo circuitu praedicabant. Simulque permulti undique publice et privatim quasi benevolentia civitatis adducti, ad concordiam cum Germanis ineundam Florentinos adhortabantur, ac se medios sequestresque offerebant, docentes[44] cum huiusmodi genere hostium nihil esse quod lucrari civitas possit; non enim urbem, non agrum habere qui victis auferatur; quod si unam modo diem in agro florentino diversentur, longe plus damni allaturos fore quam quantum nunc, ut se abstineant, sint recepturi; adderent incertos belli pugnarumque casus adversum homines desperatos et in armis exercitatissimos; adderent occupationes oppidorum, quae non difficulter possit contingere; iam vero finitimarum civitatum intuerentur exempla, quarum nulla protinus ausa sit contra tales hostes bello contendere; satis nomini gloriaeque[45] civitatis factum, quod postrema ceterarum, et non nisi derelicta ab iis[46] quae sociae periculorum esse debebant, conventionem inierit.

32   His rationibus permovere civitatem nitebantur. Sed florentinus populus alto invictoque animo cuncta prius tolerare statuit, quam Germanorum minis iactationibusque concedere; et quo maiora os-

towards them, sent envoys to the Germans to buy off harassment with money. Thus the Germans made their way peacefully through Perugian territory and approached Florence. They were a great host, and the rumor of them was terrible: it was reported that their violence had captured many towns, and many whole regions had been laid waste. The Sienese and the Pisans, as soon as they heard of the Perugians' peace agreement, followed the same policy in their turn, and agreed to pay money and to supply the Germans with victuals into the bargain.

This emboldened the Germans still further, and they began to 31 speak menacingly against the Florentines, letting it be known that they had taken so circuitous a route with the aim of attacking this city alone. At the same time there were numerous persons everywhere who both publicly and privately advised the city, as though moved by benevolence towards it, to make peace with the Germans; and they were offering themselves as intermediaries and neutral parties, instructing the Florentines that it was profitless for the city to oppose enemies of this kind. The Germans (such persons argued) had no city or lands of their own which could be taken from them when beaten; if they spent just one day in Florentine territory they would cause damage greater than the amount they would be receiving to keep away; in addition the outcome of wars and battles against desperate and highly trained men was uncertain; moreover, they might easily find their towns occupied. Let them consider now the example of the nearby cities, none of which had dared challenge such enemies to battle; it was sufficient to sustain the city's name and glory that it had been the last to come to terms, and only after being deserted by allies who should have shared in its perils.

Such were the arguments they used to win over the city. But 32 the Florentine People with high and unconquerable purpose decided it would suffer anything rather than give in to the threats and boasts of the Germans; and it held that the greater the dan-

tentabantur[47] pericula, eo pulchrius ducebat obviam proficisci. In dignitate enim atque constantia non cedendi magnam sibi gloriam fore propositam haud falso existimabat. Itaque nec pacta neque conventiones ullas audire aut tractari ab aliquo passus est; sed paratis impigre copiis, adventum Germanorum intrepidus expectabat.

33   Fama iam longe lateque vulgaverat Florentinos Germanis nequaquam concedere, sed magno elatoque animo ad resistendum parari. Atque omnium oculi in Florentinos erant conversi,[48] nec Etruriae modo, sed ceterarum Italiae partium. Admirabantur quippe homines ac praeclarum ducebant tantam animi generositatem ac praestantiam, et favebant cuncti auxiliarique festinabant. Quamobrem et a rege Siciliae et a Bernabove mediolanensi et de Patavinis Ferrariensibusque auxilia supervenere. Sed haec postmodum; ab initio autem statim civitas ipsa suas paraverat copias, ducemque his praefecerat Pandulfum Malatestam. Itaque, ubi ex perusino in senensem agrum transiisse Germanos nunciatum est, movens dux cum omnibus simul copiis obviam progressus, ad Pesam fluvium constitit, certissimo resistendi animo, si hostes advenissent. Germani contra spem sibi paratam dimicationem cernentes, in Senensi aliquandiu commorati, tandem per volaterranum vadentes agrum, in Pisanos devenere. Florentinorum quoque exercitus dux, secutus illorum motum, traductas eo copias per fines Miniatensium adversus hostem opposuit; cumque Germani ad Eram fluvium essent, ipse sub Toporio castra fecit, idoneo pugnae loco, si illi, ut iactabant, experiri fortunam maluissent. Verum hostes irrita expectatione aliquot dies in iis[49] locis commorati, tandem inde quoque abeuntes, in lucensem transiverunt[50] agrum. Eo

gers that presented themselves, the seemlier it was to go out to meet them. And certainly it was no false belief that the People would win great glory by its dignity and resolve in not giving way. Thus it allowed no one to entertain or negotiate any pacts or agreements; but it readied its troops energetically and awaited without fear the coming of the Germans.

The news now spread far and wide that the Florentines were 33 not giving in to the Germans, but were preparing to resist them with pride and great spirit. All eyes were fixed upon the Florentines, not only in Tuscany, but in the rest of Italy. Indeed, men were struck with wonder and reckoned such nobility and excellence of spirit a glorious thing. Everyone was on their side and hastened to bring them aid. On this account reinforcements arrived from the king of Sicily, from Bernabò of Milan and from the Paduans and Ferrarese. But this happened afterwards; in the beginning the city itself at once gathered its own forces, appointing Pandolfo Malatesta as their commander. So when it was announced that the Germans had moved from Perugian to Sienese territory, Pandolfo set out with all his troops at the same time to block them, halting in Valdipesa with the fixed purpose of resisting, should the enemy advance. Seeing, against their hopes, their enemy prepared for battle, the Germans remained some time in Sienese territory, then finally marched through the borders of Volterra and arrived in Pisan lands. The leader of the Florentine army tracked this movement as well, and brought his troops through the borders of San Miniato to face the enemy, and when the Germans came to Pontedera, he himself pitched camp below Montopoli, a fine place for a battle if the Germans preferred to try the fortunes of war, as they were boasting. But this expectation went unrealized, and the Germans spent several days in this place before finally leaving it, too, and passing into Lucchese territory. The Florentine forces pursued them there as well, taking up a position across from the enemy in Valdinievole. The more delay

quoque secutae Florentinorum copiae, circa Nebulam fluvium adversus hostem constitere. Quo magis intercedebat[51] morae, eo plures quotidie auxiliares Florentinis accrescebant. Nam praeter eas quas supra retulimus copias, a Bernabove quingenti equites cum Ambrosino filio, illustri adolescente, et ab Arretinis equites ducenti totidemque pedites, viri bellaces, et Neapolitanorum equites quinquaginta ex suprema nobilitate, privato spontaneoque officio; multi praeterea insignes viri civitatis gratia supervenerant. Quas ob res sublatis animis, magna erat alacritas Florentinorum in castris, magnaque vincendi fiducia, si ad pugnam veniretur.

34   Germani, ne omnino ridicule post tantas iactationes abirent, pugnam sese cupere simulabant ac magna expectatione productas copias aliquanto[52] progressi desuper ostentarunt. Sed postquam contra se alacriter iri a nostris structa acie et confligere parata viderunt, subsistentes in colle difficili et arduo, descendere in aequum locum ac potestatem confligendi facere recusarunt. In hunc modum aliquot dies irrita expectatione commorati, tandem ita abierunt Germani, ut metum trepidationemque manifestam ostenderent. Prima siquidem luce per silentium abeuntes, paucis relictis qui tabernacula incenderent, prius circa urbem Lucam se receperunt quam de illorum recessu quicquam sentiretur Florentinorum in castris. Cognita demum fuga, nostros sequi volentes dux continuit, veritus ne Pisanis, qui per id tempus Lucam tenebant, pax violaretur. Iter Germanorum ex Luca per lunensem[53] genuensemque agrum in Galliam fuit. Dux vero ac milites florentini exercitus triumphantium more post Germanorum fugam Florentiam redierunt. Ibi donatis laudatisque auxiliaribus, tandem cuncti eximia gratia dimissi sunt. Nomen certe ac[54] fama florentini populi ex hac una re mirum in modum apud cunctos accrevit, plurimamque exinde civitas est auctoritatem et gloriam consecuta.

transpired, the more reinforcements swelled the Florentine forces on a daily basis. For in addition to the forces we mentioned above, Bernabò sent five hundred cavalry with his son Ambrogino, an illustrious youth; and the Aretines sent two hundred battle-hardened cavalry and as many infantry; and fifty Neapolitan knights of the highest nobility came of their own free will out of a sense of private obligation; and many other distinguished men came besides for the city's sake. These reinforcements raised spirits, and a great eagerness came over the Florentine camp, and there was great confidence in victory if the matter should come to a fight.

The Germans did not want to depart in total ridicule after all 34 their boasting, and so, pretending they wanted a fight, after long suspense they made a show of coming down a little ways and advancing their troops. But when they saw our troops coming at them eagerly in formed lines, ready for conflict, they stood fast on their steep hill and refused to come down onto level ground and to provide an opportunity for battle. In this way they remained several days, disappointing expectations, and at length departed in such a way that they showed manifestly their fear and alarm. For departing silently at dawn, they left behind a few men to burn the tents, and took refuge near the city of Lucca²⁷ before any of the Florentines in the camps learned of their departure. When their flight at length became known, our troops wanted to pursue them but were prevented by their commander, who scrupled to violate the peace with the Pisans, at that time in control of Lucca. From Lucca the Germans took the road through the Lunigiana and Genoese territory into Lombardy. But after the flight of the Germans the commander and soldiers of the Florentine army returned in triumph to Florence. There the [foreign] auxiliaries were praised and rewarded, and finally all of them were dismissed with fervent thanks. There is no doubt that the fame and reputation of the Florentine People grew wonderfully from this one experience, and the city acquired the greatest glory and authority therefrom.²⁸

35   Non multo post reductas copias, cum Germani in Galliam[55] circa Ticinum pervenisse nuntiarentur, permota civitas ob recentissimum Bernabovis obsequium, mille equites ad illum transmisit, quibus auxiliaribus in bello uteretur. Duces vero cum equitibus missi sunt cives florentini duo, viri praestantes et bellorum non ignari.

36   Eodem anno bellum adversus Bibienam susceptum est a Florentinis ex huiusmodi causa. Tarlati et Ubertini, potentes Arretinorum familiae, licet studio partium convenirent, tamen privatis inter se odiis plurimum dissidebant. Fuerat vero utraque illarum florentino nomini inimica; siquidem ex Ubertina gente extiterant Guillielminus praesul, qui apud Campaldinum dubio[56] periculosoque certamine contra Florentinos conflixit; ex Tarlatis vero Sacon et agnati, qui multas suo tempore molestias intulerant civitati. In Saconem igitur et filios, quia recentior erat indignatio, Ubertini, eorum inimici, non alieni iam a civitatis studio putabantur. Redierant quoque aperte in gratiam per Germanorum adventum; quo quidem tempore ultro ferentes auxilium cum haud contemnenda manu Florentiam venerant, indeque ducem in castra secuti, strenuam operam navarant. Ea quidem res gratissima civitati fuit. Et accessit ad gratiam, quod paulo post reversionem exercitus, Biordus eius familiae princeps, quem ex labore castrensi adversum[57] Germanos suscepto in morbum decidisse constabat, Florentiae diem obiret. Itaque civitas, grata memorque obsequii, omnem magnificentiam ostendit in honoribus sibi exhibendis, publicoque illum funere magnificentissime[58] extulit, fratremque illius Accium militia insignivit, totam denique gentem in gratiam protectionemque suscepit.

37   Horum igitur hortatu bellum tunc adversus Bibienam susceptum est a civitate; et cura eius belli Accio Farinataeque Ubertinis

Shortly after the troops had returned, the news came that   35
the Germans in Lombardy had arrived near Pavia. Moved by
Bernabò's recent services towards it, the city sent him a thousand
cavalry that he might use them as auxiliaries in the war. Two Florentine citizens were sent out to lead the knights, excellent men experienced in warfare.

In the same year the Florentines undertook a war against Bib-   36
biena for the following reasons. The Tarlati and Ubertini, powerful Aretine families, although belonging to the same party, nevertheless had strong differences owing to private hatreds among
themselves. Both of them had been enemies of the Florentine
name, since Bishop Guglielmino, who fought against the Florentines in the critical and dangerous battle of Campaldino, was from
the Ubertini clan, while from the Tarlati had come Saccone and
his male relations, who had caused the city much grief in their
time. As the anger against Saccone and his sons was the more recent, the Ubertini, their enemies, were thought to be not un-
friendly to the city. They had also openly returned to favor thanks
to the German adventure, and indeed at that time they had willingly brought help, coming to Florence with a considerable force,
and then following the Florentine commander to his camp and de-
voting themselves energetically to the cause. This act had won
them great favor in the city. That favor had further increased because, after the return of the army, Biordo, the head of that family,
died in Florence, falling victim to a disease he was known to have
contracted from the labors he had undertaken in the field against
the Germans. Thus the city in grateful memory of his services had
shown him every honor and had carried him out for public burial
in the most magnificent way, and had knighted his brother Azzo
and taken the whole clan under its favor and protection.[29]

Thus it was at their urging that the city began the war against   37
Bibbiena, and Azzo and Farinata degli Ubertini were sent out to
take charge of the war, because they themselves possessed numer-

demandata, quod ipsi quoque circum ea loca plurima castella possidebant. Cum igitur eo missae copiae Bibienam obsedissent, Arretini pro antiquo Saconis odio ad urgendam obsidionem confestim supervenere ac seorsum castrametati suo et ipsi robore Bibienam premebant. Obsidio dura vehemensque fuit, et supra duos menses acriter repugnatum[59] est ab obsessis. Tandem, cum spem salutis nullam intuerentur, oppidani, proditis per noctem muris, hostem ex composito susceperunt. Inde pugna per oppidum fuit, et in arcem Saconiani omnes compulsi, non tamen sine certamine; in quo etiam Farinata vulnus grave periculosumque suscepit. Arx deinde obsessa ac tandem capta. Marcus et Ludovicus Saconis filii cum quibusdam agnatis Florentiam ducti sunt et carceribus asservati. Bibiena quidem per hunc modum in Florentinorum devenit potestatem. Cetera vero castella quae per agrum casentinatem Saconis filii tenebant, ad Arretinos pleraque rediere.

38   Altero dehinc anno domi forisque ab initio quies erat civitati; in Bononiensibus autem rerum motus ingens et novi belli suscitabatur materia. Eam urbem captam a praesule mediolanensi supra ostendimus. Illo autem mortuo, cum dominatio ad nepotes pervenisset, praeficitur Bononiae Olegianus, qui dux militiae in Etruria fuerat. Erat enim propinquus genere et auctoritatem habebat idoneam ad urbem conservandam; et ante mortem praesulis Bononiae praeesse consueverat, ut retinuisse magis praefecturam quam accepisse videretur. Stans igitur Bononiae Olegianus, in suspicionem dominatoribus venit. Varium certe negotium, et modo reconciliatum, modo adversum penitus et hostile habitum. Dilata per hunc modum res est usque ad hoc tempus, in quo, cum Berna-

ous castles in this area. Thus when the troops were sent there to besiege Bibbiena, the Aretines, out of their ancient hatred for Saccone, immediately joined them to press the siege. They pitched camp in a separate place and brought pressure on Bibbiena using their own resources. The siege was a hard and strenuous one and the besieged fought back bitterly for more than two months. Finally, when they saw that there was no hope of safety, the townsmen betrayed the walls by night and let the enemy in by agreement. Thereafter the battle was inside the town, and the Sacconian party were all forced back into the citadel, though not without a struggle; and in that struggle Farinata, too, received a serious and dangerous wound. The citadel was then besieged and captured. Marco and Ludovico, Saccone's sons, were brought to Florence with some of his male relatives and kept in prison. In this way Bibbiena came into the power of the Florentines. But the other castles which the sons of Saccone controlled in the Casentino were most of them restored to the Aretines.[30]

The next year the city at first enjoyed quiet in its domestic and foreign affairs, but in Bologna there was a great revolution, and fuel for a new war was ignited. Earlier we explained that that city had been captured by the archbishop of Milan. With his death, lordship passed to his nephews, and Giovanni da Oleggio was put in charge of Bologna, the man who had commanded the military forces in Tuscany.[31] He was a kinsman of the Visconti and had the necessary authority to keep control of the city; and before the archbishop's death he had been used to take charge of Bologna, so that it seemed he was keeping rather than receiving command. Being thus based in Bologna, Oleggio became suspect to his lords. The business was unstable, and at one moment he was reconciled to them, at another he was considered completely hostile to them. The situation dragged out in that way until this moment, when Bernabò had sent out an army against him. Oleggio, beset by this difficulty and being too weak to fight back, decided to surrender

38

1360

bos contra eum exercitum misisset, difficultate coactus, Olegianus, quando impar ad repugnandum esset, statuit ecclesiae romanae urbem reddere; pactusque cum legato apostolicae sedis, ut pro compensatione Firmum[60] in Picentibus sibi traderetur, Bononiam legato sponte dimisit. Id postquam Bernabos intellexit, nulla fuit mora quin bellum acrius urgeret, et copias insuper augeret ad Bononiam opprimendam. Ita bellum inter Bernabovem et legatum exoritur, magnum quidem ac grande nixu utrinque susceptum. Florentinis vero, etsi expertes erant belli, tamen propinquitas ipsa finitimi loci suspiciones varias afferebat. Erat tamen sic animata civitas, ut ecclesiam mallet quam Bernabovem in propinquo habere.

39 Eodem anno lege sancitum est, ut nemini qui dominationem alicuius oppidi dicionemve haberet, liceret magistratum Florentiae gerere. Huius ferendae legis causa fuisse creditur Nicola Azarolus,[61] qui longo intervallo Florentiam venerat. Erat enim magnus vir et multarum urbium dominator et qui regem simul ac regnum Apuliae multos annos auctoritate et sapientia gubernasset; tunc autem a legato Bononiaque redibat, magnarum rerum gratia illuc evocatus. Metuens igitur sive ipse sive civitas, ne ipsius nomen saepius iam per absentiam remissum, praesenti tunc magistratum sortiretur, generali lege de cunctis dominatoribus in omne tempus ut provideretur causa fuit. Neque enim pari iure cum aliis civibus[62] convenire sciunt qui dominari sunt consueti.

40 Principio insequentis anni Volaterrani, seditione civium conflictati, in potestatem florentini populi redierunt.

41 Semina belli pisani per haec ipsa tempora latenter quidem spargebantur, quae mox segetem armorum calamitatumque[63] uberri-

the city to the Roman Church. He made an agreement with the legate of the apostolic see to deliver Bologna voluntarily to the legate, in return for which he would be given Fermo in Piceno as compensation. After Bernabò learned of this he immediately pressed the war with still greater energy and increased his forces so as to overwhelm Bologna. Thus there arose a war between Bernabò and the legate, which was undertaken with tremendous effort on both sides. The Florentines had nothing to do with the war, but its propinquity aroused suspicions of various kinds. Nevertheless, the city's sympathies were on the side of the Church, which it preferred as a neighbor to Bernabò.[32]

In the same year it was ordained by law that no one who held 39
lordship or jurisdiction over any town would be permitted to exercise a magistracy in Florence. It is believed that the cause of this law being passed was Nicola Acciaiuoli, who had come to Florence after a long absence. He was a great man who held lordship over many cities and who had governed both the king and the kingdom of Apulia for many years with his authority and wisdom.[33] At that time he had returned from the papal legate and Bologna, having been summoned thither with great affairs in view. As his name had been passed over numerous times during his absence, either he himself or the city was afraid that he would be drawn for office at that moment.[34] This was the reason why a general law about all those holding lordships was passed for all time. For men accustomed to dominate do not know how to come together with other citizens on a basis of equal right.[35]

At the beginning of the following year, the Volterrans, buffeted 40
by civil discord, came back into the power of the Florentine Peo- 1361
ple.[36]

The seeds of the Pisan war were sown secretly during this time, 41
which soon bore a rich harvest of arms and calamity. For with the Florentines frequenting their trading center of Talamone, the hearts of the Pisans were vexed to see their own city, which had

mam produxere. Florentinis enim ad Talamonem emporium[64] ce-
lebrantibus angebantur Pisanorum animi, cernentes urbem suam,
quae portus Florentinorum esse consueverat, per illorum demigra-
tionem in solitudine destitutam. Simul enim cum florentinis negotiatoribus, ceteri quoque illiusmodi homines, secuti negotiorum
commoditatem, relictis Pisis Talamonem petierant. Pisani ergo,
navibus praedatoriis ab initio missis, Talamonis portum impedire
tentaverant. Qua in re cum sibi resisteretur a Florentinis, maiori
classe ad tutelam portus conducta, destiterunt quidem a vi aperta,
sed clam infensis animis moliebantur, ut iam fines quibus se civitates contingunt infesti a maleficiis non publica vi, sed impunitis pri-
vatorum facinoribus redderentur. Non modo enim non vetabant
delicta Pisani, sed quodam modo invitabant homines ad ea perpe-
tranda. Tantum, ut fit in populis, odium accesserat! Iam expugna-
tiones quaedam nocturnae locorum munitorum et defensiones armata vi factae audiebantur, caedesque et rapinae omnia foedabant.
His de rebus querelae saepius apud Pisanos expositae cum essent,
eo velamento excusabantur quod privati homines contra mentem
propositumque civitatis illa commisissent; eosque[65] ob haec[66] dam-
natos publice hostesque iudicatos asserebant, poenas daturos,[67] si
unquam in potestatem pisani populi devenissent. Quae cum simulata apparerent, Florentini, quo eadem ulciscerentur arte, parem li-
centiam suis largiti sunt, ac patiente republica, Pisanorum finibus
privatim referebantur clades. Haec aliquandiu continuata sic mentes utriusque populi irritaverunt, ut parum distarent ab aperto
bello. Tandem vero Petrabona castellum, quod per id tempus Pisanorum erat, per privatos quosdam occupatur. Id castellum, quia
maiusculum erat, Pisani missis copiis obsederunt, munitis maio-

formerly been the Florentines' port, abandoned in solitude owing to their departure. Other men of this kind, seeking convenience in their business dealings, had also abandoned Pisa and resorted to Talamone at the same time as had the Florentine merchants. Hence the Pisans had from the beginning sent out predatory ships in an attempt to block the port of Talamone.[37] When this was resisted by the Florentines, who hired a larger fleet to guard the port, the Pisans abandoned open violence, but plotted secretly with hostile hearts to make the borderlands between their cities unsafe from criminal activity — not by public violence, but through unpunished acts of private villainy. For not only did the Pisans not forbid these crimes, but they even in a certain way encouraged men to commit them. So far had hatred gone, as is liable to happen between peoples! Already one could hear of certain nocturnal assaults on fortified places and defensive struggles carried on with armed violence, and all was being befouled with slaughter and pillage. When complaints about these matters were laid before the Pisans, as they very often were, they excused themselves with the pretext that private individuals had committed these acts against the intention and purpose of the city; and they claimed that those responsible had been publicly condemned for these crimes and adjudged enemies, and that they would be punished if they should ever happen to come into the power of the Pisan People. These explanations being obviously fraudulent, the Florentines took their revenge using the same technique, and permitted equal license to their own men, who with the sufferance of the state inflicted great damage on the Pisans' borders in the character of private persons. After these depredations had continued for some time, the frame of mind of both peoples was so inflamed that they were close to open war. Finally the castle of Pietrabona, which at that time belonged to the Pisans, was occupied by certain private individuals. Since this castle was rather large, the Pisans sent troops to besiege

rem in modum praesidiis, et omni machinarum genere ad oppugnationem convectis.

42   Inter haec Petrus Gambacurta Pisanorum exul Florentiam venerat et discursiones quasdam suo nomine fecerat in pisanum agrum, conatus, si qua posset, in patriam regredi. Erat enim princeps factionis civium quae per id tempus deiecta premebatur. Pisani quoque ipsi Florentinorum fines impetierant, et circum Bargam oppidum cuncta vastaverant, et quasdam munitas arces occupare conati fuerant. Ita, cum iam honeste fieri posse videretur, defensio Petraebonae a Florentinis suscipitur. Missis eo copiis et praesidio quodam iuxta castellum munito, obsessos iam aperte sustentabant. Pisani quoque conspecto Florentinorum proposito, maiori nixu incubuerunt ad obsidionem urgendam. Et castra quidem sua iampridem ita munierant, ut protinus vi removeri non posse viderentur; machinis vero[68] maxime fatigabant obsessos. Tandemque[69] excitata turri lignea et moenibus castelli admota, superiecto ponte magno atrocique certamine castellum ceperunt. Maxima tamen pars hominum in proximum quod Florentini munierant praesidium evasit. In reliquos vero acerbe saevitum est a Pisanis.

43   Florentini postridie cremato praesidio copias reduxere, magno infensi dolore consiliumque damnantes suum, quod differendo ac procrastinando demum eo tempore defensionem suscipere distulissent quo iam nulla superforet defendendi spes. Corrigere deinde susceptam ignominiam properantes, contrahere maiorem in modum copias et bellum inferre Pisanis statuerunt. Tantaque fuit celeritas fervente ira, ut paucos intra dies ad mille octingentos equites, pedites vero ad quatuor millia mercede conductos in armis habuerint. His addito domestico equitatu peditatuque, fines Pisa-

it, constructing extensive fortifications and bringing up siege engines of every description.

Meanwhile Pietro Gambacurta, a Pisan exile, had come to Florence and had made certain raids on Pisan territory with the aim of returning to his country if he could. For he was the leader of a citizen faction that had been driven out at this time and was under pressure. The Pisans had also themselves attacked the borders of the Florentines and had devastated all the lands around the town of Barga, and had tried to occupy certain fortified citadels. Thus, since it seemed it could now be done with honor, the Florentines undertook the defense of Pietrabona. Sending troops there, they build a fort near the castle, now in open support of the besieged. It being obvious what the Florentines were planning, the Pisans too threw themselves into the siege with renewed effort. Indeed, they had already fortified their camps so that it seemed they could not be budged by any sudden act of violence, all the while wearing down the besieged with their engines of war. Finally, they erected a wooden tower and moved it towards the castle walls, and throwing a great bridge across them they captured the castle after a bitter struggle. Nevertheless, the greater part of the men escaped into the nearby fort which the Florentines had built. Towards the rest the Pisans acted with bitter ferocity.[38]

On the following day the Florentines burned the fort and marched their troops home, condemning in pain and anger their own ill counsel, because through delay and procrastination they had put off coming to the defense of the castle until the moment when there was no longer any hope of defending it. Making haste to wipe out the ignominy they had incurred, they decided to assemble still greater forces and make war against the Pisans. Boiling with rage, such was their celerity that within a few days they had under arms about eighteen hundred mercenary cavalry and around four thousand infantry. To these forces they added their home cavalry and infantry, and crossing the border of Pisa, they pitched

42

43

norum ingressi, circa Pecciole posuerunt castra, et castella eius regionis pleraque expugnarunt.

44   Dux erat exercitus florentini populi Bonifatius Lupus parmensis, vir magna scientia rei militaris magnaque virtute praeditus, sed ita liber ac sui animi, ut cives sibi in consilium traditos nihil protinus aestimare videretur, nulla his secreta aperiens, nihil agens ex eorum voluntate. Recte quidem. Scientia enim rei militaris vix illis qui tota vita nihil aliud meditati sunt contingit, nedum homines plebeii et otio mercaturisque assueti illam possideant. His tamen de causis Bonifatio successor datus est[70] Rodulphus Varanius camerinensis, qui suscepto exercitu ac maiorem in modum adaucto, pro magnificentia florentini populi in conspectum pisanae urbis copias ducere constituit.

45   Fossa erat interim manufacta, de qua superioribus bellis mentionem fecimus. Hanc Pisani suis custodiebant praesidiis. Varanius igitur ad fossam ducens, quamvis repugnantibus Pisanis, eam transgreditur. Ultra fossam vero plena erant omnia; quod enim confidebant Pisani prohibere transitu posse, nemo curaverat villas evacuare vel in tutum refugere. Nostri ad Cascinam primo, inde ad Sabinum castra fecere. A Sabino rursus moventes, ad ipsa prope moenia pisanae urbis profecti sunt. Ibi in conspectu ac facie urbis militaribus ad ignominiam ludis editis, ac Pisanorum copiis, quae inter ludos eruptionem fecerant, intra portam compulsis, villis aedificiisque undequaque exustis, cum satietas tandem nocendi cepisset, per eadem qua venerant vestigia retro ducentes, ad pontem Sachi fecerunt castra.

46   In his locis cum essent, literae interceptae sunt, quae ab oppido Pecciole ad Pisanos mittebantur, quibus scriptum erat omnem fere

camp near Pecciole and captured numerous castles of that region.[39]

The leader of the Florentine army was Bonifazio Lupo of 44
Parma, a man of great ability and great knowledge of military
affairs, but of such a free and independent disposition that he paid
no attention whatsoever to the citizens who had been seconded to
him as his counselors. He disclosed to them no secrets and did
nothing by their counsel. And in fact he was right to do so. For
knowledge of military affairs is unusual enough in men who spend
their whole lives doing nothing else, let alone in commoners who
are used to leisure and mercantile activities. Nevertheless, on this
account Bonifazio was replaced by Ridolfo Varano of Camerino,
who, having taken over the army and greatly enlarged it, decided
for the glory of the Florentine People to march the troops within
sight of the city of Pisa.

There was a fosse built in between which we have mentioned in 45
our account of previous wars. This the Pisans guarded with their
garrisons. Varano therefore came up to the fosse and crossed it, in
spite of Pisan resistance. All the country beyond the fosse lay in its
plenty before them. Because the Pisans trusted their ability to
block the enemy's passage, no one had taken the trouble to evacu-
ate villas or flee to safety. Our forces made camp, first at Cascina,
then at Sansovino. On the march once again from Sansovino, they
came nearly up to the very walls of Pisa. There, to shame the
Pisans, they put on military exercises right before their very eyes,
and drove the Pisan troops, who had made a sally during the
games, back inside the gates. Then they burned villas and buildings in every direction, and when they had at last had their fill of
destruction, they marched back by the very route they had come,
pitching camp at Ponsacco.

While they were in this area they intercepted letters sent to the 46
Pisans from the town of Pecciole, in which it was written that
practically all the young men of that town, in the absence of the

illius oppidi[71] iuventutem per absentiam florentini exercitus in agrum volaterranum praedandi causa profectam, biduo iam desideratam fuisse; in oppido autem paucos admodum et eos ipsos imbecilliores relictos. Itaque submitti defensores celeriter postulabant; aliter autem, si adveniant hostes, defendi oppidum[72] non posse. Dux igitur lectis literis, tabellario etiam diligenter examinato, confestim praemisit equites qui reditum illorum impedirent. Ipse vero cum reliquo exercitu secutus, oppidum obsedit, cingens undequaque ne quis regredi valeret. Post haec oppido admotis copiis, experiundi potius causa quam expugnandi spe rari defensores et inter eos feminae conspectae, certam fecere literis fidem omne quod fuerat iuventutis robur abesse.

47   Constitit postea iuventutem eius oppidi ex agro volaterrano, quo praedandi gratia fuerat profecta, concursu nostrorum aversam, maris ad littus declinasse longoque circuitu redire conatam, obsidione prohibitam se domum recipere. Ita, cum pars hostium exclusa domo, pars inclusa esset, obsidioque[73] in dies urgeretur, pactione castellum deditur,[74] nisi intra certam diem a Pisanis succurratur. Erat in eo castello arx, duaeque in ea turres ita propinquae, ut ponte coniungerentur. Praefectus earum neque pactionem receperat, nec quae oppidani fecerant probabat. Quamobrem, licet aliae partes ab oppugnatione vacarent, ad turres nihilominus pugnabatur; adauctusque iam cuniculus fundamenta alterius turris[75] succiderat, quae magno fragore prolapsa, cum super moenia oppidi[76] cecidisset, partem muri ita deiecit, ut aditum patefaceret.

Florentine army, had set out to raid Volterran territory and were expected back in two days; they had left behind in the town only a few men and those were of the weaker sort. Hence they were asking that defenders be sent swiftly to their aid; otherwise, the town could not be held if the enemy should come. Having read these letters, therefore, and carefully interrogated the messenger, the captain immediately sent ahead cavalry to block their return. He himself followed with the rest of the army and invested the town, surrounding it on all sides so that no one could get back in. After this, he moved his forces up to the town, more with the hope of testing than of capturing it, and seeing it sparsely defended, and women among the defenders, he confirmed that the letters could be relied upon and that the town's strongest and most youthful men were not present.

After this it was apparent that the young men of the town, not 47 wishing to trade blows with our forces, had gone from Volterran territory, which they had been raiding, down to the seashore and were trying to return by a circuitous route, having been prevented by the siege from returning home. Thus, with part of the enemy shut out of its home, and part shut inside, and with the siege pressing harder each day, the castle surrendered on the condition that it be not relieved by the Pisans before a certain date. There was a citadel inside this castle, and inside of the citadel were two towers set so close together that they were joined by a bridge. The commander of the towers did not accept the agreement and did not approve of what the townsmen had done. On this account, though the siege was suspended in other parts of the town, there was still fighting by the towers. A mine was dug so that the foundations of one tower fell down and collapsed with an enormous crash, and since it fell on the town walls, part of the wall was knocked over in such a way as to permit entry. So the soldiers, eager for plunder, immediately broke into the city. The unarmed townsmen called upon the good faith of the Florentine captain

Itaque eo confestim milites praedandi cupidi in oppidum irrupe-
runt. Oppidani inermes fidem ducis implorantes et oppidum sine
alia expectatione dedentes, perstabant. Quod nisi a duce praefec-
tisque properatum esset ac milites prope vi cohibiti, oppidum
nullo pactionis respectu diripiebatur. Sic quoque aegre temperatum, vociferantibus militibus praedam ad se iure belli pertinere.

48   Pecciole capto ad alia subinde castella Pisanorum dux profectus,
quaedam expugnavit; nonnulla etiam sese sponte dedentia suscepit. Sed indignatio querelaque militum ob prohibitam Pecciole
praedam cum in dies cresceret, nec duces seditionis instigato-
resque deessent, veritus dux maiorem in exercitu motum, Miniate
in oppidum reduxit. Qui vero seditionem moliebantur, ducem veriti, seorsum castrametati sunt. Ex his ad duo millia equitum
abeuntes, in societatem latrocinii coiere.

49   Per idem tempus mari quoque Pisani a Florentinis vexabantur
quatuor longis navibus. Quarum duae de Genuensibus conductae;
praeerat autem illis Perinus Grimaldi. Duas vero Nicola Azarolus
potens in regno ex Apulia miserat. Hae pluribus locis per litus
descendentes, magnas Pisanis intulerant clades, et Lilium insulam
oppidumque in illa munitissimum ceperunt. Portum quoque pisanum ingressae[77] turres expugnaverunt, et catenas ferreas quibus
portus claudebatur revulsas Florentiam transmiserunt; quae iuxta
Martis templum suspensae monstrantur pro magnificentia civitatis, quae non terra solum, sed etiam[78] mari Pisanos ulta magnifice
fuisset.

50   Per extremum eius anni Rodulpho camerinensi (quem milites
propter seditionem factam formidabant, nec dux militi, nec miles
duci satis fidebat) successor datus est Petrus Farnetius, vir egregius

and stood still, surrendering the town without any further period of waiting. And if the captain and his officers had not rushed up and almost violently restrained their soldiers, the town would have been sacked without respect for the agreement. The situation was brought under control with difficulty, with the soldiers shouting that pillage was owed them by right of war.

With Pecciole captured, the captain then set out towards other 48 castles, capturing some, and he also took a few that surrendered of their own free will. But as resentment and complaints from the soldiery about the ban on plundering Pecciole grew greater every day, and as there was no lack of leaders and instigators of discord, the captain feared a more serious upheaval in the ranks, and marched back to San Miniato. Those who were plotting sedition were afraid of the captain and encamped separately. About two thousand knights from this group left and formed a company of robbers.[40]

Around the same time the Florentines were also harassing the 49 Pisans at sea with four galleys. Two of these had been hired from the Genoese, and were commanded by Perino Grimaldi. Two had been sent from Apulia by Nicola Acciaiuoli, a powerful man in that kingdom. These fell upon many places along the coast and caused great damage to the Pisans, and they captured the island of Giglio and a fortified town on it. They also entered the port of Pisa, stormed the towers, and pulled out the iron chains that enclosed the port, sending them back to Florence. These are on display at the temple of Mars[41] for the glory of the city, which had taken magnificent vengeance on the Pisans not only on land, but also at sea.[42]

At the end of this year, Ridolfo of Camerino, whom the sol- 50 diers feared because of the revolt and who neither trusted nor was trusted by the troops, was replaced by Pietro Farnese, an outstanding fighter and among the most experienced military men of his time. So when with universal hope this man had taken charge

bello ac rei militaris per ea tempora in primis peritus. Is ergo magna spe omnium cum belli curam suscepisset, principio veris Lucam per proditionem occupare tentavit. Erat enim tunc Luca in Pisanorum potestate, ut superioribus libris ostendimus, aegreque illorum dominatum Lucenses ferebant. Re igitur arcane cum quibusdam Lucensium composita, cum duobus equitum millibus et peditibus quingentis Fucetio movens, ad constitutum tempus se circa Lucam ostendit. Sed paulo ante detecta proditio fuerat, et manus iniectae quibusdam coniuratorum. Itaque non succedentibus rebus dux e vestigio copias reduxit.

51   Barga per id tempus a Pisanis obsidebatur. Erant quoque per finitima Bargae loca defectus quidam et motus; ad quae cum Florentini Pisanique auxilia submisissent, proelium committitur, in quo praevalentibus Pisanis trecenti Florentinorum equites et pedites ducenti profligati, magnam cladem susceperunt, praefectique eorum capti sunt, et castella quae defecerant omnino amissa, et Barga duriori quam prius obsidione astricta. Ea velut ignominia tactus Farnetius, quod primae sibi res foede successerant, cum reliquis copiis agrum pisanum ingreditur, iratus quidem et sibi et hosti, certoque confligendi proposito nihil aliud meditatus quam quemadmodum acceptam cladem valeret ulcisci. Adfuitque fortuna illius coepto paene temerario. Nam, cum haud multum Pisis abesset obviosque Pisanorum equites habuisset, pedites quoque mercede conducti ac multitudo urbana studiose concurreret, pugnatum est aliquandiu dubio eventu. Tandem vero Farnetii virtus et ardor superavit, fractisque et profligatis magna strage Pisanis, plenam est victoriam consecutus. In eo proelio dux hostium captus est ac vexilla Pisanorum cum ingenti captivorum multitudine in potestatem victoris devenere. Captivos et ducem et signa milita-

of the war, he attempted at the beginning of spring to take Lucca   1363
through an act of betrayal. Lucca at that time was in the power of
the Pisans, as we have shown in previous books, and the Lucchesi
were groaning under their lordship. A conspiracy being formed
with certain of the Lucchesi, Pietro set out from Fucecchio with
two thousand horse and five hundred foot, and appeared at Lucca
at the agreed-upon time. But the plot had been discovered shortly
before, and certain of the conspirators had been seized. The conspiracy having thus failed, Pietro immediately marched his troops
back.

At this time Barga was being besieged by the Pisans.[43] There   51
were also defections and uprisings throughout the neighboring
area, and as both the Florentines and the Pisans had sent reinforcements there, a battle began which the Pisans won, putting to
flight three hundred Florentine cavalry and two hundred infantry.
It was a great disaster: their commanders were captured, the
castles which had defected were completely lost, and Barga was
bound tighter than ever by the siege. As though touched by the ignominy of this disaster, Farnese, whose first enterprise had ig-
nominiously failed, entered Pisan territory with the rest of his
troops. He was angry both at the enemy and at himself, and with
the fixed purpose of engaging the enemy he thought of nothing
else but avenging the disaster the Florentines had suffered. Fortune stood by him in this almost rash enterprise. For he was not
far from Pisa when he met the Pisan cavalry, and their hired infantry and the urban multitude also came up in support. They fought
for some time and the outcome was uncertain. But finally
Farnese's courage and ardor triumphed, and after the Pisans were
broken and put to flight with great slaughter he achieved a full victory. In this battle the enemy captain was captured and the Pisan
battle standards, along with an enormous multitude of prisoners, came into the power of the victor. With great glory Farnese
brought back to Florence the prisoners and the captain and the

ria Pisanorum capta Farnetius cum ingenti gloria Florentiam retulit. Pro quibus rebus gestis cum ab exultante populo corona laurea sibi offeretur, accipere renuit, asserens maiorum rerum triumpho illam convenire. Regressus deinde in agrum pisanum maiori apparatu quam prius, nulla vi coerceri potuit quin ad ipsa Pisarum moenia perveniret; levibusque aliquot proeliis ad portas commissis, profligatis et ibi hostibus et intra moenia compulsis, nummos argenteos in eo loco percussit, insigne habentes resupinam vulpem, quo videlicet insigni Farnetius utebatur.

52   Per idem fere tempus Barga (quod oppidum iampridem fuerat a Pisanis obsessum) liberatum est. Nam, cum equites a Farnetio missi eo pervenissent, oppidani ob auditam victoriam sublatis animis oppido egressi, magno ardore in hostem ruentes, adeo superiores fuerunt, ut et[79] castra contra se posita et praesidia omnia expugnarent. Ita ubique prospere gestis rebus,[80] gloria civitatis augebatur.

53   Sed haud multo post quasi[81] fato quodam versa retro sunt omnia, initio facto a Farnetii morte, qui in ipso victoriarum cursu pestilenti morbo correptus,[82] Miniate in oppido migravit e vita. Eius corpus magno gemitu Florentiam devectum publico funere civitas sepeliit. Haec prima turbatio Florentinorum mentes perfregit, duce optimo ac fortunatissimo repente amisso. Et supervenit confestim Anglorum gens a Pisanis conducta. Erant vero equitum supra quatuor millia, peditum vero duo millia; qui per Galliam variis bellis exercitati, tandem transmissis Alpibus in Italiam descenderant. Hos cum Florentinis militare potius optantes, propterea quod in Anglia multitudo florentinorum civium negotiaretur, ac noti amicique plurimis essent, malo consilio civitas neglexit, horrens sumptus nimios stipendiorum; militabant enim mercede ac

captured Pisan battle standards. For these deeds he was offered a laurel crown by the exultant people, but he refused to accept it, claiming that it was suited to a greater triumph than this one. Then he went back to Pisan territory with a far larger war machine than before, and no power could stop him from going up to the very walls of Pisa. After several skirmishes by the gates he put the enemy forces there to flight and forced them inside the gates. He then struck silver coins in that place bearing the sign of a wolf rampant, for this was the device Farnese used.

Around the same time Barga—the town that had long been 52 under siege from the Pisans—was liberated. For when the cavalry Farnese sent there arrived, the townsmen, emboldened by the news of victory, exited the town and rushed with great ardor upon the enemy. They bested them to such a degree that they captured the camps opposite and all the defense works. Thus, with its actions prospering everywhere, the city's glory was increasing.[44]

But not much later, as though by a kind of fate, everything 53 turned in the opposite direction. It started with the death of Farnese, who was taken with a pestilential illness in the very midst of his victories and departed this life in San Miniato. His body was borne with great mourning to Florence where it was buried by the city in a public funeral. The Florentines found the loss of this excellent and most fortunate captain extremely disturbing.[45] Immediately thereafter came the Englishmen hired by the Pisans. They numbered more than four thousand horse and two thousand foot, and having been trained in various wars throughout France, they at length crossed the Alps and came down into Italy. They would have preferred to fight alongside the Florentines because a great number of Florentine citizens did business in England and they were known to and on friendly terms with many Englishmen. But thanks to ill counsel the city took no action, dreading the excessive cost of their hire, for they were mercenary soldiers and were demanding great wages. With the Florentines behaving cooly,

magna stipendia flagitabant. Tepescentibus igitur Florentinis, Pisani meliore[83] consilio cuncta polliciti, eos sibi coniunxerunt.

54   Pisas ergo profecti Angli, magnum statim terrorem intulerunt nostris. Nam Pisani quidem rependendi ignominias avidi, quantos nunquam prius apparatus fecerunt; coniunctisque ad Anglos ceteris quas habebant copiis, domestico etiam equitatu peditatuque praecupide insequenti, haud dubie viribus superiores habebantur, praesertim cum apud Florentinos morte ducis omnia per id tempus conturbata essent. Apparatibus demum factis Pisani magna multitudine per lucensem et pistoriensem et pratensem venientes agrum, ad Piretulam duobus[84] passuum millibus ab urbe posuerunt castra. Ibi aliquot dies commorati, cum frequenter eorum agmina prope ad[85] urbem discurrissent, incendiis et rapinis omnia foedarunt; tandem exustis omnibus aedificiis ac vastatis, pisana via cum incredibili praeda magnoque captivorum agmine Pisas rediere.

55   Cum Pisis aliquot dies substitissent, illecti superiori praeda, rursus inde moventes, in agrum florentinum revertuntur. Eorum iter ad Emporium primo; inde a sinistra relicta urbe, inter Pesam et Elsam fluvios profecti, superatis collibus, quartis demum castris circa Fighinum descenderunt. In his locis, quod ea maxime diversissima sunt ab agro pisano et propterea suspicione belli plurimum vacabant, incredibilem praedam nacti sunt. Mox Fighinum expugnare adorti, haud magno labore illud ceperunt. In eo oppido stativa hostium aliquandiu fuere; unde discurrentes catervae late populabantur, multisque expugnatis oppidis, multis etiam metu desertis, trepidatio maxima cunctos pervaserat.

56   Florentinorum copiae contra hos profectae ad Ancisam constiterant, castraque iuxta oppidum ita munierant, ut ex superiore

then, the Pisans, being better advised, promised them everything, and attached the English to themselves.

The English therefore went to Pisa, and at once inflicted great   54
terror on our people. For the Pisans, eager to be recompensed for their ignominious losses, created a war machine larger than ever before; and adding the rest of their forces to the English, and with their native horse and foot following along lustily, there was no doubt that they had the more powerful forces, especially as everything lay in confusion in the Florentine camp owing to the death of their captain. When their preparations had at length been made, the Pisans came out in a great multitude through the territories of Lucca, Pistoia and Prato and pitched camp at Peretola two miles from the city. They remained there several days, and their columns made frequent raids right up to the city, befouling everything with fire and plunder. Finally, when they had burned and destroyed every building, they returned to Pisa by the Via Pisana with incredible booty and a long line of prisoners.

They stopped in Pisa for a few days; then, lured on by still   55
greater plunder, they headed out again and returned to Florentine territory. Their journey took them first to Empoli; then, leaving the city on their left, they set out between the rivers Pesa and Elsa, climbed over the hills and came down on the fourth day near Figline. In this area, which being far from Pisan territory was free from any suspicion of war, they acquired an enormous amount of booty. Then they began to attack Figline and took it with hardly any effort. The enemy were based in that town for some little time; from there raiding parties pillaged widely, and many towns were captured, and many also were abandoned out of fear; and everyone was filled with the utmost alarm.

The Florentine troops sent out against them halted at Incisa,   56
and fortified their camp next to the town in such a way that it stretched from the top of the hill all the way down to the Arno. Since their troops were in this area and skirmishes were occurring

colle ad Arnum extenderentur. In his locis cum essent copiae, et quotidie levia proelia inter utraque castra committerentur, hostes, cognito ex captivis situ castrorum, improviso supervenientes, castra nostrorum aggrediuntur. Quibus etsi resistebatur egregie, tamen, quia pro laxitate[86] castrorum non satis ampla defensorum erat manus, tandem amittuntur castra. Ne vero magna susciperetur clades, propinquitas oppidi fecit. Capti tamen permulti, in quibus et praefectus ipse copiarum fuit Rainutius Farnetius Petri frater, et commeatus impedimentaque omnia amissa. Postero deinde die hostes structam aciem oppido admoventes, transitum pervicerunt qui fossa et muro ab Ancisae[87] oppido ad Arnum claudebatur, patefactoque itinere, exustis eius vici[88] aedificiis, facultatem eundi redeundique sibi[89] paraverunt.

57   Ob haec Florentiae audita valde trepidatum est atque, ut fit in populis, alii duces ipsos, alii milites accusabant; proditos denique se credere malebant quam victos. Situs castrorum laxior et fuga quorundam spontanea[90] culpabatur; tantumque invaluit haec opinio, ut ad octingentos equites germani, quasi parum fideliter versati in castris fuerint, ignominia dimitterentur. Reliquis vero omnibus copiis in locum capti ducis Pandulphum Malatestam praefecerunt. Is enim haud multo ante domo vocatus, quasi rei militaris peritus ac partibus maxime fidus, Florentiam venerat, castrisque designandis apud Ancisam interfuerat; mox inde in urbem reversus consultandi gratia, in calamitate suscepta non adfuit.

58   Inter haec hostes, victoria elati, iactantia quadam significarunt se certa die ad portas urbis Arretina via esse venturos; proinde pararent se Florentini ad repugnandum. Hae minae hostium trepida-

every day between the two camps, the enemy, learning from captives about the siting of the Florentine defenses, came down on them without warning and attacked our camp. Although we put up a fine resistance, nevertheless the number of the defenders was not enough in proportion to the wide expanse of the encampment, and in the end the camps were lost. The nearness of the town, however, prevented a great disaster. Yet many men were captured, including the commander, Rinieri Farnese, brother of Pietro, and they lost all their baggage and supplies as well. On the following day, then, the enemy advanced towards the town in battle formation and broke through the roadway which had been closed off by a fosse and a wall from the town of Incisa to the Arno. Having opened the route, they burned the buildings in that hamlet and furnished themselves with the capacity to come and go.[46]

The news aroused great trepidation in Florence, and (as is liable to happen among peoples) some blamed the captains themselves, others the soldiers; in short they preferred to believe that they had been betrayed rather than beaten. The excessive breadth of the camps and the spontaneous flight of certain persons were held responsible, and this view gained so much ground that up to eight hundred German knights were discharged in ignominy as having conducted themselves in the field with insufficient loyalty. They put Pandolfo Malatesta in charge of the remaining troops in place of the captured captain. He had been summoned from his home not long before as a man experienced in military affairs and a loyal Guelf, and had come to Florence; he had taken part in designing the camps at Incisa, and had then come back to the city for consultations, and so missed the disaster.

Meanwhile the enemy, elated by victory, boastfully indicated that on a certain day they would arrive at the gates of the city by the Via Aretina. Accordingly, the Florentines prepared to resist them. These threats increased their fear of the enemy. On this account they posted a guard of five hundred soldiers at the church of

tionem auxere. Quamobrem et[91] ad Miniatis aedem praesidium in
supercilio urbis positum est militum quingentorum, et valli agge-
resque aliquot locis ante portam facti. Expectatus deinde eorum
adventus tanta sollicitudine, ut quidquid de superiori loco appareret, hostes adesse putarentur. Sed cum expectatio aliquot dierum
frustrata timorem ademisset ac peperisset iam securitatem, Angli
ipsi suo proprio agmine, Pisanis ad Fighinum relictis, noctu supervenerunt adeo improviso ac insperato, ut prius circa Ripolim fuerint duobus passuum millibus ab urbe quam aliquid de eorum adventu sentiretur. Ibi sublatus clamor ad urbem usque pervenit,
excitique e[92] somno cives ad portam trepidi concurrerunt. Luce demum exorta, copiae ante portam eductae constiterunt, id modo
meditantes, quemadmodum venientibus ad portam hostibus resisteretur; ultra hoc vero nihil progressae. Itaque hostes, late abacta
praeda magnoque captivorum numero coacto, incendiis multarum
villarum in oculis civium factis, nullo penitus impediente, tandem
abiere.

59   Nec multo post eadem manus Anglorum contra Arretinos profecta, usque ad moenia urbis populata est, ut eodem paene[93] tempore Fighini consistere, ac florentina Arretinaque moenia pulsare,
omnibusque ex locis praedas abigere gens Anglorum putaretur;
nec terribilius quidquam erat quam eorum nomen audire. Sed
cum finita iam aestate remeare Pisas statuissent, ne praeda captivisque onusti per difficillimos saltus quibus erat transeundum im-
pedirentur, dolum confingunt. Missis enim ad Florentinos nuntiis,
ut mense ferme ante fecerant, significarunt se pridie Idus
novembris ad Salvianum templum esse venturos; itaque priores
Florentinorum invitare ad sollemnia missarum. Haec militari iactantia nuntiata fidem adeo habuere, ut solliciti omnes diem illam

San Miniato overlooking the city, and they constructed earthworks and palisades in several places in front of the gate. Their
foe's arrival was awaited with such concern that whenever anything
appeared on the horizon the enemy was thought to be coming.
But after their expectations had been frustrated for several days
and their fears had subsided, giving place to a sense of security, a
column of the English came down upon them without warning in
the night, having left the Pisans behind in Figline. Their coming
was so sudden that they were at Ripoli, about two miles from the
city, before they were detected. The clamor that arose there spread
down to the city, and the citizens, startled from their sleep, ran in
fear to the gate. When dawn finally came, troops were marched
out in front of the gate and stood there thinking only how to resist
the enemy as he came towards the gate; beyond that place they
moved not a jot. Thus the enemy captured booty far and wide as
well as a large number of prisoners, and having put numerous villas to the torch before the eyes of the citizens with no opposition
whatsoever, they finally went away.

Shortly thereafter the same band of Englishmen went against   59
the Aretines, causing devastation right up to the walls of the city,
so that at practically the same time the English were thought to be
staying in Figline, striking at the walls of Florence and Arezzo,
and seizing booty everywhere; nothing was more terrible than the
name of the English. But as the summer had now ended they decided to return to Pisa. So as not to be hindered on the difficult
passes they had to cross, loaded as they were with spoils and captives, they thought up a trick. As they had done about a month
before, they sent messengers to the Florentines, indicating that
they would come to the church of San Salvi on the twelfth of November and they invited the Florentine priors to attend mass.[47]
This message, delivered with military braggadocio, was given so
much credence that everyone anxiously waited for that day. When
it finally came the citizens waited by the gates, as though it were a

expectarent. Quae cum tandem advenit, armati cives quasi rei certae ad portam praestolabantur; et alii iam vidisse hostes, iamque affore praedicabant; multi etiam e muris pavidi studio videndi speculabantur. At enim hostes, ea ipsa die crematis ad Fighinum castris, per asperrimos saltus ac sinuosas fauces cum omni praeda cunctisque captivis incolumes evasere. Iter eorum fere idem[94] in abeundo fuit quo prius advenerant.

60   Pisis redeuntes tanta gratulatione suscepti sunt, ut triumphare viderentur; et quoniam hiems aderat, intra urbem illis hibernare permissum est.[95] Quae quidem res permagna incommoda genuit Pisanis. Militibus siquidem intra una moenia degentibus tanta multitudine nihil liberum civibus relictum est: non urbs, non aedes, non familiae; saepiusque educere conati Pisani, nunquam parere voluerunt, modo pecuniarum defectum, modo hiemis asperitatem causantes.

61   Per eandem hiemem apud Bargam (quod oppidum rursus obsederant) iterato fracti fusique Pisani, damna non modica accepere runt, caesis[96] eorum magno numero ac signis militaribus aliquot amissis.

62   Principio insequentis anni Pisani rursus florentinum agrum maioribus quam antea copiis invadere paraverunt. Accesserat enim ad prioris[97] anni copias germanorum manus equitum trium millium noviter conductorum. Insuper multitudo Pisanorum ingens ex urbe et agro voluntaria sequebatur. His omnibus ad iter paratis per lucensem pistoriensemque et pratensem agrum magno tumultu duxere. Florentini copias quidem maiores per hiemem conductas ex Gallia et Germania expectabant; et venerat pars quaedam, non tamen tanta ut exire in apertum et castra castris auderet conferre. Itaque per oppida consistens a populationibus satis habebat hostem cohibere.

sure thing, and some were claiming that they had already seen the enemy, others that they were coming; and many also fearfully kept a lookout from the walls in their desire to see. But the enemy had burned his encampment on that very day at Figline and got away unscathed over difficult passes and winding mountain roads with all his booty and all his captives. They went back almost the same way they had come.

Returning to Pisa, they were received with so much joy and praise that it seemed they were holding a triumph; and since it was winter, they were allow to spend that season inside the city. This concession led to great distress for the Pisans. For soldiers dwelling inside a single wall in such a multitude left nothing free for the citizens: neither city, nor building, nor families. The Pisans tried repeatedly to send them out, but they would never obey, alleging now lack of money, now the bitterness of the winter. 60

During the same winter, the Pisans were for a second time broken and put to flight at Barga (since they had again besieged the town). The loss was not a slight one, as they were slaughtered in great numbers and lost several military standards.[48] 61

At the beginning of the following year, the Pisans once again prepared to invade Florentine territory with still greater forces than before. For they had added to their forces from the previous year a band of German knights, newly hired, numbering about three thousand. Furthermore, there was a great host of Pisans from the city and countryside following on a voluntary basis. Once all these forces had prepared themselves for the journey, they marched out with great uproar through the territories of Lucca, Pistoia and Prato. The Florentines were waiting for the larger forces they had hired during the winter from France and Germany, and some part of them had arrived, but not so many that they dared go out into the open and match camp to camp. So they remained stationed in the towns and considered it enough to inhibit the enemy in his acts of devastation. 62 1364

63   Cum in his essent locis Pisanorum copiae, Angli per fauces
Marinae fluvii vadentes, agrum mugellanum intraverunt. Ibi late
praedam captivosque omnis generis nacti, abegerunt. Reliquae
vero Pisanorum copiae cum Germanis ceteroque equitatu inter
Pratum et Pistorium consistebant. Placuit igitur bifariam quoque
Florentinorum copias dividere, ut aliae in urbe manentes, impetus
hostium ab ea parte, si quid conarentur, retunderent, aliae in
agrum mugellanum ad cohibendum[98] illic anglicum tumultum
proficiscerentur. Angli, aliquot dies per mugellanum agrum debacchati, tandem retro vestigia legentes per easdem Marinae fauces,
nullo prohibente, ceteras ad copias remearunt; omnibusque simul
copiis procedentes Pisani, ad Sextum et Columnatam,[99] vicos florentini agri, castra fecerunt. Florentiae vero et rumor hostium erat
et dolor atque dedecus pro agro villisque quas ante oculos incendi
vastarique ab hostibus[100] intuebantur, atque ab his hostibus quos
neque opibus neque potentia sibi pares existimabant. Ob haec
querelarum et indignationum plena erant omnia, et non succedentibus rebus dux ipse belli Pandulphus infamia laborabat. Alii nolle,
alii nescire criminabantur. Quae cum increbescerent, commeatu
petito curam eius belli ultro repudiavit.

64   Inter haec Pisani propius[101] admotis castris colles omnes qui
urbi imminent a bononiensi via ad fesulanum montem occuparunt. Inde postridie descendentes, Kalendis ipsis maiis agmine
quadrato ad urbem descenderunt; tantusque fuit impetus ut vix
quisquam extra portam esset qui non proeliando intra portam
compelleretur, ac de turribus et moenibus hostes ferirentur. Post
haec retrogressi hostes, in iisdem montibus constitere; nocteque
insecuta multis facibus discurrentes, ludos ingentibus clamoribus
inter se celebrarunt. Civitas autem trepida, utpote[102] quae non videret modo faces, verum etiam voces hostium exaudiret, insom-

Since the Pisan forces were in this area, the English pushed up 63
through the mouth of the river Marina and entered the Mugello.
There they seized and carried off booty and captives of every kind,
far and wide. The rest of the Pisan forces with the Germans and
the other cavalry stopped between Prato and Pistoia. The Florentines also decided to divide their forces in two. Some remained in
the city to blunt the attack of the enemy, if he should attempt one,
while the other set out for the Mugello to check the uproar caused
there by the English. The latter, having rampaged for several days
in that region, finally retraced their steps and rejoined the rest of
their forces, unopposed, through the mouth of the Marina. Then
all the Pisan forces simultaneously went forth and pitched camp at
Sesto and Colonnata, villages in the Florentine countryside. The
sound of the enemy came to Florence along with anguish and
shame for the countryside and its villas, which they watched being
burned and destroyed by the enemy — and by enemies whom they
reckoned their equals neither in wealth nor power. On this account there were angry outcries everywhere, and as failure succeeded failure the war captain himself, Pandolfo, came under a
cloud of infamy. Some accused him of reluctance to fight, others
of ignorance. As these charges increased, he asked for a furlough
and voluntarily disowned management of the war.

Meanwhile the Pisans moved their camp closer and occupied all 64
the hills which overlook the city from the Via Bolognese to the
mountain of Fiesole. Coming down the following day, May 1st,
they fell upon the city in a squared-off formation; and such was
the force of their attack that there was almost no one outside the
gate who was not forced inside by the fighting, and the enemy was
hit from the towers and walls. Afterwards they returned to their
stations in the mountains, and on the following night they ran
about with many torches, celebrating games among themselves
with loud cries.[49] The city, however, was in a state of fear, as it
could not only see the torches but also hear the voices of the foe;

nem transegit noctem. Et tumultus quidam ad moenia pluribus locis suscitati sunt qui metum trepidationemque augebant.

65　　Postera die hostes crematis aedificiis fere omnibus quae Fesulis, quae bononiensi via et circum ea loca fuerunt, retro moventes castra, transmisso Arno in viam pisanam omnibus copiis transiverunt. Ibi, ut prius bononiensi via fecerant, ita et pisana ad portam urbis venire conati, multis vulneribus repelluntur, consuetis iam civibus vanos metus contemnere. Quare ab ea quoque parte incendiis villarum factis, relicta tandem urbe, per dexteros profecti colles in superiorem Arnum transierunt. Inde in Arretinum agrum vadentes, usque ad moenia urbis populati sunt. Mox per Senensium fines regressi,[103] Pisas tandem rediverunt.

66　　Ante reditum harum copiarum, cum hostes circa Arretium essent, Florentini equitatu omni contra Pisas misso, cuncta circa urbem incenderunt. Inde Liburnum aggressi, cum id oppidum defensorum vacuum offendissent, ceperunt illud atque cremarunt.[104] Mox veriti ne Pisani, ad quos nova equitum manus ex Gallia supervenerat, iter interrumperent, per vulterranum agrum accelerantes, Florentiam incolumes remearunt.

67　　Cum finis esset illius aestatis, magnaeque apud Pisanos copiae forent, ac de futuri anni clade formidaretur, Florentini, sollicitatis pecunia Anglis ceterisque Pisanorum auxiliaribus ut ab illis discederent, magna impensa obtinuerunt, non tamen ut sibi coniunctae Pisanos invaderent (id enim honestate quadam militari exceperunt), sed ut neque Florentinis neque Arretinis obessent. Quod si aliis quam Pisanis bellum inferrent Florentini, adesse sibi non recusabant. Per hunc modum pars maxima copiarum a Pisanis abs-

and so it passed a sleepless night. And various uproars arose in many places near the walls, which added to their fear and alarm.

The following day the enemy burned practically every building 65 in Fiesole and in the area along the Via Bolognese, and moving their camp backwards, they crossed the Arno and came on to the Via Pisana with all their troops. There they tried to come up to the city gate by the Via Pisana, as they had done earlier by the Via Bolognese, but were thrown back with many casualties, as our citizens had by now grown used to scorning vain fears. So the enemy burned villas in that region too, and finally leaving the city behind, they passed up the Arno valley via the hills on the right. Then they invaded Aretine territory, causing devastation right up to the city walls. Next they marched back through the borders of the Sienese and finally returned to Pisa.

Before these troops had returned, while they were still near 66 Arezzo, the Florentines sent out all their cavalry against Pisa and burned everything around the city. Then they attacked Livorno (since they had found that city empty of defenders), captured it and reduced it to ashes. Then, fearing that the Pisans, to whom a fresh body of cavalry from Lombardy had come, would break off their journey [home], they galloped through Volterran territory and returned to Florence unharmed.

Since it was the end of the summer and the Pisans were in pos- 67 session of large forces, the Florentines, fearing disaster in the year to come, bribed the English and the other Pisan auxiliaries to leave them. The bribe was successful, but expensive. They did not, however, succeed in getting the mercenaries to join them and attack the Pisans (they excused themselves from this out of a sort of military honor), but they agreed not to stand in the way of the Florentines or Aretines. However, if the Florentines should attack someone other than the Pisans, they would not refuse their assistance. In this way the greater part of their forces deserted the Pisans. Only a single band of Englishmen remained with the

cessit. Manus tantummodo Anglorum[105] una remansit apud Pisanos, quam Iohannes Augus ductabat (ea fuit equitum circiter mille) et italici generis aliae copiae.

68   Florentini interea evocaverant Galeottum Malatestam, virum eximium ac peritissimum rei militaris, eumque ducem ac moderatorem bello praefecerant. Is qua die Florentiam ingressus est, receptis de more signis, sine ulla cunctatione extra urbem detulit via pisana ad secundum fere lapidem. Ibi auxilia ex Arretinis ceterisque amicis populis expectavit. Ipse vero dux per singulos dies in urbem regressus, quae sibi forent agenda cum prioribus civium consultabat. Tandem, cum omnes convenissent copiae ceteraque parata[106] forent, contra Pisanos duxit, habens peditum supra decem millia, equitum vero ad quatuor millia. Cum iis[107] copiis ad oppidum Pecciole primo, mox inde ad Cascinam constitit. In eo loco munitis castris, occasionem bene gerendae rei cum summa providentia expectabat.

69   Pisani, castra hostium sibi vicina intuentes (neque enim plus distabant a Pisis quam millibus passuum sex), proelio decernere statuerunt. Nam et populi multitudo erat ingens, praesertim iuxta urbem pugnatura, et conductorum peditum equitumque manus Florentinos spernere consueta, et superioris aestatis victoriis fidens. Aderat praeterea Iohannes Augus, peritissimus et callidissimus bello dux, qui spem eorum valde sublevabat. Cum ergo pugnare statuissent, Augus Pisis egressus ad Sabinum castra fecit; qui locus medius erat inter urbem et hostes. Ratio proelii ineundi haec fuit. Missis saepe ante equitibus ad Florentinorum castra qui tumultum suscitarent ac e vestigio fugerent, in eam consuetudi-

Pisans, commanded by John Hawkwood (it contained about a thousand knights), along with some other troops of Italian stock.[50]

68 The Florentines, meanwhile, had summoned Galeotto Malatesta, an outstanding man with great experience in war, and appointed him their commander and administrator of the war. On the very day he entered Florence, after receiving the standards in the customary fashion,[51] without any delay he went outside the city onto the Via Pisana to about the second milestone. There he awaited help from the Aretines and other friendly peoples. But the captain himself went back every day into the city to consult with the priors and leading citizens on his plan of action. Finally, when all his troops were assembled and other preparations had been made, he marched against the Pisans with a force of 10,000 foot and 4,000 horse. With these forces he stopped first at the town of Pecciole, then at Cascina. In this place he fortified his camps and with the utmost care and forethought looked for an opportunity to perform fine deeds.

69 The Pisans, seeing the enemy camp close by (and it was not more than six miles from Pisa), decided to bring the issue to a battle. They had an enormous popular host, especially as they were going to fight near the city, and their hired horse and foot were used to disregarding the Florentines, having been made confident by their victories of the previous summer. In addition they had John Hawkwood, an extremely experienced and crafty war leader, who did much to raise their hopes. So once they had decided to fight, Hawkwood left Pisa and made camp at Sansovino, a place halfway between the city and the enemy. His plan for initiating the battle was as follows.[52] He would often send horsemen up to the Florentine camp who would start an uproar, then suddenly flee. By doing this he saw to it that the Florentines acquired the habit of paying no attention to their comings and their antics. Having achieved this end by means of his clever plan, he suddenly

nem adducere curaverat, ut iam eorum adventus insultusque contemneretur. Id cum astuto consilio assecutus esset Augus, tandem post meridiano tempore subito profectus, cum omnibus copiis mirabili silentio ac dissimulatione Florentinorum castris repente supervenit. Calor erat ingens, militumque magna pars inermis vel sub tabernaculis iacebat, vel in flumine quod praeterfluit lavabatur. Cura vero aut suspicio hostis nulla per id tempus erat. Tum improvisus hostis repente ad munitiones delatus, speravit primo impetu castra perrumpere et otiosos inermesque opprimere. Arretini ab ea parte stationem habebant, qui, licet tam[108] repentino adventu perculsi, nequaquam cesserunt, sed armati simul inermesque sese hosti obiicientes, primum impetum sustinuerunt. Et iam clamor sublatus ad arma ceteros concierat, concurrebatque fortissimus quisque ad impetum retundendum. Ipse dux aetate provectus magnaeque auctoritatis milites accelerabat et pro temporis angustia hortabatur. Cum undique concurrissent,[109] et robur iam virorum adesset, non contenti munitiones defendere, eruptione facta hostem[110] invadunt ac pedem referre compellunt.

70   Augus, ubi primam aciem, contra atque ipse ratus erat, non perrupisse stationem improviso impetu conspexit, paulatim subducere agmen coepit ac sese ad Sabinum recipere.[111] Id vero tardius ex eo factum, quod maxima pars, ut magis lateret, equos dimiserat pedesque venerat ad castra perrumpenda. Itaque abeuntibus qui pone sequebantur prima acies fracta et in fugam versa obruitur a nostris, ac multa caede prosternitur.[112] Maxima vis pisani populi, utpote nocendi avida, circa primam fuerat aciem. Eorum plurima facta strages, et captivorum numerus ingens ex civibus pisanis fuit. Dux ab insequendo longius continuit, veritus insidias ob tam acceleratam hostium fugam. Caesi in prima acie

went out in the afternoon, and, with all his troops keeping wonderful silence and disguising their movements, he arrived without
warning at the Florentine camp. The heat was tremendous, and a
large part of the soldiery was unarmed or lying down in their tents
or bathing in the river that flowed nearby. There was no thought
or suspicion of the enemy at that moment. Then, suddenly, the
enemy fell upon the defenseworks, hoping to break through to the
camp with the first onslaught and crush the unarmed and resting
soldiers. The Aretines were stationed on that side, who, though
thrown back by the sudden attack, by no means gave way, but,
armed and unarmed, threw themselves on the foe and checked
their first onslaught. Now the clamor that arose drove the rest to
arms, and all the bravest men hurried to turn back the assault.
The captain himself, of great authority and advanced in years,
spurred on his soldiers, exhorting them insofar as the short time
permitted. When they had rushed together from every direction
and the flower of their strength was present, they did not rest con·
tent with holding fast behind their defenses, but made a sally and
attacked the enemy, compelling him to retreat.

When Hawkwood saw that his first line, contrary to his expec-   70
tations, had not broken through the pickets with their surprise attack, he began little by little to pull back his line of battle and to
withdrew to Sansovino. This maneuver took place the more slowly
as the greatest part of his force had left their horses behind, the
better to conceal themselves, going on foot to attack the camps.
Thus their front line, having been broken and put to flight, was
destroyed by our men who were following behind it, and it was
crushed with great loss of life. The largest force of the Pisan people, in their eagerness to cause harm, were up near the front line.
Of these there was enormous slaughter, and a huge number of the
captives were Pisan citizens. The Florentine captain kept his men
from further pursuit, fearing that the rapid flight of the enemy
concealed some plot. Eight hundred Pisans were slaughtered in

supra octingentos Pisanorum, capti ad duo millia. Augus cum reliquis copiis quae ad Sabinum refugerant, desertis castris intra Pisarum moenia se recepit.

71   Post hoc[113] Florentini propius[114] Pisas admotis copiis, ubi nemo obviam prodibat, retro moventes signa, quo captivorum impedimentis sese exonerarent, Florentiam rediere. Pisani omnes capti ad spectaculum populi curribus quadraginta quatuor per urbem devecti, tandemque carceribus traditi. His peractis dux iterum movens, pisanos fines ingreditur. Exercitus autem, postulatione duplicis stipendii et captivorum contentione male inter se concors, in seditione gravissima versabatur, adeo ut neque progredi ulterius, neque parere vellet. Ob eam rem dux pacandis sanandisque militum animis aliquot dies in primis finibus agri pisani commoratus, tandem, compositis ad aliquem modum rebus, ultra progressus, circa urbem Pisas devenit. Ibi cum hostes affligeret cladesque belli inferret, orta rursus in castris seditio, ad proelium usque processit.

72   Ea fuit causa celerioris recessus. Dux enim in discordia exercitus prope urbem hostium manere periculosum ratus, demissa parte militum, ipse cum reliquis lucensem agrum pervasit.[115] Florentiae vero multorum iam animi ad pacem inclinabantur. Nam et satisfactum dignitati putabant ob victoriam nuper habitam et tot pisanos cives spectaculo traductos et afflictum saepius eorum agrum. Et accedebat desperatio quaedam ex seditione militum coorta. Suspicio insuper nequaquam contemnenda prudentiores territabat, ne Pisani fractis desperatisque rebus urbem ac sua omnia Bernabovi dederent, tyranno potenti ac rerum novarum avido, et

the front line, and as many as two thousand were captured. Hawk-wood with the remainder of his troops took refuge in Sansovino, then abandoning his encampment, regained the walls of Pisa.[53]

After this the Florentines moved their troops closer to Pisa, 71 and when no one came out to face them, they moved their standards back, and to rid themselves of the burden of their captives, they returned to Florence. All the captured Pisans were dragged on forty-four carts through the city as a spectacle for the people, and in the end were cast into prisons. This accomplished, the captain once again set out and crossed the Pisan border. His army, however, was suffering dissension owing to its demands for double pay and to disputes about the prisoners, and was in a state of mutiny—a mutiny so serious that it refused to go on and would not obey. On this account the captain spent several days on the border of Pisan territory calming and healing the passions of his soldiers. Finally, when matters were settled after a fashion, he went on and arrived near the city of Pisa. There he set upon the foe, and was inflicting the disasters of war on them when mutiny again broke out in the camps, leading to an actual battle.[54]

That was why he beat a swift retreat. With discord in the 72 ranks, the captain felt it was dangerous to remain near the enemy city, and he dismissed part of his troops, marching with the rest towards the territory of Lucca. In Florence many minds had already turned to peace. They reckoned they had satisfied their dignity thanks to the recent victory, the numerous Pisan citizens led in triumph and the damage that had been repeatedly done to enemy territory. There was also an element of panic owing to the mutiny that had arisen in the ranks. The suspicion (which by no means was to be discounted) frightened the wiser men, besides, that the Pisans in the desperate state of their affairs would hand their city and all their possessions over to Bernabò, a powerful tyrant ever eager for innovation, who had long planned to get his hands on Tuscany. Thus talk of peace arose, and men were now

qui iampridem manus iniicere per Etruriam meditaretur. Ita mentio pacis orta est, et audire iam tolerabant pontificis romani vocem, qui per oratores suos pacem suadebat. Denique opera pontificis factum est, ut legati Pisanorum in oppidum Pisciam venirent. Ibi cum florentinis legatis congressi, de pace agere coeperunt.

73 Dum Pisciae starent legati ac de conditionibus pacis tractaretur, Iohannes cognomento Agnellus, civis pisanus, inter haec factione suorum Pisis sublevatus,[116] dominatum arripuit civitatis. Is, quia erat ex intimo Bernabovis sinu, et paulo ante ab eo redierat, nulli fuit dubium, quin ope consilioque Bernabovis haec facta essent, quo turbatam civitatem ipse arriperet. Quae causa fuit pacis maturandae. Conditiones pacis multae ac honoratae pro florentino populo fuerunt. Nam et Petrabona castellum, a quo natum ab initio bellum fuerat, per eam pacem Florentinis a Pisanis est traditum, et alia quaedam Pisanorum castella ex pacto ad solum eversa, et immunitates omnes[117] Florentinis Pisis restitutae. Praeterea in annis decem centum millia pondo auri dare Florentinis Pisani promisere, singulis videlicet annis decem millia. Accessit etiam illud honorificum, ut exercitus florentini populi in finibus Pisanorum esset cum pax facta est; utque in oppido Pisciae tractata factaque fuerit pax, loco Florentinis subiecto. Haec omnia pacem honorificam reddiderunt.[118] Populus tamen florentinus usque adeo pacem datam Pisanis aegre tulit, ut a Carolo Stroza, qui auctor suasorque fuisse pacis ferebatur, vix manus abstineret.

74 Cum finis impositus esset pisano bello, Carolus imperator in Italiam rediit, vocatus ab Urbano pontifice, quo Bernabovem perpetuum ecclesiae hostem ulcisceretur. Idem pontifex, cum transi-

willing to heed the voice of the Roman pontiff, who was urging peace through his ambassadors. Finally, through the intervention of the pope it came about that Pisan representatives went to the town of Pescia. There they met with Florentine envoys and began negotiations for peace.

While the envoys were in Pescia and the conditions of peace 73 were being negotiated, Giovanni dello Agnello,[55] a Pisan citizen, had meanwhile risen up in Pisa, thanks to a faction consisting of his supporters, and had seized the lordship of the city. Since he was an intimate associate of Bernabò's and had recently returned from his presence, no one doubted that it was with the help and advice of Bernabò that he had seized the turbulent city. This became grounds for hastening to make peace. The stipulations of the treaty were numerous and honorable for the Florentine People.[56] The castle of Pietrabona, where the war first began, was in accordance with the treaty turned over to the Florentines by the Pisans, and certain other Pisan castles were razed to the ground by agreement, and all the Florentine immunities in Pisa were restored. Moreover, the Pisans promised to pay the Florentines 100,000 florins over ten years, that is, 10,000 each year for ten years. It added to their honor that the army of the Florentine People was in Pisan territory when the peace was concluded, and that it was negotiated and signed in the town of Pescia, a place subject to the Florentines. All these circumstances rendered the peace treaty an honorable one. Yet the Florentine People were so dissatisfied with the peace given to the Pisans that they could barely restrain themselves from laying hands on Carlo Strozzi, who was reported to be responsible for the treaty and had urged its acceptance.

When the Pisan war had come to an end, the emperor Charles 74 returned to Italy, summoned by Pope Urban, to wreak vengeance on Bernabò, the perpetual enemy of the Church.[57] While Charles 1367 had been preparing for the crossing, the same pontiff implored the Florentines to send ambassadors to himself. Four leading citizens

tum Caroli[119] praeparasset, Florentini ut ad se legatos mitterent flagitavit. Missi sunt ad eum[120] quatuor e principibus civitatis. Hos pontifex multis verbis cohortatus est, ut in societatem belli adversus Bernabovem Florentini coirent. Ea per oratores domum perscripta, cum essent diligentiore consultatione habita, tandem negata est societas pontifici, eo praetextu quod pax et amicitia civitati cum Bernabove foret. Id responsum pontificem simul imperatoremque offendit; et quasi labente fundamento nihil super aedificari solidum potuit. Quamobrem imperator, qui bellum tumultuosius Bernabovi coeperat inferre, non multo post insperato pacem cum illo fecit, ac demissa magna exercitus parte, ipse cum reliquis Romam petere constituit.

75   Cum audiretur pace per Galliam facta[121] Carolum in Etruriam esse transiturum, Florentini legatis ad eum missis, qua mente quove animo esset tentavere. Fuerat protinus primo illius transitu optima gratia[122] florentinus populus apud Carolum, multaque benigne per illum indulta supra ostendimus. Sed erat suspecta pecuniarum cupiditas, praesertim indigentia coniuncta, quarum comparandarum gratia nihil non moliturus credebatur. Idque statim apparuit. Nam simul atque ad eum pervenerunt[123] legati, accusatio facta ab illo est adversus florentinum populum, quod, non contentus a se dudum concessis, iura insuper quaedam romani imperii usurpasset. Id cum querela et indignatione ab eo prolatum iram significabat et duritiem animi insigniter offensi. Erat vero id totum ars pecuniarum avertendarum. Nec multo post haec dicta iter ingressus, Lucam petiit, et a Lucensibus benigne susceptus, finitimo de loco terrorem adauxit. Equites eius atque praefecti Miniate in oppido, primo statim adventu, quasi in fronte ab eo collocati, flo-

were sent to him. These the pope harangued with many words to get them to persuade the Florentines to join an alliance against Bernabò. The ambassadors conveyed his request to Florence in written form, but after careful consultation, an alliance was finally refused the pontiff on the pretext that the city enjoyed peace and friendship with Bernabò. This response offended pope and emperor alike; and with the foundation thus unstable, nothing solid could be built upon it.[58] On this account the emperor, who had begun to make war in a rather haphazard way against Bernabò, shortly thereafter made peace with him unexpectedly, and letting a large part of his army go, he decided to head for Rome himself with the remainder.[59]

When the news came that Charles had made peace in Lombardy and was crossing into Tuscany, the Florentines sent envoys to him to test his mind and heart. The Florentine People had been in high favor with Charles from his very first expedition and they had enjoyed many privileges through his kindness, as we showed above.[60] But his desire for money was suspect, especially when conjoined with penury; and it was believed that his schemes to acquire funds would stop at nothing. And this was instantly apparent. For as soon as the envoys came to him, he made the accusation against the Florentine People that, not satisfied with what had been granted them before, they had usurped certain rights of the Roman Empire besides. This charge, which he proferred with a sense of grievance and indignation, showed the anger and hardheartedness of someone who had manifestly been offended. But the whole scene was a device to make away with money. Shortly after this declaration he started his journey and headed for Lucca. Received with kindness by the Lucchesi, he terrorized the neighboring area. His knights and commanders—whom immediately on their first arrival he stationed in the town of San Miniato, as though to affront us—began to collect plunder from Florentine territory, and then made a show of further hostile and unruly acts.

75

1368

rentino ex agro praedas abigere coeperunt, et hostilia inde tumultuosius ostentare. Ipse autem Volaterrarum ac Prati et lucensis
agri, quae a florentino populo tenebantur, restitutionem flagitabat;
nec per intercessores ab hac postulatione quibat divelli. Quare obs-
tinationem eius aspiciens, civitas conducere militem ac fines tueri
armis perrexit. Nec Florentinos solum commovit illius in Etruriam adventus, sed et alias quoque civitates novis rebus involvit.

76   Pisanis per id tempus praesidebat Iohannes cognomento
Agnus. Is Lucam ad salutandum Carolum profectus, cum ibi casu
quodam prolapsus coxam fregisset, delatus confestim Pisas rumor,
alios spe, alios metu concitavit, totaque civitas fuit in armis, prae-
valenteque diversa factione. Petrus Gambacurta, qui ad eam diem
exularat, favore suorum receptus, gubernationem reipublicae suscepit.

77   Senis quoque per haec ipsa tempora motus in republica gravissimi fuerunt, variaeque deiectiones ac fugae civium. Carolus per
hos tumultus Romam profectus, parumper ibi commoratus, dum
pontifici de rebus arcanis, quarum gratia venerat, loqueretur, tandem his[124] ut voluerat compositis, Senas regreditur. Senis autem
dum esset, in suspicionem venit quasi urbem illam alteri traditu-
rus. Quamobrem tumultu populi repente exorto paene oppressus
est; multisque suorum amissis Lucam repetiit, indeque in Galliam,
mox in Germaniam transiit.

78   Post Caroli recessum Miniatensium exules, iam pridem castellis
quibusdam occupatis, bellum oppido inferebant. Erat in eo oppido
Germanorum manus ex Caroli exercitu, cumque his oppidani
diversae factionis; sed exules favore opibusque florentini populi
nitebantur. Quod intuentes adversarii, ad Bernabovem mediola-

He himself demanded the restitution of the territories of Volterra, Prato and Lucca, which were controlled by the Florentine People, nor could he be severed from this demand by third parties. Thus, observing his obstinacy, the city exerted itself to hire soldiers and protect its borders with arms. Nor did his coming into Tuscany upset only the Florentines; it also involved other cities in civil unrest as well.[61]

Giovanni dello Agnello at that time presided over the Pisans. 76 Going to Lucca to greet Charles, he chanced to break his hip in a fall. The news was brought quickly to Pisa, arousing hope in some, fear in others. The whole city was in arms, and the opposing faction prevailed. Pietro Gambacurta, who had been in exile until that day, was restored through the favor of his supporters and took over the governance of the state.

During this time Siena, too, experienced the gravest political 77 unrest, and there were various expulsions and banishments of citizens. During these tumults Charles went to Rome, staying there a short time while he spoke with the pontiff about the secret matters on whose account he had come. Finally, having arranged these matters to his liking, he returned to Siena. While in Siena, however, he came under suspicion of planning to deliver the city to another person.[62] It was for this reason that he was nearly crushed in a sudden popular uprising; and having lost many of his men, he returned to Lucca, and from thence to Lombardy, and afterwards crossed into Germany.[63]

1369

After Charles' departure, the exiles of San Miniato, who had 78 for a long time occupied certain castles, made war on the town. A band of Germans from Charles' army was in the town, and with them were townsmen belonging to the Ghibelline faction. But the exiles relied on the favor and resources of the Florentine People. When their adversaries saw this, they fled to Bernabò of Milan and implored his aid, surrendering the town to him. Bernabò, therefore, like a man who had long been brooding on the Tuscan

nensem confugientes, illius opem implorarunt, illique oppidum tradiderunt. Bernabos igitur, ut qui rem etruscam iampridem meditaretur, ferre auxilium Miniatensibus constituit. Id vero peringrate facere visus est. Nam Florentini nuper vel ob id maxime indignationem Caroli pontificisque inciderant, quod contra ipsum tunc amicum inire foedus recusassent. Ipse vero, cum esset pax, nulla probabili causa hostem fovere ac bello implicari adversus florentinum populum haudquaquam abnuerat.

79   Florentini cognito Bernabovis proposito maiori quam antea nixu oppidum obsederunt. Nec multo post equitatus aderat Bernabovis magno quidem numero. Ducebat autem Iohannes Augus, vir clarus bello et iam inde per Italiam notus. Is audito castrorum ordine et obsidionis forma, quoniam vim afferre posse desperabat, in agro substiterat pisano, non longius tamen a Florentinorum castris quam decem millibus passuum.

80   Dux erat exercitus florentini populi Iohannes Reginus, vir egregius quidem et bellorum sciens. Qui, cum videret copias hostium morari nec ad se accedere, rectam ipse rationem secutus, standum in castris et urgendam obsidionem, nec obviam exeundum censebat, ostendens opportunitatem castrorum; unde, si adveniant hostes et conentur, cum haud dubia strage repellantur; si non adveniant, nihil eos nocere; nec vero certam exploratamque victoriam incertae dubiaeque proeliandi fortunae committendam esse. Eius consilium et rectum et prudens ferociores quidam civium in magistratu constituti ita exagitabant, ut totum illius propositum ad ignaviam timiditatemque referrent. Plebs quoque urbana ob ferociam magistratus laeta, ducis socordiam et metum pavoremque increpabat. Quod cum illi innotuisset, 'Eamus,' inquit, 'quo temeritas imperitorum iubet. Iam scient neque animum mihi neque

situation, decided to send help to the men of San Miniato. This looked like the height of ingratitude. For the Florentines had recently on this very account incurred the wrath of Charles and the pope, as they had refused to enter into a league against Bernabò, who at that time was their friend. He, on the other hand, in peacetime and with no probable cause, had been perfectly willing to support an enemy and to involve himself in a war against the Florentine People.

The Florentines understood Bernabò's plan and besieged the   79 town with redoubled effort. Shortly thereafter Bernabò's cavalry arrived in great numbers. Their leader was John Hawkwood, a distinguished soldier long famous in Italy. Having learned the disposition of the camps and the siegeworks, he despaired of applying force and stayed in the Pisan countryside, no further than ten miles from the Florentine encampment.[64]

The captain of the Florentine army was Giovanni da Reggio, a   80 distinguished man with knowledge of war. When he saw that the enemy troops were hanging back and not approaching him, he followed the correct rational course and decided to remain in the camps to press the siege, and not go out to meet the foe, possessing as he did a clear advantage in the positioning of his camps. Hence, if enemy forces should come and attack, they would undoubtedly be thrown back in slaughter; if they didn't come, they couldn't do any harm; and he ought not risk a sure and safe victory for the uncertain and doubtful fortune of battle. But certain of our more ferocious citizens who were holding magistracies upbraided him for this correct and prudent course of action, blaming it entirely on cowardice and timidity. The urban plebs was delighted at the ferocity of their magistrates and scolded the captain for his sloth and trepidation. When he was told of this he said, "Let us go where the rashness of the ignorant bids us go. They will learn then that I am lacking neither in spirit nor in sense." Thereupon at dawn he left part of his forces in camp to protect the defenses, and

consilium defuisse.' Inde prima luce copiarum parte ad tuendas munitiones in castris relicta, ipse ceteram multitudinem sub signis structam certissimo pugnandi proposito ad hostem rapit.

81   Augus vero, cum Florentinorum copias ad se venire conspexisset, suos intra munitiones continuit, volens et itinere et calore viros equosque adversariorum maxime confici. Itaque calonibus tantum et levis armaturae militibus[125] emissis, distineri[126] hostem ac defatigari imperavit. Ipse curatis suorum corporibus structam paratamque subinde aciem, cum tempus fuit, eduxit; cumque superior numero foret, et quietos in fatigatos eduxisset, perfacile vicit. Captus est in eo proelio dux florentini exercitus cum magna multitudine; caesi etiam permulti; ceteri profligati, nullo neque ordine neque duce, ut cuique sors obtulit, aufugerunt.

82   Hostes postridie sub ipsas munitiones castrorum profecti, cum eas custodiri intrepide animadvertissent, faciliorem sibi viam solvendae obsidionis arbitrati si agrum florentinum ingrederentur, relictis castris usque ad moenia paene urbis devenere, maiorem tumultum de industria ostentantes. Sed civitas in eo pertinax fuit; nulloque terrore potuit adduci quin in obsidione perstaret, confestimque reparatis copiis, magis etiam quam prius obsidionem urgeret. Evenitque haud multo post, ut Miniate per proditionem caperetur, Luperello quodam, ex minima plebe homine, per abdita ac paene invia milites noctu recipiente. Ex quo vires hostium fractae sunt, et diversae factionis homines, qui rebellandi fuerant auctores, Florentiam ducti, multitudinis concursu paene discerpti, tandem affecti supplicio periere.

83   Haud multo post Miniate receptum, Bernabovis equites sub specie auxilii Lucae commorantes, de occupanda urbe consilium

himself arranged the rest of the host under their standards and rushed off towards the foe with the firm purpose of engaging him in battle.[65]

Hawkwood, however, seeing the Florentine troops coming to- 81
wards him, kept his own forces inside their defenseworks with the intention of wearing down his adversaries' men and horses as much as possible with the heat and the effort of the journey. So he sent out only esquires[66] and lightly armed troops, ordering them to distract and wear out the enemy. He himself, having kept his troops fresh, in due course set them up in battle formation and when the right moment came, led them forth; and since his forces had numerical superiority and he was leading fresh against tired troops, he easily won. The captain of the Florentine army was captured in the battle along with a vast multitude; many, too, were killed; the rest defeated; and with no leader and no order, they each of them fled as chance allowed.

On the following day the enemy came up to the camp defenses, 82
and seeing that they were defended with spirit, they decided the easier way of raising the siege would be for them to invade Florentine territory. So leaving the camps behind, they came inland practically to the walls of the city, purposely creating a great uproar. But the city remained stubborn in the midst of this threat, and no terror could induce it to abandon the siege. Rapidly recomposing its forces, it pressed the siege even more than before. And it transpired shortly thereafter that they captured San Miniato through 1370
treachery. A certain Luparello,[67] a man of the lowest condition, let soldiers in by night through a hidden and almost impassible route. In this way the enemy forces were shattered, and the Ghibellines who had been responsible for the rebellion were dragged to Florence, where they were torn almost limb from limb by the press of the crowd, and finally were executed.[68]

Soon after the recovery of San Miniato, Bernabò's cavalry, 83
which was staying in Lucca on the pretext of helping it, started a

inierunt. Tenebat eam Caroli praefectus; nec latuit ipsum machinatio et fraus. Itaque, cum aliis se praesidiis roborasset, dimissi ab eo equites sunt honesto praetextu, quasi non amplius eorum opera indigeret. Ipse vero ad conditiones pactaque traiecit animum; pecuniaque demum accepta, urbem relinquere civibus paciscitur. Mutua ob eam rem pecunia Lucensibus data est a Florentinis, auri pondo viginti quinque millia. Missi quoque[127] eo praestantissimi civium, qui in constituenda republica moderandaque civitate adessent; nam ipsi quidem Lucenses, ut qui diu sub tyrannis vixerant, iura libertatis paene fuerant obliti. Per hunc modum libertas Lucensibus reddita est ex multis ac variis fluctuationibus. Arcem munitissimam in ea urbe a Castrucio aedificatam, quo popularius degeretur, confestim cives everterunt.

84   Eodem anno Florentinorum equites octingenti in Galliam missi, legato romanae sedis qui Bononiam tenebat auxilia tulerunt adversus Bernabovem. Fuerat enim paulo ante societas inita a Florentinis cum Urbano pontifice romano, tunc Viterbii commorante. Moverant autem Florentinos ad societatem ineundam[128] Bernabovis iniuriae circa Miniatis obsidionem illatae. Mittentes ergo in Galliam equites, legato contra Bernabovem auxilia praebuerunt.

85   Bellum per id tempus ad Regium Lepidum gerebatur; quam urbem magna vi Bernabos circumsedebat. Ille igitur, cum adventum copiarum florentini populi cognovisset, quo necessitas redeundi domum illis iniiceretur, per placentinum parmensemque agrum equitibus missis, repente circa Pisas copias ostendit. Ob eum timorem confestim ex Gallia revocati sunt equites ad legatum missi; simulque cum his sociorum equitatus accessit. Hi omnes in agrum pisanum ad hostem profecti, proelium committere properabant.[129] Sed hostis, antequam in praesentia veniretur, per eam ipsam qua

plot to occupy the city. Charles' lieutenant was in charge of the town, and these deceitful machinations did not escape his notice. So he strengthened his position with other guardsmen and dismissed Bernabò's cavalry with the honorable excuse that he had no further need of them. He then turned his attention to negotiations, and at length accepted money and agreed to leave the city to its citizens. The Florentines lent money to the Lucchesi for this purpose, a sum of 25,000 florins. They also sent there some outstanding citizens to help in setting up a republic and governing the city; for the Lucchesi, having lived for so long under tyrants, had almost forgotten the ordinances of liberty. In this way liberty was restored to the Lucchesi after numerous and varied fluctuations. The citizens immediately razed to the ground a highly fortified citadel that had been constructed in the city by Castruccio, so that they might live together more as a people.

In the same year eight hundred Florentine knights were sent to Northern Italy to bring help against Bernabò to the legate of the Roman see who held Bologna. Shortly before, the Florentines had entered into an alliance with Pope Urban, who was then at Viterbo. Bernabò's unjust actions at the siege of San Miniato had moved the Florentines to join this alliance. So by sending knights to Northern Italy they were offering help to the legate against Bernabò.[69]

84

A war was being waged at this time at Reggio Emilia, and Bernabò had surrounded that city with a great force. So when the latter learned of the arrival of troops belonging to the Florentine People, in order to force them to return home he sent cavalry through the territory of Piacenza and Parma, who appeared suddenly near Pisa. In fear of these, the knights who had been sent to the legate were immediately recalled from Northern Italy, arriving simultaneously with mounted forces from the allies. All these then headed for the enemy in Pisan territory, spoiling for a fight. But before they could arrive, the enemy returned the same way he had

85

venerat viam regressus, irrito labore longisque itinerationibus nostros fatigavit. Florentinorum sociorumque equites persecuti hostium vestigia, quaedam illis intulerunt damna ac manifestam fugae confessionem extorserunt;[130] moxque et ipsi in Galliam reversi, bellum prosecuti sunt. Certamen eius belli per aestatem longius fuit; tandemque victoria parta est adversus hostem, et obsidio Regii dissoluta. Mannus autem Donatus eques florentinus, dux earum copiarum, labore nimio confectus, in aegritudinem incidit, ex qua paulo post Patavii decessit.

86 Urbanus pontifex per haec ipsa fere[131] tempora, compositis Italiae rebus, in ulteriorem Galliam remeaverat, brevique admodum tempore supervixit. In eius locum Gregorius XI successit. Nec multo post cum Bernabove pax recepta est, et copiae sociorum solutae, equitatusque florentini populi in Etruriam rediit.

87 Per extremum eius anni oratores in ulteriorem Galliam ad novum pontificem missi pro eius assumptione gratulatum, mentem illius non satis pacatam in rebus italicis deprehenderunt. Movit autem eos maxime in Perusinos cavillatio, quos ut instar praedecessoris in gratiam habere perseveraret, adduci non poterat. Et secuta mox eius urbis occupatio suspicionem adauxit. Perusini, siquidem inopia frumenti laborantes, cum undique itinera clauderentur, legato velut expugnati victique sese dedere coacti sunt. Mansit tamen in suspicione pax; et societas quaedam cum Gregorio renovata est, in qua Pisani et Senenses et Arretini et Lucenses cum Florentinis fuerunt.

88 Factiones per haec tempora Florentiae increverant Albiciorum Riciorumque. Hae familiae erant opulentae, principesque earum familiarum, praestantes in republica viri, diversis studiis ad se alios traxerant cives. Contentionibus ac certaminibus pleraque gereban-

come, thus exhausting our forces with long journeys and useless effort. The Florentine and allied cavalry followed the tracks of the enemy, caused them some losses and forced them into an open confession of their flight. And soon they themselves went back to Lombardy to continue the war. The struggle dragged on through the summer, but at last victory against the enemy was achieved, and the siege of Reggio lifted. Manno Donati, a Florentine knight and the leader of these troops, was worn out by excessive effort and fell sick, dying shortly thereafter in Padua.

Around this same time, Pope Urban, having settled affairs in It- 86 aly, returned to France, surviving only a little while longer. Gregory XI succeeded to his place.[70] Shortly thereafter a peace was signed with Bernabò, the allied forces were dissolved, and the cavalry of the Florentine People returned to Tuscany.[71]

Around the end of this year, ambassadors were sent to France 87 to congratulate the new pontiff on his accession, and they discovered that his attitude towards Italian affairs was not wholly pacific. They were impressed particularly by his vacillation towards the Perugians, whom he could not be induced to treat with favor, as his predecessor had. The occupation of this city that soon followed increased suspicion. The Perugians were suffering from a famine and, with the roads closed all around them, were forced to surrender to the papal legate as though they had been stormed and defeated. Peace was preserved, however, in the midst of these suspicions, and an alliance of sorts was renewed with Gregory, in which the Florentines were joined by the Pisans, Sienese, Aretines, and Lucchesi.

At this time the factions of the Albizzi and the Ricci were bur- 88 geoning. These were wealthy families, and their leaders, who were 1371–72 important statesmen, were generating partisanship among the citizenry. Numerous activities were beset with struggle and competition. These factions had endured for some time in the city when the city, with excellent judgement, put an end to them. For since

tur. Hae factiones cum aliquamdiu in civitate duravissent, tandem laudabili consilio finis est illis[132] a civitate impositus. Cum enim populo, ob eas quas retulimus causas, maxime suspectus[133] esset pontificis favor, et factionum principes pro sua quisque magnitudine asciscere sibi favorem illius videretur, satietas quoque contentionum plerosque haberet[134] cives, invidia principes urgeret, quod in libera civitate popularique republica maiorem sibi quam par erat potentiam comparassent; ob haec omnia tandem lege lata, principibus earum familiarum interdictum est reipublicae administratione. Per hunc modum deturbatis auctoribus, factiones ipsae brevi conticuere.

89   Altero dehinc atque tertio anno nihil memoria dignum reperio gestum, nisi quod ubaldinae gentis castella per arces Apennini domita,[135] in potestatem florentini populi devenere; gentisque eius potentiae hic exitus fuit.

90   Per haec ipsa tempora porticus iuxta aedes publicas facta est insigni splendore ac magnificentia. Eius aedificandae gratia redemptiones domorum a possessoribus factae sunt, quae mox dirutae, spatium liberum ad aedificandam porticum praebuere.

91   Principio insequentis anni, qui fuit septuagesimus quintus supra mille trecentos, suspicio adversus pontificem iampridem concepta, magis magisque in dies augescebat, nec prius finis quam paulatim exacerbata, manifestum tandem in bellum prorupit; de quo altius repetentes, pro rei notitia quaedam memorabimus.

92   Fuerat pontificatus romanus in Gallorum manibus iam inde a Clemente VI continuatus. Hi per legatos ex Gallia missos civitates romanae ecclesiae subiectas per Italiam gubernabant. Dominatus eorum superbus erat ac paene intolerandus; nec ecclesiae tan-

the people, for the reasons we have related, held suspect the good will of the pope, and since the leaders of these factions seemed each to be seeking the pontiff's favor with a view to increasing his own importance, and also because the majority of citizens had had enough of their strife, the faction leaders became unpopular; they had acquired more power for themselves than was fair in a free city and popular republic. So finally, for all these reasons a law was passed prohibiting the leaders of these families from taking part in the governance of the state. With those responsible for them being thus cast down, the factions themselves in a short time were silenced.

For the second and third years after this I have found no deed worthy of record, except that the castles of the Ubaldini clan scattered in the fastnesses of the Apennines were brought under control and came under the power of the Florentine People; and this was the end of that clan's power.[72] 89 1373–74

During this same time the porticos near the Palazzo Vecchio were constructed with remarkable splendor and magnificence. In order to build them, houses were purchased from their possessors, which were then knocked down to make the space free to build the portico. 90

At the beginning of the next year, which was the year 1375, the suspicions the city already entertained with respect to the pontiff began to grow greater each day, and they were exacerbated little by little, not ending before they finally erupted into open war. We shall go back a little ways and record certain events in order to clarify the situation. 91 1375

The Roman pontificate had been in the hands of the French continually from the time of Clement VI onwards. These pontiffs, by means of legates sent from France, had governed the cities subject to the Roman pope throughout Italy. Their dominion was arrogant and nearly intolerable, and they yearned to subject to themselves not only the cities of the Church, but the free cities as well. 92

tum urbes, verum etiam liberas civitates sibi subdere cupiebant. Studia vero eorum non pacis erant, sed belli. Externorum hominum plena erat Italia. Arces pluribus locis per liberas civitates infinito sumptu ab illis aedificatae non libertatem, sed coactam miseramque populorum servitutem ubique testabantur. Ipsi et invisi omnibus quibus dominabantur et vicinis suspecti atque cavendi. Cum haec esset rerum conditio per Italiam, legatorumque potentia longe lateque dominaretur ac formidabilis esset, Florentini, magnis licet in suspicionibus constituti, pacem tamen et foedus cum pontifice observabant.

93   Sterilitas annonae per haec ipsa tempora supervenit civitati, et, utpote in urbe populosa, indigentia plurimum creverat, ut vix florentina plebs sustentaretur. Hae difficultates legato qui Bononiam tenebat non erant incognitae. Saepius enim iam pro amicitia et foedere rogatus, frumenti facultatem denegarat. In hac igitur tanta difficultate atque periculo, cum spes unica in segetibus esset, quae plane iam flavescebant, legatus repente omnes copias suas in Florentinos dimisit, volens itinera praecludi, et simul omnem spem futurae messis auferre. Quod nisi civitas prudenti consilio obviam iisset, iugum erat servitutis procul dubio recipiendum. Nam magnitudo copiarum tanta erat, ut a finibus arceri nulla facultas esset, praesertim repente adventantium. Hoc periculum tunc civitati imminens, non armis sed consilio depulsum est. Data siquidem grandi summa, centum triginta millium[136] florenorum, ducibus militiae, praeter legati spem, non pacati modo sed amici facti, nullam calamitatem intulere. Accessit ad ceteram indignationem Prati oppidi per eos ipsos dies detecta proditio, quam sciente machinanteque legato tentatam ferebant.

Their desire was not for peace, however, but for war. Italy was full of foreigners. Citadels constructed in many places by the free cities at enormous expense gave testimony everywhere to the straightened and wretched servitude of their peoples. The legates themselves were hated by those they dominated, and they were considered suspect and avoided by their neighbors. This being the situation throughout Italy, since the power of the legates was formidable and held sway far and wide, the Florentines, despite their apprehensions, nevertheless maintained peace and confederation with the pope.[73]

At this time the city was experiencing a dearth of grain, and, as happens in a populous city, the dearth grew so great that the Florentine plebs could scarcely bear it. These problems were not unknown to the legate who ruled Bologna. Though frequently asked to grant this out of friendship and alliance, he refused them the opportunity to acquire grain. Hence in the midst of this great difficulty and danger, when their only hope was in the crops that were now clearly ripening, the legate suddenly sent out all his troops against the Florentines with the aim of shutting off the roads and at the same time taking away all hope of a future harvest.[74] If the city had not through wise counsel blocked this plan, it would undoubtedly have put on the yoke of servitude. For the size of the legate's forces was so great that there was no chance of keeping them away from our territory, especially as they were quickly advancing. This danger then threatening the city was averted, not with arms, but with prudent counsel. An enormous sum, 130,000 florins, was given to the enemy commanders, who then, contrary to the wishes of the legate, became not only neutral but friendly, and caused no calamity. A treacherous conspiracy that was detected during those same days in the town of Prato, with the knowledge and contrivance of the legate, further inflamed the Florentines' righteous anger.

94   His ergo infensi civium animi et metu simul indignationeque commoti, adversus clericorum malignitatem insurgere statuerunt. Ea de causa magnae statim copiae paratae, octoque viri cum potestate publica creati quibus omnis cura belli demandata est. Et civitas quidem pro accepta nuper iniuria et pro repellendo in posterum libertatis periculo robuste ac celso animo ad id bellum surrexit. Octo virorum autem providentia (fuerunt enim praestantissimi ac sollertissimi viri) subsequentibus rebus confestim eluxit. Nihil enim ferociter nec propalam agendo, sed remisse arcaneque singula obeundo, monendo[137] per singulas civitates homines, et quibus erat opus, auxilia pollicendo, stragem adversariorum brevi dedere.

95   Primi omnium Tifernates ab his impulsi, contra dominatores insurgentes, iugum servitutis repulerunt. Erat in ea urbe praesidium nequaquam contemnendum. Attamen raptis armis Tifernates contra praesidium ruentes, proelium commiserunt, tandemque multis interfectis reliquos intra munimina arcis compulerunt. Eaque ipsa nocte florentini populi auxilia intra urbem recepta, una cum civibus arcem obsidentes, non multorum dierum certamine ad deditionem coegerunt.[138]

96   Qui Perusiam gubernabat legatus, ubi rebellasse Tifernates et arcem a suis teneri cognovit, coactis subito copiis ad recuperandum Tifernum eas dimisit. Id vero cum cernerent Perusini, per absentiam copiarum elati, raptis et ipsi armis, in legatum feruntur, et arcem (erat enim munitissima in ea urbe arx, ab hoc ipso legato constructa) obsederunt. Ad hos quoque submissa statim Florentinorum auxilia; et quamquam longior fuerit obsidio, tamen ad ex-

Thus the hearts of the citizenry were angered by these acts, and   94
moved at once by fear and indignation they decided to rise up
against the malice of the clergy. For this purpose they at once assembled great forces, and appointed a board of eight men with
public power, turning over to them the whole management of the
war.[75] Indeed, in response to the injury it had just received and to
ward off future dangers to its liberty, the city rose to the challenge
of this war with energy and high purpose. The wise forethought
of the Eight (who were outstanding and resourceful men) immediately shone out in subsequent events. For they did nothing that
was overly aggressive or obvious, but went about each task in a
low-key, subtle way, advising men in each of the cities and promising them whatever help they needed, thus bringing about the destruction of their enemies in a short time.[76]

The first to be influenced by them were the men of Città di   95
Castello, who rose up against their lords, throwing off the yoke of
servitude. This city had a [papal] garrison which was by no means
to be despised. Nevertheless, the inhabitants seized arms and fell
upon the garrison, in the end slaughtering many and driving the
rest inside the citadel. And on that very night, they brought into
the city help from the Florentine People, who besieged the citadel
together with the townsmen and compelled it to surrender after a
struggle lasting only a few days.

The legate governing Perugia, when he learned that Città di   96
Castello had rebelled and that its citadel was being held by his
forces, quickly pulled together some troops and sent them to recover the city. But when the Perugians saw this, they were em-
bolded by the absence of those troops to seize arms themselves
and turn them against the legate. They laid siege to the citadel (for
that city had an extremely well-fortified citadel, built by the legate
himself). To the Perugians, too, the Florentines at once sent reinforcements, and although the siege took rather longer, in the end
this city also recovered its liberty by the same process. Soon after-

tremum ea quoque civitas pari tenore suscepit libertatem. Secuta est paulo post Spoleti, Tuderti, Eugubii et Forilivii defectio; secuta et Asculi in Picentibus et Viterbii in Tuscis; nec ruinam parem meminit quisquam. Causa vero tam subitae fuit stragis mala dominatio ac infensae iampridem populorum mentes, ut primo facultas apparuit, sese in libertatem avidissime vendicantium. Nec tolerabilis sane iam erat gallorum clericorum ambitio, qui civitates Italiae servorum habebant loco, nec animos sibi conciliare hominum ulla cura fuerat, sed arcibus murisque compescere.

97   Sed super omnia mentes clericorum debilitavit et fregit Bononiae defectio, quae quidem urbs magnis Anglorum copiis tenebatur. Praeerat autem copiis Iohannes Augus. At enim, cum pro recuperatione Granaioli oppidi, quod per eos rebellaverat dies, copias eduxisset, Bononienses iampridem ab octo viris sollicitati, sumptis per absentiam copiarum animis corripuerunt arma, ac se ut ceteri in libertatem vendicarunt; et statim, ut compositum fuerat, auxilia florentini populi Bononiae adfuerunt. Copiae vero illae Anglorum eductae, ubi bononiensis motum populi audivere, Bononiam reverti non ausae, Faventiam ingressae sunt. Ea civitas in fide legati pontificisque manebat. Ob id, nec refragante populo, Angli recepti intra moenia cum essent, mirabili ducis pravitate omnia in cives fecerunt quae captis expugnatisque urbibus solent fieri. Nam et rapinae omnia propalam exposita, et viris aut pulsis aut interfectis, mulieres ad libidinem reservatae, sacraque et profana miserabiliter impieque barbarorum immanitate polluta. Urbem denique ipsam tandem omnibus nudatam, cum moenia solum parietesque superessent, sceleratus dux pecunia vendidit principibus Ferrariensium.

98   Dum haec in Italia geruntur, Gregorius pontifex romanus audita Bononiae defectione, quo ruentem ecclesiae statum repararet,

wards there followed the defections of Spoleto, Todi, Gubbio and Forlì, then Ascoli in Piceno and Viterbo in Tuscia; no one could remember a collapse equal to that one. The reason for so sudden a disaster was bad lordship and the pre-existing hostility of these peoples, who liberated themselves with great eagerness as soon as the opportunity presented itself. And indeed, the ambition of the French clerics was now intolerable. Treating the cities of Italy like slaves, they had made not the least effort to win over men's hearts and minds, but imprisoned them with walls and citadels.

But it was above all the defection of Bologna that weakened 97 and broke the spirits of the clerics. This city was being held by a large force of Englishmen commanded by John Hawkwood. But he had marched his troops out to recover the town of Granaiolo, which had rebelled during those days. The Bolognese, who had been worked on for a long time by the Eight, took heart at the absence of Hawkwood's troops, seized arms, and liberated themselves like the other peoples. Instantly, as had been agreed, the Florentine People sent help to Bologna. The English troops who had left the city, when they heard about the uprising of the Bolognese people, did not dare return, but entered Faenza instead. This city remained loyal to the legate and the pope. On this account, and with no opposition from its people, the English, thanks to the incredible perversity of their leader, once inside the walls inflicted everything on its citizens that is usually inflicted on stormed and captured cities. For everything was laid open to pillage, the men were either beaten or killed, the women raped, and things both sacred and profane were wretchedly and impiously polluted by the cruelty of the barbarians. Finally, when it had at last been stripped bare of everything, leaving only the town walls and houses, the evil captain sold the place itself to the rulers of Ferrara.[77]

While this was going on in Italy, Pope Gregory, learning of the 98 defection of Bologna, hired in France and sent into Italy six thou-

sex millia equitum et quatuor millia peditum britonum, ferocissi-
marum gentium, per Galliam scripta in Italiam misit, cumque
iis[139] legatum de latere quem Gebennensem appellabant. Ipse autem pontifex in Gallia residens censuras ac poenas contra Florentinos promulgavit. Erant autem hae permultae atque horrendae.
Itaque non contemnere placuit, maxime cum optima ratione pro-
bari posset culpam omnem in pessimos illius ministros esse refe-
rendam. Missi igitur ista de causa ad pontificem oratores duo:
Alexander Antilla et Donatus Barbadorius, viri scientia[140] iuris
clari et in agendo dicendoque in primis efficaces. Hi cum transmissis Alpibus circa flumen Rhodani ad pontificem pervenissent
tempusque dicendi illis datum esset, publico in auditorio, concursu maximo cuiusque generis hominum qui audiendi studio
convenerant, in hunc fere modum locuti fuere:

99 'Si tui, beatissime pater, sive praefecti sive legati, quos ad guber-
nandas civitates Italiae misisti, gubernationem populorum amabi-
lem ac non tyrannidem horrendam in cervices hominum fuissent
meditati, nec tibi nunc accusandi causa foret neque nobis excu-
sandi. Quippe res tranquillae pacataeque forent nec ullius queri-
monia indigerent. Immo et gubernatores populorum fidelitatem,
et populi ipsi gubernatorum moderationem debitis laudibus prose-
querentur; finitimi vero omni protinus incusatione carerent. Nunc
autem, ut par est, querela multiplex variaque insurgit, quod gubernatores fidelium populorum infidelitatem accusant; populi autem,
non ut fidelibus nec ut ingenuis, sed ut servis ac barbaris imperatum sibi conqueruntur; superbiaque et avaritia et libidinibus eorum necessario se compulsos aiunt tam miserae servitutis iugum

sand horse and four thousand foot, all belonging to that most ferocious of peoples, the Bretons, with the aim of reversing the collapse of the Papal State. With them he sent a legate *a latere*, called   1376
Gebennese.[78] The pontiff himself from his residence in France
promulgated censures and penalties against the Florentines.[79]
These were numerous and frightening. So they preferred not to
disregard them, especially since it could be proved with excellent
arguments that the whole fault should be laid at the door of the
pope's wicked ministers. Two ambassadors were therefore sent to
the pontiff for this purpose: Alessandro della Antella and Donato
Barbadori, men distinguished for their knowledge of law and
highly effective in speech and action. These men crossed the Alps
and came to the pope by the river Rhone. When they had been
granted time to speak at a public audience, they spoke approximately as follows before a vast crowd of men of every kind who
had come together in the desire to hear them.[80]

"If, Holy Father, the governors (or legates, if you prefer) you   99
sent to rule the cities of Italy had intended to impose an amiable
government and not a horrible tyranny on the necks of mankind,
there would now be no reason for you to accuse us, nor for us to
excuse ourselves. Surely, were conditions tranquil and peaceful,
there would be no cause for complaint at all. Indeed, governors
might honor with due praise the faithfulness of their peoples, and
peoples might laud the moderation of their governors; and neighbors would lack entirely any grounds for reproach. But as it is,
many and various complaints have fairly arisen, such that governors accuse loyal peoples of disloyalty, and peoples lament that
they are not treated as free and loyal persons but are ordered
about like slaves and barbarians. They say that they have necessarily been compelled by their governors' arrogance, greed and lusts
to throw off the yoke of so wretched a servitude. And we too, who
have of old been the Church's most devoted sons — we who are
now blamed as the sponsors and accomplices of the defection — we

excutere. Nos quoque, devotissimi ab antiquo ecclesiae filii, quos isti nunc quasi fautores adiutoresque defectionis criminantur, luce clarius docere possumus gubernatores illud idem nefarium servitutis iugum, quo ceteros miserabiliter premebant populos, tyrannico nimium conatu in cervices nostras extendere voluisse. Tu igitur, beatissime pater, aequissimas tuae sanctitatis aures inclina et non ut pars, sed ut iudex rectus et aequus, causam fidelium tuorum de pontificali iustitiae solio recognosce. Quo enim longius abes ac minus vel oculis inspicere malefacta gubernatorum tuorum vel auribus percipere valuisti,[141] eo magis debet Tua Sanctitas aures aequissimas nobis impertiri. Nos autem liberius de illis loquemur, quoniam certissime credimus contra voluntatem tuam illa processisse; cumque omnis legitima gubernatio gratia eorum qui gubernantur instituta sit et pro eorum utilitate, non debet Tuae Sanctitati populorum causam et iustitiam minus commendatam esse quam eorum qui a te missi sunt ad gubernandum. Atqui cogitare debebant gubernatores illi se non ad barbaros neque Saracenos, sed ad ingenuos et christianos populos gubernandos transmitti; et quo ecclesiae nomen atque religio divinius sonat, quoque alienius[142] a tyrannide armorumque violentia esse debet, eo mitius et humanius populos gubernare.

100 'Hi autem praeclari homines, obliti qui eos mittere[n]t et ad quos mitterentur,[143] ita demum se magnificos fore putarunt, ita demum vitia sua exercere posse, si vim et arma et terrorem cum misera gemendaque servitute fidelibus populis inferrent. Quid enim, quaesumus, tot arces per singulas civitates infinito paene sumptu ab illis aedificatae? Quid tot mercede conductorum militum phalanges singulis urbibus impositae? Nonne haec probant tales fuisse gubernatores, ut conscientia scelerum suorum de civium voluntate sibi fuerit desperandum, fundamentaque status sui

are able to show as clear as daylight that these governors, in the excess of their tyrannous designs, have been aiming to stretch over our necks, too, the very same wicked yoke of slavery with which they have crushed other peoples in misery. You, therefore, Holy Father, incline your Holiness's most righteous ears, and acknowledge from your pontifical seat of justice the cause of your faithful ones — not as a partisan, but as an upright and impartial judge. For as you are further off, and less able to hear or see the wicked deeds of your governors, so ought Your Holiness the more to bestow upon us a completely impartial hearing. We shall speak of them the more freely, as we believe with the utmost certainty that these acts have proceeded against your will, and since all legitimate government is instituted for the sake of the governed and for their utility,[81] the just cause of peoples should commend itself to Your Holiness no less than the cause of those whom you sent to govern them. And those governors should have reflected that they were sent out to govern free and Christian peoples, not barbarians or Saracens; and to the end that religion and the Church's name may sound with greater sublimity, to the end that it be not associated with tyranny and armed violence, they should have governed peoples with greater mildness and humanity.

"These distinguished men, forgetting who sent them and to whom they were sent, believed they would be great in no other way, that they could practice their vices in no other way, than by inflicting on loyal peoples armed violence and terror, combined with wretched, groaning servitude. Why, pray, did they construct in every city at almost unlimited expense so many citadels? Why did they impose so many phalanxes of hired troops on every city? Do not these things show that their governance was of such a kind as to compel them, in consciousness of their crimes, to despair of the good will of their citizens? Don't they prove that they had to base their position, not upon justice and benevolence, but upon the violence and wretched tyranny we use to force slaves to obey

100

collocasse non in iustitia et benignitate, sed in violenta miseraque
tyrannide, qua servos nobis parere compellimus? Haec autem, beatissime pater, a voluntate consensuque tuo semper aliena putavi-
mus et putamus. At enim superbia illorum moresque nefarii in ge-
mitum primo, moxque in desperationem populos adegerunt; nec
ullos infestiores per Italiam hostes habuit ecclesia quam gubernatores suos. Ab his et contemptus hominum superbissimi et intolerabiles rapinae et inhonestissimae cupiditates, ne dicam libidines,
exstitere. Hi populos ad defectionem[144] non verbis, sed, quod deterius est, rebus hortati sunt; hi ad inobedientiam compulerunt.
Doles tot civitates per Italiam defecisse? Gubernatoribus imputa,
qui id machinati sunt. Arma sumpta libertatemque proclamatam a
populis indignaris? Eisdem gubernatoribus adscribe, qui saevo tyrannidis iugo in furorem et arma populos adegerunt. Equi, mehercle! et elephanti, quibus non est intellectus, bonam vel malam
gubernationem discernunt, atque huic obediunt, illam non ferunt.
Nedum homines ratione praeditos haec non intelligere arbitre-
mur?

101 'Nobis autem ecclesiae devotissimis ab antiquo filiis, qui persecutiones[145] stragesque innumeras pro defensione romanorum pontificum certantes subivimus, quid isti gubernatores fecerint at-
tende. Cum fame populus noster laboraret—habemus namque civitatem populosissimam et quae plurimum importato indigeat—
cum igitur superiore anno fame laboraret populus noster, ac Bononiae ceterisque ecclesiae urbibus permagna vis frumenti superesset, neque precibus neque obsecrationibus neque lacrimis pro
infima plebe diffusis impetrare a gubernatoribus valuimus, ut de
superabundantia sua famescenti plebi nostrae, vel in aliqua saltem
particula, subvenirent, cum essemus loco proximi, cum publice socii, privatim amici. Verum haec, quamquam dura sint et inhumana
et caritatis expertia, tamen non sunt magna, si ad sequentia com-
parentur. Non contenti enim non subvenire postulantibus et indigentibus, verum etiam nostra ipsa pro tollenda[146] futuri spe adi-

us? Such means, Holy Father, we have always thought, and think now, to be foreign to your intention and consent. Yet their pride and wicked behavior has driven your peoples first to groans, then to desperation The church's worst enemies in Italy have been her own governors. It is from these men that arrogant contempt for mankind, intolerable seizures and disgraceful desires, not to say lusts, have sprung. It is they who have encouraged the peoples to defect, not by their words, but (what is worse) by their deeds; it is they who have compelled the peoples to disobey. Are you grieved that so many cities across Italy have defected? Set it down to their governors, who have schemed to this end. Are you angered that the peoples have seized arms and proclaimed their liberty? Ascribe this to those same governors, who with the brutal yoke of tyranny have driven the people to fury and arms. By heaven! even horses and elephants who lack understanding recognize good and bad rule, obeying the former and not the latter. Shall we think that human beings who have been given reason do not understand these things?

"But now listen to what these governors did to us, of old the Church's most devoted children — to us who have undergone endless persecution and slaughter in our struggles to defend the Roman pontiffs. When our people were suffering distress from famine — for we have a large population that needs to import a great deal — when, then, last year our people were suffering from famine and there was plenty of excess grain in Bologna and other cities of the Church, neither prayers nor entreaties nor tears shed for the poorest of the poor availed us the least with the Church's governors, whom we begged to help our starving populace from their own abundance — even though we were neighbors, allies in public matters and in private their friends. But this behavior, hard as it was, inhuman and devoid of charity as it was, was yet a small thing by comparison with what followed. For not content with not responding to the prayers of a people in need, your governors also, 101

mere malignitate mirabili gubernatores tui quaesiverunt. Nam, cum advenisset iam aestas, et omnis spes in segetibus esset quae iam flavescere incipiebant, scientes illi difficultates extremas nostro populo adesse, nec aliud omnino refugium quam in novis segetibus habere, repente hi praeclari gubernatores sub ficto cassationis velamine[147] universum equitatum suum incredibili multitudine contra civitatem nostram misere, ut extra vastatis agris speque frumenti adempta, intus vero fame pereuntes, quod unum restabat remedium, in eorum potestatem, id est, sub eorum servitutem ac tyrannidem, venire cogeremur. Quod nisi servasset nos primum divina benignitas, deinde pecuniarum magnitudo (centum enim et triginta florenorum millia equitibus dedimus), proditionibus dolisque subacti, in servitutem illorum miserabiliter trahebamur. Nam adversus tam repentinam vim tantasque copias improviso et inopinato supervenientes, resistendi armis facultas non erat; nec proderat servare moenia, cum intus necessarius victus deesset.

102 'Haec[148] qualia sunt, pater optime? An non stupenda, an non detestanda, an non nefaria? Hac igitur fraude malignitateque deprehensa periculumque experti, si sic posthac nos armavimus, ut iterum inferri nobis eadem pericula nequirent, utrum hoc est statum ecclesiae subvertere, an statum nostrum a periculo vindicare? Et utrum nos qui obviavimus ac restitimus illato nobis periculo, turbationis causa sumus existimandi, an illi qui periculum inferendo nos muniri adversus eorum violentiam coegerunt? Quod si aliae civitates, videntes nos armari, fiduciam assumpserunt illorum nefariis iniuriis resistendi, quis iustus iudex imputare nobis debet, cum pro defensione nostra fecerimus omnia, non pro alterius impugnatione? Haec pro nobis ipsis et iusta et legitima dixisse vide-

with incredible malignity, sought to take away even our very hope for the future. For when summer had already come, and all hope lay in the harvest which was now beginning to ripen, these men, knowing the extreme difficulties our people had to deal with, knowing that we had no other salvation than in the new harvest, these fine governors, under the fictive cloak of dismissing them from service, sent all their cavalry in incredible numbers against our city, so that, our fields devastated and all hope of supplies taken away without, and starving within, we should as a last resort be compelled to come into their power—that is, into their slavery and tyranny. And if divine benevolence had not preserved us first of all, and then an enormous sum of money (for we paid 130,000 florins to the cavalry), we should have been ground down by their deceit and betrayal and dragged wretchedly into slavery. For armed resistance was impossible in the face of such sudden violence and such great forces arriving unexpectedly and without warning, nor would guarding the walls have done any good when within them the necessary provisions were lacking.

"What sort of actions were these, Holy Father? Were they not 102 staggering, were they not contemptible, were they not wicked? If, after detecting their deceit and illwill and learning of our danger, we have thus armed ourselves to prevent them from inflicting these same perils on us again, is this act to be construed as subverting the Papal State or rather as rescuing our own state from peril? Are we, who are but blocking and resisting the danger threatening us, to be considered the cause of turmoil, or is it those who, by threatening us with danger, have forced us to defend ourselves against their violence? And if other cities, seeing us arm ourselves, have been encouraged to resist their wicked acts of injustice, what upright judge will blame us, when we have done everything in our own defense, and not to attack anyone else? What we have said on our own behalf seems both just and legitimate,

mur, et Beatitudo Tua, si recte iudicare voluerit, debet eadem comprobare.

103   'Sed quae posthac suspicio restet, libere aperiemus. Auditum est enim a nobis multa sinistra per aemulos obtrectatoresque Tuae Beatitudinis auribus instillata fuisse atque diffusa adversus devotionem fidelilatemque civitatis nostrae. Itaque necessarium videtur quae et qualis fuerit erga ecclesiam florentini populi devotio fidesque vice versa memorare. Florentinum populum, beatissime pater, si antiquae recitentur historiae, semper assertorem praecipuum romanae ecclesiae reperies extitisse; ob hoc et indignationes imperatorum gravissimas et persecutiones innumeras pertulisse. Nullus contra pontifices romanos per Italiam surrexit, qui non et florentinum populum, ut fautorem assertoremque illorum, fuerit persecutus; nec rursus ullo in loco bellatum est pro ecclesiae statu, in quo Florentinus non adfuerit in armis. Probat primi Federici persecutio, qui cum romanam ecclesiam crudeliter afflixisset, non minori saevitia Florentiam afflixit, utpote romanorum pontificum singularissimam assertricem. Probat Henrici filii persecutio identidem nobis illis de causis illata. Probat et alterius Federici, qui cum pontifices romanos exterminasset statumque ecclesiae per Italiam evertisset, ita demum hoc stabile fore putauit, si Florentinos, ecclesiae romanae studio flagrantes, e medio tolleret atque opprimeret. Itaque et carcere et tormentis et gladio et exterminatione civium et omni crudelitatis impietatisque genere in Florentinos[149] desaevivit. Successit ut in generis, sic etiam in furoris haereditatem Manfredus, qui Siciliae regnum post Federicum obtinuit. Hic rursus, ut pontifices persecutus est, ita nobis, utpote fidelissimis ecclesiasticarum partium assertoribus, bellum intulit victosque apud Arbiam maximo proelio domo pepulit extorresque patria dissipa-

and if Your Beatitude wishes to judge with rectitude, you will confirm our statement of the case.

"But let us speak frankly about the suspicions that remain. We 103 have heard that our rivals and detractors have spread and instilled in the ears of Your Holiness many perverse things, attacking the devotion and loyalty of our city. So it seems necessary in response to recall the devotion and loyalty of the Florentine People towards the Church. If old histories are related, Holy Father, you will find that the Florentine People has ever been an outstanding protector of the Roman church; and that on this account we have suffered wrath of the gravest kind from the emperors as well as innumerable persecutions. No one throughout Italy ever rose up against the Roman pontiffs without also persecuting the Florentine People as well, the popes' sponsor and defender. Again, there was no war in any place on behalf of ecclesiastical rule in which there was no armed participation by the Florentine. This is proved by the persecution of Frederick I, who having cruelly afflicted the Roman Church, afflicted Florence with no less brutality as the single most important defender of the Roman pontiffs. It is proved likewise by his son Henry, who inflicted persecution on us for the same reasons. It is proved also by the persecution of Frederick II, who having stamped out the Roman pontiffs and destroyed the position of the Church in Italy, believed that the situation would be stabilized only if he removed and crushed the Florentines, who were aflame with loyal zeal towards the Roman Church. Hence he vented his rage against the Florentines with prison and torture and the sword and killing of citizens and every kind of cruelty and impiety. Manfred, who ruled the kingdom of Sicily after Frederick, inherited this fury along with the succession of his kin. He, once again, persecuted us as he did the pontiffs, as we were the most faithful defenders of the ecclesiastical party, and he made war on us, expelling the vanquished from their home after the great battle of the Arbia, scattering them as exiles from their country; nor were

vit; nec nos ante in patriam nostram restituti sumus, quam romanus tunc pontifex in sedem suam fuerit restitutus. Sed Manfredus
ipse non impune haec egit. Nam, cum adversus illius persecutionem Carolus ex Gallia vocatus in Italiam venisset, in illa memora-
bili pugna apud Beneventum commissa florentini tunc exules suo
proprio agmine, sub vexillo quod pontifex romanus eis tamquam
devotissimis fidelissimisque donaverat, adversus Manfredum una
cum Carolo pro statu pontificum pugnavere, victoque et occiso
Manfredo, finem persecutioni gloriosissimum imposuere. Post
haec, cum huius Manfredi nepos, Corradinus, Italiam cum exercitu ingressus Romam venisset et persecutionem[150] contra ecclesiam moliretur, in quo ille proelio victus et profligatus est, nostrae
quoque civitatis auxilia interfuerunt ad persecutorem ecclesiae op-
primendum.

104   'Quid posteris temporibus ac fere nostra aetate? Cum Ludovicus Bavariae dux correptis imperatoriis fascibus magno cum exercitu in Italiam venisset, ac Romam ingressus, urbem teneret, ac
falsum pontificem cardinalesque in ea creari fecisset in magna
christianorum divisione, quisquamne magis in veri pontifices ve-
raeque romanae sedis devotione perstitit quam civitas nostra?
Quae et adversus terrorem Ludovici armatam se obtulit et adversus ambitionem fraudemque religiosorum, qui novum assumptum
ut verum pontificem praedicabant, inconcussa fidelitate constantis-
sime repugnavit. Nec[151] terror armorum, nec imminentis periculi
magnitudo, nec exempla ceterarum civitatum, quae falso pontifici
adhaerebant, populum nostrum a vera fidelitate potuerunt deflec-
tere, quamvis et bellum et obsidio gravissima a Ludovico simul
et[152] Castrucio nobis immineret.

105   'Haec et huiusmodi[153] alia permulta, cum pro ecclesia perpessus
fuerit populus noster, cum devotionis fidelitatisque studio firmo[154]
et continuato tam multa, tam gravia domi forisque, pace et bello,

we restored to our country until the Roman pontiff of that day was restored to his see. But Manfred himself did not escape punishment for these acts. For when Charles was summoned from France to oppose his persecution and arrived in Italy, in that memorable battle which took place near Benevento, the Florentine exiles of that time fought in their own formation, under a standard given them by the Roman pontiff as his most devoted and faithful followers, defending the rule of the popes along with Charles against Manfred; and with Manfred defeated and slain they put an end to his persecution in the most glorious way. Afterwards, when Corradino, the grandson of this Manfred, entered Italy with an army and came to Rome, aiming to persecute the Church, our city, too, took part in the battle where he was defeated and put to flight, in order to crush a persecutor of the Church.

"What about later times, what about events closer to our 104 times? When Ludwig, duke of Bavaria, usurped the imperial insignia and came with a great army into Italy, entered Rome, took control of the city, and caused to be created in it a false pontiff and cardinals, giving rise to great divisions among Christians, what city more than ours stood firm in its devotion to the true pontiffs and the true see of Rome? What city offered armed resistance to Ludwig's terror, and fought back with unshaken loyalty and resolve against the ambition and deceit of clergymen who proclaimed that the new pontiff was the true one? Neither fear of arms nor the greatness of the imminent peril nor the example of other cities who adhered to the false pontiff could turn our people away from its true loyalty, although we were threatened simultaneously by Ludwig and by Castruccio with war and the most grievous of sieges.

"Given these and the many other, similar sufferings our people 105 has undergone for the sake of the Church; given its steady and continuous zeal, its devoted loyalty in taking on, carrying out, and enduring on the Church's behalf so many grave trials at home and

pro ecclesia gesserit, fecerit, pertulerit, an ob haec dignus tibi[155] videtur idem populus noster, cui a tuis gubernatoribus et praefectis in extrema[156] fame subventio frumentaria denegaretur? An dignus tibi videtur populus noster, cui non solum denegetur frumentum a praefectis tuis, verum etiam in hoc ipso famis cruciatu equitatus Anglorum repente immitteretur ad segetes agrorum (quod unicum restabat diffugium[157]) pervastandas, ut per haec subdere colla ac miserae servitutis iugum suscipere cogeremur? Haec, si te volente ac iubente (quod credere non possumus) facta sunt, de sedis apostolicae, de ecclesiae romanae, de pontificis summi ingratitudine et iniuria conqueremur. Sin ipsi praefecti praeter et contra voluntatem tuam illa fecerunt, indignationem tuam ipsi promerentur, non florentinus populus, qui contra illorum nefarios conatus necessario se armavit.

106 'Quocirca, pater sanctissime, tibi ab intimis supplicamus, ut sereno tranquilloque animo causam nostram discernas; iram vero et indignationem, si quam adversus nos dolosae tibi linguae infuderunt, deponas; neque enim decet in cathedra Petri sedentem ira vel odio commoveri. Pone tibi ante oculos infantes et pueros et illam multitudinem civitatis nostrae fame laborantem, quibus non denegata modo est frumentaria subventio a praefectis tuis cum suppliciter rogarentur, verum insuper exercitus immissus ad unicam spem salutis crudeliter auferendam. Subveniat quoque tibi miserarum civitatum quae sub illorum gubernatione fuerunt, quibus veluti servis ac vilibus mancipiis imperatum est a gubernatoribus quos illis praefecisti. Moveat denique lacrimas tuas Faventia, civitas fidelis et innocens, ab equitatu praefectorum tuorum hostilem in modum direpta. O miserandam calamitatem! O sceleratum facinus! O detestandam crudelitatem! Quis non fleat, aspiciens necatos crudeliter cives, virgines ac matresfamilias ad stuprum libidinemque militum reservatas, infantium ac lactentium turbas mulieresque aetate provectas longis agminibus mendicaturas, de propria urbe laribusque depulsas? Haec sunt opera praefectorum tuorum;

abroad, in peace and in war—given all this, does it seem to you that this same people in the extremity of their need deserved to be denied a grain subvention by your governors? Do you think our people deserved not only to be denied grain by your deputies, but also, while suffering from starvation, to be set upon by English cavalry without warning in order to devastate the crops in our fields, our one remaining escape, with the aim of forcing us to bend our necks and receive the wretched yoke of servitude? If these acts were done at your behest (which we cannot believe), we should protest the ingratitude and injustice of the apostolic see, the Roman Church, and the supreme pontiff. But if it was your deputies who did these things against your will, it is they who deserve your wrath, not the Florentine People, who necessarily armed itself against their wicked enterprises.

"Wherefore, Holy Father, we beg you from the bottom of our   106
hearts to judge our cause with a serene and tranquil spirit, and to put away any wrath and indignation that treacherous tongues may have instilled in you against us; for it is not fitting that he who sits in the chair of Peter should be affected by anger or hatred. Place before your eyes infants and children and the city's common people struggling with famine, to whom your deputies not only denied a grain subsidy when they begged for it, but also sent an army besides cruelly to take away their only hope of salvation. You should think, too, of the wretched cities placed under their governance that were ordered about like slaves and low creatures by the governors whom you placed over them. Finally, you should weep over the fate of Faenza, a faithful and innocent city, pulled to pieces like an enemy by the cavalry of your deputies. O wretched calamity! O heinous crime! O despicable cruelty! Who would not weep to see its citizens cruelly slaughtered, its young girls and matrons raped by soldiers, its long lines of suckling infants and aged women going out to beg, expelled from their own city and their own homes? Such are the works of your deputies—such is their

haec illorum sanctitas ac religio! Quorum facta si tu non damnas, sed eos persequeris[158] qui adversus talia restiterunt, vide quid Deus ipse de his iudicaturus sit, et quae de huiusmodi rebus opinio in communi hominum iudicio relinquatur!'

107   Legati quidem, cum haec dixissent, finem fecerunt. Multitudo autem quae ad audiendum convenerat et corona facta in auditorio circumstabat, vehementer commoveri oratione legatorum visa est, fluxeruntque lacrimae plerisque eorum qui aderant. Nec dubium erat, si suffragio audientium res commissa fuisset, quin Florentini sententiis omnium absolverentur, ita suadenter legati dixisse visi fuerant, atque ita inflexerat animos oratio. Pontifex vero, haec animadvertens, quamquam sententia in tempus aliud differebatur, tamen nonnihil respondendum in praesentia ratus, quo animos eorum qui audiverant confirmaret, in hunc fere modum verba fecisse dicitur:

108   'Audivimus, Florentini, defensionem vestram adversus crimina per processus nostros vobis obiecta; quoque accuratior vestra fuit oratio, eo magis patet vos omnia collegisse quae vel in causa vel extra causam dici pro excusatione possunt. Et nos quidem, uti suadetis, iudices erimus recti, nec ira vel indignatione in iudicando movebimur, neque calumniis credemus, sed solummodo[159] veritati. Vos autem vice versa hortamur, ut commiserationes istas et epilogos ac cetera huiusmodi machinamenta et artes quae ad decipiendum iudicem pertinent, missa faciatis, et una simul nobiscum veritatem intueamini. Quaero igitur a vobis, cum populus vester fuerit impulsor, adiutor et auctor civitatibus ecclesiae rebellandi (nam id quidem patet et negari non potest, quod est omnibus manifestum), qua tandem ratione factum hoc a vobis defendere aggrediamini? Nempe illa ratione, quod pro tutela vestra dicitis id fecisse; sic enim quodammodo dictum fuit a vobis, ideo armasse vos, ne pericula vobis possent inferri. Haec autem verba fronte prima videntur bona et recta—cuique enim licet adversus illatam vim se

piety and moral purity! If you do not condemn their deeds, but
persecute those who resisted them, consider the judgement that
God himself will make of them, and the view of them that will
last in the common judgement of mankind!"[82]

The ambassadors ended their speech with those words. The 107
crowd that had gathered to hear and was standing around them in
the audience chamber seemed powerfully affected by the envoys'
speech, and tears flowed from many of those present. And there is
no doubt that, had the matter been submitted to a vote of the audience, the Florentines would have been absolved by universal consent. The pontiff noticed this, and although his sentence was to be
put off to another time, he nevertheless decided that some immediate response was necessary to strengthen the resolve of the audience. So he is said to have spoken approximately as follows:

"We have heard, Florentines, your defense against the charges 108
laid against you in our legal procedures; and the studied character
of your oration made it all the clearer that you have assembled every argument, relevant or irrelevant, that might be spoken in your
own defense. For our part we shall be an upright judge, as you
urge us to be, and we shall be influenced in our judgement neither
by anger nor indignation, nor shall we believe calumnies, but only
the truth. We in turn exhort you to lay aside these piteous pleas
and perorations and other rhetorical artifices suitable for deceiving
a judge, and consider the truth together with us. I ask you, then,
given that your people has been the driving force, accomplice and
author of the rebellion in the cities of the Church (for what is obvious to all is clear and undeniable), how, pray, do you set about
defending yourselves for this action? Your argument, of course, is
that you acted in self-defense; for you were in a way claiming that
you had taken up arms to prevent dangers from being inflicted on
you. At first glance these words seem good and right — for everyone is allowed to protect himself from violent attack — but still, if
someone takes up arms, not to ward off violence here and now, but

ipsum tueri—verum tamen, si arma capiat quis, non ut vim praesentem repellat, sed ut occidat eum de quo suspicatur et metuit, iam homicida est, manifesteque damnandus. Vos, Florentini, Tifernum, vos Perusiam, vos Bononiam copias vestras misistis ad arces ecclesiae expugnandas, ad gubernatores illarum deiiciendos et opprimendos. Hoc autem (pace vestra dictum sit) nequaquam est vim repellere, sed inferre; nec a sua domo propulsare violentiam, sed alienae domui violentiam facere. Tale igitur factum est vestrum, quale illius qui hominem occidit de quo suspicatur, ne sibi aliquando possit nocere; quod esse damnandum et contra leges manifestissimum est.

109   'Quamquam, quid nos de suspicione vel metu loquimur, cum appareat vos non metu vel suspicione, sed odio magis illa fecisse? Omittamus enim Bononiam, Perusiam, Tifernum, quas ad rebellandum compulistis, quarum arces expugnastis. Fuerit in propinquitate illarum aliqua vobis suspicio vel metus. At Asculum in Picentibus, et aliae illorum locorum urbes, tam procul a vobis, tam longinquae, tam distantes, nonne probant manifeste vos non suspicione vel metu, sed odio status ecclesiastici surrexisse ad illas urbes auferendas, nec minuere vires[160] ecclesiae per Italiam, sed evertere penitus ac delere funditus voluisse? Et postea vos asseritis romanae ecclesiae filios, nec intelligitis contra vos dicere, quanto gravius est filium parenti manus afferre quam extraneum? Abutimini ad omnia gubernatorum invidia, et arces per singulas urbes ab eis factas vituperatis quasi tyrannicum; denique culpam omnem defectionis in gubernatores ipsos refertis.

110   'Primum igitur, quantum ad arces pertinet, nec eas nos laudaremus, si populi semper ratione uterentur; sed ut equi otio et afflu-

to kill a man whom one suspects and fears, this becomes homicide and must be clearly condemned. You, Florentines, sent your troops to Città di Castello, Perugia and Bologna to storm citadels of the Church, to cast down and crush their governors. But such actions, with all due respect, by no means constitute a defense against violence; they are offensive. They are not like repelling violence from one's own house, but rather liking attacking another man's house. Your action resembles that of someone who kills a man he is suspicious of so as to prevent that man from doing harm to himself at some unspecified time. It is utterly clear that such an action is illegal and deserves to be condemned.

"Yet why do we speak of suspicions or fears, when it is clear 109 that you acted not so much from these motives as from hatred? Let us leave aside Bologna, Perugia, and Città di Castello, which you drove to rebellion, and whose citadels you captured. Let us grant that their propinquity was to you a source of suspicion and fear. But Ascoli in Piceno and the other cities of that region, so far from you, so distant, so remote—do they not clearly show that you rose up to take those cities from us not out of suspicion or fear, but out of hatred for Church rule? Do they not show that you wanted not to reduce the strength of the Church in Italy, but to completely overturn it and blot it out utterly? And afterwards you go on to claim that you are sons of the Roman Church, not realizing that this claim tells against you to the extent that it is a graver crime to attack a parent than a stranger. You exploit the ill-will towards the governors for every purpose, and find fault with the citadels they built in every city as signs of tyranny; finally, you throw the whole blame for the rebellion on the governors themselves.

"In the first place, then, as concerns the citadels, we, too, do not 110 commend them in cases where peoples behave rationally, but just as horses kick and become hard to handle when they have had plenty of food and rest, so peoples who have been at peace and

entia cibi intractabiles fiunt et calcitrosi, ita populi nimia interdum quiete et indulgentia insolescunt, et arcibus indigent quibus compescantur. Gubernationem legitimam omnem pro eorum qui reguntur populorum utilitate institutam esse fatemur, talemque nostram esse dicimus; neque enim sumus tyranni, nec esse volumus. Arces tamen ad populorum salutem utilitatemque pertinere credimus, ut se contineant, ut acquiescant, ut leves audacesque homines, quibus plenae sunt urbes, contra bonorum voluntatem res novas suscitare non audeant. Nam, quod ad culpam gubernatorum defectiones refertis, satis constat nobis nullum ante populum defecisse quam a vobis suadendo et pollicendo fuerit ad defectionem impulsus, ut in vobis causa sit, non in gubernatoribus nostris. Ad extremum calamitatem Faventinorum miserabiliter deplorastis; quasi vero calamitas illa non orta sit ex Bononiae rebellione! Numquam enim Angli Faventiam invasissent, si Bononia in fide permansisset. Itaque, qui rebellandi Bononiensibus causa fuerunt, iidem ipsi miserabilis Faventinorum excidii fuerunt causa. Et nostrum est de ea calamitate deque ceteris malis contra vos conqueri. Haec respondisse breviter placuit ad orationem vestram, non affirmantes sed disceptantes, iustitiam tandem facturi in sententia ferenda.'

III   Secundum has orationes mora quaedam aliquot dierum et intercapedo[161] fuit, variaeque per curiam opiniones voluntatesque. Galli siquidem omnes contra Florentinorum causam plerique sentiebant; italici vero generis cuncti pertinacissimum favorem Florentinis impertiebantur. Demum excusationibus defensionibusque reiectis sententia pontificis Florentini damnantur, et interdicto civitas subiicitur universa; in singulorum quoque bona, ubicumque reperirentur, ius asperrime constituitur. Aderant oratores floren-

treated with indulgence tend to become insolent and need citadels to keep them under control. We admit that all legitimate government is instituted for the utility of the peoples who are ruled, and we claim that our government was of this kind: we are not tyrants, nor do we wish to be. But we believe that citadels are relevant to the safety and utility of peoples, to control them and keep them quiet, and so that unstable and reckless men, of which cities are full, do not dare incite revolutions contrary to the will of the good. With respect to your blaming the governors for the revolts, it is quite obvious to us that none of these peoples defected until they were driven to defect by your urgings and promises, so that you, not our governors, are the cause of the revolts. At the end of your speech you lament piteously the calamity of the people of Faenza—but as though the origin of that calamity were not the rebellion of Bologna! For the English would never have invaded Faenza if Bologna had remained loyal. Thus, those who were the cause of the Bolognese rebellion are also the cause of the wretched destruction of Faenza. It is *we* who have grounds for remonstrance against *you* for this calamity and for other evils. We decided to make this brief response to your oration, not to confirm it but to take issue with it; and we shall in due course do justice when we pass sentence."

After these orations came an interval and delay of several days,   III
and there were various points of view and dispositions within the court. All the French were in general opposed to the Florentine case, but all the Italians held to the side of the Florentines with great tenacity. At length their excuses and defenses were rejected and the Florentines were condemned by sentence of the pontiff. The whole city-state was placed under interdict, and a right to confiscate the goods of individual Florentines, wherever they were found, was also decreed with great bitterness. The ambassadors of the Florentine People were present when the sentence was passed, and it is known that they said many things in that place with

tini populi cum sententia ferebatur, quo in loco multa facunde ac libero animo dicta ab illis fuisse constat. Et illud in primis, quod ad effigiem Dei conversus, Barbadorius (is enim maiori spiritu nitebatur) magna voce, ita ut pontifex exaudiret, 'Deus!' inquit, 'nos legati, florentini populi nomine, ab hac sententia vicarii tui inique lata, ad te tuamque aequitatem appellamus. Tu, qui falli non potes nec ira inflecteris nec servitutem populorum sed libertatem amas et tyrannos libidinesque odisti, florentino populo libertatem suam defendenti subvenies ac propitius protectorque aderis!'

112   Et res quidem curiae ita transigebantur. Britones autem, quos in Italiam missos a pontifice diximus, superatis tandem Alpibus per astensem et alexandrinum et dertonensem agrum profecti, dimensa citeriori Gallia, circiter maturationem segetum in fines Bononiensium pervenere. Florentini vero, quo ab eorum impetu Bononia defenderetur, copias omnes suas Bononiensibus transmiserunt, et Apennini aditus, quo illis in agrum florentinum veniendi facultas deesset, custodiri fecerunt.

113   Erat cum Britonibus Gebennensis legatus, de quo supra mentionem fecimus. Is ergo ficta mansuetudine fretus, nec vastari agrum neque cetera permulta quae belli natura fert permittebat fieri, et in urbem miserat qui praeteritorum omnium veniam impunitatemque offerrent. Qua quidem pollicitatione nonnullos Bononiensium in sententiam traxerat.

114   Agitatio igitur occulta ad proditionem tendebat, qua una spe Gebennensis per agrum bononiensem saepius motis castris diutius in his locis commoratus est, tentans, si qua posset, copias quae intus erant ad exeundum pellicere.[162] Intra urbem copiis praeerat Rodulphus Varanius camerinensis, vir sagaci ingenio ac bellorum

frankness and eloquence. Among the best things said was when Barbadori (who was a man of high spirit) turned to an image of God and said in a loud voice, so that the pope could hear, "O God, we, the ambassadors of the Florentine People, appeal to Thee and to thy equity against this unjust sentence of thy vicar. Thou, who cannot be deceived and are not turned from the straight path by anger, nor loveth the slavery of peoples but their liberty, Thou who dost hate tyrants and their lusts, come to the aid of the Florentine People who are defending their liberty, and protect and favor them!"[83]

Thus did affairs at the curia play themselves out. But the Bretons whom the pope had sent to Italy (as we said) at length crossed the Alps and passed through the territories of Asti, Alessandria and Tortona, and measuring the length of Cisalpine Gaul, they arrived on the borders of the Bolognese around harvest-time. The Florentines, however, to defend Bologna against their attack, sent all their troops to the Bolognese, and caused the Apennine passes to be guarded so as to remove the Bretons' ability to come into Florentine territory. 112

The legate Gebennese, whom we mentioned above, came with the Bretons. Relying on a pretense of mildness, he did not permit the fields to be devastated nor many other things to be done which war naturally brings with it, and he sent into the city men who offered pardon and impunity for all bygone deeds. And with this promise he in fact drew many Bolognese into his way of thinking. 113

Thus his secret agitation was building up to an act of betrayal, and it was with this one hope that Gebennese remained rather long in the area, moving his camps frequently around the Bolognese territory. He was trying if possible to inveigle the troops inside Bologna to come out. Ridolfo da Camerino commanded the troops inside the city, a man of keen intelligence and knowledgeable about war. Observing the enemy's delay, he surmised that the only thing they could be waiting for was an act of treachery, and so 114

sciens, qui moram hostium cernens, nihil aliud eos quam proditionem expectare coniectura suspicatus, exire copias nusquam permittebat. Unam dumtaxat meditabatur urbis custodiam, putans,
id quod erat, nisi ea potirentur urbe, omnem impetum hostibus
brevi esse casurum. Ferturque eius vox et prudens et urbana; nam
cum hostes, ipsum allicere frustra conati, tandem percontarentur
quid intus maneret cum suis copiis, quid non exiret adversus ac
pugnam capesseret, responderi iussit ideo se non exire, ne illi in-
trarent. Nec multo post agitata proditio, quoniam per huius dili-
gentiam assiduamque custodiam effectum habere nequibat, quasi
longitudine fatigata ad lucem devenit, captique proditores ac supplicio affecti irritam expectationem legato fecerunt.

115   Stantibus ad Bononiam copiis, duo Britonum equites fide suscepta, Bononiam ingressi, probra quaedam militariter contra Ita-
los[163] locuti, quoscumque nostros in singulare certamen provoca-
bant. Adversus eorum intolerabilem iactantiam, cum alii silerent,
duo primarii iuvenes sese obtulerunt: Bectus Biffolus florentinus
et Guido Ascianensis. Hi non minori verborum acerbitate contra
Britones invecti, cum minabundi se ad pugnam offerrent, data ac-
ceptaque duelli fide constitutaque ad pugnam die, insignibus equis
armisque in certamen venerunt. Locus illis[164] extra urbem datus
prope hostium castra, Gebennensi legato securitatem pollicente.[165]
Ibi quatuor pugiles magnis Italorum Gallorumque votis singuli adversus singulos congressi pugnavere. Pugna eorum fuit equestris,
effuso cursu infestis cuspidibus se petentium. Quod cum saepe[166]
egregiis animis periteque[167] fecissent, tandem[168] Biffoli virtus
prima emicuit, transfixumque hasta Gallum ad terram prostravit.
Ipse vero mox equo prosiliens, cum iacentem hostem iugulare per-

would not permit his troops to leave. His plan was simply to keep guard over the city, believing (what was in fact the case) that unless the enemy could gain control over that city, their whole attack would shortly fail. A wise and witty saying of his is passed down, for when the enemy, having tried in vain to ensnare him, finally inquired why he remained inside with his troops, why he didn't come out and engage in battle, he sent the response that he was not coming out, so that they didn't come in. Not long afterwards the planned act of treachery, which could not be carried out thanks to his care and unremitting watchfulness, came to light, as though worn out by the length of time, and the traitors were captured and punished, thus making fruitless the legate's long wait.[84]

While his troops were encamped around Bologna, two Breton 115 knights were given parole to enter Bologna. Having made certain offensive remarks of a military nature against the Italians, they challenged any of our men to a single combat. While others fell silent, two youths of high station, the Florentine Betto Biffoli and Guido of Asciano, presented themselves in opposition to the Bretons' intolerable boasting. They attacked the Bretons with no less verbal bitterness, and uttering threats they volunteered to fight them. A duel was offered and accepted, and a day for the battle was fixed. With splendid horses and arms they arrived for the contest. The place assigned was outside the city, near the enemy camp, and the legate Gebennese promised them a safe conduct. There the four champions came together to fight, one on one, supported by the hopes and prayers of the Italians and the French. They jousted at a gallop with sharpened lances; and when they had carried off numerous passes skilfully and with extraordinary spirit, Biffoli's virtue was finally the first to flash forth, and he speared his Frenchman and knocked him to the ground. He then leapt off his horse and was about to cut the throat of his prostrate enemy when Gebennese ran up and begged him to spare the man's life and keep him as a prisoner. Hearing this, Biffoli asked in the

geret, accurrens Gebennensis, parcere illius vitae captivumque servare precabatur. Id cum audiret Biffolus, interrogavit coram omnibus, num se victorem ac illius vitae necisque dominum esse
constaret. Cum id affirmaretur, contentus ea confessione, faciliter
ac benigne Gebennensi illum donavit. Restabat altera pugna, et
ipsa insignis omnique nixu agitata. Verum eius quoque is exitus
fuit. Dum se infestius petunt, ambo uno eodemque simul tempore
mutuis cuspidibus transfixi corruerunt. Sed Italus primus surrexit,
iacentemque adhuc Gallum semianimem captivum habuit. Donati
victores egregie, magna cum laude Bononiam rediere.

116   Per idem tempus apud Arretinos detecta coniuratio graviori
motu civitatem concussit. Saconis enim filii cum amicis paternis
suae factionis constituerant redire in urbem ac dominatum arripere. Erant tunc Arretini in Florentinorum societate. Itaque spes
omnis ac fiducia coniuratorum de inimicis florentini populi sume-
batur. Nec deerant copiae vel Britonum vel Anglorum qui opem in
re conficienda afferrent. Verum ea coniuratio patefacta creditur ab
ipsorum necessariis, qui sive invidia sive indignatione quod adsciti
non essent, cum aliunde rescissent, totam rem indicavere. Ob eam
capti quidam coniuratorum supplicio afficiuntur, fugati reliqui, ge-
bellinaeque factionis hominibus arma penitus honoresque reipublicae adempti. Bellum quoque ob eandem rem adversus Saconis
filios impigre resumptum.

117   Per finem eius aestatis Britones frustra bononiensi in agro commorati, tandem abeuntes Caesenam petiere. Ducebant vero eos ceterique illorum duces et Gebennensis legatus. Caesenates in potestate pontificis continuo permanserant et venienti Gebennensi
Britonibusque portas libere aperuerant. Stantibus igitur in urbe

presence of everyone whether he was clearly the victor and lord of
the man's life and death. When this was affirmed, he was satisfied
with this confession, and gave the man back to Gebennese readily
and with a good will. There remained the other fight, which was
also splendid and strenuously contested. But it too had the same
outcome. Coming together with great fury, each of the men struck
the other with his lance at one and the same time, and both fell to
the ground. But the Italian was the first to rise, and took captive
the Frenchman while he was still lying there half-dead. The victors
were given splendid prizes and returned to Bologna with great
praise.

Meanwhile a conspiracy discovered in Arezzo created serious   116
instability in that city. The sons of Saccone, together with friends
belonging to their father's faction, decided to return to the city and
seize the lordship. The Aretines at that time were allied with the
Florentines. So the conspirators derived all their hopes and confidence from the enemies of the Florentine People. And there was
no lack of Breton and English troops to furnish aid in fulfillment
of their scheme. But the conspiracy was laid bare, it is believed, by
associates of the conspirators themselves, who were envious or angry at not being privy to the scheme, and who revealed the whole
conspiracy when they found out about it from another source. On
this account certain of the plotters were captured and executed,
while the rest fled; and the men of the Ghibelline faction were
completely stripped of their arms and their honors. Owing to this
same conspiracy, war was tirelessly resumed against the sons of
Saccone.

At the end of the summer, the Bretons, after wasting their time   117
in Bolognese territory, finally left and headed for Cesena. They
were led by the legate Gebennese and the rest of their captains.
Cesena had remained continuously under papal control and freely
opened its gates to Gebennese and the Bretons when they came.
Thus it was that while staying in the city they began to commit

copiis maleficia per noctes patrari coeperunt; vexari etiam interdiu cives ac iniuriis affici. Quibus in rebus cum nil valerent querelae apud legatum factae, et quotidie magis delicta augerentur, tandem, superante patientiam magnitudine iniuriarum, in furorem Caesenates vertuntur, raptisque per iram armis Britones aggressi, supra octingentos eorum interfecerunt; reliquos vero omnes extra urbem pepulerunt.

118   Arcem in ea urbe munitissimam[169] tenebat Gebennensis, qui veritus ne civitas ad hostes deficeret, indignationem dissimulabat nihilque sinistrum de Caesenatum[170] facto loquebatur, sed eos multa perpessos indigne, merito simul necessarioque aiebat arma corripuisse; verum ea deponere tandem et ad sua redire multitudinem suadebat. His verbis confisi Caesenates, cum arma deposuissent, accitis propere Anglorum copiis et cum Britonibus coniunctis, per ipsam arcem contra populum inermem deceptumque immisit. Britones vero irati, caedem suorum ulcisci properantes, neque aetati neque sexui pepercerunt, miseram et innocuam multitudinem crudelissime trucidantes. Numerus interemptorum fuit circiter tria millia hominum, urbsque tota hostilem in modum direpta. Nec dubium fuit quin indignatio atque crudelitas Gallorum contra populos Italiae concepta, quasi facultatem nacta, in hac una urbe exprimeretur; idem factura in ceteris, si potestas adfuisset.

119   Eodem anno apud Asculum in Picentibus frequenter pugnatum est. Vendicaverat iampridem ea quoque se civitas in libertatem, sed arci praeerat Gometius quidam hispanus. Is pertinacissime illam defendebat, et a Iohanna regina Siciliae rogatu pontificis bis auxiliares copiae magno conatu eum liberaturae venerunt. Erat

misdeeds by night, and even from time to time inflicted injuries and harassment on the citizenry. As complaints lodged with the legate were of no avail against these actions, and their offenses grew greater each day, the magnitude of their injuries finally made the citizens of Cesena lose patience, and in fury they seized arms and attacked the Bretons, killing more than eight hundred of them and expelling all the rest from the city.

Gebennese controlled an extremely well-fortified citadel in that city. The legate was afraid that the city would defect to the enemy, so he disguised his indignation and said nothing critical of the Cesenans' deed, but rather said that they had suffered much unjustly and that their seizing arms had been right and necessary. But in the end he persuaded the population to lay down their arms and return to their usual tasks. Once the Cesenans, trusting his words, had laid down their arms, he quickly summoned English troops and, combining them with the Bretons, he released them from the citadel itself against the unarmed and deluded people. The angry Bretons lost no time in avenging the slaughter of their fellows and, sparing neither age nor sex, they slaughtered with the utmost cruelty the wretched and harmless populace. The number of those killed was around three thousand, and the whole city was sacked as though it were an enemy town. And there was no doubt that the savage anger the French had conceived against the peoples of Italy, as though it had found an outlet, was being vented on this one city; and the same would be vented on other cities as well if the opportunity should present itself.

In the same year there was much fighting at Ascoli in Piceno. This city, too, had for some time claimed its liberty, but the citadel was commanded by a certain Spaniard named Gomez.[85] He defended it with extreme tenacity, and at the request of the pope was twice sent reinforcements by Queen Johanna of Sicily, who made a great effort to free him. A not inconsiderable force of Florentines and their allies were at Ascoli, and these went out to meet the

118

119

Ascoli Florentinorum sociorumque non contemnenda manus, quae obviam profecta proelio commisso reginae copias profligavit. Quare Gometius, cum aliam salutis spem nullam intueretur, noctu[171] clam egressus arce, cum paucis comitibus ad Gebennensem pervenit et auxilia rogavit suscepitque. Sed dum[172] reverteretur[173] ac iam prope adesset, invasus subito ab hostibus ac damna gravia perpessus, copias amisit. Ipseque destitutus omni spe, tandem paciscitur, ut recepta uxore et filiis quos in arce reliquerat, ceteris incolumibus abire permissis, arcem dederet. Per hunc modum longo tandem labori finis impositus, et arx multis obsessa mensibus, demum recepta est et ad solum eversa.

120   Eodem anno Gregorius pontifex romanus in Italiam redire constituit, putans multum profuturum, si ipse praesens auctoritate sua rebus gerendis adesset. Habere se copiarum satis arbitrabatur Anglorum Britonumque; amicos quoque ecclesiae per Italiam superesse, quos omnes augere excitareque suo adventu cupiebat. Hac igitur ratione ductus et indignatione saucius, per autumni tempus ex Gallia movens, multis navibus Italiam petere contendit. Eius navigatio difficilis fuit, saepiusque dissipata classis, ut Genuae et Liburni et circum ea loca diutius retineretur. Ad Cornetum finis navigandi factus. Inde Romam pedestri itinere circiter Idus ianuarii pervenit, et ut faciem quandam bonae voluntatis ostenderet, ultro postulavit oratores de pace ad se mitti. Iverunt igitur ad eum Florentinorum legati, qui licet grata fronte suscepti a pontifice fuerint, tamen in re tractanda nihilo molliorem illius animum reppererunt. Itaque, mensem fere apud illum commorati oratores, cum postulata pontificis excedere modum viderentur, Florentiam vacui revertuntur.

121   In consilio autem civium cum et[174] postulata et responsa et cuncta cum pontifice agitata singillatim explicuissent animusque

queen's forces, engaged them in battle and defeated them. Hence Gomez, seeing no other hope of salvation, left the citadel secretly by night and came with a few companions to Gebennese, from whom he asked and received aid. But while he was on his way back and had already drawn near, he was attacked suddenly by enemies and after heavy losses was deprived of his troops. In despair he finally agreed to surrender the citadel, recovering the wife and children he had left in the castle, while the rest of the garrison was allowed to leave unharmed. In this way an end was finally put to long toil, and the citadel besieged for so many months was at length recovered and razed to the ground.

In the same year Pope Gregory decided to return to Italy, believing it would be greatly to his advantage if he himself were present to lend his authority to the conduct of affairs. He reckoned his English and Breton troops were sufficient, and there were also still friends of the Church left in Italy, all of whom he wished to strengthen and motivate by his coming. Induced by this reasoning and smarting with indignation, he set out from France during the autumn and strove to reach Italy in numerous ships. His voyage was a hard one, and the fleet was often scattered, so that he was held up for some time at Genoa, Livorno and nearby places. The voyage ended at Corneto. From there he came by land to Rome, arriving around the 13th of January, and in order to show a facade of good will, as it were, he voluntarily requested ambassadors be sent him to negotiate a peace. Thus the Florentines sent him envoys, who, though received by the pontiff with an outward show of favor, nevertheless discovered in the course of negotiations that his attitude had not softened in the least. Hence, having spent nearly a month with him, the ambassadors returned to Florence emptyhanded, as the pontiff's demands seemed excessive.

In Florence they laid before a council of citizens his demands, their responses, and each detail of the negotiations with the pontiff. It being evident that the pope's attitude had grown more ob-

pontificis durior[175] appareret, contrahendas maiorem in modum vires ac valentius incumbendum providendumque statuerunt. Neque enim parvum existimabatur momentum pontificis in Italiam accessio eiusque auctoritas in rebus atque praesentia. His rationibus inducti, per Bernabovem mediolanensem dedita secreto opera Anglorum multitudo, quae apud pontificem stipendio militabat, relicto pontifice ad Florentinos transivit. Hoc factum est statim ab initio anni insequentis; quae quidem res pontificis amicorumque eius plurimum fregit animos.

122   Per idem tempus octo viris, qui ad curam belli auctoritate publica delecti fuerant, prorogatum imperium est ad menses sex. Id quia saepius factum erat (nam iidem viri ab initio belli ad illud usque tempus continuaverant), magnam illis apud multos conflarat invidiam. Et carpebantur iam eorum acta et factionibus oppugnabantur. Quae cum audiisset pontifex, ad augendam octo virorum invidiam oratores suos Florentiam misit. Literae pontificis non ad magistratum, uti consueverat, sed ad populum scribebantur; ipsique oratores non alibi quam in concione populi mandata promere velle affirmabant. Data illis contio est, quamquam non ignorabatur pontificis factum missionemque illam oratorum non ad pacem, sed ad seditionem discordiamque civium spectare. Verum in civitate populari audientiam populi flagitantibus denegare vix tolerandum videbatur. Lectae igitur ad populum literae ac subinde oratores auditi. Sensus idem orationis literarumque fuit culpam a populo levare ac in gubernatores reipublicae transferre. Itaque corripi eos emendarique iubebat. Ea multi laetis auribus perceperunt propter octo virorum malivolentiam. At enim multitudo populi, quae invidia illorum honoris non tangebatur, sed

durate, the citizens decided that still larger forces should be assembled and vigorously set about making provisions to this end. They reckoned that the coming of the pope to Italy and his presence and authority in affairs was not a matter of small moment. On this account they secretly took steps, through Bernabò of Milan, to get the English host serving the pope as mercenaries to leave the pontiff and transfer its allegiance to the Florentines. This was done immediately after the beginning of the following year, and 1377 this move did much to shatter the confidence of the pope and his friends.

Around the same time, the Eight, who had been chosen by 122 public authority to conduct the war, had their powers extended for another six months. Since this had been done very often (for the same men had continued in office from the beginning of the war right down to this time), it had stirred up against them great envy on the part of many persons. Already their actions were being criticized and opposed by factions. When the pope heard this he sent ambassadors to Florence to increase the ill-will against the Eight. The pope's letters were not addressed to the magistrates, as usual, but to the people, and the ambassadors themselves confirmed that they would not present their charge anywhere else but at a public assembly. An assembly was granted them, although it was known what the pontiff was up to, and that his ambassadors' mission was not to make peace but to stir up sedition and discord among the citizenry. But it seemed scarcely tolerable in a popular state to deny those who were requesting it an audience with the people. So the letters were read to the people and afterwards the ambassadors were listened to. The substance of the speech and the letters alike was to exculpate the people and blame the governors of the republic. Thus the pope bade the latter be censured and corrected. Many were delighted to hear these words, owing to their ill will towards the Eight. Yet the mass of the people, which was unaffected by envy of the honor those magistrates held but approved

facta magnifica industriamque probabat, non satis aequo animo verba oratorum audivit. Ita frustra locuti ad populum deteriorem potius rem quam meliorem effecere. Quare haud multo post contempta pontificis auctoritate interdicti observatio sublata est ac celebrare per urbem agrumque cunctis in templis sacerdotes iussi; octo virisque in annum est imperium prorogatum. Haec omnia contumaciter facta mentem pontificis percussere, ut iam quasi domita insolentia, sentiret in potestate voluntateque exhibentium reverentiam consistere gratuitoque illam praestari.[176]

123   Per haec ipsa tempora Iohannes Arretinorum praesul rempublicam invadere conatus est. Huius rei motus a Gregorio pontifice romano[177] nascebatur, affectante annitenteque pontifice civitatem illam a Florentinorum societate disiungere. Adversus igitur hunc motum cives primo pavidi ignorantesque convenere; mox intellecto periculo, cum arma corripuissent, factio praesulis superata fractaque resedit. Ipse vero praesul Arretio pulsus est, aedesque illius crematae, et de quibusdam propinquis agnatisque eius supplicium sumptum.

124   Eodem anno Rodulphus[178] Varanius camerinensis, qui florentini dux exercitus esse consueverat, ad hostes defecit. Nam cum Fabrianum intrasset, cuius[179] oppidani ad libertatem conspirantes Florentinorum sociorumque auxilia convocarant, ipse cupiditate opportunitateque finitimi oppidi allectus, in potestate sua illud retinuit; nec flagitantibus iubentibusque octoviris dimittere Fabrianum voluerat. Hinc indignatio coorta transeundi ad hostes causa fuit. Eius transitio, quia secretorum conscius putabatur, vehementer grata fuit Gregorio, et honore ducatuque gentium illum

of their great accomplishments and hard work, heard the ambassadors' words with a degree of hostility. Thus the ambassadors' audience with the people turned out to be counter-productive. As a result, shortly thereafter, observation of the interdict was lifted in
defiance of the pope's authority, and priests were ordered to celebrate Mass in churches throughout the city and territory; and the
powers of the Eight were extended for a year. All these acts of defiance had an impact on the pope's attitude, so that he now
brought his arrogance under control, realizing that reverential respect was something freely offered, something that lay within the
power and will of those who displayed it.[86]

Around this time Giovanni, the bishop of Arezzo, tried to seize   123
possession of the state. The impulse for this uprising came from
Pope Gregory, who was trying to detach that city from its alliance
with the Florentines. At first the citizens assembled in fear and ignorance to oppose the coup; then learning of their danger, they
seized arms, and the bishop's faction, having been overcome and
broken up, was neutralized. The bishop himself was expelled from
Arezzo, his dwelling was burned down, and certain of his associates and male relatives were executed.

In the same year Ridolfo da Camerino, who had been captain   124
of the Florentine army, defected to the enemy. He had entered
Fabriano, whose inhabitants, joining together to seek liberty, had
called in aid from the Florentines and their allies. Tempted by
greed and by the opportunities presented by the neighboring
town, he kept it in his own power and would not let it go, despite
the requests and commands of the Eight. He became angry as a
result [of their interference], and this was the reason for his going
over to the enemy. His defection was deeply gratifying to Gregory,
for Ridolfo was thought to be privy to secrets, and the pope rewarded him with honors and the command of troops, putting under him fifteen hundred Breton knights. Relying on them he began aggressively to harass the peoples bordering on Camerino and

adauxit, traditis sibi britonum equitum mille quingentis. Quibus ille fretus finitimos Camerino Fabrianoque populos vexare infestius coepit. Contra vero octoviri sic indigne tulerunt illius fraudem,[180] ut ad portas plateasque urbis effigiem[181] eius cum dedecorosis vitiorum notis[182] depingi fecerint. Nec multo post, copiis contra illum missis Fabrianum ipsum, cuius gratia transitionem fecerat, sibi ademerunt.

125   Per extremum eius anni de pace cum pontifice agi[183] coeptum est, auctore ac[184] suasore Bernabove mediolanensi. Inclinabat autem pontificis animum ad pacem labascens rerum italicarum spes, minimeque respondens expectationi successus sui adventus. Rursus vero Florentinos inflectebat longitudo belli, et quod Bononienses, gratia quorum magna ex parte contentiones tantae ac tam graves erant susceptae, paulo ante cum pontifice redierant in gratiam, et arma adversus illum penitus deposuerant. Ita volentibus cunctis Serezanae conventus indicitur, oratoresque eo missi rem agitare coeperunt, praesente Bernabove ac disceptante.

126   Dum haec eo in loco[185] agitarentur, spesque foret optima rem confectum iri, supervenit pontificis inopina mors, per id maxime tempus, in quo pacis conclusio expectabatur. Gregorius enim pontifex romanus, cum ex Anania urbe Romam rediisset circiter Kalendas aprilis octavo et septuagesimo anno supra mille trecentos, intolerabili vesicae dolore interiit. Ea res nunciata conventum Serezanae dissolvit, deficiente iam auctore, ac properantibus cunctis sibi ipsis in rebus novis consulere.

127   Post huius pontificis obitum graviores casus in ecclesia subsecuti cuncta maiorem in modum turbavere, ut de pace iam cum Florentinis facienda aut de reparando per Italiam ecclesiae statu minime omnium cogitaretur. Sumpsit vero initium turbatio ex

Fabriano. The Eight were so angered by his dishonest conduct that they caused his effigy to be painted by the gates and in the piazzas of the city with shameful descriptions of his notorious moral failings. Shortly thereafter, they sent out against him troops who took Fabriano away from him, the town for whose sake he had defected.

At the end of the year peace negotiations with the pope began, 125 at the instance and urging of Bernabò of Milan. The pontiff's heart was turning to peace with the breakup of his Italian affairs, whose outcome did not correspond at all to the expectations he had had upon his arrival. The length of the war had altered the Florentine attitude as well, especially as the Bolognese, on whose account they had taken on so many serious struggles, had shortly before come back into favor with the pope and had entirely laid down their arms, opposing him no longer. Since all parties favored it, a congress was announced at Sarzana, and the ambassadors sent there began to negotiate, with Bernabò present to act as an arbitrator.

While negotiations were going on in that place, and there was 126 good hope that the matter would be brought to a close, there occurred the unlooked-for death of the pope, precisely at the time when the conclusion of the peace was expected. For the Roman pontiff, after returning to Rome from the city of Anagni around the first of April, 1378, died of an unbearable pain in his bladder. 1378 When the news was announced, the congress of Sarzana was dissolved, the man responsible for it being now dead, and everyone hastened to consult his own interests in this new state of affairs.[87]

After the death of this pontiff, the more serious crises that fol- 127 lowed threw everything into still greater confusion, so that hardly any thought was given to making peace with the Florentines or recovering the Papal State in Italy. The disturbance took its origin from the following cause. After the death of Pope Gregory and the celebration of his funeral rites, when the fathers had entered their

huiusmodi causa. Gregorio pontifice Romae defuncto solemnibusque in funere peractis, cum ingressi conclave patres de succes-
sore deligendo cogitarent, insurgens romana plebs, nullius certi
hominis impulsu, sed suopte ingenio permota, romanum pontificem ex civibus romanis[186] vel saltem ex italicis creari debere clamitabat; satis enim superque Gallos regnasse in romana sede; iam ad
cives romanos italosque redire honorem illum debere. Haec dicta
postulataque cum non inconsona rationi viderentur, augetur tumultus, crescensque multitudo palatia adusque conclaveque pervenit. Patres conterriti, quoniam romanus vel italus eligi postula-
batur, Bartholomeum archiepiscopum barensem, natione italum,
patria neapolitanum, elegerunt. Hunc et posteris diebus, cessante
iam metu, venerari ut pontificem perseverarunt. Sed fuit in illo
homine natura inquieta et dura, et tunc, praeter spem ad tantae dignitatis fastigium sublevatus, intolerabilis videbatur. Nulla patribus gratia quod se potissimum delegissent, nulla humanitas, nulla
conciliatio animorum; contumax et minabundus et asper malebat
videri, et metui potius quam diligi.

128   Ea perversitas patres coegit metu et indignatione aliorsum respicere. Itaque clam inter se de electione conquesti, cum et metum
et violentiam populi romani accusarent, abire a novo pontifice omnes ferme coeperunt, et in propinqua sese oppida recipere. Mox
hortantibus alios aliis apud Fundos Campaniae urbem conventu
facto, quasi prima electio vitiosa fuisset, alterum pontificem elegerunt. Fuit autem Fundis electus pontifex Gebennensis, ille qui
legatus in Italiam cum Britonibus transierat. Hinc iam divisio in
ecclesia, duoque simul capita fuere. Nominati sunt autem qui
Romae creatus est Urbanus; qui vero Fundis electus fuerat Clemens; divisique christianorum populi huic vel illi adhaeserunt.
Haec divisio quadraginta ferme annos in ecclesia duravit, usque ad

conclave and were giving thought to choosing a successor, the Roman plebs rose up, seemingly of their own accord and not at the instance of any identifiable person, and called vociferously for the Roman pope to be elected from among the citizens of Rome, or at least of Italy. The French (they said) had reigned for long enough, and more than enough, in the Roman see; and now was the time for that honor to return to the citizens of Rome and Italy. These demands seemed not inharmonious with reason, and so the tumult increased, and the growing mob came right up to the palace and conclave. The fathers were terrified, and since the demand was for a Roman or Italian to be elected, they chose Bartolomeo, the archbishop of Bari, an Italian from Naples. They continued to do him reverence as pope even in the days that followed, when their fears had subsided. But the man had a difficult and unquiet nature, and after being raised unexpectedly to the highest rank, he seemed to become intolerable. He gave no thanks to them for having appointed him in particular; he showed no kindness or desire for reconciliation; he preferred to appear proud and unyielding, menacing and pitiless; he would rather be feared than loved.

Such perversity compelled the fathers to look elsewhere out of   128
fear and indignation. So, complaining secretly among themselves about the election, and blaming the fear and violence caused by the Roman people, practically all of them began to leave the new pontiff and retire to a nearby town. Soon, at their mutual urging a meeting was held at the city of Fondi in Campania and, as though the first election had been flawed, they chose a new pontiff. The pope elected at Fondi was Gebennese, the legate who had come to Italy with the Bretons.[88] Hence there was now a schism in the Church, and there were two heads at the same time. The one created in Rome was named Urban,[89] while the one elected in Fondi was called Clement; and the Christian people were divided, cleaving to this or that pontiff. This schism in the Church lasted almost forty years, up to the time of Martin V, who was made pope

Martinum quintum, qui constantiensi concilio pontifex factus est, sublata penitus divisione.

129   Sed haec postea; nos ad nostra revertamur tempora. Mortuo Gregorio pontifice turbatio ecclesiae fecit ut de pace vel bello cum Florentinos non amplius cogitaretur. Itaque deposita hinc inde sunt arma tacito quodam consensu, non expressa pactione. In divisione autem ecclesiae Florentini Urbano adhaeserunt.[187]

by the Council of Constance, when the schism was completely healed.

But this happened later; let us return to the earlier time. With 129
the death of Pope Gregory, the disturbance in the Church caused
there to be no further thought of peace or war with the Florentines. Thus arms were laid down on either side by a kind of tacit
consent rather than by formal agreement. In the Schism, however,
the Florentines adhered to Urban.[90]

Note on the Text

❧❧❧

Since the publication of volume I (Books I–IV) of this text in 2001,[1] the editor has become aware of the importance of a manuscript not collated for volume I, namely codex Amiatinus 4 of the Laurentian Library. This manuscript, copied by Bruni's favorite copyist, Giovanni da Stia, contains autograph corrections (hitherto unrecognized as such), similar to those described by Paolo Viti in "Un antologia di opere di Leonardo Bruni: Il manoscritto Laurenziano 52, 5," *Rinascimento*, n. s. 33 (1993): 157–161. It also contains what appears to be an authorized list of Bruni's works, indicating that the manuscript may have been intended to serve as an authentic copy of author's archetype, now lost. The Amiatinus has now been collated for this volume and the volume to follow. On the other hand, the readings of Ashburnham 869 (M), collated for volume I, are not reported in this volume as they cannot claim any special authority and do not offer good readings not found in other manuscripts.

Collation of the Amiatinus has altered somewhat the present editor's view of the text. It seems clear that, for Books I–VI, *BCF* and *AP* belong to different families reflecting different stages in the correction and revision of the text. In a few cases *F* shares readings with *AP* and may thus represent an intermediate stage in the revision of the archetype. For Books VII–XII the situation is more complex. *BC* and *AP* still appear to represent distinct stages of revision (though *P* now seems more remote from *A*, which lacks Bruni's correcting hand for Books VII–XII). *L*, another (but much later) copy by Giovanni da Stia, represents a still later stage of the text as the collation of Book IX shows beyond doubt. *L* has several omissions and at least one sentence not found in the other

witnesses, but whether the omissions are mistakes or *pentimenti* it is not easy to decide. The extra sentence (see 7.76) reads pleonastically to modern ears, as something a modern writer might cut on revision. But it may not have seemed so to Bruni, whose writing, especially in the later books, is often rhetorically full, even redundant, and reads as though parts of it were dictated.

Choosing between variant readings offered by two manuscripts, copied within six months of each other and both corrected by the author, raises some nice questions of philological method. In general I have of course accepted all corrections made in Bruni's hand, and have usually but not always accepted corrections made by the scribes Antonio di Mario (*B*) and Giovanni da Stia (*A*), who wrote the MSS. corrected by Bruni. Giovanni was the more careful scribe and Bruni's corrections in *A* show greater care than his less frequent interventions in *B*. Bruni was a careful corrector, but not a systematic one. We cannot assume that he collated each word against his archetype — and indeed such a procedure is hardly attested for the textual scholarship of the early fifteenth century. It is entirely possible that other early copies made from the author's archetype contain correct readings not found even in the copies corrected by the author, and my apparatus reflects this state of affairs. Such problems await definitive solution. Absent a complete recension and full-dress critical edition we must fall back on Bentley's dictum, *Nobis et ratio et res ipsa centum codicibus potiores sunt.*

I am grateful to my former research assistant, Antoinette Sutto, now of Princeton University, for transferring Santini's text of Books V–XII to digital form. Paola Tartakoff, now of Columbia University, and Leah Wittington prepared collations of *B*, *C*, *F* and *P*, and I am most grateful for their help. As in the case of volume 1, I have verified personally against photographs each of the variants thus identified, and I have myself collated witnesses *A*

and *L*. My thanks also to Elizabeth Mellyn, who compiled the Index.

As announced in volume 1, Volume 3 will contain the remainder of the *History* (Books IX–XII) as well as Bruni's *Memoirs*, translated by Canon D. J. W. Bradley of Salisbury Cathedral.

A   Florence, Biblioteca Medicea Laurenziana, MS Amiatinus 4, with autograph corrections in books I–VI only. Copied by Giovanni da Stia in three separate phases: (1) Books I–VI in 1429; (2) Books VII–IX before 1438; (3) Books X–XII, c. 1440. See A. C. de la Mare, "New Research on Humanistic Scribes in Florence," in Annarosa Garzelli, *Miniatura fiorentina del Rinascimento, 1440–1525: Un primo censimento* (Florence, 1985), I, p. 499; *Repertorium brunianum*, no. 628.

B   Bologna, Biblioteca Universitaria MS 358. Books I–VI copied by Antonio di Mario in 1429; these books also contain some autograph corrections. The basis of Santini's text for Books I–VI. See vol. I, and the review of Griggio cited below in the note.

C   Florence, Biblioteca Medicea Laurenziana, Plut. 65, 5. "Antonius Marii filius Florentinus civis atque notarius transcripsit Florentiae ex originali Idibus Iunias MCCCCXLIIII." See vol. 1.

F   Florence, Biblioteca Medicea Laurenziana, Plut. 65, 3. Contains Books I–VI only. Copied by Giovanni da Stia and Antonio di Mario. See vol. 1.

L   Florence, Biblioteca Medicea Laurenziana, Plut. 65, 4. The basis of Santini's text for Books VII–XII. This is the second volume of a copy whose first volume is Plut. 65, 3 [F], containing Books I–VI. It is signed at the end (f. 113v): "Johannes Petri de Stia notarius florentinus scripsit anno domini MCCCCXLVIIII." However, Books VII–IX, written by Giovanni da Stia, Antonio di Mario, and

an anonymous scribe, are codicologically distinct from the rest of the volume and were probably copied around 1438. See J. Hankins, *Repertorium Brunianum: A Critical Guide to the Writings of Leoanardo Bruni* (Rome, 1997), no. 517.

P   For Books I–VI, copied from an uncorrected *A* (or *A*'s uncorrected source, or an uncorrected copy of *A*). Books VII-XII are less closely related to *A*.

Acc   The Tuscan translation by Donato Acciaiuoli (1473)
Sant   The edition of Santini
[ ]   Editorial deletions
< >   Editorial additions

NOTE

1. I am aware of only one substantive review, that by Claudio Griggio in *Lettere italiane* 55 (2003): 143–147, with useful comments on the presence of Dante in the early books of the *History* and new observations about the text in *B*.

Notes to the Text

꙱ꙮꙮ

BOOK V

Tit.: Historiarum Florentini
Populi liber quartus explicit;
incipit quintus *F*: incipit
liber quintus *AB*: Historie
Florentine liber quintus
incipit *P*

1. forsan *BCF*
2. Ianuenses *BCF*
3. lunensem *P*
4. fretis . . . fautoribus *P*
5. pars magna *CF* (*B illegible*)
6. coniuncti *CF* (*B illegible*)
7. obviam *om. BCF, Sant*
8. conspectu *BCF*
9. his *P, Sant*
10. nitebantur *P, Sant*
11. -que *om. P, A before correction*
12. Atque *P, A before correction*
13. agmine *AP*
14. insigni *BCF, Sant*
15. *om. AP*
16. in Arnum *Sant*
17. dederunt *A*
18. statu *ABCFP*: statui *Sant*
    (*recte*)
19. -issima *P*
20. In his] Intus *P, A before
    correction*
21. *om. AP*
22. ferme vigilia *BCF*: vigilia

ferme *P, A before deletion*
(ferme *deleted in A*)
23. conclamata *BC*
24. auxilia *BCF* (*B apparently
    corrected from* auxiliares),
    Sant: auxiliares *AP*
25. protectorem gubernatorem
    transp. AP
26. Rexque *BCF*
27. tamquam *corrected from*
    quam *by Bruni in A*: quasi
    BCF, Sant: tamquam . . .
    proclivis *om. P*
28. terraque mari *AP*: terraque
    marique *Sant*
29. -que *om. Sant*
30. rei *om. AP*
31. a Lucensibus *after*
    Calamitates *C*: *before*
    maximae *BF, Sant*
32. crederetur *BCF, Sant*
33. -erat *AP*
34. formido Pisanos *transp. AP*
35. summaque *BCF*
36. *om. BCF, Sant*
37. *om. BCF, Sant*
38. tandem *om. BCF, Sant*
39. deturbabatur *F*
40. graviorque . . . imminebat
    om. AP

41. impenderet *BCF, Sant*
42. singulis in annis *C*
43. -que *BCF, added in Bruni's hand in A: omitted by P, Sant*
44. deligerunt *A*
45. Petrus *after correction in F*
46. Erat . . . frater *om. F*
47. erat *BCF, Sant*
48. hostibus aditum *transp. BCF, Sant*
49. autem *after Ugucio BCF, Sant*
50. requiemque *after correction in A:* requietemque *BCFP*
51. illius *BCF, Sant*
52. permittant *BC*
53. descendit *AP:* descenderet *Sant*
54. ut *AP*
55. *om. AP*
56. cisalpina *F*
57. ferme *BCF, Sant*
58. prior *BCF*
59. *om. AP*
60. praefectionem *BC*
61. Dum *CP*
62. castellum *BCF, Sant*
63. lucensem *P*
64. hostis *BCF, after correction (from* hoste*) in A:* hoste *P, A before correction*
65. *Sant corrects silently to* discidit
66. pollicere *BF, before correction in C*
67. perpetuo *after* postea *BF, Sant*

68. observatum *BCF, Sant*
69. Talomeorum *BCF, after correction in A*
70. Lucae *C*
71. tunc *after* igitur *BCF, Sant*
72. -retur *BCF*
73. insuper *BCF, Sant*
74. At *CP,* B *before correction*
75. manus *BCF*
76. *BCF, added after correction by Bruni in A: om. P*
77. faciebant *BCF*
78. quidem *AP*
79. ac *om. BCF*
80. fidelissimorumque *after correction in C*
81. vident (= viderunt) *BCF:* viderent *AP*
82. rediderunt *AP:* dediderunt *CF,* B *after correction*
83. venire *F*
84. reducendis . . . copiis *AP*
85. puerorum *om. BCF*
86. tota *F*
87. pro- *BCF*
88. Pratum *C*
89. exercitus reditum] exercitum *BCF, Sant*
90. atque *AP, Sant*
91. clientum *P, Sant*
92. detrectandi *C*
93. -si utrumque *added in the margin of A in Bruni's hand: om. P*

94. conditio promissione *P*:
    promissio in conditione *BC*
95. et literis sigillisque] literis et
    sigillis *F*
96. collocato *AP*
97. Quo *C*: Quid *F*
98. fere *C*
99. locus *A*
100. eorum *C* (*see next note*)
101. illorum *BCF, Sant*
102. fieret *C*
103. civitas *added in the margin of*
    A in Bruni's hand: om. P
104. *om. BCF*
105. mihi prius *BC, Sant*: prius
    om. F
106. vacuam reperire *BCF, Sant*
107. breviter mea *A before*
    correction, BCFP, Sant
108. *Written superscript by Bruni in*
    A: om. P
109. -dum *AF, before correction in*
    B
110. *Written superscript by Bruni in*
    A: om. P
111. nemo *after* Hos *BCF, A*
    before correction
112. auderet accusare *C, before*
    correction in B
113. promptum nomen *BCF*
114. recludebatur *AP*
115. popularitate *A after correction*
    by Bruni, BCF: populariter *P*
116. et amicos] amicosque *BCF,*
    Sant

117. urbem *F*
118. ibique *BCF, Sant*
119. *BCF, added superscript by*
    Bruni in A: om. P
120. urgent (=urserunt) *BCF*:
    urgerent *AP*
121. huius *BCF*
122. circumque ea loca *om. AP*
123. Tydicius *AP*: ?Tydicius
    erased, followed by
    Pistoriensis *B*: Tydicius
    Pistoriensis *C*: Tedicius
    Pistoriensis *F*: Era in Pistoia
    uno Filippo Tedici *Acc*
124. iniuriis *added in the margin of*
    A by Bruni: om. P
125. Mox . . . faceret *omitted by*
    the scribes of AP: Mox a
    civibus revocatum *added by*
    Bruni in the margin of A
126. fuit *F*
127. agitabat *BCF, Sant*
128. Bordo *BCF, Sant*: Boldoni
    Acc
129. dimittit *AP*
130. apennino *C*
131. paludium *A, B before*
    correction: paludum *P*
132. ut *Sant: om. P, add s.s. A*
133. adduxit *AP*
134. adducere *C*
135. *om. AP*
136. *om. P: added in the margin by*
    Bruni in A
137. et *BCF*

138. praesidio *AP*
139. quisque *BCF*
140. Interim *AP*
141. destinere *F*
142. occiderunt *C*: cecidere *AP*
143. maiora sunt *BCF, Sant*
144. qua *AP*
145. decucurrerunt *BCF, Sant*
146. terrore *ACP*
147. hostes *AP*
148. cum *BCF, Sant*
149. mox *BCF*
150. expugnationem *BCF*
151. ferme *BCF*
152. rursus agmine *BCF, Sant*
153. fuerat *AP*
154. viam *BCF*
155. omnia complebat *BCF, Sant*
156. etiam *BCF*
157. transitu *after* facto *BCF*
158. milites *post* castruciani *AP*
159. continuis *C*
160. Huiusce *BCF, Sant*
161. *om. BCF, Sant*
162. *om. BCF, Sant*
163. *om. AP*
164. de *BCF*
165. *added superscript by Bruni in A: om. P*
166. quidem *P, A before correction*
167. *om. AP*
168. partium *after* diversae *P, Sant, before erasure in A*
169. omnium *BCF, Sant*: d'ognuno *Acc*: hominum *AP*

170. incensus *AP*
171. *added superscript by Bruni in A: om. P*
172. *om. BCF*
173. *added in the margin by Bruni in A: om. P*
174. *added superscript by Bruni in A: om. P*
175. *om. BCF*
176. *added in the margin by Bruni in A: om. P*
177. *added superscript by Bruni in A and B: om. FP*
178. suis nequaquam suis *BCF*
179. copias detineret] suos contineret *BCF, Sant*
180. induxit *BCF*
181. in Galliam adventu *BCF*
182. omnino *after* portis *BCF, Sant*
183. per Etruriam *om. AP*
184. hi *BCF, Sant*
185. gravissimi et sapientissimi *BCF*
186. Anseri *P*: Auferi *Sant*
187. admirari *BCF*
188. quesitus . . . obsidionem (e superiori parte) ve- *omitted in P and before correction in A*
189. e superiori parte *om. A, even after correction*
190. a me (ve)nire *before correction in A]* advenire *P (probably a scribal conjecture);* venire *added in marg. in B*

191. se BCF, A *after correction:* sed
P, Sant, A *before correction*
192. fraudium A, B *before*
correction, Sant
193. aperte inclinare AP
194. motus *after* praesul BCF,
Sant
195. Romam solum AP
196. populi nomine *om.* AP
197. unum hunc AP
198. -que BCF, *added superscript*
(by Bruni?) in A: *om.* P, Sant
199. esse *after* relictum AP
200. *om.* BCF
201. Ipse quoque] ipseque BCF,
Sant
202. Tandemque AP
203. refracta ac cremata BCF: r.
atque c. Sant
204. tubaeque simul et classica
militumque BCF, Sant: tubae
tunc et classica militum P
205. nec quidem *after correction in*
A: et quidem non BCFP, Sant
206. praedaeque intentos *om.* AP
207. rem nefariam AP
208. *om.* BCF, Sant
209. his BCFP, Sant
210. detinuit AP, tenne *Acc*
211. queat AP

212. tuba BCF
213. ubi AP
214. *corrected to* conatus *by Sant*
215. umquam *after* ex re BCF,
Sant
216. omni AP
217. simul *om.* AP
218. -retur BCF
219. maxime AC
220. possent BCF, Sant
221. *om.* BCF, Sant
222. -erant AP
223. *added in the margin by Bruni*
in A: *om.* P
224. *om.* FP
225. -que *om.* BCF
226. merum populare alterum
om. Sant
227. *om.* AP
228. videbatur BCF, Sant
229. ii AP
230. pecuniam AP
231. iisdem in locis A *after*
correction by the scribe: in *om.*
BCFP
232. pelluntur BCF
233. prodire BCF
234. Historiarum Florentini
populi liber quintus explicit
ABCF

BOOK VI

Tit: Incipit liber sextus A: Incipit
VI B: Incipit liber VI CF:

Historie Florentine liber
quintus incipit P

1. iis *BCF, Sant*
2. sine ulla cunctatione *om. AP*
3. pecunia Germanis *BCF:* Germanis *om. P*
4. de his *before* ad populum *AP:* hiis *C*
5. vobis *P, Sant*
6. his *BCFP*
7. vobis *BCFP*
8. ablatum *A*
9. -que *om. BC, Sant:* quam *F*
10. gravia *CP*
11. huius *AFP, before correction in B*
12. perveniret *CF, before correction in A*
13. acciperimus *BCF*
14. vobis *BC, Sant*
15. Pinus *FP:* Primus *C*
16. indixit *C, before correction in F*
17. iis *A:* is *C*
18. fuerunt *F, Sant, A before correction, B before correction*
19. Lucam *P, A after correction*
20. qua in urbe *F*
21. Adfuitque *BC* (-que *deleted in A*)
22. *om. AP*
23. bello *AP*
24. lucensique *CP*
25. -que *om. AP*
26. fossaque *AP*
27. *om. AP*

28. priora *AP*
29. proeliumque *AP*
30. *om. AP*
31. pedum *AP*
32. cum *BCF*
33. in potestate *s.s. in Bruni's hand in A:* potestate *om. P*
34. in praesentia *om. AP*
35. haud multo post *om. AP:* non molto di poi *Acc*
36. erat *AP*
37. dedentes *Sant*
38. apparerent *BC*
39. ac *AP*
40. contra paene *AP*
41. hi *BCF*
42. istiusmodi *BCF*
43. eius *AP*
44. *s.s. A: om. P*
45. haberet *AP*
46. ut ab illo *C*
47. admirationi cuiquam *BC*
48. tum *P:* tunc etiam *om. F*
49. communiverat *AP*
50. intra *P:* circa *F*
51. admoverant *A after correction*
52. iis *A*
53. erat *BC*
54. iis *A*
55. monimenta *A:* monumenta *BCF*
56. erat *F*
57. simul legati *BC:* legati simulque regis *F*

58. iniuriam *AP*
59. convenerant *AFP*
60. *om. AP*
61. pervenisse *AP*
62. *emended silently by Sant to* occupata; *see also below, 6.100.*
63. conversiones *BCFP, Sant: corrected to* conversationes *in Bruni's hand in A*
64. agri *F*
65. modum se *AP*
66. *added in the margin of B: om.* AFP
67. *om. AP*
68. *corrected to* componat *by Bruni in both A and B:* componit *FP*
69. promit *BCF, after correction in A (i.e., syncope for* promisit*):* promittit *P, before correction in A:* essere di bisogno *Acc*
70. -bantur *AP*
71. belli gallici belli *AFP*
72. *added by Bruni in A: om. P*
73. *om. AP*
74. tota paene *BCF*
75. hi *BCF*
76. omnibus confestim *BCF*
77. postera *BC*
78. in his locis habebat *BCF*
79. castrorum *AP*
80. Florentini et Perusini *BC, before correction in P*
81. *om. AP*

82. *om. AP, Sant*
83. multaque *Sant*
84. his *BCF*
85. urbem *AP, before correction in B*
86. redierunt omnes *BC*
87. huiuscemodi *BCF*
88. se ipsum *om. AP*
89. *Sant emends silently to* potestate: potestatem *mss.*
90. hi *BCF*
91. *erased in B, om. C*
92. cura *F, Sant*
93. cum vestrum . . . bellum *om. AP*
94. *s.s. in Bruni's hand A: om. P*
95. *s.s. in Bruni's hand A: om. P*
96. hoc *AFP*
97. concidere *AP*
98. eodem loco *AP*
99. Iam enim *F*
100. umquam *AP, Sant*
101. fuerunt equitum *A*
102. *om. BCF, Sant*
103. tetro (*s.s.*) horrendoque *A:* horrendoque tetro *P:*
104. ipse vero . . . missus *om. AP*
105. extimabatur (*sc.* aestimabatur) *BCF*
106. Florentini *P*
107. Florentinis *P*
108. habere *A*
109. *Sant silently conjectures* defessi, *perhaps correctly*

110. *om.* A
111. conquierunt *BCF*
112. tempestatem *AP, before correction in F*
113. des(a)evisset *P:* deservisset *Sant*
114. hi *BCF*
115. illorum *BCF*
116. per infimum pontem *om.* A
117. facultate *C, B before correction, Sant*
118. teneri ab eo *B, Sant*
119. etiam *C: om.* P
120. *in marg. B: om. AF*
121. iis *A*
122. Nardus *AP*
123. fuerant *BCF*
124. congressu] congressi impetu *BCF*
125. *om.* A
126. obsessis *AFP, before correction in B*
127. in dies *om.* A
128. experiri nequaquam *A*
129. -erant *AC, B before correction*
130. fluvium *AP*
131. seseque hortantes *C:* sese cohortantes *F*
132. in eo proelio *F:* eo proelio *P*
133. fuerant *BC*
134. lacerabantur *BC*
135. his *BCF*
136. *corrected to* integrum *by a second hand (Bruni's?) in B*

137. esse in civitate consueverat *C:* in civitate consueverat esse *AP*
138. aliosque *AP, B before correction:* aliasque *F*
139. his] in his *AFP, B before correction*
140. Burnellecium *ABCF*
141. hi *BCF*
142. uti *BCF:* ut *A*
143. conspicantes *A:* suspicassent *P*
144. et *A*
145. his *BCF*
146. supplicio *F*
147. discerptim *P, before correction in A*
148. nocte *AFP, B before correction*
149. corripiunt *AF*
150. Historiarum Florentini populi liber sextus explicit *BC:* . . . explicit feliciter. Deo gratias amen *F:* . . . explicit feliciter Deo gratias amen. Anno domini MCCCCXXVIIII, die XXXI, mense Decembri *A:* . . . explicit feliciter. Ego Antonius Marii filius notarius et florentinus civis absolvi Florentiae II Id. Jun. MCCCCXXVIIII. Valeant feliciter legentes *B*

BOOK VII

Tit.: Historiarum florentini
populi liber septimus
incipit. Leonardi opus lege
feliciter *AL*: Historiarum
florentini populi liber
settimus incipit *B*: Incipit
liber VII. Prosequere
feliciter *C*: Historie
Florentine liber septimus
incipit *P*

1. omnia *BC*: d'ognuno *Acc*
2. societas *C*
3. societas *C*
4. torpore *BC*
5. deiectionem *L, Sant*
6. multitudinis experiri] populi
exprobare *BC*
7. confligat atque collidat *BL*]
collidat *AC*
8. propter egregiam *om. A*
9. atque *ALP*
10. insana *P*
11. confirmare *P*
12. Hi *BCL*
13. vicinae *C before correction,
Sant*
14. -bant *AL, Sant*: diceva *Acc*
15. improbissima *BC*
16. *om. L, Sant*
17. est *after* habitus *C*
18. quo regis . . . teneretur *om.
BC*
19. recepta *L, Sant*
20. duae leges *BC*

21. toto *ACP, L before correction*
22. fuisset . . . in manibus *om.
L, Sant*
23. *om. C*
24. pro- *A*
25. *om. BC*
26. quod spatium . . . colligendi
om. L, Sant
27. eius *C*
28. quoque *A*
29. eo anno *after* oppidum *AL,
Sant*
30. laborabant *P*
31. sibi vindicantem *om. A*
32. et *B, C before correction*
33. ignorentur *ABCL*
34. *om. L, Sant*
35. igitur *C*
36. cognos- *A*
37. *after* eos *s.s. L, Sant*
38. urbem ingressa *L before
correction, Sant*
39. suscepto a suis dominio *L,
Sant*: dominatu *A*
40. *om. L, Sant*
41. causa *A*
42. re infecta *om. C*
43. patrari *P*
44. *om. A*
45. exercitu *AL, Sant*
46. tria milia *L (partly erased,
perhaps intentionally; compare
7.59)*
47. amplius non *L, Sant*

48. quae *L, Sant*
49. convenerunt *C*
50. experiri *BC*
51. -nes *C*
52. mentis *BC*
53. tamen *BC*
54. iam *C*
55. *om. BC*
56. Petrum quendam *om. BC*
57. descenderant *A*
58. concilio *Sant*
59. et *L, Sant*
60. sit *L, Sant*
61. nec enim . . . consulerem *om. L, Sant (but L has a signe de renvoie as though to insert the missing phrase)*
62. iam *C: om. A*
63. curam *A*
64. Nonnulli *A*
65. *om. A*
66. modo *after* Illud *L (added in the margin by the scribe), Sant*
67. demittantur *AL, Sant:* rimanere *Acc*
68. *om. A*
69. utique *BC*
70. diu *BC*
71. nec *CP*
72. amiciores *Sant*
73. erant *BC*
74. Et enimvero *C*
75. ac *BCL*
76. hi *BCL*

77. fuerint *AP,* B *before correction:* fuerant *L, Sant*
78. commemorant *L, Sant*
79. *om. A (and seemingly Acc)*
80. nec...ullum *ABCP,* L *before correction*
81. supra *L*
82. abusus *Sant*
83. videretur *BCL, Sant*
84. -dum *AL, Sant*
85. quampluris *BCL*
86. potestate *AL*
87. atque meditari . . . coeperunt *om. BC*
88. quoque se iis *BC*
89. hominum *BC*
90. Iis *C*
91. existimarat *C*
92. adversum *LP*
93. pollicentes *BC*
94. id *C*
95. Mediolanensium *AL*
96. ne *AL, Sant*
97. praestitistis *A*
98. deieret *ACLP,* B *before correction*
99. equitatem *sc.* aequitatem *A*
100. sequantur *L, Sant*
101. nostrum *A*
102. *om. A*
103. *om. AL, Sant*
104. in ruinam *om. AL, Sant*
105. ego *AL:* igitur *P*
106. ego *AL*
107. Haec oratio . . . consulenda

*om. ABCP, Acc. See the 'Note
on the Text'.*

108. Itaque *P*
109. urbem *BC*
110. rem *BC*
111. intellexerunt *L*
112. *om. A:* insino allora *Acc*
113. et *BC*
114. vexilli *B, C before correction*
115. strumenta *corrected from*
    instrumenta *L*
116. profundiores . . . fossas *BC:*
    profundiores . . . fossam *P*
117. *om. A*
118. ac *AL*
119. intra *P*
120. Postera vero die] Postero die
    L, Sant
121. ad id comparata *om. A*
122. vero *AL, Sant*
123. cremarunt *AL, Sant*
124. princeps *BC*
125. promoveri *P*
126. aliquis *A*
127. multaque molientes *om. A*
128. -erant *L, Sant*
129. Vocati ergo *BC:* Vocati
    igitur *P*
130. unus eorum *om. BC:*
    Richiesti adunque uno di
    loro *Acc*
131. -rentur *BCP*
132. protraxere *BCP*
133. deduxere *BC*
134. *om. BC*

135. timore *P*
136. ascendisse *BC*
137. *om. AL*
138. Sed cum pertinaciter . . .
    coactus est *om. AL, Sant,*
    Acc
139. adversum *BCL*
140. imperitis *om. BCP*
141. adversum *L, Sant*
142. Iverunt *AL, Sant*
143. erant positi *A*] erant *BLP,*
    Sant: fuerant *C*
144. insidiis *AL, Sant*
145. ingressus *P*
146. quoque *BC*
147. abeundo *C*
148. *om. BC*
149. familiarum *P, Sant*
150. Ea siquidem . . . commissa
    om. L, Sant, Acc
151. -erant *A*
152. eis *om. BC*
153. ad *BC*
154. arbitrii *L*
155. neque enim . . . decere *om.*
    C: dicere *P*
156. atque infestum . . .
    pontificis *om. L, Sant*
157. civitatium *BC*
158. die primo *AL:* die prima
    Sant
159. praeteriturique *P*
160. *om. L, Sant*
161. duce *A*
162. Gucio *L*

163. reducti *A*: perducti *L after correction, Sant*
164. *om. BC*
165. Classem *ALP, B before correction*
166. *om. BC*
167. hisdem *L*
168. iis *BC*
169. *om. BCLP, Sant*
170. bellum intulerint *A*

171. patria sunt *P*: patriae sint *Sant*
172. -aret *A*
173. nisi *AL*
174. actum sit *A*
175. intrare *A*
176. Historiarum florentini populi liber septimus explicit *AC*: Explicit liber settimus *B*: Finis *L*

BOOK VIII

Tit.: Incipit liber VIII *A*: Incipit octavus feliciter *B*: incipit octavus *C*: Historiarum florentini populi liber VIII incipit. Lege feliciter. Leonardi opus *L*: Historie florentine liber octavus incipit *P*
1. est *after* acta *BC*
2. dedito *A*
3. civitatium *B, C before correction*
4. in unum *om. BC*
5. *om. BC*
6. *sic: the scribe of C rightly objects to this usage, writing in the margin:* aut auctor aut scriptor libri erravit.
7. septem (*written out*) *A, L before correction*
8. in futurum moliri *C*: moliri *om. AL*
9. -erunt *L after correction, Sant*

10. -que *om. C*
11. fuerat *C*
12. *om. A*
13. ante *BC*
14. Atqui *Sant*
15. et *Sant*
16. -erint *P, L after correction, Sant*
17. libertatemque *Sant*
18. suis *BC, before correction in L*
19. viam *P*
20. patriam *om. ABCP*
21. redire vis] rediveris *P*
22. recte *A, before correction in L*
23. an improbentur *om. A*
24. ingressus *P, Sant*
25. -abant *L, Sant*
26. *om. A*
27. circumstantes *ABCP*
28. maxima (?) *P*: maximam *Sant*
29. *om. A*
30. habebat civitatem *P*

31. munita *BC*
32. montis *A*
33. -arunt *ABC, L before correction*
34. con- *P, F before correction*
35. peraltas *BC*
36. conabatur *L*
37. vestes *LP, Sant*
38. qui *C*
39. Pisanos *P*
40. et *L*
41. equites *after* Germani *AL*
42. *om. A*
43. his *P*
44. dicentes *A*
45. gloriae nominique *BC*
46. his *P, Santini*
47. ostendebantur *P*
48. conversi erant *BC*
49. his *AP, Sant*
50. transmearunt *C*
51. intercedebant *C, Sant*
52. aliquando *A, before correction in L*
53. lucensem *Sant*
54. et *L*
55. in Galliam] et Galli *P*
56. *om. A*
57. adversus *P*
58. -issimo *BC*
59. pugnatum *A*
60. Firmium *AL*
61. Nicola Azarolus *ABCL*: Nicola Acciauiolus *P*: Nicolas Azzarolus *Sant*

62. *om. Sant*
63. calamitatemque *AL, Sant*
64. emporiumque *P (i.e., as though* Emporium = Empoli)
65. eisque *L*
66. ob haec *om. BC*
67. daturi *AL*
68. *om. C*
69. -que *om. BC*
70. est *om. P, Sant*
71. illius oppidi *om. BC*
72. *om. L, Sant*
73. -que *om. A*
74. castellum pactione ceditur *L* (pactione *added in the margin after* castellum), *Sant*
75. *om. L*
76. *om. C*
77. ingressa *A*
78. et *L*
79. *om. A*
80. rebus gestis *L, Sant*
81. *om. A*
82. correctus *A*
83. meliori *Sant*
84. tribus *AL*
85. *om. A*
86. prolixitate *BC*
87. Ancisa *L*
88. viae *BC*
89. sibi *after* redeundique *in marg. L, om. ABCP*
90. spontaneae *A*
91. *om. A*

92. a *L, Sant*
93. *om. ABCP, Sant*
94. idem *om. BCP*
95. et quoniam . . . permissum est *om. A:* est *only omitted by L, Sant*
96. caesi *P*
97. priores *BC*
98. -dos *L*
99. -natum *Sant*
100. ab hostibus *om. AP*
101. proprius *ABL, C before correction*
102. ut *L, Sant*
103. ingressi *L, Sant*
104. cremaverunt *P, L before correction*
105. Anglicorum *AP, L before correction*
106. peracta *P*
107. his *P*
108. *om. L, Sant*
109. concurrissent undique *ABCP:* undique (*in marg., Bruni's hand?*) concurrissent ~~undique~~ *L*
110. hostem *after correction in L:* hostes *ABCP*
111. reducere *C*
112. prosternuntur *A*
113. haec *L, Sant*
114. proprius *L*
115. *om. BC*
116. Pisis sublevatus *om. BC*
117. *Sant adds* a *after* omnes

118. redderunt *BC*
119. Caroli transitum *L*
120. ad eum *om. L, Sant*
121. pacem . . . factam *L, Sant*
122. *A repeated* optima gratia *cancelled after* populus *B: after* transitu *C*
123. -erant *L, Sant*
124. iis *A*
125. *om. AL*
126. detineri *Sant*
127. Missique *A*
128. ad societatem ineundam *om. BC*
129. preparabant *P*
130. exterserunt *AL*
131. *om. CL, Sant*
132. illi *A*
133. susceptus *A*
134. plenosque haberent *A, L before correction*
135. domitas *BC*
136. centumtrigintamillium *A:* CXXX M *BCLP:* centum et triginta millium *Sant*
137. monendoque *P, Sant*
138. compulerunt *A, before correction in L*
139. his *P*
140. in scientia *A*
141. voluisti *Sant, before correction in A*
142. alienus *A, before correction in L*
143. et ad quos mitterentur *om. P*

144. ad defectionem *om.* A
145. pro- *A*
146. tollenda *added in marg. after* pro *by a second hand in* L: *om.* ABCP
147. velamento *A*
148. autem *after* Haec *AL, Sant*
149. Florentinis *A*
150. pro- *A*
151. Non *BC*
152. *Sant adds* a *after* et
153. *om. L, Sant*
154. firmissimo *Sant*
155. tibi dignus *A*
156. extra *C: B before correction*
157. refugium *Sant*
158. persequaris *L, Sant*
159. tantummodo *L, Sant*
160. statum *BC*
161. et intercapedo aliquot dierum *L* (aliquot dierum *in marg.*), *Sant*
162. pollicere *L*
163. italicos *L, Sant*
164. illi *L*
165. praestante *C*
166. saepius *AL, Sant*

167. -que *om. C*
168. tamen *BC*
169. *om. BC*
170. Caesenatium *L after correction*
171. nocte *A*
172. cum *A*
173. intueretur *C*
174. *om. A*
175. diversior *P*
176. praestare *C, B before correction*
177. *om. L, Sant*
178. *om. A*
179. cives *P*
180. illius fraudem *om. A:* eius fraudem *BC*
181. effigiemque *L*
182. cum . . . notis *om. L, Sant*
183. *om. BC*
184. atque *C*
185. in eo loco *A*
186. *om. L, Sant*
187. Historiarum florentini populi liber octavus explicit *ABC: om. PL*

Notes to the Translation

ఇ§౭ఇ

ABBREVIATIONS

ASF	Florence, Archivio di Stato
Davidsohn, *Storia*	Robert Davidsohn, *Storia di Firenze*, 8 vols. (Florence, 1977).
Perrens, *Histoire*	François Tommy Perrens, *Histoire de Florence depuis ses origines jusqu'à la domination des Médicis*, 6 vols. (Paris, 1877–83).
Stefani, *Cronaca*	Marchionne di Coppo Stefani, *Cronaca fiorentina*, ed. N. Rodolico (Città di Castello, 1903).
Giovanni Villani, *Cronica*	Giovanni Villani, *Nuova Cronica*, ed. G. Porta, 3 vols. (Parma, 1990–91).
Matteo Villani, *Cronica*	Matteo Villani, *Cronica, con la continuazione di Filippo Villani*, ed. G. Porta, 2 vols. (Parma, 1995).

BOOK V

1. I.e., the Lombard plain south of the Alps but north of the Apennines. 'Henry' is Henry VII (1274–1313), Holy Roman Emperor, for whom see 4.116 ff. in vol. 1 of this edition.

2. The Florentine year began on March 25th, the traditional feast of the Incarnation.

3. See 4.94 ff. in vol. 1. Robert of Anjou (1278–1343), King of Naples (1309–43).

4. The Castel Sant'Angelo.

5. The Subura is a valley between the Esquiline and Viminal hills.

6. Giovanni Villani, *Cronica* X, 17, 20, 24, 37, 39, 40.

7. Ibid., X, 40, 39, 43, 44–45.

8. lit. 'to the left': Bruni is seeing the situation from the Florentine perspective. Henry's plan was evidently to cross the mountainous Casentino

region above Incisa to escape the Florentine defenses below Incisa along the Arno river valley.

9. Ibid., X, 46.

10. Ibid., X, 47.

11. See 3.22, in vol. I of this edition.

12. Giovanni Villani, *Cronica* X, 48.

13. Florence, ASF, Archivio della Repubblica, Consulte 10, ff. 49, 52, and Provvisioni 16, ff. 118, 121, 134 (cited by Santini).

14. Giovanni Villani, *Cronica* X, 56.

15. Frederick II of Aragon (1272–1337), King of Sicily, third son of Peter III of Aragon and Constance of Hohenstaufen, the daughter of Manfred.

16. Ibid., X, 49.

17. See above, 2.52 ff., in volume I of this edition.

18. A town about 30 km south of Siena on the old via Francigena.

19. Cicero, *De orat.* 3.167, *Mil.* 56, *Sest.* 12; Livy 7.8.1, 10.28.1; a favorite expression with Bruni.

20. Giovanni Villani, *Cronica* X, 51, 52.

21. Ibid., X, 53.

22. See 4.106 and note 80 in vol. I.

23. Giovanni Villani, *Cronica* X, 58.

24. Ibid., X, 60.

25. For Guido Tarlati see above, 4.57, 4.88 in vol. I; for Geri Spini see 4.53, 4.88.

26. Villani, *Cronica* X, 61, 64.

27. Ibid., X, 68, 70.

28. Bruni here describes the Battle of Montecatini, 29 August 1315, a famous Florentine-Angevin defeat.

29. Ibid., X, 70–72.

30. The Provençal Bertrando di Baux, the son-in-law of King Charles II

of Anjou, called "Conte Novello" from his having been named count of Montescaglioso, Squillace and Andria in the south of Italy. He was appointed podestà and vicar of Florence by King Robert. See Giovanni Villani, *Cronica* X, 74.

31. Ibid., X, 74, 76.

32. Castruccio Castracane degli Interminelli (1281–1328), Ghibelline war leader and Signore of Lucca after 1320; Ludwig the Bavarian made him imperial vicar of Lucca in 1327 and later Signore of Pistoia. The nemesis of the Florentine People, he plays a major role in this book.

33. Ibid., X, 78.

34. Guido, count of Battifolle. See ibid., X, 79, where Villani dates Guido's appointment as vicar to 1316.

35. Ibid., X, 82, 79.

36. Ibid., X, 88, 95.

37. John XXII (pope, 7 August 1316–4 December 1334), born Jacques Duèse. He was elected pope with the backing of Philip V of France and King Robert of Naples, whose chancellor he had been before being made bishop of Avignon in 1310.

38. Ibid., X, 106.

39. Ibid., X, 111, 115.

40. Spinetta Malaspina (1282–1352), marquis, lord of the Lunigiana and Garfagnana.

41. Ibid., X, 127.

42. The Dodici Buonomini, one of the major advisory boards of the Signoria.

43. Ibid., X, 128.

44. Probably a podestà or other legal officer; in the interests of avoiding partisan justice, such men were ordinarily not natives of the towns where they served.

45. Ibid., X, 146–147, 151.

46. Ibid., X, 163.

47. Ibid., X, 187, 193.

48. Ibid., X, 205, 208–209.

49. Ibid., X, 214.

50. Ibid., X, 219.

51. Ibid., X, 219.

52. Ibid., X, 229, 271. Compare to Stefani, *Cronaca*, rbr. 366.

53. Giovanni Villani, *Cronica* X, 253.

54. Ibid., X, 233.

55. Ibid., X, 253.

56. Filippo di Fortebraccio de' Tedici, lord of Pistoia (1324); for his career see Davidsohn, *Storia* IV, 978–983.

57. See 5.41, above.

58. Giovanni Villani, *Cronica* X, 261, 269.

59. Ibid., X, 283.

60. Ibid., X, 294–295, 300.

61. Ibid., X, 301.

62. Ibid., X, 302.

63. Ibid., X, 303.

64. Ibid., X, 304–305.

65. What follows is a description of the Battle of Altopascio, 23 September 1325, a famous Florentine defeat.

66. Ibid., X, 306.

67. Ibid., X, 317–318.

68. Ibid., X, 319.

69. Ibid., X, 322, 320.

70. Ibid., X, 323. Compare Stefani, *Cronaca*, rbr. 402.

71. Giovanni Villani, *Cronica*, X, 341, 342; compare Davidsohn, *Storia* IV, 1020.

72. Acciaiuoli translates *vectigalia* as *gabelle*, i.e., customs on goods im-

ported through the gates of the city; *vectigalia* is a more general term meaning public revenues.

73. Giovanni Villani, *Cronica*, X, 324.

74. Acciaiuoli translates the Latin *praefecti* (civilian administrator or military commander) as *commissari*, implying that they were civilian commissioners sent out to oversee mercenary troops; Bruni's Latin term leaves their precise role ambiguous, perhaps intentionally. The parallel passage in Villani refers to them as *castellani*.

75. Ibid., X, 329. Charles, duke of Calabria (1298–1328), son of Robert I of Anjou.

76. Florence, ASF, Archivio della Repubblica, Provvisioni 22, f. 61 (cited by Santini).

77. Villani, *Cronica*, X, 333, 329.

78. Ibid., X, 329, 336, 338.

79. Ibid., X, 339, 348.

80. Ibid., X, 350–351.

81. Ibid., XI, 5.

82. Giovanni Caetani degli Orsini, cardinal deacon of St. Theodore, who was appointed papal legate on 17 April 1326.

83. Ludwig IV of Bavaria (1287–1347), Holy Roman Emperor and opponent of Pope John XXII, who excommunicated him in 1324. Marsilius of Padua dedicated the *Defensor pacis*, a treatise on the rights of civil authorities and attacking papal power, to Ludwig in 1326.

84. Ibid., X, 353, 356; XI, 1, 18.

85. He was crowned as King of the Lombards, by custom a preliminary to being crowned Emperor in Rome.

86. Ibid., XI, 19, 12, 31.

87. See 5.41, above.

88. Giovanni Villani, *Cronica* XI, 29–30.

89. Ibid., XI, 32.

90. Ibid., XI, 33–34.

91. Ibid., XI, 37, 48.

92. Ibid., XI, 35, 34.

93. Robert I of Anjou, "the Wise," King of Naples (1278–1343); see 4.94 ff. in vol. I of this edition.

94. Filippo di Sanguineto, son of the count of Catanzaro; see Villani, *Cronica* XI, 50.

95. Ibid., XI, 35.

96. Ibid., XI, 37, 48–49, 54–55.

97. Ibid., XI, 55, 58–59.

98. Nicholas V, antipope (12 May 1328–25 July 1330), born Pietro Rainalducci, who belonged to a group of disaffected Franciscans. He renounced the papacy in 1330 and died in 1333.

99. Ibid., XI, 69, 72.

100. Ibid., XI, 84–85.

101. Peter of Aragon (1305–42), King of Sicily, who succeeded to his father Frederick II in 1337, though he had already been proclaimed king in 1320.

102. Ibid., XI, 85, 73, 76–77, 99.

103. Ibid., XI, 86.

104. Ibid., XI, 86, 103.

105. Ibid., XI, 105, 107.

106. The Consiglio del Capitano e del Popolo (Council of the Captain and of the People), consisting of 300 popolani, and the Consiglio del Podestà e del Comune (Council of the Podestà and of the Commune), consisting of 250 citizens, including both popolani and magnates. On the reform of 1328, see Davidsohn, *Storia*, IV, 1181–85.

107. Giovanni Villani, *Cronica* XI, 110.

108. Acciaiuoli's translation adds that the place was called Montecarlo; he is presumably consulting Villani, here as elsewhere.

109. Ibid., XI, 108, 107.

110. Ibid., XI, 126.

111. Ibid., XI, 117.

BOOK VI

1. Giovanni Villani, *Cronica*, XI, 126–127.

2. Pino della Tosa, called Pinuccio, podestà of Brescia in 1311, was the main intermediary between the Germans and the Florentines; he was opposed by his kinsman Simone della Tosa, the leader of a popular faction. See Giovanni Villani, *Cronica* XI, 128.

3. ps. Cato, *Distichs* (*apud* Phaedrus, fab. 5, 8): "Fronte capillata, post est occasio calva."

4. Giovanni Villani, *Cronica*, XI, 127.

5. Ibid., XI, 128, 131.

6. Ibid., XI, 131. Acciaiuoli translates: "si venne a rinnovare gli stati e i reggimenti di Toscana."

7. Ibid., XI, 132, 134.

8. Gherardino Spinoli of Genoa. See ibid., XI, 142.

9. Ibid., XI, 134, 136, 140–141, 147.

10. Ibid., XI, 151, 155.

11. Ibid., XI, 155–156.

12. Ibid., XI, 163–164.

13. See 5.25, above. John, King of Bohemia (1296–1346), also called John of Luxembourg, was the son of the Emperor Henry VII of Luxembourg and Margaret of Brabant, and King of Bohemia after 1310. An ally of Ludwig of Bavaria, in 1330 he undertook an expedition to Italy to bring aid to Brescia, menaced by Mastino della Scala.

14. See 6.8, above.

15. Giovanni Villani, *Cronica* XI, 164, 168, 170.

16. Ibid., XI, 171, 176.

17. Pope John XXII's legate was Bertrand du Poïet, cardinal-bishop of

Ostia, the pope's nephew or possibly his son. See Giovanni Villani, *Cronica* XII, 6 and Perrens, *Histoire*, IV, pp. 87, 166.

18. 5.7–25, above.

19. Giovanni Villani, *Cronica* XI, 128, 139, 142.

20. Acciaiuoli translates: "non come confederati, né ancora come sudditi, ma come sottoposti." Bruni means that they held a status between that of allies, to be addressed as friends and equals, and conquered cities, who could be commanded as inferiors.

21. Ibid., XI, 184.

22. Acciaiuoli adds "in sul colle di Monte Carlo."

23. Ibid., XI, 202.

24. Mastino della Scala of Verona and Luigi Gonzaga of Mantua. Mastino II della Scala (1308–51), son of Alboino, was lord of Verona from 1329 to 1351, succeeding his uncle Cangrande I della Scala, the patron of Dante.

25. Obizzo III, lord of Ferrara (1317–52) and Modena (1335–52).

26. Ibid., XI, 201.

27. Ibid., XI, 212. Philip VI of Valois was king of France from 1328 to 1350. Bruni is mistaken about the close kinship between John of Bohemia and Philip VI. John's son, Charles, however, had been educated at the French court.

28. Charles IV of Bohemia (1316–78), king of Bohemia after his father's death at the battle of Crécy in 1346; crowned Holy Roman Emperor in 1355 (see below, 7.105).

29. Ibid., XI, 211, 213.

30. Niccolò d'Este, son of Alberto and grandson of Obizzo III.

31. Ibid., XI, 213, 214.

32. Ibid., XI, 215, 216.

33. Ibid., XI, 225.

34. The Baptistery, which is still adorned by a tablet marking the high point of the flood of 1333.

35. Ibid., XII, 1,4.

36. The manuscripts *AP* have the interesting variant *iniuriam* ("injury") for *ruinam*, possibly a *pentimento* on Bruni's part, though the reading is more likely to be a corruption.

37. Ibid., XII, 5, 6.

38. Ibid., XII, 8.

39. Ibid., XII, 12–15.

40. Pope Benedict XII (20 December 1334–25 April 1342), born Jacques Fournier, took vows as a Cistercian, studied theology at Paris, and afterwards served as bishop in several French towns, where he earned the reputation of being a zealous inquisitor; he was violently criticised by Petrarch for his subservience to the French and his commitment to Avignon.

41. Piero Saccone de' Tarlati (d. 1356), who had succeeded to the lordship of Arezzo in 1327, after the death of his brother Guido.

42. Ibid., XII, 19, 21, 28.

43. Uguccione da Faggiuola; see 4.106, 4.111, in vol. 1 of this edition, and above, 5.28–45.

44. Borgo San Sepolcro.

45. Giovanni Villani, *Cronica* XII, 28.

46. Ibid., XII, 30–31, 40.

47. Marsilio, Pietro and Orlando: see Perrens, *Histoire* IV, 189.

48. Giovanni Villani, *Cronica* XII, 40, 44–45.

49. Here Bruni appears momentarily to be sympathizing with the Aretine cause against the Florentine ally, Perugia.

50. Ibid., XII, 37, 41, 45.

51. Ibid., XII, 48, 49.

52. Ibid., XII. 52, 54.

53. Ibid., XII, 54, 59, 60.

54. Ibid., XII, 60.

55. Ibid., XII, 61.

56. Luchino Visconti (1292–1349), fourth son of Matteo I Visconti, later lord of Milan from 1339 to 1349.

57. Ibid., XII, 61–64.

58. Ibid., XII, 64.

59. Ubertino I da Carrara (1276–1345), lord of Padua after 1338.

60. Ibid., XII, 65–66.

61. Ibid., XII, 73, 77, 89–90.

62. I.e., the Porta San Gallo.

63. Ibid, XII, 90, 98, 100.

64. Ibid., XII, 94, 100, 114.

65. Jacopo Gabrielli of Gubbio, specially appointed under the title of Captain of the Guard; see Villani, Cronica XII, 118, and Perrens, Histoire IV, 220.

66. Giovanni Villani, Cronica XII, 118, 119.

67. Ibid., XII, 130–132.

68. Acciaiuoli translates "commessari", implying that they were military commissioners; Villani (ibid., XII, 133) calls them sindachi or legal representatives.

69. Ibid., XII, 133.

70. Ibid., XII, 134, 136–138.

71. Ibid., XII, 139.

72. The Florentine podestà was Guglielmo degli Altoviti, from a great popolano family.

73. Ibid., XII, 138–139.

74. Ibid., XII, 138–139.

75. Ibid., XII, 140.

76. Ibid., XII, 140; XIII, 5.

77. Walter VI of Brienne, "Duke of Athens" (c. 1304–1356), whose father, Walter V, lost control over the crusader duchy of Athens in 1311 to

Catalan mercenaries. There is a sarcastic allusion to him in Boccaccio's *Decameron* (2.7).

78. Bruni had made this same observation about French attitudes to popular rule in his treatise on military service, *De militia* (1420).

79. lit. "discontented with the decrees", probably referring to the Ordinances of Justice (see below, 7.4, where *constituta iustitiae* clearly refers to the Ordinances of Justice). On the origin of the Ordinances, see 4.34f. in vol. 1 of this edition.

80. Giovanni Villani, *Cronica* XIII, 1, 2. See 5.115, above.

81. lit. "before the rostra." Acciaiuoli translates "in su la ringhiera", more accurately reflecting the contemporary setting. Assemblies of the people were held in the Piazza della Signoria before the Palazzo Vecchio, which in the days of the republic had an elevated platform along one side called the *ringhiera*. There it was customary for the nine priors and the Standard-Bearer of Justice to sit in a line, getting up to address the people from a rostrum in the middle. Bruni himself gave numerous speeches and announcements from this platform in his role as chancellor.

82. Giovanni Villani, *Cronica* XIII, 3.

83. Ibid., XIII, 8.

84. Ibid., XIII, 8.

85. Ibid., XIII, 16.

86. It was a common procedure for the traditional governing bodies of Florence to summon large councils of leading citizens to advise them on any important decision, so Walter's invitation could have been seen as a conciliatory gesture, a moderation of his absolute style of rule.

87. I.e., the Duomo, which in that period was still unfinished.

88. Not because the abdication would not have been made under duress in the Casentino, but because the witnesses to the abdication in the Casentino would have been Ghibelline sympathizers, or at least non-Florentines, and therefore considered more reliable in court if the document's authenticity should be questioned.

89. Ibid., XIII, 17.

BOOK VII

1. Giovanni Villani, *Cronica* XIII, 18.

2. See 4.1, in vol. 1 of this edition.

3. Bruni's use here of the verb *antiquo*, normally "to remain in force", is non-classical.

4. The city assigned hundreds of paid public offices by lot, apportioning them equally among the sestieri. Since some of the sestieri were far more populous than others, this meant that men from the most populous sestieri had less chance to enjoy offices ("honors"). Bruni's word *tribus*, here translated "populace", was a term used for an administrative division by the Romans; the equivalent Italian term is *popolo*, not to be confused with the *popolo fiorentino* or Florentine People, for whose meaning see the Introduction in vol. 1 of this edition.

5. Giovanni Villani, *Cronica* XIII, 19. Since the Oltrarno district was where the nobility was most powerful, Bruni's implication here is that the new division of the city benefitted the nobility and their clients.

6. His fellow-nobles, as the next paragraph makes clear, not the Fourteen.

7. The interesting variant in some of the manuscripts could be translated, "rather than reproach the violence of the people."

8. The Ponte a Rubiconte.

9. The Dodici Buonomini, for whose institution see above, 5.58.

10. Bruni means that the previous scrutiny (in which the total citizen body had been screened for eligibility for offices) was redone, but in such an exacting way that the number of eligible citizens remained low. Bruni as a rule approved of such restrictions of the office-holding population, which from his Aristotelian perspective was tantamount to maximizing the virtue of office-holders.

11. Giovanni Villani, *Cronica* XIII, 20–24.

12. Ibid., XIII, 28, 25.

13. Ibid., XIII, 30.

14. Ibid., XIII, 32, 34.

15. The phrase *amplissimo consilio* implies that the claims were heard, not just before the Signoria and its advisory colleges, but also before a large number of *richiesti* (leading citizens summoned to provide additional counsel).

16. I.e., the Monte Comune, the commune's funded debt. Bruni himself was a large investor in this fund (investing 3825 florins in it according to his tax declaration of 1427), hence his evident enthusiasm for its benefits. Later, the city created other funded debts, such as the Monte dei preti to reimburse the clergy for property alienated after the War of the Eight Saints, and the Monte dei doti, an investment fund for dowries.

17. Ibid., XIII, 34, 36.

18. Matteo Villani, *Cronica* III, 106.

19. Giovanni Villani, *Cronica* XIII, 43–44.

20. The Hundred Year's War (1337–1453).

21. Acciaiuoli's translation says that the wolf entered by the Porta San Giorgio and exited by the Porta Santo Friano (Freddiano).

22. Ibid., XIII, 55–57.

23. Ibid., XIII, 73, 83.

24. Charles IV, son of King John of Bohemia, grandson of the Emperor Henry VII; see above, 6.33.

25. The Black Death of 1347–1351, the worst epidemic in European history, which killed an estimated 20 million people in Europe.

26. Giovanni Villani, *Cronica* XIII, 60, 78, 82, 84.

27. Luigi, prince of Taranto (d. 1362), brother of Robert of Anjou, cousin and second husband of Johanna, queen of Naples and Sicily. Despite Bruni, he was in fact the grandson of Charles II of Anjou; see Perrens, *Histoire* IV, 315.

28. Louis I, King of Hungary (reigned 1342–82), son of Charles I of Anjou.

29. Charles I of Anjou, King of Naples and Sicily (1266–85).

30. See 4.3, in vol. 1 of this edition. The captured son was Charles II of Anjou, king of Naples and Sicily (reigned 1285–1309), son of Charles I.

31. Charles I of Hungary (1288–1342; grandson of Charles II of Naples and Sicily), reigned in Hungary from 1307 to 1342; his claim to the throne of Hungary was in fact based on succession from his grandmother, Maria of Hungary, wife of Charles II. Charles I of Hungary's father was in fact Charles Martel of Anjou, eldest son of Charles II, King of Naples and Sicily.

32. Robert I of Anjou, "the Wise", King of Naples and Sicily (reigned 1309–43), patron of Giotto and Boccaccio.

33. See 5.115 and 6.111, above.

34. Louis I of Hungary, who succeeded his father Charles I of Hungary in 1342; Bruni gives us one Charles too many. Louis' younger brother Andreas in 1333 married Johanna I, later Queen of Naples and Sicily, and was assassinated in September of 1345 while attempting to have himself recognized as joint ruler of the Kingdom of Naples and Sicily. The tradition that Johanna orchestrated her husband's murder is not accepted by modern historians.

35. Giovanni Villani, *Cronica* XIII, 51–52, 59.

36. The aforementioned (7.33) Luigi of Tarento.

37. Giovanni Villani, *Cronica* XIII, 59, 99, 107, 111, 113, 115.

38. Matteo Villani, *Cronica* I, 1.

39. Ibid., I, 45, 46,

40. Giovanni Visconti (c. 1290–1354), brother of Galeazzo, and *signore* of Milan from 1339, archbishop of Milan from 1342.

41. Ibid., I, 79, 74–75,

42. Piero Gucci, surnamed Mucini; see ibid., *Cronica* I, 98; Stefani, *Cronaca*, rbr. 644.

43. I.e., in Bologna; see above, 7.39.

44. Matteo Villani, *Cronica* I, 97–99; II, 2.

45. The nephew or possibly the son of the Archbishop.

46. Acciaiuoli's translation tells us that this was the hill near Montughi, to the north of Florence, which shows that he was consulting Matteo Villani's *Cronica* (II, 10).

47. Ibid., II, 2–12, 14–15.

48. Ibid., II, 18–19.

49. The italicized sentence appears in one of the later manuscripts (written in 1449, but by a favorite scribe of Bruni's) and just possibly represents an authorial addition rather than a pleonastic deletion. See "Note on the Text."

50. Ibid., II, 20.

51. Acciaiuoli translates "commissari", showing that he understood these authorities (*praefecti*) to be Florentine military commissioners in charge of the troops; such men were civilians with experience of war, not *condottieri* (professional military commanders).

52. Ibid., II, 22.

53. Ibid., II, 21, 23, 29–33.

54. I.e., they were removed from the class of magnates and were officially listed as belonging to the class of *popolani*, who alone had full citizen rights; see 4.34, in vol. 1 of this edition. Santini cites Florence, ASF, Archivio della Repubblica, Provvisioni 39, ff. 35–37, which could have been known to Bruni, with his easy access to public records.

55. See above, 6.67f.

56. Matteo Villani, *Cronica* II, 36–37.

57. I.e., Borgo Sansepolcro, about thirty km east of Arezzo.

58. Ibid., II, 42.

59. Ibid., II, 43.

60. The italicized sentences are omitted in what is apparently a later redaction, if it is not a scribal error.

61. Ibid., II, 46, 52.

62. Ibid. II, 55.

63. Ibid. II, 56.

64. lit. 'fathers'; Acciaiuoli translates "cardinali."

65. Charles IV of Luxembourg (1316–1378), elected King of the Romans in 1346, crowned Holy Roman emperor in 1355; see above, 6.33. Charles's

election as King of the Romans was secured by Pope Clement V, who set him up as an anti-king against the Holy Roman Emperor, Louis IV.

66. Between Gaiole and Badia a Coltibuono in the Chianti region.

67. Matteo Villani, *Cronica*, II, 58, 64.

68. Rosso di Ricciardi de' Ricci.

69. The italicized sentence is omitted in what may be a later redaction (or a scribal error).

70. Ibid., II, 69, 79.

71. Clement VI (7 May 1342–6 December 1352), born Pierre Roger at Maumont in the Limousin, studied theology in Paris; his career was furthered by John XXII and Philip VI of France.

72. I.e., as though the agreement with Florence and her allied cities had given him an opportunity to reconcile himself with the archbishop without incurring complaint from those cities.

73. Excommunication and interdict. Clement also cancelled all the Church's legal processes against him; see ibid., III, 4 and Perrens, *Histoire* IV, 418–419.

74. Matteo Villani, *Cronica* II, 66; III, 3–5.

75. I.e., further the cause of his coronation in Rome. Charles had been elected "King of the Romans" by the electors of the Holy Roman Empire in 1346, but was not crowned Emperor until Easter Sunday, 1355, when a papal legate crowned him in Rome (the pope being then in Avignon).

76. Ibid., II, 68; III, 7.

77. Ibid., II, 70.

78. Ibid., III, 6, 11.

79. Ibid., III, 17.

80. Mercenary soldiers usually fought on a yearly contract that paid them from the beginning of the campaigning season in May until the following winter, when they would return to farming.

81. Ibid., III, 29.

82. Ibid., III, 35.

83. Ibid., III, 47. Bruni's knowledge of the terms comes from Florence, ASF, Archivio della Repubblica, Capitoli 12, ff. 94–126 (cited by Santini). The treaty was signed on 31 March 1353.

BOOK VIII

1. See 7.119, above. The treaty with Giovanni Visconti had contained a list of all those restored from exile, but owing to corruption names were being added of persons not entitled to restoration.

2. Matteo Villani, *Cronica* III, 60, 61.

3. Montréal d'Albarno, a Provençal knight and a famous condottiere. He had been a Hospitaller for a while, hence was known as "Fra Moriale" in Italy. He was executed by Cola di Rienzo in Rome in 1354 after his company had ravaged central Italy for two years (ibid., IV, 23).

4. Ibid., III, 89, 108; IV, 15, 16.

5. Charles IV of Luxembourg.

6. Ibid., IV, 27.

7. Ibid., IV, 25, 28.

8. Ibid., IV, 22, 29, 35.

9. For Neri della Faggiuola, see above, 6.50; for Uguccione, 5.28–40.

10. Matteo Villani, *Cronica* IV, 41, 44, 45, 47–49, 53–54, 61–64, 68.

11. Ibid., V, 2.

12. Ibid., IV, 76, 89; V, 14, 22.

13. Ibid., V, 73.

14. Ibid., VI, 4.

15. Ibid., VI. 11.

16. See 2.8 in volume 1 of this edition.

17. Matteo Villani, *Cronica* VII, 45.

18. 1.82–83, in volume 1 of this edition.

19. Charles I of Anjou; see 2.104 in volume 1 of this edition.

20. I.e., who were not Guelfs. Acciaiuoli translates: *o non fusse della*

università de' guelfi. The association of all Guelfs in Florence should be distinguished from the Guelf Party, a more exclusive and aristocratic body.

21. Matteo Villani, *Cronica* VIII, 24, 31–32.

22. Ibid., VI, 48, 61.

23. Probably the pass of San Godenzo, the most important route through the Alpe di San Benedetto. The ambush on the following day probably took place between San Benedetto in Alpe and the Passo di Muraglione, the most difficult part of the route.

24. Conrad Wirtinger, count of Landau (d. 1363), known as Corrado di Lando in Italy, formerly a member of Fra Moriale's band and now head of the Great Company.

25. Ibid., IV, 40, 58; V, 10, 52–53, 56, 70–72; VII, 76; VIII, 60, 72, 74–79.

26. Ibid., VIII, 14, 17.

27. Acciaiuoli adds *che si potesse sentire di loro partita,* "which might have been thought to belong to their party."

28. Ibid., VIII, 85, 97, 99; IX, 2–4, 20, 26–31.

29. Ibid., IX, 43.

30. Ibid., III, 11; IX, 47, 49, 50, 52, 61–62, 70.

31. See 7.55 ff., above.

32. Matteo Villani, *Cronica* V, 12; IX, 73–76, 102.

33. Nicola Acciaiuoli (1310–1365), Grand Seneschal of the Kingdom of Naples, and founder of the Carthusian monastery at Galluzzo outside Florence. Ibid., III, 9.

34. Ibid., X, 22–23.

35. Not equal rights inhering naturally in a subject, as in modern rights theory, but the equal right of citizens in a republic to participate in government.

36. Ibid., X, 67.

37. Ibid., VIII, 11, 63.

38. Ibid., X, 76, 83, 85, 101.

39. Ibid., XI, 2.

40. Ibid., XI, 6, 13, 15, 17–19.

41. I.e., the Florentine Baptistery.

42. Ibid., XI, 24, 30.

43. Ibid., XI, 45. Barga was a town about 20 km north of Lucca that controlled the road through the mountains to Liguria.

44. Ibid., III, 35; XI, 46, 49, 50–51, 54.

45. Ibid., XI, 59.

46. Ibid., XI, 61–63 (Filippo Villani).

47. Probably a crude joke, referring to the sacrifice of flesh and blood in the Mass.

48. Ibid., XI, 65, 67–69, 72–77 (Filippo Villani).

49. On the 1st of May the traditional spring feast of Calendimaggio was normally held in Tuscany.

50. Ibid., XI, 79, 81–82, 84–89, 95 (Filippo Villani).

51. The Florentines ordinarily held a ceremony in the Piazza Signoria upon the appointment of a new commander, in which the captain was presented with the standards, a general's baton, and other trappings of office.

52. Bruni here describes the famous battle of Cascina, 28 July 1364, which later was the subject of a battlefield piece commissioned by the Signoria from Michelangelo; the project was not finished, but copies of Michelangelo's cartoon survive.

53. Ibid., XI, 96–97 (Filippo Villani).

54. Ibid., XI, 98, 100 (Filippo Villani).

55. Ibid., XI, 101 (Filippo Villani). A Pisan merchant from a rich family, Giovanni made himself lord of Pisa in 1364, and was appointed the city's imperial vicar by Charles IV in 1368 after being expelled from that town.

56. Ibid., XI, 102 (Filippo Villani). The treaty of Pescia was signed on 28 August 1364; for the terms, see Perrens, *Histoire* V, 52.

57. Emperor Charles IV and Urban V. The latter (reigned 28 September

1362–19 December 1370) was born Guillaume de Grimoard in Lozère, took vows as a Benedictine and a doctorate in canon law, and acquired diplomatic experience while serving as a papal legate in Italy in 1352, 1354, 1360 and 1362. Austere and unworldly, he worked to put down the companies of marauding mercenaries that were harassing Italy and with the encouragement of Charles IV tried to move the papacy back to Rome from Avignon, though ultimately in vain.

58. Bruni means that without Florentine money, no papal-imperial expedition against Bernabò could be mounted.

59. Stefani, *Cronaca*, rbr. 701, 703, 706.

60. 7.14–15.

61. Stefani, *Cronaca*, rbr. 706, 708, 710.

62. I.e., the pope; see Perrens, *Histoire* V, 68.

63. Stefani, *Cronaca*, rbr. 706, 708.

64. Ibid., rbr. 710, 711, 713.

65. Ibid., rbr. 711, 713.

66. *calones*, lit. soldier-servants, probably here referring to the junior members of a lance, the three-man team consisting of a knight and his field support, which was the basic unit of Renaissance cavalry.

67. The name, appropriately enough, means "little wolf."

68. Ibid., rbr. 713, 715–717.

69. Ibid., rbr. 720, 715.

70. Gregory XI (30 December 1370–27 March 1378), born Pierre Roger de Beaufort near Limoges. A nephew of Clement VI, he was named a cardinal at the age of nineteen, then went to Perugia to study canon law under the famous jurist Baldus. He was responsible for bringing the papacy finally back to Rome, albeit in a disastrous way, as described below.

71. Ibid., rbr. 722, 754.

72. Ibid., rbr. 726, 731 735, 739.

73. Ibid., rbr. 741.

74. Because the legate's troops would burn the harvest, a common tactic.

75. This was the famous *otto di balìa,* an emergency commission with full powers to oversee the war effort; the eight members of the commission became known as the "Eight Saints," hence the war against the papacy (1375–78) became known as the War of the Eight Saints.

76. Ibid., rbr. 746, 751.

77. Ibid., rbr. 753, 756, 758.

78. Robert of Geneva, son of Count Amadeus III of Geneva, known as Gebennese in Italy. He was created a cardinal by Gregory XI in 1371. He later became the anti-pope Clement VII (see below, 8.128). A legate *a latere* (lit. "from the side," i.e. of the pope) is a cardinal commissioned for a special assignment with quasi-papal powers within the territory of his appointment.

79. Bruni's Latin terms are vague, but from other sources we know that these "censures and penalties" consisted of excommunication and interdict, i.e., expulsion from communion with the Church and suspension of the sacraments.

80. Stefani, *Cronaca,* rbr. 759, 753.

81. A broadly Aristotelian maxim; see *Politics* 3.6.

82. Santini reports that the oration of the Florentine ambassadors is based on an archival document, a diploma of 31 March 1376.

83. Ibid., rbr. 836, 754.

84. Ibid., rbr. 760.

85. Gomez Albernoz, nephew of the more famous Cardinal Albornoz, the warrior legate who recaptured the Papal States for the Avignon papacy.

86. I.e., that he could not force people to respect him.

87. Ibid., rbr. 780.

88. Clement VII, antipope (20 September 1378–16 September 1394). See 8.98, above.

89. Urban VI (8 April 1378–15 October 1389), born Bartolomeo Prignano.

90. Stefani, *Cronaca,* rbr. 782, 786.

Bibliography

❧❧❧

EDITIONS OF THE LATIN TEXT

Historiarum Florentinarum libri XII, quibus accesserunt Quorundam suo tempore in Italia gestorum et De rebus graecis commentarii, ab interitu vindicati, nec non a mendis repurgati et ex manuscriptis in lucem editi, ed. Sixtus Bruno. Strasbourg: Lazarus Zetznerus, 1610. Pp. 1–248 contains the *History*, without Bruni's preface.

[Arezzo, Accademia di Scienze, Lettere ed Arti.] *Leonardi Arretini Historiarum florentini populi libri XII. Istoria fiorentina di Leonardo Aretino, tradotta in volgare da Donato Acciaiuoli, col testo a fronte.* 3 vols. Florence 1855–60. With "Aggiunte e correzioni alla vita di Leonardo Bruni," signed by G. Mancini.

Leonardo Bruni Aretino. *Historiarum florentini populi libri XII e Rerum suo tempore gestarum commentarius.* Ed. Emilio Santini and Carmine Di Pierro. Rerum Italicarum Scriptores, vol. XIX, part III. Città di Castello, 1914–26.

ITALIAN TRANSLATION BY DONATO ACCIAIUOLI

Historia universale di Messer Lionardo Aretino. Venice, 1476. Photo-reprint, Arezzo, 1984.

Le Historie Fiorentine. Florence 1492.

Historia universale di Messer Lionardo Aretino. Venice, 1560.

La historia universale de suoi tempi di Messer Lionardo Aretino. Venice, 1561. Despite the title, this imprint contains only the *History of the Florentine People* in Acciaiuoli's translation, not the *Rerum suo tempore gestarum commentarius.*

The edition of the Accademia di Scienze, Lettere ed Arti of Arezzo, as above in section I.

Istoria Fiorentina di Leonardo Bruni, tradotta in volgare da Donato Acciaiuoli. Florence, 1861. A reprint of the previous edition, without the Latin text.

SELECTED MODERN STUDIES

Baron, Hans. *The Crisis of the Early Italian Renaissance: Civic Humanism and Republican Liberty in an Age of Classicism and Tyranny.* 2 vols. Princeton, 1955; revised edition in one volume, Princeton, 1966.

——— . *In Search of Florentine Civic Humanism: Essays on the Transition from Medieval to Modern Thought.* 2 vols. Princeton, 1988.

Brucker, Gene A. *Florentine Politics and Society, 1343–1378.* Princeton, 1962.

Cabrini, Anna Maria. "Le *Historiae* del Bruni: risultati e ipotesi di una ricerca sulle fonti." In *Leonardo Bruni cancelliere della Repubblica di Firenze,* ed. Paolo Viti, pp. 247–319. Florence, 1990.

Cipriani, Giovanni. *Il mito etrusco nel Rinascimento.* Florence, 1980.

Cochrane, Eric. *Historians and Historiography in the Italian Renaissance.* Chicago, 1981.

Davidsohn, Robert. *Storia di Firenze,* 8 vols. Florence, 1977.

Fubini, Riccardo. *Storiografia dell'umanesimo in Italia da Leonardo Bruni ad Annio da Viterbo.* Rome, 2003.

Green, Louis. *Castruccio Castracani: A Study on the Origins and Character of a Fourteenth-Century Italian Despotism.* Oxford, 1986.

Hankins, James. *Humanism and Platonism in the Italian Renaissance,* vol. 1: *Humanism.* Rome, 2003.

La Penna, Antonio. "Il significato di Sallustio nella storiografia e nel pensiero politico di Leonardo Bruni." In his *Sallustio e la 'rivoluzione romana',* 3rd ed., pp. 409–31. Milan, 1968.

Pastore Stocchi, Manlio. "Il pensiero politico degli umanisti." In *Storia delle idee politiche, economiche e sociali,* ed. L. Firpo, pp. 3–68. Turin 1987.

Perrens, François Tommy. *Histoire de Florence depuis ses origins jusqu'à la domination des Médicis.* 6 vols. Paris, 1877–83.

Rubinstein, Nicolai. *Studies in Italian History in the Middle Ages and the Renaissance.* 3 vols. Rome, 2001.

Santini, Emilio. *Leonardo Bruni Aretino e i suoi "Historiarum Florentini populi libri XII".* Pisa, 1910.

——— . "La fortuna delle *Storie fiorentine* di Leonardo Bruni nel Rinascimento." *Studi storici* 20 (1911–12): 177–95.

Ullman, Berthold Louis. "Leonardo Bruni and Humanist Historiography." *Medievalia et Humanistica* 4 (1946): 45–61. Reprinted in Ullman's *Studies in the Italian Renaissance*. Rome, 1955.

Wilcox, Donald. *The Development of Florentine Humanist Historiography*. Cambridge, Mass., 1969.

Index

References are by book and paragraph number.

Publication of this volume has been made possible by

The Myron and Sheila Gilmore Publication Fund at I Tatti
The Robert Lehman Endowment Fund
The Jean-François Malle Scholarly Programs and Publications Fund
The Andrew W. Mellon Scholarly Publications Fund
The Craig and Barbara Smyth Fund
for Scholarly Programs and Publications
The Lila Wallace–Reader's Digest Endowment Fund
The Malcolm Wiener Fund for Scholarly Programs and Publications